T0180103

Communications in Computer and Information Science 1431

More information about this series at http://www.springer.com/series/7899

Juan Carlos Figueroa-García ·
Yesid Díaz-Gutierrez ·
Elvis Eduardo Gaona-García ·
Alvaro David Orjuela-Cañón (Eds.)

Applied Computer Sciences in Engineering

8th Workshop on Engineering Applications, WEA 2021
Medellín, Colombia, October 6–8, 2021
Proceedings

Springer

Editors
Juan Carlos Figueroa-García (iD)
Universidad Distrital Francisco José de
Caldas
Bogotá, Colombia

Yesid Díaz-Gutierrez (iD)
Universidad Santo Tomás de Aquino
Bogotá, Colombia

Alvaro David Orjuela-Cañón (iD)
Universidad del Rosario
Bogotá, Colombia

Elvis Eduardo Gaona-García (iD)
Universidad Distrital Francisco José de
Caldas
Bogotá, Colombia

ISSN 1865-0929   ISSN 1865-0937 (electronic)
Communications in Computer and Information Science
ISBN 978-3-030-86701-0   ISBN 978-3-030-86702-7 (eBook)
https://doi.org/10.1007/978-3-030-86702-7

This Springer imprint is published by the registered company Springer Nature Switzerland AG
The registered company address is: Gewerbestrasse 11, 6330 Cham, Switzerland

Preface

The eighth edition of the Workshop on Engineering Applications (WEA 2021) was focused on applications in computer science, computational intelligence, IoT, bioengineering, optimization, and simulation. WEA 2021 was one of the flagship events of the Faculty of Engineering of the Universidad Distrital Francisco José de Caldas and the Informatics Engineering program of the Universidad Santo Tomás de Aquino, Colombia.

WEA 2021 was held in hybrid mode due to the COVID-19 pandemic which has changed how conferences are organized. We received 127 submissions from authors in thirteen countries on diverse topics such as computer science, computational intelligence, IoT/networks, bioengineering, operations research/optimization, and simulation systems, among others. The peer review process of all submissions was rigorous, with all reviewers providing constructive comments, and as a result of their work 44 papers were accepted for oral presentation at WEA 2021. The Program Committee organized the papers into different sections to aid the presentation and increase the impact of this volume, published in Springer's Communications in Computer and Information Sciences (CCIS) series, whose main area is Applied Computer Sciences in Engineering.

The Faculty of Engineering of the Universidad Distrital Francisco José de Caldas and the Universidad Santo Tomás de Aquino made significant efforts to guarantee the success of the conference considering that 2021 was the second consecutive year of the COVID-19 pandemic and its global effects.

We would like to thank all members of the Program Committee and the reviewers for their commitment to help in the review process and for spreading our call for papers which was a hard task due to COVID-19. We would like to thank Alfred Hofmann and Jorge Nakahara from Springer for their helpful advice, guidance, and continuous support in publicizing the proceedings. Moreover, we would like to thank all the authors for supporting WEA 2021 as without all their high-quality submissions the conference would not have been possible. Finally, we are especially grateful to the IEEE Universidad Distrital Francisco José de Caldas Student branch, the Laboratory for Automation and Computational Intelligence (LAMIC) and GITUD research groups of the Universidad Distrital Francisco José de Caldas, and the GRINTIC research group of the Informatics Engineering program of the Universidad Santo Tomás de Aquino.

October 2021

Juan Carlos Figueroa-García
Yesid Díaz-Gutierrez
Alvaro David Orjuela-Cañón
Elvis Eduardo Gaona-García

Organization

General Chair

Juan Carlos Figueroa-García   Universidad Distrital Francisco José de Caldas,
Colombia

Finance Chair/Treasurer

Julio Barón   Universidad Distrital Francisco José de Caldas,
Colombia

Technical Chairs

Crisman Martinez   Universidad Santo Tomás de Aquino, Colombia
Alexandra Silva   Universidad Santo Tomás de Aquino, Colombia

Logistic Chairs

Fernando Antonio Güiza-Jerez   Universidad Santo Tomás de Aquino, Colombia
Yesid Díaz-Gutierrez   Corporación Unificada Nacional de Educación
Superior, Colombia

Publication Chair

Germán Hernández-Pérez   Universidad Nacional de Colombia, Colombia

Program Chairs

Yesid Díaz-Gutierrez   Corporación Unificada Nacional de Educación
Superior (CUN), Colombia
Lindsay Alvarez   Universidad Distrital Francisco José de Caldas,
Colombia
Elvis Eduardo Gaona-García   Universidad Distrital Francisco José de Caldas,
Colombia
Alvaro David Orjuela-Cañon   Universidad del Rosario, Colombia

Plenary Speakers

Ana Paula Barbosa-Póvoa	Universidade de Lisboa, Portugal
Antonio Plaza	University of Extremadura (UEX), Spain
Agapito Ledezma Espino	Carlos III University of Madrid, Spain
Roman Neruda	Charles University and Czech Academy of Sciences, Czech Republic

Program Committee

Adil Usman	Indian Institute of Technology, Mandi, India
Alexandra Silva	Universidad Santo Tomás de Aquino, Colombia
Adolfo Jaramillo-Matta	Universidad Distrital Francisco José de Caldas, Colombia
Alvaro David Orjuela-Cañon	Universidad del Rosario, Colombia
Andrés Ernesto Salguero	Universidad Antonio Nariño, Colombia
Andres Gaona	Universidad Distrital Francisco José de Caldas, Colombia
Carlos Franco-Franco	Universidad del Rosario, Colombia
Carlos Osorio-Ramírez	Universidad Nacional de Colombia, Colombia
Crisman Martinez	Universidad Santo Tomás de Aquino, Colombia
DeShuang Huang	Tongji University, China
Diana Ovalle	Universidad Distrital Francisco José de Caldas, Colombia
Eduyn López-Santana	Universidad Distrital Francisco Jose de Caldas, Colombia
Elvis Eduardo Gaona-García	Universidad Distrital Francisco José de Caldas, Colombia
Fabián Garay	ESINF, Colombia
Feizar Javier Rueda-Velazco	Universidad Distrital Francisco José de Caldas, Colombia
Fernando Antonio Güiza-Jerez	Universidad Santo Tomás de Aquino, Colombia
Francisco Ramis	Universidad del Bío-Bío, Chile
Germán Hernández-Pérez	Universidad Nacional de Colombia, Colombia
Gloria Jeanette Rincón	Universidad Cooperativa de Colombia, Colombia
Guadalupe González	Universidad Tecnológica de Panamá, Panama
Gustavo Puerto-Leguizamón	Universidad Distrital Francisco José de Caldas, Colombia
Gustavo Suárez	Universidad Pontificia Bolivariana, Colombia
Heriberto Román-Flores	Universidad de Tarapacá, Chile
I-Hsien Ting	National University of Kaohsiung, Taiwan
Jair Cervantes-Canales	Universidad Autónoma de México, Mexico
Jairo Soriano-Mendez	Universidad Distrital Francisco José de Caldas, Colombia
Javier Arturo Orjuela-Castro	Universidad Distrital Francisco José de Caldas, Colombia

J. J. Merelo	Universidad de Granada, Spain
Jose Luís Gonzalez-Velarde	Instituto Tecnológico de Monterrey, Mexico
José Luis Jiménez-Useche	National Colombian Army, Colombia
Jose Luis Villa	Universidad Tecnológica de Bolívar, Colombia
Juan Carlos Figueroa-García	Universidad Distrital Francisco José de Caldas, Colombia
Lindsay Alvarez	Universidad Distrital Francisco José de Caldas, Colombia
Mabel Frías	Universidad de las Villas "Marta Abreu", Cuba
Mario Enrique Duarte-Gonzalez	Universidad Antonio Nariño, Colombia
Martin Pilat	Charles University in Prague, Czech Republic
Martine Ceberio	University of Texas at El Paso, USA
Miguel Melgarejo	Universidad Distrital Francisco José de Caldas, Colombia
Nelson L. Diaz Aldana	Universidad Distrital Francisco José de Caldas, Colombia
Oswaldo Lopez Santos	Universidad de Ibagué, Colombia
Paulo Alonso Gaona	Universidad Distrital Francisco José de Caldas, Colombia
Rafael Bello-Pérez	Universidad de las Villas "Marta Abreu", Cuba
Roberto Ferro	Universidad Distrital Francisco José de Caldas, Colombia
Rodrigo Linfati	Universidad del Bío Bío, Chile
Roman Neruda	Charles University in Prague and Czech Academy of Sciences, Czech Republic
Sebastián Jaramillo-Isaza	Universidad Antonio Nariño, Colombia
Sergio Rojas-Galeano	Universidad Distrital Francisco José de Caldas, Colombia
Vladik Kreinovich	University of Texas at El Paso, USA
Yesid Díaz-Gutierrez	Universidad Santo Tomás de Aquino, Colombia
Yurilev Chalco-Cano	Universidad de Tarapacá, Chile

Contents

Computational Intelligence

Can Communication Topology Improve a Multi-swarm PSO Algorithms? 3
José Guzmán, Mario García-Valdez, and Juan J. Merelo-Guervós

Solving Dynamical Systems Using Windows of Sliding Subproblems 13
Angel Fernando Garcia Contreras and Martine Ceberio

Landslide Susceptibility Model by Means of Remote Sensing Images
and AutoML 25
*Diego Renza, Elsa Adriana Cárdenas, Carlos Marcelo Jaramillo,
Serena Sarah Weber, and Estibaliz Martinez*

Fake Speech Recognition Using Deep Learning 38
Steven Camacho, Dora Maria Ballesteros, and Diego Renza

Automatic Classification of Energy Consumption Profiles in Processes
of the Oil & Gas Industry in Colombia 49
*Bryan Escobar-Restrepo, Juan Felipe Botero Vega,
and Juan Rafael Orozco-Arroyave*

Organizational Online Reputation Measurement Through Natural
Language Processing and Sentiment Analysis Techniques 60
*Christian Orrego, Luisa Fernanda Villa, Lina Maria Sepúlveda-Cano,
and Lillyana M. Giraldo M.*

Robust Automatic Speech Recognition for Call Center Applications 72
*Luis Felipe Parra-Gallego, Tomás Arias-Vergara,
and Juan Rafael Orozco Arroyave*

Dynamic Recognition and Classification of Trajectories in SLRecon
Adopted Artificial Intelligence in Kinect 84
*Tomas S. Gavilanez, Edgar A. Gómez, Eduardo Estevez,
and Saravana Prakash Thirumuruganandham*

Heterogeneous Acoustic Features Space for Automatic Classification
of Drone Audio Signals 97
Andrés Felipe Sabogal, Manuel Gómez, and Juan P. Ugarte

Career Recommendation System for Validation of Multiple Intelligence
to High School Students 110
    Maryori Sabalza Mejia, Carolina Campillo Jimenez,
    and Juan Carlos Martínez-Santos

Evaluation of Different Word Embeddings to Create Personality Models
in Spanish 121
    Felipe Orlando López-Pabón and Juan Rafael Orozco-Arroyave

Power Conditioner for AC PV Systems Using GA 133
    Luis David Pabon Fernandez, Edison Andres Caicedo Peñaranda,
    and Jorge Luis Diaz Rodriguez

Bioengineering

Multivariate Analysis of Adaptation Level in Low-Cost Lower Limb
Prostheses: An Unsupervised Learning Approach 147
    Gabriel Maldonado Colmenares and Jenny Kateryne Nieto Aristizabal

Carbon Monoxide Effect on Human Cardiac Tissue. In Silico Study 160
    Catalina Tobón, Geraldine Durango-Giraldo, and Juan Pablo Ugarte

Gender Recognition in Informal and Formal Language Scenarios
via Transfer Learning 171
    Daniel Escobar-Grisales, Juan Camilo Vásquez-Correa,
    and Juan Rafael Orozco-Arroyave

Towards Event-Trigger Impulsive MPC for the Treatment of T1DM
Handling Limited Resources 180
    Jhon E. Goez-Mora, Monica Ayde Vallejo, and Pablo S. Rivadeneira

Automation of Study Design Classification and Clinical Evidence Ranking
for Health Technology Assessment of Medical Devices 190
    Mabel Catalina Zapata, Juan Guillermo Barreneche,
    and Jenny Kateryne Nieto Aristizabal

Online System Based on Microservices for Rapid Diagnostic of Pathogenic
Bacteria in Seafood from Biogenic Amines Biosensors 202
    Juan M. Álvarez Q., José I. García M., and John A. Sanabria O.

Estimation of Limbs Angles Amplitudes During the Use of the Five
Minute Shaper Device Using Artificial Neural Networks 213
    Cristian Felipe Blanco-Diaz, Cristian David Guerrero-Mendez,
    Mario Enrique Duarte-González, and Sebastián Jaramillo-Isaza

SSCF-Hyperthermia Study in MCF-7 Spheroids – In Silicio 225
  Hector Fabian Guarnizo-Mendez, Angela Victoria Fonseca Benítez,
  Sandra Janneth Perdomo Lara, Sandra Johanna Morantes Medina,
  Cristian Andrés Triana Infante, Christian Camilo Cano Vásquez,
  Juan David Jaiquel Villamil, and Sebastian Mesa Zafra

Internet of Things (IoT)

Smart UTB: An IoT Platform for Smart Campus 239
  Leonardo Castellanos Acuña, Ray Narváez, Carlos Salas,
  Luz Alejandra Magre, and María José González

Development of a Short-Range Continuous Wave Radar Prototype Kit
as a Learning Tool for Theoretical and Practical Technical Training 250
  Felipe Silva Gómez, Tomás Francisco Guzmán,
  and Yolanda Parra Guacaneme

An Hybrid CPU-GPU Parallel Multi-tracking Framework for Long-Term
Video Sequences 263
  Juan P. D'amato, Leonardo Dominguez, Franco Stramana,
  Aldo Rubiales, and Alejandro Perez

Implementation of End User Radio Key Performance Indicators Using
Signaling Trace Data Analysis for Cellular Networks 275
  Hector Daniel Bernal Amaya, Elvis Eduardo Gaona Garcia,
  and Julian Camargo

Approach Pencil-on-Paper to Flexible Piezoresistive Respiration Sensor 290
  Luiz Antonio Rasia, Carlos Eduardo Andrades, Thiago Gomes Heck,
  and Julia Rasia

Maintenance Management of an Additive Manufacturing System Based
on the I4.0 Model 299
  Juan David Contreras, Jose Isidro Garcia, and Julian Gomez

Optimization and Operations Research

A Mixed-Integer Linear Programming Model for the Cutting Stock
Problem in the Steel Industry 315
  Daniel Morillo-Torres, Mauricio Torres Baena, John Wilmer Escobar,
  Alfonso R. Romero-Conrado, Jairo R. Coronado-Hernández,
  and Gustavo Gatica

Metaheuristics with Local Search Miscellany Applied to the Quadratic
Assignment Problem for Large-Scale Instances 327
  Rogelio González-Velázquez, Erika Granillo-Martínez,
  María Beatriz Bernábe-Loranca, and Jairo E. Powell-González

Linear Programming Model for Production Cost Minimization at a Rice
Crop Products Manufacturer 335
  Jairo R. Coronado-Hernández, Leonardo J. Olarte-Jiménez,
  Zulmeira Herrera-Fontalvo, and Johana Cómbita Niño

Comparison Between Amazon Go Stores and Traditional Retails Based
on Queueing Theory 347
  Jairo R. Coronado-Hernandez, Andrés F. Calderón-Ochoa,
  Ivan Portnoy, and Jorge Morales-Mercado

Analysis of Traceability Systems for Reducing the Bullwhip Effect
in the Perishable Food Supply Chain: A System Dynamics Approach 362
  Jeysser Johan Otero-Diaz, Javier Arturo Orjuela-Castro,
  and Milton M. Herrera

Exploring Efficiency and Accessibility in Healthcare Network Design 374
  Edgar Duarte-Forero and Gustavo Alfredo Bula

Scenario-Based Model for the Location of Multiple Uncapacitated
Facilities: Case Study in an Agro-Food Supply Chain 386
  Gean Pablo Mendoza-Ortega, Manuel Soto, José Ruiz-Meza,
  Rodrigo Salgado, and Angelica Torregroza

Application of the CERT Values Measurement Model for Organizational
Culture in the Management and Quality Company 399
  Claudia Yadira Rodríguez-Ríos, Abigail Calderón Narváez,
  and Santiago Cárdenas Jiménez

Engineering Applications

Methodology for the Implementation of Kalman Filters on Real
Applications 411
  Juan David Núñez, Mónica Aydé Vallejo, and Héctor Botero

Agro-Smart Caribe: Soil Moisture Measurement System 422
  Eduardo Gomez, Jorge Eliecer Duque, Alvaro José Rojas,
  Cristian Camilo Jaik, and Jose Angel Pertuz

Entrepreneurial Intention in Vocational Technical Schools in Emerging
Economies: A Case Study of Barranquilla, Colombia 435
  David Ovallos-Gazabon, Nataly Puello-Pereira, Kevin Parra-Negrete,
  and Karol Martinez-Cueto

Improvement of Visual Perception in Humanoid Robots Using
Heterogeneous Architectures for Autonomous Applications 447
  Joaquin Guajo, Cristian Alzate Anzola, Daniel Betancur,
  Luis Castaño-Londoño, and David Marquez-Viloria

Computational Design of a Road Safety Model Elaborated in Epoxy
Material Reinforced with Glass Fibers and SiO2 Addition 459
  M. Echeverri Peláez, G. Suárez Guerrero, J. Cruz Riaño,
  H. Kerguelen Grajales, and E. Vallejo Morales

Modeling, Analysis and Simulation of Curved Solar Cell's Encapsulation
Reinforcement 468
  Gabriel Espitia-Mesa, Efraín Hernández-Pedraza,
  Santiago Molina-Tamayo, and Ricardo Mejía-Gutiérrez

Variable-Prioritizing and Instrumentation for Monitoring
of an Electrically-Powered Fluvial Vessel Through a FDM
Approach 480
  Felipe Mendoza, Camilo Vélez, Santiago Echavarría,
  Alejandro Montoya, Tatiana Manrique, and Ricardo Mejía-Gutiérrez

A Framework for Multispectral Instance Classification Using Examples 493
  Camilo Peláez-García, Víctor-Alejandro Patiño-Martínez,
  Juan-Bernardo Gómez-Mendoza, and Manuel-Alejandro Tamayo-Monsalve

Advanced Engineering Control Strategies Applied to Occupational Noise
Management in Mining Dump Trucks 505
  Diego Mauricio Murillo Gómez, Enney González León,
  Hugo Piedrahíta, Jairo Yate, and Camilo E. Gómez Cristancho

Prerequisite Relationships of the OntoMath[Edu] Educational Mathematical
Ontology 517
  Alexander Kirillovich, Marina Falileeva, Olga Nevzorova,
  Evgeny Lipachev, Anastasiya Dyupina, and Liliana Shakirova

Author Index 525

Computational Intelligence

Can Communication Topology Improve a Multi-swarm PSO Algorithms?

José Guzmán[1,2], Mario García-Valdez[1,2], and Juan J. Merelo-Guervós[1,2(✉)]

[1] Tijuana Institute of Technology, Tijuana, Mexico
{jose.guzmanc19,mario}@tectijuana.edu.mx
[2] University of Granada, Granada, Spain
jmerelo@ugr.es

Abstract. Using multiple-swarm PSO is a technique used in recent years to help improve the performance of nature-inspired optimization algorithms. A distributed PSO algorithm can work in every swarm in parallel and asynchronously communicate particles between them. However, the communication design is not a trivial task because any architectural change will affect how it explores the search space and how it exploits the best particles. Nevertheless, it has been reported that the exchange of possible solutions helps optimizations algorithms to improve their performance. This paper focuses on proposing and comparing two communication policies regarding how the communication graph between swarms is organized. These policies intend to limit the communication between populations to increase per-swarm exploration and avoid premature convergence through exploring different parts of the space in different swarms. The proposed policies are chain and hypercube topologies and compare them against a simple cross-over strategy using several continuous optimization benchmark functions to assess the benefits of choosing one communication topology over another. After the experiments, the chain-based topology had a better error performance.

Keywords: Multi-swarm intelligence · Communication topologies · Multi-swarm PSO

1 Introduction

Bio-inspired optimization algorithms are intrinsically parallel, and researchers have exploited this fact since their conception. Initially, several researchers proposed a multi-population approach for Genetic Algorithms (GAs), using various architectures described in detail in classical [1] and more recent surveys r2. A typical implementation is to divide a global population into many smaller populations working in parallel and (possibly) asynchronously. Multipopulation designs have been used to solve large-scale complex optimization problems, where the search space has many locally optimal solutions [2]. Several studies are showing that multi-population optimization often outperforms single-population approaches [3,4]. Another advantage of multi-population optimization is the

© Springer Nature Switzerland AG 2021
J. C. Figueroa-García et al. (Eds.): WEA 2021, CCIS 1431, pp. 3–12, 2021.
https://doi.org/10.1007/978-3-030-86702-7_1

ability to have a parallel execution of each population, significantly improving computation time. Many proposals are using multi-threaded, parallel, and distributed processing to increase the speedup of the execution time [5,6].

One of the critical points in this technique is communication between populations, since it has been observed in various studies that the exchange of possible solutions helps optimizations algorithms to improve their performance [7]. Communication has different aspects:

- A *speed* that defines how many solutions are able to be exchanged between sub-populations.
- A *policy* in charge of selecting which solutions should be replaced by those of coming from another sub-populations.
- An *interval* or gap that establishes the frequency with which interchanges between populations take place.
- A *connection topology* that specifies the exact way subpopulations communicate.

In this work, we focus only on the connection topology aspect of the communication, because
In this paper, we propose the two communication topologies to be implemented in a even-based distributed multi-swarm Particle Swarm Optimization (PSO) algorithm. These communication topologies follow a chain and a hypercube structure on a multi-swarm. We chose these topologies for their ability to be adapted to the architecture mentioned above. They can work without altering the optimization algorithm allowing a fair comparison with other communication methods.

This paper contains the following sections: We present state-of-the-art on multi-swarm optimization in Sect. 2. In Sect. 3, we present two variants of communication topologies, to be used in an event-based architecture we also present in the section. In Sect. 4, we describe the experimental setup and results; additionally, Sect. 5 presents the conclusions for this work.

2   State of the Art

Particle Swarm Optimization (PSO) is an optimization algorithm inspired by the collective behavior of some flocks of birds and schools of fish. It was introduced in 1995 by J. Kennedy and R. Eberhart, and since then it has undergone several improvements [8]. Since then, researchers have created different versions, aimed at different purposes, developed new applications in various areas, published many studies on the effects of various parameters, and proposed great variety algorithm variants [9]. A basic version of the PSO algorithm works with a population, called a swarm, of possible solutions, which are denominated particles. They "move" in the search space according to some simple rules derived from formulas.

The movements in the particles' search space are determined by their best known locations and by the best known location of the entire swarm. These locations are supposed to get better and they will guide the swarm's movements.

The process is repeated many times, so it is expected that solution that meets the requirements will eventually be discovered, although this may not happen [10].

Multi-swarm optimization is one of the most widely known variants of Particle Swarm Optimization (PSO), and it is based the creation of multiple swarms (or sub-swarm) instead of just one. The basic flow in a multi-swarm optimization is that each sub-swarm has its own specific region to concentrate. A specific diversification method decides where and when to locate and execute this sub-swarms.

For example, Wave of Swarm of Particles [11] uses a technique on the "collision" of particles. When the particles are close to each other, they are sent into new sub-swarms, preventing full convergence between the sub-swarms. Another examples is the Dynamic Multi-Swarm-Particle Swarm Optimizer [12] that rearranges the particles from the sub-swarms (when converged) into new ones periodically, so the new iteration of sub-swarms have the advantage of starting with particles from the previous one. Locust swarms [13] are founded on a "devour and go" strategy after a sub-swarm consumes or "devours" a small fraction of the search space an explorer is deployed to search for new regions making the sub-swarm move to the new promised location ("keep going").

In contrast to typical PSO swarms, sub-swarms are fed with information about previous swarms.

These could be the positions and velocities instead of having their initial parameters to be randomly selected. Generally speaking, the development of multi-swarm systems creates a new path of design options that who were not present at the time the original PSO emerged. These design decisions now have guidelines thanks to the numerous studies on the topic, for example, tow common options are the use of non-random initial positions and initial velocities for the particles in the subs-warms helping to better results, which is not the case for individual swarms [14].

A few number of this options can be reached by relatively independent sub-components that allow different approaches to this matter to be tested. For example, the multi-swarm system UMDA-PSO [15] applies a multi-swarm hybrid approach using a diverse combination of elements from particle swarm optimization, distribution estimation algorithm, and differential evolution.

There have been some papers focused in optimizing the communication between swarms, for example the survey in reference [16] has a collection of different investigations around this subject. For example El-Abd and Kamel talked over the multiple factors that can change the overall behavior of multiple joined swarms, some of this factors were the strategy and path of communications between swarms and the number sub-swarms. Then an experiment was made applying a circular topology of communications, the results demonstrated that this approach has an overall superior performance than using a simpler technique of sharing the global best of all the swarms [17].

Another example and the source of inspiration for this paper, is one of Yongming and Xiaoping, who presented a multi-population algorithm with a chain-like structure for parallel global numerical optimization. In this approximation a few changes where applied, like a dynamic neighborhood, in order to improve the parallel optimization [18].

In the next section, we present two variants of communication topologies, to be used in an event-based architecture for the implementation of distributed population-based optimization algorithms.

3   Proposed Method

Recently, there is an interest in cloud-native, event-based architectures suitable to run locally on a personal computer or in a cloud platform service. An event-based architecture uses events to trigger and communicate between services and processes. Using an event-based architecture, we intend to carry out a series of experiments to analyze the effect of changing the communication topology in a multi-population optimization algorithm's performance. Using this type of architecture with a multi-swarm optimization algorithm is a new approach. Therefore, there is an opportunity to find a substantial variation in the performance of such an optimization algorithm by changing the way the various swarms communicate to exchange information.

3.1   EvoSwarm

First, we briefly present the overall architecture of EvoSwarm, the platform in which we implemented the distributed algorithm.

EvoSwarm follows an event-based architecture, using message queues for interprocess communication. Messages consist of small populations or swarms that are consumed by worker processes that run a local PSO for a small number of iterations. After this, the resulting swarm is pushed to another message queue to be consumed by a migration process responsible for the communication (migration) between swarm messages kept in a buffer [19].

It is worth mentioning that this architecture can be implemented using various computers in a network or using virtualization, in work we used Docker containers. Here are some of the most important features that EvoSwarm brings to the user:

- Fully capable of scalability, since more computers can be added to the network in order to manage a more significant workload.
- Independence between processes, which means that any process in the structure is completely separated from the other ones allowing more work to be done at the same time.
- It is adaptable to any population-based optimizing algorithm.

The only change made to the original version of EvoSwarm [19] was the communication policy between the populations of the multi-swarm PSO.

3.2   Proposed Communication Topologies for EvoSwarm

In the original communication policy, the architecture waited until a minimum of three populations reached the migration component. These populations are sent to a process that combines the best half of each one with the others. For example, let us name the three populations A, B, and C, then a sort method is applied to each one (based on the quality of the solution). The sorted populations are now divided into halves in preparation for the merging process, now, with three new populations, the first one has the best half of A and B, the second has the best of B and C, and the third has the best of A and C. The last step is reinserting these new populations into a queue from which the PSO processes will retake them.

The first modification, in this case, is only on the merging process. To create a chained algorithm that affects every three arriving populations, we sort the three populations. The modification consists in that the populations are only allowed to share a few members of the elite. In this case, 10. Individuals are carried into a chain structure in which a population can receive only one way of the structure and shares in another.

The second variation for the EvoSwarm structure is a hypercube; we based this one on a paper in which this topology was applied to solve a multi-reservoir of water using a multi-population algorithm [20]. The name indicates this method has a cubic structure and can only function with eight populations or more. For this paper, we only need eight populations. Once the algorithm gets filled with eight populations, the migrations algorithm needs to assign each one a place in the hypercube structure.

The structure resembles a cube, and in every one of its vertices is one population. One thing that stands immediately is the capital P because only four populations have it. In this algorithm, we divided the hypercube into two dimensions. Moreover, depending on the iteration of the experiment, the exchange of solutions is restricted.

Every iteration of an experiment changes the mode in which the populations communicate with each other. For example, in the first iteration, the eight populations can only communicate with the others in the same dimension. In the second iteration, the opposite happens, allowing them to exchange information with a population outside that dimension. With eight vertices, only two exchanges are allowed, and for the experiments on this paper, only the best 10% of solutions migrate to another swarm.

4   Experimental Setup and Results

We implemented the migration policies in Python; for the PSO algorithm, we use the Evolopy library [21], as mentioned earlier in this paper, we use the same parameters for the PSO algorithm as the EvoSwarm paper (see Table 1).

Continuing with the configuration of the experiments, Table 2 presents the parameters used in EvoSwarm; these are for the 3 cases presented in this paper.

Table 1. Parameters PSO of Evolopy library

Parameters	Values
Vmax	6
Wmax	0.9
Wmin	0.2
C1	2
C2	2

Table 2. Parameters for EvoSwarm

Dimensions	Generations	Population size	Num. Experiments	Num. population created
10	50	70	30	10
20	66	100	30	10

4.1 Benchmark Functions

In order to run the optimization experiments, we selected ten functions from the COCO benchmark. We selected these functions because in our preliminary experiments, they showed performance variations as we changed the communication topology. Here are the ten functions:

- Function 1: Sphere.
- Function 2: Ellipsoidal separable.
- Function 3: Rastrigin separable.
- Function 9: Rosenbrock rotated.
- Function 10: Ellipsoidal.
- Function 15: Rastrigin.
- Function 17: Schaffer F7, condition 10.
- Function 18: Schaffer F7, condition 1000.
- Function 21: Gallagher 101 peaks.
- Function 22: Gallagher 21 peaks

The number given to each function comes from COCO. This means that any method using the benchmark can be compared against a great variety of optimization methods. The complete collection of functions, graphics, and equations can be reviewed in reference [22].

4.2 Experimental Results

We run the experiments in a single computer using a Ryzen 5 2600x CPU and 24 GB of ram in Windows 10 Professional 64 bits, using Docker Desktop version 2.5, running ten containers. We used Python version 3.5.7. We conducted each experiment separately 30 times. The time required for each run took about 7 h. In these experiments, we are not interested in the total time required to find a solution as the changes in the algorithm did not affect the running time. In this case, we are focused on the MSE of the best solution found with the same number of function evaluations.

In ten dimensions, there are three functions in which the original topology gives better results than the topologies we propose (shown in boldface). However, once we reach twenty dimensions, the original topology obtains the worst results. Overall the chain topology gives a better MSE in 20 dimensions, only having two cases with a lower MSE than the hypercube configuration. We can see that the standard deviation of the MSE obtained by the three options only varies in few cases. In particular, the function f_{10} was difficult for this algorithm and could not find a target in any run.

In the same table, we present the results of the statistical tests of comparing both topologies against the original migration. In this case, we use a Z statistical test with an α of 0.5, giving a critical value of 1.64. Underlined results have sufficient statistical evidence to have less MSE; this means that changing the communication topology can improve, in some cases, the performance of a multi-population optimization algorithm.

Table 3. Comparison between the MSE obtained from 30 runs. We show the best results in boldface. Also, we present the statistical comparison against the EvoSwarm method, with results underlined if they are significantly better than the rest.

Dimensions	Function	EvoSwarm MSE	Chain MSE	Hypercube MSE	EvoSwarm Stdev	Chain Stdev	Hypercube Stdev
10	1	4.78611E-09	**4.45791E-09**	4.52861E-09	3.3503E-09	3.27217E-09	3.25265E-09
10	2	**3.83054E-09**	4.1792E-09	4.65155E-09	2.35352E-09	2.86765E-09	2.9481E-09
10	3	2.352927573	<u>**0.537649443**</u>	<u>0.805637277</u>	2.881847604	1.543574882	1.663900202
10	9	0.49249742	0.2527938	**0.229809004**	0.983944824	0.152990827	0.109927138
10	10	<u>**250.1738327**</u>	430.5420728	374.4359744	228.3598149	527.2651437	323.3050765
10	15	14.66500256	<u>**12.050469416**</u>	13.33777036	6.840266769	5.391630829	5.860112176
10	17	0.0923583	**0.075762972**	0.087059177	0.16646265	0.155990531	0.17433065
10	18	0.524852914	0.506412719	**0.413659866**	0.633592264	0.467805944	0.382221237
10	21	0.329852279	0.237422927	**0.20667313**	0.621910649	0.481633605	0.390914491
10	22	0.692064149	**0.514782111**	0.57179096	0.577929599	0.719118705	0.650216016
20	1	0.03594249	5.55231E-09	**5.54663E-09**	0.196865099	2.9048E-09	2.52356E-09
20	2	5.64673E-09	5.49755E-09	**5.36566E-09**	2.31813F-09	2.54807E-09	2.98753E-09
20	3	12.082746	8.746638682	<u>**7.874205319**</u>	8.54691241	7.803681637	7.808562704
20	9	**11.10349719**	11.37025195	11.49485451	1.483577297	2.321860001	1.0945346
20	10	4994.888993	**4472.971044**	5805.968994	4632.673198	2316.255771	5624.624998
20	15	58.88102471	**53.54574023**	56.38870042	20.44460373	16.99626952	20.85090795
20	17	0.788958338	0.766878619	**0.764906251**	0.43605249	0.434587453	0.487783929
20	18	2.533386188	**2.255266883**	2.559019459	1.013613907	0.930554736	1.496684622
20	21	0.901706552	<u>**0.39256696**</u>	<u>0.395204608</u>	1.040801093	0.827425128	0.672288795
20	22	3.625232097	<u>**1.518287857**</u>	<u>1.650088133</u>	3.97000465	1.64832496	1.291540717

One of the aspects we can look at is if separability is exploited by the new communication policies. Essentially, functions 1 to 3 look at that kind of thing (Sphere, Ellipsoidal and Rastrigin). In this case there is not a clear evidence that happens; as a matter of fact, the only significantly better result occurs with the Chain MSE and Hypercube. This last one is significantly better both for 10 and 20 dimensions.

Function 9 (rotated Rosenbrock), which would give us a hint on whether the new policies can follow a long path, does not offer a significant variation over the original policy.

Function 10 (Ellipsoidal) is unimodal. The only significant difference is offered by the original EvoSwarm, gut this is diluted at higher dimensions.

The next set of functions are multimodal: F15, F17 and F18 offer slight and not significant at higher level, advantages for the new policies. There's a significant difference for the Chain policy at 10 dimensions, not any more at higher dimensions.

F21 and F22 are multimodal functions; in this case, Chain and Hypercube are significantly better, although only at higher dimensions.

In general, using these functions allowed us to characterize where different communication policies might offer any advantage over the baseline policy. We will try to draw some conclusions next.

5   Conclusions

Communication policies for multiswarm PSOs have seldom been explored in the literature, despite the influence they might have in the final result. This is why, in this research, we compared three communication methods between populations of a multi-swarm system to identify an advantage resulting from these changes: EvoSwarm, Chain and Hypercube. These three methods differ mainly in the number of connections every population is going to have.

However, the experiments show that difference among results obtained by the different communication policies is not significant in most cases, but we obtained the best results at higher dimensions. Results show a weak evidence that restricting communications for higher number of dimensions might be positive, over all in multimodal functions, and when the problem space is more deceptive, as is the case with function f_3 Rastrigin Separable. In general, these are problems where the need to keep diversity high is stronger, and restriction of communication is a step in that direction. EvoSwarm, as a matter of fact, does also restrict communication, so maybe the baseline for comparison should have been a different method, using either total restriction in communications (via totally independent swarms) or total communication (via random or panmictic policy).

We should take into account that in this case, we only changed the type of communication between sub-swarms, which is only one of the policies that we can alter in this type of system. Different communication policies might need fine-tuning of other kind of parameters, to keep the exploitation-exploration balance in check; this has not been done extensively in this paper, and might be a future line of work.

In future works, other policies can be altered at the same time to see what impact they will have. With the results obtained, we can infer that the change to the communication method is relevant for this type of system in specific situations. The alteration of the different work policies in multi-swarm systems could lead to greater specialization of these in specific scenarios. We could test, for instance, adaptive policies, or even changing the number and size of swarms so that exploitation can be maintained at a higher clip in some cases. These are all lines of work that will be explored in the future.

Acknowledgment. This paper has been supported in part by projects DeepBio (TIN2017-85727-C4-2-P) and TecNM Project 11356.21-P.

References

1. Cantú-Paz, E., et al.: A survey of parallel genetic algorithms. Calculateurs Paralleles, Reseaux et Systems Repartis **10**(2), 141–171 (1998)
2. Song, H., et al.: Multitasking multi-swarm optimization, pp. 1937–1944, June 2019. https://doi.org/10.1109/CEC.2019.8790009
3. Guohua, W., et al.: Differential evolution with multi-population based ensemble of mutation strategies. Inf. Sci. **329**, 329–345 (2016)
4. Changhe, L., Trung, N., Ming, Y., Shengxiang, Y., Sanyou, Z.: Multi-population methods in unconstrained continuous dynamic environments: the challenges. Inf. Sci. **296**, 95–118 (2015)
5. El-Abd, M., Kamel, M.S.: A taxonomy of cooperative particle swarm optimizers. Int. J. Comput. Intell. Res. **4**, 137–144 (2008)
6. Nowostawski, M., Poli, R.: Parallel genetic algorithm taxonomy. In: Third International Conference on Knowledge-Based Intelligent Information Engineering Systems. Adelaide, SA, Australia (1999)
7. Blackwell, T., Kennedy, J.: Impact of communication topology in particle swarm optimization. IEEE Trans. Evol. Comput. **23**(4), 689–702 (2018). https://doi.org/10.1109/TEVC.2018.2880894
8. Kennedy, J., Eberhart, R.: Particle swarm optimization. In: Proceedings of ICNN 1995 - International Conference on Neural Networks, Perth, WA, Australia (1995)
9. Wang, D., Tan, D., Liu, L.: Particle swarm optimization algorithm: and overview. Soft Comput. **22**, 387–408 (2018)
10. Zhang, Y.-D., Wang, S., Ji, G.: A comprehensive survey on particle swarm optimization algorithm and its applications. Mat. Probl. Eng. **2015**, 1–38 (2015). https://doi.org/10.1155/2015/931256
11. Hendtlass, T.: WoSP: a multi-optima particle swarm algorithm. In: IEEE Congress on Evolutionary Computation, vol. 1, pp. 727–734 (2005). https://doi.org/10.1109/CEC.2005.1554755
12. Zhao, S.-Z., Liang, J., Suganthan, P., Tasgetiren, M.: Dynamic multi-swarm particle swarm optimizer with local search for large scale global optimization. In: IEEE Congress on Evolutionary Computation, pp. 3845–3852 (2008). https://doi.org/10.1109/CEC.2008.4631320
13. Chen, S.: Locust swarms - a new multi-optima search technique. In: Proceedings of the IEEE Congress on Evolutionary Computation, pp. 1745–1752 (2009). https://doi.org/10.1109/CEC.2009.4983152
14. Chen, S., Montgomery, J.: Selection strategies for initial positions and initial velocities in multi-optima particle swarms. In: Genetic and Evolutionary Computation Conference, pp. 53–60 (2011). https://doi.org/10.1145/2001576.2001585
15. Bolufé Rühler, A., Stephen, C.: Multi-swarm hybrid for multi-modal optimization. In: IEEE Congress on Evolutionary Computation, pp. 1–8 (2012). https://doi.org/10.1109/CEC.2012.6256566
16. Ma, H., Shigen, S., Mei, Y., Zhile, Y., Minrui, F., Huiyu, Z.: Multi-population techniques in nature inspired optimization algorithms: a comprehensive survey. Swarm Evol. Comput. **44**, 365–387 (2019)

17. El-Abd, M., Kamel, M.: Factors governing the behavior of multiple cooperating swarms. In: Proceedings of the 7th Annual Conference on Genetic and Evolutionary Computation, Washington (2005)
18. Yongming, L., Xiaoping, Z.: Multi-population co-genetic algorithm with double chain-like agents structure for parallel global numerical optimization. Appl. Intell. **32**, 292–310 (2010)
19. García-Valdez, J.-M., Merelo-Guervós, J.-J.: A modern, event-based architecture for distributed evolutionary algorithms. In: Proceedings of the Genetic and Evolutionary Computation Conference Companion, pp. 233–234 (2018)
20. Cheng, L., Chang, F.-J.: Applying a real-coded multi-population genetic algorithm to multi-reservoir operation. Hydrol. Proc. **21**, 688–698 (2006)
21. Faris, H., Aljarah, I., Mirjalili, S., Castillo, P.A., Merelo, J.J.: EvoloPY: an open-source nature-inspired optimization framework in python. In: Proceedings of the 8th International Joint Conference on Computational Intelligence, vol. 1, pp. 171–177 (2016)
22. Hansen, N., Auger, A., Finck, S., Ros, R.: Real-parameter black-box optimization benchmarking 2010: experimental setup. Research Report RR-7215, INRIA, March 2010. https://hal.inria.fr/inria-00462481

Solving Dynamical Systems Using Windows of Sliding Subproblems

Angel Fernando Garcia Contreras[✉] and Martine Ceberio

The University of Texas at El Paso, El Paso, TX 79968, USA
afgarciacontreras@miners.utep.edu

Abstract. Phenomena that change over time are abundant in nature. Dynamical systems, composed of differential equations, are used to model them. In some cases, analytical solutions exist that provide an exact description of the system's behavior. Otherwise we use numerical approximations: we discretize the original problem over time, where each state of the system at any discrete time moment depends on previous/subsequent states. This process may yield large systems of equations. Efficient tools exist to solve dynamical systems, but might not be well suited for certain types of problems. For example, Runge-Kutta-based solution techniques do not easily handle parameters' uncertainty, although inherent to real world measurements. If the problem has multiple solutions, such methods usually provide only one. When they cannot find a solution, it is not know whether none exists or it failed to find one. Interval methods, on the other hand, provide guaranteed numerical computations. If a solution exists, it will be found. Interval methods for dynamical systems fall into two main categories: step-based methods (fast but too conservative with overestimation for large systems) and constraint-solving techniques (better at controlling overestimation but usually much slower). In this article, we propose an approach that "slices" large systems into smaller, overlapping ones that are solved using constraint-solving techniques. Our goal is to reduce the computation time and control overestimation, at the expense of solving multiple smaller problems instead of a larger one. We share promising preliminary experimental results.

1 Introduction

Phenomena that change over time are abundant in nature. We model their behavior using dynamical systems, i.e., differential equations to describe how they change over time. For some real life problems, analytical solutions exist that provide an exact description of the behavior. For many other problems, such solutions do not exist, so we use numerical approximations: we *discretize* the original continuous problem over time, where each intermediate state of the system at each discrete time depends on previous and/or subsequent states. This process may result in a very large set of equations, depending on the level of granularity that is sought.

There exist many efficient and useful tools to solve dynamical systems, which might not be well-suited for some types of problems. For example, Runge-Kutta-based solution techniques do not easily handle uncertainty on the parameters,

© Springer Nature Switzerland AG 2021
J. C. Figueroa-García et al. (Eds.): WEA 2021, CCIS 1431, pp. 13–24, 2021.
https://doi.org/10.1007/978-3-030-86702-7_2

although inherent to real world measurements. Solutions are heavily reliant on an initial set of parameters. When a problem has multiple solutions, such methods do not identify how many solutions there are or whether the found solution is the best based on some criteria. When a solution cannot be found, it is not clear whether the solving technique failed to find one or none exists.

In our research, we use interval-based methods [9,10], which provide guaranteed numerical computations. These techniques guarantee that if a solution exists, it will be found, and that if none exists, it will report this with certainty. There exist two main categories of interval-based methods to solve dynamical systems: *step-based methods* that generate an explicit system of equations one discretized state at a time, and *constraint-solving techniques* that solve the entire system of implicitly discretized equations. Step-based methods are fast, but on complex systems (either because they are simulating longer times or the differential system is very non-linear), their output provides overestimated solution ranges. Constraint-solving techniques can better control the overestimation by working on the entire system at once, but will take considerably longer to report a reasonable solution range.

In this work, we introduce a heuristic approach based on the structure of a dynamical system as a constraint satisfaction problem, solving multiple smaller overlapping sub-problems. We define the parameters that determine how big the sub-problems are and how much they overlap. We test the effect that these parameters have on the quality of the interval solution and the total execution time to solve the given problem, and compare the performance against interval-based dynamical systems solvers. We conclude that our heuristic shows promise.

2   Background

2.1   Dynamical Systems

Dynamical systems model how a phenomenon changes over time. In particular, we are interested in continuous dynamical systems.

Definition 1. A continuous *dynamical system* is a pair (D, f) with $D \subseteq \mathbb{R}^n$ called a *domain* and $f : D \times T \to \mathbb{R}^n$ a function from pairs $(x, t) \in D \times T$ to $\mathbb{R}^n$.

Definition 2. By a *trajectory* of a dynamical system, we mean a function $x : [t_0, \infty) \to D$ for which $\frac{dx}{dt} = f(x, t)$.

To obtain the state equations of a dynamical system, we *integrate* its differential equations. In this research, we focus on *numerical methods* that *approximate* the actual solution. A key advantage of these methods is that they can provide good results even if the exact solution cannot be found through other methods. Their drawback is that they are not perfect and always have a margin of error that must be included in the computation. Fortunately, this error can be minimized by choosing the right type of numerical method for the problem and tweaking the parameters that generate the approximation.

2.2 Traditional Methods

Numerical methods to solve dynamical systems are usually classified in two general categories based on the type of approximation they make for the integral: explicit and implicit methods. In *explicit* methods, the state equation for a specific state involves the values of one or more previous states. To solve this kind of problem, it is possible to simply evaluate each discretized state equation in order, to obtain the values for all states in succession, as each state equation already has the values it needs from previous states. *Implicit* methods involve past and future states in their discretization. These equations cannot be solved by simple successive evaluation. They are often solved using root-finding methods, such as Newton-Rhapson. Both types of methods are used to solve dynamical system problems, either separately or synergistically.

2.3 Interval Methods

An interval is defined as: $X = [\underline{X}, \overline{X}] = \{x \in \mathbb{R} \mid \underline{X} \leq x \leq \overline{X}; \ \underline{X}, \ \overline{X} \in \mathbb{R}\}$.

Intervals represent all values between their infimum $\underline{X}$ and supremum $\overline{X}$. In particular, we can use them to represent uncertain quantities. We manipulate them in computations through the rules of interval arithmetic, naively posed as follows: $X \diamond Y = \{x \diamond y, \text{ where } x \in X, y \in Y\}$, where $\diamond$ is any arithmetic operator, and combining intervals always results in another interval. However, since some operations, like division, could yield a union of intervals (e.g., division by an interval that contains 0), the combination of intervals involves an extra operation, called the hull, denoted by $\square$, which returns one interval enclosure of a set of real values. We obtain: $X \diamond Y = \square \{x \diamond y, \text{ where } x \in X, y \in Y\}$.

We can extend this property to any function $f : \mathbb{R}^n \to \mathbb{R}$ with one or more interval parameters:

$$f(X_1, \ldots, X_n) \subseteq \square \{f(x_1, \ldots, x_n), \text{ where } x_1 \in X_1, \ldots, x_n \in X_n\}$$

where $f(X_1, \ldots, X_n)$ represents the range of f over the interval domain $X_1 \times \ldots \times X_n$, and $\square \{f(x_1, \ldots, x_n), \text{ where } x_1 \in X_1, \ldots, x_n \in X_n\}$ represents the narrowest interval enclosing this range. Computing the exact range of f over intervals is very hard, so instead we use surrogate approximations. We call these surrogates *interval extensions*. An interval extension F of function f must satisfy the following property:

$$f(X_1, \ldots, X_n) \subseteq F(X_1, \ldots, X_n)$$

Interval extensions aim to approximate the range of the original real-valued function. In general, different interval extensions can return a different range for f while still fulfilling the above property. For more information about intervals and interval computations in general, see [9, 10].

Step-Based Methods for Solving Dynamical Systems. Such algorithms use explicit discretization schemes, such as Taylor polynomials or Runge-Kutta, that must be evaluated to provide a guaranteed enclosure that includes the discretization error at every step. The solvers implement interval evaluation schemes that reduce overestimation. For example, VSPODE [7] uses Taylor polynomials for discretization and Taylor models [1,8] for evaluation; DynIBEX [4] uses Runge-Kutta discretization and evaluates its functions using affine arithmetic [5,12].

Interval Constraint-Solving Techniques. The methods used to solve a dynamical system using explicit discretization do not work for implicit discretization. We need to solve the entire system. We can do this if we treat the state equations as a system of equality constraints and the dynamical system as an interval Constraint Satisfaction Problem (CSP):

Definition 3. An interval *constraint satisfaction problem* is given by the tuple $P = (X, \boldsymbol{X}, C)$, where $X = \{x_1, \ldots, x_n\}$ is a set of n variables, with associated interval domains $\boldsymbol{X} = \{\boldsymbol{x_1}, \ldots, \boldsymbol{x_n}\}$ and a set of m constraints $C = \{c_1, \ldots, c_m\}$

The initial interval domain $\boldsymbol{X}$ represents the entire space in which a real-valued solution to the CSP might be found. With intervals, we want to find an *enclosure* of said solution. This enclosure $\boldsymbol{X^*}$ needs to be narrow: the differences between the infimum and supremum of all interval domains in $\boldsymbol{X^*}$ must be less than a parameter ϵ, representing the *accuracy* of the solution's enclosure. If the entire domain is inconsistent, it will be wholly discarded, which means that the problem has no solution.

An interval constraint solver attempts to find a narrow $\boldsymbol{X^*}$ through consistency techniques. *Consistency* is a property of CSPs, in which the domain does not violate any constraint. For interval CSPs, we want domains that are at least *partially consistent*: if they do not entirely satisfy the constraints, they may contain a solution. Figure 1 shows a visualization of the general concept behind contraction using consistency. Figure 1a shows the evaluation of a function $f(x)$ over an interval $\boldsymbol{x}$, represented by the gray rectangle $y = f(\boldsymbol{x})$. This function is part of a constraint $f(x) = -4$, whose solutions are found in the domain of $\boldsymbol{x}$; however, this interval is too wide, so it must be contracted. In this case, the range of $f(\boldsymbol{x}) \geq -4.0$ can be discarded, which creates a new interval value for the range of $f(x)$, or y', which can be *propagated* to remove portions of $\boldsymbol{x}$ that are not consistent with y'. This creates the contracted domain x', which is a narrower enclosure of the solutions of $f(x) = -4$, as shown in Fig. 1b.

Contraction via consistency is just part of how interval constraint solver techniques find narrow enclosures of solutions to systems of constraints. For example, the constraint $f(x) = -4$ shown in Fig. 1 has two solutions enclosed inside the domain $\boldsymbol{x'}$, but we need the individual solutions. Interval constraint solvers use an algorithm called *branch-and-prune*. The "prune" part of the algorithm is achieved through contraction via consistency; when "pruning" is not enough to find the most narrow enclosure that satisfies the constraints, the algorithm "branches" by dividing the domain $\boldsymbol{X}$ into two adjacent subdomains by splitting the interval value of one of its variables through a midpoint $m(\boldsymbol{x}) = \frac{\underline{\boldsymbol{x}} + \overline{\boldsymbol{x}}}{2}$. These two new sub-boxes, $\boldsymbol{X_L} = \{\boldsymbol{x_0}, \ldots, [\underline{x_i}, m(\boldsymbol{x_i})], \ldots, \boldsymbol{x_n}\}$ and $\boldsymbol{X_U} = \{\boldsymbol{x_0}, \ldots, [m(\boldsymbol{x_i}), \overline{x_i}], \ldots, \boldsymbol{x_n}\}$, are then processed using the same algorithm. This means that all sub-boxes are put in a queue of sub-boxes, as each sub-boxes and be further "branched" into smaller sub-boxes.

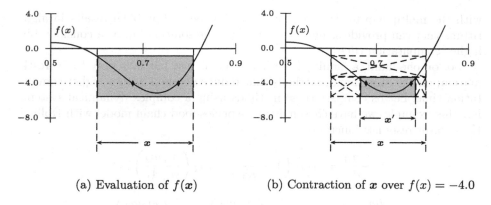

(a) Evaluation of $f(x)$ (b) Contraction of x over $f(x) = -4.0$

Fig. 1. Visual example of interval domain contraction

Interval constraint solvers such as RealPaver [6] and IbexSolve [2,3] solve systems of constraints. To solve a dynamical system, we need to generate all required state equations, and provide an initial domain containing all possible state values. While interval solvers can provide good results, when system are too large, they can be slow to find a reasonable solution. For large systems, there have been attempts at making them easier to solve, including generating an alternative reduced-order model [13], and focusing on a subset of constraints at a time [11].

2.4 Step-Based or Constraint-Based?

Step-based methods (VSPODE, DynIbex) work well, up to a point. They rely on a dynamically-computed step size aimed at minimizing the error intrinsic to the approximation. As these are interval-based methods, this means they compute an enclosure of the solution that incorporates the approximation error. This error introduces a small amount of overestimation into the solution. After computing multiple states, each with their respective computed step size h, the overestimation that accumulates at every iteration can become too large to be useful in computing a new h. If the solver cannot compute a new h, the simulation stops, even before reaching the expected final state at t_f.

Solving a full system using interval constraint-solving techniques can explore multiple realizations of the system with a desired width for the enclosure. Every state equation is evaluated multiple times, potentially increasing the contraction of the initial domain for the state variables involved. Even with a static value of h for all states, implicit approximations used increase the accuracy of the approximation.

The main reason why step-based methods are often preferred is simple: interval constraint-solving techniques are slower. Interval-based domain contractors evaluate each equation multiple times and the branch-and-prune-based algorithms used within constraint solvers create subproblems exponentially based on the number of variables. The exponential amount of subproblems combined with the multiple evaluations of each equation per subproblem results in algorithms that can provide strong guarantees on the solution but at a considerably higher computation time.

So, on one hand, a family of methods that is fast but falls pray to overestimation; on the other hand, methods that reduce domains with a higher computation time. Let us compare these methods using a complex dynamical system. For this example, we have chosen a three-species food chain model with Holling II predator response functions:

$$\frac{dm_1}{dt} = r_1 m_1 \left(1 - \frac{m_1}{K_1}\right) - a_{12} \left(\frac{m_1 m_2}{m_1 A_1}\right)$$

$$\frac{dm_2}{dt} = -d_2 m_2 + a_{21} \left(\frac{m_1 m_2}{m_1 A_1}\right) - a_{23} \left(\frac{m_2 m_3}{m_2 A_2}\right)$$

$$\frac{dm_3}{dt} = -d_3 m_3 + a_{32} \left(\frac{m_2 m_3}{m_2 A_2}\right)$$

We ran this problem with VSPODE, DynIBEX, and IBEX. We used same parameters for the system, the best settings for their respective algorithms (i.e. VSPODE and DynIBEX use dynamic step size, DynIBEX uses its most accurate Range-Kutta discretization). For IBEX, we generated a set of state equations using trapezoidal discretization, with a step size of $h = 0.01$. The dynamical system as solved up to $t_f = \{40, 100\}$ for a total of $N = 4000, 10000$ states, respectively. Figure 2 shows the plots of the solution for VSPODE and DynIBEX; there is no plot for the results of IBEX, as of the time of writing, the solver has been working for about three weeks without returning a single solution.

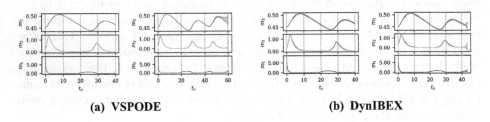

(a) VSPODE   (b) DynIBEX

Fig. 2. State enclosures VSPODE and DynIBEX when $t_f = \{40, 100\}$

The plots for $t_f = 40$ look like a single line, but actually represent narrow ranges. This is more evident in the $t_f = 100$ plots, in which overestimation starts separating the lower and upper bounds. The results for these plots do not reach all the way to $t_f = 100$: at some point between $t = 40$ and $t = 60$, the large overestimation causes these solvers to become unable to dynamically compute a new step-size h, and the solving process stops. This shows an area of opportunity: *can we find a way to reduce that overestimation without an excessive cost in computation time?* How can we apply the knowledge of one type technique to the other in order to reduce their respective flaws? In this article, we explore implementing a heuristics that improves the execution time of interval constraint-solving techniques while maintaining accuracy.

3 Problem Statement and Proposed Approach

We want to reduce the computation time and increase the accuracy of interval-based dynamical system solvers. There are instances in which a decision-maker needs accuracy under uncertainty, fast. For example, if they need to recompute the parameters of a problem on-the-fly, after an event causes the state of the problem to change dramatically and with some degree of uncertainty. Existing tools can already produce good results, often at a cost: either the method is fast but has less accuracy, or its accuracy increases at the expense of additional and potentially prohibitive computation time [14].

We believe that combining ideas from step-based methods and interval constraint solvers can yield better solutions to dynamical systems in a reasonable amount of time. In this work, we outline a preliminary approach, focused on re-examining how an interval constraint solver works through the state equations of a dynamical system: a heuristic that takes advantage of the problem's structure to speed up the solving process.

The idea is to take advantage of the structure in a dynamical system (specifically, an *initial value problem*) to create and solve subproblems made of subsets of *contiguous state variables* and their respective equations. We take the state variables $X_{\text{sub}} = \{x\,(j),\ldots x\,(j + N_w)\}$ with domains $\{\boldsymbol{x}\,(j),\ldots,\boldsymbol{x}\,(j + N_w)\}$, along the following set of state equations as a system of constraints C_{sub}:

$$g_i\,(x\,(j),\ldots x\,(j + N_w)\,, t_i) = f\,(x\,(i)\,, t_i, h)\,,\ \forall i \in \{j,\ldots j + N_w\}$$

where function g_i is a discretization of $\frac{dx}{dt}$ at t_i. We call this subproblem $P_{\text{sub}} = (X_{\text{sub}}, C_{\text{sub}})$ a *window* of size N_w. Our technique aims to speed up the computation process of interval constraint solvers by sequentially creating and solving a series of subproblems of size N_w.

The first subproblem involves the initial conditions of the problem. However, we cannot treat subsequent subproblems as smaller initial value problems, with the initial conditions taken from the last state of the previous subproblem. When doing this, we treat the new subproblem as an independent initial value problem and lose the trajectory created by the values of the states from the previous subproblem.

Our solution is to transfer multiple state values between subproblems. Solving the k-th subproblem $P_k = (X_k, C_k)$ yields a reduced domain X_k^* representing N_w states, from t_j to t_{j+N_k}. For the next subproblem, $P_{k+1} = (X_{k+1}, C_{k+1})$, we take the last o interval values of X_k^* and use them as the initial domain for the *first o* values of X_{k+1}:

$$\{\boldsymbol{x}_{k+1}\,(1),\ldots,\boldsymbol{x}_{k+1}\,(o)\} = \{\boldsymbol{x}_k\,(N_w - o),\ldots,\boldsymbol{x}_k\,(N_w)\}$$

We then solve subproblem P_{k+1} using interval constraint-solving techniques, yielding a new reduced domain used to repeat the process again. We call o the *overlap* between subproblem *windows* of size N_w. Figure 3 shows a graphical representation of how o states are transferred from one subproblem to the next.

With interval constraint solvers, a series of subproblems with a smaller number of variables is faster to solve than one with more variables: the number of subproblems generated from domain division is reduced, which speeds up the overall process. We want to find out the impact that N_w and o have in the process, both in terms of execution time, but also on the quality of said solution. Our hypothesis is that smaller sizes of N_w will be faster but with greater imation. Regarding o, we believe smaller sizes will have a similar effect.

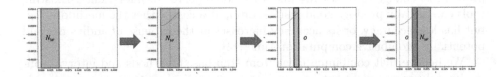

Fig. 3. Graphical plot of overlap transfer

4   Experimental Results and Analysis

4.1   Methodology

We compare the sliding windows heuristic against existing methods to solve dynamical systems using intervals (we chose VSPODE and DynIBEX), with the same three-species food chain system, with the same parameters, step size $h = 0.01$, solving up to $t_f = \{40, 100\}$. This creates two different problems to compare for: a problem with $N = 4000$ discrete times, with one state per species or a system of 12000 equations; and a problem with $N = 10000$ discrete times and 30000 equations.

We consider three metrics to compare the sliding windows heuristic against existing methods:

- *Quality of the solution (Quality)*. The solution of a given dynamical system found by an interval-based solver is given as interval values that enclose the real solutions. Due to the overestimation inherent in interval computations, the boundaries of this interval might not be a perfectly narrow enclosure. This metric is the max interval width across all state values. As we want the most narrow enclosures possible, the closer this value is to 0, the better quality the solution has
- *Total execution time (Execution time)*. The total computation time spent by each specific algorithm/solver, in seconds. This is a comparison metric for methods that provide similar results: if two methods provide equivalent overall quality, the faster is preferable. However, a method that provides wider enclosures but takes considerably less computation time might be preferable to a potential decision maker's problem (i.e. near real-time systems).

– *States until overestimation (S. Over)*. In interval computations, overestimation is inherent. When re-using interval quantities with overestimation in interval computations, the overestimation across different interval values might be compounded. When using interval computations to solve dynamical systems, the first discretized states will be narrower than states further in the simulation's future. This metric represents the first state in the simulation at which overestimation becomes too large; we consider an interval state value to be overestimated if the supremum of its interval value is 10% above its midpoint. For this metric, if a solution has overestimation, a value that is closer to t_f is better.

We also aim to explore how the sliding windows parameters affect the solution quality and execution time. We explored the following parameters/values: the *window size*: $N_w = \{20, 50\}$ the *overlap*: expressed as a percentage of N_w, $o = \{30\%, 50\%, 70\%\}$.

We implemented the sliding heuristic using the default solver in IBEX to solve each individual subproblem. We set the default solver to contract domains into solutions of width 10^{-8}, to stop the solving process after 900 s, and finally, if multiple solutions are found, we take the hull that encloses them.

4.2 Experiments

Figure 4 show the plots for all the experiments using sliding windows. Table 1 shows the comparison of metrics for DynIBEX and VSPODE against the different variations of the sliding algorithm.

4.3 Results Analysis

As shown in the metrics of Table 1, there is value for the "States until overestimation" metric any of the experiments using our slide heuristic on $t_f = 40$ because there is no overestimation up to that point – all the states are narrow, as seen in the "Quality" column.

Regarding the heuristic parameters, based on our experimental results, we conclude that, for the food chain problem, the size of the window N_w does not have a significant impact in the width of the obtained solution, though with a larger value for N_w, there is a slight improvement on the number of narrow states, as seen in the "States until overestimation" column for $t_f = 100$. The main drawback is that it requires a significantly longer computation time. Regarding o_w, its influence on the narrowness is similar to N_w's. In the results for up to $t_f = 40$, there is no significant difference in the quality of the solution, only on the execution time.

The solutions obtained by our heuristic are more relevant when compared with the solutions from other interval-based solvers. For the food chain problem, our heuristic has a later "state until overestimation" than the other two methods. This means that the slide heuristic, in all its variants, manages to return a solution that remains narrow for a longer number of states.

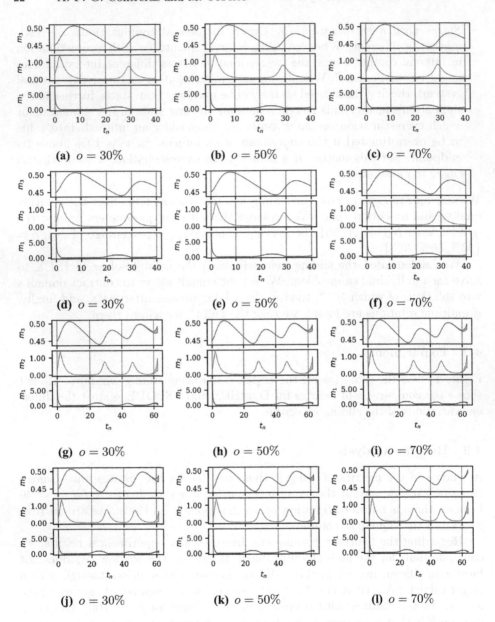

Fig. 4. (a,b,c) Plots for the sliding windows with $N_w = 20$ and $t_f = 40$. (d,e,f) Plots for the sliding windows with $N_w = 50$ and $t_f = 40$. (g,h,i) Plots for the sliding windows with $N_w = 20$ and $t_f = 100$. (j,k,l) Plots for the sliding windows with $N_w = 50$ and $t_f = 100$.

Table 1. Table of metrics

Solver	Problem 1 ($t_f = 40$)			Problem 2($t_f = 100$)		
	Quality	Exec. time	S. Over	Quality	Exec. time	S. Over
VSPODE	1.0000	3189.0619	29.09	1.5848	5351.2794	29.09
DynIBEX	0.4879	30.6470	1.50	1.1136	57.8751	1.50
$N_w = 20, o = 30\%$	6.1330E-04	313.6700	–	0.7437	741.1903	49.22
$N_w = 20, o = 50\%$	5.6379E-04	459.5741	–	0.7341	1273.4984	49.98
$N_w = 20, o = 70\%$	5.1991E-04	934.7888	–	0.7282	1346.8824	51.16
$N_w = 50, o = 30\%$	2.5693E-04	1856.3104	–	0.5853	3149.8939	50.73
$N_w = 50, o = 50\%$	2.1312E-04	2454.8584	–	0.6157	5124.8888	53.13
$N_w = 50, o = 70\%$	1.9722E-04	3258.1111	–	0.7016	5636.2485	61.64

DynIBEX is fast, but the intermediate results it reports are not as narrow, as seen in Fig. 2. Between VSPODE and our heuristic, there are two main differences: the rate at which the overestimation increases after surpassing the expected max width, and the time it takes to reach that solution. Our heuristic with a small size of N_w is faster, with a slower increase in overestimation than VSPODE. It is possible that this be due to the differences between the discretization schemes, and the current "simplified" discretization in our heuristic. Even when considering this, the similar solution quality with the faster performance shows that our approach is promising.

5   Conclusions and Future Work

Based on the results we presented, the sliding windows heuristic shows promise in providing narrower results than step-based interval solvers. It computes solutions faster than VSPODE, given the right combination of parameters N_w and o. Increasing the window size N_w produces results that will not reach overestimation until later, at the expense of much greater computational time. Increasing the overlap o has a similar effect, though not as pronounced.

We plan to further explore the potential of this technique by applying and comparing it with other challenging non-linear problems. We are looking into experimenting with different discretization schemes to reduce the error. Finally, we plan to examine how these techniques fare against other approaches that reduce the computational complexity, such as reduced order modeling.

References

1. Berz, M., Makino, K.: Verified integration of odes and flows using differential algebraic methods on high-order Taylor models. Reliable Comput. 4(4), 361–369 (1998)
2. Chabert, G.: Ibex, an interval-based explorer (2007)

3. Chabert, G., Jaulin, L.: Contractor programming. Artif. Intell. **173**(11), 1079–1100 (2009)
4. dit Sandretto, J.A., Chapoutot, A.: Validated explicit and implicit Runge-Kutta methods. Reliable Comput. **22**(1), 79–103 (2016)
5. Goubault, E., Putot, S.: Under-approximations of computations in real numbers based on generalized affine arithmetic. In: Nielson, H.R., Filé, G. (eds.) SAS 2007. LNCS, vol. 4634, pp. 137–152. Springer, Heidelberg (2007). https://doi.org/10. 1007/978-3-540-74061-2_9
6. Granvilliers, L., Benhamou, F.: Algorithm 852: RealPaver: an interval solver using constraint satisfaction techniques. ACM Trans. Math. Softw. (TOMS) **32**(1), 138–156 (2006)
7. Lin, Y., Stadtherr, M.A.: Validated solutions of initial value problems for parametric odes. Appl. Numer. Math. **57**(10), 1145 (2007)
8. Makino, K., Berz, M.: Taylor models and other validated functional inclusion methods. Int. J. Pure Appl. Math. **4**(4), 379–456 (2003)
9. Moore, R.E., Kearfott, R.B., Cloud, M.J.: Introduction to interval analysis. SIAM (2009)
10. Moore, R.E., Moore, R.: Methods and Applications of Interval Analysis, vol. 2. SIAM (1979)
11. Olumoye, O., Throneberry, G., Garcia, A., Valera, L., Abdelkefi, A., Ceberio, M.: Solving large dynamical systems by constraint sampling. In: Figueroa-García, J.C., Duarte-González, M., Jaramillo-Isaza, S., Orjuela-Cañon, A.D., Díaz-Gutierrez, Y. (eds.) WEA 2019. CCIS, vol. 1052, pp. 3–15. Springer, Cham (2019). https://doi. org/10.1007/978-3-030-31019-6_1
12. Rump, S.M., Kashiwagi, M.: Implementation and improvements of affine arithmetic. Nonlinear Theory Appl. IEICE **6**(3), 341–359 (2015)
13. Valera, L., Garcia, A., Gholamy, A., Ceberio, M., Florez, H.: Towards predictions of large dynamic systems' behavior using reduced-order modeling and interval computations. In: Proceedings of the 2017 IEEE International Conference on Systems, Man, and Cybernetics (SMC), pp. 345–350. IEEE (2017)
14. Valera, L., Contreras, A.G., Ceberio, M.: "On-the-fly" parameter identification for dynamic systems control, using interval computations and reduced-order modeling. In: Melin, P., Castillo, O., Kacprzyk, J., Reformat, M., Melek, W. (eds.) NAFIPS 2017. AISC, vol. 648, pp. 293–299. Springer, Cham (2018). https://doi.org/10. 1007/978-3-319-67137-6_33

Landslide Susceptibility Model by Means of Remote Sensing Images and AutoML

Diego Renza[1]($\boxtimes$) (iD), Elsa Adriana Cárdenas[1], Carlos Marcelo Jaramillo[1],
Serena Sarah Weber[2], and Estibaliz Martinez[3]

[1] Universidad Militar Nueva Granada, Bogotá, Colombia
{diego.renza,elsa.cardenas}@unimilitar.edu.co
[2] Universidad Católica de Manizales, Manizales, Colombia
sweber@ucm.edu.co
[3] Universidad Politécnica de Madrid, España, Spain
emartinez@fi.upm.es

Abstract. Hydrometeorological phenomena, including mass movements, are a frequent threat that can generate a great impact at different levels. In order to estimate the susceptibility to mass movements, this work contains a new proposal to estimate the susceptibility to mass movements using a supervised learning algorithm designed using AutoML (Automated machine learning). Pixel-level information from Sentinel-2 multispectral images was used to train the model, and an expert's susceptibility map was used as labels.

Keywords: Landslide · Susceptibility · AutoML · Autokeras

1 Introduction

Hydrometeorological phenomena, including mass movements, are one of the most frequent hazards that cause a large number of deaths and damage to infrastructure around the world. Particularly in Colombia, 88% of disasters are associated with the occurrence of this type of events, where about 14% of the affected houses, as well as 66% of deaths are associated with mass movements [16].

Therefore, in order to mitigate the effects generated by the occurrence of these events and to carry out a more efficient management of the territory, several types of methodologies have been proposed to assess the susceptibility to landslides, whose application depends on aspects related to the type of movements, the scale of work, the information available and the level of experience of those performing these analyses.

The main methods used in the assessment of mass movements described by [6] include Landslide susceptibility maps based on a combination of geological, topographical and land-cover conditions, inventory-based and knowledge driven methods, quantitative data-driven methods and physically based models. The heuristic method involves the direct intervention of experts to determine the susceptibility in the field or from geological and geomorphological information

J. C. Figueroa-García et al. (Eds.): WEA 2021, CCIS 1431, pp. 25–37, 2021.
https://doi.org/10.1007/978-3-030-86702-7_3

of the terrain, using GIS (Geographic Information System) tools for the elaboration of the final map. There are also bivariate, multivariate and artificial neural network-based statistical methods, as well as physical methods for assessing susceptibility to mass movement obtained from modeling slope failure processes.

Several of the studies carried out involve the use of techniques such as remote sensing. Techniques used include visual interpretation and digital analysis of aerial photographs and satellite images [3,7,8], supervised classification methods to differentiate hill-slope landslides from other terrain units [15], and use of high resolution and image fusion for landslide risk assessment [13,17].

Likewise, different types of analysis have been carried out to improve the detection processes of this type of phenomenon. For instance, the analysis of conventional methods for landslide mapping including geomorphological inventories of seasonal and multitemporal events and the application of other recent technologies involving high-resolution digital elevation models [9], analysis of the influence of tectonics on the progressive erosion of landscapes and propose a method for the classification of landscapes according to their erosional stage from the combination of geomorphic indices based on digital elevation models (DEMs) [1], the use of a joint probability model to show a measure of future landslide hazard using five model estimation procedures applied to the Chinchiná river basin, department of Caldas, Colombia [5], or the use of object oriented classification (OOA) with high resolution images to detect mass movements [12].

With respect to the use of artificial intelligence methods, different approaches have been proposed, such as the use of residual networks for landslide detection employing spectral and topographic information [19] or the use of ensembled methods [23]. For example, the assembled boosting models presented the best values in terms of performance and predictive capacity in an evaluation of machine learning methods in the vicinity of a hydrographic basin in Colombia [14].

Considering the above, this paper contains a new proposal for mass movement susceptibility using an artificial intelligence algorithm. The AutoML (Automated Machine Learning) algorithm is trained using as label the susceptibility map made by an expert from geological, geomorphological information and the use of GIS tools, and as attributes the pixel level information from Sentinel-2A multispectral images. This method is presented as an alternative to evaluate landslide susceptibility in areas where there is a lack of information such as slopes, geological or geomorphological data.

2   Study Area

The study area includes a region between "San Luis de Gaceno" and "Santa María" at the Department of Boyacá (Colombia). The geographical zone cover an area of 300 km^2; the upper left corner of the zone is placed at 4°54'44.02"N, −73°21'22.15"W, whereas the lower right corner is placed at 4°46'35.62"N, −73°10'34.46"W. The locator map is shown in Fig. 1. In the study zone, most of the area corresponds to forest cover (approximately 55%), while pasture cover corresponds to approximately 35% of the study area, and the remaining percentage is soil.

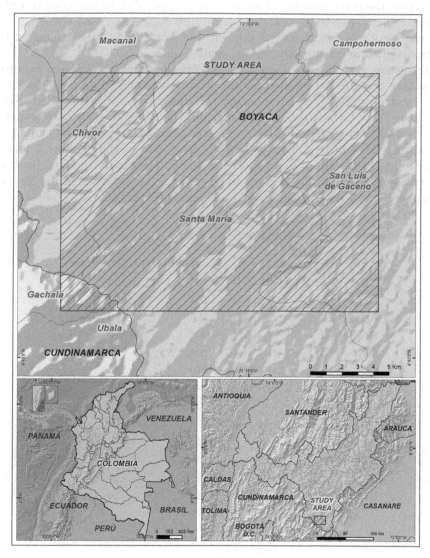

Fig. 1. Location of the study area corresponding to "San Luis de Gaceno" and "Santa María" at the Department of Boyacá (Colombia).

Once the study area has been defined, and in order to use remote sensing data, it is necessary to define the type of sensor to be used and the image bands to be selected as attributes within a machine learning model. Similarly, in order to train the supervised learning method, it is necessary to obtain a reference map (ground truth) that defines the labels of the data. These issues are presented below.

3   Image Data

Given that the determination of areas with susceptibility to landslide is a phenomenon that depends on geological, geomorphological and land cover aspects, it is necessary to consider images that include bands in different regions of the electromagnetic spectrum (ultraviolet, visible, infrared).

According to the above, a multispectral image of Sentinel-2 sensor captured in January of 2016 was selected for the study area. This image has 998×750 pixels, and it contains 13 spectral bands, including visible, Near Infra-Red (NIR), and Short Wave Infra-Red (SWIR) bands. Of the 13 bands, four have a spatial resolution of 10 meters, six bands have a resolution of 20 meters and three have a resolution of 60 meters. The radiometric resolution of the Sentinel 2 images is 12-bits, and the intensities are stored as 16-bits integers in the final product. The true color composition of the multispectral image is shown in Fig. 2a, and the general information of Sentinel-2 bands is shown in Table 1.

Table 1. Sentinel-2 bands.

Band	Description	Wavelength (nm)	Resolution
B1	Coastal aerosol	~ 443	60
B2	Blue	~ 493	10
B3	Green	~ 560	10
B4	Red	~ 665	10
B5	Vegetation Red edge	~ 704	20
B6	Vegetation Red edge	~ 740	20
B7	Vegetation Red edge	~ 783	20
B8	NIR	~ 833	10
B8A	Vegetation Red edge	~ 865	20
B9	Water vapour	~ 945	60
B10	Cirrus detection	~ 1374	60
B11	SWIR 1	~ 1610	20
B12	SWIR 2	~ 2190	20

4   Materials and Methods

The identification scheme for landslide susceptible zones is based on a supervised classification model, so it is necessary to build the reference data that will be used for training the model (ground truth), define the features that will be used in the model from the image data, and define the structure of the machine learning model that will be trained using the labels and attributes previously defined. The construction of these labels, the definition of the features and the characteristics of the proposed model are explained below.

4.1   Ground Truth Data

In order to define the reference labels that can be used to train, select and evaluate a machine learning model, a consolidated methodology was used. The susceptibility to landslide in the study area was determined by applying elements of the methodology proposed in [20,21]. The application of these methodologies allows estimating a map of susceptibility to landslide phenomena from the crossing of weighted thematic layers (variables), based on the density of unstable processes and their degree of influence.

Susceptibility to landslide is subject to several factors such as the lithological composition of the rock (geology), the denudational environment in which it is formed (geomorphology) and the type of land use that is being given to this area (land cover). The combination of these factors determines the occurrence of landslide, always taking into account the variation of the terrain, the morphogenetic environments and the degree of humidity and infiltration in the area that can affect the resistance of the material.

The variation of the lithological and structural characteristics of the study area influences the process of landslide generation, since they lead to differences in the resistance and permeability of rocks and soils. For the determination of susceptibility by geologic factor, three weighted thematic layers were assigned as shown in Eq. 1.

$$G = 0.25R + 0.25T + 0.5F_D \tag{1}$$

Where, G is the susceptibility by geologic factor, R (resistance) measures the resistance of the rocks to weathering, T (Texture) is the variable that establishes the differences in the rocks in terms of strength and directionality of mechanical properties, and F_D (fracture density) measures the regional structural discontinuities in the rock masses that decrease their resistance, increasing susceptibility to the occurrence of landslide.

Regarding geomorphology, the geomorphological units generated by the Colombian Geological Service were taken, making a more detailed delimitation of these units using a digital elevation model with a spatial resolution of 12.5 m and satellite images of the study area. Subsequently, this element was qualified according to its morphogenesis (origin of landforms, i.e., the causes and processes that shaped the landscape [20]). The susceptibility by geomorphology factor is given by Eq. 2.

$$G_m = 0.4M_g + 0.6M_m \tag{2}$$

Where G_m is the susceptibility by geomorphology factor, M_g is the morphogenesis, and M_m is the morphometry.

Regarding land use, the type of vegetation cover and land use influence soil stability, as they can reflect soil infiltration capacity and soil moisture, as well as increased resistance due to the presence of roots and protection against erosion. With respect to urban areas, there is generally no good wastewater management, hence surface runoff can increase erosion and consequently instability. In general, it can be said that the areas where most movements occur are directly related to soils without cover or bare soils, as well as the areas with the steepest slopes.

Finally, the total susceptibility was calculated from the weighting of the susceptibility obtained for geology (G), geomorphology (G_m) and cover (C) factors (Eq. 3).

$$S = 0.2G + 0.6G_m + 0.2C \tag{3}$$

In addition, taking into account that geology, geomorphology and cover factors were rated from 1 to 5, the susceptibility of the final map is also defined on the same scale, where 5 relates to the highest susceptibility. The landslide susceptibility map of the study area is shown in Fig. 2b. In this map there is a high percentage of areas with high susceptibility, mainly from the central zone to the north-west, while from the central zone to the south-east, the susceptibility presents mostly areas of medium and low susceptibility.

The map shown in Fig. 2b was obtained from the analysis of susceptibility and threat due to landslide for the study area and was carried out by an expert supported by GIS tools. The spatial and dynamic relationship of the information was made from the collection of information and observations of variables. The complexity of obtaining this type of maps leads to the evaluation of automatic learning tools that make use of easily accessible data. The following section shows the proposal for data selection to perform this task.

In accordance with the above, the susceptibility value obtained is taken as ground truth and will be used in the training process as the label for the selected attributes, as well as the label for evaluating the proposed model.

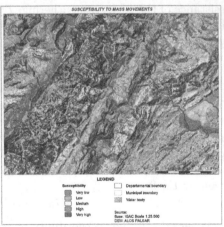

(a) Multispectral Sentinel-2 Image. 300 km² (998 × 750 pixels), RGB color composition. "San Luis de Gaceno" and "Santa María" at the Department of Boyacá (Colombia). The upper left corner is placed at 4°54'44.02"N, -73°21'22.15"W.

(b) Landslide movement susceptibility map (Ground truth)

Fig. 2. Image data and Ground truth data.

4.2 Structured Data (Input for the AutoML Model)

Although satellite images can be considered unstructured data (i.e., they do not have a rigid structure like tabular data), in this research the image was converted to structured data by considering pixel-level information. Accordingly, for each pixel position, the input attributes correspond to the pixel values of each of the image bands (i.e. the bands shown in Table 1). Having the data structured in this way (i.e., from a multispectral image) ensures that there are no null data, categorical data, or outlier data. It should be noted that bands 1, 9 and 10 were not considered as input attributes due to their low spatial resolution (60 m).

Therefore, the attributes initially selected correspond to bands 2, 3, 4 and 8 (10 m), and bands 5, 7, 8A, 11 and 12 (20 m) of Sentinel-2 Image. From these georeferenced bands of different pixel size, a new multiband file was formed, in which the 10 m bands were resampled to 20 m (nearest neighbor) maintaining the UTM WGS-84 projection.

In addition, the five susceptibility levels shown in the map in Fig. 2b were reduced to two classes: high susceptibility (for values of 5), and moderate susceptibility (for values between 1 and 4). Thus, the attributes to be evaluated include 9 bands of the original image, and the problem can be approached as a binary classification problem.

Since the input image (998 × 750 pixels) is being processed at the pixel level, the total number of examples available to train, validate and test the model is 748500 examples. Samples from this dataset were randomized and split, involving 80% samples (598800) for training, 10% samples (74850) for validation (used to tune hyperparameters) and 10% samples (74850) for testing.

4.3 AutoML Model

Automated Machine Learning (AutoML) consists of solutions to automate tasks that apply machine learning to any type of problem. AutoML solutions can include different phases of the process, from data processing to model retrieval. AutoKeras is an AutoML system based on Keras, looking for make machine learning accessible to everyone; it was developed by DATA Lab at Texas A&M University [11]. AutoKeras supports several tasks, such as image classification, image regression, text classification, text regression, structured data classification and structured data regression. This tool also allows to build customized models, specifying the high-level architecture, so that AutoKeras performs a search for the best configuration (hyperparameters).

For the present investigation, the AutoKeras AutoModel option was used, which allows defining the model according to the inputs and outputs, i.e. AutoModel infers the rest of the model. The model is fitted from a hyperparameter search space, and the fitted model can then be used as any Keras model (e.g., prediction or evaluation) [4].

To configure the AutoModel, the input was defined as structured data, and the output as a classification type. The number of trials was set to 100, the batch size to 32, the number of epochs to train each model to 10, and the search space (automatically defined by AutoKeras) involved the hyperparameters shown in Table 2. In AutoKeras, a greedy search algorithm is used to select the hyperparameters in the space, which evaluates a list of models recursively, always selecting the best model and building a hyperparameter tree from it. Once evaluated, it can generate a new set of hyperparameter values by replacing the previous ones. The evaluation and selection of the best model is repeated until the maximum number of trials is reached. This search process is greedy as it always selects the current best model and generates new models in its neighborhood [10].

Table 2. Hyperparameters in the search space for the AutoModel.

Hyperparameter	Values in search space	Best value
Normalization	[False, True]	True
Batch normalization	[False, True]	True
No. of layers	[1, 2, 3]	3
No. of units (Layer 1)	[16, 32, 64, 128, 256, 512, 1024]	256
Dropout (Layer 1)	[0.0, 0.25, 0.5]	0.0
No. of units (Layer 2)	[16, 32, 64, 128, 256, 512, 1024]	256
Dropout (Layer 2)	[0.0, 0.25, 0.5]	0.0
No. of units (Layer 3)	[16, 32, 64, 128, 256, 512, 1024]	32
Dropout (Layer 3)	[0.0, 0.25, 0.5]	0.25
Optimizer	[Adam, SGD, Adam weight decay]	Adam weight decay
Learning rate	[0.1, 0.01, 0.001, 0.0001, 2e−05, 1e−05]	0.001

After searching for the best model and the best hyperparameters for the AutoModel, based on the performances in the validation data, the model shown in Fig. 3 was obtained. The best model was obtained from the hyperparameter configuration shown in Table 2 (column 3). The description of the model and its layers is shown in Table 3. Accordingly, the model includes an input data normalization layer, batch normalization to accelerate network convergence, 2 fully connected layers of 256 units without dropout, followed by a fully connected layer of 32 units with dropout of 0.25 to reduce overfitting, an Adam optimizer with weight decay and a learning rate of 0.001 was used to train the best model.

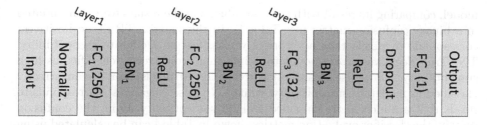

Fig. 3. Architecture of the model obtained with AutoKeras. FC: Fully Connected (Dense) layer, BN: Batch Normalization, ReLU: Rectified Linear Unit activation function.

The number of trainable parameters of the model can be seen in Table 3. In each fully connected layer, this value is calculated by taking the number of units of the previous layer (or number of inputs) multiplied by the number of units of the layer, plus the number of units of the layer. The total number of trainable parameters thus equals 77,953 (including batch normalization parameters) and the number of non-trainable parameters is 1,109.

Table 3. Summary of the model obtained with AutoKeras

Layer	No. of units	Output shape	Trainable parameters
Input	-	(,10)	0
Normalization	-	(,10)	21
FC_1 (Dense)	256	(,256)	2816
BN_1 (Batch normalization)	-	(,256)	1024
ReLU	-	(,256)	0
FC_2 (Dense)	256	(,256)	65792
BN_2 (Batch normalization)	-	(,256)	1024
ReLU	-	(,256)	0
FC_3 (Dense)	32	(,32)	8224
BN_3 (Batch normalization)	-	(,32)	128
ReLU	-	(,32)	0
Dropout	-	(,32)	0
FC_4 (Dense)	1	(,1)	33

5   Results and Discussion

Once the best model was obtained, unknown data (i.e. data that were neither used in training nor in validation) were used to evaluate its performance. These correspond to the test dataset, i.e. 74850 samples, as explained above. With each of these samples, the respective prediction was performed using the trained model, comparing its result with the real value, and the results were consolidated in a binary confusion matrix (see Table 4). In this matrix, TP (True Positives) corresponds to pixels that are correctly classified as moderate susceptibility, TN (True Negatives) corresponds to points that are correctly classified as high susceptibility, FP (False Positives) corresponds to pixels that are incorrectly classified as moderate susceptibility, while FN (False Negatives) corresponds to pixels that are incorrectly classified as high susceptibility. From the confusion matrix, the classifier evaluation metrics shown in Table 4 can be calculated using Eqs. 4–7 [18, 22].

Table 4. Confusion matrix and evaluation metrics for the test set.

		True condition	
		Moderate susceptibility	High susceptibility
Predicted condition	Moderate susceptibility	54861	15820
	High susceptibility	1541	2628
		Accuracy (ACC)	0.7681
		Precision (P)	0.7762
		Recall (R)	0.9727
		F1-Score (F$_1$)	0.8634

Thus, accuracy corresponds to the percentage of correct classifications, precision to the percentage of classifications in the positive class (moderate susceptibility) that are true positives, and recall corresponds to the proportion of positives that are correctly identified [2]. In a classification task it is desirable that P and R reach the highest possible value, while being similar to each other. The ideal value in each case is 1 and the minimum value is 0. To evaluate the balance between them, the F1 score corresponding to the harmonic mean between P and R is calculated.

$$ACC = (TP + TN)/(TP + TN + FP + FN) \tag{4}$$

$$P = TP/(TP + FP) \tag{5}$$

$$R = TP/(TP + FN) \tag{6}$$

$$F_1 = 2(P \times R)/(P + R) \tag{7}$$

According to the evaluation results, the model is able to correctly classify most of the moderate susceptibility zones. In the case of high susceptibility zones, there are pixels that are classified as moderate susceptibility, which is mainly due to the absence of slope data (e.g. a digital elevation model), or geology and geomorphology data, which were key to build the ground truth data and are not captured by a multispectral image. Beyond this, the zones detected by the model as high susceptibility largely reflect the areas classified in the elaboration of the ground truth data, as shown in the example in Fig. 4.

Fig. 4. Example of a landslide susceptibility map obtained using the proposed AutoML model for the study area. Red: high susceptibility, Violet: moderate susceptibility. (Color figure online)

Given the high variability of the susceptibility of ground truth data (Fig. 3b), the problem of identifying such zones becomes complex for a classifier fed only by multispectral data. This is reflected in the number of false negatives and positives. Hence, although the method can be used to obtain a general overview of the landslide susceptibility of an area, for greater accuracy the data must be complemented with other types of information.

6   Conclusion

The proposed model allows estimating susceptibility to mass movements, even without slope information or specific geological or geomorphological information. Since the response is obtained only from multispectral information, the susceptibility estimation is performed in a binary map (moderate or high susceptibility), while allowing to obtain such information only from one image. The model adjustment was performed using AutoML (AutoKeras) and achieved an F1 Score close to 86%.

Acknowledgment. This research was funded by "Vicerrectoría de Investigaciones–Universidad Militar Nueva Granada", grant number INV-ING-3190 of 2020.

References

1. Andreani, L., Stanek, K.P., Gloaguen, R., Krentz, O., Domínguez-González, L.: DEM-based analysis of interactions between tectonics and landscapes in the ore mountains and Eger Rift (East Germany and NW Czech Republic). Remote Sens. **6**(9), 7971–8001 (2014)
2. Ballesteros, D.M., Rodriguez-Ortega, Y., Renza, D., Arce, G.: Deep4SNet: deep learning for fake speech classification. Expert Syst. Appl. **184**, 115465 (2021). https://doi.org/10.1016/j.eswa.2021.115465
3. Beguería, S.: Changes in land cover and shallow landslide activity: a case study in the Spanish Pyrenees. Geomorphology **74**(1–4), 196–206 (2006)
4. Chollet, F., et al.: Keras. https://keras.io (2015)
5. Chung, C.J.F., Fabbri, A.G., et al.: Probabilistic prediction models for landslide hazard mapping. Photogram. Eng. Remote Sens. **65**(12), 1389–1399 (1999)
6. Corominas, J., et al.: Recommendations for the quantitative analysis of landslide risk. Bull. Eng. Geol. Environ. **73**(2), 209–263 (2014)
7. Cuervo, G.V.: Evaluacion de imagenes de satelite sar ers-1 y spot-landsat en la cartografia de movimientos en masa. In: The Use and Applications of ERS in Latin America, p. 109. ESTEC Publishing Division (1997)
8. Esper Angillieri, M.Y.: Inventario de procesos de remoción en masa de un sector del departamento iglesia, san juan. Revista de la Asociación Geológica Argentina **68**(2), 225–232 (2011)
9. Guzzetti, F., Mondini, A.C., Cardinali, M., Fiorucci, F., Santangelo, M., Chang, K.T.: Landslide inventory maps: new tools for an old problem. Earth-Sci. Rev. **112**(1–2), 42–66 (2012)
10. Jin, H.: Efficient neural architecture search for automated deep learning. Ph.D. thesis, Texas A&M University (2021)
11. Jin, H., Song, Q., Hu, X.: Auto-Keras: an efficient neural architecture search system. In: Proceedings of the 25th ACM SIGKDD International Conference on Knowledge Discovery & Data Mining, pp. 1946–1956. ACM (2019)
12. Keyport, R.N., Oommen, T., Martha, T.R., Sajinkumar, K., Gierke, J.S.: A comparative analysis of pixel-and object-based detection of landslides from very high-resolution images. Int. J. Appl. Earth Observ. Geoinf. **64**, 1–11 (2018)
13. Nichol, J., Wong, M.S.: Satellite remote sensing for detailed landslide inventories using change detection and image fusion. Int. J. Remote Sens. **26**(9), 1913–1926 (2005)
14. Ospina-Gutiérrez, J.P., Aristizábal, E.: Aplicación de inteligencia artificial y técnicas de aprendizaje automático para la evaluación de la susceptibilidad por movimientos en masa. Revista Mexicana De Ciencias Geológicas **38**(1), 43–54 (2021)
15. Paolini, L., Sobrino, J.A., Jimenez Muños, J.C.: Detección de deslizamientos de ladera mediante imágenes landsat tm: El impacto de estos disturbios sobre los bosques subtropicales del noroeste de argentina. Revista de Teledeteccion (2002)
16. de Planeación, D.N.: Indice municipal de riesgo de desastres ajustado por capacidades (2019). https://colaboracion.dnp.gov.co/CDT/Prensa/IndicemunicipalRiesgos.pdf
17. Recondo, C., Menéndez, C., García, P., González, R., Sáez, E.: Estudio de las zonas propensas a sufrir deslizamientos en los concejos de oviedo y mieres (asturias) a partir de una imagen landsat-tm y de un modelo digital de elevaciones. Rev Teledetec **14**, 49–59 (2000)

18. Rodriguez-Ortega, Y., Ballesteros, D.M., Renza, D.: Copy-move forgery detection (CMFD) using deep learning for image and video forensics. J. Imaging **7**(3), 59 (2021)
19. Sameen, M.I., Pradhan, B.: Landslide detection using residual networks and the fusion of spectral and topographic information. IEEE Access **7**, 114363–114373 (2019)
20. Servicio-Geológico-Colombiano: Documento metodológico de la zonificación de susceptibilidad y amenaza por movimientos en masa, escala 1:100.000 (2013). https://www.sgc.gov.co
21. Servicio-Geológico-Colombiano: Lineamientos técnicos para elaboración de mapas de amenaza por movimientos en masa a escala municipal y rural (2013). https://www.sgc.gov.co
22. Ulloa, C., Ballesteros, D.M., Renza, D.: Video forensics: identifying colorized images using deep learning. Appl. Sci. **11**(2), 476 (2021)
23. Wang, H., Zhang, L., Luo, H., He, J., Cheung, R.: AI-powered landslide susceptibility assessment in Hong Kong. Eng. Geol. **288**, 106103 (2021)

Fake Speech Recognition Using Deep Learning

Steven Camacho(✉), Dora Maria Ballesteros, and Diego Renza

Universidad Militar Nueva Granada, Bogotá, Colombia
{est.steven.camacho,dora.ballesteros,diego.renza}@unimilitar.edu.co

Abstract. The increase in the number of algorithms and commercial tools for creating synthetic audio has led to a high level of misinformation, especially on social media. As a consequence, efforts have been focused in recent years on detecting this type of content. However, this task is far from being successfully addressed, as the naturalness of fake audios is increasing. In this paper we present a model to classify audios between *natural* and *fake*, using an audio preparation stage that includes raw audio transformation, and a modelling stage by means of a custom Convolutional Neural Network (CNN) architecture. Our model is trained on data from the FoR dataset, which contains natural and synthetic audios obtained from several algorithms for *deepfake* content generation. The performance of the model is evaluated with different metrics such as *F1* score, *precision* (P) and *recall* (R). According to the results, the audios are successfully classified in 88.9% of the cases.

Keywords: Classification task · Convolutional neural network · Deep learning · Deepfake · Speech recognition · Synthetic audio

1 Introduction

Disinformation has been an evolving issue in recent years, transcending fake news, with algorithms and tools that allow fake audio, image and video to be generated. This type of AI-generated content is called *deepfake* [1,2], and the importance in detecting them lies in the fact that this type of content can impact different areas of society such as politics, morality and legal process. In the first case, for instance, with the decisions of citizens in electoral scenarios [2–5]. In the second case, by impacting people's lives, through, for example, pornographic videos in which the faces of famous people are used without their consent [6]. In the latter, it can be used to generate false digital evidence, impacting legal decisions [2–4].

Synthetic or fake content has been around for many years, but content generated with deep learning, i.e., *deepfake*, has only been around for a few years. In the latter case, the main advantage is the *naturalness* of the content, which has been increasing day by day. Regarding algorithms, several approaches for creating synthetic content have been proposed, as presented in Table 1. On the other hand, detection methods have also been evolving, however, there is still the

© Springer Nature Switzerland AG 2021
J. C. Figueroa-García et al. (Eds.): WEA 2021, CCIS 1431, pp. 38–48, 2021.
https://doi.org/10.1007/978-3-030-86702-7_4

Table 1. Some state-of-the-art algorithms for generating synthetic audio.

Work	Feature-based	Year
Wavenet [10]	STFT, Mel-Spectogram	2016
Tacotron [11]	SFCC, MFCC, STFT	2017
Vocoder-free text-to-speech [12]	CQCC, MFCC	2018
Deep Voice [13]	MFCC	2017
Deep Voice 2 [14]	MFCC	2017
Deep Voice 3 [15]	SFT, LFCC, LFB	2018
Controllable expressive speech synthesis [16]	SFCC, MFCC, STFT	2018
Generating MultilingualVoice [17]	SFCC, MFCC, STFT	2020

Table 2. Some state-of-the-art algorithms for detecting synthetic audio.

Work	Model-based	Year
Spectral Feature for Synthetic Speech Detection	Correlation	2017
Video Detection	LSTM	2018
Ensemble models for spoofing	CNN, SVM	2019
Generalization Of Audio Deepfake Detection	GMM, RNN, DNN	2020
Recurrent Convolutional Neural Network	RCNN	2020
DeepSonar	DNN	2020

challenge of being able to identify *deepfake* audios generated with a method that was not used in the training process of the model (known as the generalization problem) [7–9]. Table 2 shows a summary of recognition algorithms.

The methods listed in Table 1 have numerous beneficial applications that make use of synthetic audio, e.g. customizing voices for audio books and avatars, dubbing films while preserving the voice of the original actor, cloning voices to revive historical characters, among others [18–20]. However, the impact it has on forensic, political and morality issues makes it important to recognize this type of content [3]. An example of the worldwide interest in recognition algorithms was the *Facebook Challenge 2020*, in which the participants of more than 2000 teams used a dataset of 470 GB to train AI-based algorithms. Although the reported results of the winner team for internal validation was 82% in terms of *accuracy*, this value decreased to 65.18% for an external dataset [7,21]. On the other hand, the *Automatic Speaker Verification Spoofing And Countermeasures Challenge* (ASVspoof), included a sub-challengue named *speech deepfake detection sub-challenge (no ASV)* in its 2021 version [22].

Taking into account the above, in this paper we propose a model for the recognition of synthetic audio generated with artificial intelligence, which presents the following contributions:

- It is based on deep learning (DL) with a custom architecture specifically designed to the current task.
- The input data corresponding to a scatter plot of neighbouring samples. That is, the x-axis is the ith amplitude, and the y-axis is its right neighbour.

As far as we know, this is the first iteration this type of input has been used to classify fake audios.

- It is text independent and can therefore be used in a wide scenario where the voice message contains any kind of linguistic content.
- The model is trained with data from different generation algorithms, to improve data diversity and address the problem of generalization of DL-based models.

The rest of the paper is organized as follows: Sect. 2.1 explains the data preparation stage, and Sect. 2.2 describes the proposed architecture. Section 3 presents the results obtained from the evaluation and the performance of the system. Finally, Sect. 4 presents the conclusions, challenges and future work.

2   Data Preparation and Modelling

In general, a data science cycle life encompasses the following stages: understanding the problem, data preparation, modelling and evaluation. The first stage consists of getting to know the task, identifying the problems reported by other authors and the challenges that still exist. The second stage is related to data requirements, data collection, data understanding and data pre-processing (or transformation). The third stage corresponds to the training and validation process with the data obtained in the previous step. Finally, the trained model is evaluated with external data in order to obtain performance metrics. In the following, we will explain the second and third stages of the methodology used in the solution of the *deepfake* audio recognition problem.

2.1   Data Preparation

As a first step in this stage, we focus on the collection of both natural and *deepfake* audios. As a requirement, the *deepfake* audios had to come from different generation algorithms, with several examples per algorithm. One of the datasets that fulfilled the above conditions is FoR, which was released in 2019 by York University [23]. This dataset has a total of 69,316 English audios, with four sub-datasets, like a *original* and *norm* where have a same audios but with some modifications about them for example, normalized in terms of sample rate, volume and number of channels. The dataset *original* was divided into a subset that contains 92.23% of its content and its distribution in each data subset is around 78% for training, 15.6% for validation and 6.4% for testing. Table 3 shows the distribution of the original FoR dataset for each available *deepfake* generation algorithm.

An important decision in this stage is whether to work with raw or transformed data, and what type of transformation. As part of the data understanding step, different transformations were applied in search of features that could distinguish *deepfake* audios from natural audios. In the current problem, scatter plots comparing the amplitude of the sample at the ith position with the

Table 3. Data distribution of generation algorithms for FoR dataset.

Algorithm	Voices	Utterances
Deep Voice 3	1	2,645
Amazon AWS Polly	8	21,160
Baidu TTS	3	7,935
Google Traditional TTS	1	2,645
Google Cloud TTS	2	5,290
Google Wavenet TTS	2	5,290
Microsoft Azure TTS	16	42,320
Total	33	87,285

amplitude of the neighbouring sample were found to have a different behaviour between natural and deepfake audios, as shown in Fig. 1. It is worth noting that natural audios have a higher correlation between samples than in the case of *deepfake* audios, meaning that in the latter the amplitude between one sample and its neighbour changes more significantly than in the former case. Since the difference between Fig. 1a and Fig. 1b is substantial, this type of image is used as input to the AI-based model.

2.2 Modelling

In this third stage of the methodology, the design of the architecture depends strongly on the type of input data. For example, if the input is an image instead of sequential data, we can use a CNN instead of an Long short-term memory (LSTM). Therefore, our proposed model is based on CNN, since the input is an image instead of a raw audio. On the other hand, considering that the current classification task is not related to the shape of the object (as is in typical classification models) but to the scattering of the data around the *diagonal*, we select an architecture with only three convolutional blocks and two fully-connected layers (i.e., *FC-1* and *FC-2*). The input is an image of (100×100 pixels) and the output is one unit, as shown in Fig. 2.

Each convolutional block has three layers: *convolutional* (*conv*), *MaxPooling*, *dropout* and *Batch Normalization* (*BacthNorm*). In the first block, the image enters a convolutional layer of 64 filters, with *kernel size (k)* = *3* and *stride (s)* = *1*. The output is a feature map of ($98 \times 98 \times 64$). Next, the activation function ReLU is applied to the above feature map, and it enters a MaxPooling layer of 64 filters, with $k = 2$. The resulting size is ($49 \times 49 \times 64$). Third, a dropout layer of 0.1 is added to avoid overfitting. Finally, a BatchNormalization layer is included to speed up the training of the network.

The configuration in the next two *convolutional* blocks involves doubling the number of filters in each layer also changed the values of *dropout* and *padding (p)* = *same* in layer two and $s = 2$ in layer three, and the values shown in Table 4. The feature maps of the last *BatchNorm* layer are then flattened and fed into a 512-units *FC* layer. A four dropout layer is inserted again to avoid overfitting. Finally, they are connected to a unit, in the last layer, to predict the class (*real* vs. *fake.*).

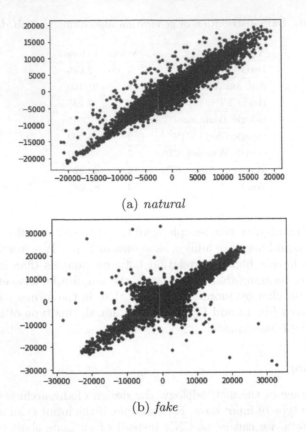

(a) *natural*

(b) *fake*

Fig. 1. Example of scatter plot of adjacent samples in audio signals.

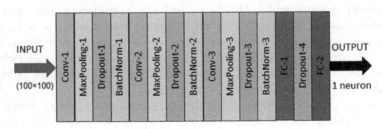

Fig. 2. Proposed deep-learning-based architecture to classify *natural/fake* speech signals.

Table 4 shows the hyperparameters of the proposed architecture. It can be noted that the number of parameters is low, at only about 3.6 million.

3   Results

This section presents the results of the proposed model, divided into three parts. The first part, Sect. 3.1, presents the conditions under which the experiments

Table 4. Description of the proposed deep-learning-based architecture to classify real/fake audio signals.

Layer	Filters	k	s	p	Output shape	Parameters
Input	–	–	–	–	(100, 100, 3)	0
Conv-1	64	3	1	–	(98, 98, 64)	1,792
MaxPooling-1	64	3	1	0	(49, 49, 64)	0
Dropout-1 (0.1)		–	–	–	(49,49,64)	0
BatchNorm-1	–	–	–	–	(49, 49, 64)	256
Conv-2	128	3	1	Same	(49, 49, 128)	73,856
MaxPooling-2	128	3	1	0	(24, 24, 128)	0
Dropout-2 (0.1)		–	–	–	(24, 24, 128)	0
BatchNorm-2	–	–	–	–	(24, 24, 128)	512
Conv-3	256	3	2	–	(5, 5, 256)	295,168
MaxPooling-3	256	3	2	0	(5, 5, 256)	0
Dropout-3 (0.2)		–	–	–	(5, 5, 256)	0
BatchNorm-3	–	–	–	–	(5, 5, 256)	1,024
Flattening	–	–	–	–	(4096, 1)	0
FC-1	–	–	–	–	(512, 1)	3,277,312
Dropout-4 (0.1)	–	–	–	–	(512, 1)	0
FC-2	–	–	–	–	(1)	513
TOTAL						3,650,433

were conducted, including both the hardware conditions and the evaluation metrics used. The second part, Sect. 3.2, presents the performance plots, and the confusion matrix. The third part, Sect. 3.3, compares the results with other state-of-the-art work.

3.1   Experimental Settings

It is important to know the hardware specifications when comparing the times obtained by different proposals, since, different hardware conditions have a significant impact on the times, even when the architecture is the same. Therefore, Table 5 presents the hardware used in the training and inference stages, specifically from three different options, the first and second with local resources, and the third, in the cloud. In both cases, the model was trained with the same number of epochs, and according to the architecture and training hyperparameters

Table 5. Hardware and timing specifications in the training and inference stages.

Device	RAM	GPU	Training time (seconds)	Inference time (seconds)
MSI	16	GTX 1050	12,384	3.36
Lenovo	8	GTX 1650	14,331	2.58
Cloud	11	–	21,177	1.12

presented in Sect. 2.2. It is noted that in the cloud, the training time was longer, but the inference time was shorter than the time with local resources.

On the other hand, considering that all proposals do not use the same evaluation metrics, you can only compare results when the same metrics have been used. For example, you may not compare an *accuracy* value reported by one study with an *F1* score reported by another study. In our case, we use four metrics widely used in the state-of-the-art in classification problems: *accuracy*, *precision*, *recall* and AUC (Area Under the Curve). The first three are obtained from true positives (TP), true negatives (TN), false positives (FP), and false negatives (FN), according to the following equations:

$$accuracy = \frac{TP + TN}{TP + TN + FP + FN} \tag{1}$$

$$precision = \frac{TP}{TP + FP} \tag{2}$$

$$recall = \frac{TP}{TP + FN} \tag{3}$$

In our case, the class equal to 1 corresponds to *natural* audios, while the class equal to 0 corresponds to *fake* audios. Therefore, TP means that *natural* audios are classified as *natural* audios; TN means that *fake* audios are classified as *fake* audios; FP means that *fake* audios are classified as *natural* audios; while FN means that *natural* audios are classified as *fake* audios. The ideal value of *accuracy*, *precision*, *recall* and AUC is 1, while 0 means that the model always classifies the audios incorrectly.

3.2   Performance of the Custom Model: Training, Validation and Testing

Figure 3 shows the results of the proposed model for training and validation in terms of *accuracy*, *precision*, and *recall*. In all cases, the number of epochs is 50.

It should be noted that, in all three graphs of Fig. 3, the validation curve follows the training curve, which means that the model is not overfitted. Additionally, a high similarity is observed between the value of P and that of R, which implies that the model is not biased by a class, and then it has a similar number of FPs as FNs. On the other hand, the summary results are shown in Table 6 for training, validation and testing. The *precision* value is slightly higher than the *recall* value, which means that there are slightly fewer misclassifications in the *fake* audios than in the *natural* audios.

3.3   Custom Model vs. State-of-the-Art

This section compares the results with those obtained in other state-of-the-art works. Some of them using the FoR or ASVSpoof dataset, while others use H-Voice [24] and Imitation datasets [25]. In DeepSonar [26], the authors use

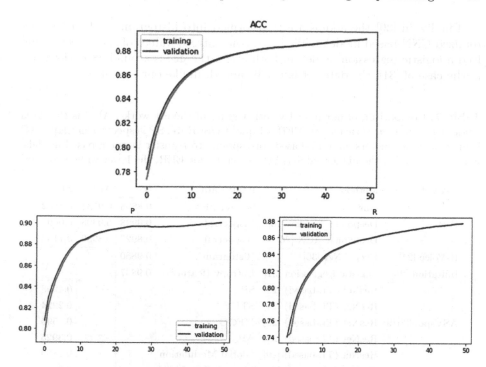

Fig. 3. Graphs of performance in terms of *accuracy*, *precision* and *recall*.

Table 6. Evaluation results of the proposed model for training, validation and testing.

	Accuracy	Precision	Recall	AUC
Training	0.8903	0.9006	0.8774	0.9542
Validation	0.8896	0.900	0.8765	0.9528
Testing	0.8898	0.9002	0.8798	0.9533

a neural network architecture, whose input corresponds to bispectral images obtained from the audios of the FoR dataset, similar to that suggested by [27]. The authors proposed two schemes (i.e., TKAN and ACN) with different results for the same input images. DeepSonar ACN's performance is similar to ours (i.e., EER around 11%).

On the other hand, in [28] the authors used an architecture based on ResNet18 but with some differences, e.g., global average pooling (GAP) was replaced by mean and standard deviation pooling layer, and changes in the filter sizes and stride values. The input is an image corresponding to a spectrogram of the speech signal, modified by a frequency mask. The obtained model was tested with the ASVspoof 2019 dataset for thirteen synthetic audio generation techniques. According to the results, the EER values were lower than 6.186%. In a similar work [29], the authors used ResNet to classify audios into bonafide and fake. They evaluate five different data transformations with results between 15.99% and 42.08% in terms of EER.

Finally, in [30] the audios are transformed into histograms and feed a customized CNN-based model; while in [31] the entropy values of the speech signal feed a logistic regression model. In both cases, the *acc* is around 98%. However, in the case of [31], the data set is not balanced, unlike our current work.

Table 7. Comparison of our model vs other state-of-the-art works. AUC is the Area Under the Curve, *acc* is accuracy, EER is Equal Error Rate, SP is spectral envelope, AP is aperiodic parameters, and TL-based corresponds to transfer learning-based models. For *acc* and AUC, the higher value is better; while, for EER, the lower value is better.

Dataset	Method	Input data	acc	AUC	EER
FoR	Our	Scatter plot	0.8898	0.9533	0.1102
	DeepSonar TKAN [26]	Bispectral	0.9998	0.9998	0.0002
	DeepSonar ACN [26]	Bispectral	0.8927	0.8930	0.1164
H-Voice [24]	Deep4SNet [30]	Histogram	0.9850	–	–
Imitation [25]	Logistic Regression [31]	Entropy (features)	0.9837	–	–
ASVspoof2019	ResNet (TL-based) [29]	SP	–	–	0.4208
	ResNet (TL-based) [29]	STFT	–	–	0.2224
	ResNet (TL-based) [29]	MFCC	–	–	0.1599
	ResNet (TL-based) [29]	AP	–	–	0.3925
	ResNet (TL-based) [29]	Global Modulation	–	–	0.1869
	ResNet (TL-based) [28]	Linear Filter Bank	–	–	0.0618

In summary, data transformation (e.g. histograms, spectrograms, bispectral, scatter plot) plays an important role in *fake* content detection. With the same architecture, performance results can vary significantly between different data transformation approaches. In addition, both customized and transfer learning-based models can provide similar results in terms of accuracy and EER (Table 7).

4   Conclusion

In this work we proposed a custom model for the classification of audios between *natural* and *deepfake*. The proposed architecture is characterized by a low number of convolutional layers with a very low number of parameters, similar to MobileNetV2. Additionally, dropout and batch normalization layers were included to avoid over-fitting. The audios were converted into scattering images, so the architecture used 2D convolutions instead of 1D convolutions, as would correspond to sequential input data. According to our results, the misclassification (around 11%) is very similar to that of *natural* audios, such as *deepfake* audios, so the model is not biased. In addition, performance is very nearly the same between training, validation and test curves. This implies that there is no overfitting and that the trained model is expected to be able to detect *deepfake* audios, in most cases.

However, for future work, we propose the following tasks: increase the amount and diversity of data (training, validation and testing), evaluate the models by transfer learning and compare them with our customized model, and include other type of data transformation (e.g. histograms, spectrograms). Furthermore, evaluate the performance of the classifier against attacks such as additive noise, re-sampling and re-quantization.

Acknowledgment. This work is supported by the "Universidad Militar Nueva Granada - Vicerrectoría de Investigaciones" under the grant IMP-ING-2936 of 2019.

References

1. Kietzmann, J., Lee, L.W., McCarthy, I.P., Kietzmann, T.C.: DeepFakes: trick or treat? Bus. Horiz. **63**(2), 135–146 (2020)
2. Paris, B., Donovan, J.: Deepfakes and cheap fakes. Data Soc. 47 (2019)
3. Ahmed, S.: Who inadvertently shares deepfakes? Analyzing the role of political interest, cognitive ability, and social network size. Telemat. Inf. **57**, 101508 (2021)
4. Lieto, A., et al.: Hello? Who am i talking to? A shallow CNN approach for human vs. bot speech classification. In: ICASSP, IEEE International Conference on Acoustics, Speech and Signal Processing - Proceedings, vol. 2019, pp. 2577–2581 (2019)
5. Yu, P., Xia, Z., Fei, J., Lu, Y.: A survey on deepfake video detection. IET Biomet. (2021)
6. Guera, D., Delp, E.J.: Deepfake video detection using recurrent neural networks. In: Proceedings of AVSS 2018–2018 15th IEEE International Conference on Advanced Video and Signal-Based Surveillance, pp. 1–6 (2019)
7. Dolhansky, B., Bitton, J., Pflaum, B., Lu, J., Howes, R., Wang, M., Ferrer, C.C.: The deepfake detection challenge dataset. arXiv preprint arXiv:2006.07397 (2020)
8. Lyu, S.: Deepfake detection: Current challenges and next steps, pp. 1–6 (2020)
9. Nguyen, T.T., Nguyen, C.M., Nguyen, D.T., Nguyen, D.T., Nahavandi, S.: Deep Learning for Deepfakes Creation and Detection: A Survey, pp. 1–12 (2019)
10. van den Oord, A., et al.: WaveNet: A Generative Model for Raw Audio, pp. 1–15 (2016)
11. Elias, I., et al.: Parallel Tacotron 2: A Non-Autoregressive Neural TTS Model with Differentiable Duration Modeling (2021)
12. Saito, Y., Takamichi, S., Saruwatari, H.: Vocoder-free text-to-speech synthesis incorporating generative adversarial networks using low-/multi-frequency STFT amplitude spectra. Comput. Speech Lang. **58**, 347–363 (2019)
13. Arik, S., et al.: Deep voice: real-time neural text-to-speech. In: 34th International Conference on Machine Learning, ICML 2017, vol. 1, pp. 264–273 (2017)
14. Arik, S.O., et al.: Deep voice 2: multi-speaker neural text-to-speech. In: Advances in Neural Information Processing Systems, vol. 2017, pp. 2963–2971 (2017)
15. Ping, W., et al.: Deep voice 3: scaling text-to-speech with convolutional sequence learning. In: 6th International Conference on Learning Representations, ICLR 2018 - Conference Track Proceedings, pp. 1–16 (2018)
16. Zhu, X., Xue, L.: Building a controllable expressive speech synthesis system with multiple emotion strengths. Cogn. Syst. Res. **59**, 151–159 (2020)
17. Maiti, S., Marchi, E., Conkie, A.: Generating multilingual voices using speaker space translation based on bilingual speaker data. In: ICASSP 2020–2020 IEEE International Conference on Acoustics, Speech and Signal Processing (ICASSP), pp. 7624–7628. IEEE (2020)

18. Zhao, Y., et al.: Voice conversion challenge 2020: intra-lingual semi-parallel and cross-lingual voice conversion. arXiv preprint arXiv:2008.12527 (2020)
19. Sisman, B., Yamagishi, J., Member, S., King, S.: An Overview of Voice Conversion and its Challenges: From Statistical Modeling to Deep Learning, pp. 1–27 (2008)
20. Mohammadi, S.H., Kain, A.: An overview of voice conversion systems. Speech Commun. **88**, 65–82 (2017)
21. Canton, C., Brian Dolhansky, J.B., Ben Pflaum, J.P., Lu, J.: Deepfake detection challenge results: An open initiative to advance AI, June 2020https://ai.facebook.com/blog/deepfake-detection-challenge-results-an-open-initiative-to-advance-ai/
22. Héctor, N., Tomi, K., Xuechen, A., Jose, M.S., Massimiliano, X.W., Junichi. ASVSPOOF 2021: Automatic speaker verification spoofing and countermeasures challenge evaluation plan (2021)
23. Reimao, R., Tzerpos, V.: FoR: a dataset for synthetic speech detection. In: 2019 10th International Conference on Speech Technology and Human-Computer Dialogue, SpeD 2019 (2019)
24. Ballesteros, D.M., Rodriguez, Y., Renza, D.: A dataset of histograms of original and fake voice recordings (h-voice). Data Brief **29**, 105331 (2020)
25. Rodriguez, Y., Ballesteros, D.M., Renza, S.: Fake voice recordings (imitation), November 2019
26. Wang, R., et al.: DeepSonar: Towards Effective and Robust Detection of AI-Synthesized Fake Voices (2020)
27. AlBadawy, E.A., Lyu, S., Farid, H.: Detecting AI-synthesized speech using bispectral analysis. In: CVPR Workshops, pp. 104–109 (2019)
28. Chen, T., Kumar, A., Nagarsheth, P., Sivaraman, G., Khoury, E.: Generalization of audio deepfake detection. In: Proceedings of the Odyssey Speaker and Language Recognition Workshop, Tokyo, Japan, pp. 1–5 (2020)
29. Gao, Y., Vuong, T., Elyasi, M., Bharaj, G., Singh, R., et al.: Generalized spoofing detection inspired from audio generation artifacts. arXiv preprint arXiv:2104.04111 (2021)
30. Ballesteros, D.M., Rodriguez-Ortega, Y., Renza, D., Arce, G.: Deep4SNet: deep learning for fake speech classification. Expert Syst. Appl. **184**, 115465 (2021)
31. Rodríguez-Ortega, Y., Ballesteros, D.M., Renza, D.: A machine learning model to detect fake voice. In: Florez, H., Misra, S. (eds.) ICAI 2020. CCIS, vol. 1277, pp. 3–13. Springer, Cham (2020). https://doi.org/10.1007/978-3-030-61702-8_1

Automatic Classification of Energy Consumption Profiles in Processes of the Oil & Gas Industry in Colombia

Bryan Escobar-Restrepo$^{(\boxtimes)}$ ⓘ, Juan Felipe Botero Vegaⓘ, and Juan Rafael Orozco-Arroyaveⓘ

GITA Lab. Faculty of Engineering, Universidad de Antioquia, Medellín, Colombia
bryan.escobarr@udea.edu.co

Abstract. Smart meters provide detailed information about energy consumption behavior for different types of users. With the aim to enable automatic decisions that directly impact the performance of the energy network and the consumption of customers, machine learning (ML) methods emerge as a reasonable alternative. The accelerated growth in the implementation of Advanced Metering Infrastructure (AMI) in Colombia allows the exploration of different ML methods to contribute in the process of automating the analysis, control, and operation of different energy systems including those related with oil and gas exploitation. This paper presents a methodology to automatically discriminate information extracted from 72 smart meter currently operating in energy networks that provide service to different processes of the oil and gas business in Colombia. The obtained results indicate that it is possible to automatically discriminate between transport vs. extraction energy systems with accuracies of up to 69.1%. Similarly, the classification between transport vs. other kinds of systems yields accuracies of up to 65.3%.

Keywords: Machine learning · Smart meters · Classification · Advanced Metering Infrastructure

1 Introduction

The implementation of smart meters has driven the development of the smart grid sector around the world. The Advanced Metering Infrastructure (AMI) is nowadays a critical part of the system due to their important role in measuring, controlling and managing energy delivery and consumption. An AMI consists of the combination of communication networks, Metering Data Management Systems (MDMS) and smart meters (see Fig. 1). The last component is the most important one especially when the energy provider wants to add reliability, efficiency and security to its electrical system/network [3].

A smart meter is an electronic device used to measure different variables including active power, reactive power, voltage and current either consumed or generated. These devices are used by utility companies to monitor the operating

J. C. Figueroa-García et al. (Eds.): WEA 2021, CCIS 1431, pp. 49–59, 2021.
https://doi.org/10.1007/978-3-030-86702-7_5

status of the power grid and to bill energy consumption. These devices bring many advantages to the electrical system. For instance the high-resolution of the collected data provides detailed information on the consumption behavior of different types of users. This information has become a fundamental basis for the use, management and optimization of the different processes that depend on the electricity market. Additionally, efficiency in the energy demand is also an important aspect that can be managed using smart meters [7,9]. Despite all positive aspects that appear when using AMIs, there are several limitations in performing different analyses upon the information generated with the smart meters. For instance the study of consumption profiles, anomaly detection, and prediction of consumption are among our interest [8], and has lead to different research projects around the world [5].

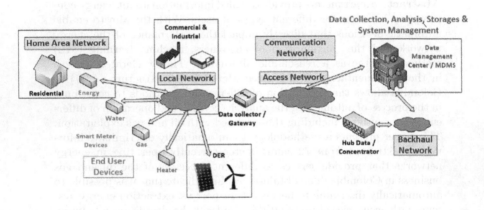

Fig. 1. Advanced metering infrastructure. Taken from [8].

An additional problem that appears when studying information collected from AMIs is the lack of labels. This limits the development of automatic systems to two main options: unsupervised learning methods or supervised methods optimized following cross-validation strategies and applying classification schemes like those where one class is compared with respect to the rest, i.e. "one vs. all".

This work applies different algorithms from the supervised learning area and analyzes their performance when classifying different measuring devices installed to monitor energy consumption of different processes of the oil & gas industry in Colombia. The rest of the paper is organized as follows: Sect. 2 describes the used database, the different stages and the algorithms implemented in the classification process. Section 3 describes the experimental settings and analyzes performance of the obtained results. Finally, the conclusions are presented in Sect. 4.

2 Methodology

2.1 Database Description

This study considers data from 72 smart meters of companies from the Colombian industry related to transport, refinery, and production of Oil & Gas. Data collected for this study include energy consumption measured every hour for three years between 2017-01 and 2019-12. The time-series include data from active power, reactive power, and power factor penalty. The data for this study was provided by IEB - Specialized Engineering[1]. Each meter is labeled according to the process to which it belongs to, as follows: "Extraction", "Biofuel", "Transport", "Administrative buildings", "Transport and storage" and "Refinery". Table 1 summarizes the number of meters per process. Note that a total of 5 devices are not associated to any of the processes.

Table 1. Data base description.

Process	# of meters
Biofuel	2
Administrative buildings	4
Extraction	22
Refinery	3
Transport and storage	3
Transport	33
Without label	5

2.2 Feature Extraction

The first step to perform the feature extraction consists in pre-processing the time series of each meter. Since there were cases of meters which did not provide data for days or even weeks, missing data were discarded. Each time series was amplitude-normalized prior to the windowing and filtering processes. After normalization, the time series are smoothed with two moving average filters one for periods of one day and another one for periods of one week. Later, the signals are filtered with a bank of 6 low-pass finite impulse response filters, with a cutoff frequency of 75% of the maximum frequency of the time series. Also, different window sizes are considered for the original time series, with the aim to cover different possible recurrent consumption patterns that may appear in the different processes considered in this study. The windows sizes included in the further experiments are 24-h, one-week, 12-h and 6-h. There was an overlap of 50% for all cases. Finally, the features set extracted from the new signals described above is listed below:

---

[1] https://www.ieb.co/energia/index.php.

- Mean energy and six statistical functionals: mean, standard deviation, maximum, minimum, kurtosis and skewness were calculated for the windows obtained.
- The Mean Squared Error and Mean Absolute Error are computed to measure the difference between each filtered time series and the original signals. Additionally, the same statistical functional described in the previous item are estimated for the filtered signals.
- The statistical functionals are also estimated for the original time series.

2.3   Statistical Tests - Based Feature Selection

The selection of features is performed by Mann Whitney U tests. Only those features that showed to be significantly different ($p \ll 0.05$) for the two classes involved on each classification experiment are included. After this statistical analysis only four features were discarded: the minimum of both moving average extractors and the minimum and maximum of the time series.

2.4   Hyper-Parameters Optimization

The hyper-parameters optimization is performed by following a nested cross-validation strategy with 4 external folds. The inner three folds used for training are distributed to optimize the hyper-parameters (i.e., development set). Those optimal parameters are tested upon the external test fold and the process is repeated until all external folds are appropriately tested. Finally, the mode over the vector of optimal hyper-parameters is taken as the optimal one with its corresponding accuracy.

2.5   Automatic Classification

Random Forest: This algorithm selects the feature that best separates and characterizes the classes, establishing it as the root of the tree. Based on this, questions are asked about the other characteristics, forming the branches until reaching the selection of the classes, which would be the leaves. The Random Forest algorithm consists of an ensemble of multiple decision trees, which are formed by Bootstrap aggregating stages. In this method small portions of the original database are randomly taken, namely the bootstrapped datasets [1]. The final decision is made based on the most voted or selected class among the decision trees [4].

eXtreme Gradient Boosting (XGBoost): The main idea of this algorithm is to obtain better classification performance by assembling several learning algorithms. In this case, XGBoost uses decision trees, which are trained in order and used as boosting trees. The objective is to correct the errors and improve the classification performed by the previous decision trees. The optimization procedure is based on the gradient descent algorithm [2]. The objective function of this algorithm is as follows:

$$f(\hat{\mathbf{X}}) = \min_{f \in \mathcal{F}} \mathbb{E}_{X|Y}(L(\mathbf{Y}, f(\mathbf{X}))) \tag{1}$$

$$f(\mathbf{X}) = \sum_{m=1}^{M} f_m(\mathbf{X}) \tag{2}$$

Where $\mathbf{Y}$ are the real labels for $\mathbf{X}$ and $f(\hat{\mathbf{X}})$ is the function f of a space of functions $\mathcal{F}$, that evaluated in $\mathbf{X}$ minimizes the expected value of $L(\mathbf{Y}, f(\mathbf{X}))$, L is a differential convex loss function, f_m is the decision tree function and M is the number of trees. The number of trees, maximum depth and learning rate of the trees need to be optimized.

Support Vector Machine (SVM): The main goal of this algorithm is to find an optimal hyper-plane so that samples of both classes are correctly classified [6]. The optimal hyper-plane is found with the following equation, which is solved as a convex optimization problem.

$$y_n \cdot (\mathbf{w}^T \phi(\mathbf{x}_n) + b) \geq 1 - \xi_n, \quad n = 1, 2, 3, \cdots, N \tag{3}$$

Where w is the vector of weights and b the bias, which defines the separation of the hyper-plane, ξ_n is a positive slack variable such that the sum of all ξ_i is the upper threshold of possible errors in the training set. N is the number of observations of the feature vector $\mathbf{x}$. $y_n \in \{-1, +1\}$ are the class labels and $\phi(\mathbf{x}_n)$ is the kernel function that maps $\mathbf{x}_n$ to a higher dimensional space where the two classes can be linearly separated. The optimization problem that needs to be solved to find the optimal hyper-plane is as follows:

$$\min_{w,b} \frac{1}{2} \|\mathbf{w}\|^2 + C \sum_{n=1}^{N} \xi_n \tag{4}$$

$$\text{subject to} \quad y \cdot (\mathbf{w}^T \mathbf{x}_n + b) \geq 1 - \xi_n$$

In this paper we considered two different kernel functions, linear and Gaussian.

3   Experiments and Results

Two experiments are performed in this paper. The first one consists in classifying between transport vs. extraction processes, and the second one is the classification between transport vs. other classes. The experiments are distributed like this for two main reasons: (1) transport and extraction are the most critical processes in the oil & gas industry, so it makes sense to think of automatic systems where most of the effort is put to discriminate between these two processes; and (2) the database that we had access to is highly unbalanced, so there are no other classes with enough data apart from transport, extraction and others. The classification systems are evaluated in terms of accuracy, precision and recall. Additionally, receiver operating characteristics curves (ROC) and detection error trade-off (DET) curves are included.

3.1   Experiment 1: Extraction vs. Transport

A total of sixty-six features were selected in the feature selection process described above. The results are shown in Table 2. Note that transport processes are better classified in all of the cases. The classifier that yields the highest precision for both classes is the Gaussian SVM, with 73.7% for "Extraction" and 75.1% for "Transport". The best average accuracy obtained in this case is 69.1%. The second best classifier is the Random Forest with an average accuracy of 60%. XGBoost shows a similar performance with an accuracy of 67.2%. The confusion matrices associated to the aforementioned results are shown in Fig. 2.

Table 2. Classification results: Extraction vs Transport.

Algorithm	Precision		Recall		Accuracy
	Extraction	Transport	Extraction	Transport	
Random Forest	63.2%	74.6%	60%	76%	69%
XGBoost	63.3%	70.2%	50%	79%	67.2%
Linear SVM	52.4%	69.2%	51%	70%	61.9%
Gaussian SVM	73.7%	75.1%	56%	79%	69.1%

With the aim to provide the reader with an illustrative figure of the distribution of the samples Fig. 3(a) shows the first two components of the resulting space after applying PCA, and Fig. 3(b) shows the distribution of the scores obtained for transport and extraction samples. Note that in this case scores refers to the distance of each sample to the optimal separating hyper-plane found with the Gaussian SVM.

Right and left side of Fig. 4 show the results more compactly by using ROC and DET curves, respectively. For the case of the ROC curves, note that although the Gaussian SVM showed the highest average accuracy, the resulting area under the ROC curve (AUC) is smaller (0.72) than the one obtained with the random forest classifier (0.76). This can be observed in the blue lines where a higher true positive rate is obtained, which the same behavior as the one observed in Table 2 where random forest showed better results when detecting the transport processes. A similar analysis can be mentioned for the DET curves (right), where blue lines (corresponding to the random forest classifier) are closer to the origin.

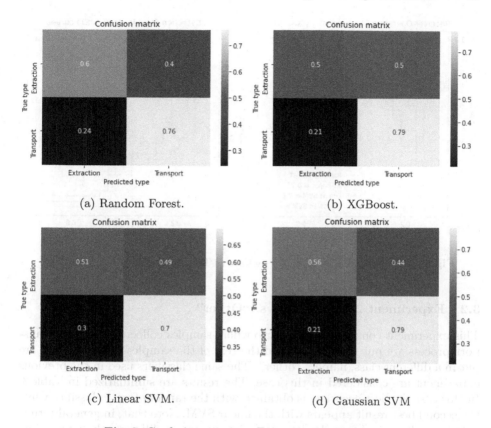

(a) Random Forest.

(b) XGBoost.

(c) Linear SVM.

(d) Gaussian SVM

Fig. 2. Confusion matrices: Extraction vs Transport

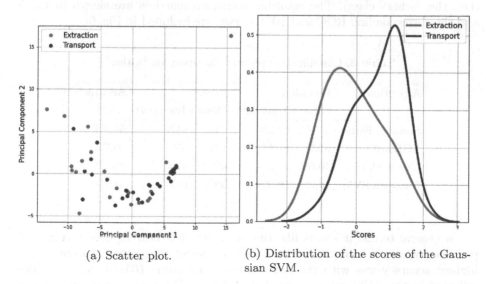

(a) Scatter plot.

(b) Distribution of the scores of the Gaussian SVM.

Fig. 3. Distribution of the scores obtained in the Extraction vs. Transport experiment.

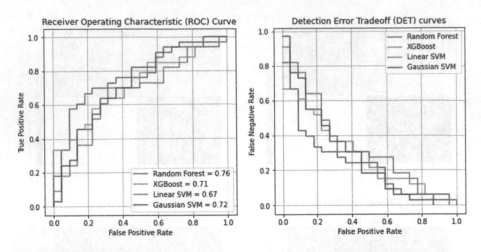

Fig. 4. ROC and DET curves: Extraction vs Transport (Color figure online)

3.2 Experiment 2: Transport vs. "Other"

This experiment considers the scenario where samples collected from the transport process are put in one class and the rest of the samples of the dataset are put in a different class, namely "other". The same classifiers used in the previous experiment are considered in this case. The results are summarized in Table 3. In this case the best accuracy is obtained with the random forest classifier while the second best result appears with the linear SVM. Note that, in general terms, better results are obtained when detecting processes different than transport (i.e., the "other" class). The resulting confusion matrices are shown in Fig. 5 and the corresponding ROC and DET curves are included in Fig. 6.

Table 3. Classification results: Transport vs. "Other"

Algorithm	Precision		Recall		Accuracy
	Other	Transport	Other	Transport	
Random Forest	67.5%	64.2%	69%	61%	65.3%
XGBoost	62.7%	61.1%	64%	55%	59.7%
Linear SVM	70.0%	58.6%	62%	67%	63.9%
Gaussian SVM	66.6%	56.3%	59%	64%	61.1%

In general terms, it seems like the linear SVM is best to detect transport processes while the random forest is best to detect the "other" samples. The highest accuracy was with the random forest algorithm (65.3%) which is also reflected in the AUC values presented in Fig. 6. The lowest performance was obtained by the XGBoost algorithm.

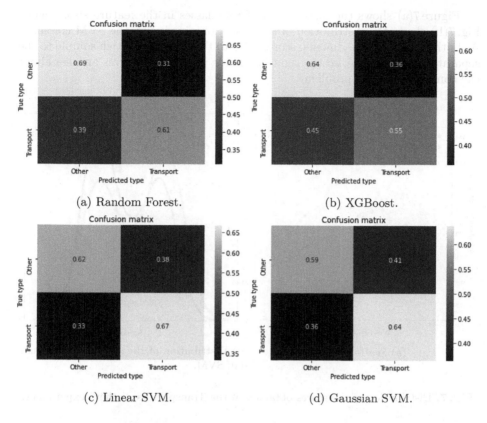

(a) Random Forest.

(b) XGBoost.

(c) Linear SVM.

(d) Gaussian SVM.

Fig. 5. Confusion matrices: Transport vs. "other".

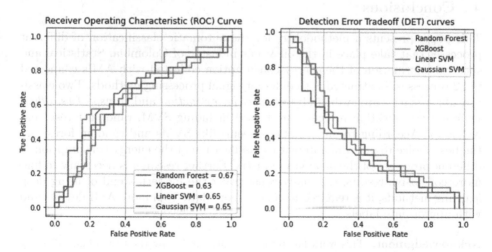

Fig. 6. ROC and DET curves: Transport vs. "other".

Figure 7(a) shows the distribution of the classes in the feature space, while Fig. 7(b) shows the distribution of the scores obtained with the SVM classifier. As in the previous experiments, scores refer to the distance of each sample to the separating hyper-plane, so the right hand side of the figure gives an idea about the complexity of the problem.

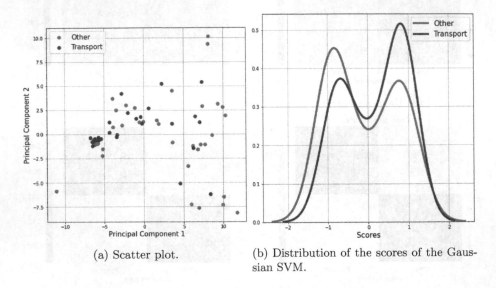

(a) Scatter plot.   (b) Distribution of the scores of the Gaussian SVM.

Fig. 7. Distribution of the scores obtained in the Transport vs. "other" experiment.

4   Conclusions

This paper presents a methodology for the automatic classification of different processes that take place in the oil & gas industry of Colombia. Statistical and spectral information of the energy consumption collected with AMIs connected to 72 processes is extracted with different signal processing methods. Two classification scenarios are evaluated: *transport vs. extraction* and *transport vs. other*. Different classification methods are tested including SVM, random forest, and XGBoost. According to our results, it seems like SVMs and random forest are the best choice to perform automatic classification of the energy consumption in different processes of the oil & gas industry. Further research is necessary to find more conclusive results, especially considering the modern trend of using deep learning methods, it is required to collect more data from more AMI devices and with appropriate labels.

Acknowledgment. This work has been partially funded by the Colombian Ministry of Science, Technology and Innovation within the framework of the call No 849-2019 (Contract No. 80740-799-2019).

References

1. Breiman, L.: Bagging predictors. Mach. Learn. **24**(2), 123–140 (1996)
2. Chen, T., Guestrin, C.: Xgboost: a scalable tree boosting system. In: Proceedings of the 22nd ACM SIGKDD International Conference on Knowledge Discovery and Data Mining, pp. 785–794 (2016)
3. Fang, X., Misra, S., Xue, G., Yang, D.: Smart grid-the new and improved power grid: a survey. IEEE Commun. Surv. Tutor. **14**(4), 944–980 (2011)
4. Ho, T.K.: Random decision forests. In: Proceedings of 3rd International Conference on Document Analysis and Recognition, vol. 1, pp. 278–282. IEEE (1995)
5. Liu, X., Heller, A., Nielsen, P.S.: Citiesdata: a smart city data management framework. Knowl. Inf. Syst. **53**(3), 699–722 (2017)
6. Schölkopf, B., Smola, A.J., Bach, F., et al.: Learning with Kernels: Support Vector Machines, Regularization, Optimization, and Beyond. MIT Press, Cambridge (2002)
7. Tasfi, N.L., Higashino, W.A., Grolinger, K., Capretz, M.A.: Deep neural networks with confidence sampling for electrical anomaly detection. In: 2017 IEEE International Conference on Internet of Things (iThings) and IEEE Green Computing and Communications (GreenCom) and IEEE Cyber, Physical and Social Computing (CPSCom) and IEEE Smart Data (SmartData), pp. 1038–1045. IEEE (2017)
8. Wang, Y., Chen, Q., Hong, T., Kang, C.: Review of smart meter data analytics: applications, methodologies, and challenges. IEEE Trans. Smart Grid **10**(3), 3125–3148 (2018)
9. Yang, J., Zhao, J., Luo, F., Wen, F., Dong, Z.Y.: Decision-making for electricity retailers: a brief survey. IEEE Trans. Smart Grid **9**(5), 4140–4153 (2017)

Organizational Online Reputation Measurement Through Natural Language Processing and Sentiment Analysis Techniques

Christian Orrego, Luisa Fernanda Villa(✉) ⓘ, Lina Maria Sepúlveda-Cano ⓘ, and Lillyana M. Giraldo M. ⓘ

Universidad de Medellín, Medellín, Colombia
cdorregos@eafit.edu.co, {lvilla,lmsepulveda,lmgiraldo}@udem.edu.co

Abstract. The set of perceptions held by various groups based on history and expectations constitutes the reputation of organizations. There are multiple correct measurements of reputation since no general definition of the concept has been reached. ORM (Online Reputation Monitoring-management) systems oversee this measurement and have a sentiment analysis component to perform this task. The literature presents different frameworks or methodologies for measurement developed by academia and industry. These proposals' common objective is to measure online reputation based on the opinions expressed by individuals close to the organization. In the absence of an automatic ORM system, it is necessary to perform this task manually within a company by a person; this can generate operational errors, delay processes, and make scalability impossible to increase the number of items reviewed (news, comments). These drawbacks can be mitigated by automating the measurement of a client's online reputation. This paper contains the development of three methodologies from the literature to explore online reputation measurement starting from Twitter and Google News information sources. The implementation results conclude that the POS-Tagger elimination methodology generates the best result compared to the coded methodologies.

Keywords: Reputation measurement · Reputation assessment · Sentiment analysis · Online reputation · Reputation management · E-reputation

1 Introduction

The most widely used definition of organizational reputation is by Fombrun [6], taking it as a perceived representation of the company based on past actions and future projections that describe the company's overall attractiveness compared to other rivals, analyzing different primary components of the organization. The proper measurement of reputation depends on the point of view from which

Supported by Universidad de Medellín, Colombia.

J. C. Figueroa-García et al. (Eds.): WEA 2021, CCIS 1431, pp. 60–71, 2021.
https://doi.org/10.1007/978-3-030-86702-7_6

the analysis is approached. There are multiple correct reputation measurements since no general definition of the concept has been reached [8].

Measuring reputation is considered a difficult task [4]. Currently, there are multiple alternatives, and finding the proper measurement method is often an obstacle for organizations since the collective perception of Stakeholders (people or organizations interested-affected by the company's decisions) must be measured, which is not possible to measure directly [4]. Stakeholders generally involved in reputation measurement are customers, investors, employees, suppliers, and the general public [9].

The most internationally recognized reputation rankings are carried out by companies specialized in the subject. Fortune magazine publishes the reputational rankings: "American most admired company" - American companies and "World's most admired companies" - international companies; the Reputation Institute, the world's leading firm in reputation research and consulting, has the RepTrak, an annual report of the companies with the best reputation worldwide [4]. The different reputation measurements take into account aspects of organizations such as human resources, financial stability, social responsibility, quality of products/services, long-term investments and innovation; and conduct surveys to the general public and managers-analysts of multiple organizations to consolidate the results [4, 8].

Today, new vulnerabilities to organizational reputation are created by advances in communication technologies, which can also be opportunities to protect and enhance reputation [8]. The development of the Internet enabled a two-way communication mechanism between users and companies, creating a low-cost channel for companies to reach users and allowing individuals to express their opinions in different communities, which can have a global impact [3].

The web is the platform that supports the evolution of online interaction, allowing the generation of content by users (UGC - User Generated Content), which can be published on multiple websites or social networks [10]. The automatic processing of UGC has different challenges generated by the incorrect use of grammar, typos, incomplete or unstructured sentences, abbreviations, ambiguity, or the use of jargon [20].

Mechanisms analyze the bidirectional relationship between users and organizations to measure online reputation. ORMs (Online Reputation Monitoring-management) are alternatives that allow the management or monitoring of companies' online reputations. Online reputation can be defined as results in a search engine, comments in social networks, ranking of customer ratings, articles, and news of the company or products/services [22].

Most of the online data is unstructured text expressed using natural language and usually requires people to be processed and analyzed. Due to the current growth of information, it is necessary to implement automatic processing of user generated content (UGC) [13].

Several organizations (medium and large) implement applications for online reputation monitoring (ORM). eBay and Amazon have embedded in their platforms ORM systems to allow customers to know the ratings and ranking users give to products; these systems were integrated to support decision making [22]. One of the tools that make up ORMs is sentiment analysis. The main objective of sentiment analysis is to extract the opinion of a product or service (entity) to obtain helpful information to summarize the polarity that the user was trying to convey (negative, positive, or neutral) [18].

The literature reviewed proposals' are presented as frameworks or methodologies, and are made by academic and industry. These proposals' common goal is to measure online reputation from individuals' opinions close to the organization. A brand's reputation can be calculated by measuring customer satisfaction based on the sentiment expressed in social networks [25].

Multiple methodologies for ORM emerged from RepLab events or used the data collections generated at these events. RepLab is an international challenge for the evaluation of online reputation monitoring-management (ORM) systems. The first RepLab was held in 2012 [2], counting on researchers and communication industries' participation to face the challenges in automating the calculation and monitoring of companies' online reputation.

The measurement of online reputation is usually performed manually inside a company by searching for information about the company that appears on the web. Because of the effort required, not all reputation analyses are performed. Only certain companies are prioritized for analysis, such as those with higher revenues, causing a loss of valuable information for the rest of the cases.

Manual validation of reputation generates additional time for employees, human errors, process delays and does not allow scalability to increase the number of items reviewed (news, comments) or extend the period being analyzed. It is necessary to solve the above drawbacks by automating the measurement of a client's online reputation. That is why this article seeks to find the principal methodologies that exist in the literature to develop them and compare the results obtained with each of them.

The rest of the article is organized as follows: Sect. 2 introduces the selection process of the methodologies analyzed, and the materials and methods. The results are presented and analyzed in Sect. 3. Section 4 summarizes and presents the conclusions of the article and future work.

2   Materials and Methods

2.1   Reputation Dimensions

The *RepTrak* framework defines seven dimensions that structure organizational reputation (Table 1). These dimensions resulted from multiple stakeholder interviews and focus groups conducted between 1996 and 2006 [7]. To date, the Reputation Institute continues to consider these same dimensions of reputation [19].

2.2   Methodology Selection

As a result of the state of the art review of the methodologies for reputation analysis, these methodologies' typical stages were consolidated in Fig. 1. The

Table 1. Reputation dimensions as defined by the *Reputation Institute*

Dimension	Description
Performance	Reflects the long-term commercial success and financial strength of a company. Attributes: profitable, good performance, and growth potential
Products/Services	Information on products/services and customer satisfaction. Attributes: value for money, responsibility for the quality, quality of products/services, and customer needs satisfaction
Innovation	New ideas and incorporation into products. Attributes: innovative company, easy to adapt to change, and launches innovative products/services
Workplace	Work environment, ability to attract, train and retain talent. Attributes: equal opportunities, employee welfare, and fair wages
Governance	Company's relationship with authorities. Attributes: ethical behavior, responsible use of power, and open and transparent
Citizenship	The company recognizes social and environmental responsibility. Attributes: protects the environment, contributes to society, and supports social causes
Leadership	Company leadership. Attributes: well organized, excellent management, solid and respected leadership, and clear vision of its future

methodologies start with the collection of a data set from the defined sources. Subsequently, the dataset is pre-processed to standardize, improve the information's quality, and guarantee the necessary initial conditions for the subsequent steps. The natural human language contained in the dataset requires transformations to be interpreted by the algorithms/models. The feature extraction stage allows the generation of a set of attributes on the information that the algorithm/model can process; the transformations' general objective is to represent the text as numbers in a matrix. The algorithm/model can be a machine learning technique or a set of steps to achieve the expected result. In the validation stage, numerical comparison of the algorithm's different performance metrics against an expected or desired value is performed; this comparison allows analysis and conclusions about the methodology.

In order to select the most appropriate methodologies for online reputation measurement, a detailed review of articles in the literature related to sentiment analysis and classification of reputation dimensions was conducted.

The criteria for selecting the methodology for measuring reputation were:

1. The methodology must use machine learning algorithms/models. This criterion is based on the fact that most of the works of other authors are based on machine learning algorithms.

2. The methodology must implement one of the algorithms/models most frequently used in the literature. The three techniques with the highest frequency are Support Vector Machine [14,20,25,26], Decision Trees/Random Forest [1,5,17,20], and Naive Bayes [11,27]. A methodology from the literature can implement multiple machine learning techniques in order to compare and select the technique that obtains the best results. Similarly, these three algorithms/models are analyzed in the systematic review conducted in [23], and for the data used, it was obtained that the best result in sentiment analysis was generated by Support Vector Machine vs. Naive Bayes, Random Forest, and Linear Regression.
3. The machine learning algorithm/model must fit the problem conditions.
   Based on the above criteria, the methodologies described in Table 2 were selected.

Table 2. Selected methodologies for reputation analysis

ID	Task	Pre-processing	Feature extraction	Model	Validation
M1 [20]	Sentiment classifier	– Stopwords removal – Replacing Hashtags and Cashtags – Mapping numbers and signs	– Word2Vec	– Random Forest – Support Vector Machines – Multilayer Perceptron	– 10-fold cross validation – Accuracy – F-score
M2 [27]	Sentiment classifier and Score computation	– Remove non-ASCII characters	– Subjectivity – Diversity – Polarity – Readability – Message length – Ranking – Customer Involved	– Naive Bayes – Deep Learning	– Standard Error
M3 [5]	Sentiment classifier	– POS-Tagging	– Bag of Words	– Random Forest	– ROC curve – F-score

2.3 Materials

Dataset. The information of the top then companies with the best reputation, based on the study carried out by Merco (*Monitor Empresarial de Reputación Corporativa*) during October 2019 and published in the *Merco Empresas* report [15], was selected to be analyzed and to collect the necessary datasets for the measurement of reputation through natural language processing and sentiment analysis.

The dataset consists of information from Twitter and Google News about the ten companies selected. The collection of the dataset was done through Twitter's exposed service (developer API), and for the Google News information, a web scraper was used, which allows generating the same results as the search compared with the results obtained by people through the Google News web page.

The Twitter dataset was collected during October, November, and December 2019, generating a total of 25,514 Tweets in Spanish, distributed by companies and dates. There are tweets and re-tweets; re-tweets were considered as input for reputation measurement because the original tweet is not necessarily in the dataset. The texts analyzed are of a maximum of 140 characters, a limitation generated by the Twitter API. The search in the Twitter service was performed using each of these companies' official accounts, through the tags at (@) and hashtag (#). The tweets mentioned through both tags were obtained for each company.

The Twitter dataset was manually labeled, classifying them in: *positive*, *neutral*, or *negative*. The average labeling time per tweet was 2.5 s; the total labeling required approximately 18 h from a subject matter expert. This person is considered an expert since he/she has performed this manual analysis of news and tweets in a service provider entity.

The classes are unbalanced, and the one with the highest representation is the *neutral* class (63.7%); this is because this social network has become a communication channel with customers, generating a large number of tweets without sentiment, that is, only informative content that cannot be considered as negative or positive for the reputation of the company.

Regarding the Google News data, this information was extracted on November 11, 2019, and January 15, 2020. The dataset was manually labeled, classifying them into the categories: positive, neutral, or negative. The average labeling time per news item was 2.5 s; the total labeling required approximately 1 h and 21 min from a subject matter expert.

The information from Twitter and Google News was unified into a single dataset used in the following stages. Table 3 shows the distribution of the resulting classes. This dataset was divided into training data (training) and test data (test) through random sampling. Partitioning is necessary to ensure that the information used for training is not used to calculate performance metrics. The information was partitioned into 70% for training and 30% for calculating the metrics (test).

Table 3. Distribution of labels in the consolidated dataset

Label	Number of observations	Train	Test
Positive - P	5100	3626	1474
Negative - N	4722	3290	1432
Neutral - NEU	17642	12308	5334
Total	27464	19225	8240

3   Results and Discussion

This section shows the detailed steps for the implementation of the previously selected methodologies and the results obtained with each one of them. Python was the tool selected to support the construction of the methodologies, using mainly the *pandas* library for data manipulation, *sci-kit learn* for creation of the learning algorithms, *NTLK* in text processing, *Stanford NLP* in some pre-processing stages, and *pickle* to store the generated models.

The training dataset was pre-processed, and the features were extracted according to the previously detailed stages. The coding of the labels was carried out using the indicator variable transformation so as not to generate a non-existent ordinal relationship.

3.1   Methodology M1

This methodology's main differentiator is in the preprocessing stage due to the proposed incorporation of Word2Vec; an algorithm used to represent the opinion to be classified (in our case, Tweet or Google News).

Pre-processing. This stage's objective is to standardize the input to improve the results in the following stages.

Feature Extraction. The authors of the methodology M1 in [20] do not detail the implementation of Word2Vec but refers to implementing the algorithm developed by Mikelov [16], referenced to complement the implementation details. The Word2Vec algorithm was previously required to be trained with context-specific data, so it was trained with all Twitter and Google News texts after the standardization and cleaning application was previously detailed.

The training was developed through the *gensim* library, expecting a vector of 300 positions (dimension) and generated through the skip-grams model as detailed in [16]. These texts are divided into sentences since to generate the vector representing the words; it takes into account the words around them. Initially, a vector of size 300 is generated for each word in the text (*Bag-of-Embeddings*), which is used to represent each word. This algorithm was trained with 37,620 sentences contained in the 27,465 texts (Twitter + Google News). The *Bag-of-Embeddings* contains 18,484 unique words.

Once the *Bag-of-Embeddings* is generated, it is applied to each of the text's words to be categorized, either the tweet or the statement of the news. The resulting text vectors are averaged to find a 300-position vector used to represent the entire tweet or news item.

Algorithm/Model. As detailed in the methodology, three classification algorithms were implemented: Random Forest, Support Vector Machine (SVM), and Multilayer Perceptron (MLP). The SVM algorithm was implemented with a

Label encoder since it is not built to accept the *One-hot* encoder because it internally implements a *one-against-one* technique, which creates $n_{classes}(n_{classes} - 1)/2$ classifiers [21]. MLP was implemented with Label and One-hot encoders. The metrics analyzed were Precision, Recall, and F-score. Since the F-score is a harmonic measure between Precision and Recall, Fig. 1 compares the three algorithms vs. this metric, generating the best results for the three classes (positive, negative, and neutral) Random Forest. The three classifiers generated the worst results for the negative label, which corresponds to the class with the lowest number of samples.

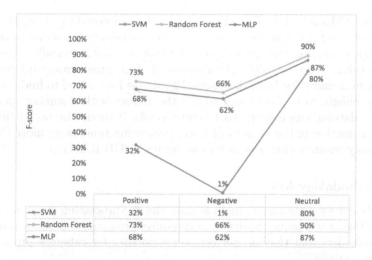

	Positive	Negative	Neutral
SVM	32%	1%	80%
Random Forest	73%	66%	90%
MLP	68%	62%	87%

Fig. 1. Comparative F-score for the M1 methodology algorithms

3.2 Methodology M2

The methodology presented in [27] uses the *TextBlob* natural language processing library to execute the feature extraction and algorithm/model stages. This library packages and uses functionalities from the *NLTK* and *pattern.en* libraries, providing tasks such as POS-Tagging, sentiment analysis, classification, and translation algorithms. Feature extraction in this methodology uses the *TextBlob* library to obtain subjectivity, diversity, polarity, and readability, but they are not yet developed for the Spanish language; at the moment, it supports English, French, and German [24]. Due to the above, it is impossible to implement the methodology fully, but this library has a classification functionality through Naive Bayes, which was used and detailed in the model/algorithm stage.

Pre-processing. The following transformations were applied to the information: standardize all text to lowercase, elimination of special characters and numbers. Only words containing the letters of the alphabet (a-z) are retained. The input to the model requires the data structured as Python tuples, so the information is structured in the "(text, label)" structure.

Feature Extraction. As previously indicated, the *TextBlob* library indicated in the methodology is not available for the Spanish language, so it is impossible to extract features as indicated by the authors. Since this library provides methods for the fast creation of classification algorithms, the function *textblob.classifiers.NaiveBayesClassifier*, programmed internally for automatic feature extraction on an input text, was used. This function is generic and does not depend on the language but the training data. By default, a simple feature extractor is used, indicating which set of words are in the document, similar to the BOW algorithm.

Algorithm/Model. The Naive Bayes algorithm proposed in the methodology was implemented through the function *textblob.classifiers.NaiveBayesClassifier*, which allows entering the data in text format and automatically detects the response variable classes. This library presented internal errors and generated problems in memory for large data sets [12]; it was impossible to find a solution for this problem, so it was chosen to use the library with a smaller amount of data. The dataset was reduced to 10,000 records, it should be noted that even with the reduction in the number of data, processing times were more than 5 h, and memory consumption was at its maximum (32GB RAM).

3.3   Methodology M3

The methodology [5] has as its main feature the pre-processing stage, in which it uses Pos-Tagger techniques to detect and remove pronouns and nouns from texts since it considers that they do not contain a polarity for category prediction in sentiment analysis.

Pre-processing. As mentioned above, the methodology proposes to implement Pos-Tagger (grammatical tagging) to identify the grammatical categories to be eliminated. The *Stanford NLP* library provides this functionality for the Spanish language.

The cleaning of the text consists of eliminating nouns (NOUN), pronouns (PRON), and proper names (PROPN) since they do not generate value in the sentiment analysis because sentiments are mainly expressed textually in adjectives (ADJ), adverbs (ADV) and verbs (VERB). Additionally, lemmatization is applied to words that are not deleted. The lemma of a word is the word that would be found as an entry in a traditional dictionary.

Feature Extraction. After data cleaning, feature extraction was applied using the BoW technique; based on the total number of texts, a dictionary of unique words was built, to later build a vector for each text of the size of the dictionary where each position represents a word and employing zeros ("0") and ones ("1") the presence or absence of the word in the text is indicated.

The BoW construction generated a dictionary of 7,114 words, causing each text's feature vector to be of this same size.

Algorithm/Model. Based on these feature vectors constructed through BoW, the Random Forest algorithm was implemented. The response variable was transformed using a *Label* encoder since it generated better results vs *One-hot* encoding.

As a summary, Fig. 2 shows the F-score metrics for each of the models/algorithms developed. As can see, the best result was generated by the M3 methodology, obtaining the best metrics for each of the classes (positive, negative, and neutral).

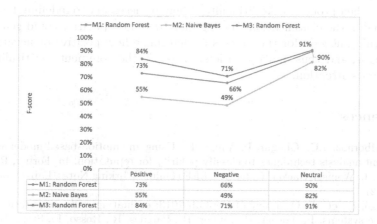

	Positive	Negative	Neutral
M1: Random Forest	73%	66%	90%
M2: Naive Bayes	55%	49%	82%
M3: Random Forest	84%	71%	91%

Fig. 2. Comparison of the F-score for the methodologies implemented for online reputation measurement

4   Conclusions and Future Works

In this paper, the development of three methodologies to explore the measurement of online reputation based on Twitter and Google News data is presented. The results of the implementation conclude that, through the three methodologies, it is possible to generate a reputation measurement that allows reducing the reaction time to a comment on Twitter or Google News; however, the M3 methodology, which makes use of POS-Tagger elimination, generates the best results compared to the coding methodologies. In general, the class that obtained the lowest results was the negative class; This class contains the fewest records. It is proposed to increase the number of records on this class to observe a possible improvement in the methodologies' metrics.

The M2 methodology, which is based on the use of *Texblob*, is discarded as a possible implementation option due to unresolved bugs in the library; it should be monitored for knowledge and testing as the Spanish language version exists.

The typical stages of these methodologies (dataset, preprocessing, feature extraction, algorithms/model, validation and analysis, and conclusions) allow building a basis for the definition of the generic methodology that allows standardizing the measurement of reputation automatically an organization.

Likewise, it was observed in the data that the highest proportion of tweets are of neutral content. The social networks may have become an additional channel of communication of companies, so the presence of emotions in these texts may not exist, given that the objective is to establish an informative communication between the customer and the company, causing the reduction of the number of comments where users express their opinions.

As future work, we propose generating a performance measurement in the execution of each of these methodologies, given that current business solutions are looking for real-time answers that reduce the time for decision-making and automate their processes. Additionally, it may be necessary to redefine the classes to be used in the classification. Having more detail on polarity could generate a more significant gain for the process to determine how positive or negative the comment is, and thus, make decisions based on the comment's criticality and prioritize its attention.

References

1. de Albornoz, J.C., Chugur, I., Amigó, E.: Using an emotion-based model and sentiment analysis techniques to classify polarity for reputation. In: Forner, P., Karlgren, J., Womser-Hacker, C. (eds.) CLEF (Online Working Notes/Labs/Workshop) (2012)
2. Amigó, E., et al.: Overview of RepLab 2013: evaluating online reputation monitoring systems. In: Forner, P., Müller, H., Paredes, R., Rosso, P., Stein, B. (eds.) CLEF 2013. LNCS, vol. 8138, pp. 333–352. Springer, Heidelberg (2013). https://doi.org/10.1007/978-3-642-40802-1_31
3. Dellarocas, C.: The digitization of word of mouth: promise and challenges of online feedback mechanisms. Manag. Sci. **49**(10), 1407–1424 (2003)
4. Eckert, C.: Corporate reputation and reputation risk: definition and measurement from a (risk) management perspective. J. Risk Financ. **18**(2), 145–158 (2017)
5. Fang, X., Zhan, J.: Sentiment analysis using product review data. J. Big Data **2**(1), 1–14 (2015). https://doi.org/10.1186/s40537-015-0015-2
6. Fombrun, C.J.: Reputation Realizing Value from the Corporate Image, vol. 1. Harvard Business School (1996)
7. Fombrun, C.J., Ponzi, L.J., Newburry, W.: Stakeholder tracking and analysis: the reptrak® system for measuring corporate reputation. Corp. Reput. Rev. **18**(1), 3–24 (2015)
8. Gatzert, N., Schmit, J.: Supporting strategic success through enterprise-wide reputation risk management. J. Risk Financ. **17**(1), 26–45 (2016)
9. Helm, S.: One reputation or many? Comparing stakeholders' perceptions of corporate reputation. Corporat. Commun.: Int. J. **12**(3), 238–254 (2007)
10. Kaplan, A.M., Haenlein, M.: Users of the world, unite! the challenges and opportunities of social media. Bus. Horiz. **53**(1), 59–68 (2010)
11. Kaptein, R.: Learning to analyze relevancy and polarity of tweets. In: CLEF (2012)
12. User grochmal - data science stack exchange. https://datascience.stackexchange.com/users/74735/grochmal. Accessed 02 June 2019
13. Manaman, H.S., Jamali, S., AleAhmad, A.: Online reputation measurement of companies based on user-generated content in online social networks. Comput. Hum. Behav. **54**, 94–100 (2016)

14. McDonald, G., Deveaud, R., Mccreadie, R., Macdonald, C., Ounis, I.: Tweet enrichment for effective dimensions classification in online reputation management (2015)
15. Merco: Ranking merco empresas colombia (2019). https://www.merco.info/co/ranking-merco-empresas?edicion=2019
16. Mikolov, T., Chen, K., Corrado, G., Dean, J.: Efficient estimation of word representations in vector space (2013)
17. Peetz, M.H., de Rijke, M., Kaptein, R.: Estimating reputation polarity on microblog posts. Inf. Process. Manag. **52**(2), 193–216 (2016)
18. Qazi, A., Raj, R.G., Hardaker, G., Standing, C.: A systematic literature review on opinion types and sentiment analysis techniques: tasks and challenges. Internet Res. **27**(3), 608–630 (2017)
19. RepTrak: Why reputation institute: The quantification of reputation (2018). https://www.reputationinstitute.com/why-reputation-institute
20. Saleiro, P., Rodrigues, E.M., Soares, C., Oliveira, E.: Texrep: a text mining framework for online reputation monitoring. N. Gener. Comput. **35**(4), 365–389 (2017)
21. Scikit-learn: 1.4. support vector machines - scikit-learn 0.24.1 documentation. https://scikit-learn.org/stable/modules/svm.html. Accessed 15 Dec 2019
22. Shuhud, M.I.M., Alwi, N.H.M., Abd Halim, A.H.: Initiating an online reputation monitoring system with open source analytics tools. In: Journal of Physics: Conference Series, vol. 1018, p. 012016. IOP Publishing (2018)
23. Singh, N., Tomar, D., Sangaiah, A.K.: Sentiment analysis: a review and comparative analysis over social media. J Ambient Intell. Humaniz. Comput. 1–21 (2020)
24. TextBlob: Extensions - textblob 0.16.0 documentation. https://textblob.readthedocs.io/en/dev/extensions.html. Accessed 01 Dec 2019
25. Vidya, N.A., Fanany, M.I., Budi, I.: Twitter sentiment to analyze net brand reputation of mobile phone providers. Procedia Comput. Sci. **72**, 519–526 (2015)
26. Yang, C., Bhattacharya, S., Srinivasan, P.: Lexical and machine learning approaches toward online reputation management. In: CLEF (Online Working Notes/Labs/Workshop) (2012)
27. Zhao, Y., Xu, X., Wang, M.: Predicting overall customer satisfaction: big data evidence from hotel online textual reviews. Int. J. Hosp. Manag. **76**, 111–121 (2019)

Robust Automatic Speech Recognition for Call Center Applications

Luis Felipe Parra-Gallego[1,2]([✉]) [iD], Tomás Arias-Vergara[1,3] [iD],
and Juan Rafael Orozco Arroyave[1,3] [iD]

[1] GITA Lab. Faculty of Engineering, University of Antioquia UdeA,
Medellín, Colombia
{lfelipe.parra,tomas.arias,rafael.orozco}@udea.edu.co
[2] Konecta Group S.A.S., Medellín, Colombia
[3] Pattern Recognition Lab, Friedrich-Alexander-Universität Erlangen-Nürnberg,
Erlangen, Germany

Abstract. This paper is focused on developing an Automatic Speech Recognition (ASR) system robust against different noisy scenarios. ASR systems are widely used in call centers to convert telephone recordings into text transcriptions which are further used as input to automatically evaluate the Quality of the Service (QoS). Since the evaluation of the QoS and the customer satisfaction is performed by analyzing the text resulting from the ASR system, this process highly depends on the accuracy of the transcription. Given that the calls are usually recorded in non-controlled acoustic conditions, the accuracy of the ASR is typically decreased. To address this problem, we first evaluated four different hybrid architectures: (1) Gaussian Mixture Models (GMM) (baseline), (2) Time Delay Neural Network (TDNN), (3) Long Short-Term Memory (LSTM), and (4) Gated Recurrent Unit (GRU). The evaluation is performed considering a total of 478,6 h of recordings collected in a real call-center. Each recording has its respective transcription and three perceptual labels about the level of noise present during the phone-call: Low level of noise (LN), Medium Level of noise (ML), and High Level of noise (HN). The LSTM-based model achieved the best performance in the MN and HN scenarios with 22,55% and 27,99% of word error rate (WER), respectively. Additionally, we implemented a denoiser based on GRUs to enhance the speech signals and the results improved in 1,16% in the HN scenario.

Keywords: ASR · Noise reduction · Speech enhancement · Speech-to-text

1 Introduction

Millions of calls answered in call centers are recorded and stored every day. The recordings are used for different purposes including to improve the Quality of

Supported by University of Antioquia.

J. C. Figueroa-García et al. (Eds.): WEA 2021, CCIS 1431, pp. 72–83, 2021.
https://doi.org/10.1007/978-3-030-86702-7_7

the Service (QoS). Typically the QoS evaluation process consists in listening to the conversations between call-center agents and customers to label whether the service requested by the customer was successfully provided or not. This procedure is usually done by humans who evaluate the service by randomly taking samples from the total set of calls. During the evaluation process, it is analyzed the reason for the call, the emotional state of both the customer and advisor, the effectiveness and promptness of the service provided by the agent, and others [18]. Although the aforementioned is the standard procedure, it has two main disadvantages: (1) it is very expensive and time consuming, and (2) only a few samples over the total calls are evaluated, so it is not possible to know about all critical calls that could negatively impact the service [18].

With the aim to make the above mentioned process more efficient, automatic systems are designed to rate the calls based on the text transcription of the spoken conversation. This is performed by using Automatic Speech Recognition (ASR) systems. Once the conversations are transcribed, several information are extracted from the resulting texts including keywords, key sentences, number and types of hesitations, specific expressions, and others. The main advantage of ASR-based systems is that they enable the analysis of all answered calls automatically. Although ASR systems are the natural way to go in order to improve QoS in call centers, their accuracy directly affects the performance of the system that rates the calls (the one that is based on text analysis). This means that transcriptions with errors could produce wrong interpretations for the QoS evaluation system. Typically, an ASR works with high performance under ideal acoustic conditions; however, many different factors reduce the ASR performance, such as the speaker's health condition and emotional state, the communication channel including the microphone and the sound card, environmental noise, and others.

This work aims of developing ASR system robust against different noisy scenarios. We first evaluate four hybrid architectures in three levels of noise: low, medium, and high. We then propose to implement a Deep Learning based-denoiser in order to clean the speech signal and thus improve the recognition performance. The denoiser is based on Complex Linear Coding (CLC), a similar approach presented in [13]. To assess the denoising technique, we re-evaluated the ASR systems' performance when passing the noisy recordings through the filter.

The rest of this paper is organized as follows: Sect. 2 presents an overview of related works; Sect. 3 describes the database; Sect. 4 introduces the methodology followed in this work; Sect. 5 shows the results obtained in this study; and Sect. 6 includes the conclusions and future work.

2   Related Works

Several techniques have been proposed in the literature to model acoustic features in ASR systems. The most typical approaches used nowadays are those based on Hidden Markov Models - Gaussian Mixture Models (HMM-GMM), and Hidden Markov Models - Deep Neural Network (HMM-DNN) [16]. HMM-GMM has played an important role in designing conventional recognizers because they are easy to train and have low computational cost [16]. Thanks to the advances in computational power and machine learning algorithms, DNN has shown excellent results in different applications including ASR. In [5] and [4], results using different acoustic models in ASR systems with different acoustic conditions are reported. Both works show that DNN-based models outperform classical methods based on GMMs. Different topologies of networks have been proposed to improve the ASR performance. In [14] three topologies are compared: (1) Recurrent Neural Network, (2) Long Short-Term Memory (LSTM), and (3) Gated Recurrent Unit (GRU). The authors used a total of 378 audio recordings from the TED talks in English. The dataset contains files for training, validation, and test. Spectrograms were used to train the acoustic model and the best WER was achieved using LSTM (65.04%). The authors reported that GRU showed similar results (67,42% WER) in a shorter period training time; GRU only ran for 5 days and 5 h while LSTM required slightly more than seven days.

More complex architectures based on end-to-end systems have been recently proposed. In [17], the authors compared different "very deep models". Convolutional LSTM with a residual connection (reConvLSTM) was also introduced in the same work. Convolutional LSTM layers basically replace multiplication operations among parameters and inputs by convolutions. Their architecture consists of 2 convolutional layers, followed by 4 ResConvLSTM and finally an LSTM Network in Network block. A total of 80 filter-banks with their deltas were used as the feature set. The Wall Street Journal (WSJ) English corpus [8] was used to train and test the network. This database contains 73 h for training and 8 h for testing. The model proposed by Zhang et al. in [17] showed a WER of 10,53%, while previous studies were around 18% in the same corpus. In the same line, the authors in [1] proposed an end-to-end system where its input is the raw speech signal. To do that, they used a convolutional filter learning based on rectangular band-pass filters. This technique is called SincNet. The authors proposed to connect SincNet to an end-to-end recurrent encoder-decoder structure using joint CTC-attention procedure. It was used WSJ corpus [8], and TIMIT corpus [3] for training and testing the model. The authors compared their system with traditional end-to-end models operating on Mel-filter-banks. For the TIMIT database, their technique did not show improvements in comparison to conventional hybrid DNN-HMM perhaps due to the small amount of available training data (less than 5 h). On the other hand, when using WSJ, their technique obtained a top-of-line WER of 4.5%, outperforming all baselines. The previous best score was 5.9% WER, which means an absolute improvement of 1.2%.

Other kinds of techniques as speech enhancement, domain adaptation, and data augmentation have also been studied with DNNs. In [7], it was proposed the problem-agnostic speech encoder (PASE), a novel architecture that combines a convolutional encoder followed by multiple neural networks, called workers, tasked to solve self-supervised problems. The aim of each worker is to generate features extracted from the original speech signal as MFCCs, log power spectrum, gammatone features, waveform speech signal, and others. The needed consensus across different tasks naturally imposed meaningful constraints to the encoder, contributing to discover general representations and hence minimizing the risk of learning superficial features. The authors performed self-supervised training with a portion of 50 h of the LibriSpeech dataset [5]; TIMIT [3], DIRHA [11] and CHiME-5 [2]. In order to validate the technique, the authors trained a hybrid DNN-HMM speech recognizer using different acoustic features such as MFCC, filter bank, gammatone, and MFCC + gammatone + filter bank. The features extracted from the PASE architecture significantly outperformed the other feature sets, with a relative improvement of 9.5% in clean speech and of 17.7% in noisy conditions using TIMIT.

3   Databases

We evaluate the proposed ASR systems using a call-center database called KONECTADB. The recordings were captured in non-controlled acoustic conditions, so we implemented a denoising technique to enhance the speech signals. We split the dataset into two parts, train and test, with the aim to optimize and evaluate the ASR system and the denoiser. The augmented version of KONEC-TADB was created by adding noise of the Demand Noise Dataset (DND).

3.1   KONECTADB

This corpus contains recordings of conversations between customers and agents of a contact-center of the Konecta Group company in Medellín, Colombia. The customers were informed that their speech was going to be recorded. Due to the nature of the service, it is assumed that the speakers in these recordings are all of legal age. The database consists of 478, 6 h of audio with a sampling frequency of 8 kHz and a 16 bits resolution. Experts in QoS annotated the recordings in the contact center. Each audio has its transcription text, the customer's gender, and its level of noise. Since the recordings were captured in non-controlled acoustic environments, this database is useful to evaluate the robustness of ASR systems against noisy conditions. Table 1 shows the demographic information of this database.

3.2   Demand Noise Dataset (DND)

The DND corpus [15] contains a variety of noise signals taken in real-world acoustic environments. The database considers two scenarios, namely "inside" environments and "open-air" environments. The inside recordings are divided into Domestic, Office, Public, and Transportation; while the open-air recordings are classified as Street and Nature. All recordings are captured with a 16-channel array of microphones sampling at 48 kHz. Thus, each environment noise recording is actually a set of 16 mono sound files.

Table 1. Demographic description of Konecta database. **LN:** Low level of noise. **MN:** Medium level of noise. **HN:** High level of noise. **Male:** Number of male recordings. **Female:** Number of female recordings

Label of noise	# of speakers	Gender distribution		Hours	
		Male	Female	Training	Test
LN	18938	19459	27313	321,0	30,3
MN	6615	7180	8191	101,4	15,9
HN	633	636	666	8,7	1,2

3.3   Data Augmentation

Clean recordings of KONECTADB are augmented by adding noise signals of the DND corpus. The noisy samples are created by randomly taking two different noises from the DND corpus associated with different Signal-to-Noise Ratio (SNR) levels: $-5, 0, 5, 10, 20,$ and $40\,\mathrm{dB}$. To achieve the selected SNR level, the noise is scaled by a factor α, which is expressed as:

$$\alpha = \sqrt{\frac{P_{s(t)}}{SNR \cdot P_{n(t)}}} \tag{1}$$

where $P_{s(t)}$, $P_{n(t)}$, and SNR are speech signal power, noise signal power, and SNR computed in linear scale, respectively.

Training and test sets were augmented separately and used to train and evaluate the denoiser described in Sect. 4.1. The data augmentation algorithm is depicted in Fig. 1.

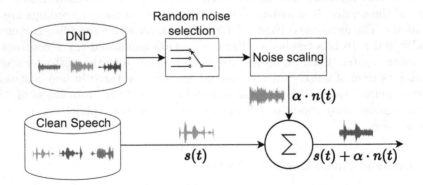

Fig. 1. Data augmentation process.

4   Methodology

Figure 2 illustrates the overall process to train and test an ASR system. At the top, it is described the training stage, and at the bottom the test one.

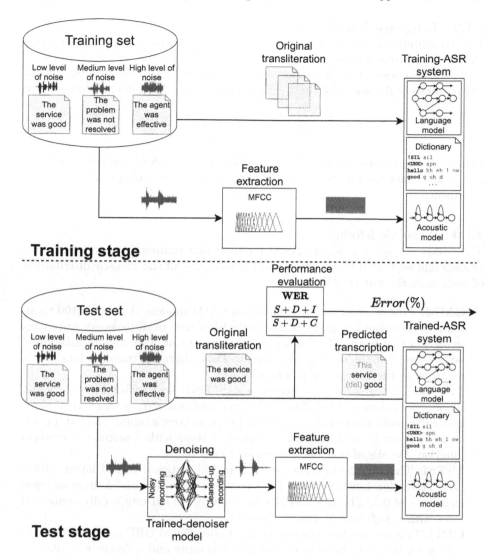

Fig. 2. General methodology followed in this study.

4.1 Training Stage

This stage encompasses feature extraction, Language Model (LM), Acoustic Model (AM), and the Dictionary.

4.1.1 Feature Extraction

This study considered a total of 40-MFCCs extracted from 40 triangular Mel-frequency bins with a window size of 25 ms and a step size of 10 ms. The spectrogram is unit-normalized.

4.1.2 Language Model

The transliteration of the training set was used to train a 3-gram language model. The probabilities of a language model can be computed by counting relative frequencies of the 3−tuples of words that belong to the training set. To estimate the probabilities of the 3−gram model, the following equation is used:

$$P(w_n|w_{n-1}, w_{n-2}) = \frac{C(w_{n-2}, w_{n-1}, w_n)}{C(w_{n-2}, w_{n-1})} \tag{2}$$

where w_n represents a word located in position n, and C represents a function that counts the number of occurrences of the word sequence defined in its argument.

4.1.3 Acoustic Model

This study considers a 3-state HMM for modeling temporal dependencies. We trained and evaluated four different models to represent the acoustic distribution of each acoustic unit (HMM state).

- **GMM:** This acoustic model is based on GMM models. A total of 100 thousand of Gaussian components and a decision tree of 4016 leaves were considered in this work. The GMMs were trained using a Maximum Likelihood estimation. This model was also used to force-align the training data and is regarded as the baseline in this study.
- **TDNN:** This architecture consists of six TDNN layers with 1536 units and a bottleneck dimension of 256. Each layer contains a frame context of three and a skip connection coming from the previous layer's input. The last TDNN layer's output is fed into a fully connected layer with a softmax activation function. Details of this method can be found in [9].
- **LSTM:** This architecture consists of four bidirectional LSTM layers with a *tanh* activation function. Each layer contains 550 units and a dropout regularization of 0.2. The last LSTM layer's output is fed into a fully connected layer with a *softmax* activation function.
- **GRU:** This architecture consists of five bidirectional GRU layers with a *relu* activation function. Each layer contains 550 units and a dropout regularization of 0.2. The last GRU layer's output is fed into a fully connected layer with a *softmax* activation function.

The forced-aligned data generated by the GMMs were used to train the DL-based models. On the one hand, the Kaldi toolkit [10] was used to train the TDNN model using Stochastic Gradient Decent (SGD) with an initial learning rate of 0.00015 and batch size of 64. On the other hand, ADAM optimizer with an initial learning rate of 0.0002 and batch size of 64 was used to train the LSTM- and GRU- based architectures using Pytorch-Kaldi framework [12]. We only considered five epochs due to computational constraints.

4.1.4 Dictionary

The dictionary contains the phone pronunciation of each word to be recognized in our model. The phone composition is performed using pronunciation rules of the Spanish language from Colombia. To build the dictionary, the most frequent words seen in the training set were selected. This study considered 20 thousand different words.

4.2 Test Stage

This involves the same processes as the training stage and also includes denoising and performance evaluation. To avoid any possible bias and to guarantee the generalization capability of the model, this process only considers recordings of the test set.

4.2.1 Denoising Model

The denoiser is thought to enhance the speech signals. We used a similar approach as the one presented in [13]. A Short-Time Fourier transform (STFT) was computed using a 25 ms Hanning window with a step size of 10 ms. The model architecture consists of a fully connected layer followed by two GRU layers and finally, two fully connected layers. The input to the model is the unit-normalized complex spectrogram. The last layer predicts the masking coefficient to denoise the complex spectrogram. The mask aims to reduce noise effects by multiplying weights closer to zero with those frequency bands that contain noise energy. The masked complex spectrogram is then transformed into the time-domain using the inverse STFT function. The complete filter process is illustrated in Fig. 3.

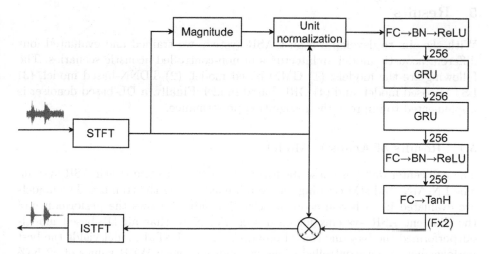

Fig. 3. Denoising process [13]. F is the number of frequency bins and $\otimes$ is the Hadamard product.

The augmented training dataset of KONECTADB described in Sect. 3 is used to train the system. The original signals are used as the ground truth during the training process of the GRU. The GRU-based denoiser is trained with Pytorch using the Adam optimization strategy with an initial learning rate of 0.0001 and a batch size of 10. Only five epochs are considered due to computational constraints.

4.2.2   Performance Evaluation

Once the ASR system is trained, this is used to convert the recordings into text transcriptions of the test set. Word Error Rate (WER) was computed to evaluate the model. This is the a well known performance measure typically used to evaluate ASR systems [6]. It is defined as follows:

$$WER = \frac{S + D + I}{S + D + C} \tag{3}$$

where,

- S: # of substitutions.
- D: # of deletions.
- I: # of insertions.
- C: # of correctly recognized words.

WER compares two text chains. This metric counts the number of operations needed to convert one text into another one. WER is computed upon the original transcription and the predicted transcription in the case of an ASR system.

5   Results

With the aim to develop a robust ASR system, we trained and evaluated four different acoustic model architectures in non-controlled acoustic scenarios. The following are the models: (1) GMM-based model, (2) TDNN-based model, (3) LSTM-based model, and (4) GRU-based model. Finally, a DL-based denoiser is implemented to improve the recognition performance.

5.1   Results of Acoustic Model

The call center database described in Sect. 3 is used to train each ASR system. The LN, MN, and HM training sets were mixed during the training. The models are evaluated in each real acoustic scenario. Table 2 shows the performance of the different ASR systems for each scenario. Note that all DL-based models outperformed the baseline (based on GMMs). The LSTM model yields the best performance in non-controlled acoustic conditions with WER values of 22, 55% and 27, 99% for MN and AN scenarios, respectively. Note that all models except the GMM-based one, obtained similar WER values in the LN condition, that is: 21, 73% for TDNN, 21, 31% for LSTM, and 21, 30 for GRU.

Table 2. Performance of the ASR systems in terms of the WER in each real acoustic conditions. **LN:** Low level of noise. **MN:** Medium level of noise. **HN:** High level of noise.

Architecture	Acoustic scenario		
	LN	MN	HN
GMM	32,10	35,54	52,47
TDNN	21,73	23,48	30,94
LSTM	**21,31**	**22,55**	**27,99**
GRU	**21,30**	22,67	28,77

5.2 Results of Denoising Process

The denoiser described in Sect. 4.1 was trained to enhance noisy speech signals. The augmented training dataset of KONECTADB was used to train the model. Two test sets are considered to evaluate the capability of the filter to suppress/remove the noise: (1) The artificially created noisy recordings (The scenario described in Sect. 3), and (2) The noisy recordings of the HN test set (Real scenario). WER values of the ASR systems are computed for the noisy and enhanced speech signals for comparison purposes. Table 3 shows the performance obtained for the DL-based ASR systems in the simulated and real scenarios. The TDNN model shows improvements in both scenarios when the denoiser is applied. In the simulated conditions, the WER goes down from 40,41% to 35,70%, and in the real noisy conditions it changes from 30,94% to 26,83% which is actually the best performance obtained for noisy conditions. For the case of the LSTM-based model in the simulated scenario, without denoising it yields the worst WER for noisy conditions (44,39%), but it improves to 38,88% after applying the denoiser. Although the improvement is relatively high (5,51 absolute percentage points), the result is still the worst among the rest obtained in that scenario. Regarding its results in the real conditions, without any denoising procedure, the LSTM yields the best WER (27,99%), however, when the denoiser is applied the WER value increases to 29,63%. A similar behavior can be observed for the GRU model, where the WER value obtained in the simulated conditions prior to the denoiser is 40,41% and it gets better to 37,27% when the denoiser is applied; however, in the real noisy conditions, its WER value gets worst in 1 absolute percentage when the denoiser is applied (from 28,77% to 29,77%).

Table 3. Performance of the ASR systems in terms of the WER before and after applying the denoiser. **Simulated:** The augmented test set. **Real:** The HN test set of KONECTADB. Values in %.

Model	Simulated conditions		Real conditions	
	Noisy	Enhanced	Noisy	Enhanced
TDNN	**40,41**	**35,70**	30,94	**26,83**
LSTM	44,39	38,88	**27,99**	29,63
GRU	40,41	37,27	28,77	29,77

6   Conclusions and Future Work

This work presented a methodology to improve the recognition performance of ASR systems. We trained and evaluated four different acoustic models in non-controlled acoustic conditions: (1) GMM-based model (Baseline), (2) TDNN-based model, (3) LSTM-based model, and (4) GRU-based model. The models were trained with recordings of a call center database, called KONECTADB. This database contains customer service telephone calls. Each recording was captured in real acoustic conditions and it was labeled in terms of its level of noise: low, medium and high. These acoustic conditions allowed us to evaluate the models in real noisy acoustic conditions. The LSTM-model achieved the best performance for medium and high levels of noise, which likely indicates that this model is the most robust in non-controlled conditions.

With the aim to improve the recognition performance, a DL-based filter was developed to clean the speech signals. The portion of KONECTADB with low level of noise was artificially contaminated with noise signals taken from Demand Noise Dataset. We trained the denoiser using the noisy recordings. Once the denoiser was trained, the ASR models were again evaluated in two scenarios: (1) Simulated (The artificially contaminated test set), and (2) the real test set with the recordings originally labeled as high level of noise. The WER was computed before and after passing the recordings through the denoiser. On the one hand, the performance of the GRU- and LSTM- based models decreased after the denoising process. But, on the other hand, the TDNN model achieved the best results when the denoiser was applied in both simulated and real acoustic scenarios. The observed improvement was 1,16% of WER with respect to the result obtained by the LSTM without any denoising strategy. For future work we consider to explore more complex architectures in the denoising process to see whether the performance can be further improved.

Acknowledgements. This work was funded by Konecta Group in association with CODI at the University of Antioquia, grant # PI2019-24110. Tomás Arias-Vergara is under grants of Convocatoria Doctorado Nacional-785 financed by MINCIENCIAS.

References

1. Agrawal, P., Ganapathy, S.: Interpretable filter learning using soft self-attention for raw waveform speech recognition. arXiv preprint arXiv:2001.07067 (2020)
2. Barker, J., Watanabe, S., Vincent, E., Trmal, J.: The fifth 'CHiME' speech separation and recognition challenge: dataset, task and baselines. arXiv preprint arXiv:1803.10609 (2018)
3. Garofolo, J.S., Lamel, L.F., Fisher, W.M., Fiscus, J.G., Pallett, D.S., Dahlgren, N.L.: Timit acoustic-phonetic continuous speech corpus LDC93S1. Web Download. Linguistic Data Consortium, Philadelphia (1993)
4. Kinoshita, K., et al.: The REVERB challenge: a benchmark task for reverberation-robust ASR techniques. In: Watanabe, S., Delcroix, M., Metze, F., Hershey, J.R. (eds.) New Era for Robust Speech Recognition, pp. 345–354. Springer, Cham (2017). https://doi.org/10.1007/978-3-319-64680-0_15

5. Panayotov, V., Chen, G., Povey, D., Khudanpur, S.: Librispeech: an ASR corpus based on public domain audio books. In: 2015 IEEE International Conference on Acoustics, Speech and Signal Processing (ICASSP), pp. 5206–5210. IEEE (2015)
6. Park, Y., Patwardhan, S., Visweswariah, K., Gates, S.C.: An empirical analysis of word error rate and keyword error rate. In: Ninth Annual Conference of the International Speech Communication Association (2008)
7. Pascual, S., Ravanelli, M., Serrà, J., Bonafonte, A., Bengio, Y.: Learning problem-agnostic speech representations from multiple self-supervised tasks. arXiv preprint arXiv:1904.03416 (2019)
8. Paul, D.B., Baker, J.M.: The design for the wall street journal-based CSR corpus. In: Proceedings of the Workshop on Speech and Natural Language, pp. 357–362. Association for Computational Linguistics (1992)
9. Povey, D., Cheng, G., Wang, Y., Li, K., Xu, H., Yarmohammadi, M., Khudanpur, S.: Semi-orthogonal low-rank matrix factorization for deep neural networks. In: Interspeech, pp. 3743–3747 (2018)
10. Povey, D., et al.: The kaldi speech recognition toolkit. Technical report, IEEE Signal Processing Society (2011)
11. Ravanelli, M., Cristoforetti, L., Gretter, R., Pellin, M., Sosi, A., Omologo, M.: The Dirha-English corpus and related tasks for distant-speech recognition in domestic environments. In: 2015 IEEE Workshop on Automatic Speech Recognition and Understanding (ASRU), pp. 275–282. IEEE (2015)
12. Ravanelli, M., Parcollet, T., Bengio, Y.: The pytorch-kaldi speech recognition toolkit. In: ICASSP 2019–2019 IEEE International Conference on Acoustics, Speech and Signal Processing (ICASSP), pp. 6465–6469. IEEE (2019)
13. Schröter, H., Rosenkranz, T., Maier, A., et al.: CLC: complex linear coding for the DNS 2020 challenge. arXiv preprint arXiv:2006.13077 (2020)
14. Shewalkar, A., Nyavanandi, D., Ludwig, S.A.: Performance evaluation of deep neural networks applied to speech recognition: RNN, LSTM and GRU. J. Artif. Intell. Soft Comput. Res. 9(4), 235–245 (2019)
15. Thiemann, J., Ito, N., Vincent, E.: Demand: a collection of multi-channel recordings of acoustic noise in diverse environments. In: Proceedings of Meetings Acoust (2013)
16. Yu, D., Deng, L.: Automatic Speech Recognition: A Deep Learning Approach. Springer, London (2015). https://doi.org/10.1007/978-1-4471-5779-3
17. Zhang, Y., Chan, W., Jaitly, N.: Very deep convolutional networks for end-to-end speech recognition. In: 2017 IEEE International Conference on Acoustics, Speech and Signal Processing (ICASSP), pp. 4845–4849. IEEE (2017)
18. Zweig, G., et al.: Automated quality monitoring in the call center with ASR and maximum entropy. In: 2006 IEEE International Conference on Acoustics Speech and Signal Processing Proceedings, vol. 1, p. I. IEEE (2006)

Dynamic Recognition and Classification of Trajectories in SLRecon Adopted Artificial Intelligence in Kinect

Tomas S. Gavilanez[1] , Edgar A. Gómez[2] , Eduardo Estevez[3] ,
and Saravana Prakash Thirumuruganandham[4(✉)]

[1] Escuela Politécnica Nacional, Mechanical Department, Quito, Ecuador
[2] Programa de Física, Universidad del Quindío, Quindío, Colombia
[3] Universidade da Coruña, Escuela Universitaria Politécnica, Ferrol, Spain
[4] Centro de Investigación en Mecatrónica y Sistemas Interactivos - MIST
Universidad Tecnológica Indoamérica, Ambato, Ecuador
saravanaprakash@uti.edu.ec

Abstract. We have proposed "SLRecon" a digital representation of the exoskeleton by Kinect software to analyze the movement of the hands and thus identifies the trajectories taken by the signs for further processing. Subsequently, the trajectories were considered for phases such as training, validation and testing of a neural network-based artificial intelligence algorithm. The network responsible for recognizing and classifying 5 important signs determined by an expert. The neural network is a multilayer perceptron that was trained using the backpropagation method. The training phase was performed with 6 subjects and additionally tested with 9 subjects. We also discussed the results from the simulation phase, which confirmed that the system achieved 99.6% efficiency in detection and classification, while it achieved 98.7% accuracy in the field test. Finally, we compared and validated our results with other methods.

Keywords: Classification · Kinect · Sign language · Recognition · Neural networks · AI · Trayectories · Motion Sensor

1 Introduction

1.1 Sign Language

Establishing successful sign language recognition, generation, and translation systems demands competence in multi-disciplinary branches, including computer vision, computer graphics, natural language processing, human-computer interaction, linguistics, and Deaf culture. A deaf or hypo acoustic person has a loss of sensitivity results from deficit in the transmission of sound via the middle ear and/or loss of transduction of mechanical vibrations into electrical nerve activity in the inner ear [1]. Performance evaluation and analysis have been a core topic

© Springer Nature Switzerland AG 2021
J. C. Figueroa-García et al. (Eds.): WEA 2021, CCIS 1431, pp. 84–96, 2021.
https://doi.org/10.1007/978-3-030-86702-7_8

in Sign Language recognition (SLR) research [2]. Around the world, there exist several types of sign languages that are subjected to the evolution of the natural process of language, that conveys sign languages are specific to each country [19]. And developing a universal library for all sign languages is a complicated task, that could be merely possible in the coming decades. Recently, Suharjito et al. [15], proposed a new Action Recognition model named i3d inception to adopt Sign Language Recognition, according to their observation on the specified i3d inception declares a 100% accuracy on training with 10 words and 10 signers with 100 classes but the validation accuracy was pretty low. Similarly, Rathi et al. [16] devised a novel 2-level ResNet50 based Deep Neural Network Architecture to classify finger spelled words obtained from the standard American Sign Language Hand gesture dataset, Their dataset was first augmented using various augmentation techniques, their Level 1 model classifies the input image into one of the 4 sets. After an image was classified into one of the sets it was provided as an input to the corresponding second level model for predicting the actual class of the image. Their model yielded an accuracy of 99.03% on 12,048 test images. We also note that, Parcheta et al. [17], applied LeNet convolutional neural network model for isolated word sign language recognition and validated their model for the "Spanish sign language db" which contains data from 92 different gestures captured with the Leap Motion sensor. On the other hand, Wilson et al. [18], reported a non-manual signals in German sign language. Their approach is based on Mouth gestures, for the recognition of certain mouth gestures they applied 3D convolutional networks for the classification as well as extraction of both spatial and temporal features, their implementation, describes on how different initialisation affect learning and classification by the network, their model produces an accuracy of around 68% on testing 10 classes of mouth gestures in German Sign Language. Considering all those research works that have been conducted on Sign Language Recognition (SLR), Consequently, in this paper, we propose the use of the SDK v1.8 tools to obtain the coordinates of the hands and determine the spatial trajectories described by the hands during a sign. Supervised training is then carried out using several people in such a way that the network can understand the differences that might exist when interpreting a sign. In Ecuador, sign language is composed of five thousand words [3] of which a small group of representative signs has been considered for this research. Following the criteria of [4], the signs considered here are: "Take", "Hello", "Good Morning", "Good Night", and "How are you?". Concerning, sign language consists of manual signs, facial kinesics, oral kinetic, dactylology, and somatic kinesics [5]. The most important component is manual signs, the trajectories of the limbs described by these signs can be obtained by a 3D Sensor. The remainder of this paper is organized as follows, we sectioned in two areas one is 3D sensor development and the second one is an Implementation of Artificial intelligence, later we discussed how we coupled these two techniques to process the 5 representative signs. Section 2 details the materials and methods used; Sect. 3 describes the results of while Sect. 4 contains the conclusions of the study.

1.2   3D Sensor

There are several 3D sensors available in the market for the application and sign language. In [6] a comparison was made between the following: Microsoft Kinect, ASUS Xtion Pro Live, Photonic E70P, IFM O3D200, and Nippon Signal FX6. For all sensors, the detected noise, error, and point rate were evaluated under different conditions such as Sensor-to-object distance, ambient lighting, and object Surface. This test determined that Microsoft Kinect and ASUS Xtion Pro Live projected light sensors have great accuracy for distances of up to 3.5 m that make them ideal for this application. Figure 1 shows the Kinect and its components. These components are used to recognize the presence of people and extract the coordinates of the skeleton. The Software Development Kit (SDK) contains libraries that allow access to Kinect data from various application development platforms such as Visual Studio. Kinect can recognize up to 6 people within the visible range, of which we can calculate the exoskeleton positions of 2 [14]. To represent the default exoskeleton, Kinect delivers the positions of 20 reference joints [7], these points are represented in Fig. 2.

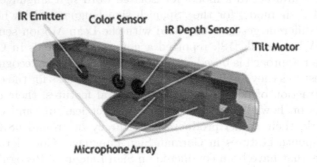

Fig. 1. Parts of Kinect

1.3   Artificial Intelligence

Intelligence is a broad branch of study that comprises several fields. Concerning [8] and [9] the most important of these branches are: fuzzy logic, genetic algorithms, and artificial neural networks. All these branches, artificial neural networks is the most used to perform the recognition and classification of patterns [29,30]. Several neural network architectures enable prediction, conceptualization, classification, and association. According to [10], Multilayer perceptron with backpropagation (BP) is one of the most established neural network architectures due to their ability to perform arbitrary nonlinear mappings. It is noteworthy to mention that common architectures for pattern recognition are: counter propagation (CP), and learning vector quantization (LVQ). The principle of CP and LVQ network operation is similar because both use a Kohonen layer for that CP is discarded in this analysis. We compared these two techniques with our backpropagation scheme. The best performance of a neural or

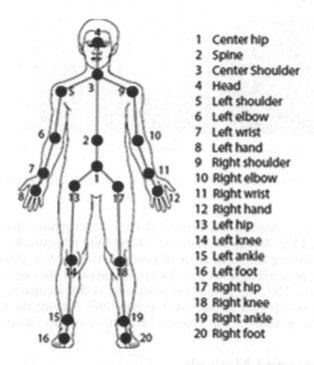

Fig. 2. Graphical representation of the skeleton

other network depends on the specific application, this could be determined by analyzing the work of [11,12], and [13], In some cases, a network had a better performance while in other cases poor performance could be observed. For this specific application, three types of networks were compared with the configuration as shown in Table 1.

Table 1. Structures and characteristic of ANN tested

Neurons number	BP_30	LVQ_30	LVQ_60
Input layer:	180	180	180
Hidden layer:	30	30	60
Output layer:	5	5	5
Training time:	1'45''	55''	12'
Number of iterations:	15	115	9
Minimum quadratic error:	2.16e−09	0.002963	0.00741
Number of neurons:	220	220	250

Looking at Table 1, it can be noted that the three networks allow the sign language to be recognized and classified, as we noted that, the minimum quadratic error is minimal; However, if we look at the confusion matrices in Fig. 3, we can

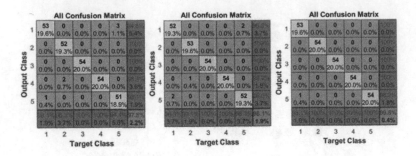

Fig. 3. Confusion Matrix ANN LVQ30, ANN LVQ 60, BP 30 (MatLab)

see that the BP network has an error of 0.4% in the training phase, compared to 2.2% of the LVQ 30 network and 1.9% of the LVQ 60 network.

After considering the three types of neural networks, it is determined that the multilayer perceptron trained by backpropagation is the one with the least quadratic error. Also, the output calculation is easier compared to the LVQ network, so it is expected to run faster in real-time. Finally, the training time required for this network is not a constraint to its implementation.

2   Materials and Methods

In this section, we detailed the system design. An HMI was developed in Visual Studio that allows us to take and export exoskeleton data in real-time, such data was used to design the Artificial Intelligence algorithm, that corresponds to a multilayer neural network trained by the backpropagation method. The design of the neural network and its training were developed in Matlab, subsequently, the weights and thresholds obtained as a result of the training were exported to the system for the relevant tests. Following section A and B describes the hardware and software that we used in the system.

2.1   Hardware

- A tripod holding the Kinetic in an appropriate position, which follows the manufacturer's recommendation was placed at 1.15 m high; while the person was 1.8 m from the sensor.
- Kinect.
- Display or projector (optional).
- ASUS brand computer with the following technical characteristics. Operating System: Windows 10 Pro, Memory RAM: 8,00 GB, Type of system: 64 bits, Processor: Intel(R) Core(TM) i-7 @ 2.40 GHz, Memory: 1 TB, Graphics card: Nvidia Geforce 940M.

2.2 Software

To create the system of HMI, we adopted the following tools, Visual Studio 2015, Matlab 2017, and the SDK for Kinect version 1.8. The user interface (HMI) was developed in Visual Studio, whereas Matlab was considered to design the neural network. We note that SDK allows Visual Studio to access the Kinect data. The following section explains the details of how the software for the systems was developed.

Data Acquisition. Analyzing the sign language dictionary the average duration of a sign was 3 s, with a minimum of 1.5 s and a maximum of 5 s. We note, Kinect is capable of generating a maximum of 30 fps (frames per second). During the test phase it was determined that the variation in the hand trajectory obtained at 30 fps was very small (0.04 m), so we established a rate of 6 sample/second. Consequently, in 5 s we generated 30 data for each coordinate(xyz). It infers that a total of 180 data will be taken for a sign.

Neural Network Design. The neural network architecture is shown in Fig. 4. The proposed neural network consists of 180 inputs, the hidden layer has 30 neurons and the output layer has 5 neurons, one for each character that should be recognized and classified. The neural network outputs are shown in Table 2. And the activation function used is shown in Eq. 1.

$$g(a) = \frac{1 - e^{-2a}}{1 + e^{2a}} \tag{1}$$

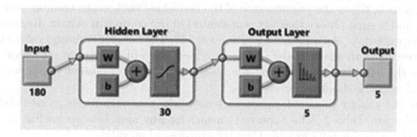

Fig. 4. Proposed neural network architecture in MatLab

Table 2. Outputs of neural network

Sign	Outputs				
Good Morning	1	0	0	0	0
Good Night:	0	1	0	0	0
Hello:	0	0	1	0	0
Take:	0	0	0	1	0
How are you?:	0	0	0	0	1

In continuation, other configurations were also tested resulting in a lower performance was observed compared to the neural network as shown in Fig. 4.

Neural Network Training. Neural network training was carried out with a total of 6 individuals. For each person, we processed nine times for every single sign, which delivers a total of 270 sign samples. The input data constructed in a manner that consists of 70% of its total content used for training, 15% of its content used for validation, and the remaining 15% partitioned for testing

HMI Design. The HMI was developed in Visual Studio, which supports multiple programming languages such as CTM, an object-oriented programming language compatible with Kinect libraries and drivers.

3 Results

It is worth mentioning that the recent work by Qinkun et al. [20] employed a multimodal fusion based on LSTM (Long short-term memory) and a Couple Hidden Markov Model (CHMM) in a framework for traduce Chinese Sign Language (CSL) Recognition. Compared to their systems, they confirmed that this can be used for automatic understanding of common phrases on CSL in the context of a vision-based system. We, on the other hand, interpreted the hand gestures using real-time trajectory analysis and our results were also useful for the hearing impaired community. Moreover, their algorithm uses a post-processing tool to interpret the input images.

Figure 5, shows the performance of the neural network in the training, validation, and testing phases that are represented in the confusion matrix. Regarding the network data, As a sum, we maintained 188 data sets for training, validation, and testing both share 41 data each. In which, data in red spaces represent the times the neural network failed; whereas, green spaces represent the times the neural network classified correctly.

In the design phase of the neural network, the outputs were established according to Table 2. The expected output for any sign is a vector-like [1 0 0 0 0]. However, outputs greater than 0.8 considered as valid.

We also noticed that the best performance was obtained in 20 epochs and this can be seen in our optimization part of the work. We added 6 more validation epochs where the gradient is reduced to 0.00018095, also the cross-entropy reduces to 0.0053684. And the figures from the optimization and cross-entropy are not included. The input data was automatically normalized by Matlab NNtool in a preprocessing phase by using the processing function "mapminmax" to scale the inputs and targets to achieve the range $[-1, 1]$, similar to [33] This data is generated in the training phase. Analyzing the diagrams in Fig. 5, it is concluded that the neural network has effectiveness in recognizing and classifying the sign language of 99.6%, a value that corresponds to 6 individuals for which it was trained. After that we made field tests, to evaluate the performance

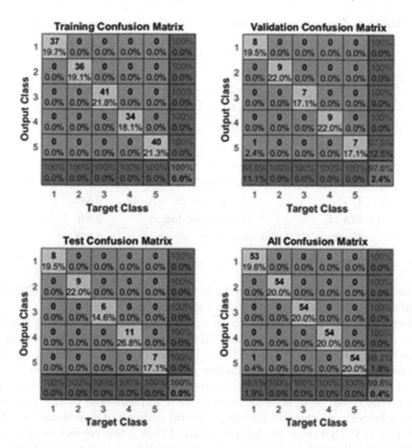

Fig. 5. Confusion matrix obtained from Matlab

of the system each person was asked to make several signs randomly (between 15 and 20). In total 227 tests were conducted with 12 different people, 3 of them were part of the training; while 9 others do not. Among the 227 tests that we conducted only three times the system did not give an adequate response, this indicates the error in recognition and classification goes to 1.32%, and we ensure that this error was generated for two reasons: (1) It can be an error of human misrepresentation while performing the sign inappropriately and also (2) it could be related to network simulation it is inevitable to have subtle errors or changes in readings in the system's network, in our case we found a value of 0.4% error as shown in Fig. 5 of the confusion matrix. Moreover, we also noticed that individual number 4 has two errors, this is unusual in comparison to the results obtained for the rest of the 11 persons. This means that person number 4 did not indicate the sign properly during the test or the system is not familiar with how to make the sign of this person, in either case, we can choose to retrain the system with this person's data to ensure greater performance. Is noteworthy to mention that, Table 3 compares the classification result of our approach

Table 3. Comparison of results on the Chanlearn Gesture dataset [22]

Method	Modalities used	Jaccard
Random Forest	RGB	0.746
MRF	Skeleton + RGB	0.826
Boosted classifier	Skeleton + Depth + RGB	0.833
3D CNN	RGB-D	0.791
3D CNN	Skeleton	0.863
Dynamic DNN	RGB-D	0.787
Dynamic DNN	Multi modal Fusion	0.879
DNN	Depth + RGB + Audio	0.881
SLVM	Multi-modal fusion	0.836
Proposed SLRecon	SDK V1.8	0.978

and the Escalera et al.'s publicly available Chanlearn Gesture dataset [22] , that evaluates the performance of the gesture recognition.

They focused several methods to intrepret the recognition, such as Random Forest, MRF, Boosted classifier, 3D CNN, Dynamic DNN, DNN, etc. with a variables combinations of RGB, Skeleton, Depth and audio modalities, and they extracted a maximum Jaccard coefficient of 0,879. Comparing our results with those of [22], it can be deduced that the technique for recording, reconstruction, discrimination, and analysis of the human body implemented by [23] in SDK V 1.8 has a better performance. Besides, a neural network of convolution is set up jointly in [21] With a multi-modal fusion SLVM that gets a coefficient of Jaccard of 0,836 that tells us the importance of using All Kinect components to remove noise from the entry of information that directly affects the outcome.

The Jaccard coefficient were calculated according to the methodology presented in [21]. The comparison of the input data with the results of our investigation was done according to the equations presented below. The Jaccard Index, is defined as follows:

$$J(s,n) = \frac{A(s,n) \cap B(s,n)}{A(s,n) \cup B(s,n)} \tag{2}$$

where A(s,n) is the ground-truth label of gesture n in sequence s, and B(s,n) is the prediction of algorithmic output for such a gesture at sequence s. The Jaccard Index J(s,n) can be seen as the overlap rate between A(s,n) and B(s,n). To compute the final score, the Jaccard Index is averaged over all gesture classes and all sequences:

$$J = \frac{1}{NS} \sum_{s=1}^{S} \sum_{n=1}^{N} J(n,s) \tag{3}$$

where N = 5 is the number of categories and S is the number of sequences in the test set. We use this mean Jaccard Index as the final evaluation criterion.

The field test identified that the best position for the person is 1.8 m from the sensor at this distance the Kinect can read all points of the skeleton.

4 Conclusions

After analyzing the sign language it is concluded that to make a sign mainly the movement of the hands is used, such movements can be represented by trajectories, this being precisely the most noticeable difference between sign and sign.

According to Ting et al. [24], they used the same 3D rendering technique for the exoskeleton, so in the same context, we recognize hands with Kinect with high performance even when ambient noise is present. This is why the Kinect and V1.8 SDK perform well for this application as it is robust against environmental interference such as light and objects.

Artificial intelligence algorithms are widely used for sign language recognition and classification [25–27] and [28], one of the most commonly used with good results are artificial neural networks [29,30], similarly genetic algorithms have wider application in parameter optimization [31], and fuzzy logic are totally dependent on human knowledge and expertise. According to M. Alaydrus et al., [32], they have discussed the fuzzy logic method in the device to translate hand signs into A-Z alphabet letters. They confirmed that their results are: The representation value of success is 84% and the percentage error is 16%. Analyzing other proposed algorithms, we conclude that using trajectories for sign language analysis is a feasible solution.

The best neural network architecture is shown in Fig. 4 with 180 neurons in the input layer, 30 neurons in the hidden layer, and 5 neurons in the output layer. This architecture achieved accuracy in the training phase of 99.6%.

The backpropagation algorithm performed well in this application; so that when trained with 270 samples, it converges quickly in 26 iterations achieving an average quadratic error of 0.0053684 and in a time not exceeding 10 s.

Field tests determined that the system can recognize and classify sign language with 98.7% effectiveness for people who were not part of the training.

The system implemented based on Artificial Intelligence and Kinect managed to recognize and classify 5 representative signs. The HMI facilitates system training and testing; it also allows to view the results.

4.1 Source of Algorithm

https://github.com/TomasGavilanez/SL-Recon.

Acknowledgement. The authors declare that there are no conflicts of interest regarding the publication of this paper. T.G.Gamboa thank for research support of the seed grant "Computational modelling of biomaterials and applications to bioengineering and infectious diseases, Universidad Technologica IndoAmerica, Ecuador", awarded to S.P.T.

References

1. Schmucker, C., Kapp, P., Motschall, E., et al.: Prevalence of hearing loss and use of hearing aids among children and adolescents in Germany: a systematic review. BMC Public Health **19**, 1277 (2019). https://doi.org/10.1186/s12889-019-7602-7
2. Eggermont, J.J.: Chapter 1- Hearing basics. In: Eggermont, J.J. (ed.) Hearing Loss, pp. 3–36. Academic Press (2017). ISBN 9780128053980, https://doi.org/10.1016/B978-0-12-805398-0.00001-3
3. FENASEC: Gabriel Román Dictionary. http://fenasec.ec/diccionario-lsec.html. Accessed 19 Nov 2018
4. Medina, M.A.: Interview, sign language: characteristics. Basic Signs Learn. **26**, 06 (2018)
5. Rodríguez, M.A.: Sign Language, Alicante: Miguel de Cervantes (2003)
6. Rauscher, G., Dube, D., Zell, A.: A comparison of 3D sensors for wheeled mobile robots. In: Menegatti, E., Michael, N., Berns, K., Yamaguchi, H. (eds.) Intelligent Autonomous Systems 13. AISC, vol. 302, pp. 29–41. Springer, Cham (2016). https://doi.org/10.1007/978-3-319-08338-4_3
7. Motiian, S., Pergami, P., Guffey, K., et al.: Automated extraction and validation of children's gait parameters with the Kinect. BioMed. Eng. **1**, 37 (2015)
8. Ponce, J.: Artificial Intelligence, Latin (2014)
9. Cruz, P.P.: Artificial Intelligence with Applications to Engineering. Alfaomega, Mexico (2010)
10. Pedro, H.T.C., Inman, R.H., Coimbra, C.F.M.: 4 - Mathematical methods for optimized solar forecasting. In: Kariniotakis, G. (ed.) Woodhead Publishing Series in Energy, Renewable Energy Forecasting, pp. 111–152. Woodhead Publishing (2017). ISBN 9780081005040. https://doi.org/10.1016/B978-0-08-100504-0.00004-4
11. Wong, W.K., Zeng, X.H., Au, K.F.: 3 - Selecting the location of apparel manufacturing plants using neural networks. In: Wong, W.K., Guo, Z.X., Leung, S.Y.S. (eds.) Woodhead Publishing Series in Textiles, Optimizing Decision Making in the Apparel Supply Chain Using Artificial Intelligence (AI), pp. 41–54. Woodhead Publishing (2013). ISBN 9780857097798. https://doi.org/10.1533/9780857097842.41
12. Mas'ud, A.A., et al.: Artificial neural network application for partial discharge recognition: survey and future directions. Energies **9**(8), 574 (2016)
13. Song, Y.H., Xuan, Q.X., Johns, A.T.: Comparison studies of five neural network based fault classifier for complex transmission lines. Electr. Power Syst. Res. **43**(2), 125–132 (1997)
14. Microsoft: Kinect for Windows Sensor Components and Specifications, Developer Network. https://msdn.microsoft.com/en-us/library/jj131033.aspx. Accessed 24 May 2018
15. Suharjito, Gunawan, H., Thiracitta, N., Nugroho, A.: Sign language recognition using modified convolutional neural network model. In: 2018 Indonesian Association for Pattern Recognition International Conference (INAPR), Jakarta, Indonesia, pp. 1–5 (2018). https://doi.org/10.1109/INAPR.2018.8627014
16. Rathi, P., Kuwar Gupta, R., Agarwal, S., Shukla, A.: Sign language recognition using ResNet50 deep neural network architecture. In: 5th International Conference on Next Generation Computing Technologies (NGCT-2019), February 2020. https://ssrn.com/abstract=3545064 or https://doi.org/10.2139/ssrn.3545064
17. Parcheta, Z., Martinez Hinarejos, C.D.: Sign language gesture classification using neural networks. In: Proceedings of the IberSPEECH, vol. 2018, pp. 127–131 (2018). https://doi.org/10.21437/IberSPEECH.2018-27

18. Wilson, N., Brumm, M., Grigat, R.R.: Classification of mouth gestures in German sign language using 3D convolutional neural networks, vol. 10, pp. 52–57 (2019). https://doi.org/10.1049/cp.2019.0248

19. In particular, oral components have been studied in Norwegian Sign Language (Vogt-Svend-sen, 1983; Schroeder, 1985), in Swedish Sign Language (Bergman, 1984), in Finnish Sign Lan-guage (Pimia, 1990), in Danish Sign Language (Engberg-Pedersen, 1993), in the Sign Language of the Netherlands (Schermer, 1985), in German Sign Language (Ebbinghaus & Hessmann, 1990), in Swiss German Sign Language (Boyes-Braem, 1984), in Italian Sign Language (Franchi, 1987), in Indopakistani Sign Language (Zeshan, 2001), in Japanese Sign Language (Torigoe & Takei, 2002). See Boyes-Braem & Sutton-Spence (2001) for a recent review. In ASL only Liddell (1980) described the mouth movement 'cs' within the study of various facial configurations

20. Xiao, Q., Qin, M., Guo, P., Zhao, Y.: Multimodal fusion based on LSTM and a couple conditional hidden Markov model for Chinese sign language recognition. IEEE Access **7**, 112258–112268 (2019). https://doi.org/10.1109/ACCESS.2019.2925654

21. Liang, Z., Liao, S., Hu, B.: 3D convolutional neural networks for dynamic sign language recognition. Comput. J. **61**(11), 1724–1736 (2018). https://doi.org/10.1093/comjnl/bxy049

22. Escalera, S., et al.: ChaLearn looking at people challenge 2014: dataset and results. In: Agapito, L., Bronstein, M.M., Rother, C. (eds.) ECCV 2014. LNCS, vol. 8925, pp. 459–473. Springer, Cham (2015). https://doi.org/10.1007/978-3-319-16178-5_32

23. Fossati, A., Gall, J., Grabner, H., Ren, X., Konolige, K.: Consumer Depth Cameras for Computer Vision: Research Topics and Applications. Springer, London (2013). https://doi.org/10.1007/978-1-4471-4640-7

24. Ting, W., Ting, Y., Tan, Y., Yong, C.: Kinect-based badminton motion analysis using intelligent adaptive range of movement index. In: 2019 IOP Conference Series: Materials Science and Engineering, vol. 495, pp. 12–17 (2019). https://doi.org/10.1088/1757-899x/495/1/012017

25. Rahaman, M.A., Jasim, M., Ali, M.H., et al.: Bangla language modeling algorithm for automatic recognition of hand-sign-spelled Bangla sign language. Front. Comput. Sci. **14**, 143302 (2020). https://doi.org/10.1007/s11704-018-7253-3

26. Hu, H., Zhou, W., Li, H.: Hand-model-aware sign language recognition. In: AAAI, vol. 35, no. 2, pp. 1558–1566 (2021)

27. Camgoz, N.C., Koller, O., Hadfield, S., Bowden, R.: Proceedings of the IEEE/CVF Conference on Computer Vision and Pattern Recognition (CVPR), pp. 10023–10033 (2020)

28. Aly, W., Aly, S., Almotairi, S.: User-independent American sign language alphabet recognition based on depth image and PCANet features. IEEE Access **7**, 123138–123150 (2019). https://doi.org/10.1109/ACCESS.2019.2938829

29. Paul, P., Bhuiya, M.A.-U.-A., Ullah, M.A., Saqib, M.N., Mohammed, N., Momen, S.: A modern approach for sign language interpretation using convolutional neural network. In: Nayak, A.C., Sharma, A. (eds.) PRICAI 2019. LNCS (LNAI), vol. 11672, pp. 431–444. Springer, Cham (2019) https://doi.org/10.1007/978-3-030-29894-4_35

30. Ko, S.-K., Kim, C.J., Jung, H., Cho, C.: Neural sign language translation based on human keypoint estimation. Appl. Sci. **9**, 2683 (2019). https://doi.org/10.3390/app9132683

31. Tyagi, A., Bansal, S.: Feature extraction technique for vision-based Indian sign language recognition system: a review. In: Singh, V., Asari, V.K., Kumar, S., Patel, R.B. (eds.) Computational Methods and Data Engineering. AISC, vol. 1227, pp. 39–53. Springer, Singapore (2021). https://doi.org/10.1007/978-981-15-6876-3_4
32. Fahmi, M.A., Alaydrus, M.: Hand signs translator using fuzzy logic method. In: 2019 International Conference on Radar, Antenna, Microwave, Electronics, and Telecommunications (ICRAMET), pp. 56–59 (2019). https://doi.org/10.1109/ICRAMET47453.2019.8980375
33. Dubdub, I., Rushd, S., Al-Yaari, M., Ahmed, E.: Application of ANN to the water-lubricated flow of non-conventional crude. Chem. Eng. Commun. (2020). https://doi.org/10.1080/00986445.2020.1823842

Heterogeneous Acoustic Features Space for Automatic Classification of Drone Audio Signals

Andrés Felipe Sabogal, Manuel Gómez, and Juan P. Ugarte(✉) ⓘ

Facultad de Ingenierías, Universidad de San Buenaventura, Medellín, Colombia
juan.ugarte@usbmed.edu.co

Abstract. The incremented use of unmanned aerial vehicles (UAV) in recent years, have leaded to security flaws that demand a solution oriented to UAV monitoring. An attractive solution to this problem is based on the analysis of UAV audio signals. Such approach aims to extract a set of acoustic features and to use them as inputs of machine learning algorithms. Current works on this topic are mainly focused in using a specific set of acoustic features, such as linear prediction and cepstral metrics. However, relevant UAV acoustic information may be missing by considering a single type of features. In this work, we propose a heterogenous acoustic features space for solving UAV automatic classification problems. Temporal, spectral and time-frequency analysis are implemented to extract features from UAV audio signals and thus building a high dimensional features space. By applying features selection techniques, the most relevant acoustic features are identified and they are used to train machine learning algorithms. Our results show that, the heterogeneous features space yields high performance in automatic UAV classification tasks of binary and multiclass type. The classification results outperform the overall classification performance of other studies using set of homogeneous features. Furthermore, the metrics extracted using the wavelet packet transform are the most prevalent in the features spaces that yield the best classification results for the binary and muticlass classification tasks.

Keywords: Unmanned aerial vehicles · Drones · Acoustic signature · Signal processing · Machine learning algorithms

1 Introduction

In the last decade, the acquisition of unmanned aerial vehicles (UAV) has increased significantly [13]. Since the manipulation of drones by civilians have received great interest, the breach of security has increased in recent years [5,23]. In order to improve the safety of outdoor and indoor spaces, UAV identification systems based on radio frequency and video have been developed [14,18,22,23]. However, these approaches demand high implementation and maintenance costs.

© Springer Nature Switzerland AG 2021
J. C. Figueroa-García et al. (Eds.): WEA 2021, CCIS 1431, pp. 97–109, 2021.
https://doi.org/10.1007/978-3-030-86702-7_9

An attractive alternative for addressing the UAV identification problem is based on the characterization of audio recordings of flying drones. For this purpose, acoustic features are extracted and used for training learning machines [28]. The usual features used in this task include cepstral measures, linear prediction, among others [2,15,28]. The implementation of a single type of features is a common decision in solving the automatic classification problem. However, such approach may lead to a loss of relevant information related with the UAV acoustics.

Bearing this ideas in mind, in this work, we test the hypothesis that a heterogeneous acoustic features space yields a good automatic classification performance of sound recordings corresponding to quadrotor UAV. For this purpose, a set of drone signals from databases freely available on the web is built. Different signal processing approaches are implemented, including time, frequency and time-frequency analysis. In this manner, a heterogeneous acoustic features space is achieved, which is evaluated in solving binary and multiclass automatic classification problems using machine learning algorithms.

2   Materials and Methods

This section presents the materials methods used in this work. The drone recordings database is described, the acoustic feature extraction methods are outlined, the feature selection techniques and the automatic classification stage are specified along with the classification performance assessment. Figure 1 depicts a diagram summarizing the methodological procedure implemented for generating an acoustic features space aiming to solve a binary and multiclass UAV classification problem.

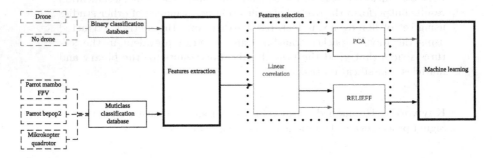

Fig. 1. Methodological scheme implemented in this work. Binary and multiclass classification problems are defined by organizing the UAV audio signals in two databases. Both databases are processed for features extraction and selection. Finally the classification problems are solved using machine learning algorithms.

2.1   Drone Audio Signals Database

The database is built using the drone recordings reported by Strauss et al. [24] and Al-Emadi et al. [1]. Theses recordings are freely available in web repositories. Strauss et al. used the MikroKopter quadrotor UAV to build the DREGON database. The recordings were acquired with a cubic array with eight microphones located bellow the drone at a sampling frequency of 44.1 KHz. Eleven recording sessions of the drone in floating and flying mode were performed in different rooms, with and without background noise. Al-Emadi et al. used two commercial UAV references, the Parrot Mambo FPV UAV and the Parrot Bebop 2. The recordings were acquired with an iPhone cellphone with the drone in floating mode at a sampling frequency of 48 KHz. Additionally, Al-Emadi et al. included audio signals from different events, such as birds, bees, human speakers, storms, vehicular traffic, among others. These recordings will be referred as the no-drone signals.

The drone recordings are arranged in signals with a duration of 1 s and a final sampling frequency of 16 KHz. Two databases are built according to the classification problem: 1) binary classification (drone/no-drone), with 993 samples that include all UAV references and 993 samples corresponding to no-drone signals; 2) multiclass classification (MikroKopter/Parrot Mambo/Parrot Bepob 2), with 331 samples per class. Table 1 summarizes the organization of the UAV recordings.

Table 1. UAV database description.

Number of signals	UAV reference	Drone mode	Classification problem
331	Parrot Mambo FPV	Floating	Binary and multiclass
331	Parrot Bebop 2	Floating	Binary and multiclass
331	MikroKopter quadrotor	Floating and flying	Binary and multiclass
933	No-drone	–	Binary

2.2   Acoustic Features Extraction

The features extraction stage is designed looking for specific characteristics of an UAV system. The subharmonic characteristic of the sound generated by the UAV propellers [9] can be quantified by frequency measures. The rotational and mechanical components of the drone generate vibration components that can be captured using time measures. Additionally, the UAV generates non stationary components that can be quantified using time-frequency techniques. By considering these criteria, the UAV acoustic features space includes 160 features that are calculated using the following approaches:

- Morphology assessment in time. The regularity of a time series can be measured using the Shannon entropy (SE). For a discrete signal $x(n)$, the normalized SE is given by the following formula:

$$SE = \frac{1}{\log N_b} \sum_k p_k \log p_k, \tag{1}$$

where p_k is the probability of occurrence of a given value in $x(n)$ and it is estimated through the histogram of the amplitudes using N_b bins. The division by $\log N_b$ yields a normalized value of SE.
- Linear predictive coding (LPC). The LPC models a discrete signal as a linear combination of its past values. This relation is formulated as an autoregressive model as follows:

$$x(n) = \sum_{p=1}^{L} a_p x(n - p), \tag{2}$$

where L is order of the autoregressive model and a_p are the LPC coefficients. The signal $x(n)$ is pre-emphasized, a Hamming window is applied and the LPC model is obtained using the Yule-Walker method using a value of $L = 10$ [25]. The 10 LPC coefficients are used as features.
- Frequency features. The discrete Fourier transform of $x(n)$ is calculated and the mean frequency, median frequency, pitch, spectral centroid and spectral spread are estimated as previously reported [4,7,19,20]. The spectral entropy is also calculated by applying the Eq. (2) to the modulus of the discrete Fourier transform.
- Mel frequency cepstral analysis. The cepstral analysis is based on humans perception of the frequency content from acoustic events. The Mel cepstrum is generated by mapping the Fourier frequency variable using the following transformation:

$$m = 1127 \log \left(1 + \frac{f}{700}\right), \tag{3}$$

where m and f are the Mel and Fourier frequency, respectively. A bank of filters is applied to the power spectrum and the energy within each band is calculated. Logarithm operation and discrete cosine transformation is applied. In this manner, the number of Mel frequency cepstral coefficients (MFCC) is equal to number of filters in the bank. In this work, 40 MFCC are extracted as features. Additionally, 40 delta cepstral coefficients (DMFCC) are calculated as the difference of two consecutive MFCC.
- Wavelet packet transform (WPT). The WPT is a time-frequency analysis that decomposes $x(n)$ into approximation and detail coefficients. Both decompositions are calculated by choosing a proper wavelet family. The approximation and detail signals are again decomposed in new wavelet levels achieving a decomposition tree. Each wavelet level halves the frequency content, where the low and high frequency half correspond to the approximation and detail signals, respectively. Further information about the WPT can be found in [8]. The WPT is applied to each signal in the database. The best wavelet tree is

determined by using and entropy criterium [6]. In short, the SE values of the wavelet node $W(a, b)$ is compared with the sum of SE values calculated from the corresponding approximation and detail signals. If the SE of upper level node is less than the sum of the SE from its approximation and detail decompositions, the node is excluded from the tree and the decomposition in that branch ends. After a visual inspection of the corresponding spectrograms of different wavelets families, looking for low aliasing events [10], the Daubechies family with 20 vanishing moments is adopted. After applying the WPT to the entire database, the 10 wavelet nodes that are recurrent in all signals are selected. The Fig. 2 shows the resulting wavelet tree. For each wavelet node, the mean frequency, median frequency, spectral centroid, spectral propagation, harmonic to noise ratio and harmonic strength are computed. In this manner, 60 WPT features are extracted from each signal.

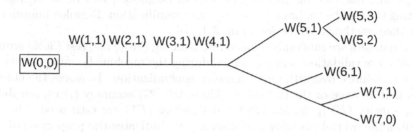

Fig. 2. Wavelet tree with 10 nodes used to characterize the drone signals.

2.3 Features Selection

Three approaches are evaluated for features selection from the raw features space.

1. The Pearson coefficient (ρ) between pairwise features is calculated. For two strongly correlated features (i.e. $\rho \geq 0.65$), only one of them is kept.
2. The Relieff algorithm generates a ranking of labeled features, in an iteratively process [21]. For each iteration, the algorithm estimates the K nearest neighbors to a given observation, rewarding the features that assign different values to neighbors with different labels and penalizing those that assign different values to neighbors with the same label. The total rewards and penalizations of each feature are accounted as weights that are used to rank the features. The value of K is set by increasing this parameter value until reaching low variation of the resulting ranking. The features space is reduced by selecting the features with the highest rank weights.
3. The Principal component analysis (PCA) is a dimensionality reduction technique, where the principal components are linear combinations of the original features [11]. The linear combination coefficients are adjusted so that, the first

principal component agrees with the largest variance in the features space. The remaining principal components are estimated using the same variance criterion, adding the linear independence condition among principal components. The number of principal components that can be calculated equals the number of features. The dimensionality reduction is achieved by selecting the components with the largest variance, in which most of the information of the original feature space is preserved. Individual principal components cannot be related with a single feature since they are linear combination of all features.

2.4 Automatic Classification and Classification Performance Assessment

Several machine learning methods are tested in this work. Support vector machines (SVM) with distinct kernel functions; the nearest neighbors algorithm with distinct distance metrics and number of neighbors; and decision trees by adjusting the number of branches at each tree ramification. Detailed information about these methods can be found in [3,12,16].

The datasets are randomly divided into training (70%) and test (30%) groups. A 5-fold cross validation is implemented during the machine learning training in order to minimize overfitting and improve generalization. To assess the classification performance of the trained machines, the [27] accuracy (Acc), sensibility (S), specificity (E), precision (Pr) and F1-score ($F1$) are estimated. The Acc quantifies the overall classifier performance, Pr indicates the proportion of corrected classifications, S represents the proportion of samples from a class that are correctly classified, E stand for the proportion of actual negative classification assignments. The $F1$ provides a unique metric that accounts for the Pr and S through its harmonic mean. For the multiclass classification problem, a given class is considered as the positive outcome and the remaining classes the negative. In this manner, three measures are obtained for the performance metric and the mean is considered as the representative value.

3   Results

In this section, the results of processing the drone database are presented. The resulting features space, the features selection and the binary and multiclass classification solutions are described.

3.1   Acoustic Features Space

The 160-dimensional features space calculated for each signal in the drone database includes: 40 MFCC, 40 DMFCC, 10 LPC coefficients, 60 WPT, mean frequency, median frequency, mean pitch, standard deviation of the pitch, spectral centroid, spectral spread, harmonic-to-noise ratio, harmonic strength, spectral and time entropy. Figure 3 depicts the histograms of representative features for the binary (top row) and multiclass (bottom row) databases. Different distribution shapes can be observed for each feature.

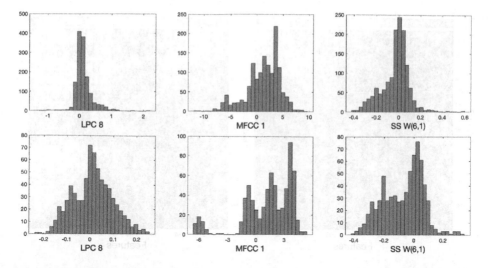

Fig. 3. Distribution of three representative acoustic features obtained from the binary (top row) and multiclass (bottom row) databases.

3.2 Features Selection

The features selection is applied in order to identify the most relevant and discriminating features. As described in the methodology, the strongly correlated features are detected. Figure 4 portrays the matrix of the absolute value of ρ for the binary (left) and multiclass (right) databases. The diagonal and lower triangular of each ρ matrix are zeroed due to the symmetry. Strongly correlated features ($\rho \geq 0.65$) are depicted in yellow and red color. For the binary classification database, 76 features (47.5%) are excluded and for the multiclass classification database, 114 features (71.25%) were excluded. Thus, the new features spaces for the binary and multiclass classification databases contain 84 and 46 features, respectively.

The Relieff algorithm and PCA are applied the outcome of the ρ selection. The Relieff algorithm results in 30 features that are detailed in Table 2. The resulting features for the binary classification mainly correspond to the WPT and cepstral analysis, whereas the multiclass classification show a more heterogeneous outcome. The PCA implementation leads to the selection of 4 principal components for both databases. Figure 5 shows the normalized variance of the first 12 principal components for the binary (left) and multiclass (right) classification. It can be seen that the variances up to the fourth principal component have a significant magnitude.

3.3 Automatic Classification

The features spaces obtained with the Relieff algorithm (30 features) and PCA (4 principal components) are used to train the learning machines described in

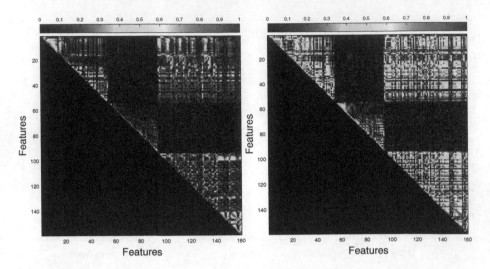

Fig. 4. Pearson correlation coefficient (ρ) matrix for the features calculated from the binary (left) and multiclass (right) classification databases. The absolute value of ρ is shown. The diagonal and lower triangular of ρ is zeroed. (Color figure online)

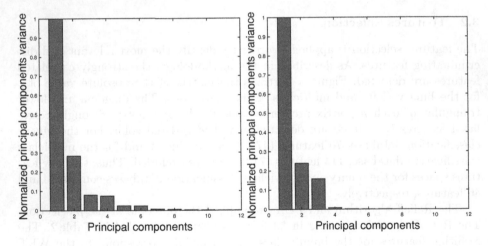

Fig. 5. Normalized variance of the first 12 principal components corresponding to the binary (left) and multiclass (right) classification databases.

the methodology. The performance metrics for the three best trained machines are shown in Tables 3 and 4 for the binary and multiclass classification problems, respectively. In both problems, the SVM fed with the Relieff features provide a good performance with all values of the performance metrics > 0.96. The binary classification problem can be properly solved with a minimum of 12 features.

Table 2. Features selection results after applying the Relieff algorithm.

Rank	Binary classification	Multiclass classification
1	Spectral spread W(6,1)	Harmonic strength
2	Spectral centroid W(6,1)	Median Frequency W(6,1)
3	Spectral spread W(2,1)	Median Frequency W(3,1)
4	Harmonic Strength	Median Frequency W(1,1)
5	MFCC 1	Spectral centroid W(6,1)
6	MFCC 22	LPC 8
7	MFCC 35	MFCC 7
8	Spectral spread W(3,1)	Time Entropy
9	Spectral centroid W(7,1)	Harmonic strength W(6,1)
10	MFCC 25	Spectral centroid W(5,1)
11	MFCC 16	MFCC 36
12	Pitch standard deviation	MFCC 40
13	MFCC 20	Spectral entropy
14	MFCC 13	Median frequency W(2,1)
15	LPC 10	Spectral spread W(7,0)
16	Spectral spread W(1,1)	Spectral centroid W(2,1)
17	MFCC 40	Harmoni strength W(5,2)
18	Spectral spread W(4,1)	LPC 9
19	MFCC 33	MFCC 38
20	MFCC 24	Spectral spread W(7,1)
21	Spectral centroid W(5,1)	Harmonic strength W(7,1)
22	Spectral centroid W(3,1)	LPC 10
23	MFCC 27	MFCC 31
24	MFCC 4	MFCC 32
25	MFCC 34	Spectral centroid W(4,1)
26	MFCC 7	Median frequency W(7,1)
27	Spectral centroid W(5,1)	DMFCC 40
28	MFCC10	MFCC 3
29	Spectral spread W(1,1)	Harmonic strength W(5,1)
30	MFCC 17	DMFCC 31

On the other hand, the multiclass classification problem requires at least 19 features. The best performance in solving the binary classification is achieved using 23 features, whereas the multiclass classification problem requires the full set of features obtained by the Relieff algorithm.

Table 3. Performance metrics for the binary classification problem. The ∗ marks the learning machine with the best performance.

Learning machine	Number of features	Features selection method	Acc	S	E	Pr	$F1$
Medium Gaussian SVM	12	Relieff	0.968	0.963	0.973	0.973	0.968
Medium Gaussian SVM∗	23	Relieff	0.982	0.973	0.990	0.990	0.982
Quadratic SVM	23	Relieff	0.9783	0.977	0.980	0.980	0.978

Table 4. Performance metrics for the multiclass classification problem. The ∗ marks the learning machine with the best performance.

Learning machine	Number of features	Features selection method	Acc	S	E	Pr	$F1$
Quadratic SVM	19	Relieff	0.991	0.987	0.993	0.987	0.987
Quadratic SVM	30	Relieff	0.991	0.987	0.993	0.987	0.987
Cubic SVM∗	30	Relieff	0.993	0.990	0.995	0.990	0.990

4   Discussion

In this work, the UAV acoustic signals are characterized using different signal processing techniques, looking for a proper description of the UAV acoustic signature. The features extraction is designed by considering functional properties of UAV that can generate relevant information embedded in the time, frequency and time-frequency domains. In this manner, a high dimensional features space is obtained which was processed using features selection techniques. The selected features proved useful in solving the automatic classification problems with high performance.

For the binary classification problem, the best performance is achieved with a 23-dimensional features space, where 39.13% of the features correspond to the wavelet analysis, 47.83% are MFCC and 4.35% are LPC coefficients. In the case of the multiclass classification, the 30 features yielding the best performance include 50% of WPT features, 23.3% MFCC and 10% LPC coefficients. The harmonic strength and the spectral centroid of node W(6,11) contain relevant information from the UAV acoustic signature, since they are observed among the five better ranked features in both classification problems.

This study included several features that characterize different aspects of the UAV acoustics. The LPC coefficients and the MFCC are the most common features reported in the literature for drones characterization [2,25]. There are studies suggesting that the most relevant UAV information can be found in the first 13 MFCC. Differently, our results show that the MFCC up to number 40 contain information for properly solving the classification problems. Such outcome agrees with other reports supporting the usefulness of MFCC [9,26,28]. Regarding the DMFCC, there are reports of improved classification performance of UAV recordings in controlled environments [9]. However, our results show no relevance of DMFCC for the binary classification, whereas they have low presence in the features space for the multiclass problem.

There are studies of automatic classification solutions using specific set of features. The classification performance yielded by MFCC is reported to be $Acc = 96.7\%$, $S = 93.7\%$ and $E = 100\%$ [2]; another study reports $Acc = 88.36\%$, $S = 90.36\%$ and $E = 86.63\%$ [17] and a third study concludes a poor performance using these features [28]. By using LPCC coefficients, the reported performance is $Acc = 75.2\%$, $S = 90.0\%$ and $E = 72.2\%$. Our classification results, based on a heterogeneous features space, outperform the overall performance of those studies. Moreover, we have evinced that time-frequency features, such as those generated through the wavelet analysis, are important in generating a good classification performance. This outcome agrees with other study, reporting good performance with another time-frequency technique (i.e. the short-time discrete Fourier transform) [28].

5   Conclusions

This work deals with the problem of generating a proper acoustic features space for solving an automatic classification task involving UAV. Although the problem of UAV automatic classification have been addressed using homogenous features, in this work we have shown that better results can be achieved by working with a heterogeneous features space, built using different signal processing approaches. For the classification problems studied in this work, the wavelet features are the most prevalent after the features selection implementation. Therefore, we suggest that the wavelet package analysis should be included in the design of solutions for drone characterization and classification.

References

1. Al-Emadi, S., Al-Ali, A., Mohammad, A., Al-Ali, A.: Audio based drone detection and identification using deep learning. In: 2019 15th International Wireless Communications & Mobile Computing Conference (IWCMC), pp. 459–464. IEEE (2019)
2. Anwar, M.Z., Kaleem, Z., Jamalipour, A.: Machine learning inspired sound-based amateur drone detection for public safety applications. IEEE Trans. Veh. Technol. **68**(3), 2526–2534 (2019)
3. Begum, S., Chakraborty, D., Sarkar, R.: Data classification using feature selection and kNN machine learning approach. In: 2015 International Conference on Computational Intelligence and Communication Networks (CICN), pp. 811–814. IEEE (2015)
4. Benesty, J., Sondhi, M.M., Huang, Y.: Springer Handbook of Speech Processing. Springer, Heidelberg (2007). https://doi.org/10.1007/978-3-540-49127-9
5. Busset, J., et al.: Detection and tracking of drones using advanced acoustic cameras. In: Unmanned/Unattended Sensors and Sensor Networks XI; and Advanced Free-Space Optical Communication Techniques and Applications, vol. 9647, p. 96470F. International Society for Optics and Photonics (2015)

6. Coifman, R.R., Wickerhauser, M.V.: Entropy-based algorithms for best basis selection. IEEE Trans. Inf. Theory **38**(2), 713–718 (1992)
7. Fernandes, J., Teixeira, F., Guedes, V., Junior, A., Teixeira, J.P.: Harmonic to noise ratio measurement-selection of window and length. Procedia Comput. Sci. **138**, 280–285 (2018)
8. Fugal, D.: Conceptual Wavelets in Digital Signal Processing: An In-depth, Practical Approach for the Non-mathematician. Space & Signals Technical Publications (2009)
9. García-Gómez, J., Bautista-Durán, M., Gil-Pita, R., Rosa-Zurera, M.: Feature selection for real-time acoustic drone detection using genetic algorithms. In: Audio Engineering Society Convention 142. Audio Engineering Society (2017)
10. Gómez, A., Ugarte, J.P., Gómez, D.M.M.: Bioacoustic signals denoising using the undecimated discrete wavelet transform. In: Figueroa-García, J.C., Villegas, J.G., Orozco-Arroyave, J.R., Maya Duque, P.A. (eds.) WEA 2018. CCIS, vol. 916, pp. 300–308. Springer, Cham (2018). https://doi.org/10.1007/978-3-030-00353-1_27
11. Jolliffe, I.: Principal Component Analysis. Springer, New York (2014)
12. Joshi, A.V.: Machine Learning and Artificial Intelligence. Springer, Cham (2020). https://doi.org/10.1007/978-3-030-26622-6
13. Meola, A.: Drone Industry Analysis: Market Trends & Growth Forecasts. Business Insider (2017)
14. Mezei, J., Fiaska, V., Molnár, A.: Drone sound detection. In: 2015 16th IEEE International Symposium on Computational Intelligence and Informatics (CINTI), pp. 333–338. IEEE (2015)
15. Mezei, J., Molnár, A.: Drone sound detection by correlation. In: 2016 IEEE 11th International Symposium on Applied Computational Intelligence and Informatics (SACI), pp. 509–518. IEEE (2016)
16. Mirjalili, S., Faris, H., Aljarah, I.: Evolutionary Machine Learning Techniques. Springer, Singapore (2019). https://doi.org/10.1007/978-981-32-9990-0
17. Ohlenbusch, M., Ahrens, A., Rollwage, C., Bitzer, J.: Robust drone detection for acoustic monitoring applications. In: 2020 28th European Signal Processing Conference (EUSIPCO), pp. 6–10. IEEE (2021)
18. Park, S., et al.: Combination of radar and audio sensors for identification of rotor-type unmanned aerial vehicles (UAVs). In: 2015 IEEE SENSORS, pp. 1–4. IEEE (2015)
19. Peeters, G.: A large set of audio features for sound description (similarity and classification) in the CUIDADO project. CUIDADO Ist Project Report **54**, 1–25 (2004)
20. Phinyomark, A., Thongpanja, S., Hu, H., Phukpattaranont, P., Limsakul, C.: The usefulness of mean and median frequencies in electromyography analysis. In: Computational Intelligence in Electromyography Analysis-a Perspective on Current Applications and Future Challenges, pp. 195–220 (2012)
21. Robnik-Šikonja, M., Kononenko, I.: Theoretical and empirical analysis of ReliefF and RReliefF. Mach. Learn. **53**(1), 23–69 (2003)
22. Schüpbach, C., Patry, C., Maasdorp, F., Böniger, U., Wellig, P.: Micro-UAV detection using DAB-based passive radar. In: 2017 IEEE Radar Conference (Radar-Conf), pp. 1037–1040. IEEE (2017)
23. Siriphun, N., Kashihara, S., Fall, D., Khurat, A.: Distinguishing drone types based on acoustic wave by IoT device. In: 2018 22nd International Computer Science and Engineering Conference (ICSEC), pp. 1–4. IEEE (2018)

24. Strauss, M., Mordel, P., Miguet, V., Deleforge, A.: DREGON: dataset and methods for UAV-embedded sound source localization. In: 2018 IEEE/RSJ International Conference on Intelligent Robots and Systems (IROS), pp. 1–8. IEEE (2018)
25. Vilímek, J., Buřita, L.: Ways for copter drone acustic detection. In: 2017 International Conference on Military Technologies (ICMT), pp. 349–353. IEEE (2017)
26. Waldekar, S., Saha, G.: Analysis and classification of acoustic scenes with wavelet transform-based mel-scaled features. Multimedia Tools Appl. **79**(11), 7911–7926 (2020)
27. Yan, X., Zhang, L., Li, J., Du, D., Hou, F.: Entropy-based measures of hypnopompic heart rate variability contribute to the automatic prediction of cardiovascular events. Entropy **22**(2), 241 (2020)
28. Yang, B., Matson, E.T., Smith, A.H., Dietz, J.E., Gallagher, J.C.: UAV detection system with multiple acoustic nodes using machine learning models. In: 2019 Third IEEE International Conference on Robotic Computing (IRC), pp. 493–498. IEEE (2019)

Career Recommendation System for Validation of Multiple Intelligence to High School Students

Maryori Sabalza Mejia[1]([⊠])(iD), Carolina Campillo Jimenez[2]([⊠])(iD), and Juan Carlos Martínez-Santos[1]([⊠])(iD)

[1] Program of Electrical and Electronics Engineering,
Universidad Tecnologica de Bolivar, Cartagena, Colombia
{msabalzam,jcmartinezs}@utb.edu.co
[2] School of Social Sciences Arts and Humanities, Universidad Nacional Abierta y a Distancia, Cartagena, BOL 130010, Colombia
carolina.campillo@unad.edu.co

Abstract. Career choice is a critical moment for any student. However, many students worldwide change of path during the first academic year. Vocational tests are tools to help students choose an upper education career by providing information about their abilities and interests. However, some of them are very difficult to apply high costs, availability, or not validated at diverse populations. Gardner's Multiple Intelligence test is a popular test that measures the brain's performance abilities in nine areas. Unlike IQ's test, Gardner Test is helpful to understand students' strengths and learning styles. Vocational tests and Multiple Intelligence test measure students' abilities and interests. This research shows the implementation of a recommendation system based on the Gardner test, we considering familiar variables and results of a basic knowledge test. For validation, we compare it with a standard vocational test. Our system recommends a top five of careers with 88.2% success and 93.3% for the top one.

Keywords: Gardner test · Education · High school · College · Machine learning · Prediction · Regression · Career

1 Introduction

One of the most crucial decisions of youth students at the end of high school is to choose an academic path. On one side, there is a society that asks you to choose something to make you happy, but the job market has particular career demands that do not always fit students' skills or vocational interests.

For these students, the completion of vocational tests will give them a deeper understanding of their skills and interests and help them make a better career choice, and reduce the desertion rate at upper education institutions during the first semesters.

© Springer Nature Switzerland AG 2021
J. C. Figueroa-García et al. (Eds.): WEA 2021, CCIS 1431, pp. 110–120, 2021.
https://doi.org/10.1007/978-3-030-86702-7_10

In Latin America, universities during the first semester of career, courses that explore topics related to introduction to university lifestyle or personal development are offer as compulsory (See [16–19]).

Contrary to this practice, in the USA, before join university, some courses that explore students' interest and improve academic deficiencies in English and Math are mainly compulsory during the first two years of College [20].

The basic knowledge test as preparation for university is standard according to the country, for example, the Programme for International Student Assessment- PISA Test [22].

PISA is an international test applied to students near the end of high school. PISA is held every three years and has assessed skills in mathematics, science, and reading. However, each country has its academic assessment skills.

In the USA it is applied the Suite of Assessments (SAT) developed by the College Board [9]. This test evaluates Reading, Writing and Language, Math, and Optional Essay.

In China, a similar test is the Gaokao [10], with the difference that this is decisive to get a place in the university. This test evaluates Chinese literature, Mathematics, and English.

In Hong Kong is the Diploma of Secondary Education Examination (HKDSE) [11]. This exam evaluates at the end of high school: Chinese and English languages, Mathematics, and Liberal studies.

In South Korea, the Suneung [12] exam is applied, which is a University School Aptitude Test. It evaluates the Korean language, Mathematics, English, and Korean history, in addition to a second foreign language and a subject free of choice.

In Colombia, this test is known as the Saber 11 test and is performed in the last year of high school and applied by the Colombian Institute for the Promotion of Higher Education-ICFES (for its Spanish acronym) [26]. The Saber 11 evaluates Math, Critical Reading, Natural sciences, English, Citizen competencies.

We propose a career recommendation system based on the Gardner test, using the results of the Saber 11 tests and some variables with information on family per student. We validated this system with the results of the EVP2 vocational test. This paper is organized as follows. Section 2 shows the research prior to this research are mentioned. Section 3 describes the theorical framework for this research. Section 4 presents the approach of this research. Section 5 explains each detail of development. Section 6 shows the results obtained. Finally, Sect. 7 contains the conclusions of this research.

2   Related Work

For this research, we took into account the career recommendation systems based on the Gardner's Multiple Intelligences test, like Shearer et al. [2] shows the practical value of applying Gardner's multiple intelligences to vocational guidance. It helps reaffirm that beyond the interests that a student may present, it will be more valuable to consider their strengths and weaknesses obtained from the multiple intelligences tests using the Multiple Intelligences Developmental Assessment Scales (MIDAS).

Kaewkiriya et al. proposed a recommendation system based on the design of rules focused on E-learning and Multiple Intelligences using a questionnaire applied to a population sample [3]. They used several algorithms (Naive Bayes, NBTree, and others) for validation, obtaining a maximum prediction percentage of 83.436%.

Two other research that also implemented Naive Bayes, Kelly et al. [1], and E K Subramanian et al. [6]. They propose an intelligent-based on multiple intelligences. Its predictive engine uses the Naive Bayes model to identify the learning characteristics of each user, like personal interests, extracurricular and curricular activities, academic information.

These interests go hand in hand with vocational abilities. Obeid et al. [4] propose a recommendation system based on ontology and improved with machine learning techniques to recommend professional careers to students.

On the other hand, Yadalam et al. [5] propose a career recommender system based on content-based filtering. This system is only for engineers students based on the qualities and activities of each student. Based on this data, each career maps through the similarity of the cosine.

Dhar et al. [7] is a comprehensive work regarding the use of machine learning techniques. According to academic performance, the recommending system, based on machine learning techniques, predicts the appropriate academic program for higher studies. Among the algorithms used are K-nearest neighbors (KNN), Decision Tree (DTs), Naive Bayes, Random Forest (RF), XGBoost, Logistic regression, and others. However, in most tests performed, RF obtained the best prediction results.

Like the research presented before, our recommendation system used machine learning techniques to recommend careers per student. However, we took into account, in addition to the basic skills in fundamental areas (Math, Critical Reading, Natural Sciences, English, and Citizen competencies), some family-related variables as part of the recommendations with a standard vocational test.

3   Theoretical Framework

This research is a recommendation system based on Gardner's multiple intelligences test and is validated using the standard EVP2 vocational test.

3.1   Test Gardner

Gardner's Multiple Tntelligences test consists of 80 questions and is part of the theory of multiple intelligences in 1983 [8]. This test affirms that a person can be intelligent in an area and should not be measured solely by their intelligence quotient (IQ), an estimator of general intelligence resulting from standardized tests.

According to Gardner, for something to qualify as intelligence, it must follow the eight "signs" of intelligence that he proposes:

- Musical-Rhythmic and harmonic: Sensitivity to recognize rhythms, tones, melody, and timbre.
- Visual-Spatial: Refers to the ability to conceptualize and manipulate large-scale spatial models.
- Linguistic-Verbal: Ability to identify words, know their meaning, order, sounds, inflections.
- Logical-Mathematical: Ability to conceptualize logical relationships between actions or symbols, helps to be deductive and detect patterns to solve problems.
- Bodily-Kinesthetic: Ability to use the whole body (or parts of it) to solve problems or create products.
- Interpersonal: Ability to interact with others, sensitivity to their moods, feelings, temperament, and motivations.
- Intrapersonal: Sensitivity to one's feelings, goals, and anxieties.
- Naturalistic: Ability to recognize and make distinctions in the world of nature.

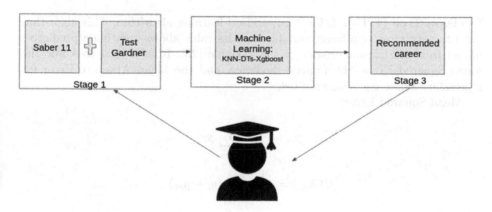

Fig. 1. Implementation

3.2   EVP2

EVP2 is a systematized professional assessment and guidance scale that provides a graphical profile of interests based on 49 careers. This test consists of 245 questions and an average response time of 30 min. The instrument has a validity of Alpha Cronbach 94% [21].

Table 1 shows EVP2 classifies the results in the test. If it falls within each established range, it recommends a high score. It is important to note that this test recommends careers from a minimum score of 56 points per career.

Table 1. EVP2

EVP2	Very low	Low	Medium	High	Very high
Score	0–34	35–45	46–55	56–70	72–100

3.3 Models

Our recommendation system consists of three machine learning models. We have used these models before, and we describe them below.

K-Nearest Neighbors (KNN). KNN is an algorithm based on instances used to predict continuous values or for classification. It is one of the simplest, and the objective is to find the closest points so that they contribute to the regression of the most distant ones [23]. Equation for the regression of k-nearest-neighbors [15]:

$$\widehat{y} = \frac{1}{k} \sum_{i=1}^{k} y_i(x)$$

Decision Tree (DTs). DT is a supervised learning algorithm. This algorithm identifies the most significant variable, and its value allows creating a predictive model from the characteristics of the variable [25]. It is crucial to know the Mean Squared Error, the Poisson deviance, and the Mean Absolute Error for regression. These equations are below.

Mean Squared Error:

$$y_m = \frac{1}{N_m} \sum_{i \in N_m} y_i$$

$$H(X_m) = \frac{1}{N_m} \sum_{i \in N_m} (y_i - y_m)$$

Half Poisson deviance:

$$H(Q_m) = \frac{1}{N_m} \sum_{y \in Q_m} \left(y \log \frac{y}{\overline{y}_m} - y + \overline{y}_m \right)$$

Mean Absolute Error:

$$median(y)_m = median_{i \in N_m}(y_i)$$

$$H(X_m) = \frac{1}{N_m} \sum_{i \in N_m} |y_i - (y)_m|$$

XGBoost. XGBoots is a reinforced tree gradient algorithm. It is a supervised learning technique that predicts a value from a set of values. This algorithm boosting to arbitrary differentiable loss functions model [24]. The equation of this algorithm seeks to minimize to the Euclidean domain [14], see below.

$$\mathcal{L}^{(t)} = \sum_{i=1}^{n} \iota\left(y_i, \widehat{y_i}^{(t-1)} + f_t(X_i)\right) + \Omega(f_t)$$

The final minimized equation, eliminating the constant parts is:

$$\mathcal{L}^{(t)} = \sum_{i=1}^{n} \left[g_i f_t(X_i) + \frac{1}{2}h_i f_t^2(X_i)\right] + \Omega(f_t)$$

Table 2. Variables

Variable	Description
Math	Score obtained in Math Saber 11 test
Critical_Reading	Score obtained in Critical Reading Saber 11 test
Social_y_Citizen	Score obtained in Social and Citizen Saber 11 test
Natural_Science	Score obtained in Natural science Saber 11 test
English	Score obtained in English Saber 11 test
Musical	Multiple Intelligence Musical-Rhythmic and harmonic
Visual	Multiple Intelligence Visual-Spatial
Linguistic-Verbal	Multiple Intelligence Linguistic-Verbal
Logical-Mathematical	Multiple Intelligence Logical-Mathematical
Bodily-Kinesthetic	Multiple Intelligence Bodily-Kinesthetic
Interpersonal	Multiple Intelligence Interpersonal
Intrapersonal	Multiple Intelligence Intrapersonal
Naturalistic	Multiple Intelligence Naturalistic
Kinship	Grandpa, Brother-in-law, Brother, Son, Stepmother, Mother, Stepfather, Father, Cousin, Nephew, Uncle
Age	Age of related relative
Occupation	Occupation or job
Educational_level	Highest educational level: Primary, secondary, technical, technological, professional

4   Our Approach

Taking into account that in Cartagena, according to the city education department, Secretaria de Educación Distrital - SED (*Secretary of District Education*) [27], Cartagena has 398 active schools. Still, only 26% (103) are public.

We obtain the database from a questionnaire and group interviews with 250 senior students in a public school in Cartagena-Colombia for this research. The public school selected during 2019 had 2649 students from Pre-K to 11th grade, so the total of senior students represented a lot of the entire school.

General and family information was collected by conducting interviews with the students. The Gardner and EVP2 test was applied. Also, we considered the Saber 11 results. We used the trial and error method for selection variables, adding variables to the system and seeing how much performance was improving.

The first test carried out was with the results of the Saber 11 test and the professional careers. Then we agree on family variables one by one: The relationship of the people with whom they live, age, occupation, level of studies. We mapped these variables to Gardner's Test results. The variables used are described in Table 2. For our system, we determine the top five careers according to the EVP2 score.

For this research, we not considered IQ and other learning because it skewed the study's objective, as well as that it does not guarantee the intelligence that a student can have more developed. So for this research, we only focus on multiple intelligences.

5   Implementation

Figure 1 shows our implementation recommendation system for careers. We used the machine learning algorithms to implement our recommendation system: KNN, DTs, and XGBoost. For train/test, we divide the data according to the Pareto 80-20 principle [13]. Our investigation was carried out in stages, which we describe below.

5.1   Stage 1: Data Preparation

In this stage, we make the data exploration and variable selection. Using the trial and error method, we added the variables in each machine learning model. We made annotations of how the prediction was improving with family variables added.

Initially, we only thought of only using the Saber 11 tests and the Gardner test results, but using only these variables, the career prediction failed. So we checked if the family variables could influence. We realized that these students have different functional families, and very few follow the father, mother, and children model.

The age of these relatives also influences because some were older siblings, so they had more responsibilities. Some of these students commented on their need to study a technical career to have an immediate job. The parent's level of education influences a large part in the student's decision to choose a technical, technological, or professional career.

5.2   Stage 2: Machine Learning Models

We validate the machine learning models using KNN, DTs, and XGBoost because these models are easy to implement. According to our data preparation, the input variables we consider Saber 11 and Gardner's test. Output variables were the results obtained in the EVP2 test. Showing the top five careers recommended to each student for each model, we compare this top with our top chosen from the races with the highest score in EVPs. Sometimes some of these algorithms fail in the top one. It is due to the model's prediction percentage. In the next session, we present the results.

5.3   Stage 3: Recommended System

We use the results of the Gardner test to validate the top five of our system. For this, we had the top of intelligence by each student. Using our top five, we verified the intelligence per student and the intelligence necessary for each career.

Some careers need up to four multiple intelligence to guarantee excellent professional performance in the occupation, so we reorganized our top five according to the careers that included all the intelligence marked by the student.

Also, this helped us choose between careers with the same score in EVP2. If one of the two careers met most of the student's intelligence, it recommends before the other careers that could not contemplate any of the student's intelligence.

6   Results

We used for the train/test a Pareto of 80-20 as mentioned above, for the validation, 250 students. We opted to remove 10% of the students to perform the validation of the recommender system. This value of 10% corresponds to a total of 25 students approx. Table 3 show the actual values.

Table 3. Pareto

Data	Number	Percentage
Train	175	70%
Test	51	20%
Validate	25	10%

According to the results in the Gardner test and the Saber 11 tests, we verify the most marked multiple intelligences in each of the students and apply the machine learning models as KNN, DTs, and XGBoost to them. For this model, we obtained a prediction of no more than 75.7%. Exactly for KNN: 71.7%, DTs: 68.7% and XGBoost: 75.7%.

The next step was to validate from the results of the EVP2 test the highest career per student. Unlike EVP2, we did not establish a minimum range of recommendations. After validating the highest careers, we took the top five by students and compared this recommendation with the one obtained in EVP2.

According to the EVP2 test, the predictor's correctness is 79.2%. However, when validated with the results of the Gardner test, the recommendation correctness increases to 88.2%.

We mapped our top five with the multiple intelligences per student. It contemplates careers were in common with all the most labeled intelligence, and the predictor rearranges the top according to that intelligence. For example, in some cases, three intelligence types predominated for a student. We validated that the top careers needed these three intelligence types, and the system recommends the top one.

Then, we chose to validate only the top one of our improved systems with the EVP2 recommendation. For the top one, we obtained a percentage of precision of 93.3%. However, in the validation test with 10% of the information, the algorithms that we used failed at least three times to predict the top one.

We can say that the few times our system did not recommend the career in the top one, it placed it in the second recommendation. We assigned a score of 100 if our top one coincided with the one recommended by EVP2. In case of being in second place 80, and in third place of 60.

7   Conclusion

This research shows the implementation of a recommendation system based on the Gardner test. We verified that it is possible to implement using familiar variables and the results of basic knowledge tests. In many countries, they are used to guarantee admission to the university.

We obtain acceptable scores in this test, correctness prediction up to 93% in the top careers. It can help confirm long-term success in the career field. Validating our system with the EVP2 test, we ensure that the EVP2 test can sometimes fail with the recommendation since it only focuses on careers with scores higher than 60 points. For example, for a student who did not obtain this score in any career, EVP2 cannot recommend.

Unlike the EVP2 test, we do consider the multiple intelligences per student. These allowed us to make the recommendation of careers to students with the highest scores. We did not establish a range like EVP2, but we were interested in the student.

We plan to design a web application for our recommendation system that schools can use during the vocational orientation for future work.

Acknowledgment. We would like to thank the anonymous WEA reviewers for their comments and feedback on the ideas in this paper and Tecnologica de Bolivar University for their support.

References

1. Kelly, D., Tangney, B.: Predicting learning characteristics in a multiple intelligence based tutoring system. In: Lester, J.C., Vicari, R.M., Paraguaçu, F. (eds.) ITS 2004. LNCS, vol. 3220, pp. 678–688. Springer, Heidelberg (2004). https://doi.org/10.1007/978-3-540-30139-4_64
2. Shearer, C.B., Luzzo, D.A.: Exploring the application of multiple intelligences theory to career counseling. Career Dev Q. **58**(1), 3–13 (2009)
3. Kaewkiriya, T., Utakrit, N., Tiantong, M.: The design of a rule base for an e-learning recommendation system base on multiple intelligences. Int. J. Inf. Educ. Technol. **6**(3), 206 (2016)
4. Obeid, C., Lahoud, I., El Khoury, H., Champin, P.A.: Ontology-based recommender system in higher education. In Companion Proceedings of the Web Conference 2018, pp. 1031–1034, April 2018
5. Yadalam, T.V., Gowda, V.M., Kumar, V.S., Girish, D., Namratha, M.: Career recommendation systems using content based filtering. In: 2020 5th International Conference on Communication and Electronics Systems (ICCES), pp. 660–665. IEEE, June 2020
6. Subramanian, E.K., Ramachandran: Student career guidance system for recommendation of relevant course selection. Int. J. Recent Technol. Eng. (IJRTE) **7**(102), 4 (2019)
7. Dhar, J., Jodder, A.K.: An effective recommendation system to forecast the best educational program using machine learning classification algorithms. Ingénierie des Systèmes d Inf. **25**(5), 559–568 (2020)
8. Gardner, H., Hatch, T.: Educational implications of the theory of multiple intelligences. Educ. Res. **18**(8), 4–10 (1989)
9. Fuess, C.M.: The College Board; its first fifty years (1950)
10. Muthanna, A., Sang, G.: Undergraduate Chinese students' perspectives on Gaokao examination: strengths, weaknesses, and implications. Int. J. Res. Stud. Educ. **5**(2), 3–12 (2015)
11. Drave, N.: Hong Kong Diploma of Secondary Education (HKDSE) English Language Level Descriptors: Stakeholder Recognition and Understanding. Learning and Assessment: Making the Connections, p. 64 (2017)
12. Kwon, S.K., Lee, M., Shin, D.: Educational assessment in the Republic of Korea: lights and shadows of high-stake exam-based education system. Assess. Educ. Princ. Pol. Pract. **24**(1), 60–77 (2017)
13. Arnold, B.C.: Pareto distribution. Wiley StatsRef: Statistics Reference Online, pp. 1–10 (2014)
14. Chen, T., Guestrin, C.: XGBoost: a scalable tree boosting system. In: Proceedings of the 22nd ACM SIGKDD International Conference on Knowledge Discovery and Data Mining, pp. 785–794, August 2016
15. Song, Y., Liang, J., Lu, J., Zhao, X.: An efficient instance selection algorithm for k nearest neighbor regression. Neurocomputing **251**, 26–34 (2017)
16. Pontificia Universidad Católica de Perú, Introducción a la vida universitaria. https://facultad.pucp.edu.pe/generales ciencias/servicio/Introduccion-a-la-vida-universitaria/. Accessed Feb 2021
17. Universidad Tecnológica Nacional, Introducción a la vida universitaria. http://www.frlr.utn.edu.ar/archivos/sec-academica/apunte-introduccion-vida-univ-ingreso.pdf. Accessed Feb 2021

18. Universidad de Chile, Introducción a la vida universitaria. https://www.uchile.cl/portal/especiales/covid19/161906/para-mechones-introduccion-a-la-vida-universitaria-online. Accessed Feb 2021
19. Universidad de los Andes, Vida universitaria. https://uniandes.edu.co/soy/guia-servicios/vida-universitaria. Accessed Feb 2021
20. Meier, K.S.: What Courses Do You Take in the First Two Years of College? https://education.seattlepi.com/courses-first-two-years-college-2691.html. Accessed Feb 2021
21. Proyeccion Humana Internacional, Escala de Valoracion y Orientacion Profesional Sistematizada. https://www.proyeccionhumanainternacional.com/evp2-escala-de-valoracion-y-orientacion-profesional-sistematizada/. Accessed Feb 2021
22. OCDE, Programme for International Student Assessment. https://www.oecd.org/pisa/pisaenespaol.htm. Accessed Feb 2021
23. Zulaikha Lateef, KNN Algorithm: A Practical Implementation Of KNN Algorithm In R. https://www.edureka.co/blog/knn-algorithm-in-r/. Accessed Feb 2021
24. xgboost.readthedocs. https://xgboost.readthedocs.io/en/latest/R-package/xgboostPresentation.html. Accessed Feb 2021
25. Tutorials Point, Decision Tree. https://tutorialspoint.dev/computer-science/machine-learning/decision-tree-introduction-example. Accessed Feb 2021
26. Instituto Colombiano para el Fomento de la Educación Superior, Educación superior y desarrollo, v-2. El instituto, Colombia (1983)
27. Cartagena Como Vamos, Informe de Calidad de Vida 2018, Módulo de Eduación. http://www.cartagenacomovamos.org/nuevo/wp-content/uploads/2019/09/Informe-Calidad-de-Vida-2018-M'odulo-Educaci'on.pdf. Accessed Feb 2021

Evaluation of Different Word Embeddings to Create Personality Models in Spanish

Felipe Orlando López-Pabón[1]([⊠]) [iD] and Juan Rafael Orozco-Arroyave[1,2] [iD]

[1] Faculty of Engineering, University of Antioquia UdeA, Medellín, Colombia
forlando.lopez@udea.edu.co
[2] Pattern Recognition Lab, Friedrich-Alexander-Universität Erlangen-Nürnberg,
Erlangen, Germany
rafael.orozco@udea.edu.co

Abstract. Research in psychology has shown that personality directly influences the way people think, feel and communicate. It also has consequences on behavior and indirectly affects work effectiveness and job performance. Automatic personality assessment has gained attention in the last decade, and one of the most common models in psychology for automatic personality analysis is the Big Five model, also called as OCEAN model. Different works that study personality traits are based on English texts; conversely, very few studies focus on creating Spanish models. This paper proposes a methodology for the automatic modeling of personality in Spanish texts. Transliterations of videos from YouTube are translated to Spanish to create and evaluate the models. Classical word embeddings are considered, including Wor2Vec, GloVe, BERT, and BETO. Classification and regression experiments are performed to predict the labels of the five traits in the OCEAN model. The results show that 3 out of the five traits can be predicted with high reliability. Additionally, embeddings created with transformer-based models (i.e., BERT and BETO) yield the highest accuracies.

Keywords: Personality traits · OCEAN model · Word embeddings · Regression · Classification

1 Introduction

Research in psychology shows that personality explains different manifestations of human beings since it greatly influences the way people think, feel, communicate and their behavior, which indirectly affects the effectiveness at work and job performance [24]. The automatic analysis of personality has gained attention and has grown a lot in the last decade for its applications in education, marketing, recommendation systems, computer-assisted tutoring systems, sentiment analysis, opinion mining, author profiling, and even in the analysis of marital happiness [8,9,12,19,20]. Researchers in psychology have studied how individuals differ, trying to find a general method to classify human behavioral traits into

Supported by University of Antioquia.

different categories. One of the most widely used models for automatic personality analysis is the Big Five model, also called as OCEAN model [5]. According to it, personality is assessed by five dimensions described as follows: **O**penness to experience: creative, curious vs. rigid, closed-mind; **C**onscientiousness: efficient, self-disciplined vs. lazy, irresponsible; **E**xtraversion: sociable, energetic vs. shy, quite; **A**greeableness: friendly, cooperative vs. selfish, unkind; **N**euroticism (the opposite of Emotional stability): insecure, nervous vs. stable, confident.

Automatic personality assessment has been evaluated with different databases, including *JamesPennebaker and Laura King's essay dataset* [14], *MyPersonality dataset* [23], Twitter data [17, 19], data from YouTube [1], among others. Some of the applied methods on these databases include natural language features (e.g., frequency of adjectives) [10], linguistic features [2], Term Frequency - Inverse Document Frequency (TF-IDF) features [18], and recently, word embeddings such as Word2Vec [22], Global Vectors for Word Representation (GloVe) [4], and Bidirectional Encoder Representations from Transformers (BERT) [7]. Regarding the classification and regression models, different approaches have been used, including Decision Trees (DT), Naive Bayes (NB), K-Nearest Neighbors (KNN), Support Vector Machine (SVM), Random Forest and Logistic Regression [1, 10, 18, 20]. Most of these studies used texts written in English to create and evaluate the methods, while few works are based on texts written in other languages, for example Italian and Brazilian Portuguese [2, 22]. It is essential to highlight that apart from the scarcity of works considering languages other than English; it is also hard to find databases open to the public. Thus, due to the difficulty in finding databases containing Spanish texts labeled with personality traits; in this work, we propose a methodology where transliterations of YouTube vlogs initially produced in English [1] are translated to Spanish, and it is used the labels according to the OCEAN model (see Sect. 2.1 for more details). Different word embeddings are extracted after the translation stage, including Word2Vec, GloVe, BERT, and BETO. Finally, the classification of different personality traits is performed with an SVM, and the prediction of different levels of manifestation of the traits is performed with an SVR. The rest of this paper is organized as follows: Sect. 2 explains the materials and methods considered in this paper; Sect. 3 introduces the experiments, results, and discussion; and finally, the conclusions and future work are presented in Sect. 4.

2 Materials and Methods

2.1 Data Base

The data used in this work correspond to transliterations of the audio extracted from vlogs of 404 YouTube users talking about various topics in front of the camera [1]. The personality scores are assigned according to the OCEAN model's five traits and are values in the range [1.9 and 6.6]. Figure 1 shows the distribution of scores for each of the five traits, where the orange dotted line corresponds to the median value of the scores. Note that the corpus contains the Emotional stability label instead of **N**euroticism, which is its opposite trait. The transliterations are originally in English and were produced by a professional company that manually transcribed the audio of the video's entire length, containing approximately 10K unique words and 240K word tokens. The labels corresponding to the five personality traits were obtained through crowdsourcing. The texts were automatically translated to Spanish using the *TextBlob* Python library, which internally uses the Google Translate API.

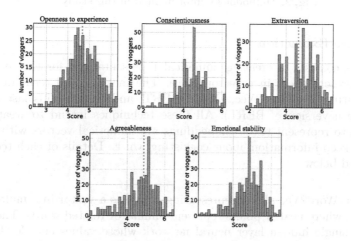

Fig. 1. Histogram for the score in the traits belonging to the OCEAN model.

2.2 Methodology

The main steps of the methodology followed in this study are shown in Fig. 2. The procedure begins with the transliterations' translation, then, the texts are pre-processed, which consists of noise removal and lexicon normalization. The third step is the feature extraction from texts considering word embeddings, and finally, regression and classification systems using Support Vector Machines are optimized to predict/classify the labels of the five traits in the OCEAN model. More details on each step are provided in the following subsections.

2.3 Pre-processing

This step consists of cleaning and standardizing the texts. Words or expressions like "uh", "um", "xxxx" are removed because these expressions were originally in the transliteration to make them as reliable as possible and to anonymize the texts. All words are converted to lower case and all punctuation marks, accents, numbers, and stop words are removed. Finally, given that there are multiple representations for a single word, lemmatization is applied to transform the words into their root form.

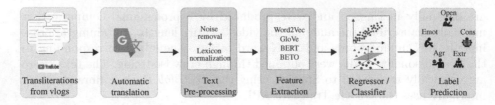

Fig. 2. Methodology implemented in this study.

2.4 Feature Extraction

This process consists of creating numerical representations for the texts that allow to represent them in a vector space. The most typical techniques used in the literature are Word2Vec, GloVe, BERT, and BETO (this last method is the Spanish version of BERT). All these techniques intend to create word embeddings to represent texts. Embeddings are numerical vectors with a fixed length that keep information about coexisting words. Details of each technique are presented below:

Word2Vec: Word2Vec allows representing words as a vector in a multidimensional space, where nearby points represent similar or related words. The model considers a single hidden layer neural network whose values encode the word representation, which can be obtained using two methods: Continuous Bag of Words (CBoW) and Skip Gram [11]. In the CBoW method, the model takes each word's context as input and tries to predict the corresponding target word according to the context. In Skip Gram's case, the input is the target word, while the outputs are the words around the target word. The input to the neural network consists of words encoded as *one-hot* vectors, and the network contains a hidden layer which dimension is equal to the embedding size. At the end of the output layer, a softmax activation function is applied so that each element of the output vector describes the probability that a specific word appears in the context.

Global Vectors (GloVe): GloVe is an unsupervised learning algorithm that allows obtaining vector representations of words by capturing local and global statistics by studying the co-occurrence of words in a corpus [15]. Given a corpus with V words, the co-occurrence matrix X will be a $V \times V$ matrix, where the $i-$th row and the $j-$th column of X, X_{ij}, denotes how many times $i-$th word has co-occurred with the $j-$th word. In Eq. 1 it can be observed the weighted mean square loss function J implemented in GloVe. This function minimizes the difference between the dot product of vectors of two words and the logarithm of their co-occurrence value:

$$J = \sum_{i,j=1}^{V} f(X_{ij})(\boldsymbol{w_i}^T \boldsymbol{w_j} + b_i + b_j - \log(X_{ij}))^2 \tag{1}$$

Where w_i and b_i are the word vector and bias, respectively for the i−th word. w_j and b_j are the word vector and bias, respectively for the j−th word. $f(X_{ij})$ is a weighting function such that assigns lower weights to rare and frequent co-occurrences values as can be seen in Eq. 2.

$$f(X_{ij}) = \begin{cases} \left(\frac{X_{ij}}{x_{\max}}\right)^{\alpha}, \text{if } X_{ij} < x_{\max} \\ 1, \text{in other case.} \end{cases} \tag{2}$$

Here, $x_{\max}$ refers to the maximum co-occurrence value that the i−th word has with the j−th, and α is a hyper-parameter that controls the sensitivity of the weights to increase co-occurrence counts.

Bidirectional Encoder Representations from Transformers (BERT): BERT makes use of Transformers, which are attention mechanisms that learn contextual relations among words (or sub-words) in a text [3]. In its general form, a Transformer includes two separate mechanisms: an encoder that reads the text input and a decoder that produces a prediction for the given task. BERT allows both left and right contexts to influence many language representations that include word predictions [3]. The Transformer architecture is composed of a stack of encoders and a stack of decoders, where the encoders are composed of a Self-Attention layer and a Feed-Forward Neural Network (FFNN). Encoders are identical in structure and are connected to decoders, which include all the elements present in an Encoder, and additionally, they have an Encoder-Decoder Attention layer between the Self-Attention layer and the Feed Forward layer.

Training Models for Word2Vec and Glove: For the case of Word2Vec and GloVe, we trained our own two models using a machine with 256 GB of RAM, 96 processing cores, and making use of the Python gensim module. Two different embeddings are created, one with an embedding dimension of 100 and other with dimension 300. For the case of embeddings with dimension 100, both models (Word2Vec and GloVe) were trained with a Spanish language corpus named WikiCorpus 2010, which contains 650 million words approximately. In the embeddings with dimension 300, the Wikipedia 2018 Corpus was considered, which contains approximately 709 million words. The Word2Vec model with an embedding size of 100 used the CBoW method and a window size of 7. While the Word2Vec model with an embedding size of 300 was trained with the Skip-Gram method and a window size of 8. In the GloVe model, for both embedding dimensions, a window size of 7 and a value of $\alpha = 0.75$ were used. The choice of window size and embedding dimension is based on state of the art, where these values provide the best results in similar tasks like the one we are addressing in this paper [6,15].

Pre-trained Models for BERT and BETO: To obtain word embeddings based on BERT, we used the WEBERT Toolkit [16], which is a Python tool typically used to obtain BERT embeddings in Spanish. For BERT embeddings, the translated version to Spanish of the corpus named Multi-Genre Natural Language Inference was used. The same framework was used to extract the BETO embeddings, which is a pre-trained BERT model that used a Spanish corpus named Spanish Unannotated Corpora. To enable direct comparisons, both BERT and BETO embeddings are 768-dimensional. Because the word embeddings are calculated per word, and the monologues correspond to spontaneous narrations (which means that the number of words is different for each vlogger), it was decided to obtain a fixed dimension vector for each subject. This was performed by taking six functional statistics from the word embeddings: mean, standard deviation, skewness, kurtosis, minimum and maximum. In summary, these are the resulting feature matrices: for Word2Vec and GloVe with dimension 100, $\mathbf{X} \in \mathbb{R}^{404 \times 600}$, for Word2Vec and GloVe with dimension 300, $\mathbf{X} \in \mathbb{R}^{404 \times 1800}$, and for BERT and BETO, $\mathbf{X} \in \mathbb{R}^{404 \times 4608}$.

2.5   Regressor and Classifier

SVM is a widely used method for automatic classification of different conditions, including personality traits [18], speech disorders [13], among others. When SVMs are used for regression they turn into SVR. The main change is that instead of predicting binary labels, a regressor is optimized to predict a real value. In this paper, we use the ε-SVR for regression and the Soft-Margin SVM [21] for classification. The decision function of a soft margin SVM is expressed according to Eq. 3, where ξ_n is a slack variable that penalizes the errors allowed in the optimization process, $y_n \in \{-1, +1\}$ are class labels and $\phi(\mathbf{x}_n)$ is a kernel function. The weight vector $\mathbf{w}$ and the bias value b define the separating hyperplane.

$$y_n \cdot (\mathbf{w}^T \phi(\mathbf{x}_n) + b) \geq 1 - \xi_n, \quad n = 1, 2, 3, \cdots, N \tag{3}$$

The optimization problem for finding the hyperplane is defined in Eq. 4, where the hyperparameter C controls the offset between ξ_n and the margin width. The samples $\mathbf{x}_n$ that satisfy the condition of equality in the Eq. 3 are called support vectors $(\mathbf{x}_m)$.

$$\begin{aligned} &\underset{\mathbf{w}, b}{\text{minimize}} \ \tfrac{1}{2} \|\mathbf{w}\|^2 + C \sum_{n=1}^{N} \xi_n \\ &\text{subject to } y_n \cdot (\mathbf{w}^T \mathbf{x}_n + b) \geq 1 - \xi_n \\ &\qquad\qquad \xi_n \geq 0 \end{aligned} \tag{4}$$

A Gaussian kernel function is considered such that the hyper parameter γ is the kernel bandwidth. More details about the optimization process can be found in [21]. For the regression process using the ε-SVR, the goal is to find a function $f(\mathbf{x})$ that has a maximum deviation of ε from the actual labels y_i [21]. The case of a linear regression is shown in Eq. 5.

$$f(\mathbf{x}) = \langle \mathbf{w}, \mathbf{x} \rangle + b \tag{5}$$

Where $\langle \cdot, \cdot \rangle$ denotes the dot product and $b \in \mathbb{R}$. The optimization problem in the ε-SVR is defined in Eq. 6 as:

$$
\begin{aligned}
\text{minimize } & \tfrac{1}{2}||\mathbf{w}||^2 + C\sum_{i=1}^{l}(\xi_i + \xi_i^*) \\
\text{subject to } & y_i - \langle \mathbf{w}, \mathbf{x_i} \rangle - b \leq \varepsilon + \xi_i \\
& \langle \mathbf{w}, \mathbf{x_i} \rangle + b - y_i \leq \varepsilon + \xi_i^* \\
& \xi_i, \xi_i^* \geq 0
\end{aligned}
\tag{6}
$$

ξ_i and ξ_i^* are slack variables, the constant $C > 0$ determines the trade-off between the flatness of $f(\mathbf{x})$ and the maximum allowed deviation ε. This corresponds to the so called ε-insensitive loss function $|\xi|_\varepsilon$, which is described as:

$$
|\xi|_\varepsilon = \begin{cases} 0 & \text{if } |\xi| \leq \varepsilon \\ |\xi| - \varepsilon; & \text{otherwise} \end{cases}
\tag{7}
$$

The hyper-parameters C, γ, and ε are optimized through a grid-search up to powers of ten in the range between $[1 \times 10^{-4}$ and $1 \times 10^4]$. A 10-Fold subject independent Cross-Validation (CV) strategy is followed. The process is repeated ten times, randomizing the samples in the database to increase the system's generalization capability. The regression systems are optimized following the same strategy as the classifier, and their performance is evaluated in terms of the Pearson's correlation coefficient (r), Spearman's correlation coefficient (ρ), Mean Absolute Error (MAE), and the Root Mean Squared Error (RMSE). Classification results are reported in terms of Accuracy, Sensitivity, Specificity, F1-score, and the area under the receiver operating characteristic curve (AUC).

3   Experiments and Results

Ground-truth labels for the five personality traits of the OCEAN model are predicted with an SVR. Additionally, the SVM classifier is trained to classify each trait individually. There is a total of 10 experiments: 5 for regression and 5 for binary classification. Each experiment is performed with the groups of features resulting from the methods explained in Sect. 2.4.

3.1   Regression Experiments

The main idea in these experiments is to predict the score on each trait of the OCEAN model. The results are reported in Table 1. Note that in four out of the five personality traits, the transformer-based methods (namely BERT and BETO) yield better results. BERT seems to be the best model for conscientiousness and extraversion, while BETO works best for agreeableness and emotional stability. The only case where transformer-based methods are not best is Openness to experience. In this case, the W2v-300 model works best, and actually, it is the only one that shows positive correlation values. This is the case with the lowest correlation coefficient values ($r = 0.13$ and $\rho = 0.12$). This likely indicates that the Openness to experience trait is the most difficult to predict among

Table 1. Regression results. Values reported as mean ± standard deviation.

Trait	Feature	r	ρ	MAE	RMSE
Open	W2v-100	−0.08 ± 0.03	−0.08 ± 0.02	0.58 ± 0.00	0.72 ± 0.00
	W2v-300	**0.13 ± 0.02**	**0.12 ± 0.03**	**0.57 ± 0.00**	**0.71 ± 0.00**
	Glv-100	−0.07 ± 0.04	−0.05 ± 0.04	0.59 ± 0.01	0.73 ± 0.01
	Glv-300	−0.02 ± 0.03	−0.01 ± 0.03	0.58 ± 0.00	0.72 ± 0.00
	Fusion-100	−0.06 ± 0.04	−0.05 ± 0.04	0.59 ± 0.00	0.73 ± 0.00
	Fusion-300	−0.02 ± 0.04	−0.02 ± 0.03	0.58 ± 0.00	0.72 ± 0.00
	Bert	−0.06 ± 0.03	−0.06 ± 0.04	0.58 ± 0.00	0.72 ± 0.00
	Beto	−0.05 ± 0.04	−0.05 ± 0.05	0.58 ± 0.00	0.72 ± 0.00
Cons	W2v-100	0.24 ± 0.01	0.25 ± 0.01	0.58 ± 0.00	0.75 ± 0.00
	W2v-300	0.24 ± 0.02	0.23 ± 0.02	0.58 ± 0.00	0.75 ± 0.00
	Glv-100	0.27 ± 0.01	0.27 ± 0.01	0.58 ± 0.00	0.74 ± 0.00
	Glv-300	0.29 ± 0.01	0.32 ± 0.01	0.57 ± 0.00	0.74 ± 0.00
	Fusion-100	0.25 ± 0.01	0.26 ± 0.01	0.58 ± 0.00	0.75 ± 0.00
	Fusion-300	0.26 ± 0.01	0.28 ± 0.01	0.58 ± 0.00	0.75 ± 0.00
	Bert	**0.36 ± 0.01**	**0.38 ± 0.01**	**0.55 ± 0.00**	**0.72 ± 0.00**
	Beto	0.36 ± 0.01	0.38 ± 0.01	0.56 ± 0.00	0.72 ± 0.00
Extr	W2v-100	0.19 ± 0.03	0.20 ± 0.03	0.79 ± 0.01	0.96 ± 0.01
	W2v-300	0.24 ± 0.03	0.23 ± 0.02	0.78 ± 0.01	0.95 ± 0.01
	Glv-100	0.26 ± 0.02	0.26 ± 0.02	0.77 ± 0.01	0.95 ± 0.01
	Glv-300	0.18 ± 0.03	0.18 ± 0.02	0.79 ± 0.01	0.96 ± 0.01
	Fusion-100	0.23 ± 0.02	0.24 ± 0.02	0.78 ± 0.01	0.95 ± 0.00
	Fusion-300	0.25 ± 0.01	0.24 ± 0.01	0.77 ± 0.00	0.95 ± 0.00
	Bert	**0.35 ± 0.02**	**0.36 ± 0.01**	**0.75 ± 0.01**	**0.92 ± 0.01**
	Beto	0.30 ± 0.01	0.30 ± 0.02	0.76 ± 0.00	0.93 ± 0.00
Agr	W2v-100	0.29 ± 0.02	0.26 ± 0.02	0.66 ± 0.01	0.84 ± 0.01
	W2v-300	0.35 ± 0.02	0.30 ± 0.02	0.65 ± 0.01	0.82 ± 0.01
	Glv-100	0.27 ± 0.02	0.24 ± 0.02	0.66 ± 0.00	0.85 ± 0.00
	Glv-300	0.24 ± 0.01	0.21 ± 0.01	0.66 ± 0.00	0.85 ± 0.00
	Fusion-100	0.30 ± 0.01	0.27 ± 0.02	0.66 ± 0.00	0.84 ± 0.00
	Fusion-300	0.37 ± 0.01	0.32 ± 0.02	0.64 ± 0.01	0.82 ± 0.01
	Bert	0.41 ± 0.02	0.38 ± 0.02	0.63 ± 0.01	0.80 ± 0.01
	Beto	**0.45 ± 0.01**	**0.40 ± 0.01**	**0.62 ± 0.00**	**0.79 ± 0.01**
Emot	W2v-100	0.13 ± 0.05	0.13 ± 0.03	0.60 ± 0.01	0.78 ± 0.01
	W2v-300	0.27 ± 0.03	0.22 ± 0.02	0.59 ± 0.00	0.75 ± 0.00
	Glv-100	0.10 ± 0.03	0.09 ± 0.03	0.62 ± 0.00	0.79 ± 0.01
	Glv-300	0.02 ± 0.03	0.01 ± 0.04	0.61 ± 0.00	0.79 ± 0.01
	Fusion-100	0.23 ± 0.02	0.24 ± 0.02	0.78 ± 0.01	0.95 ± 0.00
	Fusion-300	0.16 ± 0.04	0.12 ± 0.04	0.61 ± 0.01	0.77 ± 0.01
	Bert	0.19 ± 0.03	0.18 ± 0.03	0.60 ± 0.01	0.77 ± 0.01
	Beto	**0.28 ± 0.01**	**0.24 ± 0.02**	**0.59 ± 0.01**	**0.75 ± 0.00**

W2v: Word2Vec. Glv: GloVe. Fusion: Word2Vec + GloVe. Open: Openness to experience. Cons: Conscientiousness. Extr: Extraversion. Agr: Agreeableness. Emot: Emotional stability.

the five included in the OCEAN model. The other best correlation coefficients obtained for the other traits range between 0.28 and 0.45 for the Pearson's coefficient and from 0.24 to 0.40 for the Spearman's coefficient, indicating that, to some extent, it is possible to predict the level at which the participants express each trait. On the other hand, when comparing the performance of Word2Vec and GloVe, no clear evidence is observed to conclude whether one model is better than the other one. Conversely, when comparing 100 with 300-dimensional Word2Vec embeddings, it is clear that the greater ones yield better results. In the case of Glove embeddings, it seems like smaller embeddings work best, although no clear trend is observed. The regression results obtained in this study are in line with those reported in [22], where it is stated that no single model can provide good results for all five traits.

3.2   Classification Experiments

The scores on each trait are used to label whether a given trait is present or not, as follows: if the score is less than or equal to the median of the trait, the text is labeled as "low presence" of the personality trait; otherwise, the text is labeled as "high presence" of the personality trait. This procedure allows having a balanced number of samples along the five traits in the two defined labels. The resulting number of samples per label and trait are shown in Table 2.

Table 2. Number of subjects per trait for the classification experiments.

Trait	Number of subjects	
	Low presence	High presence
Openness	203	201
Conscientiousness	209	195
Extraversion	209	195
Agreeableness	218	186
Emotional stability	203	201

Table 3 shows the results of the classification experiments. Note that the behavior is similar to the one observed in the regression results, where transformer-based models outperformed other word embeddings. The trait with the best results is agreeableness, with an accuracy of 63.9% obtained with the BERT model. Conversely, the trait with the lowest accuracy is Openness (as it was the case in the regression experiments) with an accuracy of 52.3%. When comparing BERT and BETO results, we realize that they are quite similar in all of the traits. Additionally, the fusion of embeddings is not showing significant improvements with respect to individual models. Due to space limitations, ROC curves resulting from the classification experiments are not included in the paper. If the reader wants to have a look at them they can be found in the following repository[1].

---

[1] https://github.com/felipelopezp726/ROC-curves-personality.

Table 3. Results for classification analysis. Values reported as mean ± standard deviation.

Trait	Feature	Accuracy	Sensitivity	Specificity	F1-score	AUC
Open	W2v-100	51.3 ± 1.8	49.4 ± 4.4	53.3 ± 2.7	51.3 ± 1.8	0.52 ± 0.02
	W2v-300	52.0 ± 1.6	53.1 ± 2.6	50.9 ± 2.0	52.0 ± 1.6	0.53 ± 0.02
	Glv-100	51.2 ± 1.6	48.5 ± 3.8	53.9 ± 2.8	51.1 ± 1.6	0.50 ± 0.02
	Glv-300	50.2 ± 2.3	46.7 ± 4.7	53.7 ± 5.2	50.1 ± 2.3	0.50 ± 0.02
	Fusion-100	52.0 ± 1.3	51.7 ± 1.7	53.3 ± 2.0	52.0 ± 1.3	0.53 ± 0.01
	Fusion-300	49.5 ± 1.0	45.5 ± 3.1	53.5 ± 2.9	49.4 ± 1.0	0.50 ± 0.01
	Bert	**52.3 ± 1.7**	**49.9 ± 3.3**	**54.6 ± 3.1**	**52.2 ± 1.7**	**0.53 ± 0.02**
	Beto	51.0 ± 1.1	49.1 ± 3.0	52.8 ± 3.6	50.9 ± 1.1	0.51 ± 0.01
Cons	W2v-100	57.5 ± 1.7	65.0 ± 3.6	50.5 ± 2.8	57.3 ± 1.7	0.60 ± 0.02
	W2v-300	57.7 ± 1.3	54.9 ± 2.3	60.4 ± 2.0	57.7 ± 1.3	0.59 ± 0.01
	Glv-100	58.9 ± 1.1	60.4 ± 1.3	57.6 ± 1.9	58.9 ± 1.1	0.62 ± 0.02
	Glv-300	59.7 ± 1.0	66.9 ± 2.1	53.0 ± 1.7	59.5 ± 1.0	0.64 ± 0.01
	Fusion-100	58.9 ± 1.8	58.7 ± 2.4	59.0 ± 3.5	58.8 ± 1.8	0.61 ± 0.02
	Fusion-300	60.3 ± 0.9	65.9 ± 2.6	55.1 ± 1.9	60.2 ± 0.8	0.64 ± 0.01
	Bert	60.0 ± 1.2	57.8 ± 1.6	62.0 ± 2.8	60.0 ± 1.2	0.67 ± 0.01
	Beto	**61.3 ± 1.2**	**60.4 ± 1.9**	**62.1 ± 1.5**	**61.3 ± 1.2**	**0.65 ± 0.01**
Extr	W2v-100	56.0 ± 1.0	54.9 ± 1.5	57.1 ± 1.9	56.0 ± 1.0	0.60 ± 0.01
	W2v-300	58.5 ± 1.3	50.4 ± 2.1	66.0 ± 2.1	58.2 ± 1.3	0.61 ± 0.01
	Glv-100	59.7 ± 1.5	58.8 ± 2.4	60.6 ± 2.2	59.7 ± 1.5	0.64 ± 0.01
	Glv-300	54.7 ± 1.3	52.9 ± 1.9	56.4 ± 1.9	54.7 ± 1.3	0.57 ± 0.01
	Fusion-100	59.3 ± 1.1	56.7 ± 1.3	61.8 ± 2.4	59.3 ± 1.1	0.62 ± 0.01
	Fusion-300	57.5 ± 2.1	56.2 ± 2.6	58.8 ± 2.7	57.5 ± 2.1	0.62 ± 0.02
	Bert	**62.1 ± 1.1**	**66.9 ± 1.4**	**57.6 ± 1.8**	**62.0± 1.2**	**0.66 ± 0.01**
	Beto	59.3 ± 1.0	64.5 ± 2.6	54.4 ± 2.0	59.2 ± 1.0	0.65 ± 0.01
Agr	W2v-100	57.1 ± 1.0	53.3 ± 1.9	60.3 ± 2.3	57.1 ± 1.0	0.59 ± 0.01
	W2v-300	58.8 ± 0.7	42.3 ± 1.7	72.9 ± 1.7	57.8 ± 0.7	0.63 ± 0.01
	Glv-100	55.5 ± 2.4	48.5 ± 2.7	61.5 ± 3.3	55.3 ± 2.4	0.57 ± 0.02
	Glv-300	56.0 ± 1.5	48.5 ± 2.1	62.4 ± 2.6	55.9 ± 1.5	0.58 ± 0.01
	Fusion-100	58.3 ± 1.6	51.9 ± 2.3	63.7 ± 2.0	58.1 ± 1.6	0.61 ± 0.01
	Fusion-300	57.7 ± 1.2	50.9 ± 2.7	63.6 ± 1.3	57.6 ± 1.3	0.63 ± 0.01
	Bert	**63.9 ± 0.9**	**54.3 ± 1.8**	**72.0 ± 1.3**	**63.6 ± 0.9**	**0.69 ± 0.01**
	Beto	60.0 ± 1.3	52.6 ± 2.1	66.2 ± 1.4	59.8 ± 1.3	0.64 ± 0.01
Emot	W2v-100	53.9 ± 1.7	52.6 ± 2.5	55.1 ± 2.1	53.8 ± 1.7	0.54 ± 0.02
	W2v-300	56.3 ± 1.1	55.4 ± 1.7	57.1 ± 1.9	56.3 ± 1.1	0.57 ± 0.01
	Glv-100	55.0 ± 1.5	51.6 ± 2.3	58.5 ± 1.9	55.0 ± 5	0.56 ± 0.01
	Glv-300	52.2 ± 1.9	48.0 ± 3.2	56.3 ± 3.2	52.0 ± 1.9	0.52 ± 0.02
	Fusion-100	55.6 ± 1.6	55.0 ± 2.2	56.2 ± 1.5	55.6 ± 1.6	0.56 ± 0.01
	Fusion-300	53.5 ± 2.6	50.2 ± 2.5	56.7 ± 4.3	53.4 ± 2.5	0.55 ± 0.02
	Bert	54.1 ± 1.8	53.8 ± 2.4	54.3 ± 3.9	54.1 ± 1.8	0.55 ± 0.02
	Beto	**57.3 ± 0.7**	**55.0 ± 1.5**	**59.6 ± 2.1**	**57.3 ± 0.7**	**0.61 ± 0.01**

W2v: Word2Vec. Glv: GloVe. Fusion: Word2Vec + GloVe. Open: Openness to experience. Cons: Conscientiousness. Extr: Extraversion. Agr: Agreeableness. Emot: Emotional stability.

4   Conclusions and Future Work

Different types of word embeddings are considered to estimate the five personality traits of the OCEAN model in Spanish. Texts are obtained from translating the transliterations of the YouTube vlogs included in The YouTube Personality Dataset. Experiments show that it is possible to estimate the level at which a participant expresses the conscientiousness, extraversion, and agreeableness traits. Conversely, openness to experience is the most challenging trait, followed by the emotional stability trait. This is likely because YouTube vloggers are mainly young people, and what they like to show the most in front of the camera are gestures and words related to sociable, friendly, and critical people. The results also show similar performance to those obtained with linguistic features [2], with the additional advantage that our proposed approach does not use linguistic models that highly depend on a dictionary or a lexicon. To the best of our knowledge, this is the first work in which hand-crafted/adjusted Word2Vec and GloVe models and pre-trained Transformers models are used to generate word embeddings to estimate personality traits in Spanish. In general terms, word embeddings obtained with transformer-based models are better than embeddings obtained from other models to represent different traits; however, no single model can devise a representation of the five traits accurately. The success shown by transformer-based models may be because, although Word2Vec and GloVe are trained to differentiate content through semantic relations, they do not consider that the same word can be represented differently depending on the order of words and their context. BERT and BETO consider this situation, and the words have embeddings that depend on their position in the text and their neighbor words. To improve the results reported in this paper, we plan to work on deep learning models such as Convolutional Neural Networks (CNN) and Recurrent Neural Networks (RNN) in future work.

Acknowledgements. This work was funded by CODI UdeA, grant # PRG2017-15530.

References

1. Biel, J.I., Tsiminaki, V., Dines, J., Gatica-Perez, D.: Hi Youtube! personality impressions and verbal content in social video. In: Proceedings of the 15th ACM on International Conference on Multimodal Interaction, pp. 119–126 (2013)
2. Celli, F.: Unsupervised personality recognition for social network sites. In: Proceedings of ICDS, Valencia (2012)
3. Devlin, J., Chang, M.W., Lee, K., Toutanova, K.: Bert: pre-training of deep bidirectional transformers for language understanding. arXiv:1810.04805 (2018)
4. Giménez, M., Paredes, R., Rosso, P.: Personality recognition using convolutional neural networks. In: Gelbukh, A. (ed.) CICLing 2017. LNCS, vol. 10762, pp. 313–323. Springer, Cham (2018). https://doi.org/10.1007/978-3-319-77116-8_23
5. Goldberg, L.R.: An alternative "description of personality": the big-five factor structure. J. Pers. Soc. Psychol. **59**(6), 1216 (1990)

6. Alammar, J.: The illustrated word2vec (2019). http://jalammar.github.io/illustrated-word2vec/. Accessed 25 Mar 2021
7. Jiang, H., Zhang, X., Choi, J.D.: Automatic text-based personality recognition on monologues and multiparty dialogues using attentive networks and contextual embeddings. arXiv preprint arXiv:1911.09304 (2019)
8. John, O.P., Robins, R.W., Pervin, L.A.: Handbook of Personality: Theory and Research. Guilford Press, New York (2010)
9. Kelly, E.L., Conley, J.J.: Personality and compatibility: a prospective analysis of marital stability and marital satisfaction. J. Pers. Soc. Psychol. **52**(1), 27 (1987)
10. Mao, Y., Zhang, D., Wu, C., Zheng, K., Wang, X.: Feature analysis and optimisation for computational personality recognition. In: 4th International Conference on Computer and Communications (ICCC), pp. 2410–2414 (2018)
11. Mikolov, T., Chen, K., Corrado, G., Dean, J.: Efficient estimation of word representations in vector space. arXiv preprint arXiv:1301.3781 (2013)
12. Oliveira, R.D., Cherubini, M., Oliver, N.: Influence of personality on satisfaction with mobile phone services. ACM Trans. Comput.-Hum. Interact. (TOCHI) **20**(2), 1–23 (2013)
13. Orozco-Arroyave, J.R., et al.: Neurospeech: an open-source software for Parkinson's speech analysis. Digit. Signal Process. **77**, 207–221 (2018)
14. Pennebaker, J.W., King, L.A.: Linguistic styles: language use as an individual difference. J. Pers. Soc. Psychol. **77**(6), 1296 (1999)
15. Pennington, J., Socher, R., Manning, C.: Glove: global vectors for word representation. In: Proceedings of the 2014 Conference on Empirical Methods in Natural Language Processing (EMNLP), pp. 1532–1543 (2014)
16. Perez-Toro, P.A.: PauPerezT/WEBERT: Word Embeddings using BERT, July 2020. https://doi.org/10.5281/zenodo.3964244
17. Plank, B., Hovy, D.: Personality traits on twitter—or—how to get 1,500 personality tests in a week. In: Proceedings of the 6th Workshop on Computational Approaches to Subjectivity, Sentiment and Social Media Analysis, pp. 92–98 (2015)
18. Pratama, B.Y., Sarno, R.: Personality classification based on twitter text using Naive Bayes, KNN and SVM. In: 2015 International Conference on Data and Software Engineering (ICoDSE), pp. 170–174. IEEE (2015)
19. Rangel, F., Rosso, P., Potthast, M., Stein, B., Daelemans, W.: Overview of the 3rd author profiling task at PAN 2015. In: CLEF 2015 (2015)
20. Sarkar, C., Bhatia, S., Agarwal, A., Li, J.: Feature analysis for computational personality recognition using Youtube personality data set. In: Proceedings of the 2014 ACM Multi Media on Workshop on Computational Personality Recognition, pp. 11–14 (2014)
21. Schölkopf, B., Smola, A.J., Bach, F., et al.: Learning with Kernels: Support Vector Machines, Regularization, Optimization, and Beyond. MIT Press, Cambridge (2002)
22. da Silva, B.B.C., Paraboni, I.: Personality recognition from Facebook text. In: Villavicencio, A., et al. (eds.) PROPOR 2018. LNCS (LNAI), vol. 11122, pp. 107–114. Springer, Cham (2018). https://doi.org/10.1007/978-3-319-99722-3_11
23. Stillwell, D., Kosinski, M.: myPersonality project website (2015)
24. Tett, R.P., Jackson, D.N., Rothstein, M.: Personality measures as predictors of job performance: a meta-analytic review. Pers. Psychol. **44**(4), 703–742 (1991)

Power Conditioner for AC PV Systems Using GA

Luis David Pabon Fernandez[✉], Edison Andres Caicedo Peñaranda[✉],
and Jorge Luis Diaz Rodriguez[✉]

Universidad de Pamplona, Pamplona, Colombia

Abstract. This work presents the development of a multilevel power inverter
prototype with the use of optimized modulation which manages to significantly
minimize the harmonic content of output voltages using Genetics Algorithms.
Additionally, it integrates a DC/DC converter that allows to regulate the RMS value
of the inverter output voltage through the control of the DC bus voltage. A control
loop is implemented that allows obtaining the optimal power quality by verifying
compliance with the IEEE 1159 (1995) and IEEE 519 (1992) standards. Through
this it is possible to avoid most of the related power quality phenomena such
as sag, swell, flicker, undervoltage, etc. Finally, the prototype was successfully
implemented and verified.

Keywords: Multilevel converter · PWM · Optimization · Genetic algorithm ·
THD

1 Introduction

Photovoltaic (PV) systems are used to power loads in alternating current (AC) system,
thus the need of electrical power inverters is essential, since solar panels generate electric
power of direct current (DC) [1, 2]. The conversion of the electrical power usually uses
control strategies involving power inverters with PWM modulation [3], for this purpose.
Commonly, these techniques involve switching and harmonic distortion problems [4,
5]. To solve these problems and achieve a voltage waveform closer to a pure sinewave
waveform, with the minimum of power switching devices. The alternative of using a
new family of inverters arises: the multilevel power converters [6–8].

The idea of using multiple voltage levels to carry out electrical conversion was
proposed in 1975, nevertheless the multilevel power converter was first implemented
with the three-step inverter introduced by Nabae, Takahashi, and Akagi in 1981 [9].
Subsequently, several topologies of multilevel converters have been developed, which
have in common the elementary concept of achieving stepped voltage waves that are
closer to a sinusoidal waveform [10, 11].

To bring the waveforms of the voltages of multilevel converters even closer to pure
sinusoidal waveforms, multiple harmonic content optimization works have been carried
out [12–14]. These works pursue the elimination of harmonics, either in selective orders
[15, 16] or in a certain range or determined band [17]. However, a definitive optimum
is not achieved (the subject is currently under research).

© Springer Nature Switzerland AG 2021
J. C. Figueroa-García et al. (Eds.): WEA 2021, CCIS 1431, pp. 133–144, 2021.
https://doi.org/10.1007/978-3-030-86702-7_12

Another problem of the DC/AC conversion in PV systems is the variation of the voltage in terms of the load changes and fluctuations of the accumulator block or of the solar panels from which the inverter takes the energy [15]. In power inverters, voltage regulation can cause the output voltages to go further the limits to preserve the power quality to the load.

This work presents a prototype of a multilevel inverter that uses evolutionary techniques to optimize the harmonic content of the output voltages. As it integrates as a previous stage a DC/DC converter, that regulate the RMS value of the inverter output voltage, by means of controlling the DC bus voltage. In this way, the power quality of PV systems has been optimized, thus avoiding phenomena such as sag, swell, flicker, undervoltage, overvoltage, interharmonics, frequency deviations and DC shifts and with a minimum of total harmonic distortion (THD).

2   Two-Stage Multilevel Converter Per Phase

To mitigate the power quality phenomena associated with the RMS value, voltage control is performed on the DC bus side through a DC/DC converter. The selected converter to carry out this task is the non-inverting step-down converter of reduced elements [17]. The schematic of the CD/CD converter is shown in Fig. 1a.

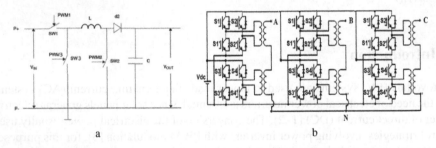

Fig. 1. Circuit a) of the DC/DC converter b) Topology of the multilevel inverter

A modification to the original topology was included, by changing a blocking diode for the switching element called SW3 in Fig. 1. This in order to carry out a simpler activation process for switch SW1, using a circuit simple bootstrap circuit.

To mitigate the phenomena associated with the waveform and to generate voltages with harmonic optimization, the multilevel inverter topology selected for this work is the common source asymmetric H-bridge cascaded converter with a 1:3 ratio and 2 power stages. The power converter generates a line voltage with a maximum of 17 steps, this topology is shown in Fig. 1b [16].

These two converters are connected in cascaded in order to obtain the electrical power inverting and conditioning prototype for PV systems that require an AC output.

3 Mathematical Modeling

3.1 Line Voltaje THD

The IEEE 519 (1992) standard defines total harmonic distortion as follows (3) [18].

$$THD = \frac{\sqrt{\sum_{n=2}^{50} h_n^2}}{h_1} \cdot 100 \tag{1}$$

Where the harmonic h_1 is the fundamental component and h_n is the peak of the harmonic n. Using this expression and previous works by the authors [13, 17], this expression becomes:

$$THD = \frac{\sqrt{\sum_{n=2}^{50} \left(\frac{1}{n}\left[\sum_{i=1}^{4}\sum_{j=1}^{Li}(-1)^{j-1}\cos n\alpha_{ij}\right]\right)^2}}{\left[\sum_{i=1}^{4}\sum_{j=1}^{Li}(-1)^{j-1}\cos 1\alpha_{ij}\right]} * 100 \tag{2}$$

Where n takes odd values not multiples of three, that is, 5, 7, 11, 13, 17, etc. and L_i are the components of the vector $L = [a\ b\ c\ d]$. which index how many angles each step has in the first quarter wave of the modulation. Similarly, the effective value can be defined in terms of harmonics as:

$$Vline_{RMS} = \sqrt{\sum_{n=1}^{\alpha} Vrms_n^2} \tag{3}$$

Replacing an upper bound $h_{max} = 50$ the Vrms is determined by Eq. 4:

$$Vline_{RMS} = \sqrt{\sum_{n=1}^{50} \frac{\left(\frac{4\sqrt{3}Vdc}{\pi n}\left[\sum_{i=1}^{4}\sum_{j=1}^{Li}(-1)^{j-1}\cos n\alpha_{ij}\right]\right)^2}{2}} \tag{4}$$

for $n = 5, 7, \ldots$ odd not multiples of three

In this way, Eq. (2) defines the THD equation as the objective function to be minimized by the optimization algorithm and Eq. (4) define the second objective equation that will search for the effective value desired by the user. In this way the algorithm will find a modulation with an RMS value. This will be defined as rated by the user and with the harmonic distortion as close to zero percent. In Eqs. (2) and (4) the harmonics evaluated are the odd and non-triple ones.

This is because harmonics multiples of three have been cancel out in line voltages, and can exist in phases. However, as the converter will be applied to a PV system where single-phase loads can be connected, the evaluation of the two functions will consider the harmonics multiples of three in order for the optimization to be carried out in both the phase and line voltages.

4   Optimization Algorithm

To obtain a power inverter that improves the quality of the energy, which should guarantee in ideal conditions that the voltage at the output of the device must be free of harmonic distortions, and at the same time be capable of maintaining the level of the constant voltage and equal to rated voltage.

With the multilevel converter, it is possible to obtain a low distortion voltage waveform with low switching, however, the switching angles must be calculated so that the harmonic distortion is low. This involves solving Eq. (2) with commutation angles by making the THD value as close to zero. However, this can cause the RMS value of the voltage to be far from the desired value. In this way, the solution of Eq. (2) must be restricted so that Eq. (4) results in a value as close as possible to the value of the desired line voltage. A technique must be used to solve this problem that allows approaching a solution that optimizes the THD value and maintains a desired RMS voltage value. The performance of the DC/DC converter is limited to correcting variations due to voltage regulation low voltage levels on the DC bus.

A multiobjective genetic algorithms were used as an optimization technique. In order to make the THD equation as close as possible to zero and the Vrms equation to as close as possible to 220 V. This will be the rated line voltage of the prototype; to achieve these objectives we will used the algorithm shown in Fig. 2.

The main fitness function will be Eq. (2) that allows the THD value to be calculated. This function should be as close as possible to zero percent, the restriction will be taken as Eq. (4) in such a way that the line voltage is as close as possible to a voltage of 220 V.

In the algorithm, the rated values of the machine are assigned first, the line voltage (V_n) and rated frequency (f_n). Then the user gives the maximum number of generations with which the multiobjective genetic algorithm must operate (Nmax), then an initial vector L is assigned to start the RMS and THD value calculations and the respective evolution. The algorithm assigns a vector of the switching angles L = [a b c d]. The vector L contains the information of how many switching angles to be generated in each of the four steps of the first quarter wave of the converter phase voltage. With this information, an initial population P(X) of 20 individuals, where X are the vectors of the created waveform.

The algorithm creates an initial population of 20 individuals that evolves in terms of the performance of the two fitness functions given by the THD and VRMS equations, in each generation of evolution. The algorithm selects the individuals with the lowest THD and whose RMS voltage value is closest to the rated value. At this stage, the use of evolutionary operators is presented, the percentage of the population to perform elitism is only 5%. The *CrossoverFraction* is the fraction of genes swapped between individuals is 0.8. The fraction of population on non-dominated front *ParetoFraction* is 0.35. In each generation these operators are applied and the evolution of the THD value is reviewed and restricted to compliance with the RMS value of the line voltage.

In this way, the algorithm will evolve until it reaches some convergence criteria, which are: if the THD and the RMS values converge or if the THD is null and the RMS value is the desired one or the maximum number of generations is fulfilled, the evolutionary part of the algorithm ends. If these conditions are not met, the algorithm applies the evolutionary operators to the population and begins with another generation.

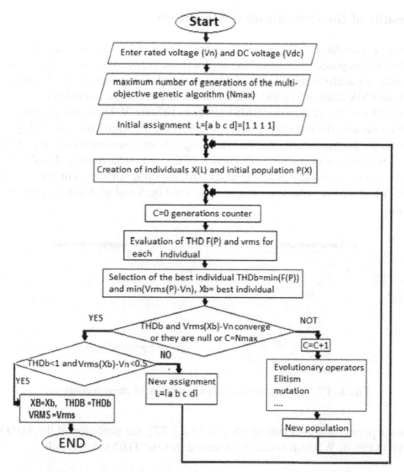

Fig. 2. Multi-objective genetic algorithm for optimization of V vs f.

If this stage ends, the algorithm verifies that the THD is less than 0.1% and that the value of the RMS line voltage approaches the desired value with a ±0.5 V margin, if this does not happen the algorithm assigns a new vector L = [a b c d] and iterate the evolutionary part again, until the conditions are met. When the conditions are achieved, the algorithm stores the vector of switching angles, the RMS voltage and the THD value in a matrix, for the given frequency.

With the help of Matlab® and the *gamultiobj* command, the algorithms corresponding to the mathematical model of the fitness functions (THD and VRMS equations) and their respective optimization using multiobjective genetic algorithms were programmed. The population size for the algorithm is taken from 20 individuals, each individual (X) made up of the total of switching angles in the first quarter wave of the phase voltage, accompanied by the vector L, which indicates the program in charge of evaluate the fitness function the angles correspond to each step. The rated value of the voltage was assigned in 220 V, the rated frequency 60 Hz, the rated voltage of the DC block of 45 V.

5   Results of the Optimization Algorithm

The vector L was determined by the algorithm as L = [5 7 9 27]. It means that the best individual is composed of 48 switching angles in the first quarter of the waveform. The phase voltage waveform modulation of this individual is shown in Fig. 4. This individual presents an RMS value of 219.99 V and a THD of 0.00006% theoretical line, in phase the THD is 0.000067% and the value RMS voltage is 127.011 V. The harmonic spectrum of this waveform with the voltage amplitude found by the algorithm is shown in Fig. 3. The phase voltage spectrum shows that there is no significant contribution of harmonics. It is seen at first glance as a zero harmonic content of the first 50 harmonics. The three-phase voltage system is generated by three phases with the same waveform of Fig. 4, but with a phase shift of 120 electrical degrees, as shown in Fig. 5 and additionally the harmonic spectrum.

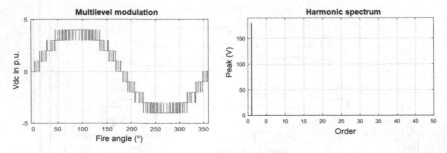

Fig. 3. PWM voltage waveform and spectrum of phase modulation.

For the population with individuals $L = [5\ 7\ 9\ 27]$, the evolution of the THD value is shown in Fig. 4. Where it is clearly observed that the THD value is null.

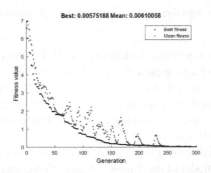

Fig. 4. Algorithm evolution for the population with individuals $\mathbf{L} = [5\ 7\ 9\ 27]$.

It takes the algorithm 300 generations to find the solution to the main function and the constraint, and it ends due to convergence as the maximum number of generations is not reached. As the variation is less than 0.00001 between two generations, the evolution is finished and when the convergence conditions are met, the general algorithm ends.

It is notable that additional steps and pulses appear in the line voltage, due to the subtraction that takes place between the phases. The phase modulation has 9 steps, while the line modulation has 17 steps, this makes the waveform closer to a sine waveform and therefore the harmonic content decreases substantially. The harmonic spectrum of the line voltages is shown in the same figure. In this spectrum it is clearly seen that the harmonic content is zero as in the phase voltages. The THD value of this calculated modulation is 0.0006% and the RMS value of the line voltage is 219.99 V.

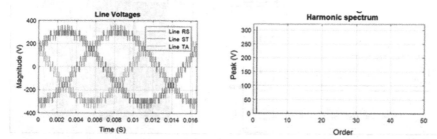

Fig. 5. PWM line voltage and spectrum of the positive sequence three-phase system.

6 Prototype Implementation

The power inverter and the DC/DC converter were implemented in a prototype of 2400 VA at rated frequency of 60 Hz. The rated input voltage is 48 V, its maximum value at the input can reach up to 70 V. The rated voltage of the line voltages is 220 V and the phase voltages 127 V. The control of the DC/DC converter and the power inverter was developed on a Virtex 5 FPGA.

6.1 Control Algorithm

To implement a voltage control that allows to preserve an optimal power quality, regardless of what happens in the load or in the accumulator block. Therefore, the DC/DC converter is connected to the power supply through the accumulator block and the output of the DC/DC converter to the multilevel power inverter. Using this as the internal connection of the prototype. The aim with this topology is that the DC/DC converter increases or decreases the value of the input voltage of the inverter. It is intended that the line voltage at the inverter output always remains the same regardless of the current required by the load, the voltage value given by the batteries or the regulation present in the prototype. The measured variable is the inverter output line voltage, this voltage is obtained with the measurement of the designed voltage sensor, which converts the RMS value of the voltage into a DC value.

The output signal of the voltage sensor is obtained using the NI USB 6009 DAQ. It is connected to a computer in which the control algorithm was developed in Labview. This algorithm has its respective graphical user interface in which the voltage set-point is assigned, in this case to a RMS voltage is 220 V. The Labview algorithm commands are communicated through the serial port to the Virtex 5 FPGA, which directly controls the DC/DC converter by increasing or decreasing the output voltage. As required by the control (Labview) of the multilevel converter, always generating the same waveform. In short, the inverter control is static, always giving the same signals so that the inverter always generates the same waveform. In this way the control loop is established. Figure 6 shows the block diagram of the different elements involved in the control of the prototype.

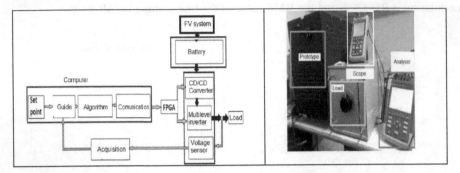

Fig. 6. Implementation of the converter a) Algorithm b) Experimental setup.

As previously mentioned, the voltage set-point was assigned to 220 V. This is adjusted by means of a graphical interface programmed in Labview®, which allows to visualize the output voltages and the reference voltage, as well as the controller actions. The Labview algorithm has the required scaling for the sensor and the output variable, as does the PID controller in the control loop.

7 Experimental Results

To validate the operation of the prototype, the converter is powered by the accumulator block of the photovoltaic system. Additionally, through the power converter, power is supplied to a three-phase load represented by a variable rheostat in order to be able to vary the operating points. The experimental setup is shown in Fig. 5b, where the elements of the system were labeled.

During the tests, the voltages and currents feeding the load were measured and the quality of the power delivered by the power converter was evaluated. In this way the voltage of the accumulator block and the current flowing from it to the prototype are measured. To evaluate the power quality of the converter, the Fluke 434 network analyzer was used, a device that has the ability to evaluate all power quality phenomena except for transient phenomena. Similarly, the NI USB 6211 acquisition card was used to capture the measurement of the line voltage from the sensor and the signal from the Fluke DP 120 voltage probe used to capture the voltage of the accumulator block and thus be able to establish the voltage profiles.

In the test the load was varied and the accumulator block was allowed to discharge deeply. With the intention of verifying the operation of the control loop and that the power quality of the output voltages and currents remain within the limits established by standards such as IEEE 1159 [19] and IEEE 519 [18]. The waveforms of the phase voltages and their harmonic spectrum were captured by the network analyzer and are shown in Fig. 7.

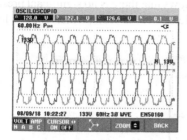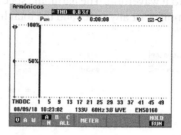

Fig. 7. Waveform and harmonic spectrum of phase voltages.

As can be seen in the figure, the three waveforms are the same. However there are small differences in the RMS value due to the construction of the transformers. The unbalance percentage of the voltages reaches just 0.6%, being well below 2% allowed in low voltage. The spectrum of the phase voltages shows that there is no significant presence of harmonics of any order and the total harmonic content is only 0.8%.

The waveforms of the line voltages are shown in Fig. 8.

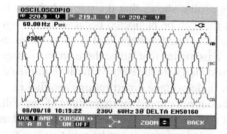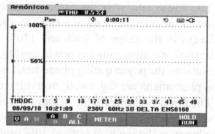

Fig. 8. Waveform and harmonic spectrum of line voltages

As can be seen in the figure, the three waves are equal in shape, presenting an almost sine waveform. However, they present different RMS values due to the differences between each of the phases due to the magnetic coupling between phases and the manual construction of the transformers. The harmonic spectrum captured by the analyzer for the line voltages is shown in Fig. 10. This spectrum, which evaluates the first 50 harmonics, shows that there is no significant presence of harmonics of any order and that the total harmonic content is less than 0.5%. This is characteristic of a pure sine waveform that guarantees an excellent quality of the power delivered by the power converter, in terms of harmonic content, it can be considered optimal.

Regarding the converter output current, the waveforms and spectrum are shown in Fig. 9.

As the converter is connected in a star connection, the line currents are equal to the phase currents, as can be seen, these are presented in an almost sinusoidal shape, with small variations. All three waveforms are identical in shape, presenting a nearly sinusoidal waveform. The harmonic spectrum shows that there is no significant presence of harmonics of any order and the total harmonic content is 1.2%, which is quite low.

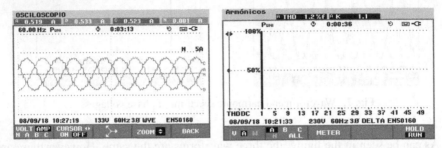

Fig. 9. Waveform and harmonic spectrum of line currents

The system of voltages are perfectly balanced in phases. Because the phase angle shows an exact 120° phase phase shift. To show the behavior of the voltage at the output of the converter, Fig. 10a shows the variation with respect to time, this figure is called the voltage profile.

The power converter line RMS volatility profile shows that the output behaves in a constant manner. Presenting a small ripple that can be neglected because the voltage is always in the range of 90% and 110% of the rated voltage that is established as the normal operating range in power quality. This means that, since there are no voltage fluctuations, the power quality phenomena associated with the RMS value are eliminated, these phenomena are sag, swell, overvoltage, undervoltage, interruptions and flicker.

The ripple presented at the output voltage does not exceed the magnitude of one volt. This ripple does not generate flickers since it is too low to be noticed by a lamp, and as it is always in the range of 90% to 10% of the rated voltage, it can be said that it is free from power quality phenomena.

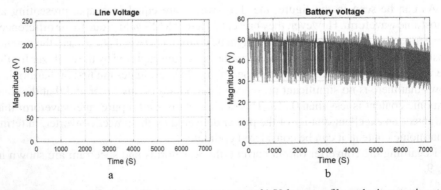

Fig. 10. a) Line voltage profile at the inverter output b) Voltage profile at the inverter input.

The voltage profile of the accumulator block during the test is shown in Fig. 10b. This shows how the input voltage to the power converter varies.

The voltage profile of the accumulator block shows that there are strong variations at the input, due to the current draw required by the prototype. The average voltage decreases as time passes, the initial value of the accumulator block is 52 V, at the end of the test the accumulator block voltage is 43 V. Despite the variations in the accumulator block and the voltage regulation that occurs over time, the voltage at the converter output remains constant over time. This means that the proposed control loop works in an adequate way, managing to mitigate the possible swell, sag, undervoltage and overvoltage that may occur due to the voltage variation of the accumulator block.

8 Conclusions

The developed prototype optimizes the power quality of photovoltaic systems by eliminating the possibility of phenomena such as sag, swell, undervoltage, overvoltage, harmonic distortion, flicker, frequency deviations, inter-harmonic, subharmonic distortion, DC component and notches. The only phenomena that the team does not cover are transitory phenomena and unbalances.

The harmonic contents found in the experimentation are very good both in the phase voltages and in the line voltages, in the same way the current also presents optimized contents, however, they do not become the same as those calculated theoretically, this is due to the presence of transformers that inject disturbances between phases and does not reproduce the pulses accurately. It is worth noting that the harmonic contents found present very low magnitudes, reaching values of 0.6%.

When implementing three-phase transformers for the H-bridge stages, the phases are coupled to each other, which generates disturbances between phases, however, this arrangement has an advantage and that is that the lack of a phase does not prevent the converter from continuing to operate. that it would work like an open star generating the third phase as a phantom phase.

In the validation, the power converter was presented at different operating points that demonstrated that the quality of the power at the output of the prototype was excellent. However, it is suggested to run a posteriori tests on the influence of the power factor on variables such as electric current.

References

1. Deshpande, S., Bhasme, N.R.: A review of topologies of inverter for grid connected PV systems. In: 2017 Innovations in Power and Advanced Computing Technologies (i-PACT), pp. 1–6 (2017)
2. Barater, D., Lorenzani, E., Concari, C., Franceschini, G., Buticchi, G.: Recent advances in single-phase transformerless photovoltaic inverters. IET Renew. Power Gener. 10(2), 260–273 (2016)
3. Gaikwad, V., Mutha, S., Mundhe, R., Sapar, O., Chinchole, T.: Survey of PWM techniques for solar inverter. In: 2016 International Conference on Global Trends in Signal Processing, Information Computing and Communication (ICGTSPICC), pp. 501–504 (2016)

4. Saleh, S.A., Rahman, M.A.: Modeling of power inverters. In: An Introduction to Wavelet Modulated Inverters, p. 1. IEEE (2011)
5. Saleh, S.A., Rahman, M.A.: Introduction to power inverters. In: An Introduction to Wavelet Modulated Inverters, p. 1. IEEE (2011)
6. Ruderman, A.: About voltage total harmonic distortion for single- and three-phase multilevel inverters. IEEE Trans. Ind. Electron. $62(3)$, 1548–1551 (2015)
7. Abu-Rub, H., Malinowski, M., Al-Haddad, K.: Multilevel converter/inverter topologies and applications. In: Power Electronics for Renewable Energy Systems, Transportation and Industrial Applications, p. 1. IEEE (2014)
8. Wu, B., Narimani, M.: Other multilevel voltage source inverters. In: High-Power Converters and AC Drives, p. 1. IEEE (2017)
9. Nabae, A., Takahashi, I., Akagi, H.: A new neutral-point-clamped PWM inverter. IEEE Trans. Indus. Appl. $IA-17(5)$, 518–523 (1981). https://doi.org/10.1109/TIA.1981.4503992
10. Koshti, A.K., Rao, M.N.: A brief review on multilevel inverter topologies. In: 2017 International Conference on Data Management, Analytics and Innovation (ICDMAI), pp. 187–193 (2017)
11. Ghosh, G., Sarkar, S., Mukherjee, S., Pal, T., Sen, S.: A comparative study of different multilevel inverters. In: 2017 1st International Conference on Electronics, Materials Engineering and Nano-Technology (IEMENTech), pp. 1–6 (2017)
12. Roberge, V., Tarbouchi, M., Okou, F.: Strategies to accelerate harmonic minimization in multilevel inverters using a parallel genetic algorithm on graphical processing unit. IEEE Trans. Power Electron. $29(10)$, 5087–5090 (2014)
13. Jacob, T., Suresh, L.P.: A review paper on the elimination of harmonics in multilevel inverters using bioinspired algorithms. In: 2016 International Conference on Circuit, Power and Computing Technologies (ICCPCT), pp. 1–8 (2016)
14. Srndovic, M., Zhetessov, A., Alizadeh, T., Familiant, Y.L., Grandi, G., Ruderman, A.: Simultaneous selective harmonic elimination and THD minimization for a single-phase multilevel inverter with staircase modulation. IEEE Trans. Ind. Appl. $54(2)$, 1532–1541 (2018)
15. Anurag, A., Deshmukh, N., Maguluri, A., Anand, S.: Integrated DC–DC converter based grid-connected transformerless photovoltaic inverter with extended input voltage range. IEEE Trans. Power Electron. $33(10)$, 8322–8330 (2018)
16. Fernandez, L.D.P., Rodriguez, J.L.D., Carvajal, M.A.J.: Three-phase multilevel inverter with selective harmonic elimination. In: 2015 Workshop on Engineering Applications - International Congress on Engineering (WEA), pp. 1–6 (2015)
17. Rodriguez, J.L.D., Fernandez, L.D.P., Garcia, A.P.: Harmonic distortion optimization of multilevel PWM inverter using genetic algorithms. In: 2014 IEEE 5th Colombian Workshop on Circuits and Systems (CWCAS), pp. 1–6 (2014)
18. IEEE Recommended Practice and Requirements for Harmonic Control in Electric Power Systems. IEEE Std 519–2014 (Revision of IEEE Std 519–1992). pp. 1–29 (2014)
19. IEEE Recommended Practice for Monitoring Electric Power Quality. IEEE Std 1159–2009 (Revision of IEEE Std 1159–1995). pp. c1–81 (2009)

Bioengineering

Multivariate Analysis of Adaptation Level in Low-Cost Lower Limb Prostheses: An Unsupervised Learning Approach

Gabriel Maldonado Colmenares[✉] and Jenny Kateryne Nieto Aristizabal[✉] [iD]

Bioinstrumentation and Clinical Engineering Research Group – GIBIC, Bioengineering Department, Engineering Faculty, Universidad de Antioquia UdeA, Calle 70 No. 52-21, Medellín, Colombia
{gabriel.maldonado,jenny.aristizabal}@udea.edu.co

Abstract. Objective: To develop an unsupervised learning approach to study the prosthesis adaptation process using functional assessment tests and their scales, health-related behaviors, and socio-demographic da-ta.

Subjects: 199 low-cost lower limb prosthesis users with below-knee and/or above-knee amputation.

Methods: For the unsupervised learning approach, different methods, such as K-Means, Agglomerative Clustering, and Fuzzy C-Means, were used to comprise clusters and classify individuals based on factors associated with the lower limb prosthesis. Davies Boulding, Dunn, and Calinski-Harabasz index as well as the Silhouette coefficient were used to validate, study, and understand the resulting clusters from the dataset.

Results: The unsupervised learning approach strategies provided patient phenotyping clusters that could be interpreted as adaptation levels in low-cost lower limb prosthesis users, while allowing the interpretation and patient phenotyping by physicians.

Conclusions : Patient care customization is important, especially in multidimensional problems. To do so, it is necessary to use historic-data-based tools, which allow better control of the current state of the prosthesis and the person's functional capacity.

Keywords: Adaptation · Amputees · Functional assessment tests · Lower-limb prostheses · Clustering analysis · PEQ-MS · Houghton · 2MWT

1 Introduction

Currently, only 10% of amputees in the world can access a prosthesis, and the population that acquires low-cost technology reports low adaptation and low adherence to the use of these accessible devices [1]. The main cause of this problem is that the diagnosis and use of prosthetic devices require both physiological and psychosocial factors along design parameters, which turn the rehabilitation process into a multidimensional [2]. Besides people's mobility being affected after lower limb amputation, there are several

© Springer Nature Switzerland AG 2021
J. C. Figueroa-García et al. (Eds.): WEA 2021, CCIS 1431, pp. 147–159, 2021.
https://doi.org/10.1007/978-3-030-86702-7_13

side effects, such as body image self-perception as well as lower participation in social and everyday activities: additionally, these factors impact the rehabilitation process [3]. Furthermore, patients from low-income countries tend to use low-cost prosthesis devices: devices costing less than 600 US dollars; moreover, there is a deficient follow-up after the initiation of prosthesis [4, 5]. Another common drawback is that there is no well-defined protocol to assess the quality and level of adaptation in these patients or a defined methodology to predict their walking ability for preventing the abandonment of the prosthesis device [3].

An efficient way to measure the current state of rehabilitation is through functional assessment scales in post-prosthetic rehabilitation, which are direct indicators of the patient's mobility capacity [6]. This tool can estimate an individual's potential to walk with a prosthesis, and nowadays, it is used by different health centers in Colombia to support the monitoring of the patient's post-prosthetic rehabilitation. These assessment scales can be obtained through self-formulated questionnaires such as the Prosthesis Evaluation Questionnaire-Mobility Scale (PEQ-MS) and Houghton questionnaire as well as performance tests such as the Two Minute Walk Time(2MWT) and Time Up and Go (TUG). Each functional assessment test provides valuable information about both the functional capacity and adaptation evaluation of the person undergoing prosthetic rehabilitation [7]. However, due to the high dependency of environmental factors along the population's characteristics, such as the different amputation cause in the Colombian population, currently, there is no well-defined standard on how to interpret and correlate different functional assessment scales in different settings specifically with low-cost prostheses [6, 7].

This lack of a standardized process makes it difficult to interpret the data collected in clinical practices and correlate it with other influencing factors such as age, physical state, health-related behaviors, and socio-economic level [2]. Given the complexity of simultaneously interpreting many variables and factors, there is a need to create tools that allow for the analysis and interpretation of these data, while extracting valuable information for the specialists. Traditionally, some of the most common analytical methods have been: Descriptive analysis, discriminant analysis, multivariate regression analysis, analysis of covariance (MANCOVA), and analysis of variance (ANOVA). These methods have been used to predict the walking ability after lower limb amputation. However, these approaches are based on a high variety success criterion such as Houghton Questionnaire Score, Daily use of prosthesis, Walking distance, TUG Score, Rivermead Mobility Index and more. In the same way, different predictive factors have been accounted for, including the cause of amputation, the amputation level, stump factors, Body Mass Index (BMI), motivation, occupation, sex, co-morbidities, psychosocial factors, social support, and other health-related behaviors [2]. This heterogeneity of methodologies, population characteristics, inclusion criteria, and outcome measures make the comparison between methods and the management of rehabilitation plans difficult in countries with populations such as Colombia.

When there is a clear need for patient phenotyping, disease subtyping, and adverse events detection; the clustering algorithms acquire great value for the development of new clinical applications [8]. K-Means, Agglomerative Clustering, Gaussian Mixture Models, and Fuzzy C-Means are unsupervised learning methods that have been used for pre-processing and pattern extraction in clinical and health-related data [9]. Besides, these techniques can determine which variables are significantly related to different outcomes like satisfaction, walking ability, and range of motion after amputation [10]. Additionally, there is evidence that unsupervised learning methods are an excellent tool for different telemedicine applications [11, 13]. Nonetheless, there is a lack of studies that applied cluster analysis in problems related with the amputee care and healthcare systems based on questionnaires [14].

This study proposes an unsupervised learning approach based on the prosthetic adaptation level considering different qualities, materials, prices, patient phenotype, among others. through clustering and statistical analysis using the PEQ-MS, Houghton, 2MWT functional assessment scores, as predictive factors.

2 Methodology

2.1 Description of Data

The population of the study was obtained from a cross-sectional study in a sample of 199 persons with lower limb amputation and users of low-cost prosthesis acquired from Mahavir Kmina: a non-profit corporation located in Colombia that helps amputee people regain their mobility and quality of life with free low-cost lower limb prosthesis devices. The data was obtained through a survey conducted to beneficiaries when they attended the corporation for device adjustment, maintenance or in a need of a prosthesis replacement, between the years 2018 and 2020. The survey consists in 42 questions that included basic demographic, medical history information, and functional assessment tests and scales.

Instances were included without age, sex, race, and amputation level restriction. The general inclusion criteria were: Participants that used low-cost lower-limb prostheses to any period and acquire the prosthesis in Mahavir Kmina Corporation made of high-density polyethylene with the foot of Jaipur. Instances were excluded in case of being first-time users without device, presenting sensory-perceptual or cognitive alteration, refusing the informed consent, and instances with very incomplete or inconsistent answers. This informed consent was designed and approved by the technical direction and ethics committees of the Mahavir Kmina Corporation and the Health Rehabilitation group of the University of Antioquia.

The design of the surveys used in the study is contemplated within the clinical practice guidelines established by the Ministry of Health and Social Protection of Colombia [6]. These guidelines suggest the use of the functional assessment tests collected in the survey (PEQ-MS, Houghton Scale, and 2MWT test) as parameters to evaluate specific aspects in the lower limb prosthesis adaptation process like mobility, self-perception and prothesis use. On the other hand, as they are factors that influence the person's daily physical activity, age, sex, amputation cause and level, occupation and the type of supports they use (walking sticks, walkers or not using them) were included the analyzes [3, 7, 15]. The description of the variables collected in the study are disposed in the Table 1.

Table 1. Description and information of the data collected.

Feature name	Description
Age	Age of the prosthesis user
Sex	Sex of the prosthesis user
Independence	3 self-reported levels over 3 different activities of daily living: 1: Independent, 2: Semi-independent and 3: Dependent
Socioeconomic level	Socioeconomic level of the user: 1: Low-low, 2: Low, 3: Medium-low, 4: Medium, 5: Medium-high, 6: High
Daily use time	Average daily prosthesis wearing time in hours
Adaptation time	Months since the start of prosthesis adaptation
Satisfaction	General level of satisfaction with the prosthesis extracted from a visual analog scale (VAS): 0 is very unsatisfied and 100 is very satisfied
Occupation	Employment status or principal activity:
Cause of amputation	3 categories were defined: Disease: (e.g., Infections, cancer, diabetes, gangrene), nonviolent accidents (e.g., car or motorbike accident, work accident) and violent accidents (e.g., gunshot, explosive mine)
Amputation level	Amputation level defined in two general categories: Below knee (BK) and above knee (AK)
Assistances user	Type of supports they use: 1: walking sticks, 2: walkers, 3: wheelchair and 4: not using them
PEQ-MS	Score of Prothesis Evaluation Questionnaire- Mobility Scale: 13 self-reported mobility related questions extracted from the original PEQ. The score is extracted from a VAS where: 0 is unable and 100 is fully capable. This test "has demonstrated good psychometric characteristics for measuring mobility and excellent reliability" [16]
Houghton score	Score of Houghton Scale: 4 self-reported questions that is widely suggested and defined as standard in the literature for classify people after the initial prosthetic rehabilitation according to walking ability category Scores $\geq$ 9: Independent community walking ability, scores from 6 to 8: Household and limited community walking ability, and scores $\leq$ 5: Limited-household walking ability [7, 16, 17]
2MWT	Result of the 2 min' walk time functional ability test: Total distance walked by the user in a period of 2 min by requesting their highest walking speed beforehand. This test has excellent test-retest reliability and internal consistency with self-reported functional ability scales and performance assessments like the Houghton score [16]

2.2 Data Analysis

Python and R were used to carry out the statistical analyzes and to explore and preprocess the data. The analysis was developed following the following flow of activities: data cleaning, exploratory and statistical data analysis, unsupervised analysis and cluster's validation, visualization, and interpretation.

Data Cleaning. The database includes multiple instances with null data, typos and inconsistent instances that were remove. The data processing pipeline includes format errors correction, automatic outliers using isolation forest and dimensional reduction analysis, imputation techniques based on regression analysis and over sampling method to maintain the volume of data in the study.

Exploratory and Statistical Data Analysis. The main objective of this stage is to generate conclusions from the data and guide the following data processing steps like feature extraction, outliers detection, and data cleaning and imputation [18]. In this stage, the level of satisfaction of a prosthesis user was used as base line model due to the high influence of satisfaction in the adaptation level [2, 3, 19]. Shapiro Wilks and Kolmogorov tests were used to test the normal distribution in the features and stratified sampling strategies were used from this distribution to generate three categories from the level of satisfaction with his prosthesis expressed by the person. From these proposed levels ANOVA and MANCOVA was used in the following sections to establish the features importance in the overall satisfaction level discrimination using a significance level of p-value $=$ 0.05 to identify statistically significant associations [20], taking into account that the features analyzed were considered as ratio data [16] and previous works have evidenced through univariate techniques such as Chi-square tests, Student's t-test and Spearman's correlation the relevance of the understanding of this associations in low-cost lower limb prosthesis users [21].

Moreover, a correlation analysis was useful to find the associations between features and redundant information in the inner questions of the test. Categorical associations were defined with the uncertainty coefficient & correlation ratio and numerical correlations were defined with the Spearman correlation coefficient. Past studies evidence strong correlations between the 2MWT test and the Houghton scale, and moderate associations between 2MWT test and the PEQ-MS, and evidence a need to propose statistical models that allow a better understanding of the relationship of the tests to each other [7]. The correlation analysis was extended to the individual questions of the PEQ-MS to evaluate associations between specific aspects of the ambulation with the prosthesis and other functional assessment tests. To reduce dimensionality of the dataset, evaluate multiples preprocessing pipelines and facilitate the visualization and interpretation of the results a dimensionality reduction analysis was tested with Principal Components Analysis [22] and u-MAP algorithm [23]. Also, the literature suggest lower dimensionality for better results in the modeling stage [24].

Unsupervised Analysis and Cluster's Validation. Unsupervised learning analysis has been applied for such varied objectives as model fitting, prediction based on groups, hypothesis generation and testing, data exploration, dimension reduction, and grouping similar entities into homogeneous groups [12, 25, 26]. In the case of prosthesis rehabilitation process the literature report a clear group definition and patient phenotyping between young and fitness prosthesis users and the advanced age users, this because there is strong evidence that younger age at amputation results in superior walking ability, however it is still possible for individuals over 90 years of age to walk independently following lower limb amputation [27]. Transition stages or subgroups in the prosthesis adaptation process, and in the clinical practice in general, can represent valuable information to build a custom rehabilitation process according to user needs, and also open the possibility of creating new telemedicine tools for prosthesis users [12, 28]. The main objective of applying these algorithms is find states of interest, transition stages or subgroups in the adaptation process of low-cost lower limb prostheses users, and assets the influence of the different features used in this study over the conformed clusters. Agglomerative hierarchical clustering, K-means, Gaussian mixture models and Fuzzy C-means algorithms were applied in three versions of the dataset: *1. All patients, 2. Below knee amputee level, and 3. Above knee amputee level* and the following internal validation metrics were used to evaluate the performance of clustering models and find the optimal number of clusters for each case: *1. Davies Boulding Index, 2. Callinsky-Harabaz Index, 3. Silhouette coefficient and 4. Dunn score* [26, 28, 29].

Visualization and Interpretation. The conformed clusters were visualized using the dimension reduction steps constructed in the preprocessing pipeline, PCA transformation and u-MAP embedding were used to visualize the distribution of the clusters and evaluate in a visual way the separability and compaction of these groups [30]. In addition, violin plots were used to study the distribution of specific features within groups and ANOVA tests were carried on to assets the significance level between the features and the conformed groups.

3   Results

Shapiro wilks and Kolmogorov test demonstrated the normal distribution of variables as satisfaction, 2MWT and PEQ-MS with 95% confidence and the Houghton Scale was transformed to a normal distribution with a box cox transformation to fulfill the assumptions of the ANOVA analysis. The Fig. 1 shows the associations map result of the correlation analysis, this representation allows a graphic understanding of the relations between numerical and categorical features used in this study. Squares are categorical associations representing uncertainty coefficient and correlation ratio (0 to 1), circles are the symmetrical numerical associations representing the Spearman correlation values (-1 to 1), and the diagonal is left blank for clarity. Following criterions reported in the literature a weak correlation was defined between absolutes values of 0 and 0.29, moderate between 0.30 and 0.49 and strong between 0.5 and 1 [7].

Satisfaction shows a strong influence by the Houghton Score ($r = 0.51$) and the main occupation/activity of the user (0.52); Moderate influence using assistances (e.g., walking stick, wheelchair) ($r = 0.49$), the PEQ-MS score ($r = 0.40$), daily hours of use ($r = 0.36$) and independence level ($r = 0.30$). The Houghton scale shows a strong positive correlation with daily hours of use ($r = 0.53$), Satisfaction ($r = 51$), and the PEQ-MS score ($r = 0.40$) and moderate correlations with the 2MWT test ($r = 0.37$), age ($r = 0.32$) and amputation cause ($r = 0.31$). In other hand, the PEQ-MS test evidence strong associations with the Houghton score ($r = 0.44$), Satisfaction ($r = 0.40$), and weak associations with de daily hour of use ($r = 0.29$) and the assistances use ($r = 0.21$).

Finally, the 2MWT shows only moderate correlations with Houghton score (r = 0.37) and weak associations with the assistances use (r = 0.29), age (r = −0.26), independence level (r = 0.26), occupation (r = 0.29), socio economic level (r = 0. 29) and satisfaction (r = 0.21).

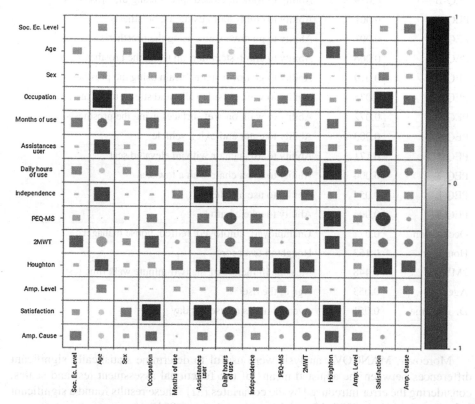

Fig. 1. Features associations using uncertainty coefficient and correlation ratio for categorical associations and Spearman correlation for numerical associations.

Associations between individual questions of the PEQ-MS were evaluated with the *"Self-perception of the ability to walk with the prosthesis"* and the results evidence strong correlations with specific aspects of the ambulation like: "Ability to walk in closed spaces using the prosthesis" (r = 0.70) and moderate correlations with the *"Ability to use a chair with a low seat"* (r = 0.48), *"Ability to go downstairs using the prosthesis"* (r = 0.47) and the *"Ability to walk on sidewalks and streets using the prosthesis"* (r = 0.45). The ANOVA test with the categorical variable of satisfaction as factor showed significance (p-value < = 0.05) for most of the questions on the PEQ-MS test, excluding the PEQJ and PEQH questions. Otherwise, the 2MWT and Houghton tests were not significant. Table 2 introduces the description of the individual questions of the PEQ-MS between the p-value resulting of the analysis of variance.

Table 2. Results of the analysis of variance using the satisfaction level as factor.

Feature	p-value	Description
PEQ-A	0.002	Self-perception of the ability to walk with the prosthesis
PEQ-B	0.019	Ability to walk in closed spaces using the prosthesis
PEQ-C	0.001	Ability to climb stairs using the prosthesis
PEQ-D	0.001	Ability to go downstairs using the prosthesis
PEQ-E	0.006	Ability to climb steep terrain using the prosthesis
PEQ-F	0.019	Ability to go down steep terrain using the prosthesis
PEQ-G	0.035	Ability to walk on sidewalks and streets using the device
PEQ-H	0.072	Ability to walk on wet surfaces using the prosthesis
PEQ-I	0.003	Ability to enter and exit a vehicle
PEQ-J	0.171	Ability to use a chair with an elevated seat
PEQ-K	0.004	Ability to use a chair with a low seat
PEQ-L	0.054	Ability to use a toilet
PEQ-M	0.006	Ability to take a bath
Occupation	0.077	Unemployed, employed, retired, house manager
Houghton	0.153	Houghton test score
2MWT	0.448	Measure in meters of the two-minute walk time test
Age	0.053	Age of the user
D. use time	0.051	Average hours of use per day

Moreover, MANCOVA analysis were useful to determine statistically significant differences between the adjusted means of the functional assessment test and scales, considering the error introduced by the covariates [31]. These results found a significant influence through the Wilks' Lambda test (p-value $= 0.001$).

Dimensional reduction analysis allowed the representation of the variation presented in the functional assessment tests and health-related behaviors, in a small number of factors. This step also remove multicollinearity in the features, making easier the modeling stage, and reducing the training time [32]. The 95% of the explained variance was reached using 17 factors from the original 30 features used in the analysis (PEQ-MS was used as the total average of the 13 questions). On the other hand, the 13 individual questions of PEQ-MS can be represented with 9 components maintaining the 95% of explained variance of data. Nonlinear transformations were applied using Uniform Manifold Approximation and Projection (UMAP), an algorithm for dimension reduction based on manifold learning and topological data analysis [23]. This method improved the compaction and separability of the different groups of patients as is evidenced in the Fig. 2, where the visualization of the UMAP embedding approach is compared with the projection using PCA.

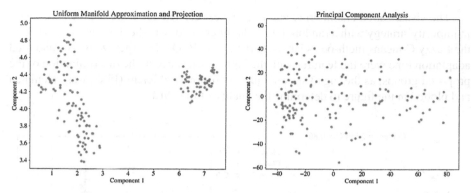

Fig. 2. Projection of the features in a 2D feature space with the UMAP embedding components (left) and the PCA components with the highest explained variance (right).

Agglomerative Hierarchical Clustering, K-means and Fuzzy C-means algorithms were trained with Python, using Scikit-learn, Scikit-fuzz and Pycaret packages. With the purpose of identify sets of clusters that are compact, with a small variance between members of the cluster, and well separated, we use 4 different index and coefficients for internal clusters validation. Silhouette coefficient and Davies Bouldin index suggest a conformation of 2 clusters in the dataset, and the Calinski-Harabasz and Dunn index suggest the conformation of 3 clusters. The results of these internal validation metrics used in 3 different clustering algorithms (Agglomerative Hierarchical Clustering (AC), K-means (KM) and Fuzzy C-means (FCM)) have been registered in the Table 3, where highlighted cells indicate the blue selection indicates the best metric found for the n-cluster, according to the criterion used by this. Only for Davies Bouldin index, a lower value will mean that the clusters are better.

Table 3. Internal validation results of Agglomerative Hierarchical Clustering (AC), K-means (KM) and Fuzzy C-means (FCM), with the Silhouette coefficient and Calinski Harabasz, Davies Bouldin and Dunn index.

Metric	Silhouette			Calinski-Harabasz			Davies Bouldin			Dunn		
Method	AC	KM	FCM	AC	KM	FCM	AC	KM	FCM	AC	KM	FCM
2 clust.	0.75	0.75	0.75	865.3	865.3	865.3	0.34	0.34	0.34	0.09	0.09	0.09
3 clust.	0.66	0.66	0.66	1246.7	1253.7	1253	0.46	0.46	0.46	0.13	0.13	0.13
4 clust.	0.61	0.62	0.62	1157.6	1176.8	1176	0.58	0.56	0.57	0.06	0.09	0.09
5 clust.	0.49	0.49	0.49	1202.7	1233.4	1229.4	0.71	0.71	0.73	0.11	0.11	0.11
6 clust.	0.42	0.50	0.51	1121.4	1169.2	846.5	0.86	0.73	0.88	0.08	0.07	0.04
7 clust.	0.42	0.43	0.38	1139.6	1168.2	1065.2	0.87	0.81	0.95	0.12	0.10	0.09
8 clust.	0.39	0.40	0.35	1115.7	1164.5	956.8	0.88	0.92	1.02	0.12	0.07	0.04

The visualization and interpretation stage were carried out using the mean decrease in impurity strategy with a random forest classifier fitted with the 3 groups generated by the Fuzzy C-means meth-od as labels. Satisfaction, PEQ-MS, Age, Daily use, and total adaptation time were the features with the highest relevance in the discrimination of the proposed groups, as the Fig. 3 shows. Fuzzy partition coefficient (FPC) was calculated and plotted in the figure to determine the quality of the cluster.

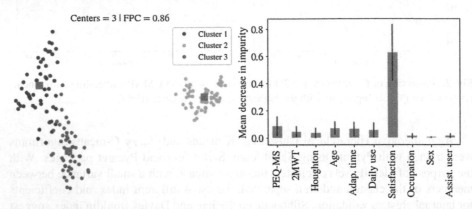

Fig. 3. Visualization and interpretation of the 3 clusters generated with the Fuzzy C-means algorithm in the UMAP projection, and the feature importance establish with the mean decrease impurity criterion.

4 Discussion

Considering the number of participants in similar works [2, 3] as well as relevance of the Mahavir Kmina corporation, which has over 3000 low-cost lower-limb prosthesis users in Latin America, we can assume that this study has an representative sample of the situation of amputees in Colombia [7].

Currently, there is no consensus of which variables and which reference value should be used to evaluate the adaptation and rehabilitation process in lower-limb prosthesis users. Moreover, there is a lack of methodologies that can propose these relevant factors and the reference values according to a specific study population. The associations found in the exploratory data analysis between the Houghton, PEQ-MS, and 2MWT tests are coherent with previous works; however, our results show that the strongest overall satisfaction was associated with the Houghton Scale as well as health-related behaviors such as the use of mobility assistances and the occupation of the user. Besides, the dimensional reduction analysis extended from the correlation analysis facilitates the understanding and modeling process of multidimensional problems such as the prosthesis adaptation process.

Consequently, the three clustering algorithms showed a similar trend in the internal evaluation metrics, and had three groups significantly separated from each other, as suggested by the Calinski-Harabasz and Dunn index value. Through the interpretation and visualization tools, these groups can be proposed as three states of adaptation in which a low-cost lower-limb prosthesis user can remain in their adaptation process with a high influence of the overall satisfaction. Although the determination of the appropriate number of groups for the problem is still on the frontier of knowledge, the possibility of identifying new states in patients through these methodologies allows for generating new tools in the monitoring and follow-up of people in the process of prosthetic rehabilitation. The modeling stage of this study is consistent with the Anderson behavioral model used in different health-rehabilitation processes, including prosthesis adaptation. This model can structure and organize healthcare management as a function of predisposing characteristics, establishing needs, and enabling resources. In this case, improving enabled resources and clinical strategies can impact the target population of these studies.

5 Conclusions

The user satisfaction is influenced by three general factors: Predisposing characteristics (e.g., the amputation level and the cause of amputation); Established need (e.g., age and occupation of the user); and enabling resources (e.g., the services offered to the users, like follow-up, maintenance, and training). To improve the results of the adaptation process, clinical policies should focus on user-centered fitting strategies supported by data science tools. Moreover, they should consider the development of monitoring systems that allow the use of prediction models, data collection for future researchers, and generation of automated reports and alerts in the evolution of prosthesis adaptation.

Although 199 participants are considered an acceptable representation considering the current state of the art, unsupervised learning algorithms can deliver more valuable results when trained with larger datasets. The development of software that integrates these components could provide remote diagnosis to patients in hard-to-reach areas and become a valuable source of data for specialists.

Acknowledgements. This work was supported by Medellín Higher Education Agency (Sapiencia) and the Ministry of Science, Technology, and Innovation of Colombia (Minciencias), and is part of a multi-disciplinary study called "Evaluation of a mixed strategy to improve the adherence of subjects amputated by Improvised Explosive Devices (IED) to the use of low-cost lower limb prostheses" with code 111580863475. We express our gratitude to the Mahavir Kmina Corporation and its entire work team, who were a great support throughout the research.

Conflict of Interest. The authors declare that there is no conflict of interest regarding the publication of this paper.

References

1. Arelekatti, V.N.M.: Detc2015–47385 Passive Prosthetic Knee for Users With Transfemoral Amputation, pp. 1–8 (2015)

2. Sansam, K., Neumann, V., O'Connor, R., Bhakta, B.: Predicting walking ability following lower limb amputation: a systematic review of the literature. J. Rehabil. Med. **41**(8), 593–603 (2009). https://doi.org/10.2340/16501977-0393
3. Baars, E.C., Schrier, E., Dijkstra, P.U., Geertzen, J.H.B.: Prosthesis satisfaction in lower limb amputees: A systematic review of associated factors and questionnaires. Medicine **97**(39), e12296 (2018). https://doi.org/10.1097/MD.0000000000012296
4. Zoellick, C.M.: Informe Mundial La Discapacidad Sobre R E S U M E N", B. R. Organ. Mund. la Salud, p. 27 (2011).
5. Biddiss, E.A., Chau, T.T.: Multivariate prediction of upper limb prosthesis acceptance or rejection. Disabil. Rehabil.: Assist. Technol. **3**(4), 181–192 (2008). https://doi.org/10.1080/17483100701869826
6. Salinas-Durán, F.A., et al.: "Guía de práctica clínica para el diagnóstico y tratamiento preoperatorio, intraoperatorio y posoperatorio de la persona amputada, la prescripción de la prótesis y la rehabilitación integral: Recomendaciones para el tratamiento de rehabilitación en adultos". Iatreia **29**(4), S-82–S-95 (2016)
7. Matamoros-Villegas, A., Plata-Contreras, J., Payares-Álvarez, K.: Correlation among tests and functional assessment scales in the follow-up of prosthetic adaptation in people with lower limb amputation. Rehabilitacion (2021)
8. Shamout, F., Zhu, T., Clifton, D.A.: Machine learning for clinical outcome prediction. IEEE Rev. Biomed. Eng. **14**, 116–126 (2021). https://doi.org/10.1109/RBME.2020.3007816
9. Chahar, R.: Computational decision support system in healthcare: a review and analysis. Int. J. Adv. Technol. Eng. Explor. **8**(75), 199–220 (2021). https://doi.org/10.19101/IJATEE.2020.762142
10. Ritter, M.A., Berend, M.E., Harty, L.D., Davis, K.E., Meding, J.B., Michael Keating, E.: Predicting range of motion after revision total knee arthroplasty. J. Arthro. **19**(3), 338–343 (2004). https://doi.org/10.1016/j.arth.2003.11.001
11. Syed Thouheed Ahmed, S., Thanuja, K., Guptha, N.S., Narasimha, S.: Telemedicine approach for remote patient monitoring system using smart phones with an economical hardware kit. In: 2016 International Conference on Computing Technologies and Intelligent Data Engineering. ICCTIDE 2016, pp. 1–4, 2016.
12. Zimina, E.Y., Novopashin, M.A., Shmid., A.V.:Application of medical data classification methods for a medical decision support system. CEUR Workshop Proceedinggs, vol. 2843 (2021)
13. Bose, E., Radhakrishnan, K.: Using unsupervised machine learning to identify subgroups among home health patients with heart failure using telehealth. CIN: Comput. Inf. Nurs. **36**(5), 242–248 (2018). https://doi.org/10.1097/CIN.0000000000000423
14. John, B., Wickramasinghe, N.: Clustering questions in healthcare social question answering based on design science theory. In: Wickramasinghe, N., Schaffer, J.L. (eds.) Theories to Inform Superior Health Informatics Research and Practice. HDIA, pp. 95–108. Springer, Cham (2018). https://doi.org/10.1007/978-3-319-72287-0_7
15. Nunes, M.A., Campos-Neto, I., Ferraz, L.C., Lima, C.A., Rocha, T.O., Rocha, T.F.: Adaptation to prostheses among patients with major lower-limb amputations and its association with sociodemographic and clinical data. Sao Paulo Med. J. **132**(2), 80–84 (2014). https://doi.org/10.1590/1516-3180.2014.1322572
16. Wong, C.K., Gibbs, W., Chen, E.S.: Use of the houghton scale to classify community and household walking ability in people with lower-limb amputation: criterion-related validity. Arch. Phys. Med. Rehabil. **97**(7), 1130–1136 (2016)
17. Houghton, A.D., Taylor, P.R., Thurlow, S., Rootes, E., McColl, I.: Success rates for rehabilitation of vascular amputees: implications for preoperative assessment and amputation level. British J. Surg. **79**(8), 753–755 (1992). https://doi.org/10.1002/bjs.1800790811

18. Sangve, S.S.B.S.M.: Clinical decision support system using SVM with the preservation of privacy. Int. J. Sci. Res 5(7), 2122–2125 (2016)
19. Biddiss, E.A., Chau, T.T.: Multivariate prediction of upper limb prosthesis acceptance or rejection. Disabil. Rehabil.: Assist. Technol. 3(4), 181–192 (2008). https://doi.org/10.1080/17483100701869826f
20. Kim, T.K.: Understanding one-way anova using conceptual figures. Korean J. Anesthesiol. 70(1), 22–26 (2017)
21. Cardona, D., Uribe, J.: Identificación de las variables cinéticas, cinemáticas y funcionales en el proceso de adaptación protésica y la rehabilitación postprotésica en", Cent. Doc. Ing. (Bl. 20–146)Colección Tesis Electrónicas, Univ. Antioquia. (2018)
22. Malembaka, E.B., et al.: A new look at population health through the lenses of cognitive, functional and social disability clustering in eastern DR Congo: a community-based cross-sectional study. BMC Public Health 19(1), 1–13 (2019)
23. McInnes, L., Healy, J., Melville, J.: UMAP: Uniform manifold approximation and projection for dimension reduction. arXiv (2018)
24. Indulska, M.: The curse of dimensionality in data quality. ACIS 2013 Proc. 2013(December), 4–6 (2013)
25. Dilts, D., Khamalah, J., Plotkin, A.: Using cluster analysis for medical resource decision making. Med. Dec. Making 15(4), 333–346 (1995). https://doi.org/10.1177/0272989X9501500404
26. Ogbuabor, G., Ugwoke, F.N.: Clustering algorithm for a healthcare dataset using silhouette score value. Int. J. Comput. Sci. Inf. Technol. 10(2), 27–37 (2018). https://doi.org/10.5121/ijcsit.2018.10203
27. Graham, L.A., Fyfe, N.C.M.: Prosthetic rehabilitation of amputees aged over 90 is usually successful. Disabil. Rehabil. 24(13), 700–701 (2002). https://doi.org/10.1080/09638280210142194
28. Windgassen, S., Moss-Morris, R., Goldsmith, K., Chalder, T.: The importance of cluster analysis for enhancing clinical practice: an example from irritable bowel syndrome. J. Mental Health 27(2), 94–96 (2018). https://doi.org/10.1080/09638237.2018.1437615
29. Malli, S., Dr. Nagesh, H.R., Dr. Joshi, H.G.: A study on rural health care data sets using clustering algorithms. Int. J. Eng. Res. 3(9), 546–548 (2014)
30. Granato, D., Santos, J.S., Escher, G.B., Ferreira, B.L., Maggio, R.M.: Use of principal component analysis (PCA) and hierarchical cluster analysis (HCA) for multivariate association between bioactive compounds and functional properties in foods: a critical perspective. Trends Food Sci. Technol. 72, 83–90 (2018)
31. Siriwardena, G.J.A., Bertrand, P.V.: Factors influencing rehabilitation of arteriosclerotic lower limb amputees. J. Rehabil. Res. Dev. 28(3), 35 (1991). https://doi.org/10.1682/JRRD.1991.07.0035
32. Islam, T., Rafa, S.R., Kibria, G.: Early Prediction of Heart Disease Using PCA and Hybrid Genetic Algorithm with k -Means, pp. 19–21 (2020)

Carbon Monoxide Effect on Human Cardiac Tissue. In Silico Study

Catalina Tobón[1]([✉]) [iD], Geraldine Durango-Giraldo[1] [iD], and Juan Pablo Ugarte[2] [iD]

[1] MATBIOM, Universidad de Medellín, Medellín, Colombia
ctobon@udem.edu.co
[2] GIMSC, Universidad de San Buenaventura, Medellín, Colombia

Abstract. The Exposure to atmospheric pollutants, such as carbon monoxide (CO), promotes the appearance of cardiovascular diseases. Studies have shown that CO blocks calcium channels, leading to a decrease of the I_{CaL} current and to a shortening of the action potential duration (APD); favoring the generation of cardiac arrhythmias. The aim of this work is to study the CO effects, at different concentrations, on the atrial and ventricular tissues using computational simulations. An equation of the CO effect on I_{CaL} was developed. It was included in two mathematical models of human atrial and ventricular cells, under normal physiological conditions. Atrial and ventricular 2D models were developed to evaluate the CO effect on the generation of reentries as an arrhythmogenic mechanism. The results show that CO blocks the I_{CaL} current in a greater fraction as its concentration increases, causing APD shortening. Such effect is larger in atrial cardiomycytes. Arrhythmic events (rotors) were generated at the high CO concentration in atrial tissue. In ventricular tissue it was not possible to generate rotors. This study provides a first step in investigating the proarrhythmic effects of CO in healthy people.

Keywords: Carbon monoxide · L-type calcium current · Action potential · In silico models · Reentries

1 Introduction

Air pollution can be defined as the presence in the atmosphere of one or more substances in sufficient quantity to cause health alterations. It is the main component of environmental pollution, causing 4.3 million premature deaths per year [1]. Between 2005 and 2010, the mortality rate increased by 4% worldwide, by 5% in China and 12% in India [1]. Latin America has not been exempted from this problem. According to the Clean Air Institute, about 100,000 people die each year in Latin America with problems related to environmental pollution [2]. The costs in 2010 were estimated at US $ 1.4 billions in China and at US $ 0.5 billions in India, according to the Organization for Economic Co-operation and Development [3]. In Europe, the estimated cost of damages (including health problems) caused by air pollution coming from the 10,000 largest polluting industries was around US $ 140–230 billions in 2009 [4]. The cost of the health impact of air pollution for developing countries was around US $ 1.7 billions in 2010 [1].

© Springer Nature Switzerland AG 2021
J. C. Figueroa-García et al. (Eds.): WEA 2021, CCIS 1431, pp. 160–170, 2021.
https://doi.org/10.1007/978-3-030-86702-7_14

In particular, air pollution increases the risk of cardiovascular disease mortality by 76% [5], where deaths are mainly related to ischemia, arrhythmias and heart failure [6–8]. Enough evidence has been found to conclude that brief exposure to high levels of pollution increases mortality in patients with a heart condition. Likewise, it has been shown that prolonged exposures reduce peoples life expectancy by several years, and increase the hospital admissions due to cardiovascular diseases [9]. Recent studies have shown a greater probability of cardiac arrhythmias appearance after exposure to atmospheric pollutants, concluding that air pollution is an acute trigger of these arrhythmias [10].

The most dangerous pollutants for health, according to the United States Environmental Protection Agency (EPA) are: nitrogen dioxide (NO_2), particulate matter (PM), sulfur dioxide (SO_2), carbon monoxide (CO) and lead (Pb). CO is a colorless and odorless toxic gas. It is generated when oxygen is not enough to carry out complete combustion. When we breathe, the CO binds to hemoglobin and it is retained in the blood, significantly reducing the capacity of carrying oxygen. The health CO effects are headache, nausea and reduced mental activity. In extreme cases, it can also cause vomiting, fainting and even death, depending on the time of exposure and the concentration levels [11]. Epidemiological studies have shown that CO exposure is closely related to hospital admissions due to cardiovascular diseases [12] and also related with cardiac mortality [13]. The CO contamination increases risk factors of heart failure, the generation and promotion of arrhythmias. Experimental studies have shown that CO causes a significant decrease in cardiac action potential duration (APD) and L-type calcium current (I_{CaL}) in cardiomyocytes [14, 15]. In general, a reduction in I_{CaL} current and APD in cardiomyocytes favors the generation and maintenance of cardiac arrhythmias [16].

Studies on the pathophysiological mechanisms by which atmospheric pollutants affect cardiovascular health would enable an improvement of prevention techniques of these pathologies. Furthermore, they would contribute to the justification of strategies to be implemented by governments to mitigate the effects of air pollution, which at this time represent high costs for health services. In this sense, in-silico studies are important tools for cardiology research, allowing access to variables that, otherwise, would be impossible to record or manipulate under experimental conditions [17].

The aim of this work is to analyze the proarrhythmic CO effects through the comparison between computational models of auricular and ventricular human tissue, under healthy conditions.

2 Methods

The methodology contemplates the development of an equation representing the CO effect on the calcium current of cardiac cells, based on published experimental studies. Such equation is introduced in mathematical models of atrial and ventricular cells by implementing the OpenCOR® software. A stimulation protocol is applied in both models to analyze the CO effects on the action potential and ionic currents at cellular level. The modified cell models are implemented in 2D tissue models using the software MATLAB® for simulating the action potential propagation in atria and ventricle. A stimulation protocol is applied for the generation of arrhythmic episodes in both tissues at different CO concentrations in order to analyze the pollutant effect. A phase singularity analysis is applied to the generated rotors to assess their dynamics. The methodology is described in detail below.

2.1 Human Cardiomyocyte Models

Two models of human cardiomyocytes were implemented: an atrial model developed by Courtemanche-Ramirez-Nattel [18] and a ventricular model O'Hara-Rudy [19]. These models consist of specific formulations for the currents and concentrations of potassium, sodium and calcium (K^+, Na^+, Ca^{2+}), mainly, and for electrogenic pumps, ion exchangers and background currents based on experimental data from human atrial and ventricular myocytes. The following equation allows the calculation of the transmembrane potential (V_m):

$$C_m \frac{dV_m}{dt} + I_{ion} + I_{st} = 0, \tag{1}$$

where C_m is the membrane capacitance, I_{st} is the external stimulation current and I_{ion} is the total transmembrane ionic current.

2.2 Model of the CO Effect on the I_{CaL} Current

Based on experimental data [14, 15], showing that CO blockades L-type Ca^{2+} channels, which can have a decremental effect on the I_{CaL} current, the Hill equation was implemented to represent the CO blocking behavior (b_{CO}) as follows:

$$b_{CO} = \frac{1}{1 + \left(\frac{14.8}{D_{CO}}\right)}, \tag{2}$$

where D_{CO} is the CO concentration in µM. The IC_{50} value for blocking the I_{CaL} current by CO was set to 14.8 µM, in agreement with experimental observations in isolated rat cells [15]. The Hill coefficient accounts for an estimate of the degree of cooperativity in the joining process. A coefficient value of 1 indicates that the binding is a independent process of the presence of other ligands. Thus, a value of 1 was assigned to this coefficient. The blocking factor was introduced into the I_{CaL} current equations in both cellular models according to the following expressions:

$$I_{CaL} = (1 - b_{CO}) \cdot g_{CaL} \cdot d \cdot f \cdot f_{Ca} \cdot (V_m - 65), \tag{3}$$

$$I_{CaL} = (1 - b_{CO}) \cdot (1 - fICaLp) \cdot PCa \cdot PhiCaL \cdot d \cdot (f \cdot (1 - nca) + jca \cdot fca \cdot nca) \\ + fICaLp \cdot PCap \cdot PhiCaL \cdot d \cdot (fp \cdot (1 - nca) + jca \cdot fca \cdot nca) \tag{4}$$

Equations (3) and (4) correspond to the atrial and the ventricular models, respectively, where g_{CaL} is the maximal I_{CaL} conductance, d is a voltage-dependent activation gate, f is a voltage-dependent inactivation gate, f_{Ca} is an intracellular calcium-dependent inactivation gate, jca is a recovery from Ca^{2+} dependent inactivation gate, nca is a fraction in Ca^{2+} dependent inactivation gate, $fICaLp$ is a fraction of channels of I_{CaL}-type phosphorylated by CaMK (Ca/calmodulin-dependent protein kinase II), PCa is the constant 0.0001 cm/s, $PCap$ is 1.1 * PCa and $PhiCal$ is a Goldmann equation.

2.3 2D Tissue Models

The simulations were carried out by developing 2D models in the commercial software MATLAB®, in order to represent the electrical behavior of atrial and ventricular tissue. These models were coupled to the cellular models described above. The 2D models consist of a 6×6 cm square mesh, composed by 192×192 elements, with a spatial discretization step of 312.5 μm.

2.4 Action Potential Propagation Model

The propagation of the action potential in the 2D models can be modeled by the following reaction-diffusion equation:

$$K\left(\frac{\partial^2}{\partial x^2} + \frac{\partial^2}{\partial y^2}\right)V_m = C_m\frac{\partial V_m}{\partial t} + I_{ion}, \tag{5}$$

where K is the diffusion coefficient of the tissue. Isotropic tissues were considered by making the conduction velocity the same in the longitudinal and transverse directions. The K value was adjusted to obtain realistic conduction velocities in atrial and ventricular tissues [20] of 60 cm/s. The solution of Eq. (5) was obtained by using a numerical scheme previously reported [21]. The integration time step was 0.01 ms.

2.5 Stimulation Protocol and Data Analysis

The unicellular models were implemented in the open-source software OpenCOR® from CellML, in order to simulate the atrial and ventricular action potentials in normal physiological conditions. The Forward Euler method was implemented with a time step of 0.01 ms for the resolution of the differential equations of the models. A S1–S1 stimulation protocol was applied at a basic cycle length of 1000 ms, for a train of 10 rectangular pulses. The pulses have 2 ms of duration and -2000 pA of amplitude for the atrial model and 0.5 ms of duration and -80 μA/μF of amplitude for the ventricular model. The applied CO concentrations ranged from 0 μM to 1000 μM. The APD at 90% of repolarization (APD_{90}), the resting membrane potential and the ionic currents amplitude were measured at the tenth action potential.

For 2D simulations, a cross-field S1 − S2 protocol was implemented [22]. The S1 stimulus was applied at a boundary of the tissue, in order to generate a plane propagation wave. Subsequently, a premature stimulus S2 was applied over a quarter of the domain and adjacent to the border where S1 was applied. The S2 stimulus occurs when the repolarization wavefront, generated by S1, passes half of the domain. The time elapsed between S1 and S2 is called the coupling interval. This protocol generates an excitation-refractoriness gradient to initialize reentries. For this work, the vulnerable window is considered as the period of time within which it is possible to generate a stable rotor for 2 s of simulation. We tested CO concentrations values from 0 μM to 1000 μM.

2.6 Phase Singularity Maps

The phase reconstruction method is widely used for studying reentries. The trajectory of the rotation center of the rotor can be observed from the phase singularity [23]. The phase reconstruction is performed from the simulated action potentials in the 2D tissues, using the Hilbert transform. The phase singularity is the point around which the phase changes by 2π rads (a complete cycle between π and $-\pi$). It is estimated through the topological charge method [23]. By plotting the phase singularity at each point in time, phase singularity maps were generated.

3 Results

The Fig. 1 shows the CO effects at different concentrations on the atrial action potential and on the I_{CaL} current.

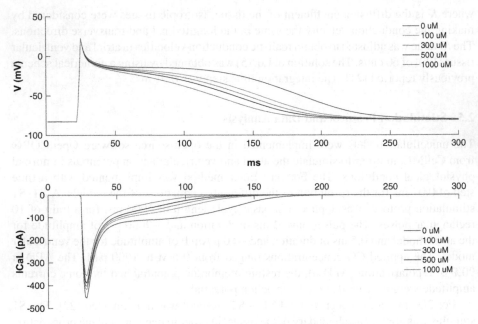

Fig. 1. Atrial I_{CaL} current and action potential for different CO concentrations.

The APD$_{90}$ and the maximum I_{CaL} peak without CO ($D_{CO} = 0$ μM) are 211 ms and -447 pA, respectively. The I_{CaL} current remains active during the action potential plateau phase. As the CO concentration increases, a reduction in the magnitude of the current and progressive inactivation is observed during the action potential plateau phase. This behavior leads to a progressive APD$_{90}$ shortening (see Table 1) and loss of the plateau phase. By applying the highest concentration of CO ($D_{CO} = 1000$ μM), the I_{CaL} peak decreased by 20.8% (-354 pA) and the APD$_{90}$ reached a value of 150 ms. The resting membrane potential did not show significant changes (≈ -83 mV).

Figure 2 shows the CO effects at different concentrations on ventricular action potential and on I_{CaL} current. The APD$_{90}$ and the maximum I_{CaL} peak without CO are 270 ms and $-1.74\ \mu A/\mu F$, respectively. As the CO concentration increases, a slight decrease of the I_{CaL} current was observed, which generates a slight APD$_{90}$ shortening (see Table 1) without loss of the plateau phase. By applying the highest CO concentration, the I_{CaL} peak decreased by 23% ($-1.34\ \mu A/\mu F$) and the APD$_{90}$ reached a value of 259 ms. The resting membrane potential did not show significant changes (≈ -88 mV).

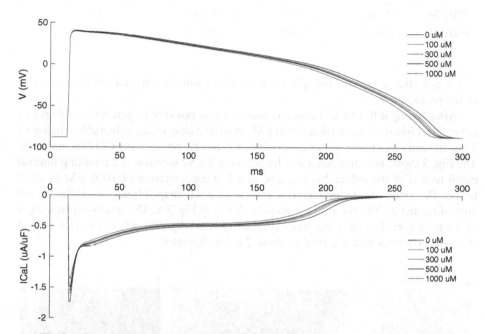

Fig. 2. Ventricular I_{CaL} current and action potential for different CO concentrations.

Table 1 shows the effects of the CO concentration on the APD$_{90}$. As the CO concentration increases, an APD shortening was observed for both models. A larger percentage of APD$_{90}$ decrease for all concentrations was observed in the atrial model. At the highest CO concentration ($D_{CO} = 1000\ \mu M$), the APD$_{90}$ reduced by 28.9% in the atrial model and 4.1% in the ventricular model. These results suggest that CO has a greater effect on atrial than ventricular APD.

The application of the S2 stimulus during the S1 − S2 stimulation protocol in the 2D models, at coupling intervals close to the refractory tail of S1, allowed the initiation of a spiral wavefront. Depending on the tissue conditions, the reentrant wave stimulates the tissue continuously at high frequency, in the waveform of a rotor; otherwise, the propagating wave is blocked by its own refractory tail and consequently extinguished. It should be noted that the latter occurs under normal physiological conditions with a CO concentration of 0 μM in both, atrial and ventricular tissue. Under such conditions, it was not possible to generate a rotor at any coupling interval, since the normal length of the

Table 1. Atrial and ventricular APD$_{90}$ at different CO concentrations. The reduction percentage is displayed.

[CO]	Atrial APD$_{90}$	% Reduction	Ventricular APD$_{90}$	% Reduction
0 μM	211 ms	–	270 ms	–
100 μM	186 ms	11.8%	267 ms	1.1%
300 μM	177 ms	16.1%	265 ms	1.9%
500 μM	168 ms	20.4%	264 ms	2.2%
1000 μM	150 ms	28.9%	259 ms	4.1%

action potential causes that the spiral wave collides with its refractory tail, terminating so the propagation.

After testing different CO concentrations, it was possible to generate stable rotors only at the highest concentration (1000 μM) in atrial tissue, with a vulnerable window of 7 ms. In ventricular tissue, it was not possible to generate rotors at any CO concentration. The Fig. 3 shows the rotor generated by applying the S2 stimulus at a coupling interval equal to half of the vulnerable window, at a CO concentration of 1000 μM in atrial tissue. The center of rotation migrates generating a star-shaped trajectory in the central area of the tissue. The rotor propagation is shown in Fig. 3A. The migratory trajectory of the rotor is evidenced in the phase singularity map (Fig. 3B), where the trajectory of the rotor tip moves within a zone of about 2 cm in diameter.

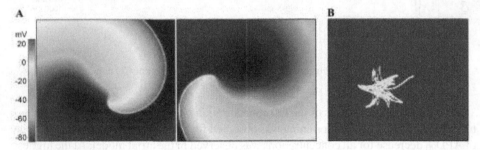

Fig. 3. A) Rotor generated by applying a CO concentration of 1000 μM in atrial tissue. The depolarizing wavefront ca be identified by the red color (20 mV). B) Phase singularity map corresponding to the trajectory of the rotor tip.

4   Discussion

Atmospheric pollution is associated with adverse cardiovascular results and may cause premature death [1]. However, this effects underlaying mechanisms are lesser-known. Epidemiological studies have related the atmospheric CO with cardiovascular diseases and with an increasing risk of cardiac mortality. It has been informed that CO, in particular, is one of the main pollutants responsible of the development of cardiovascular diseases [24, 25]. Low CO concentrations, which can be found in an urban environment, have been correlated with hospital admissions, mortality and morbidity, due to cardiovascular dysfunctions [24, 26]. Nevertheless, information about the cellular mechanisms in healthy individuals is lacking. It has been recently shown that chronic CO exposition promotes a pathological phenotype of cardiomyocytes, where, remodeling and the intracellular calcium overload would increase the arrhythmia risk [27, 28] and the myocardial ischemia-reperfusion [29, 30]. The CO ability of altering the electrophysiological activity in the heart and nervous system lead to studies about the CO regulation of specific ionic channels [31]. Such affections may occur as a direct CO action or as a CO effects on the intracellular signaling paths [15].

This work is focused on the CO effects on the L-type Ca^{2+} specific channel, the action potential duration and the rotor generation in computational models of auricular and ventricular human tissue. Our results show a CO proarrhythmic action on the cardiomyocytes, which is more prominent in auricular than in ventricular cells. Such effect includes a shortening of the action potential, mainly due to the I_{CaL} current blockade in a larger fraction according to the increment of the CO concentration. These results are consistent with experimental studies, in which, an adverse effect of the CO over the el Ca^{2+} is evinced. In a study with rats daily exposed to CO concentrations of 150–200 ppm during 12 h in 4 weeks, a pathological phenotype of cardiomyocytes through interstitial and perivascular fibrosis at the left ventricle was found [27]. Additionally, in the same work, reduction in both, the Ca^{2+} transient amplitude of diastolic intracellular calcium and the Ca^{2+} recapture, was observed. An investigation with rats isolated hearts, exposed during 4 weeks to CO-enriched air (30–100 ppm), report that prolonged CO exposition worsen the ischemic-reperfusion myocardial injuries. The outcome was a loss of myocardial function and an increment of the Ca^{2+} recapture [29]. Those aggravating effects may be explained by a reduction of the enzymatic antioxidant state of myocardium, that is related with intracellular calcium handling. A study of the CO effect on the electrical and contractile activity in isolated preparations of atrial and ventricular rat myocardium, shown that the CO causes an important shortening of the action potential duration in function atrial tissue and a significant acceleration of sinus rhythm [14]. Additionally, the CO reduces the strength of contractions and other parameters of the contractile activity. In the ventricular myocardium preparations, the exogen CO also shortens the action potential.

In our study, rotors can be generated in the auricular model due to a pronounced reduction in the action potential duration. These results are in agreements with Andre et al. [27], where, CO pollution increase the number of arrhythmic events. They suggest that the propensity to the arrhythmia may be derived from the effect on the calcium currents. It has been shown that the action potential duration reduction may generate a significant reduction of the trajectory required to the development or maintenance of reentries, which are the sustaining mechanisms of cardiac arrhythmias [32]. The action potential duration shortening in human cardiac tissue is the most likely cause of the appearance of a small number of rotors that underly the arrhythmias [33]. A limitation of this work is related with the use of 2D models. The CO effect in generating cardiac events must be assessed in 3D detailed models and conducting validation studies with patients.

5   Conclusion

The results of our simulations suggest the proarrhythmic effect of CO. By blocking the I_{CaL} current in a larger extent according to the CO concentration, the APD is shortened in atrial cardiomyocytes to a greater extent compared to ventricular cells. This behavior yields the generation of arrhythmic episodes in atrial tissue at a high CO concentration. This study is the first step aiming to investigate the electrophysiological burden of CO on the cardiac action potential and on the establishment of arrhythmogenic events in healthy people.

Acknowledgment. This work was supported by the *Ministerio de Ciencia Tecnología e Innovación* (MINCIENCIAS) from Colombia, through grant No. 120677757994. The work of Durango-Giraldo was supported by the *"Convocatoria para el fortalecimiento de proyectos en ejecución de CTeI en ciencias de la salud con talento joven e impacto regional"* of MINCIENCIAS.

References

1. OECD: The cost of air pollution. Health impacts of road transport. OECD Publishing (2014).
2. Sanchez, S., Castillo, J., Green, J., Klakamp, J.: Air pollution and health in Latin America and the Caribbean: an overview. In: Air Quality & Health Showcase. Clean Air Institute, Washington (2016)
3. OECD Environmental Outlook to 2050: The Consequences of Inaction.
4. European Environment Agency: Revealing the costs of air pollution from industrial facilities in Europe. (2011). https://doi.org/10.2800/84800
5. Miller, K.A., et al.: Long-term exposure to air pollution and incidence of cardiovascular events in women. N. Engl. J. Med. **356**, 447–458 (2007). https://doi.org/10.1056/NEJMoa054409
6. Brook, R.D., et al.: Air pollution and cardiovascular disease: a statement for healthcare professionals from the expert panel on population and prevention science of the American Heart Association (2004). https://doi.org/10.1161/01.CIR.0000128587.30041.C8
7. Finkelstein, M.: Pollution-related mortality and educational level. JAMA **288**, 830 (2002). https://doi.org/10.1001/jama.288.7.828
8. Pope, C.A., III.: Lung cancer, cardiopulmonary mortality, and long-term exposure to fine particulate air pollution. JAMA **287**, 1132 (2002). https://doi.org/10.1001/jama.287.9.1132
9. UNEP: UNEP Year Book 2014 emerging issues update. Air Pollution: World's Worst Environmental Health Risk. United Nations Environment Programme, Environment for Development, Nairobi (2014)
10. Link, M.S., et al.: Acute exposure to air pollution triggers atrial fibrillation. J. Am. Coll. Cardiol. **62**, 816–825 (2013). https://doi.org/10.1016/j.jacc.2013.05.043
11. U.S. Environmental Protection Agency: Air Quality Planning & Standards (2015)
12. Henry, C.R., Satran, D., Lindgren, B., Adkinson, C., Nicholson, C.I., Henry, T.D.: Myocardial injury and long-term mortality following moderate to severe carbon monoxide poisoning. Am. Med. Assoc. **295**, 398–402 (2006)

13. Samoli, E., et al.: Short-term effects of carbon monoxide on mortality: an analysis within the APHEA project. Environ. Health Perspect. **115**, 1578–1583 (2007). https://doi.org/10.1289/ehp.10375

14. Abramochkin, D.V., Haertdinov, N.N., Porokhnya, M.V., Zefirov, A.L., Sitdikova, G.F.: Carbon monoxide affects electrical and contractile activity of rat myocardium. J. Biomed. Sci. **18**, 40 (2011). https://doi.org/10.1186/1423-0127-18-40

15. Scragg, J.L., Dallas, M.L., Wilkinson, J.A., Varadi, G., Peers, C.: Carbon monoxide inhibits L-type Ca 2+ channels via redox modulation of key cysteine residues by mitochondrial reactive oxygen species. J. Biol. Chem. **283**, 24412–24419 (2008). https://doi.org/10.1074/jbc.M803037200

16. Dinanian, S., et al.: Downregulation of the calcium current in human right atrial myocytes from patients in sinus rhythm but with a high risk of atrial fibrillation. Eur. Heart J. **29**, 1190–1197 (2008). https://doi.org/10.1093/eurheartj/ehn140

17. Tobon, C., Saiz, J.: Modelado y simulación 3D de la fibrilación auricular y su tratamiento quirúrgico. Sello Editorial Universidad de Medellín, Medellín (2018)

18. Courtemanche, M., Ramirez, R.J., Nattel, S.: Ionic targets for drug therapy and atrial fibrillation-induced electrical remodeling: Insights from a mathematical model. Cardiovasc. Res. **42**, 477–489 (1999). https://doi.org/10.1016/S0008-6363(99)00034-6

19. Dutta, S., et al.: Optimization of an in silico cardiac cell model for proarrhythmia risk assessment. Front. Physiol. **8**, 1–15 (2017). https://doi.org/10.3389/fphys.2017.00616

20. Hansson, A.: Right atrial free wall conduction velocity and degree of anisotropy in patients with stable sinus rhythm studied during open heart surgery. Eur. Heart J. **19**, 293–300 (1998). https://doi.org/10.1053/euhj.1997.0742

21. Ugarte, J., Tobón, C., Orozco-Duque, A.: Entropy mapping approach for functional reentry detection in atrial fibrillation: an in-silico study. Entropy **21**, 194 (2019). https://doi.org/10.3390/e21020194

22. Tobón, C.: Modelización y Evaluación de Factores que Favorecen las Arritmias Auriculares y su Tratamiento Mediante Técnicas Quirúrgicas. Estudio de Simulación (2010)

23. Bray, M.A., Lin, S.F., Aliev, R.R., Roth, B.J., Wikswo, J.P.: Experimental and theoretical analysis of phase singularity dynamics in cardiac tissue. J. Cardiovasc. Electrophysiol. **12**, 716–722 (2001). https://doi.org/10.1046/j.1540-8167.2001.00716.x

24. Bell, M.L., Peng, R.D., Dominici, F., Samet, J.M.: Emergency hospital admissions for cardiovascular diseases and ambient levels of carbon monoxide results for 126 united states urban counties, 1999–2005. Circulation **120**, 949–955 (2009). https://doi.org/10.1161/CIRCULATIONAHA.109.851113

25. Stieb, D.M., Szyszkowicz, M., Rowe, B.H., Leech, J.A.: Air pollution and emergency department visits for cardiac and respiratory conditions: a multi-city time-series analysis. Environ. Heal. **8**, 25 (2009). https://doi.org/10.1186/1476-069X-8-25

26. Burnett, R.T., Cakmak, S., Brook, J.R., Krewski, D.: The role of particulate size and chemistry in the association between summertime ambient air pollution and hospitalization for cardiorespiratory diseases. Environ. Health Perspect. **105**, 614–620 (1997). https://doi.org/10.1289/ehp.97105614

27. Andre, L., et al.: Carbon monoxide pollution promotes cardiac remodeling and ventricular arrhythmia in healthy rats. Am. J. Respir. Crit. Care Med. **181**, 587–595 (2010). https://doi.org/10.1164/rccm.200905-0794OC

28. Keurs, T., Henk, E.D.J., Boyden, P.A.: Calcium and arrhythmogenesis. Physiol. Rev. **87**, 457–506 (2007). https://doi.org/10.1152/physrev.00011.2006

29. Meyer, G., et al.: Simulated urban carbon monoxide air pollution exacerbates rat heart ischemia-reperfusion injury. Physiol. Hear. Circ. Physiol. **298**, H1445–H1453 (2010)

30. Meyer, G., et al.: Carbon monoxide increases inducible NOS expression that mediates CO-induced myocardial damage during ischemia-reperfusion. Am. J. Physiol. Hear. Circ. Physiol. **308**, H759–H767 (2015). https://doi.org/10.1152/ajpheart.00702.2014

31. Wilkinson, W.J., Kemp, P.J.: Carbon monoxide: an emerging regulator of ion channels. J. Physiol. **589**, 3055–3062 (2011). https://doi.org/10.1113/jphysiol.2011.206706

32. Antzelevitch, C., Burashnikov, A.: Overview of basic mechanisms of cardiac arrhythmia. Card. Electrophysiol. Clin. **3**, 23–45 (2011). https://doi.org/10.1016/j.ccep.2010.10.012

33. Vaquero, M., Calvo, D., Jalife, J.: Cardiac fibrillation: from ion channels to rotors in the human heart. Hear. Rhythm. **5**, 872–879 (2008). https://doi.org/10.1016/j.hrthm.2008.02.034

Gender Recognition in Informal and Formal Language Scenarios via Transfer Learning

Daniel Escobar-Grisales[1]([✉]) [iD], Juan Camilo Vásquez-Correa[1,2,3] [iD],
and Juan Rafael Orozco-Arroyave[1,2] [iD]

[1] GITA Lab. Faculty of Engineering, University of Antioquia UdeA,
Medellín, Colombia
{daniel.esobar,jcamilo.vasquez,rafael.orozco}@udea.edu.co
[2] Pattern Recognition Lab., Friedrich-Alexander-Universität,
Erlangen-Nürnberg, Germany
[3] Pratech Group, Medellín, Colombia

Abstract. The interest in demographic information retrieval based on text data has increased in the research community because applications have shown success in different sectors such as security, marketing, heathcare, and others. Recognition and identification of demographic traits such as gender, age, location, or personality based on text data can help to improve different marketing strategies. For instance it makes it possible to segment and to personalize offers, thus products and services are exposed to the group of greatest interest. This type of technology has been discussed widely in documents from social media. However, the methods have been poorly studied in data with a more formal structure, where there is no access to emoticons, mentions, and other linguistic phenomena that are only present in social media. This paper proposes the use of recurrent and convolutional neural networks, and a transfer learning strategy for gender recognition in documents that are written in informal and formal languages. Models are tested in two different databases consisting of Tweets and call-center conversations. Accuracies of up to 75% are achieved for both databases. The results also indicate that it is possible to transfer the knowledge from a system trained on a specific type of expressions or idioms such as those typically used in social media into a more formal type of text data, where the amount of data is more scarce and its structure is completely different.

Keywords: Demographic information retrieval · Gender recognition · Transfer learning · Recurrent neural networks · Convolutional neural networks

1 Introduction

Demographic information retrieval consists in recognizing traits from a human being such as age, gender, personality, emotions, and others. Typically the main

Supported by University of Antioquia.

J. C. Figueroa-García et al. (Eds.): WEA 2021, CCIS 1431, pp. 171–179, 2021.
https://doi.org/10.1007/978-3-030-86702-7_15

aim is to create a user profile based on unstructured data. The retrieval of such information has different applications in forensics, security, sales, marketing, health-care, and many other sectors [9]. In e-commerce scenarios, this type of information provides advantages to companies in competitive environments because it allows to segment customers in order to offer personalized products and services which strengths their marketing strategies [4,8]. Although most of the demographic factors are explicitly collected through the registration process, this approach could be limited given that most of potential customers in online stores are anonymous. The automatic recognition of demographic variables such as gender can help to overcome these limitations [5].

Text data from customers can be obtained via transliterations of voice recordings, chats, surveys, and social media. These text resources can be processed to automatically recognize the gender of the users. Different studies have applied Natural Language Processing (NLP) techniques for gender recognition in text data, mainly from social media posts. In [12,13] the authors used Term Frequency-Inverse Document Frequency (TF-IDF) to extract features from tweets in the PAN17 corpus [16], and reported accuracies for gender classification around 81%. The authors in [3] used extracted features from TF-IDF as well as specific information only available in social media posts such as the frequency of female- and male-emojis. The authors reported an accuracy of 83.2% in the PAN17 [16] corpus for gender recognition. Although the high accuracy reported in the study, the methodology would not be accurate to model text data written in more formal scenarios such as customer reviews, product surveys, opinion posts, and customer service chats, which have a different structure compared to the texts that can be found in social media data. In other study [11], the authors proposed a system to classify the gender of the persons who wrote 100,000 posts from Weibo (Chinese social network similar to Tweeter). The system was based on a Word2Vec model, which achieved an accuracy of 62.9%. The authors compared the performance of their model with human judgments, which accuracy was 60%. This fact evidences that the problem of recognizing gender in written texts is very hard even for human readers. Wod2Vec models were also considered in [1] for gender recognition in the PAN17 corpus. The authors reported an accuracy of 69.5% for the Tweets in Spanish. There are some studies focused on gender classification using Deep Learning (DL) methods. However, when considering texts in Spanish, the number of studies is relatively small [9,11]. In [10], the authors proposed a methodology based on Bidirectional Gated Recurrent Units (GRUs) and an attention mechanism for gender classification in the PAN17 corpus. The authors worked with a Word2Vec model as input for their DL architecture and reported accuracies of up to 75.3%.

According to the reviewed literature, gender classification based on text data has been mainly explored in social media scenarios, where the language is informal and the documents do not follow a formal structure [6]. These types of documents use a number of language variants, styles, and other content like emojis that help to accurately recognize different demographic information. There is a gap between models trained on formal and informal written language because a trained model with formal language data for a specific purpose will not achieve comparable results on an informal language scenario, or vice-versa [7]. Due to this reason, it is important to validate trained models for gender recognition in both types of languages: formal and informal. In addition, the recognition of demographic variables such as gender are under-explored in documents with a more formal structure.

This paper proposes a methodology based on Recurrent Neural Networks (RNNs) and Convolutional Neural Networks (CNNs) for gender recognition in informal and formal language scenarios. First, the models are trained and tested in the PAN17 corpus, which is a traditional dataset for gender classification in Tweets. The models originally trained using the PAN17 corpus are re-trained using a transfer learning strategy with data from call-center conversations, which are structured in a more formal language. Accuracies of up to 75% are obtained, indicating that the proposed methodology is accurate for gender classification in documents written in formal and also in informal languages. Moreover, fine-tuned models using transfer learning show that despite the noise and lack of structure in documents written in informal language, they can be used to improve the accuracy of gender classification.

2 Materials and Methods

2.1 Data

PAN17: We are particularly working with the Spanish data of the corpus, namely PAN-CLEF 2017 [16]. In this database, there are variants of Spanish from seven countries: Argentina, Chile, Colombia, Mexico, Peru, Spain and Venezuela. The training set is composed by texts from 600 subjects from each country (300 female). Since each subject has 100 Tweets, there is a total of 4200 subjects and 420000 Tweets in the dataset. The test set comprises data from 400 subjects from each country (200 female) for a total of 2800 subjects and 280000 Tweets. For the sake of comparison with previous studies, we kept the original train and test sets. The training set was randomly divided into 80% for training and 20% to optimize the hyper-parameters of the models (development set). All data distribution was performed subject independent to avoid subject specific bias and to guarantee a better generalization capability of the models.

Call Center Conversations: This corpus contains transliterations of conversations between customers and agents from a customer service center of a pension administration company in Colombia. Texts are manually generated by a group of linguistic experts based on the audio signals from the customers. Similarly, the label of the gender is assigned based on the audio recordings processed by the linguists. Formal language is typically used by the customers when asking for a service, making a request, asking about certificates, and other questions about the service provided by the company. This database comprises 220 transliterations of different customers (110 female). The average number of words for each conversation is 602, with a standard deviation of 554.

2.2 Deep Learning Architectures for Gender Classification

We consider two DL architectures in this case: an RNN with Bidirectional Long Short Term Memory (LSTM) cells, and a CNN with multiple temporal resolutions. These networks are trained with data from the PAN17 corpus. Then, a transfer learning strategy is applied to recognize gender from the call center conversations data.

Bidirectional Long Short Term Memory: The main idea of RNNs is to model a sequence of feature vectors based on the assumption that the output depends on the input features at the present time-step and on the output at the previous time-step. Conventional RNNs have a *causal* structure, i.e., the output at the present time step only contains information from the past. However, many applications require information from the future [15]. Bidirectional RNNs are created to address such a requirement by combing a layer that processes the input sequence forward through time with an additional layer that moves backwards the input sequence. Traditional RNNs also exhibit a vanishing gradient problem, which appears when modeling long temporal sequences. LSTM layers were proposed to solve this vanishing gradient problem by the inclusion of a *long-term* memory to produce paths where the gradient can flow for long duration sequences such as sentences of a Tweet, or the ones that appear in a conversation with a call-center agent [17]. We proposed the use of a Bidirectional LSTM (Bi-LSTM) network for our application. These architectures are widely used for different NLP tasks such as sentiment analysis in social media and product reviews [2,14,18]. A scheme of the considered architecture is shown in Fig. 1.

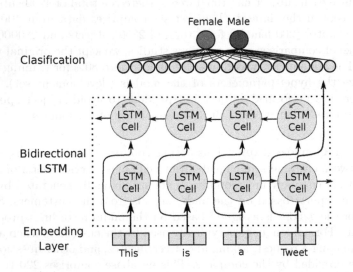

Fig. 1. Bi-LSTM architecture for gender classification in a Tweet.

Words from the data are represented using a word-embedding layer. The input to the Bi-LSTM layer consists of k d-dimensional words-embedding vectors, where k is the length of the sequence. The final decision about the gender of the subject is made at the output layer by using Softmax activation function.

Convolutional Neural Network (CNN): CNN-based architectures are designed to extract sentence representations by a composition of convolutional layers and a max-pooling operation over all resulting feature maps. We proposed the use of a parallel CNN architecture with different filter orders to exploit different temporal resolutions at the same time. Details of the architecture can be found in Fig. 2. The output from the word-embedding layer is convolved with filters of different orders (n) and that correspond to different number of the n in n-grams. The proposed CNN computes the convolution only in the temporal dimension. After convolution, a max-pooling operation is applied. Finally, a fully connected layer is used for classification using a Softmax activation function.

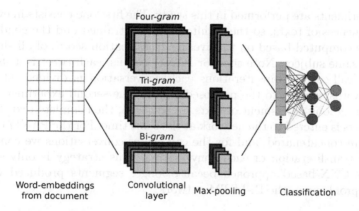

Fig. 2. CNN architecture for gender classification in a Tweet.

2.3 Training

The networks considered in this work are implemented in Tensorflow 2.0, and are trained with a sparse categorical cross-entropy loss function using an Adam optimizer. An early stopping strategy is used to stop training when validation loss does not improve after 10 epochs. The embedding dimension d is set to 100. The vocabulary size for the tokenizer is set to 5000 for the PAN17 corpus and 1500 for the call-center conversations. The difference between the two vocabulary sizes is given because the number of unique words present in the training sets of each database. Hyper-parameters are optimized upon the validation accuracy and the simplest model.

2.4 Transfer Learning

We tested two approaches for the call-center conversations data: (1) training the network only using the data from the corresponding corpus, and (2) training the model via transfer learning by using a pre-trained model generated with the PAN17 corpus. For the transfer learning approach, the most accurate model for the PAN17 data is fine-tuned, but freezing the embedding layer in order to keep the tokenizer and a bigger vocabulary. Experiments without freezing the embedding layer were also performed but the results were not satisfactory. The motivation for using transfer learning is to test whether the knowledge learned by a model trained with text data in informal language is useful to improve gender classification systems based on text with formal language, since it is generally common to collect large amounts of data with informal structure through social media, but it is difficult to collect written documents with a formal structure.

3 Experiment and Results

Two experiments are performed in this study. The first one consists in evaluating short sequences of texts, so the architectures are trained and the gender of the subject is computed based on the average classification scores of all short texts from the same subject. Note that for PAN17 corpus, each tweet is a short text, while for call-center transliterations each conversation is divided into chunks with 60 words, similar to the proposed in [10]. The second experiment consists in evaluating long assessment of texts. In this case, the complete text data from the subjects is entered to the network at the same time. For the PAN17 corpus all Tweets are concatenated, and for the call-center conversations we consider the complete transliteration of each conversation. This strategy is only evaluated using the CNN-based approach because longer segments produced vanishing gradient problems in the Bi-LSTM network.

Experiments with PAN17: The results obtained for the PAN17 corpus (informal language) are shown in Table 1 for both approaches, short and long texts evaluation. Bi-LSTM and CNN networks are considered. The best results are obtained using the strategy with long texts in the CNN. There is an improvement of up to 4% in the accuracy per subject with respect to the accuracy obtained with short texts. The improvement in the F1-score is around 2%.

Experiments with Call-Center Conversations: The results observed for the call center conversations (formal language) are shown in Table 2. The results include those obtained with and without applying transfer learning. The results also include the ones obtained using short and long texts. The results for this corpus are obtained following a 10-fold cross-validation strategy due to the small size of the corpus. The highest accuracy is obtained here also with the long texts, similar to the results obtained with the PAN17 corpus. In addition, note that the accuracy improves in up to 20% when the transfer learning strategy is applied

Table 1. Results of the gender classification in the PAN-CLEF 2017 database.

	Short texts		Long texts
	Bi-LSTM	CNN	CNN
Accuracy per Tweet	60.5	61.1	–
Accuracy per subject	71.3	71.9	**75.9**
Precision	68.6	81.1	**75.6**
Recall	72.0	68.0	**76.1**
F1-Score	70.8	73.9	**75.8**

with respect to the accuracy obtained without using the pre-trained models. Note also that models using transfer learning show a smaller standard deviation which likely indicates that these methods are more stable.

Table 2. Results of the gender classification in the call-center conversations data. **TL:** transfer learning.

	Short texts				Long texts	
	Bi-LSTM Without TL	Bi-LSTM With TL	CNN Without TL	CNN With TL	CNN Without TL	CNN With TL
Accuracy per text	52.7 ± 6.43	51.6 ± 5.07	57.9 ± 9.20	58.3 ± 6.48	–	–
Accuracy per subject	54.2 ± 10.1	56.4 ± 12.1	65.9 ± 12.7	62.9 ± 14.9	55.9 ± 11.9	**75.0 ± 6.18**
Precision	65.3 ± 29.2	55.0 ± 13.8	52.0 ± 22.2	61.1 ± 17.9	54.6 ± 25.4	**77.2 ± 8.12**
Recall	53.3 ± 22.7	56.7 ± 13.2	70.4 ± 17.2	64.6 ± 15.2	54.9 ± 34.8	**72.1 ± 10.4**
F1-Score	55.2 ± 19.8	55.2 ± 11.9	57.8 ± 19.9	61.1 ± 15.7	48.5 ± 24.0	**73.8 ± 6.06**

4 Conclusions

We proposed a methodology for automatic gender classification based on formal texts such as those available in social media posts, and based on formal texts collected in call center conversations. Different deep learning models are evaluated including one on Bi-LSTMs, another one based on CNNs and a transfer learning approach, which is pre-trained with data collected from social networks. The transfer learning method is fine-tuned to improve the accuracy of the model designed for text classification in formal languages. The results indicate that it is possible to classify the gender of a person based on his/her written texts with accuracies of about 75% in informal and formal language scenarios. The use of a transfer learning strategy improved the accuracy in scenarios where it is more difficult to collect data like in call-center conversations, indicating that this strategy is suitable for companies or sectors where it is not possible to create large datasets from scratch. The models using transfer learning are also more stable and generalize better than others where the neural networks are trained from scratch. This is very positive since it is possible to benefit from the large amounts of text data that are available in other domains like the social networks. The proposed approaches can be extended to other applications related to demographic information retrieval such as age recognition, geographic location, personality of the subjects, and others, which would allow the building of more complete and specific author/customer profiles.

Acknowledgments. This work was funded by the company Pratech Group S.A.S and the University of Antioquia, grant # PI2019-24110. We would like to thank the Natural Language Engineering Laboratory of the Universidad Politécnica de Valencia for providing access to one of the databases used in this work.

References

1. Akhtyamova, L., Cardiff, J., Ignatov, A.: Twitter author profiling using word embeddings and logistic regression. In: Conference and Labs of the Evaluation Forum (CLEF) (Working Notes) (2017)
2. Arras, L., Montavon, G., Müller, K.R., Samek, W.: Explaining recurrent neural network predictions in sentiment analysis. arXiv:1706.07206 (2017)
3. Basile, A., et al.: N-gram: new groningen author-profiling model. arXiv:1707.03764 (2017)
4. Dogan, O., Oztaysi, B.: Gender prediction from classified indoor customer paths by fuzzy C-medoids clustering. In: Kahraman, C., Cebi, S., Cevik Onar, S., Oztaysi, B., Tolga, A.C., Sari, I.U. (eds.) INFUS 2019. AISC, vol. 1029, pp. 160–169. Springer, Cham (2020). https://doi.org/10.1007/978-3-030-23756-1_21
5. Fernandez-Lanvin, D., de Andres-Suarez, J., Gonzalez-Rodriguez, M., Pariente-Martinez, B.: The dimension of age and gender as user model demographic factors for automatic personalization in e-commerce sites. Comput. Stand. Interfaces **59**, 1–9 (2018)
6. González Bermúdez, M.: An analysis of twitter corpora and the differences between formal and colloquial tweets. In: Proceedings of the Tweet Translation Workshop 2015, pp. 1–7. CEUR-WS.org (2015)
7. Gu, J., Yu, Z.: Data annealing for informal language understanding tasks. arXiv:2004.13833 (2020)
8. Hirt, R., Kühl, N., Satzger, G.: Cognitive computing for customer profiling: meta classification for gender prediction. Electron. Mark. **29**(1), 93–106 (2019). https://doi.org/10.1007/s12525-019-00336-z
9. Hsieh, F., Dias, R., Paraboni, I.: Author profiling from Facebook corpora. In: Proceedings of the Eleventh International Conference on Language Resources and Evaluation (LREC 2018) (2018)
10. Kodiyan, D., et al.: Author profiling with bidirectional RNNs using attention with GRUs. In: Conference and Labs of the Evaluation Forum (CLEF), vol. 1866. RWTH Aachen (2017)
11. Li, W., Dickinson, M.: Gender prediction for Chinese social media data. In: Conference Recent Advances in Natural Language Processing (RANLP), pp. 438–445 (2017)
12. Markov, I., Gómez-Adorno, H., Sidorov, G.: Language-and subtask-dependent feature selection and classifier parameter tuning for author profiling. In: Notebook for PAN at Conference and Labs of the Evaluation Forum (CLEF) (2017)

13. Martinc, M., Skrjanec, I., Zupan, K., Pollak, S.: Pan 2017: author profiling-gender and language variety prediction. In: Conference and Labs of the Evaluation Forum (CLEF) (Working Notes) (2017)
14. Minaee, S., Azimi, E., Abdolrashidi, A.: Deep-sentiment: sentiment analysis using ensemble of CNN and Bi-LSTM models. arXiv:1904.04206 (2019)
15. Otter, D.W., et al.: A survey of the usages of deep learning for natural language processing. IEEE Trans. Neural Netw. Learn. Syst. (TNNLS) **32**(2), 604–624 (2020)
16. Rangel, F., Rosso, P., Potthast, M., Stein, B.: Overview of the 5th author profiling task at pan 2017: gender and language variety identification in twitter. In: Working Notes Papers of the Conference and Labs of the Evaluation Forum (CLEF), pp. 1613–0073 (2017)
17. Torfi, A., Shirvani, R.A., Keneshloo, Y., Tavvaf, N., Fox, E.A.: Natural language processing advancements by deep learning: a survey. arXiv:2003.01200 (2020)
18. Trofimovich, J.: Comparison of neural network architectures for sentiment analysis of Russian tweets. In: Computational Linguistics and Intellectual Technologies: Proceedings of the International Conference "Dialogue", pp. 50–59 (2016)

Towards Event-Trigger Impulsive MPC for the Treatment of T1DM Handling Limited Resources

Jhon E. Goez-Mora⬤, Monica Ayde Vallejo⬤,
and Pablo S. Rivadeneira$^{(\boxtimes)}$ ⬤

Facultad de Minas, Universidad Nacional de Colombia, Medellín, Colombia
{jegoezm,mavallejov,psrivade}@unal.edu.co

Abstract. Tight control of blood glucose is a difficult task in patients with type I diabetes. Nowadays, the artificial pancreas is becoming an auspicious treatment for them. It consists of an insulin pump, a continuous glucose monitoring (CGM) sensor, and a control strategy running on a portable device. However, it faces many challenging issues, including limited resources such as insulin supply and battery power capacity. This paper examines this problem within the model predictive control (MPC) framework. The standard impulsive zone MPC formulation has been modified by adding an event-trigger feature and two new constraints that help extend the battery life and the insulin reservoir. The event-trigger scheme allows the new formulation to decide at which time instants it is necessary to compute a control action. In addition, when battery life and insulin supply are below the established limits, the two constraints become active, providing more time to the treatment than the standard strategy. The performance of this new proposal is assessed through several simulations, obtaining promising results that deserve further research.

Keywords: Artificial pancreas · Model predictive control · Type 1 diabetes · Limited resources

1 Introduction

Type I diabetes mellitus (T1DM) is an autoimmune disease that destroys the pancreatic β−cells and generates a deficiency in insulin hormone production, which is necessary for the processing and regulation of blood glucose (BG) [1]. Consequently, the body stores large amounts of glucose causing damage to several organs, veins, and nerves, deteriorating them to the point of becoming lethal. This condition leads people with T1DM to depend on exogenous insulin, which must be supplied according to each patient's insulin requirements; for instance, after meal intake or before exercising [2]. The T1DM treatment consists of multiple daily injections of insulin. Nowadays, this treatment is supported by CGM sensors which provide a measurement every 5 min; this allows the treatment's effectiveness [3,4].

The artificial pancreas (AP) is the solution proposed from the control engineering community to address this problem. The AP is an insulin pump enhanced

J. C. Figueroa-García et al. (Eds.): WEA 2021, CCIS 1431, pp. 180–189, 2021.
https://doi.org/10.1007/978-3-030-86702-7_16

with a CGM sensor and a control strategy and it tries to emulate the normal functioning of the pancreas, dosing the correct amount of insulin when required. The core of the AP is a controller that computes insulin doses based on glycemia measurements and runs on an embedded system into a portable device. Three types of control strategies have been extensively used in the literature: fuzzy control, proportional-integrative-derivative control (PID), and model predictive control. [5].

Although the commercial pump MiniMed 670G already has an integrated basal PID control, the most developed strategy for the AP in the academic community is the MPC, which has proven to perform significantly better than others control strategies [6–8]. One advantage of the MPC is the inclusion of physical constraints, such as the partial and total amount of insulin delivered; this represents a great improvement because the insulin supply is restricted. In addition, this control strategy's algorithm obtains its accuracy from an optimization process. However, its main disadvantages are the prediction model to be used and the computational effort required, which, in general, is greater than that required by the other approaches. A higher computational effort involves a higher energy consumption, which becomes relevant specially when they are running a portable device as in the AP case. To handle limited resources on portable healthcare devices has always been a challenge. This AP application demands efficient operations and high precision in the control applied to patients [9].

In this work, an MPC approach is formulated to regulate BG considering the idea of implementing the artificial pancreas in a portable device that carries a battery with a limited energy capacity, that is continuously consumed by the calculations and injection of the insulin. Furthermore, the insulin reservoir decreases with each dose, especially if the patient has low insulin sensitivity, which increases the magnitude of the dose and makes the reservoir have to be renewed more frequently.

The standard impulsive zone MPC formulation given in [10] is modified by adding an event-trigger (ET) strategy and two new constraints to extend the battery life and the insulin reservoir. The event-trigger component allows the new strategy to decide at which time instants the MPC optimization problem needs to be solve. The two constraints become active when predefined limits are trespassed, this allows the strategy to save battery life and insulin supply, which is traduced to more time with treatment than the standard strategy. The performance of the new proposal was evaluated through several simulations assuming that a Raspberry Pi 3 embedded system [15], a stepper motor with gearbox, and electric energy sensors are used.

2   Model of the Patient with Diabetes Mellitus Type I

The mathematical model that describes the glucose-insulin dynamics is the AP's core, especially for model-based controllers as the MPC. In this paper, an adaptation of the model described in [11] is used as prediction model. This is a physiological grey box model based on five compartments to represent glucose dynamics, insulin absorption and action, and meal absorption dynamics. This model stands out since it adequately represents the equilibriums of a patient with T1DM and has a long-term validation. The model state space representation is as follows:

$$\dot{x}(t) = Ax(t) + Bu(t) + B_r r(t) + E, x(0) = x_0,$$

$$A = \begin{pmatrix} -\theta_2 & -\theta_3 & 0 & \theta_4 & 0 \\ 0 & -\frac{1}{\theta_5} & \frac{1}{\theta_5} & 0 & 0 \\ 0 & 0 & -\frac{1}{\theta_5} & 0 & 0 \\ 0 & 0 & 0 & -\frac{1}{\theta_6} & \frac{1}{\theta_6} \\ 0 & 0 & 0 & 0 & -\frac{1}{\theta_6} \end{pmatrix}, \quad B = \begin{pmatrix} 0 \\ 0 \\ \frac{1}{\theta_5} \\ 0 \\ 0 \end{pmatrix}, \quad B_r = \begin{pmatrix} 0 \\ 0 \\ 0 \\ 0 \\ \frac{1}{\theta_6} \end{pmatrix}, \quad E = \begin{pmatrix} \theta_1 \\ 0 \\ 0 \\ 0 \\ 0 \end{pmatrix}.$$

$$(1)$$

The five state variables are: x_1, the glycemia (mg/dl); x_2 and x_3, the delivery rates of insulin in the blood and interstitial space compartments, respectively (U/min); and x_4 and x_5, the delivery rates of carbohydrates in the stomach and guts compartments, respectively (g/min). The inputs are u, the exogenous insulin (U/min), and r, the carbohydrate amount due to meal intakes (g/min). The output of the system corresponds to glycemia, *i.e.* y(t) = Cx(t), with $C =$ (1 0 0 0 0). All parameters of the model have physiological interpretation which can be seen in Table 1, and their values have been identified from the UVA/Padova cohort of 10 adults.

Table 1. Parameters description of the model.

Parameter	Description	Units	Value
θ_1	Hepatic auto-regulation	1/min	1.27
θ_2	Insulin sensitivity	mg/dl/U	0.0034
θ_3	Carbohydrate bioavailability	mg/dl/g	44.223
θ_4	Endogenous glucose production at zero-insulin level	mg/dl/min	2.308
θ_5	Time-to-maximum of effective insulin concentration	min	56.001
θ_6	Time-to-maximum appearance rate of glucose	min	21.84

3   Impulsive Model Predictive Control for T1DM

With the knowledge that insulin doses are administered as small spaced pulses, rather than a continuous or a discrete input, the consideration of the system as an impulsive control strategies (ICS) is appropriate to emulate the real treatment of T1DM. Then the model in (1) is rewritten in the form:

$$\dot{x}(t) = Ax(t) + B_r r(t) + E, \quad x(0) = x_0, \ t \neq \tau_k,$$
$$x(\tau_k^+) = x(\tau_k) + Bu(\tau_k), k \in N,$$
$$y(\tau_k) = Cx(\tau_k),$$

$$(2)$$

where $t \in R$ denotes time, τ_k, $k \in N$ denotes the impulse time instants, and τ_k^+ the limit from the right as t approaches to τ_k; $x \in X \subseteq R^{n_x}$, $u \in U \subseteq R^{n_u}$, and $y \in R^{n_y}$ are the (constrained) state vector, the (constrained) impulsive control inputs, and the measured variables of the system, respectively.

The discrete sequence in (2), that relates the state at time τ_k^+ with the state and the impulsive input at times τ_k can be expressed by a primary underlying discrete-time subsystem (UDS) to describe the original system (2) at times τ_k [12], which is:

$$x^\bullet(k+1) = A^\bullet x^\bullet(k) + B_u^\bullet u^\bullet(k) + B_r^\bullet r^\bullet(k) + E^\bullet, \qquad (3)$$

where $A^\bullet = e^{AT}$, $B^\bullet = e^{AT}B$, $B_r^\bullet = \int_0^T e^{As} ds B_r$, $E^\bullet = e^{AT}E$, $x^\bullet(0) = x(\tau_0)$, and T is a fixed sampling time defined as $T = \tau_{k+1} - \tau_k$.

Based on this discrete system, an optimization problem is posed using the cost function described in Eq. 4, which minimizes the total amount of insulin and the deviation of glycemia from the desired target. In this case, the target is $\overline{y} = 90\,\text{mg/dl}$, which is a healthy value inside a region called normoglycemia ranging from 70 to 120 mg/dl. However, glycemia usually fluctuates inside the normoglycemia zone, and therefore, a slack variable δ is added to the function cost as optimization variable to permit such fluctuation. The cost function $V(y, u, \delta)$ read as:

$$V(y, u, \delta) = \sum_{i=1}^{H_p-1} ||y^\bullet(i) - \overline{y} + \delta||_Q^2 + \sum_{i=0}^{H_u-1} ||u^\bullet(i)||_R^2 \\ + ||y^\bullet(H_p) - \overline{y} + \delta||_S^2, \qquad (4)$$

where k indicates the actual time instant, H_p the prediction horizon, H_u the control horizon, and $|| \cdot ||_P^2$ denotes a quadratic term penalized with matrix P. The weighting matrices Q, R and S are chosen as strictly positive definite matrices of appropriate dimensions. The constrained optimization problem to be solved at time k by the MPC is given by.

$$\min_{u,\delta} V(y, u, \delta)$$

$$s.t.$$

$$\begin{aligned} &x^\bullet(0) = \hat{x}^\bullet, \ r(0) = r^\bullet, r^\bullet(i+1) = 0, && j \in I_{1:H_p-1}, \\ &x^\bullet(i+1) = A^\bullet x^\bullet(i) + B^\bullet u^\bullet(i) + B_r^\bullet r^\bullet(i) + E^\bullet, && j \in I_{0:H_p-1}, \\ &y^\bullet(i) = Cx^\bullet(i), \\ &u_{min} \leq u(i) \leq u_{max}, \ |\delta| \leq \delta_{max}, \end{aligned} \qquad (5)$$

where $r^\bullet \neq 0$ when the meal is announce, $u_{min} = 0$ is the lower bound of u, u_{max} is the upper bound settled as 7.5 U (since the insulin pump has a maximal rate of delivery of 1.5 U/min), and δ_{max} determines the length of the zone, which is measured around y. It should be notice that $x^\bullet(0) = \hat{x}^\bullet$ is the state at time k, which must be estimated since that only glycemia is measured. Therefore, the following estimator is included

$$\hat{x}^\bullet(k+1) = A^\bullet \hat{x}^\bullet(k) + B^\bullet u^\bullet(k) + B_r^\bullet(k) + E^\bullet + L(y^\bullet(k) - C\hat{x}^\bullet(k)). \qquad (6)$$

where matrix L is chosen so that the estimator is stable. Here, the standard Kalman filter algorithm is used to obtain the estimation. CGM noise was added to simulations using the description in [13].

3.1   Event-Trigger Scheme and Constraints to Handle Limited Resources

The artificial pancreas is envisioned to be implemented in embedded systems working in portable devices with limited life battery, limited amount of insulin, and limited computing capacity (specially relevant when control-estimation algorithms become more complex). Therefore, the control algorithms must incorporate additional features to extent to the maximum the battery life and the insulin reservoir.

In this paper, an event trigger scheme and two constraints are added to the MPC formulation 5 to take into account the limited resources.

Firstly, the event-trigger feature is incorporated to decide if the MPC problem must be solved at a time instant k. This constraint will help to save power because it is not necessary to solve the optimization problem in each time instant to achieve the control goals which allow the device to operate for more time and give the patient greater clearance to recharge the battery. The idea is to use the predicted sequence of controls already computed in the precedent time instant. The generation of this event is based on the difference between the output prediction $\tilde{y}$ and the actual measured output [14]. The MPC problem is solved when this difference is greater than some tolerance ϵ or when the predicted control sequence is exhausted, that is

$$\|y(k) - \tilde{y}(k)\| \geq \epsilon \quad or \quad k \geq k_l + H_u. \tag{7}$$

with k_l the initial time instant of the actual predicted control sequence. Along with the event-trigger strategy, the first constraint added accounts for the battery life of the portable device. It will become active when the remaining battery life falls below to the 15% of the total energy battery, and it read as

$$\sum_{i=1}^{H_u} \alpha u^{\bullet}(i) \leq W_{min} - W_{act} - W_{proc}. \tag{8}$$

The left part of Eq. 8, i.e. $\sum_{i=1}^{H_u} \alpha u_i^{\bullet}$, is the projection of the energy system consumption due to insulin injection for the control horizon H_u. It is assumed that the portable device works using a stepper motor with a gearbox. The coefficient α defines the relationship between the necessary steps of the motor to inject an specific insulin amount, i.e. it defines the energy consumption W (mWh) of the stepper motor to apply one unit of insulin (U).

In the right part of Eq. 8, the term W_{proc} denotes the energy consumption due to processor computations to generate the insulin dose at time k. It is assumed that the time (t^*) to find the solution of the optimization problem is the same in all time instants k, and therefore, the value of $W_{proc} = W_p t^*$ results constant, where W_p is the energy consumed by the processor at each time k.

The term W_{act} is the total energy consumption of the battery at time instant k, which is calculated as the total energy available in the battery (mAh) minus a constant consumption due to the basic functioning of the embedded system multiplied for the sampling time, and minus the energy consumed by generating the control action at time k and the application of such dose by the portable device.

Finally, the term W_{min} represents the minimal battery life safe value that can be reached during the horizon prediction Hp, considering the basic consumption of the embedded system and the control computation in the prediction horizon.

The second constraint added attempts to prolong the insulin supply and is activated depending on insulin consumption. Normally, the insulin used in treatments is a short-acting insulin called U-100, and each reservoir contains 300 units. The constraint will become active when the injected insulin reaches a specified percentage, and it is incorporated into the MPC formulation by changing the value of the upper bound u_{max}. This variable is changed to the 3% of its nominal value when the insulin consumption reaches the 80% of its full capacity (i.e., 240 U), and it is changed to 2% when reaches 90%.

In summary, the new event trigger MPC to solve at each time k is given by

$$\textbf{If } |y(k) - \tilde{y}(k)| \leq \epsilon \ \textbf{ or } \ k \geq k_l + H_u \ \textbf{ then } \ \textbf{solve}$$

$$\min_{u,\delta} \ V(y, u, \delta)$$
$$s.t.$$

$$
\begin{aligned}
&x^\bullet(0) = \hat{x}^\bullet, \ r(0) = r^\bullet, r^\bullet(i+1) = 0, && j \in I_{1:H_p-1}, \\
&x^\bullet(i+1) = A^\bullet x^\bullet(i) + B^\bullet u^\bullet(i) + B_r^\bullet r^\bullet(i) + E^\bullet, && j \in I_{0:H_p-1}, \\
&y^\bullet(i) = Cx^\bullet(i), \\
&u_{min} \leq u^\bullet(i) \leq u_{max}, \ |\delta| \leq \delta_{max}, \\
&\textbf{if } insulinsupply \leq 20\% \ \textbf{then} \\
&u_{max} = 0.03u_{max}, \\
&\textbf{else } \ \textbf{if } insulinsupply \leq 10\% \ \textbf{then} \\
&u_{max} = 0.02u_{max}, \\
&\textbf{if } batterylife \leq 15\% \ \textbf{then} \\
&\alpha \sum_{i=1}^{H_u} u^\bullet(i) \leq W_{min} - W_{act} - W_{proc}.
\end{aligned}
\tag{9}
$$

4   Results and Discussion

This paper considered specific hardware elements, although the performance was assessed only by simulation. It is understood that the portable device is equipped with a Raspberry Pi 3 B embedded system, a micro stepper reduction motor with a gearbox generating 30 rpm maximum, and a 6800 mAh–capacity lithium-ion polymer battery. The energy consumption measurements of the embedded system at rest and processing were taken off-line with the "Gravity: I2C Digital Wattmeter" sensor. Based on these elements, the energy consumption terms of the new constraints resulted as follows $\alpha = (1657.22051 \, step/U)$ $(0.01333 \, mWh/step) \approx 22.0907 \, mWh/U$, $G_{proc} = (600 * 2.7833 \times 10^{-4} * H_u) \approx 1.7$ mWh, and $W_{act} = 1500 * 0.083333$ mWh.

The sampling time was chosen as $T = 5$ min, and the controller tuning parameters used for the application were: $H_p = 80$, $H_u = 10$, $Q = 100$, $R = 1 \times 10^5$, $S = 1 \times 10^5$. The reference was chosen as 90 mg/dl, and $\delta_{max} = 10$. The simulation time was 26 h, and the total available insulin units were assumed to be 43 U. The initial glycemia was taken as $x_1(0) = 180$ mg/dl, and three meal intakes were considered at 7am with 51 g, at 12 pm with 73 g, and at 7 pm with 70 g.

The performance of the new strategy was evaluated by the following metrics: i) the consumed insulin units, ii) the energy consumed, iii) the state of glycemia, and iv) the times that the optimization problem was solved.

To assess the new proposal's performance and the effect of each constraint, four simulations were carried out for the simulation scenario described above keeping the same tuning. The first one evaluated only the effect of the ET strategy given by 9, the second one explored the energy consumption constraint, the third one evaluated the insulin consumption constraint, and the last one the complete strategy. In all cases, the results were compared against the standard MPC given by Eq. 5.

In Fig. 1 is illustrated the first simulation for ϵ values ranging from zero (standard strategy) to 1.1. Both MPC formulations stabilize the patient with a similar performance and metrics, for instance, the insulin consumption was approximately 45.5 U for any value of ϵ. However, the total energy consumed was in the range of 1074.8 mAh ($\epsilon = 0$) and 768 mAh ($\epsilon = 1.2$) mAh, saving approximately 28% of energy. This is expected since that the optimization problem was computed only 183 times for $\epsilon = 1.1$, while 312 times for $\epsilon = 0$. However, hypoglycemia events occur more frequently when $\epsilon \geq 1.1$. Also, it was observed that for all values of ϵ, there are glycemia values above the hyperglycemia threshold, specially after the meal intakes. But, they were not considered as hyperglycemia events since they did not last more than 40 min.

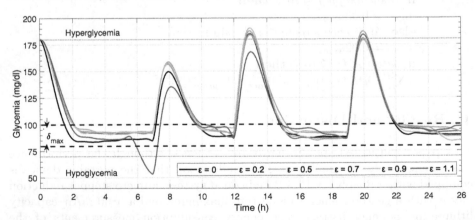

Fig. 1. Performance illustration of the event-trigger component for several ϵ values.

In Fig. 2, shows the MPC behavior including the energy consumption constraint. As it was designed, when the battery life was below 15%, the constraint 8 became active. As a result, smaller doses were computed achieving an energy saving of 4.5% and equivalently, the treatment was sustained for almost one more hour. After the battery's depletion, the time to reach the hyperglycemia zone was greater using the constraint, giving the patient more time to replace the battery and the insulin reservoir.

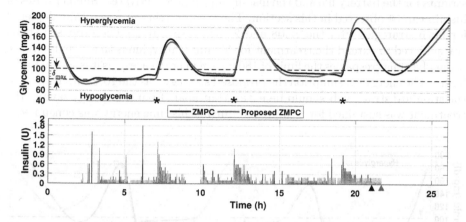

Fig. 2. Performance of the MPC including the battery energy constraint. The symbol * represents the meal intakes.

In Fig. 3, the effect of the restriction in the insulin supply is shown. It was assumed that the insulin reservoir had 43 units. The standard MPC (black line) and the one considering this constraint (blue line) exhausted the 43 units at 23.17 h and 24.42 h (marked in the figure with the triangle black and blue), respectively. Although the treatment was extended due to the constraint for 1 h and 15 min more, a non severe hyperglycemia episode occurred.

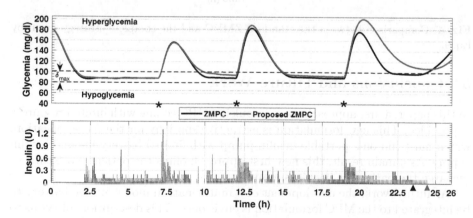

Fig. 3. Performance of the MPC considering the restriction for insulin supply activated at 80 and 90% of the total reservoir. The symbol * represents the meal intakes. (Color figure online)

Finally, the complete strategy's performance, i.e. the MPC including the ET component and the two constraints, is illustrated in Fig. 4. At the beginning, the standard MPC gets to steer the glycemia to the normal zone faster than the proposed strategy due to the fact that, the control is not updated using new measurements. After that, the performance of both strategies is similar, until the constraints for the battery life and the insulin supply were activated. Smaller doses of insulin can be observed in this section. The insulin reservoir was totally depleted for both strategies after the 22.08 and 23.5 h, respectively. The proposed strategy achieved to extend the treatment for 85 min (this value is the time difference when glycemia trespasses the limit of 180 mg/dl in both cases), as it is shown in the figure. The energy consumption the proposed strategy was the 10% with respect to the standard strategy. It should be notice that apart from this energy saving, the treatment was sustained for 85 min, and during this time energy was consumed.

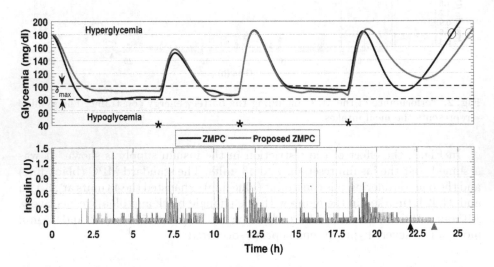

Fig. 4. Comparison between the standard ZMPC and the complete strategy given by Eq. 9.

5   Conclusions and Future Work

In this paper, a first approach to an impulsive MPC coping with limited resources is provided. This new formulation is attractive specially for the AP application, which must run on a portable insulin pump with limited battery life and insulin supply. As a main result, this new first approach offers the patient more time to recharge the battery or insulin supply.

As future work, the development of a mathematical model for the battery to be integrated to the MPC formulation is envisioned. This description allows us to optimize both, the glycemia goals and the consumption of energy in the device but further analysis is necessary. Also, designing of better event-trigger strategies for impulsive MPC in the framework of the artificial pancreas will be specially studied.

References

1. Gondhalekar, R., Dassau, E., Doyle, F.J.: Periodic zone-MPC with asymmetric costs for outpatient-ready safety of an artificial pancreas to treat type 1 diabetes. Automatica **71**, 237–246 (2016). https://doi.org/10.1016/j.automatica.2016.04.015
2. Toffanin, C., Aiello, E.M., Del Favero, S., Cobelli, C., Magni, L.: Multiple models for artificial pancreas predictions identified from free-living condition data: a proof of concept study. J. Process Control **77**, 29–37 (2019). https://doi.org/10.1016/j.jprocont.2019.03.007
3. van den Boom, T., De Schutter, B.: Optimization in Systems and Control. TUDelft 194 (2007)
4. Jung, C.A., Lee, S.J.: Design of automatic insulin injection system with Continuous Glucose Monitoring (CGM) signals. In: 3rd IEEE EMBS International Conference Biomed Heal Informatics, BHI 2016, pp. 102–105 (2016)
5. Colmegna, P., Garelli, F., De, B.H., Sánchez-peña, R.: Automatic regulatory control in type 1 diabetes without carbohydrate counting. Control. Eng. Pract. **74**(2017), 22–32 (2018). https://doi.org/10.1016/j.conengprac.2018.02.003
6. Pinsker, J.E., Lee, J.B., Dassau, E., et al.: Randomized crossover comparison of personalized MPC and PID control algorithms for the artificial pancreas. Diabetes Care **39**(7), 1135–1142 (2016). https://doi.org/10.2337/dc15-2344
7. Doyle, F.J., Huyett, L.M., Lee, J.B., Zisser, H.C., Dassau, E.: Closed-loop artificial pancreas systems: engineering the algorithms. Diabetes Care **37**(5), 1191–1197 (2014). https://doi.org/10.2337/dc13-2108
8. Radziuk, J.: The artificial pancreas. Diabetes **61**(9), 2221–2224 (2012). https://doi.org/10.2337/db12-0647
9. Benatti, S., et al.: A versatile embedded platform for EMG acquisition and gesture recognition. IEEE Trans. Biomed. Circuits Syst. **9**(5), 620–630 (2015)
10. Villa Tamayo, M.F., Caicedo Álvarez, M.A., Rivadeneira, P.S.: Handling parameter variations during the treatment of type 1 diabetes mellitus. In: Silico Results. Mathematical Problems in Engineering (2019). https://doi.org/10.1155/2019/2640405
11. Ruan, Y., Wilinska, M.E., Thabit, H., Hovorka, R.: Modeling day-to-day variability of glucose-insulin regulation over 12-week home use of closed-loop insulin delivery. IEEE Trans. Biomed. Eng. **64**(6), 1412–1419 (2017). https://doi.org/10.1109/TBME.2016.2590498
12. Rivadeneira, P.S., Gónzalez, A.H., Ferramosca, A.: Control strategies for non-zero regulation of impulsive linear systems. IEEE Trans. Autom. Control **63**(9), 2994–3001 (2018)
13. Vettoretti, M., Facchinetti, A., Sparacino, G., Cobelli, C.: Type-1 diabetes patient decision simulator for in silico testing safety and effectiveness of insulin treatments. IEEE Trans. Biomed. Eng. **65**(6), 1281–1290 (2018)
14. Chakrabarty, A., Zavitsanou, S., Doyle, F.J., III., Dassau, E.: Event-triggered model predictive control for embedded artificial pancreas systems. IEEE Trans. Biomed. Eng. **65**(3), 575–586 (2018)
15. Goez-Mora, J.E., Villa-Tamayo, M.F., Vallejo, M., Rivadeneira, P.S.: Performance analysis of different embedded systems and open-source optimization packages towards an impulsive MPC artificial pancreas. Front. Endocrinol. **12**(April), 1–15 (2021). https://doi.org/10.3389/fendo.2021.662348

Automation of Study Design Classification and Clinical Evidence Ranking for Health Technology Assessment of Medical Devices

Mabel Catalina Zapata[1]([✉]), Juan Guillermo Barreneche[1,2][iD],
and Jenny Kateryne Nieto Aristizabal[1,2][iD]

[1] Bioinstrumentation and Clinical Engineering Research Group - GIBIC,
Medellín, Colombia
mcatalina.zapata@udea.edu.co

[2] Bioengineering Department, Engineering Faculty, Universidad de Antioquia UdeA,
Calle 70 No. 52-21, Medellín, Colombia

Abstract. The Health Technology Assessment (HTA) is an important tool to support the health technology incorporation and selection process in a whole health system. In the specific case of medical devices, evaluation is a challenge due to factor such as rapid innovation, the learning curve of users, among others. In most Colombian hospitals, where the HTA process exists, the clinical evaluation (safety, effectiveness and efficacy) of health technology is based on data generated through literature searching (or literature systematic review) and clinical experience, this process can be complex and time-consuming. The reduction in workload, time, and risk of bias in the literature review process is possible through automation techniques and Natural Language Processing (NLP), not only in the medical domain but also where big volumes of text must be analyzed. This work aims to compare different techniques to classify Random Controlled Clinical Trials (RCT) and Systematic Reviews (SR), and to explore NLP methods for prioritizing title and abstracts screening for literature review in the HTA process. A ranking strategy was proposed and applied in an HTA report, the total articles for the screening process were halved. The best performance for the classification was obtained by using a Support Vector Machine, specifically, sensitivity and specificity were 0.98 and 0.91 (RCT) and 0.93 and 0.97 (SR). Even though a good search strategy is a fundamental part to obtain the clinical evidence for the assessment process, where screening task is almost as important, and prioritizing methods as proposed can reduce the processing time and the researchers can focus on the analysis of relevant information. In the last years, many efforts have been made to guide the good practices in clinical studies reports and researchers have been receptive but there are still publications with unclear study design, in which the automatic classification can lighten this task for the review process.

Keywords: Health technology assessment · Natural language processing · Medical devices · Systematic review · Random controlled trial

J. C. Figueroa-García et al. (Eds.): WEA 2021, CCIS 1431, pp. 190–201, 2021.
https://doi.org/10.1007/978-3-030-86702-7_17

1   Introduction

The Health Technology Assessment glossary defines the HTA as "the systematic evaluation of the properties and effects of health technology, addressing the direct and intended effects of this technology, as well as its indirect and unintended consequences, and aimed mainly at informing decision making regarding health technologies" [1]. The hospital-based (HB) HTA means performing HTA activities tailored to the hospital context to support decision-making on investment and implementation of new health technologies. It can be carried out by a team of hospital professionals or external experts [2]. The HB-HTA brings some benefits for institutions like providing scientific evidence to support both clinical practice and decision-making management in hospitals [3]. Also, to adopt the most suitable technology according to local criteria like patients, organizational structure, and financial capacity for acquisition. For the medical device context, the product lifecycle, clinical evaluation, user issues, costs, and economic evaluation make it necessary a different approach to developing the right assessment [4]. Furthermore, the HTA in the hospital context helps to achieve the standards of accreditation of the Joint Commission and Colombian Technical Standards and Certification Institute for the Accreditation of Healthcare Organization [5].

The HTA process can be developed over two methodologies, primary data, and secondary data. The first one denotes the data obtained from clinical studies like clinical trials, observational studies, and diagnostic accuracy studies. Secondary data refers to evidence obtained from primary studies or research like reviews, reports, scientific papers, and among others [6]. In most Colombian hospitals, the decision-making is based on HTA from secondary data, although HTA is a low disseminated practice in the country. A central part of this process is the systematic review of clinical evidence which is time-consuming and depending on the clinical issue, it can be complex to gather evidence to make a decision [7,8]. The objective of a systematic review is to collect the best evidence and summarize the findings in order to respond to specific research questions. Clinical trials have been considered the gold standard evidence for HTA and other processes like Evidence-Based Medicine (EBM) practice, however, identifying previous systematics reviews from a specific topic is also important for HTA [9]. In 2015, was held the first meeting of the International Collaboration for the Automation of Systematic Reviews (ICASR) [7]. The present work shows that Natural Language Processing (NLP) and Machine Learning (ML) are useful tools to perform that automation [7,10,11].

NLP includes a wide variety of methodologies such as word counting, statistical analysis, Named Entity Recognition (NER), word embedding methods, among others. J. Marchall et al. [12] presented an approach based on N-grams of titles and abstracts of papers to identify Randomized Controlled Trials (RTC's). This work outperforms search filters, specifically the Publication Type (PT) tag for PubMed articles. It is important to note that PT filter is not always available for all articles and even other models have shown probably wrong PubMed tags for RTC [13]. N-grams strategy was also used by A. Cohen et al. [13], to automatically predict the risk of bias in RTC, those algorithms had the same performance as human reviewers on extracting text for risk of bias judgments. Encouraged by the results shown by K. Weinberger [14], to solve the problem about a large feature space, J. Marchall et al. used a hashing function, which maps texts to vectors of fixed dimensions.

In a systematic review, after applying a search strategy, it is necessary a study selection based initially on screening titles and abstracts versus the inclusion criteria to prioritize the most relevant studies [9]. Text mining techniques are commonly used for this purpose, in many studies, the features were represented with word counting techniques like Bag Of Words (BoW) and Term Frequency – Inverse Document Frequency (TF-IDF) [15]. TF-IDF is also used in other domains of NLP such as text sentiment classification [16], keywords extractions [17], and prioritizing of documents [18]. Nevertheless the methods based on word occurrence produce sparse matrices with a lot of zero elements which can reduce the performance of the algorithms. Regarding to semantic analysis, word embeddings methods have demonstrated better performance [19]. In 2018, Bidirectional Encoder Representation from Transformers (BERT) which uses attention mechanisms [20], become the State-Of-The-Art (SOTA) in several NLP applications [21]. This model uses WordPiece embeddings, which transforms words into predetermined fixed dimension vectors, the vocabulary is constituted by 30,522 tokens. Based on BERT, others models have been released on specific domains, such as SciBERT and BioBERT. The first uses the same architecture but it is trained with a biomedical domain corpus (1.14 M of papers, 18% computer science – 82% biomedical), which have different embeddings for their scientific corpus, denominated SCIVOCAB [22]. BioBERT keeps BERT architecture and vocabulary but also changes the corpus and adds PubMed abstracts and PMC full-text abstracts. It improves performance in NER, relation extraction, and question answering [23]. This work aims to evaluate the automation of clinical trials and systematic review identification in the HTA process, and proposes an automated evidence ranking or prioritizing of references from the results of a PubMed search. It is illustrated in Fig. 1

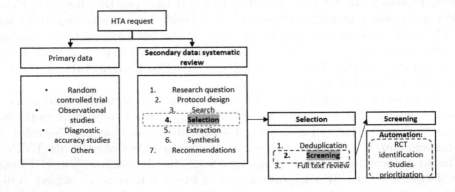

Fig. 1. Automatable tasks for HTA proposed in this work

Both tasks are based on the NLP methods for titles and abstracts. Suitable search strategies are not the interest of this paper. The structure of this document is as follows: Sect. 2 describes the database of collected articles, then, the used algorithms for text classification and techniques for prioritizing studies are presented. Section 3, 4 and 5 describe the results, discussion, and main conclusions, respectively.

2 Materials and Methods

2.1 Data Collection

Through a manual search, 49 reports of HTA were gathered and from the description of the clinical studies included in each of these, the database was raised. 523 clinical studies were collected from those reports, which evaluated medical devices intended to diagnose or treat some cardiovascular condition, within these are magnetic resonance imaging systems, left ventricular assist devices, ultrasound imaging technologies, etc. Technology, population, comparison, and outcomes assessed from each HTA report were extracted. Table 1 summarizes the data collected. Dataset was raise manually because HTA reports are not yet standardized, and there is not an updated repository for these.

Table 1. HTA reports and study design of studies included in the database

HTA reports	49
Included studies *	556
Included studies (unique)	523
Random Controlled Trials	143
Systematic reviews	97
Observational and diagnostic accuracy studies	283

*Some HTA reports included the same study to evaluate the technology of interest in each instance, respectively.

The time-frame for included studies were 1995 to 2015, language was restricted to English, and keywords for search were: Radiographic Fluoroscopic Systems, Angiography Interventional; Cardiovascular Scanning Systems, Ultrasonic, Cardiac; Intravascular Scanning Systems, Ultrasonic, Cardiac; Intravascular Magnetic Resonance imaging computed tomography scanners; Scanning Systems; Gamma-Camera; Positron emission tomography (PET); Surgical robotic systems; Electrocardiographs, Cardiac Electrophysiology. Those devices were chosen based on Cardiovascular and Stroke Endpoint Definitions for Clinical Trials [24].

2.2 Study Design Identification

Three different approaches for feature extraction were proposed, uni- and bigrams occurrence, BERT, and SciBERT embeddings from titles and abstracts.

Normally, a classification task based on word counting methods is not scalable because the algorithm will depend on the training vocabulary and each time a new word is presented to the system it will not be recognized. For this reason, the hashing trick is used for feature extraction, this method finds the token string name into a feature integer index mapping. Statistic features for BERT and SciBERT embeddings were computed through WEBERT [25], which are the mean, standard deviation, kurtosis, skewness, minimum and maximum values for each neuron of models.

For the classification task, the Support Vector Machine (SVM) algorithm seeks a hyperplane that separates different classes, this hyperplane is chosen in order to maximize the distance between decision boundary and all of the samples. The hyperplane is a subspace of dimension $n - 1$, where n is the number of features that represent the classes, in this case, $n = 4608$ for BERT and SciBERT embeddings (mean, standard deviation, kurtosis, skewness, minimum and maximum values for 768 neurons) and $n = 2^{20}$ for N-grams (with hashing trick). In most cases, data are not completely separable, so a penalty is added to misclassified samples.

The performance evaluation metrics used were precision, recall, specificity, and area under the receiver operating characteristic curve or ROC curve.

These performance metrics are defined as follows:

$$Recall(Sensitivity) = \frac{TruePositive}{TruePositive + FalseNegative} \tag{1}$$

$$Precision = \frac{TruePositive}{TruePositive + FalsePositive} \tag{2}$$

$$Specificity = \frac{TrueNegative}{TrueNegative + FalsePositive} \tag{3}$$

The ROC curve plots the True Positive Rate (Recall) vs False Positive Rate (1- Specificity). In classification, a perfect model will have an area under the ROC curve (AUC) of 1, and a smaller value of AUC means the classification does not have any prediction capability.

2.3 Clinical Evidence Ranking

The first filter applied in systematic reviews can be a high workload process due to the amount of data obtained, to classify data into included or excluded studies is even hard for review experts. In this work we propose a different method to reduce the workload, it consists of ranking (prioritization) the evidence so that the firsts n documents contain the major amount of information (or most relevant information) to make a decision. In this way, it would not be necessary to screen the total documents because the last positions are likely to be excluded from studies. The number n will depend on the total data collected.

The Term Frequency – Inverse Document Frequency (TF-IDF) is a measure related to the occurrence of a word or term in an entire text, on information retrieval this weight is commonly associated with the importance of that word in the document collection. This weight $W_{(x,y)}$ is obtained applying:

$$W_{(x,y)} = tf_{(x,y)} * log\frac{N}{df_x},\tag{4}$$

$tf_{(x,y)}$: frequency of x in y
df_x: documents with the term x
N: Total documents

If stopwords are not removed, their weight will be low and high values will be representing the less common or most important terms.

Cosine Similarity is another technique used to compare documents; on information retrieval, it could rank documents regarding a vector of query words. Documents are compared with term frequency vectors (terms can be N-grams of one, two, or more words). Cosine similarity is given by:

$$sim(x, y) = (x.y)/|x||y|\tag{5}$$

Where, x, y are vectors for comparison and, $|x|$ is the Euclidean norm of vector $x = (x_1, x_2, \ldots, x_p)$, defined as $\sqrt{(x_1^2 + x_2^2 + \ldots, +x_p^2)}$

The sim(x,y) is the cosine of the angle between vectors x and y. A 0 value indicates a 90° angle between vectors, which means dissimilarity and 1 indicates 0° angle (or parallels vectors) and the major similarity possible.

For this approach, the search strategy of the HTA report: Use of Biventricular Pacing in Atrioventricular Heart Block [26] was reproduced. Then the ranking based on TF-IDF and Cosine similarity was made and compared with the included studies in the report.

3   Results

3.1   Study Design Identification Results

The training-testing data balance was 70%–30% for all experiments in SVM and DT. The RTC class was constituted by 143 samples and 143 samples were randomly selected from the other studies (in order to balance the classes). In order to get the best performance the parameters kernel, C, and gamma (for non-linear kernel) were tuned in the SVM case. Depth, samples required to split, and minimum numbers to be a leaf node were tuned in the DT case. The final parameters used in both cases are illustrated in Table 2.

The classification was performed using features extracted from titles and abstracts of the documents; uni- and bi-grams occurrence, BERT and SciBERT embeddings were used and evaluated, and each algorithm was launch for three methodologies. The feature vectors were normalized using the 'L2' norm. Stopwords removal was made in the hashing trick case but not for BERT and SciBERT embeddings. The best results for Random Controlled trials (RTC) classification are shown in Table 3.

Table 2. SVM and DT tuned parameters

Algorithm	Parameter	Arrangement
SVM	Kernel	Linear, radial basis function*, polynomial
	C	1, 10, 100*, 1000
	Gamma	1e-2*, 1e-3, 1e-4
	Degree of freedom	1, 2, 3, 4, 5
DT	Depth	8*, 10, 12, 16
	Samples required to split	2*, 3, 4, 5
	Minimum numbers to be a leaf node	1*, 2, 5, 10, 15

* Better performance for SVM RCT classification

Table 3. Random Controlled trials classification results

	SVM + BERT	SVM + SciBERT	SVM + Hashing vec	DT + BERT	DT + SciBERT	DT +Hashing vec	DT + Hashing vec
Accuracy (mean) (std)	0.922 0.027	0.861 0.046	0.926 0.023	0.776 0.040	0.761 0.048	0.897 0.047	0.856 0.036
Precision (mean) (std)	0.866 0.038	0.841 0.054	0.906 0.041	0.776 0.055	0.750 0.060	0.881 0.058	0.882 0.064
Recall (Sensitivity) (mean) (std)	0.951 0.021	0.891 0.044	**0.951 0.013**	0.774 0.051	0.784 0.056	0.912 0.049	0.822 0.040
Specificity (mean) (std)	0.866 0.038	0.841 0.054	**0.906 0.041**	0.776 0.055	0.750 0.060	0.881 0.047	0.881 0.064
AUC (mean) (std)	0.972 0.014	0.923 0.013	**0.974 0.014**	0.776 0.040	0.762 0.048	0.897 0.047	0.855 0.036

Best results in bold

The SR class was constituted by 97 samples and 97 samples were randomly selected from the other studies. The best results for the Systematic Review (SR) classification are shown in Table 4.

3.2   Clinical Evidence Ranking Results

In order to expose the final results about the ranking obtained, a HTA report was selected, "use of biventricular pacing in atrioventricular heart block" [26]. In that report the PICO strategy summarized as follow; Patients: Patients with a third-degree heart block, Intervention: Biventricular pacing, Comparison: Right ventricular pacing, Outcomes: LV function and ventricular dyssynchrony, quality of life score and 6 min walk test, mortality or hospitalization. The search strategy used was: (Biventricular pacing [Title/Abstract] OR cardiac re-synchronization therapy [Title/Abstract] OR biventricular pacemaker [Title/Abstract]) AND (heart block[Title/Abstract] OR AV block [Title/Abstract] OR atrioventricular block[Title/Abstract] OR AV-block [Title/Abstract] OR bradycardia [Title/Abstract]). 367 articles were collected and finally 8 were included.

Table 4. Systematic review classification results

	SVM + BERT	SVM + SciBERT	SVM + Hashing vec	DT + BERT	DT + SciBERT	DT + Hashing vec
Accuracy (mean) (std)	0.934 0.034	0.852 0.026	0.911 0.009	0.757 0.052	0.794 0.049	0.856 0.036
Precision (mean) (std)	0.905 0.060	0.881 0.043	0.988 0.018	0.751 0.070	0.823 0.076	0.882 0.064
Recall (Sensitivity) (mean) (std)	**0.976** **0.019**	0.812 0.035	0.829 0.008	0.767 0.077	0.750 0.047	0.822 0.040
Specificity (mean) (std)	0.905 0.060	0.881 0.043	**0.988** **0.018**	0.751 0.070	0.823 0.076	0.881 0.064
AUC (mean) (std)	**0.983** **0.011**	0.930 0.023	0.977 0.013	0.757 0.052	0.793 0.048	0.855 0.036

Best results in bold

To establish a prioritization of the 367 articles, a ranking based on the weighted sum of TF-IDF index is proposed. The words were chosen based on the technology assessed: biventricular pacing, and primary outcome measured: Left Ventricular Fraction, three different weights vectors were proposed. These parameters are illustrated in Table 5.

Table 5. Parameters used for evidence prioritization

	Key terms	Vector w
1	Random	NA
2	'biventricular pacing', 'left ventricular', 'ventricular ejection', 'ejection fraction'	[0.25, 0.25, 0.25, 0.25]
3	'biventricular', 'left', 'ejection', 'fraction'	[0.7, 0.05, 0.2, 0.05]
4	'biventricular pacing', 'left ventricular', 'ventricular ejection', 'ejection fraction'	[0.5, 0.125, 0.25, 0.125]

Once the sum is obtained, the articles are ranked in descending order. Figure 2 shows the percentage of documents with clinical evidence that is necessary screening to analyze the most relevant information in this HTA report, according to words and vectors summarized in Table 5. Where the relevant information refers to the included studies of the HTA report, i.e. 8 documents for this case.

To compare the TF-IDF ranking presented above, the cosine similarity between 367 articles was calculated. There were no significant reductions in the percentage of articles to screening.

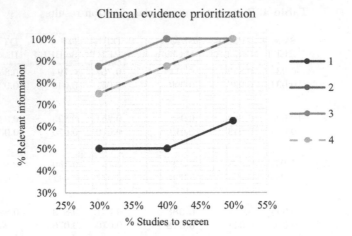

Fig. 2. Results of clinical evidence prioritization based on TF-IDF and key terms

4   Discussion

From Table 4 and Table 5, it is observed that SVM classifier achieved better classification than DT algorithm, for both RCT and SR studies (AUC = 0.983 and 0.974). Regarding RCT, the hashing trick got better performance than embeddings, SciBERT was slightly better than the BERT, it could be due to the specific medical domain vocabulary was used to train the SciBERT model. Although transformers are the SOTA for NLP, it is a more powerful tool for understanding tasks like question-answering and semantic textual similarity, in the classification task presented in this study. The results showed that classical methods are a good strategy for feature extraction. Compared to I. J. Marchall [11], who uses the Clinical Hedges dataset (49025 articles from the years 2000 and 2001), this work (with 523 articles, from 1995 to 2015) presents really good results. They stated that standardized and explicit article reports according to CONSORT guidelines (updated in 2010) [27], could improve the performance of ML and traditional filters. The present work with articles published between 1995 and 2015 probes this theory, given that similar results have been reproduced with significantly fewer samples.

In this work not only is presented the automatic identification of RCT but also SR, it is important because these studies can replace the ongoing review or represent the analysis of several RCT on the topic of interest. This two design are the most important due to its methodological rigor.

Figure 2 shows that the three proposals (2, 3, and 4) for important words and values of w achieved to prioritize the relevant information in a way that half of the studies retrieved summarizes the total information to 'make a decision'. The line 1 represents the relevant information (62,5%) in the half of documents in random order, i.e. the order given by PubMed, there is a significant difference with the results obtained for the proposed ranking (lines 2, 3 and 4). With these results, the good match between a suitable search strategy and a prioritizing method is probed.

Although the literature review tends to be a standardized process, for HTA is not always developed with the same rigor, so that in a HTA process the relevant evidence depends on parameters like patients, intervention (technology), comparison, and outcomes, thus the necessary evidence to make a decision will depend on a specific research questions and researchers' judgments. Then, like is proposed by G. Kontonatsios [11], the review can be stopped when researchers decided it, according to the low likelihood that the remainder studies represent relevant information or the time is over to make a decision. Cosine similarity measure indicates that the 367 articles gathered have close features, and differences between included and not included studies are not significant. According to this measure, does not make sense to find a method which predicts or ranks exactly the included studies, at least for this specific task. For HTA of medical devices is important to choose the right keywords based mainly on intervention (focused on technology) of interest to obtain a good prioritization of references in the search stage.

5 Conclusions

The SOTA on NLP and ML has shown there are sophisticated algorithms that generally have a high computational cost and do not always represent better performance. Classical methods such as TF-IDF, cosine similarity measure, and n-grams occurrence can provide solutions to improve tasks like a literature review. Even though a good search strategy is a fundamental part to obtain the clinical evidence for the assessment process, screening task is also important. A good strategy for prioritizing references was presented, it could reduce screening and the researchers could focus on the relevant information. In this approach the vector w is given by the researcher's experience and HTA report data, this method is proposed to support a process and not for replace the human criteria. Future work aims to reproduce search strategies from others HTA reports and measure the performance of the method proposed. In this way, it could be possible to find a pattern in workload reduction and to enhance the use of this kind of tools in HTA.

In recent years, many efforts have been made to guide the good practices in clinical studies reports and researchers have been receptive, but there are still many documents with unclear study design, at this point, the automatic classification can lighten this task in the review process. Finally, NLP is a powerful tool to help clinical stakeholders in clinical evidence analysis and reduce time spent in non-relevant information review. To keep growing the dataset will allow dealing with algorithms such as neural networks and could improve the current results.

Acknowledgements. The authors would like to thank to Bioinstrumentation and Clinical Engineering Research Group (GIBIC).

References

1. HTAi INAHTA: Health technology assessment (2020)
2. Lach, K., et al. The AdHopHTA Handbook, p. 222 (2015)
3. Cicchetti, A., Marchetti, M., Dibidino, R., Corio, M.: Hospital based health technology assessment. worldwide survey. HTAi Interest Sub-Group Hospital Based HTA 2008 (2008)
4. Polisena, J., et al.: Health technology assessment methods guidelines for medical devices: how can we address the gaps? The International Federation of Medical and Biological Engineering perspective. Int. J. Technol. Assess. Health Care **34**(3), 276–289 (2018)
5. Gómez, J.G.B., Castro, A.E.M., Ruiz, L.B., Arango, M.A.T.: La evaluación de nuevas tecnologías en salud en hospitales: revisión narrativa. Medicina UPB **35**(2), 120–134 (2017)
6. Barreto, J.O., Toma, T.S., Pereira, T., Vanni, T.: Síntese de evidências para políticas de saúde (2017)
7. Beller, E., et al.: Making progress with the automation of systematic reviews: principles of the international collaboration for the automation of systematic reviews (ICASR), pp. 1–7 (2018)
8. Rathbone, J.: Automating systematic reviews. Centre for Research in Evidence-Based Practice, May 2017
9. Centre for Reviews and Dissemination: Cdrs guiance for undertaking reviews in health care. Centre for Reviews and Dissemination, University of York (479), pp. 6–16 (2009)
10. O'Mara-Eves, A., McNaught, J., Thomas, J., Miwa, M., Ananiadou, S.: Using text mining for study identification in systematic reviews: a systematic review of current approaches. Syst. Rev. J., 1–22 (2016)
11. Kontonatsios, G.: A semi-supervised approach using label propagation to support citation screening. J. Biomed. Inf. **72**, 67–76 (2017)
12. Marshall, I.J., Noel, A., Joël, S., James, K., Byron, T.: Machine learning for identifying randomized controlled trials: an evaluation and practitioner's guide **479**, 602–614 (2018)
13. Cohen, A.M., et al.: Automated confidence ranked classification of randomized controlled trial articles: an aid to evidence-based medicine. J. Am. Med. Inform. Assoc. **22**(3), 707–717 (2015)
14. Weinberger, K., Attenberg, J., Org, A.S.: Feature hashing for large scale multitask learning (2009)
15. Olorisade, B.K., de Quincey, E., Brereton, P., Andras, P.: A critical analysis of studies that address the use of text mining for citation screening in systematic reviews (2016)
16. Das, B.: An improved text sentiment classification model using TF-IDF and next word negation (2018)
17. Science, C., Engineering, S.: Text classification using keyword extraction technique **3**(12), 734–740 (2013)
18. Qaiser, S., Ali, R.: Text mining: use of TF-IDF to examine the relevance of words to documents text mining: use of TF-IDF to examine the relevance of words to documents, July 2018
19. Manning, C., Pennington, J., Socher, R.: Glove: global vectors for word representation Jeffrey **31**(6), 682–687 (2017)

20. Vaswani, A., et al.: Attention is all you need. In: Advances in Neural Information Processing Systems, (NIPS), pp. 5999–6009, December 2017
21. Devlin, J., Chang, M.-W., Lee, K., Toutanova, K.: BERT: pre-training of deep bidirectional transformers for language understanding (MLM) (2018)
22. Beltagy, I., Lo, K., Cohan, A.: SciBERT: a pretrained language model for scientific text, pp. 3613–3618 (2019)
23. Lee, J.: BioBERT: a pre-trained biomedical language representation model for biomedical text mining. Bioinformatics **36**(4), 1234–1240 (2020)
24. Hicks, K.A., et al.: 2017 cardiovascular and stroke endpoint definitions for clinical trials. Circulation **137**(9), 961–972 (2018)
25. Perez-Toro, P.A.: Word embeddings using BERT. (Version V0.0.1) (2020)
26. Saab, L., Suarthana, E., Almeida, N., Dendukuri, N.: Use of biventricular pacing in atrioventricular heart block (2016)
27. Moher, D., et al.: Consort 2010 explanation and elaboration: updated guidelines for reporting parallel group randomised trials. BMJ (Clinical research ed.) **340** (2010)

Online System Based on Microservices for Rapid Diagnostic of Pathogenic Bacteria in Seafood from Biogenic Amines Biosensors

Juan M. Álvarez Q.[1]([✉])[iD], José I. García M.[2], and John A. Sanabria O.[1][iD]

[1] Escuela de Ingeniería de Sistemas, Universidad del Valle,
Cali, Valle del Cauca, Colombia
{juan.alvarez.quinonez,John.sanabria}@correounivalle.edu.co
[2] Escuela de Ingeniería de Mecánica, Universidad del Valle,
Cali, Valle del Cauca, Colombia
jose.i.garcia@correounivalle.edu.co

Abstract. Currently, the seafood industry demands strict quality standards for the acceptance of products in international markets. In this context, rapid detection of pathogenic bacteria is a pressing need in the fishing industry. In this sense, this work integrates the advances of information and communications technologies to facilitate the management of information on the concentration of pathogenic bacteria in sea products that reach a fishing port. For this, the proposed system integrates a series of low-cost biosensors with a distributed information architecture based on microservices. To achieve the results, initially, several pathogen bacteria detection systems were analyzed. Subsequently, both the relevant information variables were defined from a biogenic amines biosensor selected as the modes of operation of the proposed system. Then, the structure of the online information system and the characteristics of the interfaces were defined considering different types of users. To follow, a dynamic model was generated to show the evolution of the states of the system. Finally, the proposals were evaluated, showing the advantages from the functional, economic, and use potential uses.

Keywords: Fishing industry · Pathogenic bacteria · Biogenic amines biosensor

1 Introduction

Biogenic amines (BAs) are organic nitrogen compounds of important significance as quality/safety index for the food industry due to their association with microbial activity (e.g. food spoilage) and toxicological considerations in public health [1]. Particularly, rapid assessment of BAs is an important technological need for handcrafted and small-scale fisheries located in undeveloped regions of the world -currently comprising nearly 48 million tons of annual catch worldwide,

© Springer Nature Switzerland AG 2021
J. C. Figueroa-García et al. (Eds.): WEA 2021, CCIS 1431, pp. 202–212, 2021.
https://doi.org/10.1007/978-3-030-86702-7_18

which lack sufficient data-based decision-making support to optimize management along the food continuum [2,3].

Biosensors for food quality assessment is a growing field with promising potential for rapid and low-cost detection of molecular biomarkers [4,5]. Even though performance characteristics of these type of devices is often not comparable with standard laboratory techniques (such as HPLC, GC, and PCR), they offer competitive advantages in the context of developing countries, including the possibility for local manufacturing, low-cost, portability, and user-friendly operation. Biosensors impact can be potentiated through coupling with online data-management systems, which turns into a powerful tool for generating big data with high spatial and temporal resolution. Generated data can be further integrated with different stakeholder information-frameworks to support an evidence-based decision.

In this sense, currently, software engineering suggests a way to develop applications through micro-services, which are automated and independently deployed software items that communicate with each other through message exchange [6]. This application construction offers advantages such as the reduction in external dependencies usage and the increased speed on design, development, and release of services. In the food industry, there have been some outstanding software tools, like "A user-friendly general-purpose predictive software package for food safety" [7] and MicroHibro [8]. This evidence shows that the use of microservices is a trending approach in application development.

Considering different conditions of seafood production, the design of the diagnostic tools is extremely useful for estimation of quality and for identifying human health risks, or another application. Authors as [9] present a technological integration towards the traceability of quality assurance in seafood in points of gathering and recollection. This value increase permits offer products and services with a high-quality index, generating competitive advantage. [10] identifies the advantages of technology in the industry of capture, consumption, and commercialization of seafood, especially in the identification and traceability of factors that assure sustainable development. Likewise [11–13] identify an advantage of this integration aimed to increase the quality of minimizing health risks. [14] analyze the management processes on the value chain in sea products. Indicating information management as a relevant trait [15].

To face the biggest world health calamity, [16] describes the COVID-19's impact on society and the environment, and the plausible ways to control the disease, emphasizing on the generation of means to improve the relationship between humans and nature. In this sense, [17] presents a model for bacterial risk due to spray transmission on the seafood distribution point. For this, the information system was related to data about viral dissemination, dispersion, airborne deposition, biological decomposition, pulmonary deposition, and por sonal infection. This evidences the advantages of the usage of microservices on the seafood information management system. Specifically, usage of online systems and cloud architectures has been increased, due to an increase in sanitary restrictions and quarantines. This research is presented a microservice-biosensors integration aim to reduce the mobility of people taking and analyzing samples. As depictec in Fig. 1, this system is a plausible tool for quality food engineers working from their homes. Herein, we present an innovative technological synergy between a recently developed low-cost biosensor for BAs detection [18] with a microservices based data-management system with specific capabilities for: (i) compiling biosensor's output, (ii) computing biosensor´s performance, (iii) estimating BAs levels in fish samples, (iii) comparing BAs levels with regulatory frameworks of the food industry and public health, (iv) informing the user, and (v) keeping records in the cloud.

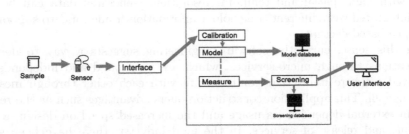

Fig. 1. Proposed system overview

The most relevant result of this approach was to develop a systematic infrastructure to ease the access of information regarding the quality of a seafood product, enabling to automate the assessment process and reducing the time and costs for the producers.

2   Related Works

The growing demand for food and public health requires open source solutions. As stated by [5] the standard microbiological methods for testing require long times. This makes biosensors a promising alternative for screening harming bacteria in food samples. Further iterations on biosensor technology [4,18] which use some local sourced and low cost materials, deliver an affordable solution to gather data which can be used to infer information regarding the safety and quality of food to consumers who lack access to chemical testing laboratories.

On the other hand, microservices architectures are a novel manner for optimize the software development and deployment using Fine-grained service interfaces, independently deployable services and RESTful resources [19].

This work is an adaptation of the architecture presented on [20] in order to test the flexibility of the aforementioned architecture aimed deliver a software platform which can collect data from biosensors and return the condition assessment of the food sample.

3 Methodology Framework

The methodological procedure is derived from the works of García et al. [21] and Caratar et al. [22].This procedure is intended to build the proposed solution in a systematic way, as depicted in Fig. 2.

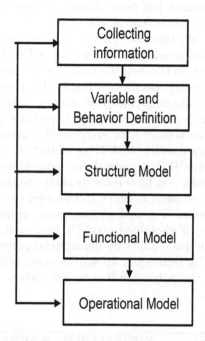

Fig. 2. Outline of methodological framework.

3.1 Collecting Information

In this stage, it was necessary to collect information related to the current system of attention to identify its behavior, mode of operation, resources, and interactions between them, parameters, and variables. For this purpose, it was considered a set of six types of detection targeting several pathogenic bacteria which are detailed in [4].

3.2 Variable and Behavior Definition

Considering the information gathered on the previous stage and the results on [5], which evidenced the use of BA biosensors for rapid detection of pathogenic bacteria in food samples, the selected variable for the study was the BA concentration. In addition, other information with the relation to geographic location and type of seafood was considered.

3.3   Structural Model

From the results from earlier steps, it was identified the technical resources, such as, biosensors fabrication, legal restrictions regarding to food conditions in different countries, potentials users, among others. This information allowed to define the system architecture and the user interface structure.

Once the model approach has been defined, a structural assessment is conducted to determine how to implement the system.

The working scheme of a biosensor involves a 3-step process: i) biorecognition; ii) transduction; iii) signal acquisition, is depicted on Fig. 3. In the biorecognition step, a molecular interaction between the target and a macromolecular structure on the sensor results in highly specific binding. In the transduction step, selective binding of the target produces a change in energy state of the system. Transduction can be inherent (such as a change in impedance due to antibody [Ab]–antigen binding in immunoassays), or engineered (cascade reactions involving Förster resonance energy transfer [FRET] as a function of nucleotide binding in polymerase chain reaction [PCR] or addition of exogenous reagents). Nanomaterials that enhance transduction have recently shown to significantly improve the performance of biosensors. Most research has focused on materials that improve electron or photon mobility (e.g. carbon nanotubes, graphene sheets, nanometals, metal oxides and other photocatalysts) [5]. Recent discoveries allow any lab to directly write conductive circuits on commercial polymers (polyimide) with a single laser setup. The technique, known as laser, scribed graphene (LSG), converts sp3 carbon in the polyimide film to sp2 carbon, which is the allotrope found in graphene [18].

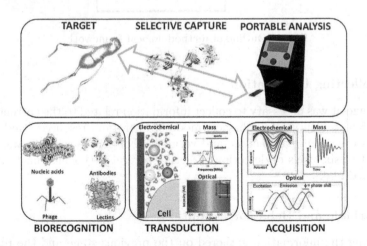

Fig. 3. Working scheme of biosensor.

Biosensors were fabricated via LSG using a low-cost apparatus and locally sourced materials, and compared to electrodes fabricated with analytical grade chemicals. Material analysis of LSG showed a stitched morphology, with an average LSG thickness of approximately 60 m. The type of copper used for metallization significantly affected the morphology and electrochemical properties of the nanoscale structure, which is not surprising. The mesotube structures formed with locally sourced copper material (from an agricultural store in Cali, Colombia) contained copper/iron alloys, as well as potassium/chloride crystals. Which deliver a good response to BA, specially histamine within 4–7 s.

3.4 Functional Model

The conceptual model definition, established the relations between the variables and available resources found previously, having in count the process to analyze a sample (depicted in Fig. 4), an automatization procedure was determined. Due to this procedure can be split in specific task, an approach in microservices were adopted.

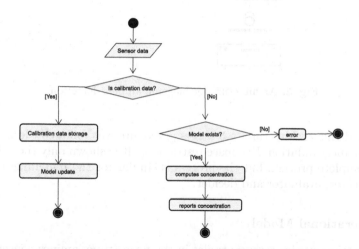

Fig. 4. Flowchart of the food sample evaluation process.

In this architecture the food samples are measured by a sensor and received by an observer microservice, and according to a Boolean variable it determines if the data goes to a calibration service or to the evaluation service. The calibration service takes the data of concentration and current as a time series and correlates them using a linear regression algorithm to generate the sensor model. The evaluation service uses the sensor model to compute the concentration and send the data to a decider service. The decider service suggests actions to do with the food under analysis based on the concentration and the regulations. The decision taken by the user interface service. Also, there is a storage service to keep the model parameters (determined by the calibration service) and the amine concentration regulations for a set of countries.

With the purpose of materialize the before mentioned data flow, it is proposed the architecture depicted in Fig. 5. Which is an adaptation of architecture proposed on [20].

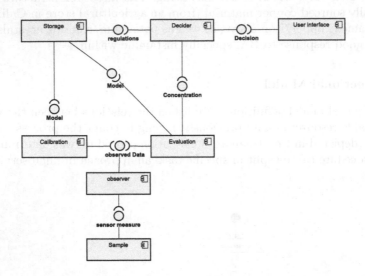

Fig. 5. Architecture for biogenic amines detection.

To build this architecture, a 3 stages procedure was followed: design, implementation and validation. For space restrictions, it is shown only the calibration service complete process, but the process is similar for the remaining microservices: observer, evaluator and decider.

3.5   Operational Model

The calibration service receives tuples in the form (time, amines concentration, current) and based on the knowledge of an expert and after a linear regression process it is converted to a linear polynomial which relates the amines concentration Vs current, additionally this service delivers the detection threshold and the saturation threshold. Those data are the detection model. The overview of the process is shown in the Fig. 6.

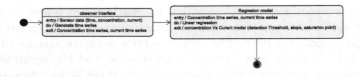

Fig. 6. Calibration microservice state machine.

Although microservices can be built in different programming languages, Python was chosen because the simplicity of the syntax, also it has several tools and libraries to simplify processes like data treatment [23], database connections [24] and interfaces to expose and consume data [25]. With the purpose of keep a light communication channel between observer, calibration and evaluation services, those services use the MQTT protocol. This microservice connects to a MQTT channel ("fresh/sensor"), and anytime that a message arrives it is parsed and computed into a concentration mode.

4   Results

To validate the information, it was conducted a series of sensor calibration experiments. The data was processed on a spreadsheet and on the calibration microservices. Figure 7 shows the comparison between experimental data (blue line) and calibration microservices model (red line). The comparison shows that microservices model must be adjusted to concentration spikes produced due to the increase of concentration.

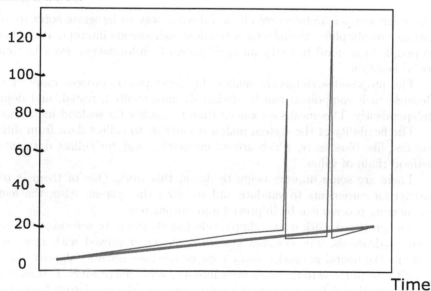

Fig. 7. Result comparison between experimental data and system computed data (Color figure online).

Biosensors deliver electrical signals related to the biogenic amines' concentrations in food samples, as is detailed in [18]. Such data is received by a classification service that discriminates if the data is a calibration data or a measure.

In the first case, the data goes to a calibration which produces an evaluation model. In the second case, according to the evaluation model, the data are received by an evaluation service that computes the concentration of the biogenic amine. The results of the evaluation are sent to a decision aid service which determines the aptitude of the evaluated sample. Lastly, all data is stored by a registry service.

Given the characteristics of the process, it can be separated into specific tasks. Each task is performed by a microservice. Thus, the proposed solution is a hierarchical, microservices based architecture. In the lower level, there is a data classifier, which determines if the incoming data corresponds to calibration or to a measure. The second level is composed by a calibration microservice, which processes the calibration data to produce a model for each sensor, and the data evaluator, which determines the amines level of a sample based on the model. The third level is an interpreter service which according to the amines level and the regulations it decides if the sample is suited to be consumed, if it needs some preserving process or if is not suitable for human consumption. And the top layer has the storage service.

5   Discussion

The microservices architecture offers a flexible way to integrate software applications and simplifies the interfaces to allow components interoperation. Letting to people in seafood industry an agile access to information, even in times of social isolation.

The proposed architecture makes the development process more efficient. Because each component can be designed, implemented, tested, and deployed independently. This means a reduced time to market for seafood industries.

The flexibility of the system makes it suitable to collect data from different sources, like biosensors, which are an interesting way for collect data into the seafood chain of value.

There are some improvements to do on this work. One of them is to run further measurements to validate and stabilize the system. Also, the features engineering process can be improved and automated.

The proposed work uses a simple rule based system to screening the results with conditionals. The decision system could be improved with more robust systems like neural networks, fuzzy logic or machine learning algorithms.

with the purpose to turn this work into a commercial product. It should adapt the information delivered for this architecture into the regulatory frameworks.

References

1. Costa, M.P., Rodrigues, B.L., Frasao, B.S., Conte-Junior, C.A.: Biogenic amines as food quality index and chemical risk for human consumption. In: Food Quality: Balancing Health and Disease, pp. 75–108. Elsevier (2018). https://linkinghub. elsevier.com/retrieve/pii/B978012811442100002X

2. FAO: Improving our knowledge on small-scale fisheries: data needs and methodologies. In: Fisheries and Aquaculture Proceeding, vol. 56 (2017)
3. Purcell, S.W., Pomeroy, R.S.: Driving small-scale fisheries in developing countries. Frontiers Mar. Sci. **2** (2015). https://doi.org/10.3389/fmars.2015.00044/abstract
4. Vanegas, D.C., Gomes, C.L., Cavallaro, N.D., Giraldo-Escobar, D., McLamore, E.S.: Emerging biorecognition and transduction schemes for rapid detection of pathogenic bacteria in food. Compr. Rev. Food Sci. Food Saf. **16**(6), 1188–1205 (2017). https://doi.org/10.1111/1541-4337.12294
5. Vanegas, D.C., Gomes, C.: Biosensors for indirect monitoring of foodborne bacteria. Biosens. J. **5**(1) (2016). https://www.omicsonline.com/open-access/biosensors-for-indirect-monitoring-of-foodborne-bacteria-2090-4967-1000137.php?aid=74017
6. Bogner, J., Zimmermann, A.: Towards integrating microservices with adaptable enterprise architecture. In: 2016 IEEE 20th International Enterprise Distributed Object Computing Workshop (EDOCW), pp. 1–6. IEEE (2016)
7. Halder, A., et al.: A user-friendly general-purpose predictive software package for food safety. J. Food Eng. **104**(2), 173–185, May 2011. https://linkinghub.elsevier.com/retrieve/pii/S0260877410005686
8. González, S.C., et al.: 'MicroHibro': a software tool for predictive microbiology and microbial risk assessment in foods. Int. J. Food Microbiol. **290**, 226–236, February 2019. https://linkinghub.elsevier.com/retrieve/pii/S0168160518307700
9. Regattieri, A., Gamberi, M., Manzini, R.: Traceability of food products: general framework and experimental evidence. J. Food Eng. **81**(2), 347–356 (2007). https://linkinghub.elsevier.com/retrieve/pii/S0260877406006893
10. Crona, B., et al.: China at a crossroads: an analysis of china's changing seafood production and consumption. One Earth **3**(1), 32–44 (2020)
11. Shao, H.H., et al.: Simultaneous determination of nitrate, nitrite and polyphosphates in seafood by ion chromatography. Food Sci. **20** (2014)
12. Zhang, S., Yin, H., Li, Q.X.: An review on research advance of important poisonous materials in seafood. J. Trop, Oceanogr. **6** (2007)
13. Zhu, B., Zhou, J.H., Yang, Z., Zhao, L.Q.: Study on rapid-detection of heavy metal mercury in fresh and lively seafood by test paper. Chin. J. Mar. Drugs **30**, 49–54 (2011)
14. Liu, P., Zhou, Y.Q., Zang, L.J.: Investigation of heavy metal contamination in four kinds of fishes from the different farmer markets in Beijing. Huan Jing Ke Xue = Huanjing Kexue **32**(7), 2062–2068 (2011)
15. Gui-Di, Y., Zheng, J.P., Huang, H.X., Guo-Min, Q., Jin-Hua, X., Feng-Fu, F.: Speciation analysis of arsenic in seafood with capillary electrophoresis-UV detection. Chin. J. Anal. Chem. **37**(4), 532–536 (2009)
16. Chakraborty, I., Maity, P.: Covid-19 outbreak: migration, effects on society, global environment and prevention. Sci. Total Environ. **728**, 138882 (2020)
17. Zhang, X., Ji, Z., Yue, Y., Liu, H., Wang, J.: Infection risk assessment of covid-19 through aerosol transmission: a case study of south china seafood market. Environ. Sci. Technol. (2020)
18. Vanegas, D., et al.: Laser scribed graphene biosensor for detection of biogenic amines in food samples using locally sourced materials. Biosensors **8**(2), 42 (2018). http://www.mdpi.com/2079-6374/8/2/42
19. Zimmermann, O.: Microservices tenets: agile approach to service development and deployment. Comput. Sci. Res. Dev. **32**(3), 301–310 (2016)

20. Alvarez Q., J.M., Sanabria O., J.A., Garcia M., J.I.: Microservices-based architecture for fault diagnosis in tele-rehabilitation equipment operated via internet. In: LATS, pp. 1–6 (2019)
21. Melo, J.I.G., Roy, A.G.M., Junqueira, F., dos Santos Filho, D.J., Miyagi, P.E.: Modeling the supervision of manufacturing system considering diagnosis and treatment of fault. In: IECON 2010–36th Annual Conference on IEEE Industrial Electronics Society, pp. 2168–2173. IEEE (2010)
22. Caratar-Chaux, J.F., Cano-Buitrón, R.E., Garcia-Melo, J.I.: Productive process improvement to elaborate cane train baskets, using coloured petri nets. Dyna 85(206), 105–113 (2018)
23. Varoquaux, G., Buitinck, L., Louppe, G., Grisel, O., Pedregosa, F., Mueller, A.: Scikit-learn. GetMobile Mob. Comput. Commun. 19(1), 29–33 (2015)
24. Hackett, B.: Pymongo (2020). https://pypi.org/project/pymongo/
25. Ronacher, A.: Flask (2020). https://pypi.org/project/Flask/

Estimation of Limbs Angles Amplitudes During the Use of the Five Minute Shaper Device Using Artificial Neural Networks

Cristian Felipe Blanco-Diaz, Cristian David Guerrero-Mendez,
Mario Enrique Duarte-González, and Sebastián Jaramillo-Isaza[✉]

Faculty of Mechanical, Electronics and Biomedical Engineering,
Antonio Nariño University, Bogotá, Colombia
{cblanco88,crguerrero69,mario.duarte,sebastian.jaramillo}@uan.edu.co

Abstract. Biomechanical studies are essential in health research areas, such as rehabilitation, kinesiology, orthopedics, and sports. For example, they provide information to elaborate on patients' diagnostics or improve athletes' performance. In recent years, deep learning and other computational methods have started to be used to quantify new biomechanical parameters or perform deeper data analysis. Motion capture is one of the methods commonly used in biomechanical studies. For this method, video-based and marker-based systems are the gold standards; nevertheless, those systems are typically quite expensive. Moreover, experimental errors in data capture are frequently related to the occlusion of the markers during motion capture. Data missed is solved by increasing the number of cameras to cover more angles or by using predetermined interpolation algorithms. However, the last method could fail to predict all the marker data missed, and both options increase the cost of the data analysis. For solving those kinds of problems, novel computational methods could be used. This study aims to implement an artificial neural network (ANN) to estimate the limb angle amplitude during the execution of a movement from a single axis (X-axis). For training and validating the ANN model, the data and features from the Five-Minute Shaper machine (a physical conditioning device) are used. The obtained results include RMSE values smaller than 3.2 (Minimum RMSE of 0.96) and CC values close to 0.99. The predicted values are very close to the experimental amplitude angles, and, according to the Two-sample Kolmogorov-Smirnov test, the experimental and the estimated amplitude angles follow the same continuous distribution ($p - value > 0.05$). It is shown that these methods could help researchers in biomechanics to perform accurate analysis, reducing the number of needed cameras and avoid problems due to occlusion by only needing information from a specific axis.

This work was supported by the Faculty of Mechanical, Electronics and Biomedical Engineering of Antonio Nariño University in Bogotá Colombia for the Program of Biomedical Engineering.

J. C. Figueroa-García et al. (Eds.): WEA 2021, CCIS 1431, pp. 213–224, 2021.
https://doi.org/10.1007/978-3-030-86702-7_19

Keywords: Artificial neural networks · Biomechanical analysis · Limb joints angles · Five minutes shaper · Computational modeling in biomechanics · Lower and upper limbs

1 Introduction

Biomechanical movement analyses have been essential for the management of neurological and orthopedic pathologies, where different kinematic and kinetic studies provide vital information for health professionals and even show the evolution of treatment, especially in real-time [4, 10]. According to the above, several biomechanical systems have been introduced (diversified scales, low and high-cost tools): electromyography, dynamometry, weight platforms, among others [1].

The latest decades have increased the use of computational intelligence in the evaluation and analysis of biomechanics information. In this way, Artificial Neural Networks (ANN) has been used in biomechanics analysis due to their potential to classify and predict new data at different fields and situations [2]. In addition, the ANN has the capacity of generalizing the information, tolerate noisy inputs, removing redundancies in the input data, and dealing with different types [16, 18]. Among the applications in biomechanics, it is important to highlight its use to predict joint amplitudes and moments [9, 12], improve the data acquisition [15], determinate biomechanical postures [7] and others [14, 17]. These applications impact daily exercises as gait, running, and devices to improve physical conditions.

Deep learning has also been applied in the field of kinematic motion with the aim of generating tools to improve biomechanical analysis [3, 11, 16]. For example, in [19], neural networks have been used for estimating the amplitude angles in the squat exercise by using electromyography (EMG) signals. As a result, the Root Mean Square Error (RMSE) and Pearson correlation coefficient (CC) were estimated. An average of five (5) for the RMSE and 0.99 for the CC were obtained.

There are several types of physical conditioning devices in the market, and, among them, the Five Minutes Shaper (FMS) that use the subject's weight to muscle toning, principally in the abdominal area. The FMS is a device that activates several muscles in the body in different proportions and involves the wrist, elbow, and knee joints. The principal activated joint is the knee due to the lower limbs are displaced by the knee following the machine's support to generate the movement. In addition, the most activated joint amplitude is the hip due to it acts as the center for stabilizing the trunk in the device [5].

Markers occlusion, when acquiring data in biomechanical laboratories, can cause problems with the data integrity and generated false diagnostics [8]. One solution to improve the acquisition and reduce the occlusion is to put more cameras in the biomechanical laboratories. However, these cameras have a high price in the market due to the kind of features used in data acquisition. Another method to fix the tracking failure is by using temporal continuity of a point trajectory, assuming rigid bodies of the volunteers' segments and manually digitizing the correct position [13].

There are new researches about using new devices to improve the study of kinematics parameters in the physical condition and the problems with the marker occlusion. This study aimed to estimate, through an Artificial Neural Network (ANN), the angle of amplitude of two joints around the upper and lower limbs when the subjects use the FMS device in the easy level from just one axis information. For this, features obtained of only X-axis kinematics information and some anthropometric features of ten (10) subjects were used as input of the ANN.

The neural network correctly estimated these angles with Root-Mean Squared Error (RMSE) between 0.5 and 2 and Correlation Coefficient (CC) close to 0.99. A Two-sample Kolmogorov-Smirnov test analysis shows that the amplitude angles estimation models do not have a significant difference ($p - value > 0.05$) compared to the gold standard information. This tool allows the reduction of cameras and diminishes the occlusion problem by only needing information from one specific axis.

This article is organized as follows: Section 2 presents the experimental methods, Section 3 presents the results obtained for each model. Finally, the last section presents the discussion, conclusions, contribution of the results, and futures works.

2   Experimental Methods

2.1   Five Minutes Shaper Device

The Five Minutes Shaper (FMS) is a fitness device used for total body workouts. This device has six different levels adjustable through the inclination angle to the floor. These levels are cataloged in easy, intermediate, medium, difficult, hard, and extreme, as shown in Fig. 1. The FMS is commonly used for muscle toning in the abdominal area and increases physical conditioning due to its use of the subject's weight to performs the exercises. The subjects moved the lower limbs through the knee machine's support until reaching the maximum limit located to 65 cm from the knee support and then return to the initial position. In this study, only the easy level with an inclination of 15 degrees is considered.

2.2   Data Collection

In this study, the experimental protocol consisted of registering ten healthy volunteers (five men and five women) who used the Five Minutes Shaper device (FMS) at the easy level of around 30 s. Table 1 shows the anthropometric parameters of each subject and the average values.

The FMS places the subjects in ventral decubitus posture by supporting the arms and knees on the device. The outline of the implemented protocol is presented in the Fig. 2. Each participant performed a survey to know the fracture history, surgical procedures, frequency in physical activity development, and physical conditioning level. This survey was taken as an indicator to establish the

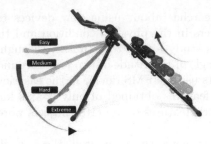

Fig. 1. An image of the Five Minutes Shaper Device used in the experimental protocol.

inclusion criteria, which is healthy subjects and without physical conditioning. The subjects were selected if they practice physical training routines less than once a month. In addition, each one signed an informed consent considering the recommendations established in the Helsinki declaration.

Table 1. Anthropometric parameters of each subject

Subjects	Weight (kg)	Height (m)	Age (years)
Man 1	75	1.80	22
Man 2	65	1.71	21
Man 3	59	1.68	19
Man 4	88	1.82	18
Man 5	62	1.69	20
Woman 1	55	1.57	18
Woman 2	68	1.75	19
Woman 3	50	1.50	19
Woman 4	55	1.67	18
Woman 5	62	1.66	20
Average	63.9 ± 11.1	1.7 ± 0.1	19.4 ± 1.4

Markers were placed on the left side of the subjects following the International Society of Biomechanics (ISB) recommendations for registering the biomechanical activity. The selected joints were the wrist, elbow, shoulder, hip, and knee and were labeled as follows: LW, LE, LS, LH, and LK, respectively, as shown in the Fig. 2. In addition, the used markers have a diameter of approximately 2 cm. The 2D video recording was in the sagittal plane to quantify the joints amplitude. For this, a Basler AG scA640-70gc high-speed camera system with a capture frequency of 70 fps located 2 m distance from the subjects is used. For extracting the position of markers, the free software Kinovea (software for biomechanical analysis) is used. A single trial is registered for each subject, i.e., a cycle where the subject goes up and down. Nevertheless, the cycle for the analysis is extracted where the movement nature is noted for each subject.

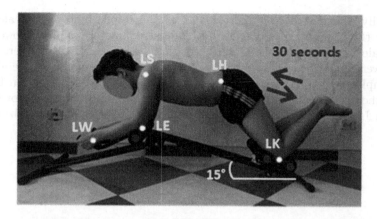

Fig. 2. Experimental protocol for collecting data. The FMS device is configured at the easy level.

2.3   Processing Signals

According to the experimental design, the continuous data were segmented into one cycle per person when the subject normally executed the movement. The markers' positions are stored as signals in a $10 \times M$ matrix. The rows correspond to the X and Y axis positions of the five markers, and M stands for the number of samples. In this work, 801 samples were used.

Subsequently, the matrix was reduced by using only the information of the axis with more variance (for this movement, Y-axis information was discarded), and thus the main extracted features consisted of the difference between the position of the markers of interest (LK, LH, LS, and LE), whose angles between them correspond to the joint amplitude of the movement (upper and lower joint amplitude), and a reference marker, corresponding to the one with less movement (LW). Model 1 was trained and evaluated only with features extracted from markers. For models 2–6, these features were complemented with data from subjects such as weight, sex, height, age, and anthropometric segment length (see Table 2).

Table 2. Features used to train and test the different ANN models

Features Models	LK-LW	LH-LW	LS-LW	LE-LW	Height	Sex	Weight	Age	Segment Length
Model 1	X	X	X	X					
Model 2	X	X	X	X	X				
Model 3	X	X	X	X		X			
Model 4	X	X	X	X			X		
Model 5	X	X	X	X				X	
Model 6	X	X	X	X					X

Finally, the true outputs correspond to the upper limb angle, calculated through the X and Y position of the LE-LS-LH markers, and the lower limb angle, calculated through the X and Y position of the LS-LH-LK markers. These angles were quantified following the Eq. 1, where α corresponds to the angle of limb amplitude either lower or upper, a is the vector formed between LS and LE for the upper limb, and LS-LH for the lower limb, and b is the vector formed between LS and LH for the upper limb and LH-LK for the lower limb, respectively.

$$\alpha = cos^{-1} \left(\frac{\bar{a} \cdot \bar{b}}{|\bar{a}| \cdot |\bar{b}|} \right),$$ (1)

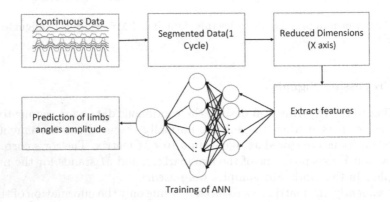

Fig. 3. Block Diagram of the processing of signals, feature extraction, and training of ANN for prediction of limbs angles amplitude

2.4   Neural Network Structure

The processed input features were given to a three-layer feed-forward neural network whose schematic view is shown in Fig. 3. The Levenberg–Marquardt algorithm was used for network training because the gradient descent algorithm may fall into a local optimum, and network outputs may never converge towards the targets. All the estimated results by the proposed model have been performed using the Leave-one-out cross-validation. The sigmoid function was selected as the network transfer function from the input layer to the hidden layers [19]. The output layer corresponds to the estimated limb amplitude angle. Ten (10) neural network structures were evaluated with different number of iterations in order to choose an optimal neural network for this study. For this purpose, only the input data corresponding to biomechanical variables (Model 1) and an output corresponding to the inferior angle were used. The different configurations were: 3 configurations with 1 Hidden Layer of 2, 5 and 10 respectively (C_1–C_3), 3

Configurations with 2 Hidden Layers: 5×5, 10×5 and 5×10 respectively (C_4–C_6), and 4 configurations with 3 hidden layers: $5 \times 5 \times 5$, $10 \times 5 \times 5$, $5 \times 10 \times 5$ and $5 \times 5 \times 10$ respectively (C_7–C_{10}). The different structures were compared and evaluated through the RMSE metric (see Eq. 2) and all processing was implemented in MATLAB software (version 2020a, MathWorks, Inc).

2.5   Metrics

The Root Mean Square Error (RMSE) and Pearson Correlation coefficient (CC) were used to evaluate the neural network estimation. Equations 2 and 3 define the metrics, where $\hat{\theta}_i$ is the estimated limb amplitude angle, θ_i is the actual limb angle amplitude angle at the sampling time i, and N is the length of the data for the angle amplitude.

$$RMSE = \sqrt{\frac{\sum_{i=1}^{N}(\hat{\theta}_i - \theta_i)^2}{N}} \tag{2}$$

$$CC = \frac{\sum_{i=1}^{N}(\theta_i - \bar{\theta})(\hat{\theta}_i - \bar{\hat{\theta}})}{\sqrt{\sum_{i=1}^{N}(\theta_i - \bar{\theta})}\sqrt{\sum_{i=1}^{N}(\hat{\theta}_i - \bar{\hat{\theta}})}} \tag{3}$$

2.6   Statistical Analysis

The statistical analysis evaluates which estimation method has a significantly lower error than the others. First, a Kolmogorov-Smirnov analysis was performed to confirm that the behavior of the data has a high probability of having a normal distribution. Subsequently, a Two-sample Kolmogorov-Smirnov test was performed. The null hypothesis is that the estimated amplitude angles and the true value of the amplitude angles follow the same continuous distribution. On the other hand, the alternative hypothesis is that they follow different continuous distributions. The analysis was performed in Matlab with the function *kstest2* where the criterion for the significant analysis was a p-value of 0.05 [6].

3   Results

In the Table 3 is possible to see the RMSE for the different configurations of Neural Network using biomechanical features and the lower limb amplitude angle, with this information is possible to choose a optimal configuration for this study. The C_3 (1 Hidden Layer with 10 neurons) with 400 iterations was selected to perform the analysis, because this configuration had less error than the others.

Table 3. RMSE for the different configurations of Neural Network using biomechanical features and the lower amplitude angle.

\Configurations Number of Iterations	C_1	C_2	C_3	C_4	C_5	C_6	C_7	C_8	C_9	C_{10}
100	2.82	1.82	**1.25**	3.06	3.68	1.89	5.79	5.55	5.48	4.61
200	2.73	1.67	**1.18**	3.48	3.59	1.78	5.61	5.34	5.41	4.33
300	2.91	1.72	**1.24**	3.36	3.57	1.81	5.33	5.16	5.46	4.24
400	2.88	1.67	**1.12**	3.11	3.25	1.96	5.36	5.08	5.34	4.10
500	2.77	1.68	**1.12**	3.17	3.22	1.71	5.24	5.37	5.42	4.32

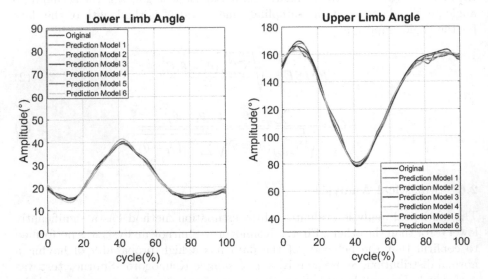

Fig. 4. Experimental upper and lower limb amplitude angle versus neural network estimation of each model for a female subject

Figures 4 and 5 show the results of estimating the upper and lower limb angles of two subjects (female and male) who performed the exercise in the Five Minute Shaper. In these figures, the blue line indicates the original limb angles; the red line indicates the angle estimated by the ANN model 1; and so on, as indicated in the figures' legends.

Figures 4 and 5 show that the estimated angles, using ANNs, are quite similar to the original limb angle during the movement of the exercise in the Five Minute Shaper. These facts can also be verified by the Table 4, in the Figs. 6 and 7 that show the calculated RMSE metric through the Eq. 2. On the other hand, the table 4 shows the calculated CC through the Eq. 3 for all the trained estimation models.

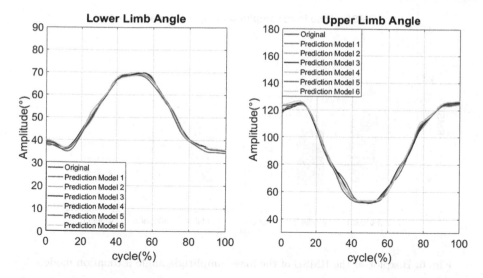

Fig. 5. Experimental upper and lower limb amplitude angle versus neural network estimation of each model for a male subject

Table 4. Estimated RMSE and CC metrics for the six models used for predicting the angles of the limbs

Lower limb angle			Upper limb angle		
Model	RMSE	CC	Model	RMSE	CC
1	1.2531	0.9885	1	3.1820	0.9857
2	1.0948	0.9915	2	2.6268	0.9883
3	0.9587	0.9936	3	2.4291	0.9916
4	1.1655	0.9918	4	2.6461	0.9895
5	1.0299	0.9948	5	2.7423	0.9855
6	1.1811	0.9861	6	2.6719	0.9906

The Kolmogorov-Smirnov statistical analysis for a sample showed that the behavior of the models has a high probability of having a normal distribution. When performing the Two-sample Kolmogorov-Smirnov test analysis between the amplitude angle estimated and the True amplitude angles, it is verified, for all models, that they follow the same continuous distribution ($p-value > 0.05$).

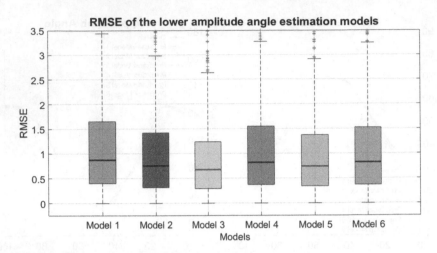

Fig. 6. Boxplot of the RMSE of the lower amplitude angle estimation models

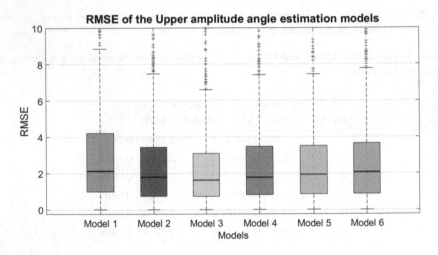

Fig. 7. Boxplot of the RMSE of the upper amplitude angle estimation models

4   Discussion and Conclusion

The are several computational methods for fixing missed data from markers' failures. This work shows that using neural networks is a promising way to evaluate the tracking results and improve data analysis in biomechanics.

It is possible to conclude, through the Table 4, that the models have quite acceptable performance for the estimation of the amplitude angles of the upper and lower limbs during the execution of the exercise in the Five Minute Shaper. Model 3 showed the best performance with an RMSE of 0.9587 and CC of 0.9936 and RMSE of 2.4291 with CC of 0.9916 for lower and upper limb amplitude, respectively. Model 1 had the worst performance with RMSE of 1.2531 and CC of 0.9885 for lower limb amplitude and RMSE of 3.1820 and CC of 0.9857 for upper limb amplitude, respectively. The results support the conclusion that the physical variable related to sex may have a greater influence on the estimation of the angle, so it is recommended to investigate this variable further. Although the models have different behaviors from each other, it is highlighted that the six proposed models can be applied for estimating the upper and lower limb amplitude angle. The statistical analysis verified that the estimated values and the true samples of angle follow the same continuous distribution ($p - value >$ 0.05).

This study demonstrated that a multilayer neural network with a simple structure could estimate the limb angle while performing a simple athletic movement through features obtained in a single axis of interest even though the movement is registered in two dimensions. This approach can be used in real-time biomechanical analysis. It allows decreasing physical resources such as the number of cameras, reducing the marker occlusion problem and acquiring biomechanical information without requiring a controlled environment. To our knowledge, kinematic estimation of human motion using artificial intelligence during multi-limb tasks in the real-load situation has not been fully studied.

This study is preliminary work and thus requires further examination. For example, in future studies, several athletic tasks with more participants can increase the generalizability of the network. In addition, future studies can use simpler models of refreshment that allow the estimation of the angles of the limbs, use less computationally expensive algorithms, and the option of using these models with other types of movements, possibly in 3D-type acquisition.

Acknowledgment. The authors would like to thank the Antonio Nariño University, particularly the Faculty of Mechanical, Electronic, and Biomedical Engineering for the support in this study.

References

1. Ashok, T.S., et al.: Kinematic study of video gait analysis. In: 2015 International Conference on Industrial Instrumentation and Control (ICIC), pp. 1208–1213. IEEE (2015)
2. Bartlett, R.: Artificial intelligence in sports biomechanics: new dawn or false hope? J. Sports Sci. Med. 5(4), 474 (2006)
3. Blanco Díaz, C.F., Quitian-González, A.K., Jaramillo-Isaza, S., Orjuela-Cañón, A.D.: A biomechanical analysis of free squat exercise employing self-organizing maps. In: 2019 IEEE Colombian Conference on Applications in Computational Intelligence (ColCACI), pp. 1–5. IEEE (2019)
4. Van den Bogert, A.J., Geijtenbeek, T., Even-Zohar, O., Steenbrink, F., Hardin, E.C.: A real-time system for biomechanical analysis of human movement and muscle function. Med. Biolog. Eng. Comput. 51(10), 1069–1077 (2013)
5. Endo, Y., Sakamoto, M.: Correlation of shoulder and elbow injuries with muscle tightness, core stability, and balance by longitudinal measurements in junior high school baseball players. J. Phys. Ther. Sci. 26(5), 689–693 (2014)

6. Fadlallah, B., Fadlallah, A., Razafsha, M., Karnib, N., Wang, K., Kobeissy, F.: Chapter 6 - Robust detection of epilepsy using weighted-permutation entropy: Methods and analysis. In: Kobeissy, F., Alawieh, A., Zaraket, F.A., Wang, K. (eds.) Leveraging Biomedical and Healthcare Data, pp. 91–106. Academic Press (2019). https://doi.org/10.1016/B978-0-12-809556-0.00006-X

7. Gholipour, A., Arjmand, N.: Artificial neural networks to predict 3d spinal posture in reaching and lifting activities; applications in biomechanical models. J. Biomech. **49**(13), 2946–2952 (2016)

8. Kaptein, B., Valstar, E., Stoel, B., Rozing, P., Reiber, J.: A new type of model-based roentgen stereophotogrammetric analysis for solving the occluded marker problem. J. Biomech. **38**(11), 2330–2334 (2005)

9. Kipp, K., Giordanelli, M., Geiser, C.: Predicting net joint moments during a weightlifting exercise with a neural network model. J. Biomech. **74**, 225–229 (2018)

10. Lu, T.W., Chang, C.F.: Biomechanics of human movement and its clinical applications. Kaohsiung J. Med. Sci. **28**, S13–S25 (2012)

11. Plazas Molano, A.C., Jaramillo-Isaza, S., Orjuela-Cañon, Á.D.: Self-organized maps for the analysis of the biomechanical response of the knee joint during squat-like movements in subjects without physical conditioning. In: Figueroa-García, J.C., Duarte-González, M., Jaramillo-Isaza, S., Orjuela-Cañon, A.D., Díaz-Gutierrez, Y. (eds.) WEA 2019. CCIS, vol. 1052, pp. 335–344. Springer, Cham (2019). https://doi.org/10.1007/978-3-030-31019-6_29

12. Mundt, M., David, S., Koeppe, A., Bamer, F., Potthast, W., Markert, B.: Joint angle estimation during fast cutting manoeuvres using artificial neural networks. ISBS Proc. Arch. **37**(1), 101 (2019)

13. Nakano, N., et al.: Evaluation of 3D markerless motion capture accuracy using openpose with multiple video cameras. Frontiers Sports Active Living **2**(50) (2020)

14. Nandy, A., Mondal, S., Prasad, J.S., Chakraborty, P., Nandi, G.: Recognizing & interpreting Indian sign language gesture for human robot interaction. In: 2010 International Conference on Computer and Communication Technology (ICCCT), pp. 712–717. IEEE (2010)

15. Papic, C., Sanders, R.H., Naemi, R., Elipot, M., Andersen, J.: Improving data acquisition speed and accuracy in sport using neural networks. J. Sports Sci., 1–10 (2020)

16. Shahid, N., Rappon, T., Berta, W.: Applications of artificial neural networks in health care organizational decision-making: a scoping review. PloS one **14**(2), e0212356 (2019)

17. Trost, S.G., Zheng, Y., Wong, W.K.: Machine learning for activity recognition: hip versus wrist data. Physiol. Meas. **35**(11), 2183 (2014)

18. Walczak, S.: Neural networks in organizational research: applying pattern recognition to the analysis of organizational behavior. Organ. Res. Methods **10**(4), 710 (2007)

19. Zangene, A.R., Abbasi, A.: Continuous estimation of knee joint angle during squat from sEMG using artificial neural networks. In: 2020 27th National and 5th International Iranian Conference on Biomedical Engineering (ICBME), pp. 75–78. IEEE (2020)

SSCF-Hyperthermia Study in MCF-7 Spheroids – In Silicio

Hector Fabian Guarnizo-Mendez[(✉)], Angela Victoria Fonseca Benítez,
Sandra Janneth Perdomo Lara, Sandra Johanna Morantes Medina,
Cristian Andrés Triana Infante, Christian Camilo Cano Vásquez,
Juan David Jaiquel Villamil, and Sebastian Mesa Zafra

Universidad El Bosque, Bogotá, Colombia
{hguarnizo,afonsecab,perdomosandraj,smorantes,ctrianai,ccanov,
jjaiquel,smesaz}@unbosque.edu.co

Abstract. Electromagnetic hyperthermia is an alternative treatment for cancer
that has been carried out as an adjuvant to other cancer treatments such as
chemotherapy and radiotherapy; this study shows the interaction between a cell
culture of three dimensional MCF-7 spheroids (Michigan Cancer Foundation-7)
inside a culture media and the electromagnetic radiation generated by a set of
two applicator antennas. This study was performed by using an electromagnetic
simulation model. The cell culture was modeled by using its conductivity and
permittivity parameters and was placed in a 24-cell plate. The distribution of the
electric field was analyzed in both, the culture media and the 3D spheroid culture
MCF-7 when they were illuminated by the two applicators in different scenarios
regarding the input power of the applicator and the distance between the cell culture and the applicator. Temperature behavior was analyzed from the electric field.
Moreover, standardization of spheroids using microplates coated with Ultra-Low
Attachment (ULA) surface for 3D cell culture (Corning® Costar®) through two
methods, with and without the Geltrex™ LDEV matrixes is presented. The preliminary results indicate that the electric field is significantly more focused over
the 3D spheroids in a scenario when the applicators are located 4 cm apart from
the cell culture and are excited with a power of 5 W, in this scenario configuration
the effect of hyperthermia will be successfully obtained for the 3D spheroids.

Keywords: 3D spheroid culture MCF-7 · Electromagnetic hyperthermia ·
Applicators

1 Introduction

Cancer is a disease characterized by the uncontrolled growth and spread of abnormal
cells. About one in six deaths is caused by cancer [1]. In 2020, It was estimated 19
292 789 new cases of cancer. In these new cases 11.7% correspond to breast cancer. In
both men and women, breast cancer causes 6.9% of deaths worldwide [2]. Immunother-
apy, stem cell transplantation, radiotherapy, chemotherapy, targeted medicine therapies

© Springer Nature Switzerland AG 2021
J. C. Figueroa-García et al. (Eds.): WEA 2021, CCIS 1431, pp. 225–236, 2021.
https://doi.org/10.1007/978-3-030-86702-7_20

and surgery (lumpectomy, mastectomy, and axillary lymph node dissection) are standard treatments used to tackle breast cancer [3]. Along with the treatments mentioned above, electromagnetic hyperthermia is another treatment that is being implemented. Hyperthermia treatment involves direct electromagnetic radiation over the tumor area to increase its temperature to 39–45 °C, where tumor cell death by apoptosis is induced [4]. The main challenge in the hyperthermia treatment is to effectively increase the tumor temperature while the surrounding tissues temperature as little as possible [5]; the electromagnetic hyperthermia combined with other standard treatments is an alternative with a promising prognosis [6]. Currently, hyperthermia is under study in human patients and in human breast cancer cell lines [7].

To obtain a cell culture, first, the cells of a plant or an animal are withdrawn. Second, withdrawn cells are placed in a favorable artificial environment for their growth. Cells are withdrawn from the tissue directly, alternatively, they can be unbundled by mechanical or enzymatic means before culturing or they can stem from a cell line that has already been established [8]. In [9], it is presented a categorization of 84 breast cancer cell lines, this characterization has been carried out according to three receptors (ER, Estrogen Receptor, PR, Progesterone Receptor, HER2, Human Epithelial Receptor 2). Among the 84 cell lines presented in [9], it is of particular interest the human breast adenocarcinoma cell line MCF-7 (Michigan Cancer Foundation-7), this cell line has been used for more than 40 years as a standard model in cancer research in vitro [10] and it is one of the most used as a model for the investigation of processes that impact patient care [11].

On the other hand, in conventional monolayer cultures it has been observed that the cytotoxic effects obtained are not similar to those obtained in vivo [12].

The 3D growth of cell lines is considered a model closer to the tumor in vivo to perform drug selection or assess antitumor treatments [13] because cell-cell interactions are generated in this system [14], there is a production and extracellular matrix deposition [15]. 3D models of tumor spheroids are used in the experimental evaluation and screening of conventional chemotherapeutics. These chemotherapeutics are used in the treatment of lung cancer, breast cancer, head and neck cancer, and ovarian cancer [16]. Janati [17] has reported a thermally enhanced dose with radiofrequency combined with hyperthermia and external mega-voltage X-rays in spheroids in the DU145 prostate cancer cell line.

Hyperthermia as evidenced in different studies cause direct damage to cancer cells and sensitize them to other treatment modalities (such as chemotherapy and radiotherapy) [18], in these cases hyperthermia is an adjuvant treatment [4].

Verification of a positive response to cancer treatment is carried out through cell death. Cell death is the "irreversible degeneration" of vital cell functions (especially ATP (adenosine triphosphate) production and preservation of redox homeostasis) that culminates in loss of cell integrity (permanent permeabilization of the plasma membrane or cell fragmentation) [19].

Hyperthermia on cell lines is carried out by using electroporation ECM 830 (microsecond pulsed electric field), an incubator, an UHR-2000 microwave beam thermo device, A RF-capacitive system (Celsius TCS), Iron oxide magnetic nanoparticles, X-ray, laser, photothermal technique.

In this paper, the distribution of the electric field (simulated) in the cell culture (3D spheroid culture MCF-7 (Michigan Cancer Foundation-7) and culture media) was analyzed. The cell culture was in a 24-cell plate (Fig. 2a). Moreover, temperature behavior was analyzed from the electric field. The cell culture was illuminated with two applicators at 2.45 GHz. The applicators were located at 2 cm and 4 cm over cell culture and were excited with a power of 1W, 5W and 10 W. The applicators were developed in SIW (substrate integrated waveguide) technology. Furthermore, standardization of spheroids using microplates coated with Ultra-Low Attachment (ULA) surface for 3D cell culture (Corning® Costar®) through two methods, with and without the Geltrex™ LDEV matrixes is presented.

2 Methodology

The electromagnetic simulation was carried out using the finite element method (FEM) solver of ANSYS Electronics®. Cell culture was modeled by 3D spheroid culture MCF-7 and culture media. The simulation setup is presented in the Table 1.

Table 1. HFSS configuration setup

Properties	Values
Maximum number of passes	10
Maximum delta S	0.01
Maximum converged passes	3
Order of basis function	Mixed order

The maximum delta S values and maximum converged passes values were chosen to improve the mesh accuracy and the convergence. Mixed order basis function was chosen because 3D spheroid culture MCF-7 and culture media have different electrical properties (conductivity (σ) and permittivity (ε)). Mixed order assigns a lower order (base function elements) where the fields are weaker, and a higher order (base function elements) where more precision is required.

Table 2 display the electrical properties of 3D spheroid culture MCF-7 and culture media implemented in the electromagnetic simulation based on the properties presented in [20] for a frequency of 2.45 GHz.

Table 2. Electrical properties of 3D spheroid culture MCF-7 and culture medium

	Relative permittivity	Conductivity
3D spheroid culture MCF-7	23	1.2
Culture media	72.81	2.7

3 Applicator

The cell culture was illuminated with two equal applicators at 2.45 GHz developed in SIW technology, Fig. 1 shows the applicator.

This applicator is conformed of 3 parts. First, a cavity designed by using the analysis equations of waveguides and rectangular cavities [21]. TE_{101} mode is the cavity resonance mode. Second, a transition from microstrip to SIW cavity as described in [22] is used in the cavity's top wall. A 50-microstrip line is coupled to the coplanar waveguide (CPW) cavity access. Third, a meandered slot antenna printed on the cavity's bottom wall [23], meandered slot antenna is equivalent to a magnetic dipole antenna of $\lambda/2$. It is designed to operate at $f_0 = 2.45$ GHz.

The impedance of meandered slot antenna is obtained by using the expressions of Janaswamy and Schaubert (low permittivity ε_r) [24], the slot was designed according to [25].

This applicator is one of the applicator prototypes which are being developed for a hyperthermia system for the treatment of breast cancer. It has linear polarization and frequency selectivity due to the cavity.

Applicators were developed in the substrate Rogers TMM 6 (tm), this substrate has a permittivity (ε) of 6.3 and an electrical strength (dielectric strength) of 14.6 MV/m.

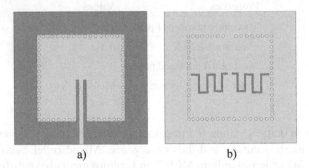

a)   b)

Fig. 1. SIW technology applicator at 2.45 GHz. (a) Top view. (b) Bottom view

4 Results

The cell culture was illuminated with two applicators at 2.45 GHz (Fig. 2a) for three different conditions, namely, with input power values of 1, 5 and 10 W. The applicators were located at 2 cm and 4 cm over the cell culture (Fig. 2a). 3D spheroid (0.5 cm diameter) culture is located in the center of the culture media, this location is due to cell culture feature (Fig. 2b), both 3D spheroids culture and culture media are located inside a 24-well plate (Fig. 2a).

The distribution of the electric field in both culture media and 3D spheroids culture was obtained on the 4 rows (Fig. 2a) of the 24-well plate.

The distribution of the electric field in both culture media and 3D spheroids culture located on row 1 (Fig. 2a) is presented in Fig. 3. The applicators were located at 2 cm

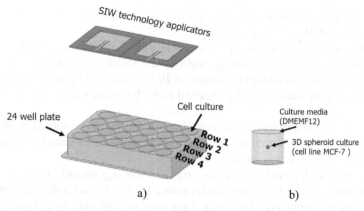

Fig. 2. 3D model. (a) Applicators located over cell culture. (b) Cell culture

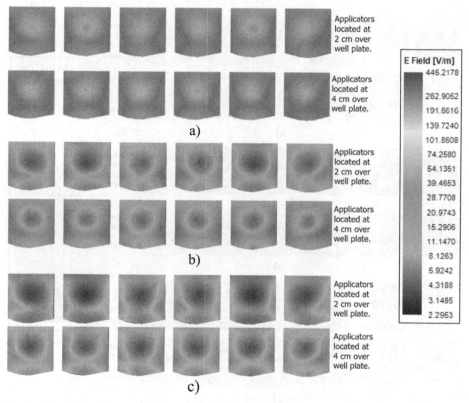

Fig. 3. Distribution of the electric field in both culture media and 3D spheroids culture located on row 1 (Fig. 2a), (a) the applicators were excited with a power of 1 W, (b) the applicators were excited with a power of 5 W, (c) the applicators were excited with a power of 10 W.

and 4 cm over the cell culture (Fig. 3a–c). The applicators were excited with a power of 1 W (Fig. 3a), 5 W (Fig. 3b) and 10 W (Fig. 3c).

Figure 3c shows that the electric field was absorbed by both, the culture media and the 3D spheroids culture when the applicators were located at 2 cm and 4 cm over the cell culture and were excited with a power of 10 W. This result is undesirable because the increase in temperature will be obtained in both culture media and 3D spheroids culture.

In Fig. 3a, it is observed that the electric field was poorly absorbed by the culture media and the 3D spheroids culture when the applicators were located at 4 cm over the cell culture and were excited with a power of 1 W.

In Fig. 3b, it is depicted how the electric field was significantly more absorbed by the 3D spheroids while the culture media interacted weakly with the electromagnetic radiation with the applicators located at 4 cm over the cell culture and excited with a power of 5 W, this result is important because in this scenario the temperature will be focused in the 3D spheroids, and therefore the effect of hyperthermia will be obtained.

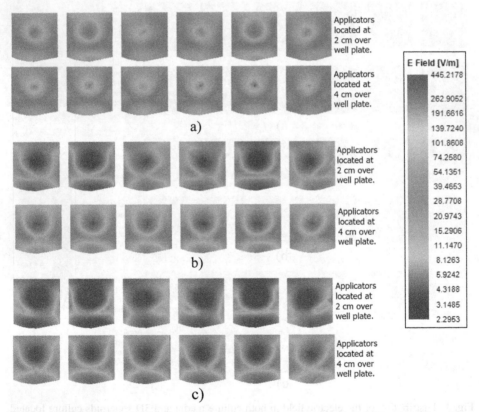

Fig. 4. Distribution of the electric field in both culture media located and 3D spheroids culture located on row 2 (Fig. 2a), (a) the applicators were excited with a power of 1 W, (b) the applicators were excited with a power of 5 W, (c) the applicators were excited with a power of 10 W.

The distribution of the electric field in both culture media and 3D spheroids located on row 2 (Fig. 2a) is presented in Fig. 4. The applicators were located at 2 cm and 4 cm over the cell culture (Fig. 4a–c). The applicators were excited with a power of 1 W (Fig. 4a), 5 W (Fig. 4b) and 10 W (Fig. 4c).

Figure 4a shows that the electric field was absorbed weakly by both, the culture media and 3D spheroids when the applicators were 2 cm and 4 cm apart from the cell culture and were excited with a power of 1 W, however, the magnitude of the electric field was significantly more focused in the 3D spheroids than in the culture media, this result is interesting because the temperature increment will be focused in the 3D spheroids, therefore achieving the desired hyperthermia effect.

In Fig. 4c, it is observed that the electric field was significantly absorbed by both culture media and 3D spheroids when the applicators were located at 2 cm and 4 cm over the cell culture and were excited with a power of 10 W. This is an undesirable result because the increase in temperature will be obtained in both media.

In Fig. 4b, it is depicted how the electric field was significantly more absorbed by the 3D spheroids while the magnitude of the electric field was weak in the culture media. In

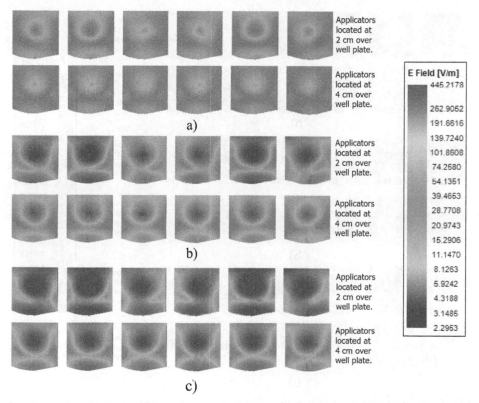

Fig. 5. Distribution of the electric field in both culture media and 3D spheroids culture located on row 3 (Fig. 2a), (a) the applicators were excited with a power of 1 W, (b) the applicators were excited with a power of 5 W, (c) the applicators were excited with a power of 10 W.

this scenario the applicators were 4 cm apart from the cell culture and were excited with a power of 5 W, this is an interesting scenario that results in a temperature increment of the 3D spheroids only.

Generally, the magnitude of the electric field is more intense in both, the culture media and the 3D spheroids located on row 2 compared to row 1 because row 2 is located below the center of the applicators ("main radiation zone" of the applicator).

The distribution of the electric field in both culture media and 3D spheroids located on row 3 (Fig. 2a) is presented in Fig. 5. The applicators were located at 2 cm and 4 cm over the cell culture (Fig. 5a–c). The applicators were excited with a power of 1 W (Fig. 5a), 5 W (Fig. 5b) and 10 W (Fig. 5c).

In Fig. 5, it is displayed that the distribution of the electric field on row 3 in both culture media and 3D spheroids is similar to that observed in row 2 (Fig. 4). This behavior is due to the fact that row 2 and row 3 are localized below the center of the applicators ("main radiation zone" of the applicator).

The distribution of the electric field in both culture media and 3D spheroids located on row 4 (Fig. 2a) is presented in Fig. 6. The applicators were located at 2 cm and 4 cm

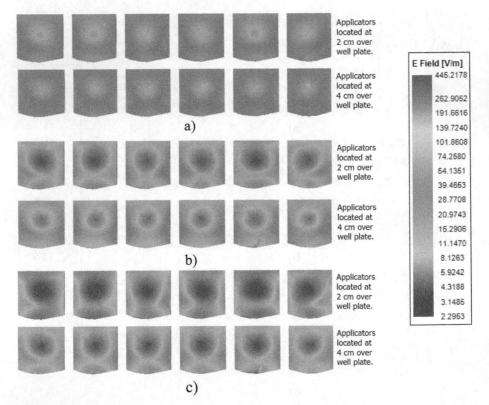

Fig. 6. Distribution of the electric field in both culture media and 3D spheroids culture located on row 4 (Fig. 2a), (a) the applicators were excited with a power of 1 W, (b) the applicators were excited with a power of 5 W, (c) the applicators were excited with a power of 10 W.

over the cell culture (Fig. 6a–c). The applicators were excited with a power of 1 W (Fig. 6a), 5 W (Fig. 6b) and 10 W (Fig. 6c).

In Fig. 6, it is depicted how the distribution of the electric field on row 3 in both culture medium and 3D spheroids is similar to that observed in row 1 (Fig. 3). This behavior is due to the fact that row 2 and row 3 are localized below the center of the applicators ("main radiation zone" of the applicator).

5 Cell Culture Conditions

The results presented in Sect. 4 were obtained through simulation of the interaction between the cell culture and the electromagnetic waves radiated by the antenna applicator, all the simulations were performed for 3D spheroids centered inside a culture media on a 24-well plate. This section describes the culture conditions in which the 3D spheroids of the MCF-7 line are being currently developed.

5.1 Culture of MCF-7 Cell Line

Currently, cell culture standardization is being carried out, that is, human breast epithelial adenocarcinoma cells MCF-7 (ATCC) were seeded as monolayer culture, cells were maintained in Dulbecco's modified Eagle's medium F12 (DMEM F12) supplemented with 10% fetal bovine serum (FBS-Gibco), and 1% antibiotics penicillin/streptomycin/amphotericin b (Lonza) at 37 °C in a humidified atmosphere with 5% CO_2.

5.2 MCF-7 Cell Line-Derived Spheroids

Spheroids were obtained using Microplates coated with Ultra-Low Attachment (ULA) surface for 3D cell culture (Corning® Costar®) through two methods, with (Fig. 7a) and without (Fig. 7b) the Geltrex™ LDEV matrix. MCF-7 cells were seeded at a density of 1.000, 2.000 5.000, and 10.000 cells/well in ULA 96-well plates. Spheroids were cultured in DMEM F12 (Dulbecco's Modified Eagle's Medium/Nutrient Mixture F-12) supplemented with 10% fetal bovine serum (FBS-Gibco) and 1% antibiotics penicillin/streptomycin/amphotericin b (Lonza). Spheroids were incubated in a humidified atmosphere and 5% CO_2 at 37 °C. After 4 day spheroid formation was determined under an inverted microscope.

5.3 Morphological Parameter Estimation

Spheroid formation was assessed through a light microscope Zeiss Imager.M2BX connected to a digital camera CCD monochromatic AxioCam HRm. Morphology parameters (diameter, solidity, convexity, sphericity, and volume) were assessed with AnaSP image analysis software. Tridimensional reconstruction with ReVisp software was made. Spheroids with more sphericity and larger diameter will be chosen to be used in this study.

Morphology parameters (diameter: It is calculated with the diameter of the circle that has the same area as the cross-sectional area of the analyzed spheroid; solidity; It is related to the cohesion of the cells that make up the spheroid about its density; convexity: the index allows the integrity of the spheroid to be determined before treatment; and volume: calculated as the number of voxels) will be obtained by image analysis. The software converts images gray levels to make the segmentation of the spheroids and finally achieve a binary mask that allows extracting the morphological parameters through equations. It is important to highlight that these parameters will be evaluated only in in vitro conditions. Because they are treatment effect predictors, any decrease of sphericity may be due to loss of spheroid integrity. It can be related to losing cell-cell or cell-matrix adhesion. Additionally, all parameters correlate with other assays.

The magnitude of the diameter of the spheroid has been used to carry out the electromagnetic simulation, the diameter of 0.5 cm has been used because with it the best cohesion of the cells was obtained. Likewise, the value of the permittivity and the conductivity of the spheroid has been considered to carry out the electromagnetic simulation.

5.4 Evaluation of Cell Culture Formation

Spheroid formation was evaluated with a light microscope (10×). The results showed that spheroids with morphological characteristics more spherical were obtained using the method without the Geltrex™ LDEV matrix (Fig. 7b). Three-dimensional cell culture models like spheroids; allow accurately mimic treatment responses in vivo. Because of this, we proposed to generate and standardize a breast cancer 3D crop to know how hyperthermia affects cell viability, morphological and structural organization of the tumor cells. We found that a better method to MCF-7 spheroids is using ULA only, without any matrix.

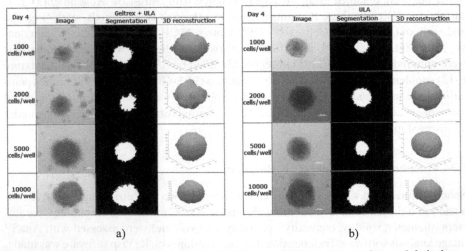

a)   b)

Fig. 7. Spheroids of MCF-7 cultured (a) with Geltrex and ULA, segmentation, and their three-dimensional reconstruction. (b) Cultured with ULA only, segmentation and their three-dimensional reconstruction.

Figure 7(a) shows that the most representative images of the spheroids seeded at three cells numbers (1000–2000–5000 and 10000). Scale bar 200 μM. Note that density color schematically shows the location of the voxels within the three-dimensional figure.

Figure 7(b) shows that the most representative images of the spheroids seeded at three cells numbers (1000–2000–5000 and 10000). Scale bar 200 μM. Note that density color schematically shows the location of the voxels within the three-dimensional figure.

6   Conclusions

This paper presented the simulated distribution of the electric field in both 3D sphe-roid culture MCF-7 and culture media when they were illuminated by a set of two applicators with input power values of1 W, 5 W and 10 W. Located at a distance of 2 cm and 4 cm from the cell culture. The results indicate that the magnitude of the electric field was greatly focused in the 3D spheroids MCF-7 when the applicators were located at 4 cm over the cell culture and were excited with a power of 5 W, in this case, the best effect of electromagnetic hyperthermia in the 3D spheroids MCF-7 was obtained.

Spheroids with the best spherical morphological characteristics were obtained using Ultra-Low Attachment (ULA) only. The three-dimensional reconstruction shows spheroids as more homogeneous and circular.

Currently, a study of the distribution of the electric field (simulated) in the cell culture when the applicators are located at other distances (different at 2 cm and 4 cm) is being carried out. Furthermore, different applicators are being used.

References

1. A. C. Society: American Cancer Society. Cancer Facts & Figures 2020, American Cancer Society, pp. 1–52 (2020)
2. I. A. for R. on Cancer and W. H. Organization: International Angency for Research on Cancer, World Health Organization, Globocan 2020 (2020)
3. Hadi, F., et al.: Combinatorial effects of radiofrequency hyperthermia and radiotherapy in the presence of magneto-plasmonic nanoparticles on MCF-7 breast cancer cells. J. Cell. Physiol. **234**(1), 20028–20035 (2019)
4. Datta, N.R., et al.: Local hyperthermia combined with radiotherapy and/or chemotherapy: recent advances and promises for the future. Cancer Treat. Rev. **41**(9), 742–753 (2015)
5. Iero, D.A.M., Crocco, L., Isernia, T., Korkmaz, E.: Optimal focused electromagnetic hyper-thermia treatment of breast cancer. In: 2016 10th Eur. Conference Antennas Propagation, EuCAP 2016, pp. 1–2 (2016)
6. Mallory, M., Gogineni, E., Jones, G.C., Greer, L., Simone, C.B.: Therapeutic hyperthermia: the old, the new, and the upcoming. Crit. Rev. Oncol. Hematol. **97**(2015), 56–64 (2016)
7. Chicheł, A., Skowronek, J., Kubaszewska, M., Kanikowski, M.: Hyperthermia – description of a method and a review of clinical applications. Rep. Pract. Oncol. Radiother. **12**(5), 267–275 (2007)
8. Dopico, A.: Atcc, Invitrogen: Cell Culture Basics Handbook, Atcc **39**(6) (2014)
9. Dai, X., Cheng, H., Bai, Z., Li, J.: Breast cancer cell line classification and Its relevance with breast tumor subtyping. J. Cancer **8**(16), 3131–3141 (2017)
10. Comşa, Ş, Cîmpean, A.M., Raica, M.: The story of MCF-7 breast cancer cell line 40 years of experience in research. Anticancer Res. **35**, 3147–3154 (2015)

11. Sweeney, E.E., McDaniel, R.E., Maximov, P.Y., Fan, P., Craig Jordan, V.: Models and mechanisms of acquired antihormone resistance in breast cancer: significant clinical progress despite limitations. Horm. Mol. Biol. Clin. Investig. **9**(2), 143–163 (2012)

12. Johnson, J.I., et al.: Relationships between drug activity in NCI preclinical in vitro and in vivo models and early clinical trials. Br. J. Cancer **84**(10), 1424–1431 (2001)

13. Thoma, C.R., Zimmermann, M., Agarkova, I., Kelm, J.M., Krek, W.: 3D cell culture systems modeling tumor growth determinants in cancer target discovery. Adv. Drug Deliv. Rev. **69–70**, 29–41 (2014)

14. Baker, B.M., Chen, C.S.: Deconstructing the third dimension – how 3D culture microenvironments alter cellular cues. J. Cell Sci. **125**(13), 3015–3024 (2012)

15. Kimlin, L.C., Casagrande, G., Virador, V.M.: In vitro three-dimensional (3D) models in cancer research: An update. Mol. Carcinog. **52**(3), 167–182 (2013)

16. Eguchi, H., Akizuki, R., Maruhashi, R., Tsukimoto, M.: Increase in resistance to anticancer drugs involves occludin in spheroid culture model of lung adenocarcinoma A549 cells. Sci. Rep. **8**(1), 151–157 (2018)

17. Esfahani, A.J., Mahdavi, S.R., Shiran, M.B., Khoei, S.: The role of radiofrequency hyperthermia in the radiosensitization of a human prostate cancer cell line. Cell J. **19**, 86–95 (2017)

18. Mocna, M.: Hyperthermia in oncology. AIP Conf. Proc. **958**, 256–257 (2007)

19. Galluzzi, L., et al.: Molecular mechanisms of cell death: recommendations of the nomenclature committee on cell death 2018. Cell Death Differ. **25**(3), 486–541 (2018)

20. Hussein, M., Awwad, F., Jithin, D., El Hasasna, H., Athamneh, K., Iratni, R.: Breast cancer cells exhibits specific dielectric signature in vitro using the open-ended coaxial probe technique from 200 MHz to 13.6 GHz. Sci. Rep. **9**(1), 4681 (2019)

21. Pozar, D.M.: Microwave Engineering. Wiley India, New Delhi (2017)

22. Hao, Z.C., Hong, W., Chen, X.P., Chen, J.X., Wu, K.T.J.C.: Multilayered substrate integrated waveguide (MSIW) elliptic filter. IEEE Microw. Wirel. Compon. Lett. **15**(22), 95–97 (2005)

23. Hong, W., Member, S., Behdad, N., Member, S., Sarabandi, K.: Size reduction of cavity-backed slot antennas. IEEE Trans. Antennas Propag. **54**(5), 1461–1466 (2006)

24. Gupta, K.C., Garg, R., Bahl, I.J.: Microstrip lines and slot lines (1979)

25. Bohórquez, J.C., et al.: Planar substrate integrated waveguide cavity-backed antenna. IEEE Antennas Wirel. Propag. Lett. **8**, 1139–1142 (2009)

Internet of Things (IoT)

Smart UTB: An IoT Platform for Smart Campus

Leonardo Castellanos Acuña$^{(\boxtimes)}$, Ray Narváez, Carlos Salas,
Luz Alejandra Magre, and María José González

Universidad Tecnológica de Bolívar, Cartagena de Indias, Colombia
{lmagre,mgonzalez}@utb.edu.co

Abstract. The Internet of Things (IoT) aims to create applications to improve people's quality of life using novel protocols, sensor networks, cloud computing, middlewares and other technologies. These applications can be used in several contexts such as industry, agriculture or smart cities. On university campuses, applications based on IoT can also be implemented. The applications can be focused on monitoring people's behavior, smart buildings, or sustainable environments. Generally, IoT applications are not designed and developed in a standardized way. Besides that, university campuses do not have a platform to manage and deploy these applications easily. This work presents Smart UTB, an IoT platform designed by using the Industrial Internet Reference Architecture (IIRA) and focused in the management and deployment of IoT applications towards sustainability in a smart campus.

Keywords: Internet of Things · Smart campus · Reference architecture · Environmental sustainability · Sustainability in higher education

1 Introduction

As we are living through the fourth industrial revolution, focusing mainly on the use and development of the Internet of Things (IoT), we are discovering the great advantages that it can give us in several fields and situations. One of these fields is environmental monitoring. Environmental monitoring gives key tools to those university campuses that point to sustainability within their institutional policies. Starting from the commitments and progress made by Higher Education Institutions (HEI) in the Stockholm Declaration [28], Talloires Declaration [25] and other declarations signed by universities around the world since the late 19th century [22], pointing to the incorporation of sustainability principles both in education, research and the physical space itself.

The Universidad Tecnológica de Bolívar (UTB), specifically, in order to strengthen its commitment to environmental sustainability, joins the UI Green-Metric World University Ranking in 2019, an initiative of the Universitas Indonesia with around 779 participants and ranking 486 [27].

© Springer Nature Switzerland AG 2021
J. C. Figueroa-García et al. (Eds.): WEA 2021, CCIS 1431, pp. 239–249, 2021.
https://doi.org/10.1007/978-3-030-86702-7_21

The main objective of this work is to implement IoT solutions to the UTB campus in order to get the most of its capabilities, such as environmental monitoring. The article proposes a platform open to members of the University (Students and faculty members), so they are able to monitor environmental variables or add more sensors to the network for their own projects. Thus, this platform is a key tool for achieving the strengthening of the UTB as a sustainable campus, which offers its community a safe space consistent with the education provided and an accurate timely decision making process.

The paper is organized as follows: Sect. 2 discusses research in the field and their approaches. Section 3 shows the selected architecture for this work. Section 4 presents the implementation of the platform. Finally, Sect. 5 describes the conclusions of this work.

2   Related Work

The term Internet of Things (IoT) was coined by the work done by the MIT Auto-ID Center in 1999. In that work, an infrastructure was designed based on RFID [12]. However, just in the last few years this term has been popularized in several contexts. IoT allows users to interconnect heterogeneous physical devices gathering data to create many applications and services.

From a technical point of view, IoT is a paradigm that needs the integration of several technologies to be used: Machine to machine (M2M), cloud computing, big data, communication protocols and wireless sensor networks (WSN). Zhou et al. [31] presents a set of features and requirements to integrate those technologies:

- Data management: The "things" (devices) generate a huge quantity of data that need to be stored and managed.
- Web based interfaces: The "things" (devices) require this to exchange information and to integrate different applications.
- Interoperability: The "things" are heterogeneous. However, they must communicate between all devices.
- Real time: IoT applications can be classified into real time and no real time.
- Dynamic network: IoT will integrate several heterogeneous devices. The devices can be connected or disconnected at any moment.
- Everything as a service (XaaS): If the number of connected devices grows, then the number of applications will grow too. These services must be available to be used and reused.
- Security: IoT needs global accessibility and connectivity, which means anybody can access it in any moment and from any place. This increases the range of attacks for the IoT applications and networks.
- Privacy: Any IoT application must respect users' privacy.

IoT communication technologies enable the connection of heterogeneous devices and the creation of specific services. The tool that allows that communication is called protocol. Different protocols can be used in IoT applications according to several standards. Al-Fuqaha et al. [2] shows a list of the most relevant protocols, here we show some of them:

- HyperText Transfer Protocol (HTTP): This is the protocol that transfers most of the information used on the Internet. One of the development architectures based on this protocol is REST (REpresentational State Transfer). REST allows exchanging data between different clients and servers on HTTP in an easy way. REST enables the implementation of a non-state architecture. In other words, an action on a resource does not depend on another action.
- Constrained Application Protocol (CoAP): CoAP defines a web transfer protocol based on REST to implement HTTP functionalities. However, CoAP uses UDP (not TCP) by default, which is important to modify IoT applications. Additionally, CoAP modifies some functionalities of HTTP to achieve the IoT requirements such as low energy consumption and operations in presence of noisy links.
- Message Queue Telemetry Transport (MQTT): MQTT is a message protocol that was introduced by Andy Stanford-Clark from IBM and Arlen Nipper from Arcom (now EUROTECH) in 1999. MQTT aims to connect embedded devices and networks with applications and middlewares. The connection operation uses a routing mechanism and one-to-one, one-to-many and many-to-many. MQTT consists of three basic components: Subscriber, publisher and broker. A device can be registered as a subscriber for specific topics in order to be informed by the broker when the publishers publish on a topic. The publisher acts as the generator of the information. Then, the publisher transmits the information to the stakeholders (subscribers) through the broker.

The potentialities offered by IoT allow to develop a big number of applications. These applications can improve people's quality of life and can be deployed in different contexts: Health, agriculture, transport, sustainability and others. In the next subsection, we talk about the Internet of Things in sustainable applications, specifically for smart campuses.

2.1 Sustainability and IoT

Since 1962, when Rachel Carson published her book "Silent Spring" [3], talking about the concern around pesticides negative environmental effects on ecosystems and human health, it has become increasingly important to talk about the impacts from anthropogenic activities in both rural and urban areas, their ecosystems and population itself, as well as efforts to achieve a healthy environment.

Besides, during the United Nations Conference on the Human Environment, in 1972 [28], Higher Education Institutions were encouraged to incorporate educational programs into their curriculum that would generate knowledge around the problems of economic and population growth and environmental crisis. With the aim of achieving society awareness and strong environmental policies, based on the efforts from universities and the education system in general [7].

It was not until 1987 that a concept emerged and that would become important to understand the need to take action on all those impacts that Carson [3], Meadows et al. [13], and many other authors, society sectors, agendas, and statements [4,10,19,21]; have demonstrated, debated and questioned. Considering the consequences of an economic and population growth that must consider its environment and importance for a society that depends on it for its survival. This concept is sustainable development, which is the "development that meets the needs of the present without compromising the ability of future generations to meet their own needs" [16].

Added to the efforts made by these authors and Agendas, Stockholm Declaration [28], the Millennium Development Goals [17], current Sustainable Development Goals and its 2030 Agenda [18], have been focused on the achievement of sustainable development worldwide, but also in strengthen Sustainability in Higher Education (SHE), specifically. In recent decades, a series of sustainability rankings have been born [9,14,22,30], evaluating aspects such as environmental management policies themselves, education in sustainability and research carried out by the Higher Education Institutions (HEI). Among these rankings is the UI GreenMetric World University Ranking, which is an initiative launched in 2010 by the Universitas Indonesia to recognize those universities that were making efforts to reduce environmental impact and combat climate change, and establish a uniform and attractive system where universities could numerically measure their progress and compare themselves with other committed universities worldwide [27].

Several works related to sustainability have been developed in the last few years. Xiaojun et al. [29] noted that doing an empirical analysis of air pollution with an automatic monitoring system with high precision and forecasting features is too expensive, so they present an IoT system that reduces the hardware cost to 1/10 and the information collected allows use of a neural network to the forecasting task.

Ahmed et al. [1] show WaterGrid-Sense as a node based on LoRa to monitor and control a smart water management system. It is a full stack node with all the components integrated in a single board. Besides, they conducted two experiments with good results related to power consumption and communication reliability.

If we talk about smart campuses applications, Marchetti et al. [11] present an initiative to create a sustainable campus where low cost technologies are used for monitoring environmental parameters such as carbon dioxide, humidity and temperature in the classrooms of the University of Ferrara. Other systems have been developed in order to monitor ultra-fine particles (PM2.5) in the campus using LoRaWAN [20]. This is done with the objective of testing the quality of the air which can affect people in the campus. Rodrigues [23] uses LoRaWAN also, several devices were distributed inside a university campus to monitor harmful gas emissions to people's health and generate alerts for the academic community and the campus administration to improve the quality of campus' environment.

MQTT protocol has also been used for these applications, Muladi [15] shows a system to monitor air quality in a campus using MQTT. To develop that system, a wireless sensor network was created using Arduino and Raspberry Pi and the collected information is visualized using a web application.

We have seen that these applications have been implemented in a variety of platforms, using various protocols to offer some kind of information to the users. In our approach, we created a platform that could allow students at the University to create their own application towards sustainability. Giving more flexibility when it comes to the use of sensors and the way each user receives the information. Also, by making the programming part easier, students can focus on work on a useful application for the campus.

3   Architecture

To be able to implement our proposed solution, first we need to design an architecture that can manage all the users, teams and IoT applications that we want to deploy. In this section we describe the proposed architecture for the development of the platform.

Reference architectures have been developed to establish a set of rules to develop IoT systems in a standardized way. IIRA (Industrial Internet Reference Architecture) is a reference based on functional aspects of IoT applied to industry [8]. IIRA identifies common architectural issues on IoT systems and classifies the issues on viewpoints with the stakeholders. This reference architecture defines four viewpoints: Business, Use, Functional and Implementation.

Business and Use viewpoints are focused on the stakeholders and the description of activities on several system's components. On the other hand, Functional and Implementation viewpoints are related with the requirements, features and design of typical IoT systems. IIRA presents an architectural pattern of three tiers which show the details of the required components and technologies to develop an IoT System. This pattern mixes most of the components from functional domains and is made up of an Edge Tier, a Platform Tier, and an Enterprise Tier.

On the Edge Tier, the control domain is implemented. The control domain represents a set of functions with sensors and actuators. Basically, several devices collect data in this tier. On Platform Tier the information and operation domains are implemented. This tier is related to data management and storage, and with this information, the system tasks can be optimized. Finally, Enterprise Tier implements applications of specific domains, supports system decisions and provides user interfaces.

This work presents an architecture based on the three-tier architectural pattern of IIRA. Figure 1 shows the details of the architecture, and its components are described in the next paragraph.

On the Edge Tier, several devices are sensing data and actuators can be activated according to the system's rules. Besides, the devices can be connected to the platform using IoT protocols through the APIs. The data is processed and

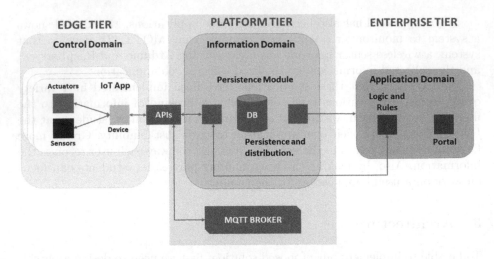

Fig. 1. Designed architecture for the system based on [8]

analyzed on the information domain, pipelines can be used to improve real-time data processing. The information analysis is sent to the operation domain. After that, the operation domain makes decisions according to the rules established by the stakeholders, then it sends the decision to the control domain. On the Enterprise tier, a customized dashboard shows relevant information to the final user and provides a set of tools to create the system's rules. Those rules are used by the operation domain to make decisions.

The proposed platform was designed in a standardized way, this allows to add more features and services in the future. Also, the use of IIRA in this work can be used as a guide for other IoT developers.

4   Implementation

In order to implement the platform according to the architecture described before, we selected ThingsBoard [26] version 3.1.0. Thingsboard is an open source framework to develop IoT platforms. This framework was chosen given that it has all the system modules needed for the proposed architecture. It provides a set of tools for device creation, user management, rules definition and application management. Moreover, this framework offers support to several IoT protocols such as HTTP, MQTT, Sigfox or CoAP, giving the possibility to scale this platform to these communication protocols. Thingsboard also allows the users to define rules through what they call "nodes". The users can create alarms, send emails when it is triggered, and other functionalities that make it easier for students to create their own smart campus application.

On the other hand, an IoT indoor air application was developed to validate the use of the platform. The application aims to monitor the quality of the air but also to generate alarms in case it is required. The variables to be sensed are

CO2, temperature and humidity, which are commonly used for this task [11,15, 24]. Next, it was necessary to select the right hardware for this app. The app includes two NodeMCU (a development card based on ESP8266 processor), two sensors MQ135 to measure CO2 and two sensors DHT11 to measure humidity and temperature. Also, it is important to say that the devices are located in different locations, which is one of the great features that IoT offers.

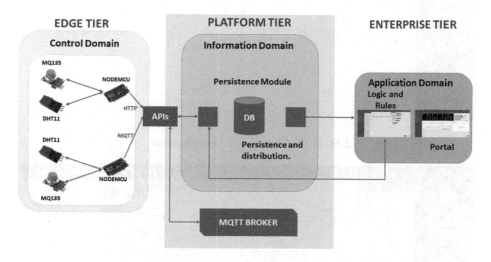

Fig. 2. Proposed IoT indoor application.

Figure 2 shows the architecture of the proposed app. Each NodeMCU has a MQ135 and a DHT11 connected. One of them sends the data to the platform using a HTTP API, and the other one sends the data using a MQTT API. The use of different protocols aims to demonstrate the interoperability of the platform. The information is processed and then shown in a customizable dashboard (See Fig. 3).

The platform provides a tool to set several alarms, depending on the application. In this case, six alarms were created in order to test this feature. Figure 4 presents how the alarms were configured using a visual tool, if the measured values are greater than a threshold, then the alarm is activated. This visual tool allows a user with little knowledge on programming to configure the alarms by themselves. Although this is a simple example, more advanced alarms can be configured with some coding on the tool. Finally, the alarm that was generated can be seen from the dashboard and that an email was sent to the stakeholders (Fig. 5). In this test, the alarms were configured to be triggered when the CO_2 and humidity values were higher than a certain threshold (in this case it was below the reference values established by current regulations [5,6], so we could test the alarm functionality).

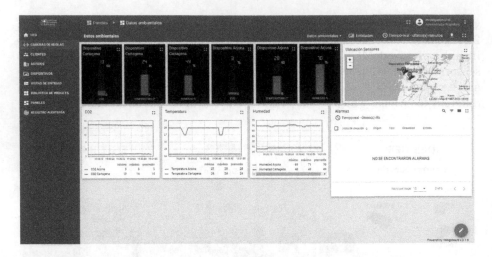

Fig. 3. Dashboard of the application.

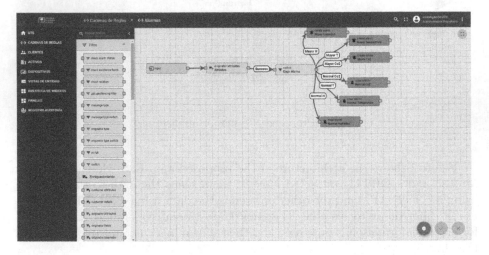

Fig. 4. Set of alarms for the IoT application.

The proposed platform was developed following a reference architecture, which allows additional features to be easily added later. Additionally, the platform offers an inter-operable environment, because devices can communicate using different protocols such as MQTT or HTTP. Finally, several applications can be developed in this way and may be integrated to the platform using the available APIs, in order to provide the student community information about the campus and make decisions to improve it.

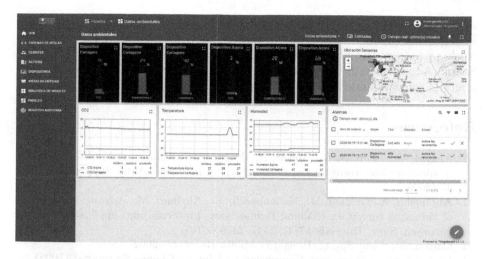

Fig. 5. Dashboard with the activated alarms.

5   Conclusions

The Internet of Things is a novel paradigm that allows to create applications which aim to improve the people's quality of life. These applications can be deployed on several fields such as health, industry, agriculture, and others. This work is focused on the concept of a smart campus, where several IoT applications can gather data and give relevant information about some conditions of the campus. In general, applications on IoT need the integration of several technologies, devices, protocols and web applications. This forces the developer to have knowledge and duplicate his efforts in building the mechanisms to allow the integration, neglecting the main task of developing the application.

This work presents Smart UTB, a platform for the deployment and management of Internet of Things applications on a smart campus. This platform was designed and developed in a standardized way, specifically using the guidelines described on IIRA. The platform enables users to create work groups to manage their own IoT application, this is ideal in a university environment where we can find several academic groups.

The applications that can be managed in the platform can be focused on several fields, the only requirement is that the protocol must use the devices. In order to offer an inter-operable platform, two APIs are available, one for the HTTP and another for the MQTT protocol. On the other hand, the developers of the application can set alarms from the platform if it's necessary.

To validate the use of the platform, an IoT indoor air application was developed. The devices use both protocols supported by the platform to demonstrate the interoperability. Several alarms were configured also.

The design and the development of the platform and the IoT app presented in this work can be used for the IoT community to build applications using reference architectures. Besides, the smart campus platform can be used by the student community to deploy applications or test the concept of IoT. As future work, we propose to add support to other IoT protocols such as LoRA, CoAP and Sigfox. Additionally, it would be important to test the scalability of the solution and add some analytic features to improve campus decision-making process.

References

1. Ahmed, U., Mumtaz, R., Anwar, H., Mumtaz, S., Qamar, A.M.: Water quality monitoring: from conventional to emerging technologies. Water Supply **20**(1), 28–45 (2020)
2. Al-Fuqaha, A., Guizani, M., Mohammadi, M., Aledhari, M., Ayyash, M.: Internet of things: a survey on enabling technologies, protocols, and applications. IEEE Commun. Surv. Tutorials **17**(4), 2347–2376 (2015)
3. Carson, R.: Silent Spring. Houghton Mifflin Harcourt (2002)
4. United Nations Framework Convention on Climate Change Secretariat (1992)
5. Decree 1594 of 1984 (1984). https://www.minambiente.gov.co/images/Gestion IntegraldelRecursoHidrico/pdf/normativa/Decreto_1594_de_1984.pdf
6. The Ministry of Environment and Sustainable Development: Decree 3930 of 2010 (2010). https://www.minambiente.gov.co/images/normativa/decretos/2010/dec_3930_2010.pdf
7. Gomez, C., Botero, C.M.: The greening of higher education: a case study in three institutions in Medellin, Colombia. Gestion y Ambiente **15**(3), 77–88 (2012)
8. IIC: The industrial internet of things volume g1: Reference architecture (2017)
9. Jajo, N.K., Harrison, J.: World university ranking systems: an alternative approach using partial least squares path modelling. J. High. Educ. Policy Manag. **36**(5), 471–482 (2014)
10. Kyoto Protocol (1997)
11. Marchetti, N., Cavazzini, A., Pasti, L., Catani, M., Malagù, C., Guidi, V.: A campus sustainability initiative: indoor air quality monitoring in classrooms. In: 2015 XVIII AISEM Annual Conference, pp. 1–4. IEEE (2015)
12. Mattern, F., Floerkemeier, C.: From the internet of computers to the internet of things. In: Sachs, K., Petrov, I., Guerrero, P. (eds.) From Active Data Management to Event-Based Systems and More. LNCS, vol. 6462, pp. 242–259. Springer, Heidelberg (2010). https://doi.org/10.1007/978-3-642-17226-7_15
13. Meadows, D., Randers, J., Meadows, D.: Limits to Growth: The 30-Year Update. Chelsea Green Publishing (2004)
14. Moed, H.F.: A critical comparative analysis of five world university rankings. Scientometrics **110**(2), 967–990 (2016). https://doi.org/10.1007/s11192-016-2212-y
15. Muladi, M., Sendari, S., Widiyaningtyas, T.: outdoor air quality monitor using MQTT protocol on smart campus network. In: 2018 International Conference on Sustainable Information Engineering and Technology (SIET), pp. 216–219. IEEE (2018)
16. United Nations: Our common future (1987). https://sustainabledevelopment.un.org/content/documents/5987our-common-future.pdf
17. United Nations: Millennium development goals (2000). https://www.un.org/millenniumgoals/
18. United Nations: Millennium development goals (2015). https://www.un.org/sustainabledevelopment/sustainable-development-goals/

19. United Nations: Sustainable development goals knowledge platform (2020). https://sustainabledevelopment.un.org/conferences
20. Park, J., Oh, Y., Byun, H.H., Kim, C.K.: Low cost fine-grained air quality monitoring system using LoRAWAN. In: 2019 International Conference on Information Networking (ICOIN), pp. 439–441. IEEE (2019)
21. UNEP: The montreal protocol (2020). https://www.unenvironment.org/ozonaction/who-we-are/about-montreal-protocol
22. Ragazzi, M., Ghidini, F.: Environmental sustainability of universities: critical analysis of a green ranking. Energy Procedia **119**, 111–120 (2017)
23. Rodrigues, P.L., dos Santos Rabello, R., Cervi, C.R.: An application to generate air quality recommendations and alerts on a smart campus. In: Stephanidis, C. (ed.) HCII 2019. CCIS, vol. 1033, pp. 507–514. Springer, Cham (2019). https://doi.org/10.1007/978-3-030-23528-4_69
24. Sastra, N.P., Wiharta, D.M.: Environmental monitoring as an IoT application in building smart campus of universitas udayana. In: 2016 International Conference on Smart Green Technology in Electrical and Information Systems (ICSGTEIS), pp. 85–88. IEEE (2016)
25. University Leaders for a Sustainable Future: The taillores declaration (1990). http://ulsf.org/talloires-declaration/
26. ThingsBoard: Thingsboard open-source IoT platform (2017). https://thingsboard.io
27. UIG: Ui greenmetric world university ranking (2019). http://greenmetric.ui.ac.id/what-is-greenmetric/
28. UNESCO: The stockholm declaration (1972). https://www.ipcc.ch/apps/njlite/srex/njlite_download.php?id=6471
29. Xiaojun, C., Xianpeng, L., Peng, X.: IoT-based air pollution monitoring and forecasting system. In: 2015 International Conference on Computer and Computational Sciences (ICCCS), pp. 257–260. IEEE (2015)
30. Yudkevich, M., Altbach, P.G., Rumbley, L.E.: Global university rankings: the "olympic games" of higher education? Prospects **45**(4), 411–419 (2015)
31. Zhou, J., et al.: Cloudthings: a common architecture for integrating the internet of things with cloud computing. In: Proceedings of the 2013 IEEE 17th International Conference on Computer Supported Cooperative Work in Design (CSCWD), pp. 651–657. IEEE (2013)

Development of a Short-Range Continuous Wave Radar Prototype Kit as a Learning Tool for Theoretical and Practical Technical Training

Felipe Silva Gómez(⊠), Tomás Francisco Guzmán(⊠), and Yolanda Parra Guacaneme(⊠)

Corporación de Alta Tecnología para la Defensa (CODALTEC), Bogotá, Colombia
{fsilva,tguzman,yparra}@codaltec.com

Abstract. Radar technology is a topic of interest today because of its many applications such as autonomous vehicles, security systems, health monitoring, among others. Practical training in this technology is not always possible because commercial systems are in closed enclosures, so they are not easy to explore; some learning kits are not affordable for institutions. This paper presents an LFMCW radar prototype kit for teaching and practical training in this technology. This kit allows the user a detailed approach to the hardware and software of a radar, and it describes the practical experience carried out by students and instructors of an academic institution using the prototype kit from two teaching levels: classroom training and outdoor practical training.

Keywords: LFMCW radar · Practical learning system · Radar technology education · Embedded systems · Radar signal processing

1 Introduction

Use of radar technology is increasing in different applications and equipment that people use in their everyday life. Topics such as improving the driving experience of vehicles [1], managing parking spaces in malls [2], reinforcing perimeter surveillance in critical infrastructures, driving autonomous platforms with advanced driver assistance systems [3], and controlling vital signs in medical applications [4, 5], among others are examples of its applications. Knowledge and teaching of this technology are essential for its correct adoption and use to create technological innovations.

LFMCW (Linear Frequency-Modulated Continuous Wave) radars are among the most widely used technologies for many reasons: their performance, their architecture and less complex hardware, their low consumption and power emission, and a relatively low cost compared to other types of radars [6].

Radar technology is an area of specialized knowledge that, except for postgraduate programs, is not wide enough in terms of diffusion. It is rare to have physical tools for practical learning, perhaps by requiring specialized laboratory equipment that is not always available in learning centers [7]; usually, the most used tools are simulation software that does not offer the same experience with physical elements [8].

J. C. Figueroa-García et al. (Eds.): WEA 2021, CCIS 1431, pp. 250–262, 2021.
https://doi.org/10.1007/978-3-030-86702-7_22

This document describes a radar kit prototype as a practical teaching tool; its purpose is to help with improving knowledge about this valuable technology, as a complete kit for practices; it has the advantage of not needing the use of specialized laboratory equipment. The designed prototype includes commercially available elements, except for the Graphical User Interface Software; it is designed specifically for this radar application. This strategy allowed to work with reliability and get a fair price for the kit, which is an adequate condition to have an accessible learning tool.

The prototype was developed with SENA (Servicio Nacional de Aprendizaje). It is a public institution for education and training and contributed to the project with the pedagogical part to build the learning elements used in the kit. The joint work with SENA included a theoretical-practical introductory course to radar technology and the learning guides for practical teaching for instructors and students. The kit has the elements to deploy and store the radar components, it has the hardware for the assembly and operation of an LFMCW K-band short-range radar, and it has a Graphical User Interface Software to visualize the monitored area and the detected targets.

2   LFMCW Radar Overview

Radars use radio-frequency waves to detect objects and estimate their distance, direction, and speed [9]. Radars are active sensors as they generate their signal to detect objects in their field of view. There are two main types of radar: pulsed radar and continuous-wave radar. Depending on the application, one or the other is proper.

Continuous-wave radars constantly send a signal at a given frequency and, by the Doppler effect, they can detect moving objects. When the signal emitted by the radar collides with the object located within its field of view returns a radio frequency echo; these two signals, the radiated and the received waves, combine to get the difference that represents the change in frequency due to the Doppler effect of the moving target, which allows estimating the target speed. To find the range or distance of the target, the continuous wave signal experiments a change in its parameters of amplitude or frequency in such a way that it is "marked" to see its beginning and end. This mark lets to obtain the round-trip time value of the signal to calculate the distance to which the target is.

LFMCW radars are continuous wave radars that use linear frequency modulation to estimate the target range and Doppler shift [10]. The resulting signal from the mixture between the transmitted signal and the echo is known as the beat signal fb and the time difference Δt is a measure of the distance to the target.

The beat frequency fb is:

$$f_b = \frac{4Rf_m\Delta f}{c} \tag{1}$$

Where R is the range or distance to the target, fm is the modulation frequency, Δf is the peak frequency deviation, c is the speed of light and Δt time difference between the sent signal and the echo.

3   Methodology and Development

The project involves two milestones: the radar prototype and the technical training. The following sections describe each one of these.

3.1 Radar Prototype

The design and fabrication of a radar requires several different areas of expertise. The planning of the project included a separation of activities related to each one of these areas.

Radar System. In Fig. 1 there is a hierarchical map of the areas required to create the prototype. Hardware includes electronic circuits: power supply, interface board, sensor, and processor board. Hardware also includes mechanical components such as the radar enclosure with the internal supports for the circuits and the accessories required for the system integration, such as cables, power cords, hard case, Wi-Fi router, and radar tripod. The software includes the Graphical User Interface Software, which runs on a laptop PC and serves as an interface for the user to interact with the radar, showing targets over a map background along with main radar functions. The embedded software runs on the Processor Board inside the radar case, processing the radar signal in real-time with the help of a real-time operating kernel. Before testing the radar processing algorithms inside the radar device, the research team developed a complete mathematical model and simulation software; this exercise allowed the designers to check calculations and do offline analyses not possible to do within the embedded system.

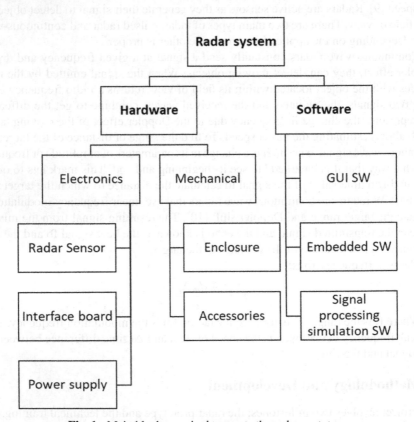

Fig. 1. Main blocks required to create the radar prototype.

The prototype is a monostatic, non-rotatory Linear Frequency Modulated Continuous Wave radar operating in the K-band frequency. Signal processing is embedded software in a dual-core processor of the series Zynq7000. Each core has assigned one task, and this division keeps enough resources for all processes. This processing approach is known as Asymmetric Multiprocessing Real-Time Operating System because it uses a Real-Time Operating System in each one of the cores. Figure 2 shows this division of tasks between processors. There is an Ethernet interface that communicates the results of internal processes (plots, tracks) to the laptop with Graphical User Interface (GUI) Software through Transfer Control Protocol (TCP). GUI software interacts with the user in a personal computer that receives information from the radar. It sends different control commands to the radar, such as turn on/off, power change, frequency channels, among others.

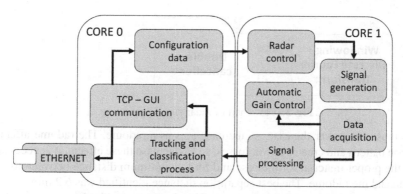

Fig. 2. Asymmetric Multiprocessing Real Time Operating Systems with two cores.

Signal processing takes the signals from the electromagnetic sensor and turns them into information. Figure 3 presents a flowchart of this process; radars bring data from I and Q channels from this data. The process begins with keeping only the positive ramp and applying a DC filter to remove the signal offset. Automatic Gain Control (AGC) increases the dynamic range of the signal. On one hand, when the signal amplitude is weak the AGC amplifies it; however, when the signal is strong the AGC does not amplify it to avoid ADC saturation. A first Discrete Fourier Transform is applied to get a signal distance profile. Double canceller acts as a clutter removal filter to remove static targets such as walls or trees. Then A new DFT is applied in the second dimension, called the Doppler DFT. It sorts signals by target speed. A magnitude operation followed by a CFAR (Constant False Alarm Rate) detector is applied to get target detection. A single target could create multiple detections, so it is necessary to do a group process to get the plots to send to the GUI software.

Radar Enclosure. Keeping in mind that the radar prototype must work in outdoor environments, it is necessary to have a proper enclosure for the radar to support the performance even in conditions such as rain, direct sunlight, or dust that can damage the electronic circuits or create a drift in system parameters such as the radiation pattern. For these reasons, it was chosen as a generic IP55 enclosure to protect internal systems and circuits. There were three main challenges in this design: 1) Radar electromagnetic

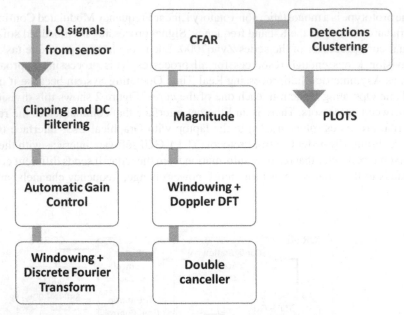

Fig. 3. Flowchart of radar signal processing.

waves must cross over the case, so the case acts as a radome. The radome affects the radiation pattern and creates power losses, so to decrease these effects, it is necessary to select the proper material for the case and find an optimum distance between the radar antenna and the radome. The best separation distance identified was 6.2 mm.

2) Accommodation of Printed Circuit Boards (PCB) inside the case according to size restrictions. It creates the need of having internal supports for the boards. Figure 4 shows the view of PCB circuits inside the case without the internal supports for a clearer view. 3) Create conditions for temperature dissipation so that radar will not overheat in operation.

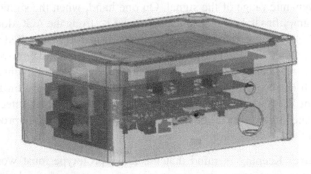

Fig. 4. 3D model of the radar enclosure with internal circuit boards.

Graphical User Interface (GUI) Software. The radar system requires a tool to show detected targets in its field of view to the user, in this case, to instructors or students.

Therefore, a desktop application running on a laptop was designed and developed for this purpose, called GUI software. This software exchanges information with the radar through the network interface. The software has two main functionalities: control and visualization. The software can control radar sensor functions such as turning on and off, initializing radiation, increasing or decreasing the radiated power level and selecting the frequency channel. The user can fill in other fields such as the coordinates of the scene, true north, the unit selection system, establishing a connection with radar, among others.

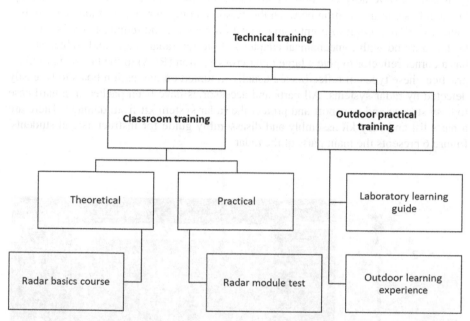

Fig. 5. Map of the different parts of technical training.

The visualization consists of a screen that shows plots and targets from the radar, and the user can load a satellite map of the operating scenario to show in the background. It has main functions such as zooming in and out, moving the screen, a distance measurement tool, and a rotating map. User can save scenarios for future sessions. Figure 6 and Fig. 7 show the views of the GUI software.

An Interface Communication Protocol was created for the exchange of messages between the GUI software and the radar. GUI software is written in C# language with the use of Microsoft Maps WPF library which allows the use of Bing maps to locate plots and tracks with their coordinates over a background map. Even though only one radar prototype was developed, the GUI software can add up to 32 radar devices, which could be connected simultaneously. The software was created following an MVVM design pattern (Model – View – ViewModel) to have a modular and scalable solution.

The main functions of GUI software are: 1) create or edit surveillance areas, which is the physical area that is going to be evaluated with the radar. 2) Add, configure, edit, remove, connect, or disconnect radar devices. 3) Toolbars functions as measuring distance, clean previous measures, zoom in and out, center the map, map panning, and map rotation. 4) Display in real-time plot and tracks from the radar, also showing their properties as position, speed, direction. 5) Save or open previous scenarios with the surveillance areas and radar configuration, so there is no need to reconfigure radar on each use.

Accessories. The kit includes a set of accessories to make sure the complete integration of all subsystems. First, the kit includes the necessary cables, adapters, and connectors such as the AC/DC adapter, a power cord, Ethernet cables, and accessories for the laptop. For wireless communication between the personal computer and the radar system, two routers work in a point-to-point communication network and require line of sight. The kit has a tripod with a mechanical adapter to hold the radar safely and stable. The kit has a corner reflector to give a large radar cross-section (RCS) to the targets in outdoor practice; these types of reflectors are usually mounted on navigation boats to be easily detected by radar systems. All parts and accessories have been packed in a hard case to easy storage and transport and protect the radar system kit from damage. There are a parts list and easy kit assembly and disassembly guide for instructors and students. Figure 6 presents the main parts of the radar.

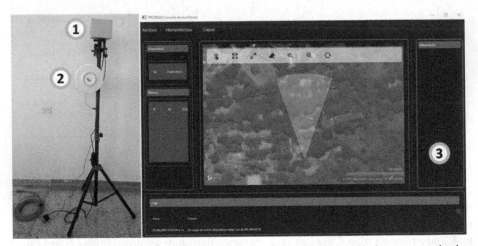

Fig. 6. Main parts of the radar system kit: 1) radar, 2) point-to-point wireless communication device, 3) GUI software.

Prototype Test Protocol. According to the project scope, the research team designed a test protocol to verify the proper functionality of the radar prototype. The protocol has a set of 19 requirements for the prototype, so it involves 19 tests, including methods such as visual inspection, datasheet inspection, measuring with instruments, practical demonstrations, analysis, and certification.

3.2 Technical Training

With the prototype developed, there are two possible different levels of training: classroom training and outdoor practical training. It is highly recommended to begin classroom training before outdoor practical training to ensure that the learning experience is as rewarding as possible. Figure 5 shows the different parts of technical training.

Classroom Training. The classroom training has the goal of teaching the fundamentals of radar technology. This learning includes the prototype of this project as a tool of training. SENA took care of selecting fifteen people among instructors and students to receive the knowledge in the classroom. This level comprises a theoretical part and a practical part.

The theoretical part consists of a basic radar course, which has two stages: the first has the purpose of learning the basic knowledge about radar systems, their classification, their history, and understanding of the equations and models for the radar technology are. Radar processing, current/future radar technologies, and applications are topics from the beginning of the second stage of the course.

The practical part in the classroom is the last topic of the second stage. It consists of a radar module test which includes an introduction to Python programming to test an elemental commercial continuous-wave radar transceiver to see its functionality. This stage is the first contact with a small radar module easy to plug in and use to promote curiosity in students, who can see how to practice the theoretical concepts learned with this technology. This moment let the students understanding and manipulation signal and data radar processing algorithms.

Outdoor Practical Training. The second level of technical training aims to test the radar prototype previously designed and developed in this project. This practice level has two components: the laboratory learning guide and the outdoor learning experience.

The research team designed the laboratory learning guide after the guidance given by SENA for the structuring of learning guidebooks to start the practice with the radar prototype. This guide has different sections for students to let them know what the activities are.

First, the guide describes the parts, components, and materials available in the radar kit, describing in detail what are the functionalities of each one of them with text and images. Then, the lab learning guide continues with detailed assembly and installation instructions for deploying the radar system, describing the process step by step with illustrative text and photos. In addition, the guide describes the steps for making power connections, network connections, and connecting to the laptop with graphical user interface software that interacts with the end-user.

The guide has a chapter dedicated exclusively to the Graphical User Interface Software to teach the student all steps to add a radar device, configure its main functionality, and run the device to view the radar detection. The last part of the lab learning guide explains target detection tests. These tests belong to the second part of the outdoor practical training.

This guide describes the steps required for users to identify and implement the radar prototype, set up the test to develop, and run the test. In the same way, at the end of the tests, users can disassemble and store the kit elements correctly.

The outdoor learning practice is the second part of outdoor practical training, and it has a direct relation with the target detection tests of the laboratory learning guide.

As a work strategy to check the proper functioning of the prototype and the usefulness of the laboratory learning guide, the users of the prototype interact in practice with it, execute its deployment, and test its operation to detect targets according to the learning guide.

The outdoor learning experience allows students to interact with the radar prototype and understand its complexity. The developed prototype is transportable, and its elements let its easy and rapid deployment in different test sites.

It was necessary to conform work crews to start the target detection activities: one group had the aim to deploy the prototype and its connections, another group was in charge to run the laptop with Graphical User Interface Software, and another team acted as targets in different dynamics of movement, directions, and speeds of travel.

The first activity aims to recognize how to run the prototype and detect a target (person). For this activity, a person places in front of the radar, and then he starts walking away radially. In the Graphical User Interface, students find the distance in which the target appears and the range in which it is no longer detected. Reflective cones take place on the testing area to show where the object appears on the Graphical User Interface and the point at which it disappears. The students can measure the distances between the radar and the cones and compare the ranges in the Graphical User Interface. This comparison lets to check the correct operation of the radar and the GUI.

The idea of the second activity is to detect a target larger than a person. The students can emulate this kind of target with the corner reflector (included in the radar kit). The procedure is like the first activity: a person moves in front of the radar carrying the corner reflector. In this activity, the student must see and analyze how the size or type of target influences radar detection.

The third activity includes two people, who must walk in front of the radar, moving away from each other constantly, and in the graphical user interface it to observe and recognize when one or two targets are detected, depending on the separation between them. This exercise let to analyze the distance resolution of the radar.

In the fourth activity, two people will move in front of the radar and stop at some point (within the radar coverage area) until the radar does not detect them and they are not displayed in the graphical user interface. This exercise lets to differentiate the detection of moving targets and static targets. The users can experiment with different movements, directions, and speeds to see their behavior on screen.

4   Results

The first result of this project consists of a short-range radar system kit as a learning tool for theoretical and practical technical training. This kit has all subsystems that integrate the radar, starting from the GUI software, through the communications system, the processor, and the radar sensor. The GUI software allows the radar operator or end-user (teacher or student) to see the different detections in the field of view of the radar in a coverage map, and control de radar sensor with actions such as turning on-off, initializing radiation, increasing decreasing the radiated power level, selecting the frequency channel, among other functions. The kit includes a corner reflector to emulate bigger targets due to its larger radar cross-section (RCS). This kind of reflector facilitates target detection for radar, and it is a didactic tool for learning.

This prototype provides a solution to develop field practices in which instructors can teach the principles and basics about LFMCW radars, identify how radars detect targets in the field of view, recognize how the GUI software works in radar systems, and test the theoretical knowledge through practice.

Once the radar prototype finished its design and development phases, the research team applied a protocol to test the main characteristics of the radar to confirm the correct functionality of the system. The protocol includes features like, for example, operation frequency, radiated power, performance in terms of range, and azimuth, among others. Figure 7 shows the scenario for the outdoor test protocol. Table 1 summarizes the main characteristics of the radar prototype.

The second result of this project is the learning experience that took place in the facilities of SENA. The research team carried out a demonstration of the radar system kit with the prototype ready to work. Thirteen students and two instructors of technical careers related to electronics and telecommunications from the educational institution participate in this demonstration.

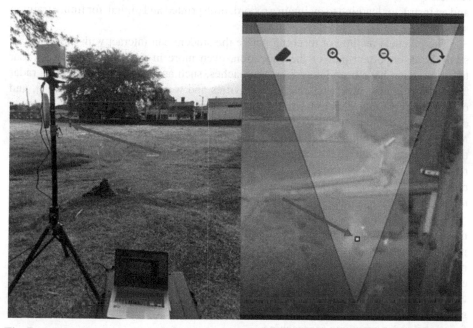

Fig. 7. Outdoor test protocol: the graphical user interface software shows the detection of a person who was walking in the radial direction to the radar.

Table 1. Main specifications of the radar prototype.

Parameter	Value	Parameter	Value
Central Transmitter Frequency	24.125 GHz	Max range	60 m persons
Bandwidth	250 MHz	Range resolution	3 m
Horizontal beamwidth	30° (±15°)	Weather protection	IP55
Vertical beamwidth	20° (±10°)	Weight	2.5 kg
Max output power EIRP	20 dBm (100 mW)	Radar dimensions	190 × 150 × 85 mm

This activity included a short lesson about radar technology in the classroom, and an outdoor demonstration of the assembly, operation, and disassembly of the radar system kit. The goal of this event was to see in practice the topics learned in the classroom. The event was well-received, and a learning activity was held for the first time at this institution focused on radar systems. The added value was that, since this institution contributed financial resources to the project, this kit was delivered to the institution through instructors to continue with this type of training activities, not only in educational matters but also in training activities for the job. The research team provide the guidelines and an instructor learning to maintain a record, both printed and digital, for future training sessions.

The practical method of teaching where the student can interact with the object of study is an important part of the education, even more in engineering. As for radar teaching, there have been lately new approaches, such as a teaching method for radar artillery equipment involving practical activities and work under simulation [11], and one of the most innovative teaching projects of radar engineering, which is the open design of a Doppler radar system used for the Massive Open Online Course of the Massachusetts Institute of Technology [12]. With this design and without a high budget, the students can build a basic radar using metal cans as antennas. The work presented in this document helps as a practical tool for radar technology teaching and provides not only the basic core of the radar but also the enclosure and all accessories that let to do tests and operations outdoors checking the results in real-time.

Even though there are many universities with undergraduate programs in telecommunications or electronics engineering, radar equipment is not often for teaching. The main reasons are that commercial radar systems are not available to explore and do not allow signal manipulation, and commercial systems created for radar teaching are expensive. In addition, radar technology is just a topic of these programs, and expensive equipment could be underused. For instance, in Colombia, there are no graduate programs specifically in radar technology. As a result, the research team developed a fully functional radar prototype for teaching.

5 Conclusions

To develop the project demanded the acquisition and strengthening of new capacities of a specialized technical nature by the research group in fields such as modeling, simulation, design, and manufacture of electronic, mechanical, and radiofrequency subsystems, as well as digital signal processing, the use of embedded systems with the real-time operation and front-end applications for displaying information to the user.

The goal was to increase the knowledge in training with SENA through the experience in a learning environment and providing a functional radar prototype with laboratory guides. The radar kit lets students become familiar with this type of system in specific surveillance applications. Besides, they understand the process and principles of operation in radar systems. Students and instructors revealed interest in radar technology and the lack of knowledge on these topics.

The radar prototype performed satisfactorily within the intended academic scope. The research team executed the test protocol both in the laboratory and in the field, and it allowed not only to test the system but also to characterize it. This process showed positive results against the requirements set before the design.

The training tool in this type of technology is possible to lead to other academic institutions, not only at a technical level but also at a professional level. Accordingly, this training tool lets to improve the academy and scientific education of students from different branches of engineering such as electronics, mechanics, electromechanical, telecommunications, computing, or similar.

Acknowledgment. This project was performed at the researching center Corporación de Alta Tecnología para la Defensa – CODALTEC with the participation of SENA-CISM (Centro de Industria y Servicios del Meta), the SENNOVA staff and financed by SENA and CODALTEC under the grant "Convenio Especial de Cooperación n° 0206 de 2018 entre el Servicio Nacional de Aprendizaje – SENA, Tecnología e Innovación Inversiones S.A.S. y Corporación de Alta Tecnología para la Defensa – CODALTEC".

References

1. Swami, P., Jain, A., Goswami, P., Chitnis, K., Dubey, A., Chaudhari, P.: High performance automotive radar signal processing on TI's TDA3X platform. In: 2017 IEEE Radar Conference, RadarConf 2017, pp. 1317–1320 (June 2017). https://doi.org/10.1109/RADAR.2017.7944409

2. Garcia, J., Zoeke, D., Vossiek, M.: MIMO-FMCW radar-based parking monitoring application with a modified convolutional neural network with spatial priors. IEEE Access **6**, 41391–41398 (2018). https://doi.org/10.1109/ACCESS.2018.2857007

3. Gusland, D., Torvik, B., Finden, E., Gulbrandsen, F., Smestad, R.: Imaging radar for navigation and surveillance on an autonomous unmanned ground vehicle capable of detecting obstacles obscured by vegetation. In: 2019 IEEE Radar Conference (RadarConf) (April 2019). https://doi.org/10.1109/RADAR.2019.8835514

4. Fletcher, R.R., Kulkarni, S.: Wearable Doppler radar with integrated antenna for patient vital sign monitoring. In: 2010 IEEE Radio and Wireless Symposium, RWW 2010 – Paper Digest, pp. 276–279 (2010). https://doi.org/10.1109/RWS.2010.5434220

5. Obadi, A., Soh, P., Aldayel, O., Al-Doori, M., Mercuri, M., Schreurs, D.: A survey on vital signs detection using radar techniques and processing with FPGA implementation. IEEE Circuits Syst. Mag. **21**(1), 41–74 (2021). https://doi.org/10.1109/MCAS.2020.3027445

6. Xiong, R., Feng, X., Zheng, H., Chen, Z.D.: Linear FMCW radar system for accurate indoor localization and trajectory detection. In: 2020 International Conference on Computing, Networking and Communications, ICNC 2020, pp. 741–745 (February 2020). https://doi.org/10.1109/ICNC47757.2020.9049799

7. Liang, G., Lv, G., Meng, Y.: Discussion on informatization teaching of certain radar transmitter. In: AIP Conference Proceedings, vol. 1834, no. 1, p. 020009 (April 2017). https://doi.org/10.1063/1.4981548

8. Kulie, M.S., Ackerman, S.A., Bennartz, R.: Integrating Web-Based Technological Classroom Tools into an Undergraduate Radar and Satellite Meteorology Course (2007)

9. Eide, E., Rosshaug, I.H., Seatex, K.A., Undheim, R.: Master of Science in Electronics Design of a Linear FMCW Radar Synthesizer with Focus on Phase Noise (2012)

10. Mahafza, B.R.: Radar Systems Analysis and Design Using MATLAB, 3rd ed. (2013)

11. Liang, G., Lv, G., Huang, X., Wang, L.: Teaching method research of practical course of certain artillery radar equipment. In: Proceedings – 2020 International Conference on Artificial Intelligence and Education, ICAIE 2020, pp. 398–401 (June 2020). https://doi.org/10.1109/ICAIE50891.2020.00098

12. Kolodziej, K.E., et al.: Build-a-radar self-paced massive open online course (MOOC) (April 2019). https://doi.org/10.1109/RADAR.2019.8835726

An Hybrid CPU-GPU Parallel Multi-tracking Framework for Long-Term Video Sequences

Juan P. D'amato[1,2]([✉]), Leonardo Dominguez[1,2], Franco Stramana[1,3],
Aldo Rubiales[1,3], and Alejandro Perez[1,3]

[1] PLADEMA, Universidad Nacional del Centro de la Provincia de Buenos Aires,
Tandil, Argentina
[2] National Council Scientific Technical Research, CONICET,
Buenos Aires, Argentina
[3] Comisión de Investigaciones Científicas, CICPBA, Buenos Aires, Argentina

Abstract. The automatic evaluation of video content is today one of the biggest challenges in computer Vision. When the purpose is to work with static surveillance cameras, where most of the time the scenes do not change, a full Convolutional Network (CNN) approach seems to require too much CPU effort, specially when the objects are slightly moving between different frames. On the other side, visual tracking has seen great recent advances in either speed or accuracy but still remain scarce when have to deal with long videos where new objects constantly come into the scene and others disappear.

In this paper, we present a parallelization scheme to handle multiple instances of object tracking. The main purpose is reduce overall processing time. The idea is to use already pre-trained CNNs for discovering objects and a parallel multi-tracker for following them, using both CPU and GPU devices.

Our multi-tracker framework consists of three main components, a movement detector, an object classification and a tracker. The detector is used as an initialization for trackers. When there are plenty of objects in the scene, the other two components are incorporated for reducing CPU effort. The first one is a *scheduler* than prioritizes tracking those objects that seems more relevant than the others. The second one, is a GPU memory handler, that lets adapt the framework to different hardware configuration. We evaluate this framework in different cases and cameras configurations, reaching reasonable speed-up and confidence.

Keywords: Video processing · GPGPU · Object tracking · CNN

1 Introduction

Visual object tracking plays a crucial role in computer vision and a critical role in visual surveillance [1]. Despite great successes in recent decades, robust real-time tracking is still a challenge, as in visual tracking still exists many factors including object deformation, occlusion, rotation, illumination change, pose variation,

© Springer Nature Switzerland AG 2021
J. C. Figueroa-García et al. (Eds.): WEA 2021, CCIS 1431, pp. 263–274, 2021.
https://doi.org/10.1007/978-3-030-86702-7_23

among others. The new algorithms trend toward improving tracking accuracy using deep learning-based techniques (e.g., [2]).

Such algorithms, unfortunately, often suffer from high computational effort and hardly run in real-time or requires a lot of power consumption, situation that not seems suitable for sustainable smart cities. Researchers have been proposing efficient visual trackers like [3,4], represented by the series of algorithms based on correlation filters. While easily can run at real-time, these trackers are usually less robust than deep learning-based approaches. In this context, it is a likely to have the better of both worlds, having a trade-off between speed and accuracy.

Additionally, today for smart cities, a bunch of new different hardware is available, having a reasonable CPU at less than 50 dollars, compared to a high performance processing server that could cost at least 2,000 dollars. This cheap equipment are very interest and help to think in a massive distributed processing network, as propose in [5], but have different limitations that have to be over passed in order to be useful for Computer Vision.

Finally, other challenges arise in surveillance systems:

1. In long video scenes, new objects constantly come into the image and other ones leave. In these cases, it is essential to have algorithms that handle when new objects are discovered.
2. In general, many different class of objects are present (people, vehicles, animals) in every image. Each one, moves at different speed, depending its class. In general, people moves smoothly, in contrast, vehicles could move faster. These cases typically require to be handled by different tracking strategies, adapted to movement speed.
3. Convolutional Networks (CNNs) are not perfect. Even tough they can detect with high precision different objects at different scales, they suffer when objects are constantly displacing and changing its orientation.
4. GPGPU capabilities limitations. Multi-thread and GPGPUs computing has already benefited computer vision system. There are plenty of CNN implementations that uses too much vRAM, that restricts its portability against different platforms (ARM, intel). The idea here is to use a multi-platform approach based on OpenCL.

The main purpose in this work is to present a multi-tracker framework that could handle complex scenes with many different objects in real time. This framework takes long-video sequences from surveillance systems, registering moving objects on a distributed platform. With some similar ideas presented in [6], the idea is to reach a high frame rate (above 20FPS) using both parallel CPUs and GPUs. The proposed framework has three main components: the detection module, the scheduler and the trackers. The detector itself is based on CNNs framework that will identify all potential objects in an image with their corresponding class. Despite obtaining excellent performance, the application of such algorithms is severely restricted by the high cost of extracting features in each frame. To deal with such limitation, the idea is to apply a fast tracker for each new detection, that updates objects position and confirms its prediction with a new detection. When the amount of objects is rather high (more than 20), this task could be even more expensive than the detection itself. For that reason, a task scheduler is required to distribute the available computation power.

As many times the scenes remain unchanged (there are no movement), a fast Background Subtracion Algorithm (BGS) could also be used as an activation or deactivation of the pipeline. All these parts will interact through synchronized images queues. To process all these tasks, both the CPU and GPU of a computer will be exploited. The framework is illustrated in Fig. 1.

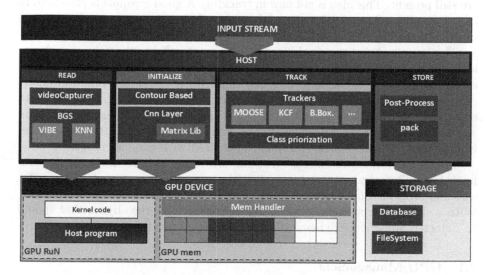

Fig. 1. Architecture of the framework.

2 Related Work

The techniques of detection of events used in Video-Surveillance systems are mainly based on quickly discriminating of movement from a fixed video camera. Research works as [7], describe the most common algorithms to detect and track objects. In [8], there is a special comparison between the different algorithms of basic detection, concluding that their combination may be absolutely useful to diminish false positive rates; while keeping the time and rate of true positives. The background subtraction commonly used classify shadows as a part of the objects, what alters both size and shape of the objects, affecting consequently the efficacy of such algorithms [9]. Also, it hinders some other procedures which need the result of the detection of objects, such as classification or tracking of the trajectory and also, analysis of certain behavior: loitering, vandalism, traffic law braking, among others. This problem also affects those techniques based on characteristics [10].

By contrast, trackers usually are based on searching similar regions respect to the target. For this task, various object appearance modeling approaches have been used such as [11], other inspired by deep features in visual recognition like

[12,13]. Recently, correlation filters have drawn increasing attention in visual tracking. [14] propose a filter tracker as sum of squared error (MOSSE), achieving a high frame rate but punishing accuracy. [4] introduce kernel space into correlation filter that result in the well-known Kernelized Correlation Filters (KCF) tracker.

In all these cases, the idea is to first try to detect the objects in the scene based on a inference algorithm and some time later confirm that the same objects are still present. This idea is not new in tracking. A good example is presented in [2], in which tracking results are validated per frame to decide which detection shall progress.

The proposal in our work is to combine tracking algorithms with re-identification ones, based on neural networks. As it is possible that many objects are present in the scene, and tracking algorithms could be computationally expensive, the idea is to include some metric that could dynamically helps to choose the best tracking parametrization, which means, choosing an algorithm and tracking frequency. This combination can helps to reach high performance, while mostly all the scene is constantly evaluated with good accuracy.

In [15] the formulate different tracking strategies in different hardware configuration. They evaluate multiple algorithms application of such trackers for cars and propose some combination that could run according to the capabilities. With a similar purpose, our solution takes into account the objects that should be detected and choose dynamically the most convenient tracking algorithm.

2.1 GPU Management

To reduce memory consumption in single-GPU detection, there are some existing ideas and work like Leveraging host RAM as a backup to extend GPU device memory. CUDA, for example, enables Unified Memory with Page Migration Engine so that unified Memory is not limited by the size of GPU memory. Of course, this method can bring a severe performance loss, as GPUs are more focused on transferring data than processing it.

Another way is using a run-time memory manager to virtualize the memory offloading the output of each layer and pre fetching it when necessary, which can only be applied to the layer-wise CNN models, not to sequence models. A Memory-efficient RNN is proposed by [16]. However, for those sequence models with attention mechanism, the attention layer actually requires much more memory space than LSTM/GRU.

There are also some other optimization methods, such as Memory-Efficient DenseNets [17] with significantly reducing memory consumption. However, this is applicable for special cases. In this paper, a general based approach "swap-out/in" handler is proposed, which is targeted for any kind of neural network. To pursue more memory optimizations, memory-efficient attention algorithm are designed.

3 Proposal

As was named at the beginning, the proposed framework is composed by three main components:

1. an identifier: identifier tries to identify objects present in the frame with their corresponding class. Detected objects are used as input to the trackers.
2. a set of trackers: responsible of locating and updating the position of each object in each frame.
3. an (adaptable) scheduler: responsible for distributing computation priority among available trackers

In this work, it is considered that tracking is much faster than identifying and are not fully dependent, so both components could work asynchronously. The identifier tries to find a set of potential objects from an image and a tracker is created and assigned to each object. Such mechanism triggers a temporal tracking drift that is corrected during processing. Also, each tracked object is independent of the other, so a second level of parallelism could be exploited.

To improve performance, several separated threads are allocated for the different software components, like video reading, tracking, classifying and storing. The components are connected each other through several synchronized queues.

An input queue is first used to read frames from a file or stream. A frame is chosen from this queue, and passed through the next processing one. Once this frame is processed and objects detected, both structures are passed to the tracker component that follows up every object until they leave the scene. Finally, but also important is storing. The fourth thread is responsible for taking all objects and stored someway, either in the local file system or in remote databases. For dealing these cases, a storage task runs asynchronously collecting all data obtained from the multi-tracker. Objects are encoded in a format proposed in [18].

As it is expected to be a very flexible framework, some important designing marks should be taken in consideration

1. The inference network and tracking algorithms should be selected according to application (it is no the same a traffic video that a retailing one) and available computational resources.
2. The trackers should be robust to small light changes and to occlusion.
3. The objects detection step can be implemented in many ways, from fast object moving segmentation to CNN inference. When the scenes are not crowded, a simple movement segmentation should be more effective.

Each item is detailed in the following sections.

3.1 Initialization and Tracking

Initialization task has the responsibility to take a frame from an input queue and return a set of potential objects with their corresponding location or bounding box. Objects could be classified in that moment (determining their class, as vehicle, person, animal among other) using a CNN or just identifying them as a set of connected components in the foreground mask and deferring the classification step once they are stored. These both strategies has their corresponding advantages and disadvantages that will be discussed later.

In any case, the input for the trackers are a set of bounding box indicating the objects that have to be followed through the consequent frames until they leave the scene. For each frame, each tracker must update their corresponding object state and compute the new location. If during this step the tracking fails, it is possible that the object was occluded or has to be removed. In both cases, a parameter indicating that the object is "alive" is decreased. Once this parameter reach to ZERO, it should be considered as "dead" and moved to the store task.

Contour Based Initialization. In a scene taken from a static surveillance camera, static objects has non-value. For that reason, a background subtraction algorithm could easily segments pixels in movement from the static ones. Once these pixels are obtained, they are merged into "blobs"; grouping pixels that are in contact with their neighbours. A contour based algorithm to be used for this step. If blobs are too small, they could be discarded.

CNN Initialization. Using a trained network, a set of objects are extracted from the input image. Very depth networks, such as Yolo or Resnet, are more precise and could detect almost all objects in the scene (both static or movable ones). The CNN predicts the location and bounding box of the objects with their corresponding class, that is used as input for the next stage.

3.2   GPU Management

With the purpose of having an adaptable multi-platform framework, we develop a memory handler that dynamically allocates and organizes the amount of available memory. Every time a GPU operation requires memory, the Handler checks if it is already allocated. In case not, a copy from host to device is carried out. In other case, the handler returns the actual buffer. If the amount of memory is not enough, the handler removes those buffers that are not used in that moment. After several operations, the handler could clear less used buffers and keeps the most used ones.

3.3   Multi-tracking Scheduling and Update

Every frame, the list of active tracker should evaluate if the object is moving and update their position. As it was named, updating each tracker has a relative high computation effort. For instance, updating the position of a KCF tracker, takes about 20 ms for each frame for each. When there are many objects in the scene (above 10), the total computation effort is not enough to attend to each tracker each frame.

On the other side, every object is not moving at same speed or not moving at all. Even more, due to perspective effect, further objects seems to move slower in pixels space. For those reasons, we consider that is not strictly necessary to update the objects' position on every frame but if a tracker is not updated thoroughly, the observed object could be lost. To manage these situation, the movement of the objects is defined by three terms:

- the Object class (vehicles move faster than persons)
- the position in the space (further objects seems to move slower)
- its own behaviour (object could be stop or in movement).

To avoid tracker starvation, a fourth parameter is included, modeling the time since last update. With these information, we propose a criteria for distributing the available computation capabilities among the active trackers: the higher the priority, the more probable to be updated. The criteria is described in 1:

$$Priority(O) = \alpha * class(O) + \beta * pY(O) + \gamma * rS(O, MK) + \epsilon * timeSinceU(O) \quad (1)$$

Where pY is a function dependent of the camera perspective. The farther the object is, the slower its movement. $Class$ is a function that gives a score to each class. rS indicates if the object is moving or not. Using the movement mask MK and the object bounding box R, with 2

$$moving(O, MV) = \begin{cases} 1 : nonBlank(MV[R]) \geq thresholdMove \\ 0 : inOtherCase \end{cases} \quad (2)$$

For handling multi-tracking, we implemented a tracker scheduler. This scheduler computes the $Priority$ of each pair tracker-object and sort them in decrease order. Using a backpack strategy, those that has the higher priorities are first assigned to be update. If there is available computation time, the next trackers are included.

To avoid starving objects, the more time the tracker awaits to update, $timeSinceU$, the higher the priority. On each new frame, the scheduler computes the priority and updates only those trackers that have a higher one. With these scheme, objects that are not moving but were detected during the initialization, have very low priority and should not be tracked ever.

On each frame, it is checked whether there are new objects or if they are the same that are being tracked from previous frames. To support this, a main history list of objects is kept. After a new detection, the list is updated. If there are new objects, a tracker is assigned to each one. On the other side, trackers update the position. If objects could not be tracked during last frames, they are removed from the list. The algorithm is presented here:

4   Experiments

Our framework is implemented in C++ and it can runs on several hardware configurations, supporting Intel, NVidia and AMD GPUs. As each GPU memory allocation request in the framework requires to pass through the Handler,

Algorithm 1. Multi-tracking update

```
1:  procedure UPDATETRACKERSSTATE(newObjects, histObjects)
2:      for d ∈ new do
3:          t ← initTracker(d.box)
4:          keep ← push(t)
5:      for d ∈ histObjects do
6:          if d.life ≤ 0 then
7:              keep ← remove(d)
8:      return keep
9:  procedure UPDATE                              ▷ this runs on a synchronized thread
10:     History ← new()
11:     while true do
12:         Objects, frame ← dequeue(queueTrack)
13:         active ← UpdateTrackersState(Objects, History)
14:         for frame.index ≤ Window do                    ▷ Process next frames
15:             computePriorities(active)
16:             while t ← active do
17:                 if t.priority > threshold then
18:                     couldUpdate ← t− > update(R, frame) ;
19:                     if couldUpdate = True then
20:                         t.setNewPosition(t.objectRectangle)
21:                     else                    ▷ Probably, the object has left the scene
22:                         d− > life− = 1
```

---

we implemented an own OpenCL version of YOLO and VIBE BGS. Other third party libraries, like the tracking one, that could also used GPUs are not considered in this work.

For evaluating the capabilities of this framework, several t studies that were carried up:

1. Memory management configurations: different memory limitations are studied. As the idea is to have a deeper network, only those CNNs that used more of memory are evaluated.
2. Priorization parameters on long sequences. For evaluating how the framework adapts to different situations, different parameters are considered, such as the different initialization schemes.

We have selected the pre-trained Yolo v4 networks for inference [19]. Other traffic objects segmentation networks are also useful.

4.1   Considerations

As in [6], different classification interval initialization interval I may affect both the accuracy and efficiency. A smaller I means more frequent verification, which requires more computation and thus degrades the efficiency. A larger I, on the contrary, may cost less computation but could make loosing targets while their appearance change quickly. The first initialization interval was set to 20.

At the same time, in the priority metric proposed, the component based on object position varies mainly on perspective. As each scene is observed in different point of view, the function should be rectified before using it. Before applying the algorithm, the camera has to be calibrated. For this purpose, the class and normalized Y position of each object in the image is evaluated. For several frames, the size and location of the objects is obtained and represented, as can be shown in Fig. 2. After this study is carried for each object class, it was determined that the slope of the mean line is used as input in the Eq. 1.

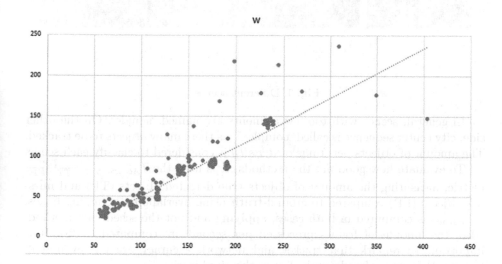

Fig. 2. Car speed variation respect to Y coordinate.

Respect to objects trackers, it was first consider MIL [20] and KCF [4]. Compared to MIL, KCF is more efficient while less accurate in short time interval. Though KCF runs faster than MIL, it performs less accurately in short time, hence significantly increasing the amount of lost objects. By contrast, MIL is more accurate in short time, and finally leads to efficiency in computation.

4.2   Scheduling Parameters

In this framework, it is required to be efficient and accurate most of the time, even in hard cases. To show the effects of managing the multi-tracks, different scenes with a particular configuration were evaluated. In such cases, the scheduling algorithm should give more importance to vehicles rather than people, also considering perspective correction. For this purpose, we evaluate several frames from different moments taken on a street corner or routes, either during night or early morning. The used cases are shown in Fig. 3.

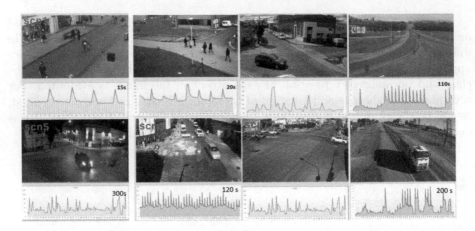

Fig. 3. Different scenes.

In general, scenes with too few elements are named "simple". On the other side, city center sequence is called "complex", as there many objects to be tracked. The amount of objects per frame or *density* is considered to classify each scene.

To evaluate how good are the methods, it is used the $T_{Accuracy} = \frac{TP}{(TP+FP)}$ metric, measuring the amount of objects true detected objects (TP) and missing objects (FP) compared to ground-truth using overlapping bounding boxes. $T_{Accuracy}$ is computed in both cases, applying and not the scheduling method. Also, the amount of frames processed per second are computed (FPS). It is important to remark that tracker and network accuracy are not evaluated, because they were already evaluated in the cited works.

Finally, we present in 4.2 a resume of different scenarios, measuring processing speed, scene complexity and detection accuracy.

		Non scheduled		Scheduled	
Scene	Density	FPS	Accuracy	FPS	Accuracy
1 (street)	1.3	2.9	0.64	**7.26**	0.508
2 (street)	1.5	6.4	0.93	**8.84**	0.84
3 (corner)	0.45	9	0.81	**12.03**	0.76
4 (route)	0.2	26	0.95	**28**	0.95
5 (corner)	0.1	38	1.0	**38**	1.0
6 (crowded corner)	1.17	3.1	0.82	**5.27**	0.79
7 (avenues)	0.75	5.1	0.79	**6.85**	0.77
8 (route)	1.17	12	0.9	**15**	0.89

It is observed that when density is bigger than 0.5, the scheduled algorithm always improves the performance, about a 50%. In some situation, like scene 1, it punishes the accuracy. That case should be evaluated in depth.

5 Conclusions

In this work, a novel parallel tracking and framework that combines correlation kernel-based tracking and deep learning-based classification is presented. We propose a metric that taking into account objects behaviour, can choose which objects should be observed more frequently. The videos have been processed and visualized in real time since the algorithm has relative computational low cost. The solution shows promising results on thorough experiments. Moreover, it is worth noting that it is a very flexible framework and our implementation is far from optimal. We believe there are great rooms for future improvement and generalization.

Future works will attempt to incorporate the automatic adaptation of the weights of each tracker, considering the variation of the intensity of the movement when processing the video, and adding some other considerations, like darker areas where the algorithm has difficulty and in general lost objects. Another challenge aims to achieve that the parameters of the algorithm automatically adapt to different times of the day.

Acknowledgement. This work was partially supported by the National Council Research of Argentina (PICT 2016 - 0236) and (PICT 2020 - 005).

References

1. Kruegle, H.: CCTV Surveillance: Video Practices and Technology. Butterworth-Heinemann, Newton (2014)
2. Kalal, Z., Mikolajczyk, K., Matas, J.: Tracking-learning detection **34**(7), 1409–1422 (2012)
3. B. Babenko, Yang, M.-H., Belongie, S.: Robust object tracking with online multiple instance learning **33**(8), 1619–1632 (2011)
4. Henriques, J.F., Caseiro, R., Martins, P., Batista, J.: High-speed tracking with kernelized correlation filters. CoRR abs/1404.7584 (2014)
5. D'Amato, J.P., Dominguez, L., Perez, A., Rubiales, A., Stramana, F.: Generación de servicios digitales en ciudades inteligentes a partir de las capacidades de los sistemas de cámaras. RISTI - Revista Iberica de Sistemas e Tecnologias de Informacao (27), 566–578 (2019)
6. Fan, H., Ling, H.: Parallel tracking and verifying: a framework for real-time and high accuracy visual tracking. In: 2017 IEEE International Conference on Computer Vision (ICCV), pp. 5487–5495 (2017)
7. Legua, C.: Seguimiento automático de objetos en sistemas con múltiples cámaras (2013)
8. Shaikh, S.H., Saeed, K., Chaki, N.: Moving object detection using background subtraction. In: Moving Object Detection Using Background Subtraction. SCS, pp. 15–23. Springer, Cham (2014). https://doi.org/10.1007/978-3-319-07386-6_3
9. Azab, M., Shedeed, H., Hussein, A.: A new technique for background modeling and subtraction for motion detection in real-time videos. In: IEEE International Conference on Image Processing, pp. 3453–3456 (2010)
10. Hadi, R., Sulong, G., George, L.: Vehicle detection and tracking techniques: a concise review. Sig. Image Process Int. J. (SIPIJ) **5** (2014)

11. Bao, C., Wu, Y., Ling, H., Ji, H.: Real time robust l1 tracker using accelerated proximal gradient approach. In: CPVR, vol. 3 (2012)
12. Krizhevsky, A., Sutskever, I., Hinton, G.E.: ImageNet classification with deep convolutional neural networks. In: Advances in Neural Information Processing Systems, vol. 25. Curran Associates, Inc. (2012)
13. Nam, H., Han, B.: Learning multi-domain convolutional neural networks for visual tracking. CoRR abs/1510.07945 (2015)
14. Bolme, D.S., Beveridge, J.R., Draper, B.A., Lui, Y.M.: Visual object tracking using adaptive correlation filters. In: 2010 IEEE Computer Society Conference on Computer Vision and Pattern Recognition. (2010) 2544–2550
15. Greco, A., Saggese, A., Vento, M., Vigilante, V.: Vehicles detection for smart roads applications on board of smart cameras: a comparative analysis 20(99), 1–13 (2021)
16. Wang, Z., Lin, J., Wang, Z.: Accelerating recurrent neural networks: a memory-efficient approach. IEEE Trans. Very Large Scale Integr. (VLSI) Syst. 25(10), 2763–2775 (2017)
17. Pleiss, G., Chen, D., Huang, G., Li, T., van der Maaten, L., Weinberger, K.Q.: Memory-efficient implementation of DenseNets. CoRR abs/1707.06990 (2017)
18. Stramana, F., D'amato, J.P., Dominguez, L., Rubiales, A., Perez, A.: Object extraction and encoding for video monitoring through low-bandwidth networks. In: Figueroa-García, J.C., Garay-Rairán, F.S., Hernández-Pérez, G.J., Díaz-Gutierrez, Y. (eds.) WEA 2020. CCIS, vol. 1274, pp. 431–441. Springer, Cham (2020). https://doi.org/10.1007/978-3-030-61834-6_37
19. Redmon, J.: Darknet: Open source neural networks in C. http://pjreddie.com/darknet/ (2016)
20. Babenko, B., Yang, M.H., Belongie, S.: Visual tracking with online multiple instance learning. In: 2009 IEEE Conference on Computer Vision and Pattern Recognition, pp. 983–990 (2009)

Implementation of End User Radio Key Performance Indicators Using Signaling Trace Data Analysis for Cellular Networks

Hector Daniel Bernal Amaya[1,2]([⊠]), Elvis Eduardo Gaona Garcia[1]([⊠]),
and Julian Camargo[1]([⊠])

[1] Grupo de Investigación en Telecomunicaciones (GITUD),
Facultad de Ingeniería, Bogotá, Colombia
hdbernala@mail.udistrital.edu.co, {egaona,
jcamargo}@udistrital.edu.co
[2] Maestría en Ingeniería Industrial, Universidad Distrital Francisco
Jose de Caldas, Bogotá, Colombia

Abstract. Mobile telecommunications markets are highly competitive and Dynamic population with mobile service is more than 100%, operators must take care of customers and prevent complaints. Mobile customers performance measurements to identify complaints by subscriber can be made with New Standard 3GPP TS32.321. This standard includes Subscriber traces for all network elements, this paper presents the process of creation of End User Performance indicators from subscriber traces in a real LTE operator using python and Databases. Indicators proposed for mobile customers are based on 3GPP TS32.250 network indicators but adapted during parsing to be calculated by (UE) User equipment to propose a better Customer Experience Index. This novel method is to get indicators using traces for customers and also for the network as a whole. Comparison of key performance indicators between network level against user indicators were created. Customer Experience Index for ERAB Accessibility is proposed and main components impacting the customer experience were identified by using machine learning techniques.

Keywords: Mobile telecommunication · Customer experience index · Real time trace analysis · Customer complaint behavior

1 Introduction

The mobile telecommunications market is a competitive and dynamic market where market penetration has already exceeded 100%, acquiring new customers and keeping existing ones is an arduous and costly task [1]. One way of achieving new customers is Churn, which consists of customers switching from one mobile operator to another or the registration of new customers, however, with a penetration of more than 100% in today's mobile markets, growth through Churn or new customers has been reduced.

J. C. Figueroa-García et al. (Eds.): WEA 2021, CCIS 1431, pp. 275–289, 2021.
https://doi.org/10.1007/978-3-030-86702-7_24

Thus, the telecommunications market has focused on keeping existing customers and making them loyal customers. Previous research has studied the main factors why customers complain to mobile operators [1]. In these studies, it has been observed that customers complaints are a probable cause of service desertion either to terminate the service or to switch to the competition. Past analysis have concluded that it is important to maintain high customer loyalty, Infrastructure services in general cannot prevent occurrence of failures and customers should have enough loyalty to stay even if service has failures [2], so that customer should discards the effort to change company and could consider that the conditions that will have in another provider would not generate greater benefit. To achieve customer loyalty, CCB (Customer Complaint Behavior) models have been developed, as well as Churn prediction models. These customer behavior prediction models seek to anticipate customer complaints by identifying the main dissatisfaction factors. Using these models, telecom companies can plan the management of "quality of experience" to avoid customer desertion through proactive actions, the second chance, to improve service, gifts, or benefits to unsatisfied customers.

These models are based on the databases available of operators in different platforms, such as network indicators, customer complaints database and other information available to the operator that allows the identification of the root cause of the change of operator or customer complaints.

Radio Access Networks Mobile technologies (2G, 3G, 4G, 5G) are necessary for different solutions associated to Industry 4.0 and Internet of things (IoT) [3], where the "users" are mainly machines that requires connectivity and good performance. Different qualities of service are required for different devices as mission critical services, ultra-low latency, high density and each type of solution require the measurement of performance by UE (User Equipment) to identify issues related to specific devices or solutions.

Network Operators have high volume of information and different variables that can influence customer complaints and churn, machine learning techniques, computing power and large databases have allowed identification of root causes for customer complaints [4–7]. Implementation of real-time experience indicators by subscriber has being used and Customer Experience indexes have been proposed [8, 9].

3GPP through the technical specification of equipment and subscriber traces [10] has enabled traces generation by user. Real-time experience indicators using customer data (radio traces) has been documented by Chen [11], where the author propose the "Data Customer Experience Index" and the "Voice Customer Experience Index". Chen concludes that there is still a lot of work to be done such as CEI (Customer Experience Index) formulas including more network factors and training data.

In following chapters are described the steps followed by us to implement customer indicators: first the description of trace activation in eNodeBs, later traces decoding and parsing, creation of counters from messages, creation of more complex KPIs and finally the results and analysis for customer experience index proposed.

2   Trace Activation and Data Parsing

2.1   eNodeB Trace Activation

The traces were enabled in 19 eNodeBs in cellular service provider following technical equipment specifications, eNodeBs activated will send one file per minute to centralized FTP server with raw traces information.

Trace Files generated by eNodeBs include all messages with ASN1 format as established in standard 3GPP32.423 [12]. Traces include three protocols S1, X2 and Uu, as established in [13] shown in Fig. 1.

2.2   ETL System for Decoding and Load

Subsequently, a system of extraction, transformation, and loading (ETL) of traces was implemented using Python and the open-source library "pycrate" for the decoding network messages encoded in ASN1 [14] according to the standard. ETL perform the hourly load of messages in database. The messages required for customer indicators are created from the traces.

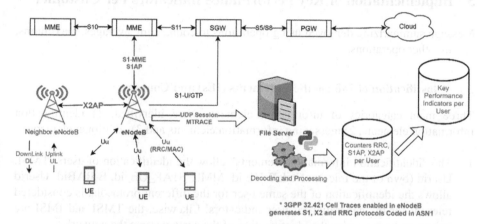

Fig. 1. Dataflow topology

Decoding system was implemented reading binary files using standard description for file header as established in [14]. During decoding process were found the following information: message Length, Length of data packet, Timestamp, eNodeB identifier, Cell identifier, User identifier for eNodeB, Protocol, Direction (DL/UL), PDU (packet Data Unit) and Message Type.

PDU is different for each protocol, for RRC decoder required is ASN1 UPER, for X2AP and S1AP decoder required is APER. Protocol information elements are obtained from PDUs:

- From RRC were obtained following Information Elements according to protocol definition [15]: dedicatedInfoNAS, NASDecoded, IMSI, RRC LTEtypemessage,

RRCestabcause, RRCRelcause, RRCTMSI, RRCMMEc, PCellRSRP,PCellRSRQ, RRC_NAS_OLD GUTI_TMSI, RRC_NAS NEW_GUTI_TMSI, RRC_NAS EPS_ATTACH_TYPE_EPSID, ESMType, EMMType.

- From S1AP were obtained following fields according to protocol definition in [16]: S1APMessage, procedureCode, uEaggregate MaximumBitRateUL, uEaggregateMaximumBitRateDL, e_RAB_ID, qCI, gTP_TEID, transportLayerAddress, lAC, cell_ID, pLMNidentity, m_TMSI, mMEC, tAC, eNB_UE_S1AP_ID, mME_UE_S1AP_ID and
- From X2AP were obtained following fields: X2AP_mME_UE_S1AP_ID, New-eNB-UE-X2AP-D, X2AP_Old eNB_UE X2AP_ID, X2AP_TargetCell_ID, Source-CellECGI, HandoverReportType, X2AP_cause_radionetwork, transport, protocol or misc.

A database of messages was generated, it is necessary to transform this database to generate the radio indicators and measure the performance of the radio network for each customer.

3 Implementation of Key Performance Indicators Per Customer

Message summarizing deployed using operations to count, sum, averages, maximums, among other operations.

3.1 Classification of Information Elements (IEs) and Counters

Three main categories of information elements were identified: 1) identification information elements, 2) messaging information elements and 3) additional elements.

1) The "identification information elements" allow the identification of users: TMSI, Userid (own of the trace), eNodeB UE id, MME_S1AP_UE_id, E-RABid. Userid allows the identification of the same user for the different protocols, is considered relevant for the generation of user indicators. Likewise, the TMSI and IMSI are important because give the identification of the customers on the network.
2) The "messaging information elements" are all the messages of the protocols decoded, these messages are the information necessary for counting attempts, successes and failures for all the procedures of the protocols. Indicators of "success rate" or "failure rates" can be obtained.
3) The "message attributes" provide more information about the message context. Within this type of messages are the measurements of radio indicators such as RSRP (Reference Signal Received Power), RSRQ (Reference Signal Received Quality), ERAB release causes and call establishment reason (Table 1).

Table 1. LTE attachment and call setup message flow obtained using traces decoded

ID	USERID	DIR-PROTOCOL-MSG TYPE	MESSAGE	ESMMSG	EMMMSG
91346	0x1EE4	UL-RRC-ULCCCH	rrcConnectionRequest		
91348	0x1EE4	DL-RRC-DLCCCH	rrcConnectionSetup		
91351	0x1EE4	UL-RRC-ULDCCH	rrcConnectionSetupComplete	PDN connectivity request	Attach request
91352	0x1EE4	UL-S1AP-ALL	initialUEMessage	PDN connectivity request	Attach request
91353	0x1EE4	DL-S1AP-ALL	downlinkNASTransport		Authentication request
91354	0x1EE4	DL-RRC-DLDCCH	dlInformationTransfer		Authentication request
91356	0x1EE4	UL-RRC-ULDCCH	ulInformationTransfer		Authentication response
91357	0x1EE4	UL-S1AP-ALL	uplinkNASTransport		Authentication response
91358	0x1EE4	DL-S1AP-ALL	downlinkNASTransport		Security mode command
91359	0x1EE4	DL-RRC-DLDCCH	dlInformationTransfer		Security mode command
91360	0x1EE4	UL-RRC-ULDCCH	ulInformationTransfer		Security mode complete
91361	0x1EE4	UL-S1AP-ALL	uplinkNASTransport		Security mode complete
91364	0x1EE4	DL-S1AP-ALL	InitialContextSetupRequest		
91365	0x1EE4	DL-RRC-DLDCCH	securityModeCommand		
91366	0x1EE4	DL-RRC-DLDCCH	ueCapabilityEnquiry		
91367	0x1EE4	UL-RRC-ULDCCH	securityModeComplete		
91368	0x1EE4	UL-RRC-ULDCCH	ueCapabilityInformation		
91369	0x1EE4	DL-RRC-DLDCCH	rrcConnectionReconfiguration	Activate default EPS bearer context request	Attach accept
91371	0x1EE4	UL-RRC-ULDCCH	rrcConnectionReconfigurationComplete		
91372	0x1EE4	UL-RRC-ULDCCH	ulInformationTransfer	Activate default EPS bearer context accept	Attach complete
91373	0x1EE4	UL-S1AP-ALL	uplinkNASTransport	Activate default EPS bearer context accept	Attach complete
91374	0x1EE4	UL-S1AP-ALL	InitialContextSetupResponse		
91375	0x1EE4	UL-S1AP-ALL	UECapabilityInfoIndication		
91409	0x1EE4	UL-RRC-ULDCCH	measurementReport		

3.2 Key Performance Indicators

Network Indicators were used as reference [17], however these formulas are not completely valid for customer indicators. Following is the list of KPIs defined in our proposal:

Indicator	Formula	Description and components
Initial E-RAB (enhanced radio access bearer) accessibility	$ERAB\ Init\ Acc_i$ $$= \frac{\sum_{uid \in i} RRCStpSucc_i}{\sum_{uid \in i} RRCStpAtt_i}$$ $$\times \frac{\sum_{uid \in i} S1EstSucc_i}{\sum_{uid \in i} S1EstAtt_i}$$ $$\times \frac{\sum_{uid \in i} ERABinStpSucc_i}{\sum_{uid \in i} ERABinStpAtt_i} \quad (4)$$	This KPI shows the probability for an end-user to be provided with an E-RAB at request Indicator includes all setup phases RRC establishment, UE S1 context setup and E-RAB setup, where: uid: User identification for an specific user i: user identification of the message on the trace $ERABinStpSucc_i$: Count of Messages 'Initial Context Setup Request' Downlink from MME to eNB for all QCI on S1AP Messages for userid i $ERABinStpSucc_i$: Count of Messages 'Initial Context Setup Response' Uplink from eNB to MME for all QCI on S1AP protocol for userid i $RRCStpAtt_i$: Count of Messages 'rrcConnectionRequest' Uplink from UE to eNB by UL-CCCH channel for all establishment causes for userid i $RRCStpSucc_i$: Count of Message 'rrc Connection Setup Complete' Uplink from UE to eNB by UL-DCCH channel for userid i $S1EstAtt_i$: Count of S1AP "Initial UE Message" for userid i and all S1AP messages 'PathSwitchRequestAcknowledge' that are the incoming services to the cell by Handover X2 $S1EstSucc_i$: S1 signalling is considered success when is received the first S1AP message including the S1AP UE ID assigned

(continued)

(*continued*)

Indicator	Formula	Description and components
E-RAB abnormal drop ratio	$$ERAB\ Drop\ Rate\ by\ Abnormal\ cause_i = \frac{\sum_{uid \in i} AbnRelease_i}{\sum_{uid \in i} AllRelease_i} \quad (5)$$	Drop Rate by Abnormal conditions based on existing messages where: *uid:* User identification for an specific user on traces *i:* user identification on the trace *AbnRelease_i:* Count of all ERAB releases by abnormal cause (failure) S1AP messages 'UE Context Release Command', 'E-RAB Release Command' with cause in information element 'tx2relocoverall-expiry', 'failure-in-radio-interface-procedure', 'radio-connection-with-ue-lost' or 'transport-resource-unavailable', *AllRelease_i.:* Count of Messages 'UE Context Release Command', 'E-RAB Release Command' on S1AP protocol,
Mobility success rate	$$Mobility\ Success\ Rate_i = \frac{HOExeSucc_i}{HORequest_i} \times 100\%$$	Mobility definition according to standard is defined as the completion of the two phases of Handover, Handover Preparation and Handover Execution: *HOExeSucc_i:* Count of successful Handovers executed by userid i. Incoming message 'uEContextRelease' in X2AP protocol. Message requesting release because Handover has been completed in target eNodeB *HORequest_i:* Count of Handover Request from eNB source to Target eNodeB f userid i
Average RSRP (dBm)	$$RSRP(\text{dBm}) = IE\ value - 140\ \text{dBm}$$	In traces the measurement is received by Information Element. RSRP is the Reference Signal Received Power as measurement of coverage level based on reference signal as the linear average over the power contributions (in [W]) of the resource elements that carry cell-specific reference signals within the considered measurement frequency bandwidth

(*continued*)

(*continued*)

Indicator	Formula	Description and components
Average RSRP (dBm)	$RSRQ(\text{dBm}) = \frac{(\text{IE value} - 40)}{2\,\text{dB}}$	RSRQ is defined as the ratio N × RSRP/(E-UTRA carrier RSSI), where N is the number of Resource Blocks of the E-UTRA carrier RSSI measurement bandwidth. Roughly speaking the differencbetween total RSSI and Reference signal carried by all RBs

Indicators calculated by customer in table above were taken directly from standard. Only exception is the E-RAB Abnormal Drop Ratio that has a different definition in standard. E-RAB Drop ratio by user defid in our proposal is the rate of abnormal releases per user in following table are the abnormal releases as observed (Table 2):

Table 2. UE context release causes per message for a specific day

Cause	Release Cause	Release Type	S1FlowMessage	Sum
Radio	user-inactivity	Normal	UEContextReleaseRequest	216485
NAS	detach	Normal	UEContextReleaseCommand	53131
Misc	unspecified	Normal	UEContextReleaseCommand	47890
Misc	unspecified	Normal	UEContextReleaseRequest	11
Radio	interrat-redirection	Normal	UEContextReleaseRequest	43854
NAS	normal-release	Normal	E-RABReleaseCommand	37
NAS	normal-release	Normal	UEContextReleaseCommand	7834
Radio	cs-fallback-triggered	Normal	UEContextReleaseRequest	2209
Radio	release-due-to-eutran-generated-reason	Normal	UEContextReleaseRequest	667
Radio	radio-connection-with-ue-lost	AbNormal	UEContextReleaseRequest	458
Radio	transport-resource-unavailable	AbNormal	E-RABReleaseIndication	25
Radio	transport-resource-unavailable	AbNormal	UEContextReleaseRequest	369
Radio	failure-in-radio-interface-procedure	AbNormal	UEContextReleaseRequest	43
Radio	tx2relocoverall-expiry	Normal	UEContextReleaseRequest	6

Other Key Performance indicators established in 3GPP 32.250 were not implemented for the following reasons:

IP Throughput: decoding issues, not clearly identified the fields on trace.

IP Latency: Standard defines IP Latency in eNB from reception of a packet by S1 and transmission by air interface (uu). This KPI cannot be obtained directly from traces and features used.

Cell Availability: cell availability is a pure network KPI relative to time in service of cells (network) and not related to users.

4 Results

4.1 Hardware Usage and Processing

The implementation of the system for the Extraction, Transformation and Load (ETL) of cellular network traces for 19 cells was achieved. Messages processed per cell are in average 1.8 million per day, storage usage was 6.6 GB. After creating a database normalized, database size was reduced to 2.8 GB for the 19 cells.

In Table 3 can be observed that the main contributor in volume of messages are the PCCH messages, checking in detail PCCH Channel is a common channel used by all the sectors on the same TAC (Tracking Area Code) for paging purposes. These messages could be processed for only one cell per TAC and reduce hardware resources.

Number of messages required for the implemented indicators (excluding PCCH) are 530.000 per cell per day. Size in database for one day is 801 MB per day for all 19 cells, average of 42 MB per cell per day.

In terms of processing the transformation using Python had a processing rate of 1.98 s per file in average. The processing of messages per minute consumes 70% of one CPU core of 64bit-2.39 GHz processor and 600 MB of RAM.

Table 3. Average Messages per day per cell

Protocol Name	Message Type	Qty Messages	Average messages per cell per day
RRC	PCCH	24 056 470	**1 266 130**
RRC	ULDCCH	2 236 705	117 721
RRC	DLDCCH	2 159 959	113 682
RRC	ULCCCH	443 690	23 352
RRC	DLCCCH	443 613	23 348
S1AP	ALL	3 885 156	204 482
TRACE	ALL	817 642	43 034
X2AP	ALL	144 207	7 590
Grand Total		**34 187 442**	**1 799 339**

With current implementation as reference, we can estimate Hardware usage in a network of 5000 cells as shown in Table 4. It is important remark that final usage can vary and will depend of the number of active users.

Table 4. Hardware estimation for network of 5000 cells

Cells	Processing time per core (seconds/file)	Files for all cells (files/hour)	RAM(GB) per core*	Total Minutes required to process one hour of files per CPU core (min)
19	1.98	1140	0.6	37.62 min
5000	1.98	300000	0.6	9900 min
	Processor Cores to process all files in 60 mins			9900 min /60mins = 165 cores
	Minimum Processor core CPU required (#cores)			165 cores
	Minimum RAM required (GB)			0.65GB/core x 165 cores = 99 GB
	Minimum SQL Storage per day (GB)			0.042GB/Cell x 5000 cells = 210 GB
	Minimum Readings per second (I/O)			60 kB/min x 5000 cells / 60 s = 5000 kB/s

Based on the formulas and criteria established in the previous points, following indicators were obtained grouped per Customer, Cell id and day, for a period of one week. Dataset obtained is shown in Table 5.

Table 5. Complete list of KPIs obtained using traces 3GPP 32.321 at user level

Total_InitERAB_Accessibility	ERAB_ABNORMAL_RELEASE_RATE
ERAB_STP_SUCC	tx2relocoverallExpiry_Release
ERAB_STP_ATT	RadioFailure_release
ERAB_STP_SR	Radio_UELost_release
S1CONTEXT_ESTAB_SUCC	Transport_release
PATH_SWT_REQ_ACK	AbnormalRadioReleases
InitialUEMessage	TotalReleases
InitialS1Context_STP_SR	avgdBmRSRP_avgdBm
RRC_CONN_REQUEST	avgWRSRP_mW
RRC_STP_COMPLETE	avgWRSRP_dBm
RRC_CONN_STP_SR	maxRSRP_dBm
X2_HO_REQUEST	minRSRP_dBm
X2_HO_COMPLETE	avgRSRQ
X2_HO_SR	maxRSRQ
RRC_RE_ESTAB_REQUEST	minRSRQ
RRC_RE_ESTAB_COMPLETE	RRC_RE_ESTAB_SR
RRC_RE_ESTAB_REJECT	

Customer Experience indicator proposed for ERAB Accessibility and network indicator are in following table (Table 6):

Table 6. Customer experience index proposal

Indicator	Formula	Description and components
Customer experience index ERAB access	$CEI\ ERABAccess_{c,j}$ $= \frac{\sum_{i=1}^{N}\left(ERAB\ Init\ Acc_{i,j,c}\right)}{N}$	• $CEI\ ERABAccess_{c,j}$: is the Customer Experience Index for LTE service Accessibility for users in cell c during day j • $ERAB\ Init\ Acc_{i,j,c}$: is the ERAB accessibility for user i, in cell c during day j • N: number of users in cell c for day j
Network ERAB access	$Network\ ERAB\ Init\ Acc_{c,j}$ $= \frac{\sum_{i=1}^{N} RRCStpSucc_{i,c,j}}{\sum_{i=1}^{N} RRCStpAtt_{i,c,j}}$ $\times \frac{\sum_{i=1}^{N} S1EstSucc_{i,c,j}}{\sum_{i=1}^{N} S1EstAtt_{i,c,j}}$ $\times \frac{\sum_{i=1}^{N} ERABinStpSucc_{i,c,j}}{\sum_{i=1}^{N} ERABinStpAtt_{i,c,j}}$ (4.b)	$Network\ ERAB\ Init\ Acc_{c,j}$: is the ERAB Network Accessibility for cell c during day j

4.2 Comparison Between Network Indicator and Customer Experience Indicator

Customer Experience Index for ERAB Accessibility is the average experience for all users. Network accessibility indicator is the formula (4) for whole network element.

Comparison between cell (network) performance and user performance was made graphically as can be observed in Fig. 2 in one cell stats for seven days where network KPI was calculated and compared to user performance on the cell for all users during the same period. As can be observed a group of subscribers are not having good performance compared with cell KPI.

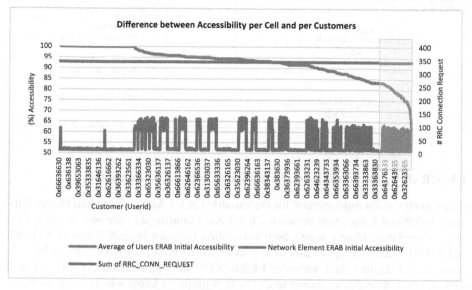

Fig. 2. Initial ERAB accessibility per user

To validate the observation statistical significance test was applied for the two methods to measure the ERAB Accessibility by network and by user, Hypothesis to validate is if both methods have the same average (Table 7).

Average Comparison of the two samples using "T test" allows us to conclude that average performance measurement by customer (CEI ERABAccess) is different to the average of Network indicator (Network ERAB Init Acc).

On average Customer indicator gives higher values than network indicators. However, some customers may have bad experience with bad access to the service as observed. For 14 of 133 samples the Customer experience Index is worse than Network KPI. Operator quality plans are required to improve the end user experience for such users. Mitigation plan or evaluation to include these users in retention from commercial point of view could be applied.

In a real discussion between customers about cellular network performance the perception of this group would be more influenced for users with worse service without take in account that some users may have more or less call attempts. This approach allow to identify and take actions before than users start to complaint to the operator or the social circle.

Table 7. T-test mean comparison network indicator vs. customer experience index.

Mean Comparison between CEI ERAB Access and Network ERAB initial Accessibility			
Hypothesis: $H_0: \mu_{Network} = \mu_{users}$ $H_1: \mu_{Network} \neq \mu_{users}$	*Stats*	*CEI ERABAccess*	*Network ERAB Init Acc*
	count	133	133
Where: $\mu_{Network}$: is the average of all *ERAB Init Acc$_{c,j}$* for the all C cells and M days: $$\mu_{Network} = \frac{\sum_{c=1}^{C}\sum_{j=1}^{M} Network\ ERAB\ Init\ Acc_{c,j}}{M \times C}$$ μ_{users}: is the average of all *ERAB Init Acc$_{c,j}$* for the all C cells and M days: $$\mu_{users} = \frac{\sum_{c=1}^{C}\sum_{j=1}^{M} CEI\ ERABAccess_{c,j}}{M \times C}$$	*mean*	94.0833	92.063172
	std	4.381966	5.107144
	T-Student Test Statistic	3.46 is not in the 99% of critical value H_o *is rejected* for $\propto = 0.01\ with\ range\ [-2.59, 2.59]$	
	P-value	0.0006252 *small value H_1 is accepted*	

4.3 ERAB Initial Accessibility Performance Network Main Factors

Factor analysis was implemented for the variable ERAB Accessibility and factors indicated in Table 8 Correlation between ERAB Accessibility per user and all other variables. Correlation Matrix shows high correlation between InitialS1Context_STP_SR and ERAB Accessibility. In this case it is expected because ERAB Accessibility is composed of the first three variables ERAB_STP_SR, InitialS1Context_STP_SR and RRC_CONN_STP_SR as shown in Eq. 4, It is useful to know which component has more impact on dependent variable ERAB Accessibility.

Table 8. Correlation matrix between ERAB accessibility per user and independent variables

Correlation Matrix	Total _InitERAB_ Accessibility	ERAB_STP _SR	InitialS1Con-text_STP_SR	RRC_CONN _STP_SR	X2_HO_SR	RRC_RE_ESTAB_R EQUEST	RRC_RE_ESTAB_S R	avgdBmRSRP_avg dBm	avgRSRQ	cantMeasure-ments
Total_InitERAB_Accessibility	1.00	0.37	0.88	0.28	0.04	-0.01	-0.01	-0.05	0.00	-0.03
ERAB_STP_SR	0.37	1.00	-0.01	0.12	0.01	-0.01	0.00	-0.15	-0.07	0.06
InitialS1Context_STP_SR	0.88	-0.01	1.00	-0.05	0.04	0.00	-0.02	0.06	0.07	-0.09
RRC_CONN_STP_SR	0.28	0.12	-0.05	1.00	0.03	-0.03	0.01	-0.19	-0.14	0.09
X2_HO_SR	0.04	0.01	0.04	0.03	1.00	-0.08	0.05	-0.02	0.00	-0.01
RRC_RE_ESTAB_REQUEST	-0.01	-0.01	0.00	-0.03	-0.08	1.00	-0.61	0.04	-0.02	0.16
RRC_RE_ESTAB_SR	-0.01	0.00	-0.02	0.01	0.05	-0.61	1.00	-0.05	0.05	-0.20
avgdBmRSRP_avgdBm	-0.05	-0.15	0.06	-0.19	-0.02	0.04	-0.05	1.00	0.18	-0.11
avgRSRQ	0.00	-0.07	0.07	-0.14	0.00	-0.02	0.05	0.18	1.00	-0.10
cantMeasurements	-0.03	0.06	-0.09	0.09	-0.01	0.16	-0.20	-0.11	-0.10	1.00

Conceptually, the relationship between factors has been hypothesized that the relationship between factors influence Customer Experience for ERAB Accessibility. Linear Regression was applied to the postprocessed dataset for a week of data for all users with more than 20 RRC Connection Request per day.

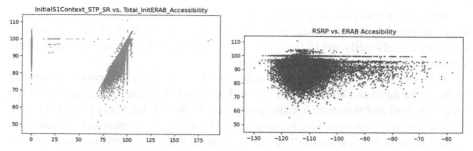

Fig. 3. Initial RAB accessibility vs. RSRP per EUTRAN cell

From Linear Regression results, can be concluded that there is strong multicollinearity between variables. However, the objective is the identification of the main factors related to the ERAB Accessibility per user. In this case It is observed that main factors of influence of ERAB Accessibility is the InitialS1Context_STP_SR. Multicollinearity issue might be related to the short number of variables (Fig. 3).

Dependent Variable	coefficient	std err	t	P>|t|	[0.025	0.975]	Hypo-thesis	Result
const	-184.4093	0.074	-2485.483	0	-184.555	-184.264	H1	Accepted
ERAB_STP_SR	0.9267	0	1988.144	0	0.926	0.928	H1	Accepted
InitialS1Context_STP_SR	0.981	0.00E+00	5196.384	0	0.981	9.81E-01	H1	Accepted
RRC_CONN_STP_SR	0.934	0.001	1559.946	0	0.933	0.935	H2	Accepted
X2_HO_SR	-0.0013	0	-7.597	0	-0.002	-0.001	H2	Accepted
RRC_RE_ESTAB_REQUEST	-0.0023	0.001	-1.587	0.112	-0.005	0.001	H3	Rejected
RRC_RE_ESTAB_SR	-5.82E-05	3.41E-05	-1.704	0.088	0	8.73E-06	H3	Rejected
avgdBmRSRP_avgdBm	-2.40E-03	0.00E+00	-12.339	0	-0.003	-2.00E-03	H4	Accepted
avgRSRQ	0.0013	0.001	2.33	0.02	0	0.002	H4	Accepted
cantMeasurements	0.0001	6.90E-05	1.631	0.103	-2.27E-05	0		Rejected
Regression Results								
Method:	Least Square					R^2	0.999	
No. Observations	31424					R^2 Adjusted	0.999	
Condition Index	16400*							

* Condition Index is large. This might indicate that there are strong multicollinearity or other numerical problems
H1: ERAB_STP_SR,InitialS1Context_STP_SR and RRC_CONN_STP_SR impacts positively Total_InitERAB_Accessibility
H2: Mobility Success Rate by X2 interface X2_HO_SR impacts positively. Bad performance of mobility will also impact negatively ERAB Accessibility
H3: RRC_RE_ESTAB_REQUEST and RRC_RE_ESTAB_SR impact negatively ERAB Accessibility
H4: RSRP and RSRQ measurements should impact positively ERAB Accessibility

5   Conclusions

In this work, we reach the implementation of a system for the extraction, transformation and load of cellular network traces was developed. Hardware and processing consumption was identified. From our results, we estimate the possible hardware consumption for a network of 5000 Cells.

The system of indicators created at the network level can be implemented for any eNodeB hardware supplier that complies with the 3GPP32.421 standard. Currently, the indicators are generated by the cellular network equipment and have some variations between vendors, networks have started to handle different hardware vendors through Open RAN and network densification with microsites. It is concluded that it is an advantage to have a trace-based, vendor-independent system of indicators that allows uniform monitoring of both network indicators and customer experience indicators.

This work proposes a Customer Experience index for ERAB Accessibility per customer. Indicator based on indicators previously standardized by 3GPP at network elements such as eNodeBs and LTE cells. Proposed aggregation by customer will provide a better assessment of customer experience.

This work proposes a novel use of indicators that had been previously standardized by 3GPP for network elements such as eNodeBs and LTE cells, for aggregation at the Customer level and thus have a better assessment of the service being provided by the network for each customer. Key performance indicators per customer help operators to identify network zones where KPI per cell is good but disparity of performance between users is high, zones where traditional optimization indicators are good, but with the new method may require action plans.

In terms of customer experience, the difference between the quality of service perceived by the customers and network performance is considerable for some groups of users that have considerable traffic but bad performance. Customer Experience Index proposed for ERAB or Service Accessibility of Radio Main component impacting ERAB accessibility is the S1 Context Setup phase. More indicators and correlation between factors can be made in future works. New counters can be added from the source for any procedure of Radio Access Network.

References

1. Garín-Muñoz, T., Gijón, C., Pérez-Amaral, T., López, R.: Consumer complaint behavior in telecommunications: the case of mobile phone users in Spain. In: 25th European Regional Conference of the International Telecommunications Society (ITS), Brussels, Belgium (2014)
2. Hirschman, A.: Exit, Voice and Loyalty: Responses to Decline in Firms, Organizations. Harvard University Press, Cambridge, MA (1970)
3. Aguilar, L.J.: tecnologías Facilitadoras de la industria 4.0. In: Industria 4.0, Bogotá, Alfaomega, pp. 59–65 (2019)
4. Qualcomm: Making 5G NR a Reality. Qualcomm Technologies Inc., San Diego, CA, USA (2016)
5. Vafeiadis, T., Diamantaras, K.I., Sarigiannidis, G., Chatzisavvas, K.: A comparison of machine learning techniques for customer churn prediction. Simul. Model. Practice Theory **55**, 1–9 (2015). https://doi.org/10.1016/j.simpat.2015.03.003
6. Shin, H.C.S.: Response modeling with support vector machines. Expert Syst. Appl. **30**(4), 746–760 (2006). https://doi.org/10.1016/j.eswa.2005.07.037
7. Lee, H., Shin, H., Hwang, S., Cho, S., MacLachlan, D.: Semiupervised response modeling. J. Interact. Market. **24**(1), 42–54 (2010). https://doi.org/10.1016/j.intmar.2009.10.004
8. Lessmann, S., Voß, S.: A reference model for customer-centric data mining with support vector machines. Eur. J. Oper. Res. **199**(2), 520–530 (2009). https://doi.org/10.1016/j.ejor.2008.12.017
9. Diaz-Aviles, E.: Towards real-time customer experience prediction for telecommunication operators. In: IEEE International Conference on Big Data, Santa Clara, CA (2015)
10. Keramati, A., Jafari-Marandi, R., Aliannejadi, M., Ahmadian, I., Mozaffari, M., Abbasi, U.: Improved churn prediction in telecommunication industry using data mining techniques. Appl. Soft Comput. **24**, 994–1012 (2014). https://doi.org/10.1016/j.asoc.2014.08.041
11. 3GPP TS32.421: Subscriber and equipment Trace, France (2020)

12. Yang, C.-Y.: A practical approach with big data analysis for customer-driven network optimization. In: Asia-Pacific Network Operations and Management Symposium, Matsue, Japan (2019)
13. Choi, C.: Predicting Customer Complaints in Mobile Telecom Industry Using Machine Learning Algorithms. Purdue University, West Lafayette, Indiana (2018)
14. TS32.423: Subscriber and equipment trace; trace data definition and management release 15. 3GPP, Sophia Antipolis Cedex, France (2018)
15. 3GPP TS36.401 V12.2: Architecture description. 3GPP, Valbonne, France (2015)
16. ITU_X.690: ASN.1 encoding rules: specification of basic encoding rules (BER), canonical encoding rules (CER) and distinguished encoding rules (DER). In: Series X: Data Networks and Open System (2002)
17. TS36.423: X2 Application Protocol (X2AP). 3GPP, Sophia Antipolis Cedex, France (2014)
18. TS36.331: Radio Resource Control (RRC) Release 12. 3GPP, Sophia Antipolis Cedex, France (2015)
19. TS36.413: S1 Application Part Protocol (S1AP) Release 12. 3GPP, Sophia Antipolis Cedex, France (2014)
20. 3GPP TS32.450: 3GPP32.250 Key Performance Indicators (KPI) for Evolved Universal Terrestrial Radio Access Network (E-UTRAN) Release 16. Valbone, France (2020)

Approach Pencil-on-Paper to Flexible Piezoresistive Respiration Sensor

Luiz Antonio Rasia[1]([⊠])(iD), Carlos Eduardo Andrades[1](iD), Thiago Gomes Heck[1](iD), and Julia Rasia[2](iD)

[1] Regional University of the Northwest of the State of Rio Grande do Sul, Ijuí, Brazil
{rasia,thiago.heck}@unijui.edu.br
[2] Center for Rural Sciences - CCR, UFSM – Federal University of Santa Maria, Santa Maria, Brazil

Abstract. The technologies based on paper and flexible material allow developing devices for diagnostic tests of the type Point-of-Care - PoC. These technologies enable the development of sensor devices and actuators for tests and diagnostics in humans and animals, since the materials used are thin, light, flexible and inexpensive, when compared with traditional Silicon technologies. These sensor platforms or devices are simple to manufacture, batch production, easy to use and are environmentally friendly. The pencil on paper allows the produced of many types of sensors, in special, sensors that using the piezoresistive effect for individual monitoring of human breathing.

Keywords: Flexible and stretchable sensors · Wearable sensors · Respiration sensors · Graphite film

1 Introduction

Paper as a substrate is a new field of interest for electronics and a new opportunity for the development of new devices due to its low cost, lightness, flexibility and biocompatible and recyclable nature.

The literature [1–3] indicates that it is possible to deposit different materials on paper substrates. In this work, pencil graphite obtained by mechanical exfoliation is used, without the use of chemical solvents. This technique is known as GoP – Graphite on Paper or PoP – Pencil on Paper, as shown in Fig. 1 [1–8].

In this article, we intend to introduce the procedure for manufacturing and developing humidity sensors for applications in masks for human breathing.

Humidity sensors, in particular, are being applied in industrial processing and environmental control, domestic applications, the automotive industry, the medical field, precision agriculture, industry in general and a wide variety of other applications [7]. The literature [1] shows that flexible electronic devices have the potential for different applications, including human movement detection and wearable thermal therapy.

© Springer Nature Switzerland AG 2021
J. C. Figueroa-García et al. (Eds.): WEA 2021, CCIS 1431, pp. 290–298, 2021.
https://doi.org/10.1007/978-3-030-86702-7_25

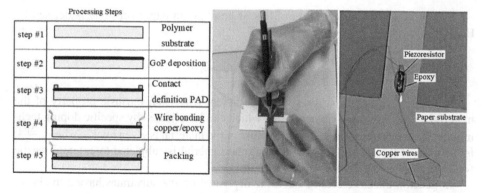

Fig. 1. Description of the manual processing steps of graphite sensor and sensor encapsulate

Otherwise, rapid diagnosis can have wide applications in different areas, such as medical clinic, food safety, environmental monitoring and veterinary medicine, among others. PoC – type diagnostic tests are easy to use, fast and inexpensive, especially in countries with limited resources, hence the importance of new methodologies for the manufacture of sensor devices. PoC diagnostics facilitate disease detection and control, treatment monitoring and make it possible to address global health problems. Technologies based on platforms that use paper, flexible material and graphite films enable new devices in the area of PoC diagnostics [4].

Piezoresistive mechanical stress sensors on flexible substrates that can convert mechanical deformations through variations in electrical resistance provide a simple and practical detection tool in the area of health monitoring, human movement detection, personal health, man-machine interface and so-called electronic skin.

Flexible electronic devices on paper substrate are a great innovation as it is biocompatible, recyclable and biodegradable. Among the devices that can be manufactured are mechanical strain gauges, force and pressure sensors that use thin films of graphite pencil. Graphite sensors on flexible polymeric substrates can be applied in the manufacture of different devices, such as wearable devices, sensors for internet of things, bioengineering and applications in several other areas of science and technology [5, 6].

1.1 Fundamental Concepts

The fundamental component of the sensors for mass, pressure, acceleration, inertia, among others is the strain gauge because its function is to convert mechanical loads into an electrical signal, that is, it is from this device that the environment variables are measured can be controlled.

In order to explore an organic material for making a sensor device chose to use the graphite making up 2B pencil trace on paper substrate according to Eq (1).

$$R = \rho \frac{L}{wt} \tag{1}$$

Where, ρ, is the resistivity of the material, L, is length, w, is width and, t, the thickness of the deposited film.

The piezoresistive effect in thin films of graphite on paper substrate is defined by Eq. (2).

$$\frac{\Delta \rho_{ij}}{\rho} = \pi_{\pi ijkl} T_{kl} \tag{2}$$

Where, $\pi_{\pi ijkl}$, is the piezoresistive coefficient tensor, an intrinsic property of the material chosen as sensor elements, and which can be adjusted by specific doping techniques. The mechanical stress in the structure of the material is given by, T_{kl}, where, $\frac{\Delta \rho_{ij}}{\rho}$, is the ratio of the electric resistivity when the material is subjected to external tensile forces or mechanical deformations [5].

In general, the structures of the films deposited on the substrates have a thickness much smaller than the thickness of the substrate itself $t_s \gg t_f$ therefore; the mechanical stresses are transmitted integrally from the substrate to the film according to the theory of small deflections as shown in [9].

The sensitivity factor, GF, is dependent on the crystallographic orientation of the material, this case, graphite and is related to the piezoresistive coefficient through the Young's modulus, E, given by Eq. (3).

$$GF = \pi_{ij} E \tag{3}$$

Equation (3) shows the sensitivity of the graphite sensor element.

1.2 Characteristics of the Paper Substrate

Paper is a biodegradable and abundant material, it has been used for centuries for printing, packaging, and liquid absorption. The paper is porous, consisting of a hydrophilic network of interwoven cellulose fibers. This network defines the mechanical and fluid properties of the material. In recent years, paper has become increasingly interesting as a material in new applications.

Figure 2 illustrates the structure of the cellulose fibers in a schematic way and a SEM – scanning electron microscopy of the paper with 430× magnification. The small white dots next to the paper fibers indicate residues due to the production processes of the sheets.

Cellulose fibers in paper are wooden cells (or pieces of wood) which can even have 2 mm to 5 mm long and 20 μm to 40 μm wide, depending on their natural origin. The cellulose-based cell wall consists of small fibrils, which in turn are made of microfibers with a diameter of about 3 nm to 20 nm. While the amorphous parts between fibrils consist mainly of hemicelluloses and lignin, microfibrils consist of chains of cellulose that partially form crystalline regions of cellulose and are held together by hydrogen bonding [10].

The level or degree of crystallinity of the cellulose fibers as well as the number of free hydroxyl groups are of fundamental importance for the absorption of water by the paper. As a result, it is hygro-expandable and the tension of the deposited graphite film.

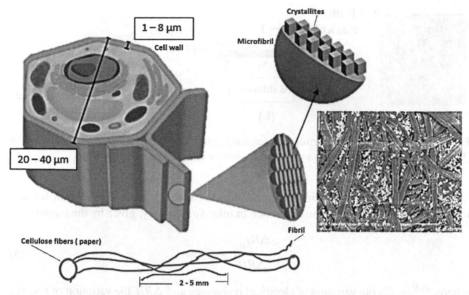

Fig. 2. Schematic representation of the cellulose fiber structure adapted [10] and view of a sheet of white sulfite paper seen in the SEM

The ratio between the dimensional variation, resulting from a change in the moisture content and its initial dimension, defines the hygroexpansibility of the paper according to Eq. (4) [11].

$$\varepsilon_h = \left(\frac{\Delta_l}{l_0}\right) \times 100 \tag{4}$$

where, ε_h, hygroexpansibility of the paper in %, Δ_l, variation in length and, l_0, initial length of the sample.

Cellulosic fibers are hygroscopic and absorb water quickly. However, under equilibrium conditions, the humidity of the paper depends on the relative humidity as well as the ambient temperature.

The fibers absorb water internally and, on the surface, so that they expand when they absorb and contract when they lose water. This expansion and contraction effect is transmitted to the deposited graphite film, changing its electrical resistance due to the piezoresistive effect shown in Eq. (2) [9].

The humidity of the paper decreases with increasing temperature and increases with relative humidity, in balance with the environment. Therefore, a graphite piezoresistor deposited on this substrate presents a mechanical deformation that can be measured, indicating the relative humidity absorbed by the paper, in this case, by the humidity sensor.

The resistivity variations of the piezoresistor are amplified and delivered to the analog input of a microcontroller system which performs adjustments, filters, and performs mathematically and computationally the electrical voltage signals corresponding to relative humidity. This principle is used to detect the breathing of humans. Figure 3 illustrates the possible arrangement for the sensor if placed in a breathing mask.

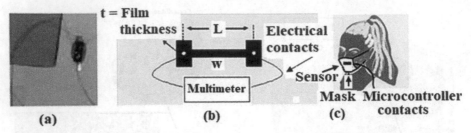

Fig. 3. Experimental arrangement of the respiration sensor. (a) Photograph of encapsulated sensor (b) geometric model of the piezoresistor and (c) sensor device in a disposable mask

The sensitivity of the sensing element is defined as the ratio of the relative difference in electrical resistance over the difference in relative humidity, given by the equation,

$$S = \frac{\Delta R/R_0}{\Delta RH} \times 100\% \tag{5}$$

where, $\Delta R/R_0$, is the variation of electrical resistance and ΔRH the variation of relative humidity.

1.3 Characteristics of the Graphite Film

Graphite is constituted of infinite layers of carbon formed by sp^2 hybridization. In each layer, the sheet of graphene, a carbon atom bonds to three other atoms, forming a flat arrangement of fused hexagons. Sp^2 hybridization occurs with carbon atoms making a double bond [5]. Figure 4 illustrates the structure of the graphite and shows the homogeneity of the film after thermal annealing on the paper substrate. This figure was obtained by SEM with 180x magnification.

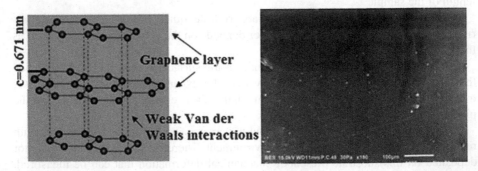

Fig. 4. Graphite structure and SEM film deposited on paper

Due to the relocation of π electrons graphite can conduct electricity and therefore has electrical resistivity. In diamond, for example, this movement of the electrons is very small making it slightly conductive of electrical current.

The extreme anisotropy makes graphite a mineral with peculiar properties, being responsible for an electrical resistivity of 5×10^3 $\Omega \cdot m$ in the direction perpendicular to the plane and 5×10^{-6} $\Omega \cdot m$ in the direction parallel to the plane.

Unlike other materials, graphite undergoes a process called "relaxation resistivity", that is, resistivity depends on the intrinsic characteristics of the material itself [12].

2 Results and Discussions

Flexible and extensible detection electronics for wearable devices and health monitoring are complex integrated systems, composed of flexible substrates, special conductive films, detection materials and, occasionally, encapsulation materials. As such, special attention is needed to the individual functions of each constituent component, their interactions and how these interactions affect the performance of the system and its biocompatibility to prevent infections or contamination.

Wearable devices require durable and compatible substrates for various scenarios of both invasive and, in this work, non-invasive application in human health care.

In this work, two characterizations of electrical sensitivity of graphite piezoresistors were obtained, due to the paper's hygroexpandability with the variation of relative humidity, RH, as shown in Fig. 5 and Fig. 6.

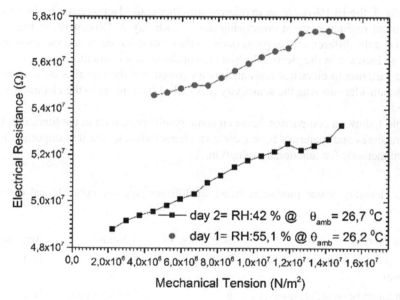

Fig. 5. Variation of electrical resistance of sample with 55.1% and 42% RH

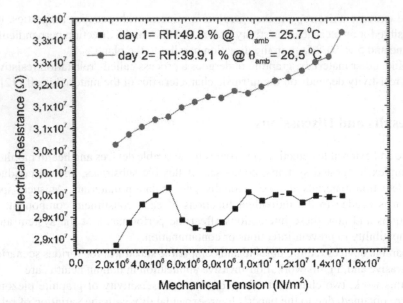

Fig. 6. (a) Variation of electrical resistance of sample with 49.8% and 39.9% RH

In Fig. 5, the 13.1% decrease in relative humidity caused an increase in the variation of electrical resistance when comparing day 1 with day 2. Otherwise, in Fig. 6 it is verified that the difference of approximately 10% relative humidity and variation of 1 °C caused an increase in the electrical resistance of the sensor element.

The variation in electrical resistance is measured and the signal is conditioned via a microcontroller showing the sensitivity (mV/%RH) according to the electrical supply voltage.

Table 1 shows a comparison between some results presented in the literature. However, processes and materials have their own characteristics, and it is important to use different methods for functional evaluation.

Table 1. Humidity sensor parameters based on different types of materials and deposition processes.

Material/process	Sensibility, S%	Substrate	Reference
Graphene (CVD – MLG – multilayer graphene)	7–27	Epoxy	[13]
Carbon nanotube on cellulose paper	6	Cellulous paper	[14]
Nanocrystalline graphite	0.0334	Silicon	[15]
Pencil-trace/pencil-drawn	8.34	Weighing paper	[16]
Graphite on paper	4.17	Cellulous paper	[this work]

3 Conclusions

The results of this work are promising and contribute to the care of human health it allows the development of disposable respirators with possible monitoring of the absorbed oxygen rate, based on the hypo-expandability of the paper with humidity and the piezoresistive effect of the film graphite.

The sensor element studied must subsequently undergo a test stage following the protocols of the health area.

Flexible detection electronics will change conventional medical diagnostic methods and revolutionize medical instruments by making them portable, wearable, remote and possibly low cost.

Acknowledgments. The authors thank the Regional University of the Northwest of the State of Rio Grande do Sul and the Foundation for Research Support – FAPERGS and CNPq for financial support.

References

1. Dinh, T., Phan, H., Qamar, A., Nguyen, N., Dao, D.: Flexible and multifunctional electronics fabricated by a solvent-free and user-friendly method. RSC Adv. (2016). https://doi.org/10.1039/C6RA14646E
2. Mahadeva, S.K., Walus, K., Stoeber, B.: Paper as a platform for sensing applications and other devices: a review. ACS Appl. Mater. Interfaces (2015). https://doi.org/10.1021/acsami.5b00373
3. Gabbi, R., Rasia, L.A., Valdiero A.C., Gabbi, M.T.T.: An aproach for computational simulation of the elements piezoresistives of graphite. Int. J. Develop. Res. 19150–19155 (2018)
4. Shafiee, H., et al.: Paper and flexible substrates as materials for biosensing platforms to detect multiple biotargets. Sci. Rep. **5**, 8719 (2015). https://doi.org/10.1038/srep08719
5. Rasia, L.A., Leal, G., Koberstein, L.L., Furlan, H., Massi, M., Fraga, M.A.: Design and Analytical Studies of a DLC Thin-Film Piezoresistive Pressure Microsensor. In: Figueroa-García, J.C., López-Santana, E.R., Villa-Ramírez, J.L., Ferro-Escobar, R. (eds.) WEA 2017. CCIS, vol. 742, pp. 433–443. Springer, Cham (2017). https://doi.org/10.1007/978-3-319-66963-2_39
6. Rasia, L.A., Pedrali, P.C., Furlan, H., Fraga, M.A.: Design and Characterization of Graphite Piezoresistors in Paper for Applications in Sensor Devices. In: Figueroa-García, J.C., Duarte-González, M., Jaramillo-Isaza, S., Orjuela-Cañon, A.D., Díaz-Gutierrez, Y. (eds.) WEA 2019. CCIS, vol. 1052, pp. 577–583. Springer, Cham (2019). https://doi.org/10.1007/978-3-030-31019-6_48
7. Chen, Z., Lu, C.: Humidity sensors: a review of materials and mechanisms. Sens. Lett. **3**, 274–295 (2005). https://doi.org/10.1166/sl.2005.045
8. Lin, C.-W., Zhao, Z., Kim, J., Huang, J.: Pencil drawn strain gauges and chemiresistors on paper. Sci. Rep. **4**(3812), 2–6 (2014). https://doi.org/10.1038/srep03812
9. Rasia, L.A., Pedrali, P.C., Valdiero, A.C.: Characterization of piezoresistive sensors of graphite on paper substrate. In: 16th LACCEI International Multi-Conference for Engineering, Education, and Technology: "Innovation in Education and Inclusion", 19–21 July 2018, Lima, Peru. https://doi.org/10.18687/LACCEI2018.1.1.327

10. Tobjörk, D., Österbacka, R.: Paper electronics. Adv. Mater. **23**, 1935–1961 (2011). https://doi.org/10.1002/adma.201004692

11. Mohammadzadeh, A., Barletta, M., Gisario, A.: Manufacturing of cellulose-based paper: dynamic water absorption before and after fiber modifications with hydrophobic agents. Appl. Phys. A **126**(5), 1–11 (2020). https://doi.org/10.1007/s00339-020-03577-4

12. Lu, W., et al.: Voltage-induced resistivity relaxation in a highdensity polyethylene/graphite nanosheet composite, [S.l.], pp. 860–863 (2007). https://doi.org/10.1002/polb.21111

13. Popov, V.I., Nikolaev, D.V., Timofeev, V.B., Smagulova, S.A., Antonova, I.V.: Graphene based humidity sensors: the origin of resistance change. Nanotechnology **28**(35) (2017). https://doi.org/10.1088/1361-6528/aa7b6e

14. Han, J.-W., Kim, B., Li, J., Meyyappan, M.: Carbon nanotube based humidity sensor on cellulose paper. J. Phys. Chem. C. **116**, 22094−22097 (2012). https://doi.org/10.1021/jp3080223

15. Ling, T.Y., et al.: Sensing performance of nanocrystalline graphite based humidity sensors. IEEE Sens. J. 25539 (2019). https://doi.org/10.1109/JSEN.2019.2905719

16. Zhang, J., et al.: Pencil-trace on printed silver interdigitated electrodes for paper-based NO_2 gas sensors. Appl. Phys. Lett. **106**, 143101 (2015)

Maintenance Management of an Additive Manufacturing System Based on the I4.0 Model

Juan David Contreras[1]([📧]) [iD], Jose Isidro Garcia[2] [iD], and Julian Gomez[2]

[1] Pontificia Universidad Javeriana Cali, Cali, Colombia
juandavid.contreras@javerianacali.edu.co
[2] Universidad del Valle, Cali, Colombia
{Jose.i.garcia,gomez.julian}@correounivalle.edu.co

Abstract. Currently, novel industrial organizations have emerged supported by the Industry 4.0 model. This digital transformation encourages a technological integration where addictive manufacturing plays a resale role. In this sense, this work focuses on the definition of an addictive manufacturing industrial environment under the Industry 4.0 model that integrates a value-based platform. The model presented strengthens maintenance management allowing new scenarios, such as: self-maintenance and remote maintenance.

Keywords: Industry 4.0 · 3D printer · Asset administration shell

1 Introduction

The digital transformation model defined by the Industry 4.0, which aims to increase value in the sustainable production of goods, has driven the productivity, flexibility and mobility of customized mass production. This model supports the synergic integration between nine technological pillars. 1) Industrial Internet of Things (IIoT), focused on the connectivity of objects and systems; 2) Big Data, used to process large and complex datasets for decision-making; 3) Horizontal and vertical integration of systems both internally and externally; 4) Simulations which establishes analytical techniques and optimization algorithms. 5) Cloud Computing, offering specialized computational environments that can be shared between multiple users, 6) Augmented Reality (AR) enabling human-machine interaction to facilitate specific tasks such as maintenance and training; 7) Autonomous Robots in charge of tasks that can be complex, repetitive or even dangerous for humans; 8) Additive manufacturing introduces mass production techniques through printing technology and 9) Cyber security contributes with prediction models for digital systems [8]. Although these technologies have had an individual development, their integration into data processing and industrial processes bestow novelty to Industry 4.0, particularly in emerging economies. This industrial model offers an environment for the rapid development of products along with a flexible and smart production system, as a response to the

© Springer Nature Switzerland AG 2021
J. C. Figueroa-García et al. (Eds.): WEA 2021, CCIS 1431, pp. 299–311, 2021.
https://doi.org/10.1007/978-3-030-86702-7_26

complexities of current products, processes and environments, derived from the growing demand of customized items with decreasing lifecycles [8]. Hence, the model enables enhancements to satisfy customer requirements, through a flexibility in different dimensions, inside and outside organizations and optimized decision-making as well as the creation of new services, bringing forth a sustainable production to benefit society and nature [16].

Additive manufacturing allows the creation of structures in a layered deposition process that is reshaping the industry due to its capacity to deliver net products in short time periods with nearly any waste in materials [14]. In [20], the authors define some of the potential benefits of additive manufacturing such as: straight design-to-component production, generation of pieces with higher customization level without additional costs from tools or product, functional design that allows to build complex inner features; production of lightweight and flexible components with hollow structures; direct production to its net (or nearly final) form with little to no additional processing; potential to reach zero-waste production through maximized use of materials; significant reduction in the general development of products and delivery times which leads to faster market transfer; smaller operational footprint towards the production of a variety of parts; on-demand production and excellent scalability. As a result, the acceptance of this technology has translated into market growth. In 2014, its market was estimated at \$4 billion USD, expected to grow by \$21 billion in 2021 [19]. In [5], significant contributions are presented to additive manufacturing in Industry 4.0 such as customization, design, development, virtual prototyping and inventory, waste reduction, time reduction, increase in flexibility and customer satisfaction. Although this technological pillar has shown a growing trend, there is little evidence of growth in value-based services such as maintenance. This means, despite the great growth in the adoption of 3D printing by SMEs and makers, the technical support services associated with this market have not grown at the same rate as the demand, this in part because 3D printer vendors are not direct manufacturers, but distribution partners. Traditionally, The technical performance of productive systems has been improved in terms of maintenance, through economic savings and new strategies such as remote maintenance or self-maintenance [8]. The former establishes an environment where maintenance is independent from the geographical location of experts and devices. The latter defines a set of maintenance strategies integrated within control systems. Furthermore, the processing of industry 4.0 information makes it possible to detect and verify patterns that can establish a prediction of the abnormal states of a system both horizontally and vertically, in favor of predictive maintenance [6]. Predictive maintenance is based on statistics and the estimation of functional degradation of a mechanical element [18].

A systematic review of 47 articles focused on predictive control in Industry 4.0 is presented in [23]. In [11], different tasks of production management and maintenance are identified and classified in the technological integration proposed in Industry 4.0. Additionally, [17] presents a summary of the potential application of the Industry 4.0 pillars to the maintenance process. The authors in [10] perform an analysis including 68 articles and identify the growing contribution of maintenance to the sustainability goal of Industry 4.0.

Based on the previous statements, the present work exposes the structure of a hybrid, predictive and proactive maintenance system of 3d printers based on Industry 4.0, focused on the architecture of maintenance management and not on fault detection algorithms. The objective of this project is to integrate 3D printer owners and systems, predictive maintenance tools and technicians on an industry 4.0 value-based services platform. This is presented as a solution for the gap between the growing demand for technical assistance for the maintenance and repair of 3D printers and the poor formal provision of these services. In this sense, two different scenarios are analyzed whilst showing evidence of the benefits of the proposed architecture.

2   Industry 4.0

Since 2015, the Reference Architectural Model for Industry 4.0 (RAMI 4.0) has established itself as a unified environment focused on classifying standards and methods of the Industry 4.0 model. The ecosystem is based on three axis. The vertical axis represents the interoperability dimension and defines a six-level structure for IT components. The horizontal left axis that defines the different processes that participate in the lifecycle or value flow, based on regulation IEC 62890. The horizontal right axis presents a structure of roles and responsibilities regarding the product generation environment according to regulation IEC 62264 / IEC 61512 [7]. As a result, RAMI 4.0 defines a network of components interconnected by the "administration Shell" which contains the data of the virtual representation of an object in the real world with its own features and functionalities [21]. A more detailed description of the different viewpoints in RAMI 4.0 is included in [22].

2.1   Asset Administration Shell

The AAS is an information system than integrates the interoperability dimension of RAMI 4.0, representing a relevant feature of a cyber-physical component of Industry 4.0 as seen in Fig. 1 where a non-Industry 4.0 component lacks the AAS, thus restricting its interoperability in the Industry 4.0 ecosystem. The Administration Shell encompasses three aspects: functional, information and communication, allowing a virtual description of the elements, assets and objects including software and documentation, among others. A detailed description of the AAS is discussed in [2,3].

According to [3], The AAS can be mapped to several data format to make possible to share information between different AAS throughout the area covered by the entire RAMI4.0 model, some of this accepted data formats are OPC UA Information models, AutomationML, XML, JSON and RDF, and each format has its respective application scenario being OPC UA the target format for information models in the domain of production operations. Figure 2 shown

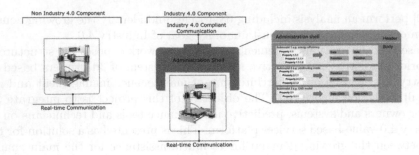

Fig. 1. Comparison between Industry 4.0 components and non-Industry 4.0 components

the mapping between some elements of the AAS metamodel and the OPC UA information model.

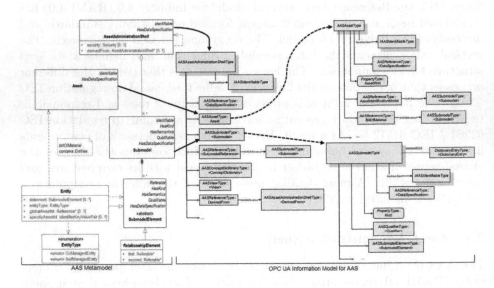

Fig. 2. Mapping from AAS metamodel to OPC UA information model. Source: [3]

OPC UA (Open Process Communications Unified Architecture) is a data exchange standard developed by OPC Foundation and standardized in IEC 62541. According to SOA principles, OPC UA presents a smoothly coupled architecture which facilitates the interconnection of heterogeneous components distributed both horizontally and vertically within an industrial organization, using internet as a communication channel. Furthermore, OPC UA handles quality features considered to be relevant in an industrial environment such as security, structured information model and automatic discovery functions [9]. In [15], OPC UA is compared to other industrial communication protocols such as

ROS, DDS and MQTT, showing the strengths of OPC UA in terms of semantic information modelling and high performance. These factors have led OPC UA to become a suitable infrastructure in the implementation of the communication layer within the Industry 4.0 model [13]. A detailed description of the OPC UA architecture, the addressing of components and the offered services is presented in [12]. In conclusion, RAMI 4.0 outlines a general reference framework of the architecture of an Industry 4.0 system comprised by the interconnection of I4.0 components, which are created by adding to an asset an AAS that represents it virtually. Lastly, the AAS can be implemented in different forms, yet the information models of OPC UA deliver enhanced support and a higher development level.

3   Architecture of the VBS Platform

Value-Based Services (VBS) are an application scenario of the Industry 4.0 published in the Platform Industry 4.0 [1]. In this report, they define VBS as: "The process data, state of the production sources and the use of products are the raw materials for future models and commercial services".

This new business model represents a migration of the industrial model towards the Industry 4.0 (see Fig. 3). In the traditional supply chain, a machine operator (owner of one or more production machines) only contacts a machine provider (entity in charge of selling machines) to acquire a machine or receive technical service in case of failure. In contrast, according to the new VBS model, the machine operator can access new services while the VBS platform operator (entity in charge of the I4.0 machine management) offers them online to the value-based service provider (entity in charge of finding and developing the VBS). Hence, the VBS operator identifies new services for the machine operator and opportunities to widen the provider's portfolio.

The Platform Industry 4.0 in [4] proposes certain business model development scenarios on three levels: remote supervision of machines, individual optimization of machines and production scheduling. The first level allows a customer to have access to the virtual representation of the machine (or AAS) that contains the technical information, variable values and alarms within a monitoring-oriented environment. The second level allows to remotely establish the optimal operation parameters, perform diagnosis on component status and remote/on-site solution in case of failure event. The last level focuses on optimizing the work of a set of interrelated machines. The present project revolves around the first and second levels of the model, focusing in the management of maintenance for 3D printers.

The system architecture proposed to improve the maintenance through a VBS platform is represented with a Sysml diagram (see Fig. 4) that involves three inner blocks: the 3D printer, a single-board computer (SBC) and the VBS platform. In the printer block, the controller behavior is depicted along with the various electronic devices, sensors and actuators, involved in the operation and data acquisition, the controller manages the energy supply of the extruder using a PID controller to reach or maintain the required temperature, which is sensed

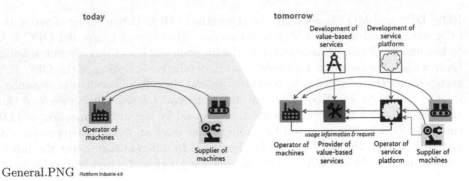

today

tomorrow

Development of value-based services

Development of service platform

Operator of machines

Supplier of machines

usage information & request

Operator of machines

Provider of value-based services

Operator of service platform

Supplier of machines

General.PNG Plattform Industrie 4.0

Fig. 3. VBS platform example. **Source:** [4]

through a thermistor. The same method is used to control the temperature of the heated bed. Furthermore, the controller receives instructions in the form of G and M codes through the serial port, which are executed on a hardware and software level in the printer. The following variables are sent through this port: indirect positions (X, Y and Z), extruder motion and operation temperatures.

In order to read the non-functional variables of the 3D printer which are necessary for the predictive maintenance, two sensors were added: a temperature sensor and a vibration sensor in the stepper motors. These sensors communicate with the SBC using the I2C communication protocol. The inner block of the single-board is comprised by three sections: serial connection app, I2C connection app and OPC-UA server. The first two manage the communication through serial port and I2C respectively, while the third one allows the implementation of the AAS with the respective variables and methods as well as the documentation of the 3D printer. The OPC UA server is exposed through the SBC so that the platform sets a connection with the virtual representation of the machine through an OPC UA client. The client app is in charge of sending the history data to the cloud database and working in tandem with the VBS platform.

The functions of the platform are synthesized in four blocks. Firstly, the data analyzer is a software in charge of feeding the data and detecting the failures or miscalibrations based on deterministic models, as well as integrating machine learning models for predictive maintenance. Secondly, the visualizer software is in charge of presenting relevant information through a graph-based web interface that uses the technical information of the printer and alarm history records. Nest, the notifier software block is in charge of generating a report of the machine operation and sending it to the user, offering technical support service. Finally, the fixer block helps the staff in the diagnosis of the printer through reports that include previous failure events, resolved cases and false reports.

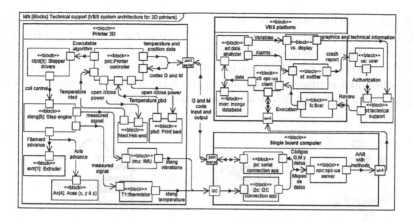

Fig. 4. Platform architecture

4   Maintenance Management

Based on the previously described VBS platform, different maintenance scenarios are discussed in this section. As a general overview, a failure or malfunction in the 3D printer is detected by the VBS platform through data capture from the 3D printer operation. After applying the industry 4.0 standardization framework, data captured from the printers is highly structured and interoperable, which eases their automatic integration into the maintenance and supervision system. Furthermore, the automatic operation of the data analysis system makes it independent from a supervised data visualization system which would be inefficient due to the increase in the number of connected devices.

Figure 5 shows the data processing throughout the elements of the information system. Firstly, raw data is generated from the printers based on sensors and the control hardware of the machine. These data are transmitted to the SBC via serial communication and I2C as explained in Sect. 3. In the SBC, a software unit receives the data and records it in an OPC UA server, involving standardized information models which are automatically generated by XML metadata structures in the form of AAS. Thus, the AAS not only contains the information derived from the sensors but also the parameters of each individual machine. A representation of the information structure that comprises the AAS is presented in Fig. 6, that serves as a simplified instance of the AAS metamodel shown in Fig. 2. Submodels are depicted as the information blocks that comprise the AAS and correspond to standardized metadata structures or blocks created by the user for specific company projects. In this application, the identification submodel based on the DIN SPEC 91406 standard is integrated. This submodel allows to unequivocally identify the represented asset. The CNC Systems submodel is also integrated based on the OPC 40502 specification, which is usually designed for subtractive manufacturing CNC devices but can be adjusted to CNC devices such as 3D printers to represent features (axis, drivers, controllers and communication channels). In order to enable the smart management of the device, the condition monitoring submodel is integrated based on the VDMA 24582 standard in which the variables gathered from the sensors and printer controller are mapped. Lastly, a documentation submodel is integrated that allows swift access to the user manual. As non-standardized models, a negotiation and contact submodel is proposed that allows the VBS platform to include information that facilitates the delivery of maintenance services.

Raw Data:
- Temperature
- Vibration
- Run time ...

Structured Data:
- OPC UA information model
- XML
- Asset Administration Shell

Information and knowledge:
- Fault detection and diagnostics
- Reinforcement learning models
- Analytics and visualization

Fig. 5. Data processing throughout the elements of the information system

From an implementation point of view, two possible alternatives are presented. One consists on programming the OPC UA server to generate the structures of the information models that describe the metadata structure in XML format both for the AAS and for every submodel. Another option involves the AASX Package Explorer tool that can create the AAS in graphic form, by importing the corresponding submodels. In both cases, a previous manual configuration of the information is required followed by the execution and deployment of the OPC UA server.

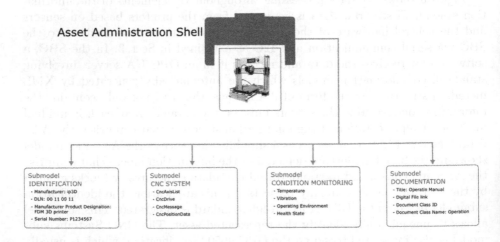

Fig. 6. AAS submodels for 3d Printer

4.1   Scenario 1: On-Site Technical Support

In this first scenario, the analysis platform detects a failure or miscalibration in the printer that requires on-site support from a technician based on the information delivered by the AAS. These events are mostly mechanical such as lack of tension in the belts, sensor failure or damaged electronics. Subsequently, a sequence of Interactions is initiated as shown in Fig. 7. The platform creates a report and sends it to the printer owner who reviews it and authorizes the support service. If the service is not authorized, the process concludes. Otherwise, the platform checks for available technicians and factors variables such as average service time and user reviews. The report is sent to the technician with the best review and if he refuses to offer support then the process is repeated until a technician is found. When the technician concludes with the maintenance or calibration of the 3D printer, he must determine whether the diagnosis delivered by the analysis system was accurate as well as notify of any other malfunctions that were previously undetected. The information is used by the platform to structure the data and send it to the reinforcement learning model so it can improve future predictions. Afterwards, a customer service evaluation is requested to update the technician review score.

In this scenario, the customer can also initiate the workflow by reporting a failure or malfunction without a detection being issued by the analysis system. This allows to improve future predictions.

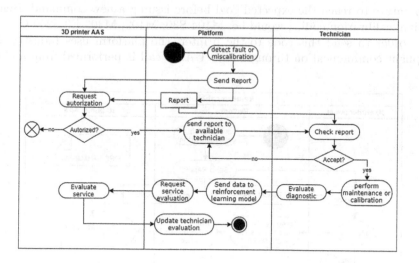

Fig. 7. Activity diagram for on-site scenario

4.2   Scenario 2: Automatic Remote Calibration

In this scenario, the VBS platform detects a failure or miscalibration based on data analysis, yet it is determined that on-site support is unnecessary. A remote operation can be performed to correct the malfunction using the AAS communication channel. Some of the most common repairs or calibrations that can be handled remotely are:

- Errors in temperature control that can be solved through PID control-based calibration using auto-tuning or flexibilization of the error conditions.
- Errors in the progression of the extruder and along the axis, can be corrected by changing parameters such as steps/mm and maximum acceleration.
- Other errors that can be handled by the printer owner such as an improper adhesion to the heated frame. This one can be solved remotely by programming a new sequence of automatic level adjustment.

Figure 8, corresponds to an activity diagram that presents a simplified version of the actor's functions in this scenario. As in scenario n° 1, the VBS platform detects the malfunction or improvement opportunity, delivers a report and requests authorization from the owner to perform calibration or repair-related changes. Once the authorization is issued, the platform generates a sequence of codes that can be executed to solve the detected incidents. For instance, if the temperature of the extruder is not constant or takes too long to be stabilized then code "M303 E0 S200 C8" can be launched for auto-tuning of the temperature PID controller parameters. However, this only works correctly if the extruder is at room temperature beforehand so the command "M104 S30" must be sent first to cool off the extruder followed by "M109" so that the printer waits for the temperature to reach the expected goal before issuing a new command. Hence, the final calibration coding would be: M104 S30; M109; M303 E0 S200 C8.

In order to send this code to the printer, the platform uses Industry 4.0-compliant communication through OPC UA. A call is performed from a client

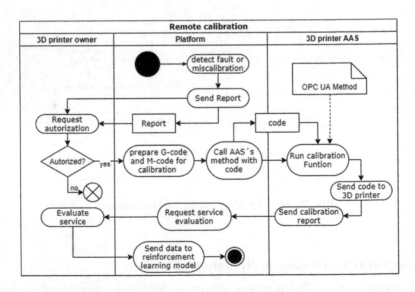

Fig. 8. Activity diagram for remote calibration scenario

PC to an OPC UA method available in the printer AAS. This method calls a function that receives the code as an input and sends it through the serial port to the 3D printer once it is available. After the calibration is concluded, the AAS generates an activity report that includes the final PID parameters and the total time of the task. Lastly, the platform requests a service assessment in order to gather user feedback and improve the predictions of the machine learning model.

In a future work, the results of a simulation model will be presented in which the performance of the system is evaluated and indicators such as times, synchronization between modules and impact on production.

5 Conclusions

Additive manufacturing represents one of the fastest growing technologies in the last decade and one of the pillars of the Industry 4.0. In this context, this document presents the architecture of a 3D printing system considering the industry 4.0 model and a VBS platform. The homogenization of this cyber-physical environment facilitated maintenance management. Where, two scenarios were treated. The first one exemplifies the process where an evaluation and maintenance by an expert operator is required from the identification of a failure state by the system control system. The second presents the execution of a maintenance service regardless of the location of the machine or expert operator.

Compared to traditional predictive maintenance systems where production systems operate locally and limited data is fed to each company's network, systems based on industry 4.0 allow data to be safely integrated between several companies without requiring manual work. to structure the data. This is especially important in the field of 3D printing, where many SMEs and makers have a small amount of equipment and geographically disparate data integration is required to make production systems work efficiently.

The VBS platforms aim to generate value for customers and suppliers by analyzing the data generated by the use of Industry 4.0 components (assets + AAS). In this project, the scenario of technical support for maintenance of 3D printers was evaluated, which allowed generating value for 3D printer owners from all the benefits associated with predictive maintenance, and also allows generating value for maintenance service providers at the same time. That seeks operational excellence from the continuous feedback of results.

As future work, it is proposed to work in new scenarios such as integration with a 4.0 logistics system that allows managing the procurement of spare parts based on data analysis and the use of augmented reality as assistance to the technician or to the owner himself during calibration or repair on-site.

References

1. Anderl, R., et al.: Aspects of the research roadmap in application scenarios. Plattform I4. 0 (2016)

2. Bader, S., Berres, B.: Details of the Asset Administration Shell - Part 2. Technical report, Federal Ministry for Economic Affairs (2020)
3. Barnstedt, E., Bedenbender, H.: Meik Billmann: Details of the Asset Administration Shell - Part 1. Technical report, Federal Ministry for Economic Affairs (2018)
4. Bauer, K., Diemer, J., Hilger, C., Lowen, U., Michels, J.: Benefits of application scenario value-based service. Technical report, Federal Ministry for Economic Affairs and Energy (BMWi) (2017)
5. Butt, J.: Exploring the interrelationship between additive manufacturing and industry 4.0. Designs **4**(2), 13 (2020)
6. Chukwuekwe, D.O., Schjoelberg, P., Roedseth, H., Stuber, A.: Reliable, robust and resilient systems: towards development of a predictive maintenance concept within the industry 4.0 environment. In: EFNMS Euro Maintenance Conference (2016)
7. Contreras, J.D., Garcia, J.I., Pastrana, J.D.: Developing of industry 4.0 applications. International Journal of Online Engineering, vol. 13, no. 10 (2017)
8. Di Bona, G., Cesarotti, V., Arcese, G., Gallo, T.: Implementation of industry 4.0 technology: new opportunities and challenges for maintenance strategy. Procedia Comput. Sci. **180**, 424–429 (2021)
9. Ferrari, P., Flammini, A., Rinaldi, S., Sisinni, E., Maffei, D., Malara, M.: Impact of quality of service on cloud based industrial IOT applications with OPC UA. Electronics **7**(7), 109 (2018)
10. Franciosi, C., Iung, B., Miranda, S., Riemma, S.: Maintenance for sustainability in the industry 4.0 context: a scoping literature review. IFAC-PapersOnLine **51**(11), 903–908 (2018)
11. Garcia, S.G., Garcia, M.G.: Industry 4.0 implications in production and maintenance management: an overview. Procedia Manuf. **41**, 415–422 (2019)
12. Leitner, S.H., Mahnke, W.: OPC UA-service-oriented architecture for industrial applications. ABB Corp. Res. Center **48**, 61–66 (2006)
13. Muller, M., Wings, E., Bergmann, L.: Developing open source cyber-physical systems for service- oriented architectures using OPC UA. In: 2017 IEEE 15th International Conference on Industrial Informatics (INDIN), pp. 83–88. IEEE (2017)
14. Oliveira, J., Santos, T., Miranda, R.: Revisiting fundamental welding concepts to improve additive manufacturing: from theory to practice. Progress Mater. Sci. **107**, 100590 (2020)
15. Profanter, S., Tekat, A., Dorofeev, K., Rickert, M., Knoll, A.: OPC UA versus ROS, DDS, and MQTT: performance evaluation of industry 4.0 protocols. In: 2019 IEEE International Conference on Industrial Technology (ICIT), pp. 955–962. IEEE (2019)
16. Rajput, S., Singh, S.P.: Connecting circular economy and industry 4.0. Int. J. Inform. Manag. **49**, 98–113 (2019)
17. Silvestri, L., Forcina, A., Introna, V., Santolamazza, A., Cesarotti, V.: Maintenance transformation through industry 4.0 technologies: a systematic literature review. Comput. Ind. **123**, 103335 (2020)
18. Spendla, L., Kebisek, M., Tanuska, P., Hrcka, L.: Concept of predictive maintenance of production systems in accordance with industry 4.0. In: 2017 IEEE 15Th International Symposium on Applied Machine Intelligence and Informatics (SAMI), pp. 000405–000410. IEEE (2017)
19. Thompson, M.K., et al.: Design for additive manufacturing: trends, opportunities, considerations, and constraints. CIRP Ann. **65**(2), 737–760 (2016)
20. Tofail, S.A., Koumoulos, E.P., Bandyopadhyay, A., Bose, S., O'Donoghue, L., Charitidis, C.: Additive manufacturing: scientific and technological challenges, market uptake and opportunities. Mater. Today **21**(1), 22–37 (2018)

21. Velasquez, N., Estevez, E., Pesado, P.: Cloud computing, big data and the industry 4.0 reference architectures. J. Comput. Sci. Technol. **18**(03), e29–e29 (2018)
22. Wang, Y., Towara, T., Anderl, R.: Topological approach for mapping technologies in reference architectural model industrie 4.0 (rami 4.0). In: Proceedings of the World Congress on Engineering and Computer Science, vol. 2, pp. 25–27 (2017)
23. Zonta, T., da Costa, C.A., da Rosa Righi, R., de Lima, M.J., da Trindade, E.S., Li, G.P.: Predictive maintenance in the industry 4.0: a systematic literature review. Computers & Industrial Engineering, p. 106889 (2020)

Optimization and Operations Research

A Mixed-Integer Linear Programming Model for the Cutting Stock Problem in the Steel Industry

Daniel Morillo-Torres[1], Mauricio Torres Baena[1], John Wilmer Escobar[1,2],
Alfonso R. Romero-Conrado[3], Jairo R. Coronado-Hernández[3($\boxtimes$)],
and Gustavo Gatica[4]

^{1} Pontificia Universidad Javeriana - Cali, Cali, Colombia
{daniel.morillo,mauricio1torres,jwescobar}@javerianacali.edu.co
^{2} Universidad del Valle, Cali, Colombia
john.wilmer.escobar@correounivalle.edu.co
^{3} Universidad de la Costa, Barranquilla, Colombia
{jcoronad18,aromero17}@cuc.edu.co
^{4} Universidad Andrés Bello, Santiago, Chile
ggatica@unab.cl

Abstract. A mixed-integer linear programming (MILP) model is proposed for solving a one dimension cutting stock problem (1D-CSP) in the steel industry. A case study of a metallurgical company is presented and the objective is to minimize waste in the cutting process of steel bars, considering inventory constraints and the potential use of the resulting leftovers. The computational results showed that an optimal solution was always found with an average improvement in waste reduction of 80%. There was no significant difference when comparing results between the complete model and the model without inventory constraints.

Keywords: Cutting stock problem · Mixed-integer linear programming · Steel bars · Industrial application

1 Introduction

Cutting stock problems (CSP) are one the most studied optimization problems in literature due to their high complexity and wide usage in industrial applications [2, 19].

Wascher [26] describe a CSP as: given a set of large objects (input, supply) and a set of small items (output, demand) (all of them defined with n number of geometric dimensions), the objective is to build subsets with one or more items and assign them to one of the large objects, holding the geometric constraints. In practice, this is commonly translated into the optimization of material usage (material waste reduction) in processes like cutting, trimming, or die-cutting.

Some classifications of CSPs are considered as highly complex problems (NP-Hard). It is possible to find an optimal solution for a small-sized CSP instance;

© Springer Nature Switzerland AG 2021
J. C. Figueroa-García et al. (Eds.): WEA 2021, CCIS 1431, pp. 315–326, 2021.
https://doi.org/10.1007/978-3-030-86702-7_27

however, these instances are unusual in real industrial planning decisions [7]. Heuristic approaches have been widely studied and allowed to find feasible solutions for large-scale instances in a wide variety of production-related problems [19,20]. Recently, with the advances in data processing, computing, and relaxation methods, some real problems can now be solved using exact approaches [6].

The aim of this paper is to show the application of a mixed-integer linear programming (MILP) model for solving real instances of a one-dimensional cutting stock problem (1D-CSP). The objective is to minimize the waste in a steel bar production process considering the geometric constraints and the inventory availability.

A case study is presented and includes instances from one of the most important metallurgical companies in Colombia. In this country, the steel industry shares approximately 10% of the national economy. Also, it generates approximately 12.12% of the country's total sales and nearly 13.44% of its jobs.

This paper is organized as follows: Sect. 2 includes a brief description of the 1D-CSP. A literature review is presented in Sect. 3, the case study is presented in Sect. 4, and the proposed solution approach is outlined in Sect. 5, including the description of the proposed MILP model. Computational results for the generation and solution of instances, and a brief comparison of solution methods are shown in Sect. 6. Finally, the main conclusions are summarized in Sect. 7.

2 Problem Description

The 1D-CSP is one of the most popular combinatorial optimization problems, and it is a generalization of the well-known Bin Packing Problem (BPP). According to Kantorovich [14], the 1D-CSP is defined as follows: given two-element sets, a large object set ($I = \{1, ..., i, ..., u\}$) and a small item set ($J = \{1, ..., j, ..., m\}$), all of them in one geometric dimension. The first set is the input of the problem (e.g., raw material), and the second set is the output (e.g., finished product). Each object has an integer capacity c, i.e., geometric limitations such as width or height. The items have an integer demand d_j and a geometric size (width or height) w_j. The BPP is a specific case of the 1D-CSP when the demand of each item j is equal to one ($d_j = 1$). Both problems are NP-hard in the strong sense, and the demonstration was done through the transformation from 3-Partition problem.

3 Literature Review

There are several variants of the cutting and packing problem. However, a common objective is obtaining a set of items that fit into given stock objects [3,4,12,15]. In this section, we focus on the main contributions for solving the 1D-CSP, which is closely related to the problem presented in the case study in Sect. 4.

In 1960 [14], an integer linear programming model for the 1D-CSP was proposed. However, only small-size instances could be solved by this model due to the considerable amount of cut combinations.

Later, Gilmore [11] proposed an integer linear model for the CSP, based on the "pattern" concept. A pattern is one of all combinations of items that can fit into an object, holding the geometric constraints. Compared with the model proposed by [14], the patterns-based model had a better integrality gap without symmetric solutions. However, the major drawback of this model was that the number of patterns grew exponentially.

Dyckhoff [8, 9] was one of the first authors that proposed a typology of cutting and packing problems. This topology considers four characteristics: Dimensionality, Kind of assignment, Assortment of large objects, and Assortment of small items. However, some problems can be classified into several categories, and two different problems could fit into the same category.

Valerio De Carvalho [22] proposed an arc-flow based formulation for the CSP. The objective function was to minimize the flow of an acyclic directed graph $G = (V, A)$, where a complete path represents each pattern. The main disadvantage of this exact algorithm was the growing number of constraints.

In 2007 Wascher [26] proposed a new classification based on [9], adding a new criterion: the shape of the small items. The difference between these typologies is that the first one presents a complete problem hierarchy. Pure, basic, intermediate, refined, standard, non-standard, and special problems are considered.

Several studies have tried to improve the performance of Integer Programming models using Column Generation (CG) [16], Brand and Bound (B&B), Branch and Price [23], and Cutting Plane (CP) approaches [24].

Rothe et al. [21] proposed a two-stage three-dimensional guillotine cutting stock problem with usable leftover, allowing rotating items.

In 2018, a comparative study of exact methods for the bi-objective 1D-CSP was studied by [10]. The proposed bi-objective model aims to minimize the frequency and the number of different cutting patterns, being these conflicting objectives. However, with the contributions in exact algorithms, 1D-CSP large-scale instances cannot be optimally resolved in a reasonable computational time.

Therefore, CSPs have been also addressed using approximate methods. These procedures do not guarantee an optimal solution but can achieve a near-optimal solution in short computational time. The approximate methods applied to the 1D-CSP are grouped into two sets: heuristic methods [5, 19, 25] and meta-heuristics approaches [1, 13, 27].

Some specific cases in the steel industry include efforts from Moussavi et al. [18] who presented an optimization approach for minimizing the cutting waste from reinforcing bars in the construction of concrete structures. The model considers lap splicing patterns flexibility, and results showed improvements up to 55.7% in steel waste reduction.

Maher et al. [17] showed the implementation results of a control system for the steel reinforcements industry. The system merged a one-dimensional cutting stock algorithm and a leftover control algorithm.

Despite the high complexity of the 1D-CSPs, some real instances could deal with a significant number of patterns through constraints associated with the cutting process. Some of those instances can be optimally solved using integer programming. In this paper, a cutting pattern generation procedure is proposed and a solving method was validated for large instances in reduced computational times.

4   Case Study

The case study takes place in a metallurgic company in the state of Valle del Cauca, Colombia. The company has a steel production capacity of 1800 tons per month. The cutting process begins when an order arrives, and it contains the demand of a given number of bars of different sizes (small items).

The company implemented an empirical cutting procedure (Company Method) to minimize the number of different item sizes per lot. For example: There are two orders: the first order contains 20 pieces of 6 m, and the other order contains 35 pieces of 12 m. Under this method, the company will produce the total number of 6-m pieces consecutively and then produce the total number of 12-m pieces. This cutting method generates high amounts of waste.

There are some particular considerations of the cutting process that must be taken into account:

1. The demand for small items is known and grouped by customer.
2. There is limited space for storage in the production area.
3. Each cut could be performed in a steel bar (large object) of 6 m, 9 m, 10 m, 11 m, 12 m or 14 m.
4. The length of the cuts could be as long as the assigned steel bar.
5. A cutting pattern can include a maximum of two types of small items.
6. The exceeding material in the cutting process is classified as *waste* or *leftover* depending on the piece's length. Leftovers are pieces that can be used to make other cuts in the next production cycle, and the waste is material that has to be discarded.

5   Solution Approach

The process for obtaining a solution for the 1D-CSP is shown in Fig. 1. A set of feasible cutting patterns was generated using the information of orders of small items (bars of different sizes) and inventory records of large objects (quantities and specifications of standard steel bars). The feasible patterns were generated considering all geometric constraints and were set as parameters in the proposed MILP model. Finally, a 1D-CSP solution was obtained for every order.

5.1   Cutting Patterns Generation Algorithm

Formally, a pattern p can be defined by an integer array $(a_{1p}, a_{2p}, ..., a_{mp})$, where each a_{jp} is the number of copies of item j that are contained in p. Patterns are feasible when they fulfill the geometric constraints.

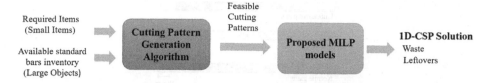

Fig. 1. Solution approach for the 1D-CSP.

Algorithm 1. Pattern generation algorithm

Require: Demand, Standard_Length
Ensure: Feasible Patterns
  Initialize L, m, n
  for i in Standard_Length **do**
    for j in Demand **do**
      while $i - (L^*j) \geq 0$ **do**
        P_m = Generate Pattern$_m(L)$
        \\Patterns with just one item
        Initialize $Leftover = i - (L^*j)$
        Initialize $Z = L + 1$
        while $Leftover - (Z^*j) \geq 0$ **do**
          T_n = Generate Pattern$_n(Z)$
          \\Patterns with two items
          n++, Z++
        end while
        L++
      end while
    end for
  end for
  print P_m, T_n

Figure 2 shows some cutting pattern representations. Unfeasible Patterns are not allowed (in this case, the pattern included more than two different types of small items). Special Patterns have leftover, Normal Patterns have waste material, and Efficient Patterns have neither leftover nor waste.

Algorithm 1 was used to generate feasible cutting patterns, according to geometric constraints, and taking into account the particular considerations of the cutting process (Sect. 4). Cutting patterns are generated considering the use of leftovers and with a maximum of two types of small items in a single cutting pattern. This constraint allows reducing the complexity of the problem, reducing the total number of feasible solutions.

5.2 Proposed MILP Model

The following Mixed Integer Linear Programming model has been proposed to improve production planning efficiency and minimize the total steel waste.

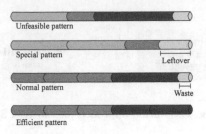

Fig. 2. Pattern representations

Sets

- $S = \{1, ..., s, ..., q\}$ set of special patterns.
- $N = \{1, ..., n, ..., m\}$ set of normal patterns.
- $I = \{1, ..., i, ..., b\}$ set of small items.
- $P = \{6, 9, 10, 11, 12, 14\}$ set of large objects, i.e. available lengths $[meters]$.
- $K_l \subset S \mid l \in P$ subset of special patterns with object of length l.
- $J_l \subset N \mid l \in P$ subset of normal patterns with object of length l.

Parameters

- N_n: waste generated by each normal pattern n.
- E_s: trim loss generated by each special pattern s.
- D_i: quantity to produce from each required bar i
- CN_{in}: quantity of bars i obtained by using the normal pattern n.
- CE_{is}: quantity of bars i obtained by using the special pattern s.
- $C_l \mid l \in P$: quantity of bars of length l available in inventory.

Variables

- X_n: number of times the normal pattern n is used.
- Y_s: number of times the special pattern s is used.

Objective Function and Constraints

$$Minimize: z = \sum_{n=1}^{m} N_n * X_n + \sum_{s=1}^{q} E_s * Y_s \tag{1}$$

s.t.

$$\sum_{n=1}^{m} CN_{in} * X_n + \sum_{s=1}^{q} CE_{is} * Y_s = D_i, \quad \forall i \in I \tag{2}$$

$$\sum_{n \in J_l} X_n + \sum_{s \in K_l} Y_s \leq C_l, \quad \forall l \in P \tag{3}$$

$$n = \{1, \ldots, m\}, \quad s = \{1, \ldots, q\}, \quad X_n, Y_s \in \mathbb{Z}_+ \tag{4}$$

The objective function (1) aims to minimize the total waste and trim loss generated by the cutting process. Constraint (2) ensures the demand fulfillment. Constraint (3) ensures production must be done with the available objects in inventory for each type of standard length. Finally, the expressions in (4) define the sets and the domain of decision variables. Two versions of the MILP model were considered: a complete model and a model without the inventory constraint (3).

6 Results

This section is divided into two parts: the first one shows the results of the proposed model in the applied case, the second part extends the experimentation to larger simulated instances.

6.1 Steel Waste Reduction in the Applied Case

An optimal solution was always found for both models: complete and without inventory constraints. The models were programmed using c++ and solved with CPLEX 12.2 through AMPL 3.5. Hardware specifications included a computer with an Intel Core i5 processor with 1.8 GHz, 8 Gb RAM. The average number of integer variables in the complete model was 8000, and the average number of constraints was 50.

According to the solution of the MILP model, waste N_n is expressed in meters. Table 1 shows the weight conversion factor for steel bars according to their diameter.

Table 1. Weights of steel bars according diameter

Diameter	Weight (Kg/m)
1/4"	0.45
3/8"	0.56
1/2"	0.994
5/8"	1.552
3/4"	2.235
7/8"	3.042
1"	3.973
1"	6.404

A set of six random production orders was selected and the steel waste was calculated considering the cutting patterns obtained from the company method (Sect. 4), the complete MILP model, and the MILP model without inventory constraints.

Figure 3 shows a summary of the obtained results. The vertical axis's left side shows the steel waste in kilograms, and the right side shows the percentage of improvement (PI) in steel waste reduction. In Eq. (5), w_c represents the waste generated using the company method, and w_{MILP}, represents the waste generated with the complete MIP model.

$$PI = \frac{w_c - w_{MILP}}{w_c} * 100 \tag{5}$$

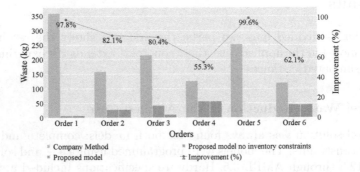

Fig. 3. Computational results.

According to every solution method, the horizontal axis shows the obtained results of steel waste for the six random production orders.

Results showed that the complete MIP model outperforms the company method in all instances. The average improvement was 80%, with a minimum of 55.3%, and a maximum of 99.6%. There were no significant differences between the complete model and the model without inventory constraints.

6.2   Computational Complexity Experiments

A total of 100 random instances were generated to perform the computational experiments. The instances included all the possible combinations of 10 types of Large Objects (LE, by its Spanish acronym) and a set of 10 types of small items (LD, by its Spanish acronym). The instance generation considered the minimum values for LD and LE, which increased by 12 centimeters to obtain the 10 types of parts. The maximum and minimum quantity of each part was randomly generated based on the range of actual demands.

Figure 4 shows the average time (in seconds) spent to create all cutting patterns as a function of LD and LE. Due to the limitations of the cutting process, the pattern generation procedure was efficient. Although the largest instances only took about 80 s to be generated, the number of patterns began to grow exponentially, resulting in plain text files with more than 300 MB of pattern information. This increasing trend in the number of LD and LE dependent patterns is observed in Fig. 5, reaching one million patterns.

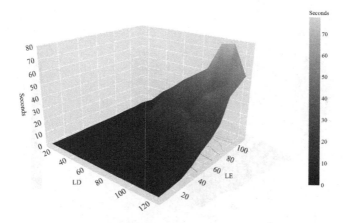

Fig. 4. Average time (s) to create cutting patterns.

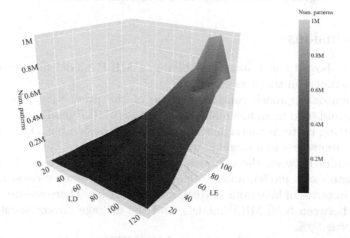

Fig. 5. Number of generated patterns as a function of LE and LD.

Despite a large number of patterns, the proposed linear programming model can solve them quickly, as can be seen in Fig. 6. The maximum time obtained for the largest instance was 2 s. However, the memory usage of the model before solving (loading it into RAM) was significantly high. It can use more than 8 Gb of memory in the largest instances. This memory usage was the main limitation of the experimentation and the reason for not making larger increments in the generation of LDs and LEs. For example, with increments of 14 centimeters, the problem could not be loaded into memory.

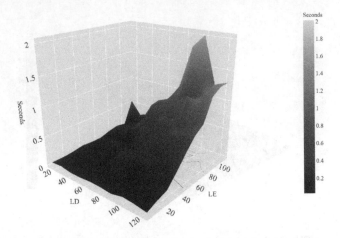

Fig. 6. Number of patterns as a function of LE and LD.

7   Conclusions

This paper showed the results of applying a MILP model for solving actual 1D-CSP instances in the steel industry.

The solution approach considered some of the production process's main limitations and used them to simplify the proposed MILP model. The number of feasible cutting patterns was significantly reduced, considering a limited number of different references in a single pattern.

The results between the empirical method implemented by the company, the complete exact model, and the model without inventory constraints were compared in terms of kilograms of steel waste per order. There was no significant difference between both MILP models, and the average improvement in waste reduction was 80%.

The pattern generation algorithm and the MILP model were experimentally proven to be efficient, solving instances of more than one million patterns in less than 2 s. As a limitation, the memory usage is very high, preventing the execution of larger instances. Large-scale optimization methods (such as column generation, where the explicit use of all variables is not required.) are recommended, considering the memory usage limitations.

Future work opportunities include considering the integration of the MILP models into a production planning web application. Also, some additional efforts should consider alternative strategies to reduce production costs and improve the solution of large-scale instances with a larger number of constraints.

References

1. Benjaoran, V., Bhokha, S.: Three-step solutions for cutting stock problem of construction steel bars. KSCE J. Civ. Eng. **18**(5), 1239–1247 (2014). https://doi.org/10.1007/s12205-014-0238-3

2. Benjaoran, V., Sooksil, N., Metham, M.: Effect of demand variations on steel bars cutting loss. Int. J. Constr. Manag. **19**(2), 137–148 (2019). https://doi.org/10.1080/15623599.2017.1401258
3. Cheng, C.H., Feiring, B.R., Cheng, T.C.: The cutting stock problem - a survey. Int. J. Prod. Econ. **36**(3), 291–305 (1994). https://doi.org/10.1016/0925-5273(94)00045-X
4. Cherri, A.C., Arenales, M.N., Yanasse, H.H., Poldi, K.C., Gonçalves Vianna, A.C.: The one-dimensional cutting stock problem with usable leftovers - a survey. Eur. J. Oper. Res. **236**(2), 395–402 (2014). https://doi.org/10.1016/j.ejor.2013.11.026
5. Cui, Y., Yang, Y.: A heuristic for the one-dimensional cutting stock problem with usable leftover. Eur. J. Oper. Res. **204**(2), 245–250 (2010). https://doi.org/10.1016/j.ejor.2009.10.028
6. Dell'Amico, M., Furini, F., Iori, M.: A branch-and-price algorithm for the temporal bin packing problem. Comput. Oper. Res. **114**, 104825 (2020). https://doi.org/10.1016/j.cor.2019.104825
7. Delorme, M., Iori, M.: Enhanced pseudo-polynomial formulations for bin packing and cutting stock problems. INFORMS J. Comput. **32**(1), 101–119 (2020). https://doi.org/10.1287/IJOC.2018.0880
8. Dyckhoff, H.: New linear programming approach to the cutting stock problem. Oper. Res. **29**(6), 1092–1104 (1981). https://doi.org/10.1287/opre.29.6.1092
9. Dyckhoff, H.: A typology of cutting and packing problems. Eur. J. Oper. Res. **44**(2), 145–159 (1990). https://doi.org/10.1016/0377-2217(90)90350-K
10. Filho, A.A., Moretti, A.C., Pato, M.V.: A comparative study of exact methods for the bi-objective integer one-dimensional cutting stock problem. J. Oper. Res. Soc. **69**(1), 91–107 (2018). https://doi.org/10.1057/s41274-017-0214-7
11. Gilmore, P.C., Gomory, R.E.: A linear programming approach to the cutting stock problem-Part II. Oper. Res. **11**(6), 863–888 (1963). https://doi.org/10.1287/opre.11.6.863
12. Golden, B.L.: Approaches to the cutting stock problem. AIIE Trans. **8**(2), 265–274 (1976). https://doi.org/10.1080/05695557608975076
13. Jahromi, M.H., Tavakkoli-Moghaddam, R., Makui, A., Shamsi, A.: Solving an one-dimensional cutting stock problem by simulated annealing and tabu search. J. Ind. Eng. Int. **8**(1), 24 (2012). https://doi.org/10.1186/2251-712X-8-24
14. Kantorovich, L.V.: Mathematical methods of organizing and planning production. Manag. Sci. **6**(4), 366–422 (1960). https://doi.org/10.1287/mnsc.6.4.366
15. Lackes, R., Siepermann, M., Noll, T.: The problem of one-dimensionally cutting bars with alternative cutting lengths in the tubes rolling process. In: IEEE International Conference on Industrial Engineering and Engineering Management, pp. 1627–1631. IEEE Computer Society, Department of Business Information Management, Technische Universität Dortmund, Dortmund, Germany (2012). https://doi.org/10.1109/IEEM.2012.6838022
16. Lemos, F.K., Cherri, A.C., de Araujo, S.A.: The cutting stock problem with multiple manufacturing modes applied to a construction industry. Int. J. Prod. Res. **59**(4), 1–19 (2020). https://doi.org/10.1080/00207543.2020.1720923
17. Maher, R.A., Melhem, N.N., Almutlaq, M.: Developing a control and management system for reinforcement steel-leftover in industrial factories. IFAC-PapersOnLine **52**(13), 625–629 (2019). https://doi.org/10.1016/j.ifacol.2019.11.091
18. Moussavi Nadoushani, Z.S., Hammad, A.W., Xiao, J., Akbarnezhad, A.: Minimizing cutting wastes of reinforcing steel bars through optimizing lap splicing within reinforced concrete elements. Constr. Build. Mater. **185**, 600–608 (2018). https://doi.org/10.1016/j.conbuildmat.2018.07.023

19. Pitombeira-Neto, A.R., Prata, B.d.A.: A matheuristic algorithm for the one-dimensional cutting stock and scheduling problem with heterogeneous orders. Top **28**(1), 178–192 (2020). https://doi.org/10.1007/s11750-019-00531-3

20. Romero-Conrado, A.R., Coronado-Hernandez, J.R., Rius-Sorolla, G., García-Sabater, J.P.: A Tabu list-based algorithm for capacitated multilevel lot-sizing with alternate bills of materials and co-production environments. Appl. Sci. (Switzerland) **9**(7), 1464 (2019). https://doi.org/10.3390/app9071464

21. Rothe, M., Reyer, M., Mathar, R.: Process optimization for cutting steel-plates. In: Liberatore, F., Parlier, G.H., Demange, M. (eds.) ICORES 2017 - Proceedings of the 6th International Conference on Operations Research and Enterprise Systems, vol. 2017-Janua, pp. 27–37. SCITEPRESS - Science and Technology Publications, Institute for Theoretical Information Technology, RWTH Aachen University, Kopernikusstraße 16, Aachen, 52074, Germany (2017). https://doi.org/10.5220/0006108400270037

22. Valério De Carvalho, J.M.: Exact solution of bin-packing problems using column generation and branch-and-bound. Ann. Oper. Res. **86**(0), 629–659 (1999). https://doi.org/10.1023/a:1018952112615

23. Vance, P.H., Barnhart, C., Johnson, E.L., Nemhauser, G.L.: Solving binary cutting stock problems by column generation and branch-and-bound. Comput. Optim. Appl. **3**(2), 111–130 (1994). https://doi.org/10.1007/BF01300970

24. Vanderbeck, F.: Computational study of a column generation algorithm for bin packing and cutting stock problems. Math. Program. Ser. B **86**(3), 565–594 (1999). https://doi.org/10.1007/s101070050105

25. Varela, R., Vela, C.R., Puente, J., Sierra, M., González-Rodríguez, I.: An effective solution for a real cutting stock problem in manufacturing plastic rolls. Ann. Oper. Res. **166**(1), 125–146 (2009). https://doi.org/10.1007/s10479-008-0407-1

26. Wäscher, G., Haußner, H., Schumann, H.: An improved typology of cutting and packing problems. Eur. J. Oper. Res. **183**(3), 1109–1130 (2007). https://doi.org/10.1016/j.ejor.2005.12.047

27. Yang, C.T., Sung, T.C., Weng, W.C.: An improved tabu search approach with mixed objective function for one-dimensional cutting stock problems. Adv. Eng. Softw. **37**(8), 502–513 (2006). https://doi.org/10.1016/j.advengsoft.2006.01.005

Metaheuristics with Local Search Miscellany Applied to the Quadratic Assignment Problem for Large-Scale Instances

Rogelio González-Velázquez[1], Erika Granillo-Martínez[2]([✉]),
María Beatriz Bernábe-Loranca[1], and Jairo E. Powell-González[1]

[1] Facultad de Ciencias de la Computación, Benemérita Universidad Autónoma de Puebla,
Prol. 14 sur Esq. Av. Sn. Claudio, C.P 72590 Puebla, Mexico
jairoe.powell@viep.com.mx
[2] Facultad de Administración, Benemérita Universidad Autónoma de Puebla, Av. Sn. Claudio,
C.P 72590 Puebla, Mexico

Abstract. The quadratic assignment problem (QAP) is classified as an NP-hard problem, so metaheuristic procedures are often used to solve it. QAP is a classic combinatorial optimization problem with real applications, for example in supply chain, logistics, manufacturing, finance, among others. In this article, to search for QAP solutions, the design of a program code for the Greedy Randomized Adaptive Search Procedure (GRASP) metaheuristic was implemented with three different neighborhood structures contained in k-exchange mode in order to perform the local search. The experimental procedure was applied for large-scale test instances available from QAPLIB. Finally, the results of the approximations to the optimal solutions are reported.

Keywords: Metaheuristics · NP-hard · k-exchange · Neighborhood

1 Introduction

Metaheuristic procedures are a class of approximation methods, designed to solve difficult combinatorial optimization problems [1]. Optimization problems are based on choosing the best configuration from a set of feasible solutions to achieve an objective [2] and are divided into two categories: problems with continuous and discrete variables. For this case, the second category will be taken that tries to find an objective that is taken within a finite and discrete set, an integer, a set of integers, a permutation or a graph. The two types of problems have different solution methods, however, combinatorial optimization problems belong to the second category [2] as an example, Greedy Random Adaptive Search Procedures (GRASP).

GRASP is an iterative procedure where each step consists of a construction phase and an improvement phase. In the construction phase, a constructive heuristic procedure is applied to obtain a good initial solution. This solution is improved in the second phase by a local search algorithm. The best of all the solutions examined is the final result [3, 4].

© Springer Nature Switzerland AG 2021
J. C. Figueroa-García et al. (Eds.): WEA 2021, CCIS 1431, pp. 327–334, 2021.
https://doi.org/10.1007/978-3-030-86702-7_28

The main contribution of this work is based on the experimentation and analysis of the results in the method, obtaining a good initial solution and subsequently improving it.

This paper is organized as follows: Sect. 1, contains an introduction to this work, in Sect. 2, related work is presented. In Sect. 3, the formulation for the quadratic Assignment Problem (QAP); Sect. 4, shows the metaheuristics, Sect. 4.1, contains a description of GRASP, as well as the design of the pseudocode, subsequently in Sect. 4.2 the use of GRASP for the Quadratic Assignment Problem.

Section 5, shows the experiments that were done, and the results that were obtained, respectively. Finally, in Sect. 6, it will find a discussion, conclusions and future work.

2 Related Work

The Quadratic Assignment Problem (QAP) is a combinatorial optimization problem that consists in finding an optimal allocation of n resources to n locations in order to minimize the cost of transportation, additionally, two matrixes are needed, one for the requirements of the units to be transported and the second is the cost of transport per unit between the localities.

QAP was proposed by [5] in 1957. Later in 1976, Shani and González proved that QAP is an NP-complete problem [6]. So far, optimal solutions have been found using exact methods for instances of size 30 [7]. The QAP is used in many applications such as: computer keyboard design, manufacturing programming, airport terminal design, and communication processes. An exact branch and bound algorithm is used with some variants to solve the QAP and was proposed by [7], however, recently solutions were proposed with different metaheuristics techniques such as [8, 9]: genetic algorithms, simulated annealing, tabu search [10] and GRASP [3, 11]. In [12] implemented GRASP in parallel for QAP.

Other works related to the search for QAP solutions are based on the particle swarm algorithm, recombination of operators for genetic algorithms and stagnation aware cooperative parallel to local search [13, 14].

QAP in large instances is a notably hard problem to find a solution to and the performance of metaheuristic algorithms varies, as mentioned in [15] where two algorithms are compared with results that depend on the size of the problem.

In [16] simulated annealing, particle swarm optimization, genetic algorithms, iterated local search, tabu search and crow search algorithms are implemented and compared in massive parallel processing units to solve QAP for large instances. Another example of parallel processing can be seen in [17] where this metaheuristic is implemented with Tabu search to work with large size QAP.

3 Formulation for the Quadratic Assignment Problem

The QAP consists of finding an optimal allocation that minimizes the cost of transporting materials, among n facilities in n locations, considering the distance between locations and the flow of materials between facilities. The QAP can be formulated by a combinatorial optimization model (CP).

Given a set N = {1, 2,.., n} and two symmetric matrices of size $n \times n$ where: $F = (f_{ij})$ y $D = (d_{kl})$, a permutation p $\in$ Π_N must be found that minimizes

$$\sum_{i=1}^{n} \sum_{j=1}^{n} f_{ij} d_{p(i)p(j)} \tag{1}$$

Where Π_N is the set of all permutations of N, F is the material flow matrix between facilities and D is the distance matrix between cities.

4   Metaheuristics

The major drawbacks that heuristic techniques face is the existence of local optimum that are not absolute. If during the search there is a local optimum, the heuristic could not continue the process and would be "trapped" at the same point. In order to solve the problem, it is recommended to restart the search from another initial solution and verify that the new search explores other paths.

Most combinatorial optimization problems are specific problems, so a heuristic technique algorithm that works for one problem is sometimes not useful for solving other problems. However, in recent times. general purpose heuristics called metaheuristics have been developed that try to solve the above drawbacks. Most metaheuristics are developed with neighborhood search methods.

The word metaheuristics was coined [1] at the same time that the term Tabu Search emerged (1986). A metaheuristic is a master strategy that guides and modifies other heuristics to generate better solutions than are normally presented by other methods [18].

There are several successful metaheuristics in solving combinatorial problems. The Greedy Randomized Adaptive Search Problem (GRASP) metaheuristic is one of the most recent techniques, it was originally developed [19] at the time of studying coverage problems of high combinatorial complexity [3]. Each iteration in GRASP generally consists of two steps: the construction phase and the local search procedure. In the first stage, an initial solution is built that is later improved by post-processing to perfect the solution obtained in the first stage until obtaining a local optimum.

There are works where this metaheuristic is applied for optimization problems in big data [20]. Additionally, there are other variants such as: GRASP-path relinking, GRASP-reactive, GRASP-parallel, GRASP-hybrids with some other metaheuristics whose search is based on neighborhoods [21].

4.1   Greedy Randomized Adaptive Search Problem GRASP

A GRASP is an iterative process, each iteration consists of two steps: the construction phase and the local search procedure. In the first, an initial feasible solution is construct, later it is improved by means of an exchange procedure until obtaining a local optimum [4].

Once the two phases have been executed, the solution obtained is stored and another iteration is carried out, each time saving the best solution that has been found so far. An algorithm that exemplifies metaheuristics is shown in Fig. 1.

```
Procedure GRASP
    InputInstance();
    While (stop criterion not satisfied) do
        ConstructSolutionGreedyRandomizeAdaptative();
        Post-proccesing();
        UpdateSolution();
    End {While}
    Return (Best solution)
End {GRASP}
```

Fig. 1. Generic GRASP pseudocode.

The general description of the main components of GRASP are: The Greedy component that uses a myopic algorithm for the selection of the components that guide the construction of solutions, the Randomized used for the random selections of an elite list of candidates that determine the path of search, the Adaptive has the mission of updating each result obtained from the components of the solution that is built [22].

4.2 GRASP for the Quadratic Assignment Problem

The GRASP design has been used by some researchers to solve the QAP for different instances [1, 4, 6]. It should be noted that the solutions are a permutation of length n, summarizing the procedure as follows: Initial construction phase: stage 1, generation of a list of candidates, which has previously been restricted by two parameters, then one is randomly taken of these candidates from which the first 2 assignments are derived. Stage 2, the remaining $n-2$ assignments are added in relation to the Greedy procedure, once the process is finished, the permutation is completed, producing a feasible solution. Phase 2 of improvement: the solution generated from phase 1 is taken as the initial solution of some local search procedure, at the end of the procedure, a local optimal solution will be obtained, which could also be globally optimal.

The neighborhood structures used are: 2-exchange, N* and λ-exchange. In practice, the flow matrixes are taken, as well as the distance matrix and their elements are listed separately. The flows (matrix) are ordered from highest to lowest and the distances from least to greatest, both lists are restricted with a parameter $0 < \alpha < 1$, they are multiplied generating a new list of elements of the form $f_{ij} * d_{kl}$ that contains large flows and short distances. This list is restricted with a parameter $0 < \beta < 1$, with these operations you have a restricted list of candidates (CRL), from this list an element of the form is randomly selected $f_{ij} * d_{kl}$, producing the first assignment pair (i, k), (j, l), interpreted as facility k is assigned to location i and facility l is assigned to location j. Finally $n-2$ components remain to be assigned, again with a greedy we calculate the C_{ik} costs with respect to the 2 assignments against the remaining possible assignments, another CRL is formed and one of these candidates is selected with which the third assignment is generated and so on. Until completing the permutation of n components called initial solution S0 which is subjected to phase 2, called improvement phase, this is an iteration of GRASP [23].

5 Results

This section shows the results obtained for instances taken from [24], the instances dimensions are greater than 42 up to 100 considering as a great scale. A data table is shown for each of the three implemented neighborhood structures. It also shows three comparative tables of the neighborhood structures in terms of the number of iterations, the execution time TCPU and the percentage in which they reach the optimal or best known value. Likewise, a table with the GAP percentages is presented.

All the results shown in this section were obtained by restricting the list of candidates (RLC) with the parameters $\alpha = 0.2$ and $\beta = 0.3$, which were determined experimentally. The neighborhood topologies is discussed in [3, 25] in which the size of the neighborhood is commented as follows: for 2-exchange is C_n^2, λ-exchange, for the size is $\frac{n^3}{24}$, N^* is $\frac{n^4}{8}$, finally, the pseudocode algorithms for the previous neighborhood structures are shown in [3].

Table 1. GRASP results with local search λ-exchange, Skorin-Kapov instances

Instance	Neighborhood	Option	BKV	BFV GRASP	Error %	TCPU
Sko 42	λ-exchange	Random	15812	15966	0.97	36380
Sko 49	λ-exchange	Greedy 2 stage	23386	23596	0.90	64381
Sko 56	λ-exchange	Greedy 2 stage	34458	34694	0.68	121372
Sko 64	λ-exchange	N. initial Sol.	48498	48686	0.39	207061
Sko 72	λ-exchange	Random	66256	66686	0.65	282684
Sko 81	λ-exchange	Random	90998	91772	0.85	462095
Sko 90	λ-exchange	Greedy 2 stage	115534	116582	0.91	797597
Sko 100a	λ-exchange	Random	152002	153208	0.79	1064643
Sko 100b	λ-exchange	Greedy 2 stage	153890	155188	0.84	1251686
Sko 100c	λ-exchange	Random	147862	149074	0.82	11543734
Sko 100d	λ-exchange	Greedy 2 stage	149576	150958	0.92	1245131
Sko 100e	λ-exchange	Random	149150	150454	0.87	1141179

Table 2. GRASP results with local search 2-exchange, Skorin-Kapov instances

Instance	Neighborhood	Option	BKV	BFV GRASP	% error	TCPU
Sko 42	2-exchange	Random	15812	15922	0.70	28288
Sko 49	2-exchange	Greedy 2 stage	23386	23594	0.89	64184
Sko 56	2-exchange	Random	34458	34840	1.11	96746
Sko 64	2-exchange	Greedy 2 stage	48498	49002	1.04	197513
Sko 72	2-exchange	Random	66256	66794	0.81	281584
Sko 81	2-exchange	Greedy 2 stage	90998	91640	0.71	537896
Sko 90	2-exchange	Random	115534	116448	0.79	757746
Sko 100a	2-exchange	Random	152002	153012	0.66	1162220
Sko 100b	2-exchange	Random	153890	154916	0.67	1262583
Sko 100c	2-exchange	Greedy 2 stage	147862	148736	0.59	1290115
Sko 100d	2 exchange	Greedy 2 Stage	149576	150800	0.82	647448
Sko 100e	2 exchange	Greedy 2 stage	149150	150724	1.06	1372944

Table 3. GRASP results with local search N*, Skorin-Kapov instances

Instance	Neighborhood	Option	BKV	BFV GRASP	Error %	TCPU
Sko 42	N*	Random	15812	15950	0.87	351405
Sko 49	N*	Greedy 2 stage	23386	23554	0.72	606638
Sko 56	N*	Random	34458	34780	0.93	1318201
Sko 64	N*	Greedy 2 stage	48498	48912	0.85	192592
Sko 72	N*	Random	66256	66830	0.87	289931
Sko 81	N*	Random	90998	91868	0.96	489550
Sko 90	N*	Greedy 2 stage	115534	116176	0.56	860121
Sko 100a	N*	Random	152002	152942	0.62	2186983
Sko 100b	N*	Random	153890	154928	0.67	1060393
Sko 100c	N*	Random	147862	148854	0.67	1094756
Sko 100d	N*	Random	149576	150772	0.80	1197065
Sko 100e	N*	Random	149150	150704	1.04	961112956

6   Conclusions

The results of Tables 1, 2 and 3 shows that GRASP is a robust metaheuristic in the search for solutions to NP-hard problems. The solutions reached in the work are compared with the best known values according with QAPLIB [24]. As shown in Tables 1, 2 and 3 and in the % error column, the results obtained oscillate between 0.56 and 1.11 in error percentage. The seventh column shows the execution time for each instances in milliseconds, which is a reasonable computing time for large-scale instances.

Within the research it was shown that for the Sko 42 instance case, the best implementation was 2-exchange, in the case of Sko 64 the best combination was λ-exchange and for Sko 90 the best execution was Greedy 2 stage. Talking about the case of matrices of size 100 that represent the largest scale, the results are considered favorable because the error is less than 1%, only in the case of the Sko100e instance the maximum error is 1.06.

In the present document, the results obtained were carried out in the Java programming language for the three local searches with GRASP and were executed on an Intel i7 processor. Therefore, with the results shown, the usefulness of metaheuristics to solve highly complex problems was verified, as well as the verification to obtain approximate optimal solutions, given the inefficiency of the exact methods.

As future work, it is proposed to implement the metaheuristic variable neighborhood search (VNS) with the neighborhood structures 2-exchange, N* and λ-exchange as an improvement phase for GRASP to form a hybrid GRASP-VNS.

References

1. Díaz, A.D., Glober, F., Ghaziri, H.M., Gonzalez, J.L., Moscato, P., Tseng, F.T.: Optimización Heurística y Redes Neuronales en Dirección de Operaciones e Ingeniería. Ma-drid (1996)
2. Cela, E.: The Quadratic Assignment Problem: Special Cases and Relatives. Tesis doctoral. Institut für Mathematik B Technische Iniversität Graz, Graz, Austria (1995)
3. Li, Y., Pardalos, P.M., Resende, M.G.C.: A Greedy Randomized Adaptative Search Pro-cedure for the Quadratic Assignment Problem. In: Pardalos, P.M., Wolkowicz, H. (eds.) Quadratic Assignment and Related Problems, Vol. 16 of DIMACS Series on Discrete Mathematics and Theoretical Computer Science, pp. 237–261. American Mathematical Society, Rhode Island (1994)
4. Resende, M., Pardalos, P., Li, Y.: Algorithm 754: Fortran subroutines for approximate solution of dense quadratic assignment problems using GRASP. ACM Trans. Math. Softw. 22(1), 104–118 (1996). https://doi.org/10.1145/225545.225553
5. Koopmans, T.C., Beckmann, M.J.: Assignment problems and the location of economic activities. Econometrica 25, 53–76 (1957)
6. Sahni, S., Gonzalez, T.: P-complete approximations problems. J. Asssoc. Comp. Machine 23, 555–565 (1976)
7. Roucairol, C.: A parallel branch and bound algorithm for the quadratic assignment problem. Discrete Appl. Math. 18(2), 211–225 (1987). https://doi.org/10.1016/0166-218X(87)90022-9
8. Zhou, Y., Hao, J.K., Duval, B.: Frequent pattern-based search: a case study on the quadratic assignment problem. IEEE Trans. Syst. Man Cybern. Syst. (2020)
9. Hafiz, F., Abdennour, A.: Particle swarm algorithm variants for quadratic assignment problems—a probabilistic learning approach. Expert Syst. Appl. 44, 413–431 (2016)
10. Skorin-Kapov, J.: Tabu search applied to the quadratic assignment problem. ORSA J. Comput. 2(1), 33–45 (1990). https://doi.org/10.1287/ijoc.2.1.33
11. Chmiel, W., Kadłuczka, P., Kwiecień, J., Filipowicz, B.: A comparison of nature inspired algorithms for the quadratic assignment problem. Bull. Pol. Acad. Sci. Tech. Sci. 65(4) (2017)
12. Pardalos, P.M., Pitssoulis, L.S., Resende, M.G.C.: A parallel GRASP implementation for the quadratic assignment problem. In: Ferreira, A., Rolim, J. (eds.) Parallel Algorithms for Irregularly Structured Problems – Irregular 1994, pp. 111–130. Klower, Boston (1995)

13. Aksan, Y., Dokeroglu, T., Cosar, A.: A stagnation-aware cooperative parallel breakout local search algorithm for the quadratic assignment problem. Comput. Ind. Eng. **103**, 105–115 (2017)
14. Tosun, U.: A new recombination operator for the genetic algorithm solution of the quadratic assignment problem. Procedia Comput. Sci. **32**, 29–36 (2014)
15. Saifullah Hussin, M., Stützle, T.: Tabu search vs. simulated annealing as a function of the size of quadratic assignment problem instances. Comput. Oper. Res. **43**(2), 286–291 (2014)
16. Kumar, M., Sahu, A., Mitra, P.: A comparison of different metaheuristics for the quadratic assignment problem in accelerated systems. Appl. Soft Comput. **100**, 106927 (2021). https://doi.org/10.1016/j.asoc.2020.106927
17. Dokeroglu, T., Sevinc, E., Cosar, A.: Artificial bee colony optimization for the quadratic assignment problem. Appl. Soft Comput. J. **76**, 595–606 (2019)
18. Mishmast, H., Gelareh, S.: A survey of meta-heuristic solution methods for the quadratic assignment problem. Appl. Math. Sci. **46**(1), 2293–2312 (2007)
19. Feo, T.A., Resende, M.G.C.: Greedy randomized adaptive search procedures. J. Global Optim. **6**, 109–133 (1995)
20. Palmieri, F., Fiore, U., Ricciardi, S., Castiglione, A.: GRASP-based resourced re-optimization for effective big data access in federated clouds. Futur. Gener. Comput. Syst. **54**, 168–179 (2016)
21. Festa, P., Resende, M.G.C.: GRASP: basic components and enhancements. Telecommun Syst. **46**, 253–271 (2011). https://doi.org/10.1007/s11235-010-9289-z
22. El Mouayni, I., Demesure, G., Bril-El Haouzi, H., Charpentier, P., Siadat, A.: Jobs scheduling within Industry 4.0 with consideration of worker's fatigue and reliability using Greedy Randomized Adaptive Search Procedure. IFAC-PapersOnLine **52**(19), 85–90 (2019). https://doi.org/10.1016/j.ifacol.2019.12.114
23. Riffi, M.E., Saji, Y., Barkatou, M.: Incorporating a modified uniform crossover and 2-exchange neighborhood mechanism in a discrete bat algorithm to solve the quadratic assignment problem. Egypt. Informat. J. **18**(3), 221–232 (2017)
24. Burkard, R.E., Karisc, S.E., Rendl, F.: QAPLIB – A Quadratic Assignment Problem, Library, http://www.imm.dtu.dk/~sk/qaplib/ins.html
25. Obdelkafi, O., Idoumghar, L., Lepagnot, J., Brévilliers, M.: Data exchange topologies for the DISCO-HITS algorithm to solve the QAP. In Siarry, P., et al. (eds.) ICSIBO, LNCS 10103, pp. 57–64 (2016). https://doi.org/10.1007/978-3-319-50307-3_4

Linear Programming Model for Production Cost Minimization at a Rice Crop Products Manufacturer

Jairo R. Coronado-Hernández, Leonardo J. Olarte-Jiménez,
Zulmeira Herrera-Fontalvo[(⊠)], and Johana Cómbita Niño

Universidad de La Costa, Barranquilla, Colombia
{jcoronad18,lolarte1,zherrera1,jcombita2}@cuc.edu.co

Abstract. Companies in general must establish processes that generate profitability at lower costs. Manufacturing of rice crop protection products requires major investments and resource planning, including infrastructure, raw materials, technology, human resources, tests and trials, among others, which represents a major challenge. This paper proposes a methodology that aims to minimize production costs taking different factors into consideration. The first section identifies and describes the variables required for modeling. In the second section a linear programming model is formulated to determine the optimal function in terms of cost reduction. Lastly, the model was applied at a real company, producing satisfactory results in terms of an improved production plan and an 11% cost reduction, while enabling viewing the variables with greatest impact, such as storage and shift programming, with cost reductions of 68% and 44%, respectively. The purpose is to assist companies in this industry in applying mathematical programming models to solve problems and enable better resource planning to improve profitability.

Keywords: Lineal programming · Rice crop · Production · Cost reduction · Production planning

1 Introduction

Worldwide, companies that manufacture crop protection products have experienced substantial growth, and the industry is forecast to grow at an annual rate of 5.5% up to 2026 [1]. This represents a challenge for the industry in terms of adapting to the market's needs and adjusting their administrative and operating structures to take advantage of this expected growth. In this context, companies must make efficient use of their resources and select suitable production plans to meet growing demand, with well-trained human resources, investment in technology and leadership for decision-making.

Manufacturers in this and all industries seek to obtain sustainable profits for their shareholders, and consequently always seek to avoid increases in costs and expenses and to reduce product manufacturing costs, in other words, to do more with less [2].

J. C. Figueroa-García et al. (Eds.): WEA 2021, CCIS 1431, pp. 335–346, 2021.
https://doi.org/10.1007/978-3-030-86702-7_29

Businesses currently use several approaches to increase profitability, including reducing the cost of supplies, optimizing the use of technology, more sophisticated information systems, improving personnel skills, reducing storage areas, and reducing shifts, among others [3]. The literature includes a wide variety of approaches and planning models based on the economics of each industry [4] aimed at increasing profitability.

This study is motivated by the above, with the aim of contributing to increasing profitability at the intervened company by designing an improved production plan, by means of a lineal programming model, based on the aggregated planning methodology, to enable better operational control and cost reductions, using as starting point the company's information and quantitative variables, historic demand, operating costs and production capacity, among others.

This study basically consists in integrating mathematical models in the solution of the actual problems faced by an economic sector, with the purpose of finding an optimal solution, additionally enabling an analysis of all the variables used to run the model, providing details on how it was developed and validating the results against the company's data, to demonstrate substantial cost reductions and manufacturing alternatives, with an improved production plan, obtaining a satisfactory result from the proposal.

2 State of the Art

Production, acquisitions planning and logistics are complex tasks at companies with several production and/or storage sites [5]. In order to achieve their production objectives and make adequate use of their resources, companies must adequately plan and control their production activities [6].

Production planning covers all the resources needed for production [7], and as a strategic decision it implies the assignment of aggregate production resources for aggregate groups of products. It is carried out in a manufacturing environment to make efficient use of these production resources to satisfy sales opportunities for finished products [8].

Production planning management can solve problems such as non-optimal production quantities, production cost ranges, production bottlenecks and unplanned production conditions [9].

Production planning activities seek to balance market needs against the optimal use of the resources available in different industries [10]. Currently, in many cases it fails to offer reliable production plans. One of the reasons is that the transition times represent a substantial proportion of the delivery time, and they are difficult to predict because they are subject to a large number of volatile and partly unknown factors [11].

Industrial processes generally involve complex manufacturing operations, and therefore require adequate decision-making support for the effects of aggregate production planning [12]. Aggregate Planning is a medium-term production planning method, covering all aspects from raw materials, labor and finished products in the medium time range to fulfill the orders [13].

Lineal Programming is used to describe optimization problems to enable finding optimal solutions in an effective manner. Unlike other heuristic models, linear programming finds an optimal solution that satisfies an objective function [14], and interested parties can use linear programming to identify the alternative route that best achieves their objectives [15]. This type of model is applied in different contexts and to find optimal solutions with parameters that comprise a system, such as specific aspects associated to an activity of a production process, as in the case of [16], who proposes a mixed-integer linear programming (MILP) model to minimize waste in the current process of cutting marble slates, with the selection of marble blocks, taking into account the cutting sequence of the slate. Other studies have focused on logistics aspects, such as the minimization of transportation costs, such as the model proposed by [17], who proposes an optimal production distribution solution from 2 production sites to 9 distributors.

Other approaches aligned with this study are related to the distribution of production activities or results, seeking the minimization of costs or waste, or the maximization of benefits or profits, through the optimization of resources. [18] proposes a mixed-integer linear programming (MILP) model to minimize costs of installation, stock outages and pending orders, in which the model aims to program production, batch size and plastic automotive components, to which end he takes into consideration the capacity of minimum and maximum stock levels and penalizes stock outages. In this study, the problem to be addressed is programming and sizing of optimal batches in flexible injection machines in parallel, applied to an automotive plastic components manufacturer.

A similar study is that by [19], who uses a mixed integer linear programming model with the main objective of minimizing production times taking into consideration an optimal number of workstations. The aim was to minimize costs and increase the production capacity of a truck assembly line at an automotive manufacturer in Indonesia, with a lean manufacturing approach and use of time study methods to obtain information for the model. Also, [20] proposes a linear programming model that establishes an optimal planting plan based on the assignment of food or diets at a dairy farm, minimizing feeding costs to the milk-producing herds.

Specifically in the case of rice crops, [21] proposes a linear programming model to optimize sales revenues of the Rejo Asri Gapoktan farmer cooperative, which has problems managing tools and machines to balance trade revenues and expenses. Using the Simplex method to optimize profits, it was found that the overall benefit obtained was 42,494,670 rupees (Indonesian currency), a major financial achievement for the farmer cooperative.

As in the above case studies, this study seeks to provide a solution to a specific need of a company in terms of the optimal use of resources, but in this case, it involves planning and the minimization of productions costs for rice crop protection products. Through the linear programming model, an optimal solution is sought from the analysis of variables determined in the model for cost reduction and an improved production plan, taking into account that resource management is an important aspect for planning production in this sector. In the literature review, no studies aligned with the study sector were found.

3 Methodology

The proposed methodology seeks to minimize production costs at a company that produces substances used in rice crops. The methodology involves 3 phases or stages. Firstly, the problem is identified and delimited, and an assessment is made of the background and main causes, to then describe the variables required for modeling. Next, the linear programming model is formulated to determine with optimal function with the objective of reducing production costs and thereby improving the company's effectiveness and productivity. To this effect, the LP Gusek specialized software for solving problems is used, which maximizes or minimizes the inputs to obtain optimal solutions. Lastly, the company's industrial data is input to run the model and obtain actual results, which enables replicating the use of the model (See Fig. 1).

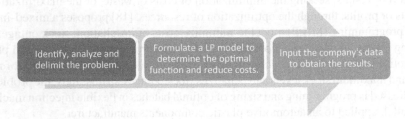

Fig. 1. Diagram of the methodological process.

4 Formulation of the Mathematical Model

The aim of a linear programming model is to optimize (minimize or maximize) a linear function, called an objective function, whose variables are subject to restrictions expressed by means of a system of equations or inequations, which enables making decisions on their impacts in any case study.

In the case of this study, the aim was to minimize production costs, including and considering variables such as machines, demand, types of products, direct manufacturing and overhead costs, cost of storage and labor. Including the variables in the model will enable making decisions on the number of units to be produced and how many to units to keep in storage to obtain the best result. Consequently, the following linear programming model was developed (Table 1):

Table 1. Set, parameters, variables.

Set
j: Products$\{P1, P2, P3, P4, P5\}$

Parameters
$D_{(j,i)} = $ *Demand for product j in period i*
$S_{(j)} = $ *Initial stock of product j*
$S_{max} = $ *Maximum warehouse storage capacity*
$V_{(j)} = $ *Volume of product j*
$TPmax_{(i)} = $ *Max. production time in period i*
$T_{(j)} = $ *Time to manufacture product j*
$P_{(j)} = $ *Setup time for product j*
$B_{(j)} = $ *Production cost of product j*
$C_{(j)} = $ *Storage cost of product j*
$CP_{(i)} = $ *Cost of workshift in period i*
$CM_{(j)} = $ *Setup cost for product j*

Variables
$x_{(j,i)} = $ *Units of product j made in period i*
$y_{(j,i)} = $ *Units of product j stored in period i*
$w_{(i)} = $ *Number of work shifts in period i*
$v_{(j,i)} = \{1$ *if setup is made*, 0 *otherwise*$\}$

- *Objective function:*

$$MinZ = \sum_{j}^{J} \sum_{i}^{I} \left(B_{(j)} * x_{(j,i)}\right) + \sum_{j}^{J} \sum_{i}^{I} \left(C_{(j)} * y_{(j,i)}\right)$$
$$+ \sum_{i}^{I} \left(CP_{(i)} * w_{(i)}\right) + \sum_{j}^{J} \sum_{i}^{I} \left(CM_{(j)} * v_{(j,i)}\right) \quad (1)$$

- *Restrictions:*

Stock balance:

$$S_{(j)} + x_{(j,1)} - D_{(j,1)} = y_{(j,1)}, \forall j \quad (2)$$

$$y_{(j,i-1)} + x_{(j,i)} - D_{(j,i)} = y_{(j,i)}, \forall j, \forall i \geq 2 \quad (3)$$

Maximum storage capacity:

$$\sum_{j=1}^{CARD(j)} V_{(j)} * y_{(j,i)} \leq S_{max}, \forall j, \forall i \quad (4)$$

Maximum production capacity:

$$\sum_{j=1}^{CARD(j)} (P_{(j)} * v_{(j,i)} + T_{(j)} * x_{(j,i)}) \leq TPmax_{(i)} * w_{(i)}, \forall_j, \forall_i \tag{5}$$

Non − negative:

$$x_{(j,i)}, y_{(j,i)}, w_{(i)} \geq 0, \forall_j, \forall_i \tag{6}$$

Binary variable, 1 *if setup is made*, 0 *otherwise*:

$$v_{(j,i)}\{1, 0\} \tag{7}$$

Activación de preparación de máquinas:

$$x_{(j,i)} \leq BigM * v_{(j,i)} \tag{8}$$

5 Validation of the Mathematical Model

5.1 Case Study Company

This manufacturing company is located in Colombia and belongs to the agro-chemical industry. It also has presence in other countries in the Americas and is dedicated to manufacturing rice crop protection products. Consequently, it expects substantial growth and market acceptance, thanks to the quality of its products and because rice is a major commodity consumed worldwide. It is strategically located in Colombia to benefit from the country's maritime shipping routes, which facilitates both local and international distribution, as well as the reception of imported raw materials for production. It has a good commercial strategy and a well-known global brand, as well as strategic partnerships with distributors and rice plantation owners, to promote solid growth in the market.

5.2 Problem

Companies in the agro-chemical industry depend heavily on the stability of their sector, because demand and production in Colombia are substantially affected by unforeseeable factors such as the weather. In order to remain in the market, they must incur in substantial costs and maintain large stocks of non-ordered products on hand in order to be able to manage adequate lead times. Consequently, production planning represents a major challenge, in terms of managing resources and establishing work plans, including programming the shifts and personnel involved in the process; the quantities of the different types of products to be produced each month; inventory turnover so as not to overburden the warehouse with unsold and non-ordered products, and scheduling overtime shifts to cover stock outages, as well as other factors that increase uncertainty and are intrinsically associated with the process.

Based on the above, the purpose is to propose an alternative with the support of linear programming models to find an optimal solution to minimize production costs, taking into consideration all the above factors.

5.3 Implementation

The statistics for the subproblem are 77 equations, 100 integer variables, 30 of which are binary variables. The coding for the solution of the problem was done on the AMPL Software using the GLPK solver, in a computer with an AMD Ryzen 3 2.6 Ghz processor and 8 GB of RAM. The computational time to generate each point was 5.5 s: Using the model, savings of $ 550,687,281 were found in total costs.

The last 6 months of the previous year were used as baseline for the study, for the effects of forecasting the linear programming model for the current period. The following input data of the model is shared in the following Appendix Link 1.

Input Data:

1. Demand: Quantity of products requested by customers each month. (See Appendix 1)
2. Initial inventory: Stock of products available for sale at the start of each period. (See Appendix 2)

$$Units\ produced - Demand = Initial\ Stock, month\ 1 \qquad (9)$$

$$Prev\ Initial\ Stock + Units\ produced - Demand$$
$$= Initial\ Stock\ P \geq 2, for\ month\{2, 3, 4, 5, 6\} \qquad (10)$$

3. Maximum storage capacity: Maximum space available to store products in cm^3. (See Appendix 3)

$$Height \times Length \times Depth = CA_{max} \qquad (11)$$

4. Volume: Volumetric measurement of each product for storage. (See Appendix 3)

$$Height \times Length \times Depth = Product\ type \qquad (12)$$

5. Maximum production time: The number of minutes available in each month for production. (See Appendix 4)

$$Days\ month \times T.480\ min = TP_{max} \times Shift \qquad (13)$$

$$Days\ month \times 1,440\ min = TP_{max} \times Month \qquad (14)$$

6. Time to manufacture the product: Number of minutes required to manufacture each type of product. (See Appendix 5)

$$\frac{Run\ time(min)}{Number\ of\ Units\ Produced} = TF \times P \qquad (15)$$

7. Product changeover time: Number of minutes required to clean the machine for the next production run.

$$T.A \leq 30\ min \qquad (16)$$

8.   Manufacturing cost: The cost to manufacture one unit. (See Appendix 1)

$$CFT = MP + CIF + G.OPER. \tag{17}$$

$$\frac{Total\ manufacturing\ cost}{Number\ of\ Units\ Produced} = CP \times UNIT \tag{18}$$

9.   Storage cost: The cost of storing one unit of each product. (See Appendix 1)

$$\frac{Storage\ cost}{Number\ of\ units\ stored} = CA \times UNIT \tag{19}$$

10. Work shift cost: Labor cost of one shift. (See Appendix 1)

$$Cost\ of\ shift \times Shifts\ per\ month = CT \tag{20}$$

11. Setup cost the machine: The cost of preparing the machine for the next run. (See Appendix 1)

$$Setup\ cost \times No.\ of\ changes\ in\ month = CM \tag{21}$$

The total costs and times were calculated for each product, and the times were expressed in terms of minutes.

5.4   Comparison of the Proposed Model to the Current Planning System

Verification was performed using the actual data from the previous semester compared to the results of the mathematical model, with the aim of minimizing the production costs involved in manufacturing the 5 products.

Satisfactory results were found in the comparison, producing an 11% reduction in overall costs, as displayed in Fig. 2, which indicates the change in cost by type during the 6 months of production (See Fig. 2).

Storage cost displayed a cost reduction of 64% in the amount of $29.673.353, against current cost of $46.327.373 and modeled cost of $16.654.020.

Setup cost displayed a cost reduction of 33% in the amount of $5.237.477, against current cost of $15.712.431 and modeled cost of $10.474.954.

Work shift cost displayed a cost reduction of 12% in the amount of $2.554.135, against current cost of $21.863.799 and modeled cost of $19.309.664.

Production cost displayed a cost reduction of 11% in the amount of $513.221.316, against current cost of $4.774.584.746 and modeled cost of $4.261.363.430.

The data modeling produced an improved production programming for the next 6 months, for the effects of viewing a better alternative to help fulfill the objectives in terms of expected demand and cost reduction (See Tables 2 and 3).

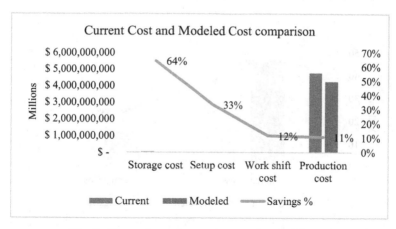

Fig. 2. Comparison of current cost and modeled cost.

Table 2. Forecast of units produced by type of product for 6 months (Current Process).

Product	Month 1	Month 2	Month 3	Month 4	Month 5	Month 6	Total
Prod. 1L	0	0	0	4.008	0	1.188	5.196
Prod. 4L	1.500	0	0	3.000	0	1.800	6.300
Prod. 20L	750	150	2.400	2.000	3.613	5.902	14.815
Prod. 60L	0	316	140	0	74	200	730
Prod. 200L	294	200	15	100	500	674	1.783

Table 3. Forecast of units produced by type of product for 6 months (Modeled Process).

Product	Month 1	Month 2	Month 3	Month 4	Month 5	Month 6	Total
Prod. 1L	0	0	0	706	0	4.476	5.182
Prod. 4L	1.488	0	0	2.061	1596	0	5.145
Prod. 20L	0	0	3.325	1.693	1.928	5.798	12.744
Prod. 60L	464	0	0	0	0	0	464
Prod. 200L	269	0	0	169	639	632	1.709

The benefits of the new planning from linear programming are reflected in the costs of storage and setup, with reductions of 64% for storage and 33% in setup (see Fig. 3).

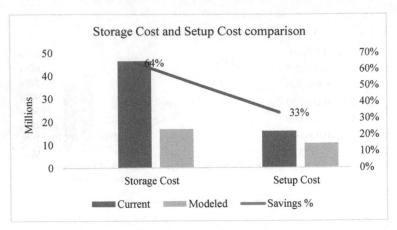

Fig. 3. Comparison of reduction of storage costs and setup costs.

The above demonstrates the effectiveness of the model, which produced suitable information for decision-making.

6 Sensitivity Analysis

A sensitivity analysis was carried out to determine how the variations of some parameters affect total production costs, storage costs, work shift cost, setup cost, and the optimized total cost. This analysis is carried out by making variations by $-50, -25, +25$, and 50% in the values of the parameters: manufacture time, production cost per product, maximum production time, work shift cost by period, and setup time. The data of the parameter's variation and sensitivity analysis results are shared in the following Appendix Link 2.

The table in Appendix 9 shows the results of the parameters variation in the costs of the proposed model, which allows us to analyze the influence of these parameters on the model results. For the total production costs, there is a significant influence $B_{(j)}$ that represents the production cost for each product, observing changes by increasing and decreasing the values for the five products, with a directly proportional behavior.

In storage costs, a significant influence is observed in three of the five parameters analyzed. A growth in storage costs is observed by increasing the manufacturing time $T_{(j)}$. However, this behavior isn't proportional to the time of decreasing the time. Regarding the maximum manufacturing time TP_{max}, a significant influence is observed in the variation of its values per period, showing a decreasing behavior when increasing the time and increasing when decreasing it. In the case of preparation time $P_{(j)}$, it proportionally influences variations above and below this time, showing a significant influence.

Additionally, it can be observed how work shift costs are sensitive to changes in some of the parameters under study, such as manufacturing time $T_{(j)}$ and work shift cost CP. In the case of the maximum manufacturing time TP_{max}, an inversely proportional behavior is observed, due to with increasing time a decreasing behavior is observed and when decreasing it is increasing.

Furthermore, the cost of preparation is sensitive to changes in some parameters. As the manufacturing time increases $T_{(j)}$, the values increase proportionally, as well as decreasing them. In the case of maximum manufacturing time TP_{max}, the cost increases by increasing it by 25% and 50%, keeping the same value ($ 11,971,400). As the percentage decreases, the cost rises to 25% and then decreases to 50%, with an atypical behavior that does not follow a pattern. There is only a variation in setup costs as the setup time $P_{(j)}$ parameter decreases.

Finally, from the results obtained in the sensitivity analysis on the total cost of the model, it can be concluded that the parameter that has the most significant influence is the production cost of each product $B_{(j)}$, followed by the time of manufacture $T_{(j)}$.

7 Conclusions

Mathematical models are able to solve real company programs and everyday events in an optimal manner, enabling making informed decisions that reduce uncertainty and error. This tool offers numerous benefits, including improved forecasting and use of resources, detecting shortcomings or restrictions, a basis for decision-making, reducing costs, anticipating future events, optimal solutions, among many other benefits.

As with other linear production models, this study shows how improved production planning based on demand enables obtaining obtain economic benefits, thereby improving business profitability and making better use of resources, in terms of deciding what, how much and when to produce. The adequate definition of the system's parameters and variables enabled obtaining a lineal model to minimize costs and optimize resources, which helped achieve a considerable cost reduction in terms of product storage by 64%, setup cost by 33%, the number of work shifts per month by 12%, and production cost by 11%. Overall costs decreased by 11%, which will represent a substantial forecast economic benefit for production in the next 6 months.

Future projects could take into consideration other parameters to provide a broader picture of the production process and help minimize other product costs, such as distribution costs, distribution programming and storage area availability.

References

1. Market Research. https://marketresearch.biz/report/crop-protection-chemicals-market/. Accessed 29 Mar 2021
2. Universidad ESAN. https://www.esan.edu.pe/apuntes-empresariales/2016/07/reduccion-de-costos-con-eficiencia/. Accessed 29 Mar 2021
3. Camino Financial. https://www.caminofinancial.com/es/como-reducir-los-costos-de-produc cion-de-tu-empresa/. Accessed 29 Mar 2021
4. Paredes Roldán J.: Planificación y control de la producción, 1ra edn. IDIUC, Instituto de Investigación Universidad de Cuenca (2001)
5. Frontoni, E., Marinelli, F., Rosetti, R., Zingaretti, V.: Optimal stock control and procurement by reusing of obsolescences in manufacturing. Comput. Ind. Eng. **148** (2020). https://doi.org/10.1016/j.cie.2020.106697
6. Peña, I., Santa Cruz, R.: Modelo de Planeación de la Producción para una Empresa Agroindustrial. Acta Nov. **1**(2), 181–189 (2001)

7. Cáceres, D., Reyes, J., García, M.: Modelo de Programación Lineal para Planeación de Requerimiento de Materiales. Rev. Tecnológica ESPOL – RTE **28**, 24–33 (2015)
8. Sabah, B., Nikolay, T., Sylverin, K. T.: Production planning under demand uncertainty using Monte Carlo simulation approach: a case study in fertilizer industry. In: Proceedings of the 2019 International Conference on Industrial Engineering and Systems Management, IESM, pp. 1–5 (2019). https://doi.org/10.1109/IESM45758.2019.8948112
9. Marimin, M., Zavira, R.: Production planning of crude palm oil: a study case at X Co. IOP Conf. Ser.: Earth Environ. Sci. **472**(1) (2020). https://doi.org/10.1088/1755-1315/472/1/012047
10. Valencia, E.T., Lamouri, S., Pellerin, R., Dubois, P., Moeuf, A.: Production planning in the fourth industrial revolution: a literature review. IFAC-PapersOnLine **52**(13), 2158–2163 (2019). https://doi.org/10.1016/j.ifacol.2019.11.525
11. Schuh, G., Prote, J.P., Sauermann, F., Franzkoch, B.: Databased prediction of order-specific transition times. CIRP Ann. **68**(1), 467–470 (2019). https://doi.org/10.1016/j.cirp.2019.03.008
12. Hahn, G.J., Brandenburg, M.: A sustainable aggregate production planning model for the chemical process industry. Comput. Oper. Res. **94**, 154–168 (2018). https://doi.org/10.1016/j.cor.2017.12.011
13. Charoenponyarrat, D., Somboonwiwat, T.: Aggregate planning in canned pineapple production lines. In: 2018 5th International Conference on Industrial Engineering and Applications, ICIEA 2018, pp. 349–354 (2018). https://doi.org/10.1109/IEA.2018.8387123
14. Nahmias, S.: Análisis de la producción y las operaciones, 5ta edn. The McGraw-Hill Companies Inc., Mexico (2007)
15. Schito, J., Moncecchi, D., Raubal, M.: Determining transmission line path alternatives using a valley-finding algorithm. Comput. Environ. Urban Syst. **86** (2021). https://doi.org/10.1016/j.compenvurbsys.2020.101571
16. Baykasoğlu, A., Özbel, B.K.: Modeling and solving a real-world cutting stock problem in the marble industry via mathematical programming and stochastic diffusion search approaches. Comput. Oper. Res. **128** (2021). https://doi.org/10.1016/j.cor.2020.105173
17. Prifti, V., Dervishi, I., Dhoska, K., Markja, I., Pramono, A.: Minimization of transport costs in an industrial company through linear programming. IOP Conf. Ser. Mater. Sci. Eng. **909**(1) (2020). https://doi.org/10.1088/1757-899X/909/1/012040
18. Andres, B., Guzman, E., Poler, R.: A novel MILP model for the production, lot sizing, and scheduling of automotive plastic components on parallel flexible injection machines with setup common operators. Complexity **2021**, 1–16 (2021). https://doi.org/10.1155/2021/6667516
19. Yudhatama, J., Hakim, I.M.: Truck assembly line reconfiguration to reduce cycle time with lean manufacturing approach in the Indonesian automotive industry. IOP Conf. Ser. Mater. Sci. Eng. **1003**(1) (2020). https://doi.org/10.1088/1757-899X/1003/1/012101
20. Bellingeri, A., Gallo, A., Liang, D., Masoero, F., Cabrera, V.E.: Development of a linear programming model for the optimal allocation of nutritional resources in a dairy herd. J. Dairy Sci. **103**(11), 10898–10916 (2020). https://doi.org/10.3168/jds.2020-18157
21. Asmara, S., Rahmawati, W., Suharyatun, S., Wibowo, S.A.: Optimalization of upja revenue (business provider services) rice cultivation using linear programing analysis in seputih raman district, central Lampung. IOP Conf. Ser. Earth Environ. Sci. **355**(1) (2019). https://doi.org/10.1088/1755-1315/355/1/012087

Comparison Between Amazon Go Stores and Traditional Retails Based on Queueing Theory

Jairo R. Coronado-Hernandez[1], Andrés F. Calderón-Ochoa[1(✉)], Ivan Portnoy[1], and Jorge Morales-Mercado[2]

[1] Department of Productivity and Innovation, Universidad de la Costa, 080001 Barranquilla, Colombia
{jcoronad18,acaldero1,iportnoy}@cuc.edu.co
[2] Supermercados Megatiendas, Cartagena, Colombia
jmorales@megatiendas.com.co

Abstract. The Amazon Go Store model's introduction posed a breakthrough in the shopping market due to its ground-braking approach, in which customers exercise the so-called self-service checkout. Although many qualitative analysis studies can be found, along with some quantitative approaches, a literature review on this matter shows a lack of comparative analysis between this model and traditional retail models using queueing theory, which could provide powerful insight into the improvements introduced by Amazon Go Store system. This work sets out the path to quantitative approaches for such comparison, as it aims to provide a performance analysis through queueing theory. The article compared two queueing systems; a traditional retail store vs. the Amazon Go Store. Both systems were analyzed as queueing stochastic networks. First, the traditional retail store was modeled as a two-stage (shopping and payment) network. On the other hand, the Amazon Go Store was modeled as a single-stage (shopping + payment) network. Both systems were assessed in two case scenarios: a high-demand typical day and a low-demand typical day. The implemented methodology allowed obtaining, for both compared systems, the key performance indicators (KPIs) such as the cycle time (CT), work in process (WIP), and the throughput (TP), revealing that the Amazon Go Store model exhibits better performance regarding the WIP and CT. Therefore, the Amazon Go Store model renders a higher-quality, more cost-effective service in the retail sector.

Keywords: Queuing theory · Markovian model · Jackson networks · Retail shopping · Amazon Go Store

© Springer Nature Switzerland AG 2021
J. C. Figueroa-García et al. (Eds.): WEA 2021, CCIS 1431, pp. 347–361, 2021.
https://doi.org/10.1007/978-3-030-86702-7_30

1   Introduction

A supermarket is a commercial enterprise that provides a service instead of an own product in the usual sense. Conversely, the supermarket adds value to existing products acquired from suppliers located far between, assembled in regional factories, or distributed in local stores. These products are finally sold to local customers, sparing them the need to go long distances to find the variety of supplies they need [1].

The queueing models apply to a variety of systems, including supermarkets [2–6]. Such models have been used to study supermarkets through different approaches. Some studies address the efficient management of supermarket queues [7, 8], the queueing theory-based analysis of checkout points' operations [9], the mathematical analysis of multiple-server, single-queue models and multiple-server, multiple-queue models [10], the assessment of the queueing theory application on the checkout systems in supermarkets [11], among other matters. A well-known queueing model for supermarkets is the single-server, n-queues model. Customers arrive at the supermarket following a Poisson process with an arrival rate λ_n, where λ (subject to $0 < \lambda < 1$) is a constant. Upon arrival, each customer uniformly heads to one of the waiting lines (queues) randomly and with replacement, and then he or she joins the shortest waiting line (queue) among those available (ties are broken choosing the nearest of the shortest queues available). Customers are served according to the first-in-first-out (FIFO) dynamic [1].

An indicator of service quality in a supermarket is the residence time, which plays a significant role and influences the customers' shopping decision, as too long residence times lead them to do something else and come back later [12], or even discourage them from shopping, thus generating a significantly negative impact on the profits. Also, the number of customers in the queue has a similar impact on the shopping incidence [13]. The study of the diverse waiting line systems and their performance has drawn particular attention in the literature. Multiple works have addressed the study of the phenomena in different commercial settings, elucidating how these phenomena influence the service quality and profits in supermarkets [14–16].

As of 2018, the Amazon Go Store supermarkets were launched [17], implementing the so-called self-service checkout, in which customers serve themselves. This new system introduces an utterly novel shopping dynamic relying on the Just Walk-Out technology (JWOT), which utilizes artificial intelligence (AI)-based technologies called AIPARS (AI-powered automated retail stores). AIPARS technologies and machine learning and image recognition techniques are meant to be the next breakthrough for in-person retail markets [18–20].

The self-service checkout system's dynamic goes as follows: the customers must install an app on their cellphones, a code outputting the app on the cellphone is scanned at the store's entrance, then the customers are tracked in real-time during the shopping, as the list of products put in the cart is recorded, and finally, the customers can leave the store without heading to a checkout line as they are automatically charged. This technology eliminates the need for waiting lines and checkout servers [21, 22].

We conducted a literature search using the Scopus database. The period to retrieve data was set as 2018 to 2021. The research data includes journal articles published before March 5, 2021. Five search Boolean queries were used: TITLE: (Amazon Go Store AND (Queuing Theory OR Queuing Theory) OR Performance), TITLE: (Amazon Go Store AND (Queuing System* OR Queuing System*) OR Performance), TITLE: (Amazon Go Store AND (Queueing OR Queueing OR Performance), TITLE: (Amazon Go Store AND Traditional AND (Supermarket OR Store OR Retail)), TITLE: (Amazon Go Store AND Jackson Networks).

The retail-related search showed that literature lacks research addressing the quantitative estimation of Amazon Go Store supermarkets' performance based on queueing theory. Therefore, this article's purpose is to model and estimate the performance of Amazon Go Store's queueing system, comparing its KPIs with those of traditional retail. The manuscript is organized as follows: Sect. 2 explains in detail the methodology used for the study, Sect. 3 shows the results obtained for both retail models, and finally, Sect. 4 presents the conclusions and future work related to this research.

2 Methodology

The methodology of this work comprises four steps explained in detail below:

Step 1 – Data Gathering and Tabulation: Data was retrieved from a primary source (i.e., traditional retail) through direct quantitative-oriented observation by the research team, gathering it on an hourly basis. The measured variables include the time between customers' arrivals at the supermarket $\frac{1}{\lambda_1(t)}$, the self-service residence time $\frac{1}{\mu_1(t)}$, the average arrival rate to a server $\lambda_2(t)$, the servers' service rate $\mu_2(t)$, and the number of available servers n. Data was gathered for both a high-demand day and a low-demand day. Data is further tabulated as in Table 1.

Step 2 – Systems Modeling: Both queueing systems (traditional retail and Amazon Go Store) were mathematically modeled. Subsections 2.1 and 2.2 explain such mathematical models in detail, along with the assumptions and parameters considered for either system.

Table 1. Table array used for data gathered from traditional retail.

Time	Stage 1				Stage 2					
	High demand		Low demand		High demand			Low demand		n(t) (Customers)
	(s)	(min)	(s)	(min)	(Customers/h)	(Customers/h)	n(t)	(Customers/h)	(Customers/h)	
7:00 a.m	24,39	50	56,29	36,38	23,52	38,70	7	28,20	48,00	3
8:00 a.m	17,04	71,2	61,71	46,88	10,26	12,78	20	7,32	48,00	7
9:00 a.m	25,40	87,31	62,31	36,29	10,74	14,16	29	8,58	8,94	12
10:00 a.m	26,94	89,79	66,12	37,06	8,70	9,54	29	10,62	14,52	16
11:00 a.m	23,93	78,61	109,80	37,06	14,76	100,02	29	9,84	14,82	15
12:00 p.m	52,48	77,23	92,26	37,25	7,38	7,86	31	7,20	15,60	12
1:00 p.m	27,54	74,84	108,70	36,36	4,74	8,58	23	8,58	10,98	9
2:00 p. m	26,22	46,68	84,54	26,11	12,84	17,40	21	12,90	20,28	8
3:00 p.m	25,21	52,54	64,75	28,00	8,70	9,90	25	18,66	21,96	8
4:00 p.m	30,57	53,27	63,08	23,75	21,18	23,70	21	12,24	19,62	9
5:00 p.m	17,22	59,91	93,99	33,73	15,54	16,20	15	5,22	20,94	10
6:00 p.m	25,07	34	110,15	23,60	13,80	24,84	18			11

2.1 Traditional Retail Model

The traditional retail was considered as a two-stage open Jackson Network. An M/M/∞ (self-service) model is used for Stage 1, while the n-queue Stage 2 uses an M/M/1 model with a time-varying number of servers, set empirically by the store's manager/staff as a response to online demand. For Stage 1, times between arrivals are assumed to fit an exponential behavior, and self-service times are also assumed exponential and equivalent to having infinite parallel servers. As for the customers, once within the system, they serve themselves without heading to queues. For Stage 2, the customers' arrival rate to the servers is also assumed exponential, and so are the service times with a service rate μ_2. Figure 1 depicts an operations diagram of the two-stage model proposed for the traditional retail.

According to Taha [23], the M/M/∞ model (as in Stage 1) has an unlimited number of servers, as customers act as their own servers with continuous arrival rates (λ) and service rates (μ), so that: $\lambda_n = \lambda$, and $\mu_n = n\mu$, for $n = 0, 1, 2, \ldots$. On the other hand, the M/M/1 model (as in Stage 2) features independent and exponentially distributed arrival and service times with a single server, infinite system capacity, and follows the FIFO dynamic.

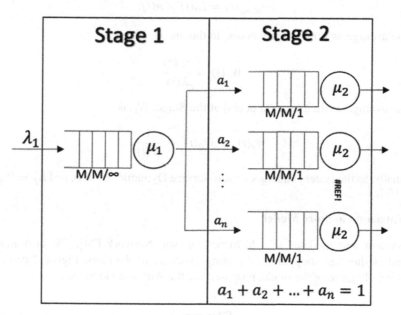

Fig. 1. Operations diagram of the two-stage model proposed for the traditional retail.

The model's underlying equations are now presented. For Stage 1, the utilization factor, ρ, is computed as in Eq. (1):

$$\rho(t) = \frac{\lambda(t)}{\mu(t)} \tag{1}$$

The average number of customers in the node, L_s, is:

$$L_s(t) = L_q(t) + \frac{\lambda(t)}{\mu(t)} \tag{2}$$

The average waiting time (in hours) at the stage, W_s, is:

$$W_s(t) = W_q(t) + \frac{1}{\mu(t)} \tag{3}$$

For Stage 2 (checkout), the utilization factor is also computed using Eq. (1), and the average number of customers in the node, L_q, is calculated as in Eq. (2) as well. The total number of customers at the node, $L_{s_{total}}$, is further calculated as in Eq. (4).

$$L_{s_{total}}(t) = L_s(t) \times n(t). \tag{4}$$

The average waiting time (in hours) in the queue, W_q, is:

$$W_q(t) = \frac{L_q(t)}{\lambda(t)} \tag{5}$$

The average waiting time (in hours) at the Stage, W_s, is:

$$W_s(t) = W_q(t) + \frac{1}{\mu(t)} \tag{6}$$

Finally, as the system undergoes a self-service Dynamic: $L_s = \rho$, and $L_q. = W_q = 0$.

2.2   Amazon Go Store Model

This system was modeled as a M/M/∞. Jackson Network [24]. The customers are charged as they are shopping and putting products in the carts. Figure 2 depicts the operations diagram of the model proposed for the Amazon Go Store.

Stage 1

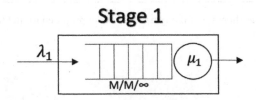

Fig. 2. Operations diagram of the model proposed for the Amazon Go Store.

Step 3 – Calculating the Key Performance Indicators (KPIs): The KPIs were calculated for both queueing models using Little's Law. According to Little and Graves [25], the TP is defined as a system's average production rate per unit time, the WIP is the inventory between the beginning and the end of a product's route, and the CT is the average time elapsed from liberation to the start of the product's routing. These KPIs are mathematically defined in Eqs. (7)–(9).

$$TP = \lambda Stage1. \tag{7}$$

$$WIP = L_s Stage1 + L_{s_{total}} Stage2 \tag{8}$$

$$CT = \frac{WIP}{TP} \tag{9}$$

Step 4 – Results Comparison. Once the KPIs were calculated for both systems, their performance is assessed and compared according to those indicators (TP, CT, and WIP).

3 Results

From the traditional retail model, Tables 2 and 3 are obtained. Table 2 presents the outcomes for Stages 1 and 2 in the high-demand scenario. Table 3 presents the outcomes for Stages 1 and 2 in the low-demand scenario.

Table 2 contains the hourly values for parameters and variables of the traditional retail system for the high-demand scenario, which exhibit a dynamic behavior and inform on the system performance, providing quantitative information to compare this system with the Amazon Go Store.

Analogously to Tables 2 and 3 contains the hourly values for parameters and variables of the traditional retail system for the low-demand scenario. Such information will be further used to perform a quantitative comparison (performance-wise) with the Amazon Go Store.

The Amazon Go Store model comprises a single stage in which both the shopping and payment are made simultaneously during the service time (see Fig. 2). This model was implemented using the same parameters featured by the traditional retail model. From the Amazon Go Store model, results for the high-demand and low-demand scenarios are presented in Tables 4 and 5, respectively.

Tables 4 and 5, analogously to Tables 2 and 3, show the hourly values for parameters and variables of the Amazon Go Store system, which will further inform on the system's performance and allow its comparison with the traditional retail system.

Table 2. Traditional retail model outcomes for the high-demand scenario.

High demand - Stage 1								High demand - Stage 2								
Time	$\frac{1}{\lambda_1(t)}$ (s)	$\lambda_1(t)$ (Customers/h)	$\frac{1}{\mu_1(t)}$ (s)	$\mu_1(t)$ (Customers/h)	$\rho_1(t)$	Ls(t) (Customers)	Ws(t) (h)	$\lambda_2(t)$ (Customers/h)	$\mu_2(t)$ (Customers/h)	$\rho_1(t)$	Ls(t) ((Customers)	Lq(t) (Customers)	Ws(t) (h)	Wq(t) (h)	n(t) (Units)	$Ls_{Total}(t)$ (Customers)
7:00 a.m	24,39	147,63	50	1,2	123,03	123,03	0,83	23,52	38,7	60,78%	1,55	0,94	0,07	0,04	7	10,85
8:00 a.m	17,04	211,33	71,2	0,84	250,78	250,78	1,19	10,26	12,78	80,28%	4,07	3,27	0,4	0,32	20	81,43
9:00 a.m	25,4	141,73	87,31	0,69	206,24	206,24	1,46	10,74	14,16	75,85%	3,14	2,38	0,29	0,22	29	91,07
10:00 a.m	26,94	133,66	89,79	0,67	200,01	200,01	1,5	8,7	9,54	91,19%	10,36	9,45	1,19	1,09	29	300,36
11:00 a.m	23,93	150,44	78,61	0,76	197,1	197,1	1,31	14,76	100,02	14,76%	0,17	0,03	0,01	0	29	5,02
12:00 p.m	52,48	68,6	77,23	0,78	88,3	88,3	1,29	7,38	7,86	93,89%	15,38	14,44	2,08	1,96	31	476,62
1:00 p.m	27,54	130,72	74,84	0,8	163,05	163,05	1,25	4,74	8,58	55,24%	1,23	0,68	06	0,14	23	28,39
2:00 p.m	26,22	137,3	46,68	1,29	106,82	106,82	0,78	12,84	17,4	73,79%	2,82	2,08	0,22	0,16	21	59,13
3:00 p.m	25,21	142,83	52,54	1,14	125,07	125,07	0,88	8,7	9,9	87,88%	7,25	6,37	0,83	0,73	25	181,25
4:00 p.m	30,57	117,76	53,27	1,13	104,55	104,55	0,89	21,18	23,7	89,37%	8,4	51	0,4	0,35	21	176,5
5:00 p.m	17,22	209,12	59,91	1	208,81	208,81	1	15,54	16,2	95,93%	23,55	22,59	1,52	1,45	15	353,18
6:00 p.m	25,07	143,63	34	1,76	81,39	81,39	0,57	13,8	24,84	55,56%	1,25	0,69	0,09	0,05	18	22,5
PROM.		144,56		1		154,6		12,68	23,64							

Table 3. Traditional retail model outcomes for the low-demand scenario.

Low demand - Stage 1 / Low demand - Stage 2

Time	$\frac{1}{\lambda_1(t)}$ (s)	$\lambda_1(t)$ (Customers/h)	$\frac{1}{\mu_1(t)}$ (s)	$\mu_1(t)$ (Customers/h)	$\rho_1(t)$	Ls (t) (Customers)	Ws (t) (h)	$\lambda_2(t)$ (stomers/h)	$\mu_2(t)$ (Customers/h)	$\rho_1(t)$	Ls (t) (Customers)	Lq (t) (Customers)	Ws (t) (h)	Wq(t) (h)	n(t) (Units)	$Ls_{Total}(t)$ (Customers)
7:00 a.m	56,29	63,96	36,38	1,65	38,78	38,78	0,61	28,2	48	0,59	1,42	0,84	0,05	0,03	3	4,27
8:00 a.m	61,71	58,33	46,88	1,28	45,57	45,57	0,78	7,32	48	0,15	0,18	03	0,02	0	7	1,26
9:00 a.m	62,31	57,77	36,29	1,65	34,95	34,95	0,6	8,58	8,94	0,96	23,83	22,87	2,78	2,67	12	286
10:00 a.m	66,12	54,45	37,06	1,62	33,63	33,63	0,62	10,62	14,52	0,73	2,72	1,99	0,26	0,19	16	43,57
11:00 a.m	109,8	32,79	37,06	1,62	20,25	20,25	0,62	9,84	14,82	0,66	1,98	1,31	0,2	0,13	15	29,64
12:00 p.m	92,26	39,02	37,25	1,61	24,23	24,23	0,62	7,2	15,6	0,46	0,86	0,4	0,12	0,05	12	10,29
1:00 p.m	108,7	33,12	36,36	1,65	20,07	20,07	0,61	8,58	10,98	0,78	3,58	2,79	0,42	0,33	9	32,18
2:00 p.m	84,54	42,59	26,11	2,3	18,53	18,53	0,44	12,9	20,28	0,64	1,75	1,11	0,14	0,09	8	13,98
3:00 p.m	64,75	55,6	28	2,14	25,95	25,95	0,47	18,66	21,96	0,85	5,65	4,8	0,3	0,26	8	45,24
4:00 p.m	63,08	57,07	23,75	2,53	22,59	22,59	0,4	12,24	19,62	0,62	1,66	1,03	0,14	0,08	9	14,93
5:00 p.m	93,99	38,3	33,73	1,78	21,53	21,53	0,56	5,22	20,94	0,25	0,33	0,08	0,06	0,02	10	3,32
6:00 p.m	110,15	32,68	23,6	2,54	12,86	12,85	0,39	16,44	17,82	0,92	11,91	10,99	0,72	0,67	11	131,04
PROM.		47,14		1,86				12,15	21,79							

Table 4. Amazon Go Store model outcomes for the high-demand scenario.

High demand

Time	$\frac{1}{\lambda_1(t)}$ (s)	$\lambda_1(t)$ (Customers/h)	$\frac{1}{\mu_1(t)}$ (s)	$\mu_1(t)$ (Customers/h)	$\rho_1(t)$	Ls (t) (Customers)	Ws (t) (h)
7:00 a.m	24,39	147,63	50,00	1,20	123,03	123,03	0,83
8:00 a.m	17,04	211,33	71,20	0,84	250,78	250,78	1,19
9:00 a. m	25,40	141,73	87,31	0,69	206,24	206,24	1,46
10:00 a.m	26,94	133,66	89,79	0,67	200,01	200,01	1,50
11:00 a.m	23,93	150,44	78,61	0,76	197,10	197,10	1,31
12:00 p.m	52,48	68,60	77,23	0,78	88,30	88,30	1,29
1:00 p.m	27,54	130,72	74,84	0,80	163,05	163,05	1,25
2:00 p.m	26,22	137,30	46,68	1,29	106,82	106,82	0,78
3:00 p.m	25,21	142,83	52,54	1,14	125,07	125,07	0,88
4:00 p.m	30,57	117,76	53,27	1,13	104,55	104,55	0,89
5:00 p.m	17,22	209,12	59,91	1,00	208,81	208,81	1,00
6:00 p.m	25,07	143,63	34,00	1,76	81,39	81,39	0,57
Average		**144,56**		**1,005**		**154,596**	

Table 5. Amazon Go Store model outcomes for the low-demand scenario.

Low demand

Time	$\frac{1}{\lambda_1(t)}$ (s)	$\lambda_1(t)$ (Customers/h)	$\frac{1}{\mu_1(t)}$ (s)	$\mu_1(t)$ (Customers/h)	$\rho_1(t)$	Ls (t) (Customers)	Ws (t) (h)
7:00 a.m	56,29	63,96	36,38	1,65	38,78	38,78	0,61
8:00 a.m	61,71	58,33	46,88	1,28	45,57	45,57	0,78
9:00 a.m	62,31	57,77	36,29	1,65	34,95	34,95	0,60
10:00 a.m	66,12	54,45	37,06	1,62	33,63	33,63	0,62
11:00 a.m	109,80	32,79	37,06	1,62	20,25	20,25	0,62
12:00 p.m	92,26	39,02	37,25	1,61	24,23	24,23	0,62
1:00 p.m	108,70	33,12	36,36	1,65	20,07	20,07	0,61
2:00 p.m	84,54	42,59	26,11	2,30	18,53	18,53	0,44
3:00 p.m	64,75	55,60	28,00	2,14	25,95	25,95	0,47
4:00 p.m	63,08	57,07	23,75	2,53	22,59	22,59	0,40
5:00 p.m	93,99	38,30	33,73	1,78	21,53	21,53	0,56
6:00 p.m	110,15	32,68	23,60	2,54	12,86	12,86	0,39
Average		**47,14**		**1,86**			

The KPIs (TP, WIP, and CT) were calculated for both models. Results are shown in Table 6 for both the high-demand and low-demand scenarios.

Table 6. KPIs obtained for traditional retail and Amazon Go Store.

| | Traditional retail | | | | | | Amazon Go Store supermarket | | | | | |
| | High demand | | | Low demand | | | High demand | | | Low demand | | |
Time	WIP (Customers)	CT (h)	TP (Customers/h)	WIP (Customers)	CT (h)	TP (Customers/h)	WIP (Customers)	CT (h)	TP (Customers/h)	WIP (Customers)	CT (h)	TP (Customers/h)
7:00 a.m	133,87	0,91	147,63	43,05	0,67	63,96	123,03	0,83	147,63	38,78	0,61	63,96
8:00 a.m	332,21	1,57	211,33	46,83	0,8	58,33	250,78	1,19	211,33	45,57	0,78	58,33
9:00 a.m	297,31	2,1	141,73	320,95	5,56	57,77	206,24	1,46	141,73	34,95	0,6	57,77
10:00 a.m	500,37	3,74	133,66	77,2	1,42	54,45	200,01	1,5	133,66	33,63	0,62	54,45
11:00 a.m	202,12	1,34	150,44	49,89	1,52	32,79	197,1	1,31	150,44	20,25	0,62	32,79
12:00 p.m	564,92	8,24	68,6	34,51	0,88	39,02	88,3	1,29	68,6	24,23	0,62	39,02
1:00 p.m	191,44	1,46	130,72	52,24	1,58	33,12	163,05	1,25	130,72	20,07	0,61	33,12
2:00 p.m	165,95	1,21	137,3	32,52	0,76	42,59	106,82	0,78	137,3	18,53	0,44	42,59
3:00 p.m	306,32	2,14	142,83	71,18	1,28	55,6	125,07	0,88	142,83	25,95	0,47	55,6
4:00 p.m	281,05	2,39	117,76	37,52	0,66	57,07	104,55	0,89	117,76	22,59	0,4	57,07
5:00 p.m	561,99	2,69	209,12	24,85	0,65	38,3	208,81	1	209,12	21,53	0,56	38,3
6:00 p.m	103,89	0,72	143,63	143,9	4,4	32,68	81,39	0,57	143,63	12,86	0,39	32,68
Average	303,45	2,1	144,56	77,89	1,68	47,14	154,6	1,07	144,56	26,58	0,56	47,14

Finally, Table7 summarizes the improvements (as percentages of KPIs change) achieved by the Amazon Go Store model compared to the traditional retail model regarding the TP, WIP, and CT.

Table 7. KPIs comparison; Amazon Go Store vs. traditional retail.

Time	Traditional retail vs. Amazon Go Store – High demand		Traditional retail vs. AMAZON GO STORE – Low demand	
	% Improvement WIP	% Improvement CT	% Improvement WIP	% Improvement CT
7:00 a.m	91,90	91,90	111,02	111,02
8:00 a.m	75,49	75,49	102,76	102,76
9:00 a.m	69,37	69,37	918,38	918,38
10:00 a.m	39,97	39,97	229,55	229,55
11:00 a.m	97,52	97,52	246,33	246,33
12:00 p.m	15,63	15,63	142,46	142,46
1:00 p.m	85,17	85,17	260,33	260,33
2:00 p.m	64,37	64,37	175,45	175,45
3:00 p.m	40,83	40,83	274,35	274,35
4:00 p.m	37,20	37,20	166,08	166,08
5:00 p.m	37,15	37,15	115,42	115,42
6:00 p.m	78,34	78,34	1119,38	1119,38
Average	**50,95**	**50,95**	**293,05**	**300,93**

The implications of the results are discussed in the following section.

4   Discussion

The performance assessment revealed that, compared to the traditional retail, the Amazon Go Store achieved better CT and WIP, as shown in Table 7. When implementing the Amazon Go Store model, the WIP changed from 303,45 (for the traditional retail model) to 154,6 customers, yielding an improvement of 50,95% during high-demand days. Moreover, for low-demand days, the WIP changed from 77,89 to 26,58 customers, a 293,05% improvement. On the other hand, the CT changed from 2,1 to 1,07 h in high-demand days and 1,68 to 0,56 h in low-demand days, achieving 50,95% and 300,93% improvement, respectively. Nevertheless, the TP remained unchanged for both systems in both demand scenarios, as observed in Table 7. That is the reason why the TP improvement was not included in Table 7. Figure 3 shows a comparative chart for the WIP's time evolution for both systems in both demand scenarios, while Fig. 4 shows the same for the CT.

Fig. 3. Hourly WIP comparison: traditional retail vs. Amazon Go Store.

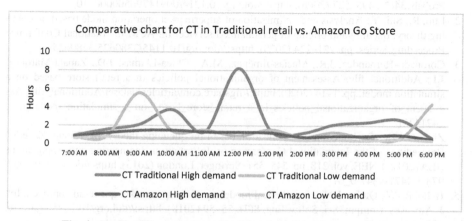

Fig. 4. Hourly CT comparison: Traditional retail vs. Amazon Go Store.

5   Conclusions

A literature review on M/M/∞ queues applied in the supermarket's context revealed that there is relatively little information on this matter. Moreover, no work was found to quantitatively compare the Amazon Go Store's performance with that of traditional retail. Therefore, this work compared, based on queueing theory, the systems for the traditional retail and the Amazon Go Store using the throughput (TP), cycle time (CT), and the work in process (WIP) as performance indicators.

Results showed a better performance for the Amazon Go Store regarding the WIP and CT, while the TP remained the same for both systems. The improvements found in the Amazon Go Store system arise from the fact that this system does not involve a checking-out stage since customers are automatically charged as they shop. Thus, this quantitative study concludes that, overall, the Amazon Go Store model achieves important improvements regarding the customers' residence time at the supermarkets. In addition, this article sets out the path for future quantitative-oriented studies aiming to analyze and compare new upcoming shopping paradigms with the currently existing regarding their performance.

Future works should give more attention to quantitative approaches to elucidate the Amazon Go Store model's drawbacks and advantages. This article contributes to creating a quantitative-oriented body of knowledge on this issue. Moreover, future works should propose changes to improve the performance of both Amazon GO and traditional retail regarding their performance (measured through the KPIs) and propose novel, more adequate performance metrics that can adapt more flexibly to new upcoming shopping paradigms. Finally, future works could characterize the AIPARS individually to determine which technologies impact the most on supermarkets' performance.

References

1. Luczak, M.J., Mcdiarmid, C.: On the maximum queue length in the supermarket model. Ann. Probab. **34**(2), 493–527 (2006). https://doi.org/10.1214/00911790500000710
2. Luo, R., Shi, Y.: Analysis and optimization of supermarket operation mode based on queuing theory: queuing and pricing of personalized service. In: ACM International Conference Proceeding Series, pp. 221–224 (2020). https://doi.org/10.1145/3380625.3380635
3. Coronado-Hernández, J.R., Macías-Jiménez, M.A., Chica-Llamas, J.D., Zapata-Márquez, J.I.: Additional file. Assessment of organizational policies in a retail store based on a simulation model, pp. 1–14 (2020). https://figshare.com/articles/dataset/Additional_file_Ass essment_of_organizational_policies_in_a_retail_store_based_on_a_simulation_model_/ 14214251
4. Zhao, T., He, C.: Supermarket application based on queueing theory. In: Zhong, Z. (eds.) Proceedings of the International Conference on Information Engineering and Applications (IEA) 2012. LNEE, vol. 218, pp. 545–551. Springer, London (2013). https://doi.org/10.1007/ 978-1-4471-4847-0_67
5. Bello, R.-W., Otobo, F.N.: Hypothetical modeling of a supermarket queue-an approach. Int. J. Adv. Res. Comput. Sci. Softw. Eng. **8**(7), 55–59 (2018). https://doi.org/10.23956/ijarcsse. v8i7.815
6. Jhala, N., Bhathawala, P.: Analysis and application of queuing theory in Supermarkets. Int. J. Innov. Res. Sci. Eng. Technol. **6**(9), 6 (2017). https://doi.org/10.15680/IJIRSET.2017.060 9021
7. Igwe, A., Onwuere, J.U.J., Egbo, O.P.: Efficient queue management in supermarkets: a case study of Makurdi Town, Nigeria. Eur. J. Bus. Manag. **6**(39), 185–192 (2014)
8. Morabito, R., De Lima, F.C.R.: A Markovian queueing model for the analysis of user waiting times in supermarket checkouts. Int. J. Oper. Quant. Manag. **10**(2), 165–177 (2004)
9. Priyangika, J., Cooray, T.: Analysis of the sales checkout operation in supermarket using queuing theory. Univ. J. Manag. **4**(7), 393–396 (2015)
10. Prasad, V., Vh, B., Koka, T.A.: Mathematical analysis of single queue multi server and multi queue multi server queuing models: comparison study. Glob. J. Math. Anal. **3**(3), 97–104 (2015)
11. Koeswara, S., Kholil, M., Pratama, Z., Hendri: Evaluation on application of queuing theory on payment system in the supermarket 'saga' Padang Pariaman West Sumatra. In: IOP Conf. Ser. Mater. Sci. Eng. **453**(1), 012045 (2018). https://doi.org/10.1088/1757-899X/453/1/012045
12. Artalejo, J., Falin, G.: Standard and retrial queueing systems: a comparative analysis. Rev. Matemática Complut. **15**(1), 101–129 (2002). https://doi.org/10.5209/rev_rema.2002.v15.n1. 16950
13. Lu, Y., Musalem, A., Olivares, M., Schilkrut, A.: Measuring the effect of queues on customer purchases. Manage. Sci. **59**(8), 1743–1763 (2013). https://doi.org/10.1287/mnsc.1120.1686

14. Li, K., Pan, Y., Liu, B., Cheng, B.: The setting and optimization of quick queue with customer loss. J. Ind. Manag. Optim. **16**(3), 1539–1553 (2020). https://doi.org/10.3934/JIMO.2019016
15. Xing, W., Li, S., He, L.: Simulation model of supermarket queuing system. In: 2015 34th Chinese Control Conference (CCC), vol. 2015-Septe, pp. 8819–8823 (2015). https://doi.org/10.1109/ChiCC.2015.7261032
16. Chai, C.F.: Problem analysis and optimizing of setting service desks in supermarket based on M/M/C queuing system. In: Qi, E., Shen, J., Dou, R. (eds.) The 19th International Conference on Industrial Engineering and Engineering Management. Springer, Heidelberg (2013). https://doi.org/10.1007/978-3-642-38391-5_88.
17. Ives, B., Cossick, K., Adams, D.: Amazon Go: disrupting retail? J. Inf. Technol. Teach. Cases **9**(1), 2–12 (2019). https://doi.org/10.1177/2043886918819092
18. Polacco, A., Backes, K.: The Amazon Go concept: Implications, applications, and sustainability. J. Bus. Manag. **24**(1), 79–92 (2018)
19. Pillai, R., Sivathanu, B., Dwivedi, Y.K.: Shopping intention at AI-powered automated retail stores (AIPARS). J. Retail. Consum. Serv. **57**(August), 102207 (2020). https://doi.org/10.1016/j.jretconser.2020.102207
20. Chuawatcharin, R., Gerdsri, N.: Factors influencing the attitudes and behavioural intentions to use just walk out technology among Bangkok consumers. Int. J. Public Sect. Perform. Manag. **5**(2), 146–163 (2019). https://doi.org/10.1504/IJPSPM.2019.099091
21. Shekokar, N., Kasat, A., Jain, S., Naringrekar, P., Shah, M.: Shop and go: an innovative approach towards shopping using deep learning and computer visión. In: 2020 Third International Conference on Smart Systems and Inventive Technology (ICSSIT), pp. 1201–1206 (2020)
22. Wankhede, K., Wukkadada, B., Nadar, V.: Just walk-out technology and its challenges: a case of Amazon Go. In: International Conference on Inventive Research in Computing Applications, ICIRCA 2018, vol. Icirca, pp. 254–257 (2018). https://doi.org/10.1109/ICIRCA.2018.8597403
23. Taha, H.A.: Operations Research an Introduction. Pearson Education Limited 2017, New York (2017)
24. Jackson, J.R.: Networks of waiting lines. Oper. Res. **5**(4), 518–521 (1957)
25. Little, J.D.C., Graves, S.C.: Chapter 5 Little's Law. Oper. Manag. **115**(December), 81–100 (2008). https://doi.org/10.1007/978-0-387

Analysis of Traceability Systems for Reducing the Bullwhip Effect in the Perishable Food Supply Chain: A System Dynamics Approach

Jeysser Johan Otero-Diaz[1]([⊠]), Javier Arturo Orjuela-Castro[1]([⊠]),
and Milton M. Herrera[2]([⊠]) [iD]

[1] Universidad Distrital Francisco José de Caldas, Bogotá, Colombia
jjoterod@correo.udistrital.edu.co, jorjuela@udistrital.edu.co
[2] Universidad Militar Nueva Granada, Bogotá, Colombia
milton.herrera@unimilitar.edu.co

Abstract. Traceability system (TS) is part of safety and quality assurance strategy in the perishable food supply chains (PFSC). TS plays an essential role in supporting food logistics system. The TS can provide precise real time information about products and to contribute to alleviate the bullwhip effect. However, the mistakes planning of TSs can influence on bullwhip effect along PFSC. This paper explores strategies for mitigating the bullwhip effect on supply chain performance through a simulation model. A simulation model was developed to assess performance measures in PFSC such as inventory, transport, loss of food, and shortages.

Keywords: Traceability systems · Bullwhip effect · System dynamics · Perishable food supply chain

1 Introduction

The management of transport, inventory, storage and distribution processes are determined by the behavior of information and material flows throughout the supply chain [1]. Although the flow analysis is relevant for integration in supply chains, the lack of information systems and uncertainty concerning the demand hamper integration and coordination among the actors in the chain. Indeed, several studies have showed that the shortage of information limits decision-making processes at the operational, tactical, and strategic levels [2]. Besides, uncertainty in demand affects the quantity of products in inventory, the costs, and the quality of the products and the capacity of the chain's response [3]. In this context, the role of the information flow associated with traceability system (TS) plays an important role in the study and analysis of the bullwhip effect, especially in the perishable food supply chain (PFSC) [3].

The phenomenon of the bullwhip effect is a result of the inadequate management of information flows associated with the uncertainty of demand [4]. The chain's variable and uncertain behavior ends up affecting the operations of retailers, wholesalers, distributors and manufacturers within the PFSC [5]. The phenomenon of the bullwhip effect within

© Springer Nature Switzerland AG 2021
J. C. Figueroa-García et al. (Eds.): WEA 2021, CCIS 1431, pp. 362–373, 2021.
https://doi.org/10.1007/978-3-030-86702-7_31

the PFSC is associated with two types of causes: (i) behavioral (anticipation of shortages and advance purchases) and (ii) operational (consolidation of orders, delays in delivery times, and mistakes in planning of the demand). In addition, the bullwhip effect produces a series of consequences related to the increase in inventory security levels, a deficit in customer service and a decrease in sales [6].

In this context, the problem questions that guide this article are: ¿What are the technological tools used in the configuration of the traceability system and what are the motivators that justify the implementation of traceability systems in the perishable food supply chain? On the other hand, how has the problem of the whip effect and traceability systems in the perishable food supply chain been analyzed from a system dynamics perspective in the literature? This phenomenon has been investigated in different works, from different perspectives [6, 7].

The integration of the PFSC in technology has been made possible by the development of logistics 4.0. In this sense, the traceability systems have the ability to track and trace products, in each of the links of the PFSC which allows the location and control of traceable units, through the flow of information and materials [8]. The information flows are the result of the monitoring, capture and tracing of products throughout the PFSC, these flows have an important characteristic, as they flow in each of the links, the adhered information will be greater, allowing the incorporation of variables that facilitate access to information in the operational, tactical and strategic areas throughout the PFSC [9].

In the same way, the material flows have a relationship with the information, since by giving access to it to the agents who intervene in each link of the PFSC, it will be possible for them to make better decisions for the management of operations and logistics, thus the information and material flows will have a coordination and mitigating the causes in the generation of the bullwhip effect [10]. The article is divided into the following sections including this introduction. Session 1 presents an overview of the literature review of the main concepts that the article addresses. Session 2 presents the modeling methodology used to address the problem. Finally, the results and conclusions are discussed in Session 3.

2 Background

2.1 The Bullwhip Effect

Causes in the Generation of the Bullwhip Effect
The causes of bullwhip effect generation are categorized into behavioral and operational [11] in other cases these causes are considered general without categories [12]. Table 1 presents the main causes identified in the literature review.

The behavioral causes in the generation of the bullwhip effect are considered by the literature as strategic decisions that impact the chain, the demand forecast is one of them, the lower the precision of the historical data, the greater the imprecision in the demand [13]. Variation in prices is a behavioral cause, aspects such as promotions for large orders, inventory policies are included in this category [14] together with information not shared in the same way they are considered behavioral causes [11]. Operational causes are categorized into order batches [12] operational cost, and lead time [16].

Table 1. Causes categorized in the literature. Authors.

	Causes of the generation of the bullwhip effect	Authors
Behavioral	Demand forecasting	[1, 19, 20]
	Price fluctuation	[3, 4, 21]
	Ordering and inventory policy	[1, 4, 19, 22]
	Information sharing	[11, 21, 23]
Operational	Cost	[16, 20]
	Order batching	[3, 24, 25]
	Lead time	[1, 11, 16]

2.2 Overview of Traceability System

Traceability systems allow the tracking of objects, elements or information [20]. The information captured through the traceability systems is established through the design and structure of these systems. In the design of the traceability systems, factors such as the characteristics of the traceable objects, the objective or the need for the system, such as the food safety, food quality [21] and product control [22]. Furthermore, other studies highlight the importance of establishing the motivator for the design of a TS [23] which can be guided by regulations and safety [20]. The characteristics (perishable, frozen foods) [24] and properties (e.g.; temperature) of traceable products [27] as well as, the structure of a TS is associated with the technologies that will be integrated (RFID, internet of things, QR, blockchain). These technologies allow the reception of information and support decision making. Therefore, a traceability system allows the flow of information throughout the perishable food supply chain (PFSP).

There are motivators in the PFSC that justify the development of a traceability system, motivators have been identified such as legislation, food safety, quality assurance [22], international certifications, globalization of trade [20] communication throughout PFSC, process efficiency, cost reduction, social analysis, government financing [23] sustainability, production optimization. [21, 24] identify as characteristics, the amplitude, depth, precision, access and reliability in the identification of the plotting unit. Among the identified TS properties are the traceable resource unit, assignment of identifiers to traceable units, the registration of product properties directly or indirectly, mechanisms of access to information.

2.3 Literature Review – System Dynamics and Bullwhip Effect

For the development of the literature review, the approaches established by [26]. Were followed. The systematic review considered the databases Scopus, IEEE, Science Direct, Proquest, Web of Science, and Google Scholar. The reviewed articles cover the periods 1997 to 2020, as identified in Fig. 1.

The first search filter is associated with the words bullwhip effect, traceability, traceability systems, SC, PFSC, system dynamics. In total 124 articles were reviewed; the categorization is made according to the type of article for the bullwhip effect and traceability in the PFSC.

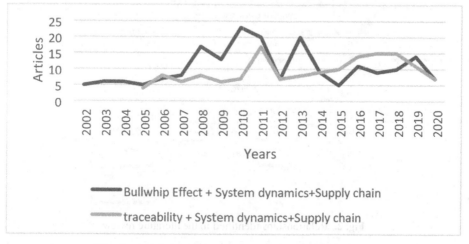

Fig. 1. Articles published per year with search equations

From the literature review, it was found that simulation with system dynamics (SD) is one of the most widely used approaches in the study of the bullwhip effect, as shows in the Fig. 2. This approach allows the analysis of the behavior of information and material flows over time and its effects on inventories and order orders [1]. Several studies using SD modeling propose strategies based on simulation scenarios for variables such as demand information, inventory orders, turnover, shortage [10, 15] performs an analysis based on scenarios for demand, current, stationary and stochastic, which allows estimating the quantities to order from suppliers and formulating inventory policies to face changes in demand behavior. [12] identifies some factors that affect the PFSC when it is presented, such as response times, operating costs. [17] Apply systems dynamics to examine the causes of the bullwhip effect and options to mitigate the bullwhip effect in terms of inventory policies [6]. Proposes the beer game, a didactic model to understand the causes and behavior of the bullwhip effect.

Among the techniques most used to study the problem of the bullwhip effect, is the dynamics of systems (SD), for their characteristics help to understand from the structural basis the representation of systems. [25] identify factors such as demand information, inventory orders, turnover, and shortage, using a SD model which affect and generate the bullwhip effect in the PFSC. The use of system dynamics goes beyond the measurement or quantification of the bullwhip effect, [21] addresses its use to estimate the quantities to order and inventory, [15] apply the system dynamics to examine the causes of the bullwhip effect and the options to mitigate it through inventory policies [18] Analyze how the bullwhip effect is generated and behaves, it is addressed under the beer game.

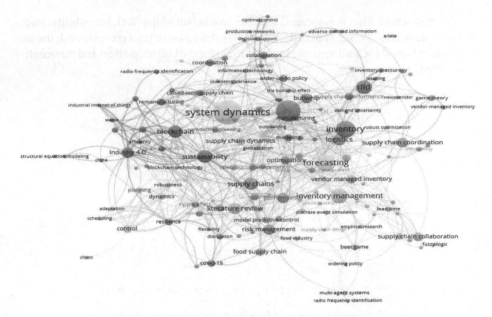

Fig. 2. Relationships identified in the literature review

3   System Dynamic Modeling: Case Study in the Mango Supply Chain

For the analysis of the SD model, the mango supply chain was identified, in Colombia the departments with the highest production are Cundinamarca, Tolima and Magdalena, The scenarios proposed for the analysis of the bullwhip effect in the PFSC are the actual chain and the chain with the implementation of the traceability system along the links, taking into account bar code and RFID technology. For the development of the causal model, the approaches proposed by [4, 30], are followed, which consist of defining the problem, variables, and design of the causal loop diagram (CLD).

3.1   Dynamic Behavior Hypothesis

According to the literature review, a dynamic hypothesis of the behavior of the bullwhip effect in the perishable food supply chain and traceability systems is proposed, which is used to design a CLD: "The implementation of a traceability system in the perishable food supply chain will allow the constant flow of information in the links, increasing the quality and demand of food, letting agents to make better decisions mitigating the bullwhip effect."

Causal Loop Diagram

A CLD is the representation of the system structure and the relationship of the main system variables. This closed-loop relationship can be either reinforce (R) or balance

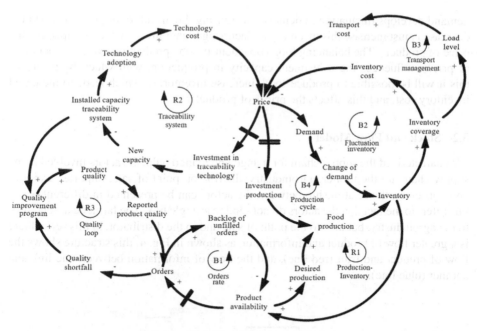

Fig. 3. Causal loop diagram. Authors.

(B). Figure 3 presents the CLD proposed for the problem, it consists of 3 reinforcing loops and 4 balancing loops.

The reinforcing loop (R1) establishes the dynamics of production and inventory, an increase in inventory allows for product availability, this availability manages to maintain the desired production levels for increased food production. The reinforcing loop (R2) represents the behavior of the traceability system, investment in traceability technology allows new capacity to exist for the system, the less investment there is, the less new capacity there will be, in turn to increase the installed capacity of the traceability system should increase the adoption of technology, the higher the adoption, the higher the technological cost will be generated, impacting the prices of the products and the decrease in investment in traceability technology. The reinforcing loop (R3) exhibits the quality behavior, the higher the quality of the products, the greater the information on the quality of the product will be transmitted, this allows the decrease due to quality deficit, increasing the improvement of the quality program, and This increases the quality of the products. The reinforcing loop (R4) identifies the dynamics of transport. The consolidation of large quantities of inventories in means of transport occupying their maximum capacity reduces transport costs, influencing the behavior of prices, increasing sales, generating delays in these orders, which leads to increased inventories in order to fulfill orders. The balancing loop (B1) identifies the behavior of orders, an increase in the number of orders causes orders to accumulate and to be delayed, this accumulation of orders decreases product availability, generating an increase in orders. The balancing loop (B2) represents the dynamics of the fluctuation of demand and inventories, at lower established prices, greater demand for product, this increase in demand develops fluctuation in demand, decreasing the inventory of product, when the decrease I must increase this inventory by incurring higher inventory costs impacting the price of products. The balancing loop (B3) identifies the production cycle, the behavior of prices, influences the investment capacity in production, with which by means of this it will be possible to produce food, increase inventories, which leads to increased inventory cost, and this affects the prices of products.

3.2 Stock and Flow Model

We characterized the supply chain for mango and mango pulp, the actors involved in the supply chain are the farmer, agroindustry, distributor, point of sale, importer, exporter and consumer, the relationship between the actors can be presented in different ways, this refers to the fact that the actors do not send to a single link. The farmer can send fruit to the agroindustry, but also to the point of sale and to the distributor, in this sense there is a greater flow of product and information as shown in Fig. 4, this structure shows the flow of product and fruit (red line), and the flow of information between one link and another (blue line).

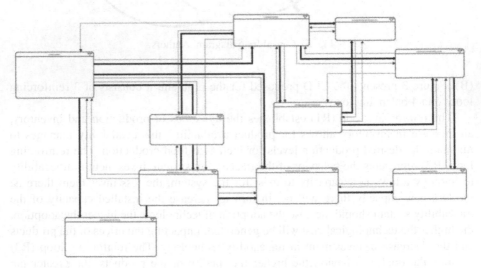

Fig. 4. Model structure for the perishable food supply chain (Color figure online)

The stock-and-flow diagram was developed according to the structure proposed by [29]. This structure links the inventories, transportation, and losses, allowing to analyze the effects of the information. Figure 5 identifies the agroindustry link, which receives fruit from the farmer, generates losses both in transportation and in inventory, shipments are established according to the delivery and arrival rates characterized in each link. The delivery rate is established with the farmer's inventory, the percentage destined from the farmer to the agroindustry, the shortages of fruit from the farmer to the agribusiness, and the orders from the agribusiness, in the same way, for the arrival rate, the transportation of fruit from the farmer to the agroindustry is established, and the delivery times determined from the loading times and transit times. As the agroindustry is a link where the mango fruit is transformed, it has a production rate, determined according to the orders of the distributor and the point of sale, the percentages of fruit for product, and the consumption of fruit per unit of product, likewise the production delays establish the inventory levels of finished product.

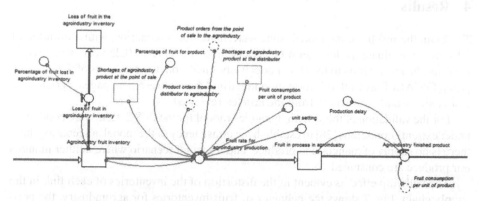

Fig. 5. Stock and flow model for the agroindustry

For the analysis of the behavior of the bullwhip effect in the perishable food chain, a scenario is established in which it is proposed to evaluate the chain without traceability, another scenario in which traceability is implemented, in this system the technology chosen is RFID. Likewise, a third scenario of the supply chain with BAR CODE technology is evaluated, and a final scenario of the chain in which the actors who market fruit implement BAR CODE, and the actors who market mango products implement RFID. The structure of the TS proposed by [30], makes it possible to evaluate the change of technology along the chain, the capacity of the actors under implementation of the

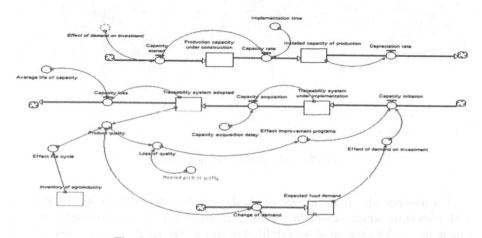

Fig. 6. Stock and flow model for traceability system

system, the quality of the product, thus making it possible to determine the expected demand of the actors and greater effectiveness in inventory management, which mitigates the bullwhip effect in the food supply chain. Hence, Fig. 6 shows the structure of the traceability system.

4   Results

To obtain the results of the model, runs were made for 4 scenarios, with a duration of 10 years, to evaluate the long-term behaviors, likewise a DT of 0.25 years was used in the runs, the information to feed the model is obtained from the databases of the research group GICALyT, as well as information identified from government pages, agricultural associations, and information from the articles reviewed.

For the validation of the system dynamics model for the PFSC, tests were conducted under extreme conditions [28] to establish the consistency of the model, a scenario where there is no supply of mangos and produce, and a second scenario where neither mangos nor produce are consumed.

The bullwhip effect is evident in the distortion of the inventories of each link in the supply chain, Fig. 7 shows the behavior of fruit inventories for agroindustry, the periodicity of shipments by the farmer and the distributor to the agroindustry is determined according to the weather conditions for mango harvest in the region where it is grown. Through the implementation of traceability systems, it can be identified that RFID technology in fruit inventories generates better results for the farmer and the distributor, compared to product inventories with a 1% reduction for the point of sale. Similarly, for BAR CODE technology, the logistical performance of inventories establishes a reduction in the chain, and regulates the consequences of the bullwhip effect.

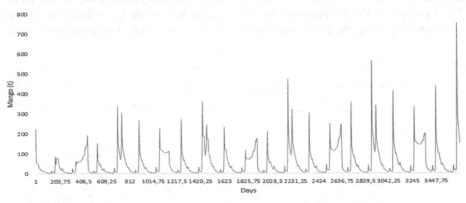

Fig. 7. Fruit inventory for agroindustry

For transportation in the mango chain, the Fig. 8 shows the behavior of the chain with respect to transportation, the logistic performance in the transport sector in relation to the implementation of traceability systems shows that the combination of BAR CODE and RFID technologies is ideal to guarantee stable transport levels along the chain, which minimizes transport losses in the supply chain. For the distributor link, the implementation of traceability represents an increase in transport levels, which leads to the identification of tradeoffs to mitigate this impact on transport.

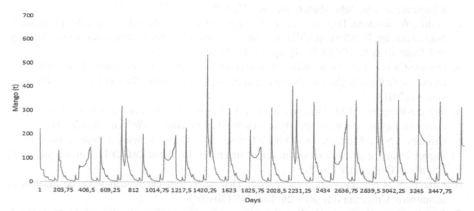

Fig. 8. Fruit transport for agroindustry

Under the implementation of traceability systems it is identified that losses in inventories and transportation decrease when using a combination of BAR CODE and RFID technologies, for the farmer and the fruit distributor, this added to a quality approach of the traceability system where storage and transportation conditions are controlled, This will preserve the food over time, preventing fruit losses from increasing along the supply chain of perishable foods, and each link will be ordered according to the information of the traceability system, reducing the percentage of mango losses.

5 Conclusion

A system dynamics model is proposed to analyze the behavior of the bullwhip effect under the implementation of the TS with bar code and RFID technology, the scenarios allow establishing policies for the management of inventories, transportation, and the reduction of losses in transportation and inventory. However, the mitigation of the bullwhip effect will not be effective in all links of the supply chain, and some points in the chain will be negatively affected by mango harvesting times and transportation delays along the chain, increasing the complexity of the structure. The adoption of traceability systems by the actors in the supply chain for the mitigation of the bullwhip effect, benefits the chain in general terms, a trade off must be found between fruit losses for inventories and transportation, product quality, and implementation capacity with which all actors can obtain a benefit from the investment in technology.

For future work, it is proposed to analyze the behavior of the bullwhip effect in other types of perishable foods, as well as the analysis of other types of technologies within logistics 4.0 such as the Internet of things, Blockchain, as well as the analysis of the behavior of asymmetries in the information generated by the use of different technologies and their consequence in relation to the bullwhip effect.

References

1. de Almeida, M.M.K., Marins, F.A.S., Salgado, A.M.P., Santos, F.C.A., da Silva, S.L.: Mitigation of the bullwhip effect considering trust and collaboration in supply chain management: a literature review. Adv. Manuf. Technol. **77**, 495–513 (2015)
2. Ardila, W., Romero, D., Gonzalez, F.: Estrategias para la gestión de riesgos de la Cadena de Suministro. In: Twelfth LACCEI Latin American and Caribbean Conference for Engineering and Technology (LACCEI 2014), pp. 22–31 (2014)
3. Orjuela-Castro, J.A.: Incidencia del diseño de la cadena de suministro alimentaria en el equilibrio de flujos logísticos. Doctoral dissertation, Universidad Nacional de Colombia-Sede Bogota (2018)
4. Herrera-Ramirez, M.M., Orjuela-Castro, J.A.: Perspective of traceability in the food supply chain: an approach from system dynamics. Revista Ingenieria **19**(2), 63–84 (2013)
5. Cifuentes, N.R., Mendez, J.S., Orjuela-Castro, J.A.: Consecuencias del efecto bullwhip al implementar la estructura vendor managed inventory. In: Tenth LACCEI Latin American and Caribbean Conference (2012)
6. Canella, S., Ciancimino, E., Framinan, J., Disney, S.: Los cuatro arquetipos de cadenas de suministro. Universia Bus. Rev. **26**, 134–149 (2010)
7. Liu, P., Chen, S., Yang, H., Hung, C., Tsai, M.: Application of artificial neural network and SARIMA in portland cement supply chain to forecast demand. In: Fourth International Conference on Natural Computation, pp. 97–101 (2008)
8. Zhigang, Z.: Applying RFID to reduce bullwhip effect in a FMCG supply chain. In: 2011 International Conference on E-Business and E-Government (ICEE), pp. 1–4 (2011)
9. Wen-li, W., Yao-wen, X.: Simulation of supply chain network based on discrete-continuous combined modeling. In: International Conference on Computational Aspects of Social Networks, vol. 10, no. 160, pp. 699–702 (2010)
10. Derbel, M., Chabchoub, H., Hachicha, W., Masmoudi, F.: Measuring the impact of (s, S) ordering policy on the bullwhip effect by means of simulation optimization. In: International Conference on Advanced Logistics and Transport, no. 10, pp. 482–487 (2013)
11. Fransoo, J.C., Wouter, M.J.: Measuring the bullwhip effect in the supply chain. Supply Chain: Int. J. **5**(2), 78–89 (2000)
12. Derbel, M., Hachicha, W., Masmoudi, F.: A literature survey of bullwhip effect (2010–2013). In: International Conference on Advanced Logistics and Transport, pp. 173–178 (2014)
13. Novitasari, N., Damayanti, D.D.: Systematic literature review and improved model for mitigating bullwhip effect. In: 5th International Conference on Industrial Engineering and Applications, pp. 531–535 (2018)
14. Dejonckheere, J., Disney, S.M., Lambrecht, M.R., Towill, D.: Transfer function analysis of forecasting induced bullwhip in supply chain. Int. J. Prod. **78**(2), 133–144 (2002)
15. Le, M., Yingying, Z., Lu, Z.: Research on the impact of products exchange policy on bullwhip effect of remanufacturing closed-loop supply chain, pp. 3590–3596. IEEE (2017)
16. Sucky, E.: The bullwhip effect in supply chains-an overestimated problem? Int. J. Prod. Econ. **118**, 311–322 (2009)
17. Dominguez, R., Cannella, S., Framinan, J.M.: The impact of the supply chain structure on bullwhip effect. Appl. Math. Model. **39**, 7309–7325 (2015)
18. Lee, H., Padmanabhan, V., Whang, S.: The bullwhip effect in supply chains. Sloan Manag. Rev. **38**, 93–102 (1997)
19. Wangphanich, P., Kara, S., Kayis, B.: A simulation model of bullwhip effect in a multi-stage supply chain. In: IEEE International Conference on Industrial Engineering and Engineering Management, pp. 365–379 (2007)

20. Tian, F.: An agri-food supply chain traceability system for China based on RFID & blockchain technology. In: 13th International Conference on Service Systems and Service Management (ICSSSM), pp. 1–6 (2016)
21. Rincon, D.L., Ramirez, J.E.F., Castro, J.A.O.: Hacia un Marco Conceptual Común Sobre Trazabilidad en la Cadena de Suministro de Alimentos. Revista Ingenieria **22**(2), 161–189 (2016)
22. Herrera-Ramírez, M.M., Orjuela-Castro, J., Sandoval-Cruz, H., MartínezVargas, M.A.: Modelado dinámico y estratégico de la cadena agroindustrial de frutas. Universidad Piloto de Colombia, Bogota (2017)
23. Ren, J.: RFID enable food supply chain traceability and safety. In: International Conference on Logistics, Informatics and Service Sciences (LISS), pp. 1–5 (2015)
24. Bao, X.-Y., Lu, Q., Wu, S.-J., Wang, Y.: Application of mid-based RFID handset in food traceability. In: International Conference on Machine Learning and Cybernetics, vol. 1, pp. 410–413 (2011)
25. Liu, P., Liu, W., Li, Q., Duan, M., Wang, Y., Dai, Y.: A research on tracing code of culture of food safety traceability based on RFID and improved EPC. In: International Conference on Logistics, Informatics and Service Sciences (LISS), pp. 1–6 (2016)
26. Kitchenham, B.: Procedures for performing systematic reviews. Joint technical report (2004)
27. Ramírez, S.A., Peña, G.E.: Analysis of chaotic behaviour in supply chain variables. J. Econ. Finan. Adm. Sci. **16**(31), 85–107 (2011)
28. Sterman, J.D.: Business Dynamics: Systems Thinking and Modeling for a Complex World. McGraw Hill, Mexico (2000)
29. Orjuela, J.A., Caicedo, A.L., Ruiz, A.F., Jaimes, W.A.: External integration mechanisms effect on the logistics performance of fruit supply chains: a system dynamics approach, vol. 10, no. 2, pp. 311–322 (2016)
30. Herrera, M.M., Orjuela, J.A.: An appraisal of traceability systems for food supply chains in Colombia, vol. 12, no. 1, pp. 37–50 (2021)

Exploring Efficiency and Accessibility in Healthcare Network Design

Edgar Duarte-Forero[1,2]([✉]) [iD] and Gustavo Alfredo Bula[1] [iD]

[1] Universidad Nacional de Colombia, Bogotá, Colombia
{eduartef,gabula}@unal.edu.co
[2] Universidad Libre, Bogotá, Colombia
edgarl.duartef@unilibre.edu.co

Abstract. Healthcare network design has a critical role in achieving sustainability goals because of their possibilities as drivers for wellness and patient-driven care. Healthcare systems with limited resources require not only to improve access for patients but also to define facilities location and limit operation expenditures. In this work, a study was conducted to understand the relation between accessibility and cost-efficiency in healthcare networks. A mathematical model is proposed to evaluate optimization consequences on accessibility for patients and location-related costs for networks. The proposed model defines the location of facilities and servers, the allocation of patients, and the configuration of network links. A computational study used a randomly generated instance with multiple service levels and covering distances. Each scenario is evaluated regarding accessibility and cost-efficiency concluding that those are conflicting objectives in an optimization approach.

Keywords: Healthcare network design · Accessibility · 2SFCA · MILP

1 Introduction

Healthcare Networks (HNs) provide services to promote community wellness through interconnected resources (public or private) such as facilities, specialized equipment, healthcare professionals, or administrative staff. From a logistic perspective, incoming patients use the resources allocated on the network nodes in order to be serviced. Nevertheless, the flow of patients across HNs experience frequent interruptions that cause long waiting lists for consultations, poor service quality, or repeated medical visits. This is known as fragmentation and is mainly due to complex administrative processes and wrong logistic decisions.

Aiming fragmentation reduction, HNs must satisfy multiple criteria such as accessibility, opportunity, continuity, and equity, among others [10]. Accessibility considerably influences system fragmentation because it defines how easy it is for a patient to receive services from a specific predefined place during the first and subsequent contacts with servers.

© Springer Nature Switzerland AG 2021
J. C. Figueroa-García et al. (Eds.): WEA 2021, CCIS 1431, pp. 374–385, 2021.
https://doi.org/10.1007/978-3-030-86702-7_32

Healthcare Network Design deals with the configuration of network components to provide suitable service levels for the population. Previous works show that operations research techniques provide adequate solutions for the design of healthcare networks [2]. Most of those works consider optimizing objective functions of cost-efficiency[1] and coverage. One of the limitations with this approach is that it does not explore the influence of network design optimization in system accessibility for patients [1, 16].

This paper aims to examine accessibility and cost efficiency in Healthcare Network Design. The main contributions of the paper are as follows: a mathematical optimization model that provides an in-depth look at these measurements in multiple scenarios; inclusion of a gravity-based method to estimate patient access; and cost-efficiency metrics including allocation of servers and transfer and transportation of patients. The proposed mathematical model is formulated based on previous works for HNs design, but in this case it also includes the optimization of accessibility as an objective function.

The remainder of the paper is organized as follows. Section 2 provides an overview of relevant literature and positions this paper. In Sect. 3, it is proposed a formulation for Healthcare Network Design that includes cost efficiency and accessibility. Section 4 highlights the solution method and computational results. Finally, Sect. 5 states concluding remarks.

2   Overview of the Literature

This section states the concept of accessibility and its measurement in healthcare location, and the main trends for Healthcare Network Design using mathematical modeling techniques. Subsequently, we delimit the scope of the paper and locate it in the research field.

2.1   Accessibility Measurement

In the healthcare field, accessibility is defined as the level of spatial availability of services [12] and a system is considered as accessible if required services are available whenever and wherever the patient may need them.

Literature review presents multiple accessibility measurements [4, 16]. This paper focuses on accessibility as a function of the movement of patients to receive attention in the HN. Gravity models are used to measure accessibility in health care systems incorporating variables of supply capacity, population size, and impedance functions that depend on the travel cost. This approach considers that accessibility of a demand point is the weighted sum of supply-to-demand ratios of all nearby suppliers. The Two-Step Floating Catchment Area (2SFCA) method allows for a more general solution for this problem where supply-to-demand ratios and their sums for each population location represent its accessibility [9]. 2SFCA method has been employed to analyze spatial access to healthcare services in a number of studies during recent years [8, 17].

---

[1] In this study, the concept of cost-efficiency refers to the sum of location related costs for patients and service managers.

2.2   Healthcare Network Design

Designing a healthcare network involves making decisions about the supply and demand. For the first one, decision-makers must define facilities location, its capacities and, connections between them, among others. Demand related decisions include the allocation of patients to specific facilities and servers for their treatments. Those decisions shall consider multiple criteria including travel distance for patients, specialties of servers, demand patterns, resource availability, and capacity of facilities.

A great deal of previous research into Healthcare Network Design has focused on specific applications areas such as calculation of available professionals [5], enabled beds and other service capacity measurements for healthcare networks. Regarding optimization objectives, reviewed literature emphasize on minimizing costs for server allocations, travel times, and installed capacity costs [3,11]. Service level specifications are also included by some authors in order to minimize waiting times [15] and lost demand [13].

Two aspects emerge from the studies discussed so far. Firstly, the need to examine the healthcare network design problem from a combined perspective of facility location and network design. Secondly, the possibility of exploring the relationships between cost-efficiency and accessibility in HNs. The following section integrates these aspects with the formulation of a mathematical model for the design of healthcare networks.

3   Healthcare Facility Location Network Design Problem

In general, the Healthcare Facility Location Network Design Problem (HFLNDP) deals with the location of a set of healthcare servers at some available facilities to satisfy the needs of patients subject to constraints of quality of service, capacity management, and patients flow, among others. It also aims to define the necessary connections among users and servers to allow patients flow [14]. Figure 1 shows a hypothetical network where three groups of patients with different required treatments have to choose one from the available facilities (medical centers). Each considered facility has a group of servers of different specialties. The links represent the connections and possible allocations between places of residence and facilities and between the servers for patient referrals.

Consider a patient from group A that visits facility $f1$. A general practitioner attends the case and, with a certain probability, passes a referral to a specialist in $f2$. After that, the patient will have to visit the specialist in $f2$ who may then send a new referral to $f3$ for a medical test. Results of this test will be sent from $f3$ to the specialist in $f2$. Finally, in a new appointment, the specialist will formulate recommendations to the patient according to the diagnosis. Similar flows may take place with patients for treatments B or C. This study considers just one hypothetical flow of patients for a specific group.

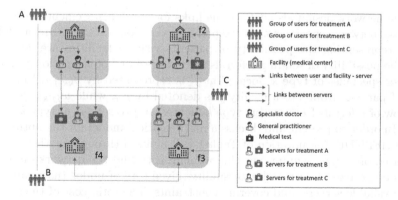

Fig. 1. Model of a hypothetical network

The proposed model for the HFLNDP determines (i) the selected facilities, (ii) the allocation of servers to facilities, (iii) the allocation of patients to servers, and (iv) the required links for referrals. The constraints include demand covering, capacity management at servers and facilities, flow of patients and referrals across links, and service level for patients[2].

The model considers a HN as a graph with a set of nodes and links. Let I denote the set of population zones indexed by i, $i \in I$. J denote potential facility locations indexed by j, $j \in J$. Finally, K represents the set of medical specializations for patient treatments indexed by k, $k \in K$. It is assumed that population at demand nodes I generate a stream of deterministic and inelastic demand denoted by h_i. Every server allocated to a facility j provides a specialized service k with a patient capacity c_{jk}. A facility at j has a maximum number of servers for specialty k denoted by s_{jk}. Coverage parameters a_{ij} and $b_{jj'}$ represent the possibility of visiting j from i, and j' from j, respectively. In addition, the distance commonly traveled by patients between demand regions i and facilities j is denoted by d_{ij}. There is also a cost for every referral between servers represented by $e_{jj'}$.

In this model, it is assumed that specialty $k = 1$ corresponds to the first level of attention commonly provided by a general practitioner. Additionally, specialists ($k \geq 2$) cannot refer patients to general practitioners. The patient entering the network has to select a facility for a first appointment ($k = 1$). Then, the practitioner may assume the treatment or refer the case to a specialist ($k \geq 2$). The selection of subsequent specialists depends on the parameter $t_{kk'}$ representing the percentage of patients referred from specialty k to k'. The number of available facilities for the first appointment is defined as Service Level and is modeled with the parameter q_i.

---

[2] Service level refers to the number of available facilities for first appointments.

The network design also defines the links for patient movement and referrals of cases between specialists. Corresponding decision variables are as follows. Links representing the possibility of patients visiting facilities are denoted by z_{ij}. The possibility of sending referrals from a specialist of type k located at j to another specialist of type k' located at j' is represented by $v_{kk'jj'}$. Finally, the flow of patients from i to a facility j is denoted by y_{ij}, while $w_{jj'kk'}$ represents the flow of referrals from servers type k located at j to servers of type k' located at j'. In order to present and discuss a mathematical model for the optimization of the HFLNDP, the notation of Table 1 will be used throughout this section.

Based on these assumptions, the problem is to find the network design that fulfills objectives of cost and accessibility, given sets of nodes (users and facilities), available servers, and covering constraints. The total cost of the system is modeled by the sum of transportation costs for patients (TCP), allocation costs at facilities (ACP), and referring costs of patients among servers (RCS). Those components are formulated as follows:

$$TCP = r * \sum_{ij} d_{ij} y_{ij} \tag{1}$$

$$ACS = \sum_{jk} f_{jk} x_{jk} \tag{2}$$

$$RCS = u * \sum_{jj'kk'} w_{jj'kk'} e_{jj'} \tag{3}$$

Accessibility measurement is formulated using the Two-Step Floating Catchment Area (2SFCA) method [9]. The reason that 2SFCA is selected is because of its predominance as a proper measurement of accessibility for healthcare locations [8,17]. It measures the accessibility of a demand location i considering the supply and a threshold of availability for those services and demand. The procedure for computing the measure value is shown next.

Step 1. Given a solution for the HFLNDP, for each location j, and a service k, search all demand locations i that are within a threshold travel distance from location j. Threshold distances a_{ij} depend on decision-maker criteria. Calculate the server-to-population ratio, R_{jk} as follows:

$$R_{jk} = x_{jk} / \sum_i (a_{ij} h_i) \quad \forall jk \tag{4}$$

Step 2. For each demand location i, search all server locations j that are within a threshold travel distance (a_{ij}) from location i and sum up the ratios at these locations.

$$A_{ik} = \sum_j a_{ij} * R_{jk} \quad \forall ik \tag{5}$$

Table 1. Notations of sets, parameters and decision variables for the HFLNDP.

Symbol	Description
Sets	
I	Set of users demand nodes. $i \in \{1, 2, ... |I|\}$
J	Set of potential facilities. $j \in \{1, 2, ... |J|\}$
K	Set of services required by users. $k \in \{1, 2, ... |K|\}$
Parameters	
d_{ij}	Distance on link (i, j)
$e_{jj'}$	Referral cost on link (j, j')
f_{jk}	Fixed cost of resource k at j
h_i	Demand of users at node i looking for a first appointment
a_{ij}	Equal to 1 if and only if $i \in I$ can be covered by $j \in J$
$b_{jj'}$	Equal to 1 if and only if $j \in J$ can be covered by $j' \in J$
c_{jk}	Capacity of a specialist of type k located at facility j to attend users
s_{jk}	Maximum number of specialists of type k that can be hosted at facility j
q_i	Minimum number of facilities to choose from for a first appointment from i
$t_{kk'}$	Percentage of users referred from specialty k to specialty k'
r	Traveling cost for users visiting servers
u	Referring cost of users between servers
Decision variables	
x_{jk}	Number of servers of type k allocated at facility j
y_{ij}	Number of users allocated from region i to facility j
z_{ij}	Binary variable equal to 1 if and only if users travel from i to j
$w_{jj'kk'}$	Number of users referred from a specialist type k at facility j to a specialist k' at a facility j'
$v_{jj'kk'}$	Binary variable equal to 1 if and only if a specialist type k at facility j refers patient to a specialist k' at a facility j'

The larger the index value A_{ik}, the better accessibility at this location. Equation 4 calculates an initial ratio for every service location and Eq. 5 sums up different ratios within a threshold distance for every demand location. Finally the whole accessibility of a system is the sum of every A_{ik}.

$$TAS = \sum_{ik} A_{ik} \qquad (6)$$

Special attention must be given to the modeling of links activation. Binary variables z_{ij} and $w_{jj'kk'}$ change if and only if there is flow of users between i and j, and between jk and $j'k'$ respectively. A ceiling function provides this formulation establishing limits for z_{ij} with the quotient of the flow y_{ij} and its maximum possible value $\sum_i h_i$. The following equation represents the implementation of this ceiling function for z_{ij}.

$$\frac{y_{ij}}{\sum_i h_i} \leq z_{ij} \leq \frac{y_{ij}}{\sum_i h_i} + 0.999 \quad ; \forall ij; z_{ij} \in \{0, 1\} \qquad (7)$$

Regarding the case of referrals (flows from j to j'), the implementation of the ceiling equation stands as follows:

$$\frac{w_{jj'kk'}}{\sum_i h_i} \leq v_{jj'kk'} \leq \frac{w_{jj'kk'}}{\sum_i h_i} + 0.999 \quad ; \forall jj'kk', v_{jj'kk'} \in \{0,1\} \tag{8}$$

The resulting mathematical formulation for the HFLNDP is as follows:

$$\text{maximize} \quad Z_1 = TAS \tag{9}$$

$$\text{minimize} \quad Z_2 = TCP + ACS + RCS \tag{10}$$

$$\text{subject to} \quad \sum_j y_{ij} = h_i \ \forall i \in I, \tag{11}$$

$$z_{ij} \leq a_{ij} \ \forall i \in I, j \in J, \tag{12}$$

$$v_{jj'kk'} \leq b_{jj'} \ \forall(j,j') \in J, (k,k') \in K, \tag{13}$$

$$\sum_i y_{ij} \leq c_{jk}x_{jk} \ \forall j \in J, k = 1, \tag{14}$$

$$\sum_{jk} w_{jj'kk'} \leq c_{j'k'}x_{j'k'} \ \forall(j') \in J, k' \in K, k' \neq 1, \tag{15}$$

$$\sum_{j \in J} z_{ij} \geq q_i \ \forall i \in I, \tag{16}$$

$$x_{jk} \leq s_{jk} \ \forall j \in J, k \in K, \tag{17}$$

$$t_{1k'} * \sum_i y_{ij} = \sum_{j'} w_{jj'1k'} \ \forall(j,k') \in K, \tag{18}$$

$$t_{k'k''} * \sum_{jk} w_{jj'kk'} = \sum_{j''} w_{j'j''k'k''} \ \forall(j'j'') \in J, (k',k'') \in K, \neq 1),$$
$$\tag{19}$$

$$y_{ij} \leq z_{ij}c_{jk}x_{jk} \ \forall i \in I, j \in J, k = 1, \tag{20}$$

$$y_{ij} \leq zij * \sum_i h_i \ \forall i \in I, j \in J, \tag{21}$$

$$y_{ij} \geq (zij - 0.999) * \sum_i h_i \ \forall i \in I, j \in J, \tag{22}$$

$$w_{jj'kk'} \geq v_{jj'kk'} * \sum_i h_i \ \forall(jj') \in J, (kk') \in K, \tag{23}$$

$$w_{jj'kk'} \geq (v_{jj'kk'} - 0.999) * \sum_i h_i \ \forall(jj') \in J, (kk') \in K, \tag{24}$$

$$y_{ij} \geq 0 \ \forall i \in I, j \in J, \tag{25}$$

$$z_{ij} \in (0,1) \ \forall i \in I, j \in J, \tag{26}$$

$$w_{jj'kk'} \geq 0 \quad \forall(j,j') \in J, (k,k') \in K, \tag{27}$$

$$v_{jj'kk'} \in (0,1) \quad \forall(j,j') \in J, (k,k') \in K, \tag{28}$$

$$x_{jk} \geq 0 \quad \forall j \in J, k \in K \tag{29}$$

The proposed model is formulated with two objective functions. Equation 9 sets the objective for maximizing the system accessibility and Eq. 10 minimizes the sum of traveling costs for patients, referral cost between servers and the fixed costs of servers at facilities.

Equation 11 ensures that every user must receive attention and Eq. 12 states that there can be a flow of patients from i to j if and only if the facility at j covers patients from i. Similarly, Eq. 13 allows referrals of patients from j to j' if and only if there is coverage between facilities at j and j'. Equations 14 and 15 verify the fulfillment of servers capacity requirements. Service level for patients is considered in Eq. 16 where the minimum number of available facilities is represented by q_i. The maximum number of servers for every facility is stated by Eq. 17.

The flow of patients across general practitioners and specialists is modeled by Eqs. 18 and 19, respectively. The activation of links in the network is constrained by Eqs. 21, 22, 23 24. Equations 25 to 29 define the mathematical nature of every variable in the model.

4   Computational Experiments

An implementation of the mathematical model for HFLNDP was coded in Python programming language supported by the Pyomo optimization modeling language [7] and solved using commercial optimization solver (Gurobi) [6] with a randomly generated instance. Table 2 presents parameter values for the constructed instance.

Table 2. Values of parameters for random instance

Param.	Values
$|I|$	8
$|J|$	14
$|K|$	5
d_{ij}	Euclidean distances between nodes i, j with random positions $\sim$ U(0,1)
$e_{jj'}$	Uniform random values for each pair i, j with random positions $\sim$ U(0,1)
f_{jk}	$\sim$ U(1,2)
h_i	$\sim$ U(5,8)
a_{ij}	Defined according to covering distances of 1.4, 1.0, 0.8, 0.6, 0.5 and 0.4
b_{ij}	Defined as 1.4
c_{jk}	$\sim$ U(40,100)
s_{jk}	$\sim$ U(8,12)
$t_{kk'}$	Randomly generated for each level k and considering that $t_{k,k'} \geq t_{k+1,k'+1}$

Experiments considered two factors: (i) covering distance for first appointment (a_{ij}), and (ii) service level (represented by the sum of available facilities for first appointments: $\sum_i q_i$). Covering distance was included with six levels: of 1.4, 1.0, 0.8, 0.6, 0.5 and 0.4. Second factor was explored defining levels for available facilities ranging from 13 to 21. This quantity was distributed among demand regions according to its population size.

Experiments consisted in solving the mathematical model separately for the objective functions defined in Eqs. 9 and 10. Figure 2 illustrates the effect of minimizing costs and the corresponding accessibility of different scenarios. The lower the costs, the lower the accessibility. There is no evidence of an influence of service level in either of the objectives. Conversely, higher values of covering distance corresponded to lower values for costs and accessibility. From that point of view, the decision to decrease costs affects the accessibility of patients. Therefore, conflicts arise when reducing costs in a HN because that would cause a reduction of accessibility and a reduction of covering distances increases costs.

An additional set of experiments was done to maximize accessibility. Results indicate that the higher values of covering distances, the higher costs obtained (Fig. 3). The maximization of accessibility can be accompanied by lower costs with shorter covering distances. If covering distances are to be higher, accessibility is reduced and costs increase significantly. The optimization model seeks for increasing accessibility by allocating the maximum possible number of servers in facilities. Obviously, this strategy brings higher costs.

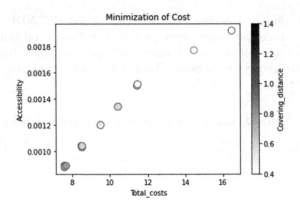

Fig. 2. Minimization of costs

Results guide towards the inclusion of covering distances as an influential parameter in network design. When minimizing costs, increasing covering distances allows a reduction of the costs in the system and a markdown on accessibility. On the contrary, when maximizing accessibility, increasing covering distances conveys an increase in costs. Consequently, decision-makers shall find balances among those measures that may preserve the access for patients and the cost efficiency for the system.

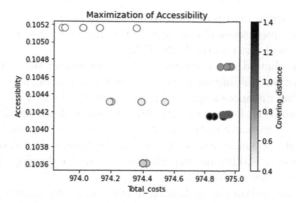

Fig. 3. Maximization of accessibility

Additional tests were performed with the comparison of optimal values for accessibility and costs on every scenario. Figure 4 represents the space of objective functions included in the experiments. This analysis suggests a conflicting nature between accessibility and cost-efficiency. In every scenario, a reduction in system cost resulted in an overall decrease of accessibility. This statement leads to the need of additional studies in order to find proper equilibrium among those objectives.

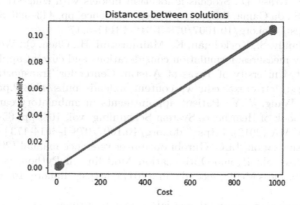

Fig. 4. Space of objective functions

5   Conclusions

A formulation for the Healthcare Facility Location Network Design Problem (HFLNDP) was proposed to analyze the relation among accessibility and cost efficiency. The scope of the study consisted in separately experiment with the minimization of network costs and the maximization of accessibility. Network costs included patient transportation, allocation of servers and transfer or referrals. Accessibility measurement consisted in the implementation of the Two Steps Floating Catchment Area method (2SFCA).

Experiments showed that the minimization of costs for the system conducted to a reduction of accessibility for patients. When maximizing accessibility, longer values of covering distances required higher costs for the system. Shorter covering distances produced lower costs and higher values of accessibility. This study considered service level as a factor and it was modeled as the number of available facilities for first appointments. Nevertheless, the results do not reflect its influence on accessibility. Additional experiments should be developed considering a wider range of options for its levels.

Finally, the analysis of the conflicting nature among accessibility and costs for the system supports the need for additional studies to explore the multi-objective dimension of healthcare network design. In addition to accessibility and costs, further objectives may be included in future studies: congestion, continuity and equity, among others.

References

1. Aboolian, R., Berman, O., Verter, V.: Maximal accessibility network design in the public sector. Transp. Sci. **50**(1), 336–347 (2016)
2. Ahmadi-Javid, A., Seyedi, P., Syam, S.S.: A survey of healthcare facility location. Comput. Oper. Res. **79**, 223–263 (2017)
3. Berman, O., Krass, D.: Stochastic location models with congestion. In: Laporte, G., Nickel, S., da Gama, F.S. (eds.) Location Science, pp. 443–486. Springer, Cham (2015). https://doi.org/10.1007/978-3-319-13111-5_17
4. Bhat, C., Handy, S., Kockelman, K., Mahmassani, H., Chen, Q., Weston, L., et al.: Accessibility measures: formulation considerations and current applications. Technical report, University of Texas at Austin. Center for Transportation Research (2000). https://ctr.utexas.edu/wp-content/uploads/pubs/4938_2.pdf
5. Gupta, D., Wang, W.Y.: Patient appointments in ambulatory care. In: Hall, R. (ed.) Handbook of Healthcare System Scheduling, vol. 168, pp. 65–104. Springer, US, Boston, MA (2012). https://doi.org/10.1007/978-1-4614-1734-7_4
6. Gurobi Optimization, LLC: Gurobi optimizer reference manual (2020)
7. Hart, W.E., et al.: Pyomo-Optimization Modeling in Python, vol. 67. Springer Science & Business Media, second edn. (2017). https://doi.org/10.1007/978-3-319-58821-6
8. Luo, J.: Analyzing potential spatial access to primary care services with an enhanced floating catchment area method. Cartographica **51**(1), 12–24 (2016)
9. Luo, W., Wang, F.: Measures of spatial accessibility to health care in a gis environment: synthesis and a case study in the chicago region. Environ. Plann. B Plann. Des. **30**(6), 865–884 (2003)
10. Mendes, E.V.: Las Redes de Atención de Salud. Organización Panamericana de la Salud, Brasilia (2013)
11. Paraskevopoulos, D., Gürel, S., Bektaş, T.: The congested multicommodity network design problem. Transp. Res. Part E Logistics Transp. Rev. **85**, 166–187 (2016)

12. Phillips, D.R.: Health and Health Care in the Third World. Longman Scientific & Technical, Harlow, Essex, England, Longman Development Studies (1990)
13. Pouraliakbari, M., Mohammadi, M., Mirzazadeh, A.: Analysis of maximal covering location-allocation model for congested healthcare systems in user choice environment. Int. J. Ind. Syst. Eng. 28(2), 240–274 (2018)
14. Rahmaniani, R., Ghaderi, A.: A combined facility location and network design problem with multi-type of capacitated links. Appl. Math. Model. 37(9), 6400–6414 (2013)
15. Vidyarthi, N., Kuzgunkaya, O.: The impact of directed choice on the design of preventive healthcare facility network under congestion. Health Care Manag. Sci. 18(4), 459–474 (2015)
16. Wang, F.: Measurement, optimization, and impact of health care accessibility: a methodological review. Ann. Assoc. Am. Geogr. 102(5), 1104–1112 (2012)
17. Zhou, X., Yu, Z., Yuan, L., Wang, L., Wu, C.: Measuring accessibility of healthcare facilities for populations with multiple transportation modes considering residential transportation mode choice. ISPRS Int. J. Geo-Inform. 9(6), 394 (2020)

Scenario-Based Model for the Location of Multiple Uncapacitated Facilities: Case Study in an Agro-Food Supply Chain

Gean Pablo Mendoza-Ortega[1]($\boxtimes$) , Manuel Soto[2] , José Ruiz-Meza[3] ,
Rodrigo Salgado[1], and Angelica Torregroza[1]

[1] Corporación Universitaria del Caribe, Sincelejo, Colombia
{gean.mendoza,rodrigo.salgado,angelica.torregroza}@cecar.edu.co
[2] Universidad Tecnológica de Bolívar, Cartagena, Colombia
mjsoto@utb.edu.co
[3] Universidad de La Sabana, Chía, Colombia
joserume@unisabana.edu.co

Abstract. Supply chains for agricultural products have taken on great importance in recent times due to the need that exists for consumers to acquire fresh products in excellent quality conditions. In the design of supply networks for this type of product, the location of facilities and allocation decisions are among the most relevant decisions in operations management, which in many cases involve aspects of uncertainty. This research proposes to plan the distribution of multiple agro-food products taking into account the location and capacities of producers, potential location of facilities and variations in crop yields. A scenario-based optimization model for the location of multiple uncapacitated facilities is developed. The model is tested in the cassava agro-food chain in Sucre, Colombia. First, the description for the construction of the scenarios for the uncertainty associated with the yield per hectare of cassava crops is presented. Next, the mixed integer programming model (MIP) for the location of uncapacitated facilities (UFLP) is presented. The aim of the model is to minimize operational distribution costs. The results of the case study were obtained with the help of the CPLEX Solver integrated in GAMS in low computational time. A reduction of costs by almost 60% of the distribution costs is obtained.

Keywords: Agro-food supply chain · Facility location · Mixed integer programming · Scenario-based optimization

1 Introduction

The supply chain (SC) of a typical product starts with material input, followed by production, and finally, distribution of the final product to customers [1]. In [2] define that a SC is composed of all parties involved, either directly or

---

Corporación Universitaria del Caribe.

J. C. Figueroa-García et al. (Eds.): WEA 2021, CCIS 1431, pp. 386–398, 2021.
https://doi.org/10.1007/978-3-030-86702-7_33

indirectly, with the sole function of satisfying the customer. Similarly, in [3] define the SC as a network of retailers, distributors, transporters, warehouses, and suppliers involved in the production, distribution, and sale of a product to the consumer. In [4] classify SC-related activities into four areas such as sourcing, production, inventory, and transportation/distribution. Therefore, the SC is a distribution network composed of facilities and transportation flows between these facilities. This network fulfills functions such as suppliers, factories, warehouses, distribution centers, among others. Supply Chain Management (SCM) efficiently integrates suppliers, manufacturers, warehouses, and retailers. SCM aims to ensure that products are produced and distributed in the correct quantities, at the locations, and at the time, to minimize system-wide costs while meeting service level requirements [5].

Most studies focus on SCMs dedicated to manufacturing products and services, and only a few studies focus on agricultural products in food supply chains [6]. Therefore, SCM for agricultural products has become relevant in the last decade as Agri-Food Supply Chains (ASC). Unlike other SCMs in ASCs, there is a continuous and significant change in product quality [7]. In addition, products are perishable, prices are sensitive, and high quality is demanded [8]. For SCs involving fresh foods, distribution planning is complex due to the nature and source of the product, the rival interaction between the SC, and the marketplace [9].

Location decisions are strategic and are hard to make for an efficient SC design. In addition, deciding where to locate leads to high facility costs [10]. Therefore, localization problems vary according to the particularity of the cases, the objective, and the constraints that seek to minimize, equalize, or maximize problems. In the literature, this type of problem is called Facility Location problem (FLP) [11]. One of the variants of this model is the uncapacitated FLP (UFLP), called by other names such as uncapacitated, simple, and optimal [12].

Optimization models for ASCs are deterministic or under uncertainty, depending on the type of information in the problem [13]. Several researchers present stochastic approaches to deal with uncertainty for ASC models. However, its application is limited compared to deterministic models [6]. The uncapacitated multiple-warehouse location optimization model proposed in this paper is efficient for handling stochastic interval parameters limited to a range of variance. Additionally, the model presents optimal results of a real case for the cassava supply chain in the department of Sucre, Colombia. The application of operations research in real cases generates complex problems. However, there are alternatives and solution strategies that allow obtaining optimal or efficient results. A statistical analysis of the yield behavior of cassava crops (industrial and sweet) in the last ten years is performed for the case study. The intervals are grouped according to [14], taking the class mark as the scenario value. A tree with 16 possible scenarios in the yields of sweet and industrial cassava crops is constructed. The study problem is solved using the General Algebraic Modeling System (GAMS) software with the CPLEX solver, generating optimal results in low computational times. Another differentiating factor of the study carried out in the cassava agro-food chain is to consider the crop yield with a probabilistic behavior due to its dependence on environmental factors. This type of consideration allows for early warning of food safety management [14].

The remainder of this document is structured as follows. Section 2 provides a brief review of the literature. Section 3 defines the mathematical model. Section 4 presents the elements of the cassava agro-food supply chain as a case study. Section 5 details the experimental results. Finally, the conclusions of the model, the case study, and future research lines are summarized in Sect. 6.

2   Related Literature

The FLP is a combinatorial optimization problem[15] that aims to minimize the location and service cost associated with facilities [16]. One of the variants of this problem is UFLP, which is Np-hard framed within binary optimization [17]. This variant considers that the capacity of the facility is unlimited, giving fulfillment of all customer demand [17,18]. Some UFLP models aim to optimize transportation costs and minimize opening costs [19]. In addition, to consider more realistic situations, uncertainty is included in some parameters, such as demand [16]. Different approaches have been developed in the literature to solve this type of problem, such as mixed integer programming [20], dynamic programming [21], and quadratic programming [19]. These techniques are efficient with the simple structure of the problem and generate results in low computational times [17]. However, given the Np-hard nature, some approximate methods have been developed.

To solve the UFLP, [12] apply Tabu Search (TS) by obtaining efficient solutions on a test data set from the literature. The results are compared with optimal solutions to check the efficiency of the algorithm. Similarly, [15] apply TS and compare it with approaches such as the Lagrangian method showing better results. For real cases, [22] solve the UFLP by implementing a discrete variant of the metaheuristic called Unconscious Search (US). This approach presents three steps: construction, construction review, and local search. The results obtained show a high performance compared to other algorithms. [17] develop an improved scatter search (ISS) based on the scatter search algorithm (SS). The method presents improvements oriented to the application of different techniques of crossover and mutation of the best solutions found in the local search. The algorithm is compared with other metaheuristics such as Genetic Algorithm (GA), Particle Swarm Optimization (PSO), Artificial Bee Colony (ABC), Differential Evolution (DE), Tree-Seed Algorithm (TSA), and Artificial Algae Algorithm (AAA), showing better solutions.

2.1   Optimization Model Under Uncertainty

Network design models involving uncertainty aspects are divided into three main groups: i. conditions where the uncertainty factor is considered. ii. models based on the probabilistic approximation that represents random variables with known probability distributions. iii. scenario-based approximation [23]. In the latter approach, a discrete number of scenarios of the random parameters represents the uncertainty of the SC. Similar to [24], a scenario tree representing the possible realizations of the stochastic parameters is constructed. Each path from the root to one of the leaves represents a particular scenario; a scenario is a realization of the uncertain parameter along the stages at a given time [25]. For the probability associated with each scenario, [26] states that Ω represents the set of all possible outcomes of the experiment. Also, probability is defined as an application such as and $P(\Omega) = 1$ y $P(A_1 \cup A_2) = P(A_1) + P(A_2)$.

3   Model Description

The uncapacitated location model for distribution planning in an agri-food supply chain presents the following assumptions. i. there are multiple products, ii. the location of producers (suppliers), distributors, processing plants, and warehouses is known. iii. the yield of products per hectare cultivated has a stochastic behavior. iv. warehouse capacities are infinite. v. flows are allowed only between two consecutive echelons in the chain, and no flows are allowed between elements of the same echelon, nor skipping echelon. vi. production and transportation costs are deterministic. The entire quantity of sweet cassava flows to the distributors through the warehouses. Finally, the shipment from the warehouses to the customers uses vehicles with a capacity of 30 tons. The index, parameters, and decision variables used in the formulation of the model are detailed below (Tables 1 and 2).

Equation (1) minimizes distribution costs in logistics operations from producers to distributors and processors through the facilities. Constrain (2) and (3) guarantees that no flow takes values above the possible quantities to be produced. Constrains (4) and (5) ensure demand compliance. Constrains (6) and (7) limit the number of facilities to be opened. Constrains (8) and (9) give viability to fixed cost generation in open facilities. Finally, constrains (10), (11) and (12) correspond to the restrictions of non-negative and binary admissible values for decision variables.

$$Minz = \sum_{i \in L} \sum_{q \in Q} \sum_{h \in H} \sum_{k \in K} \sum_{e \in E} \frac{P}{V_e} \times QV_{iqhke} \times \varphi_e$$

$$+ \sum_{j \in L} \sum_{q \in Q} \sum_{h \in H} \sum_{k \in K} \sum_{e \in E} \frac{P}{I_e} \times QI_{jqhke} \times \varphi_e + \sum_{i \in L} \sum_{q \in Q} \sum_{h \in H} \sum_{k \in K} \sum_{e \in E} CT1_{iqh} \times QV_{iqhke} \times \varphi_e$$

$$+ \sum_{j \in L} \sum_{q \in Q} \sum_{h \in H} \sum_{k \in K} \sum_{e \in E} CT2_{jqh} \times QI_{jqhke} \times \varphi_e + \sum_{i \in L} \sum_{q \in Q} \sum_{h \in H} \sum_{k \in K} \sum_{e \in E} \frac{QV_{iqhke}}{30} \times CV \varphi_e$$

$$+ \sum_{j \in L} \sum_{q \in Q} \sum_{h \in H} \sum_{k \in K} \sum_{e \in E} \frac{QI_{jqhke}}{30} \times CV \varphi_e + \sum_{q \in Q} CFA_q \times Y_q \quad (1)$$

Table 1. Model parameters.

Symbol	Meaning
$l \in L$	Set of producers/product ($l = 1, 2, 3, ..., L$)
$i \in L^1$	Subset of sweet cassava producers ($L^1 \subset L$)
$j \in L^2$	Subset of industrial cassava producers ($L^2 \subset L$)
$q \in Q$	Set of facilities ($q = 1, 2, 3, ..., n$)
$k \in K$	Set of processors ($k = 1, 2, 3, ..., t$)
$h \in H$	Set of distributors ($h = 1, 2, 3, ..., s$)
$e \in E$	Set of scenarios ($e = 1, 2, 3, ..., w$)
g_i	Maximum capacity of sweet cassava producers i
g_j	Maximum capacity of industrial cassava producers j
V_e	Yield in tons per hectare of sweet cassava crop according to the scenario e
I_e	Yield in tons per hectare of industrial cassava crop according to the scenario e
D_h	Distributor demand h
D'_k	Processors demand k
$CT1_{iqh}$	Cost of transporting the product between the producers i through the facility q to the distributors h
$CT2_{jqh}$	Cost of transporting the product between the producers j through the facility q to the distributors h
CFA_q	Fixed cost to open a facility q
CV	Vehicle preparation cost
M	Maximum number of facilities allowed to be opened
P	Fixed production cost associated with planting requirements and crop assistance for the product
$\varphi_e : 0 \leq \varphi_e \leq 1$	Scenario probability e. For $e \in E : \sum_{e \in E} \varphi_e = 1$

Table 2. Decision variables.

Symbol	Meaning
QV_{iqhke}	Represents the flow from the producer i to the distributor h or processor k through the facility k on the scenario e
QI_{jqhke}	Represents the flow from the producer j to the distributor h or processor k through the facility k on the scenario e
Y_q	Binary variable. $Y_q = 1$ if the facility is open. $Y_q = 0$ otherwise
$Y1_{qh}$	Binary variable. $Y1_{qh} = 1$ if the facility q is assigned to serve the distributor h. $Y1_{qh} = 0$ otherwise
$Y2_{qk}$	$Y2_{qk} = 1$ if the facility q is assigned to serve the processor k. $Y2_{qk} = 0$ otherwise

s.t.

$$\sum_{q\in Q}\sum_{h\in h}\sum_{k\in K} QV_{iqhke} \leq V_e \times g_i, \ \forall\, l \in L, \ e \in E \tag{2}$$

$$\sum_{q\in Q}\sum_{h\in h}\sum_{k\in K} QI_{jqhke} \leq I_e \times g_j, \ \forall\, l \in L, \ e \in E \tag{3}$$

$$\sum_{i\in L} QV_{iqhke} \leq D_h \times Y1_{qh}, \ \forall\, q \in Q, \ h \in H, \ k \in K, \ e \in E \tag{4}$$

$$\sum_{j\in L} QI_{jqhke} \leq D'_k \times Y2_{qk}, \ \forall\, q \in Q, \ k \in K, \ e \in E \tag{5}$$

$$\sum_{q\in Q} Y1_{qh} \leq M \ \forall\, h \in H \tag{6}$$

$$\sum_{q\in Q} Y1_{qk} \leq M \ \forall\, k \in K \tag{7}$$

$$Y1_{qh} = Y_q, \ \forall q \in Q, \ h \in H \tag{8}$$

$$Y2_{qk} = Y_q, \ \forall q \in Q, \ k \in K \tag{9}$$

$$QV_{iqhke} \geq 0, \ \forall\, i \in L, \ q \in Q, \ h \in H, \ k \in K, e \in E \tag{10}$$

$$QI_{jqhke} \geq 0, \ \forall\, j \in L, \ q \in Q, \ h \in H, \ k \in K, e \in E \tag{11}$$

$$Y_q, Y1_{qh}, Y2_{qk} \in \{0,1\}, \ \forall q \in Q, \ h \in H, k \in K \tag{12}$$

4   Description of the Case Study

The Department of Sucre, Colombia, is agriculturally oriented. The agricultural sector is the second-largest contributor to the Gross Domestic Product (GDP). One of the most representative crops of Sucre is the cassava [27]. Cassava is a plant that supplies a high-carbohydrate tuber. Two types of cassava are grown in Sucre, industrial and sweet, most of the M-Tai and Venezuelan varieties, respectively; the latter is for human consumption. The product flow begins with the production of cassava roots during the cultivation stage. At this stage, there is seed selection, sowing, crop maintenance, and finally, harvesting. There is a great uncertainty linked to crop yields due to the variety of soils, environmental conditions, and the level of technical labor. Harvesting is generally in rural areas that are difficult to access, so it is necessary to transport the crop in tractor vehicles to the municipalities and store it in the open air. Subsequently, once the required quantity is available, the cassava roots are transported in larger trucks. Purchasing agents plan the sweet cassava process. The activities correspond to the purchase and sale of different distribution centers located mainly in Sincelejo, Corozal, Cartagena, and Barranquilla. One of the biggest problems in the SC is storage without the necessary measures to maintain product quality.

On the other hand, industrial cassava is transported to processors to obtain native starch used as raw material in various sectors. A by-product of cassava is cassava chips for animal feed production. Currently, the scheduling of cassava root harvesting and distribution activities depends mainly on the empirical experiences of producers and purchasing agents. It is difficult to achieve an optimal scheduling sequence and operation of the SC due to the limitations of human judgment. Therefore, it is necessary to formulate a multi-facility location optimization model to improve logistics operations. This model aims to minimize the total costs of the system, model the uncertainty present in the chain, and improve the food safety of the product. Therefore, it includes an echelon between producers, processing plants, and distributors. Figure 1 shows a diagram of the cassava agri-food supply chain in Colombia. The echelons demarcated by the dots are those that have direct relevance in the department of Sucre.

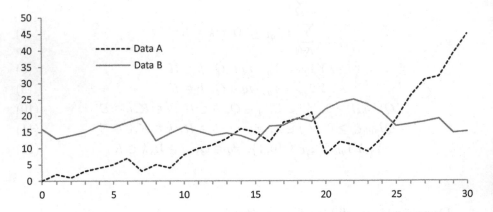

Fig. 1. Agro-food supply chain structure of cassava in Colombia.

4.1 Identification and Determination of Uncertain Parameters

This research uses the scenario analysis methodology as shown in Sect. 2.1 to recreate the yield variability of sweet and industrial cassava crops. The analysis of sweet cassava crop yield variations for 2007–2017 is in Fig. 2(a). The average is in the range of 8 to 12 tons/ha. As time has passed, yield variations have decreased. For industrial cassava, the average is in the range from 15 tons/ha to approximately 18 tons/ha (see Fig. 2(b)). In addition, the crop has not varied considerably between the years included in this period. However, in 2012, no yield information was obtained for this crop, as reported by Agronet [28].

The yield behavior of sweet and industrial cassava crops in Sucre presents a variability associated with a degree of uncertainty. Based on this, it is necessary to build scenarios to represent the uncertainty [29]. Statistical analysis was performed in Statgraphics Centurion XVII software. Figure 2(c) shows the histogram of sweet cassava yields grouped into four intervals [30]. The height of the bars denotes the absolute frequency of the yield data, representing the

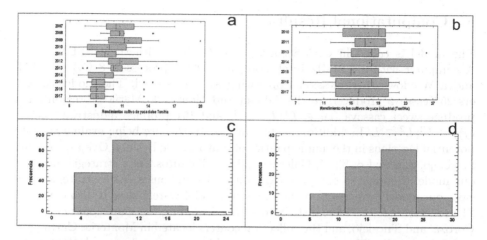

Fig. 2. Cassava crop yields (2007 to 2017) and Frequency histogram for the yield of sweet cassava crop.

probability for the scenarios. There is a higher height in the range between 8.25 and 13.5 and a class mark or midpoint of 10.875 ton. The histogram of industrial cassava yields is shown in Fig. 2(d). The interval with the highest height equivalent to 33 data points in the range 17.5–23.7 and a class mark or midpoint of 20.625. Subsequently the scenario tree is developed by taking the class marks of each interval as an event of the possible outcomes (i.e., there are four intervals for sweet cassava yield and four intervals for industrial cassava yield, leading to 16 scenarios in total, represented as $RDYD_n$ and $RDYI_m$; where n and m = 1, 2, 3, 4). The probabilities are shown in Table 3.

Table 3. Scenario probability.

Scenarios	Yield sweet C (Ton/Ha)	Yield industrial C (Ton/Ha)	Probability of events YD	Probability of events Yi	Scenario probability
E1	5.625	8.125	0.331	0.1333	0.04415
E2	5.625	14.375	0.3312	0.32	0.10598
E3	5.625	20.625	0.3312	0.44	0.14573
E4	5.625	26.875	0.3312	0.1067	0.03534
E5	10.875	8.125	0.6104	0.1333	0.08137
E6	10.875	14.375	0.6104	0.32	0.19533
E7	10.875	20.625	0.6104	0.44	0.26858
E8	10.875	26.875	0.6104	0.1067	0.06513
E9	16.125	8.125	0.0519	0.1333	0.00692
E10	16.125	14.375	0.0519	0.32	0.01661
E11	16.125	20.625	0.0519	0.44	0.02284
E12	16.125	26.875	0.0519	0.1067	0.00554
E13	21.375	8.125	0.0065	0.1333	0.00087
E14	21.375	14.375	0.0065	0.32	0.00208
E15	21.375	20.625	0.0065	0.44	0.00286
E16	21.375	26.875	0.0065	0.1067	0.00069

5   Computational Results

The model is coded in GAMS software and solved with the CPLEX solver. A computer with a 2.2 GHz Intel Core I5 - 5200U processor, 8 GB of RAM, and a Windows 10 Professional operating system is used. The model considers 254 cassava producers in the Sabana and Montes de María subregions. 103 produce sweet cassava $(i) i \in L^1; L^1 \subset L$ and 151 produce industrial cassava $(j) j \in L^2; L^2 \subset L$. In addition, eight warehouses (Q) are being evaluated, with potential locations in the municipalities of San Juan de Betulia, Ovejas, Corozal, Sincelejo, San Pedro, Sincé, Galeras, and Los Palmitos. As a strategic decision, our model proposes to open a maximum of 4 warehouses. As a strategic decision, our model proposes to open a maximum of 4 warehouses. It also considers 21 processors (K) and five distributors (H), including the municipal markets of Corozal and Sincelejo, and the collection centers located in Monteria, Cartagena, and Barranquilla. The parameters and variables correspond to production costs, transportation costs, availability of area for growth, demand, and production quantities closely linked to yields in each of the scenarios. The period considered in this case study is four months (October, November, December, and January). This period corresponds to the cassava root harvest in the department of Sucre.

Yield variability of sweet and industrial cassava crops generates two conditions. The first corresponds to an average yield scenario called ESC PROME. Yield variability of sweet and industrial cassava crops generates two conditions. The first corresponds to an average yield scenario called ESC PROME. The second condition corresponds to 16 scenarios, called ESC PROB that contemplate the variability and probability associated with each one (Table 4). For ESC PROME, the objective function generates distribution costs of $ COP 36,068'981,374. A total of three warehouses are opened. The solution is obtained in 388 iterations, a relative GAP of 0.5%, and a computational time of 1.92 s.

For ESC PROB, the objective function minimizes distribution costs by COP $ 58,718'387,753 with the opening of four warehouses. The solution has 9755 iterations, a relative GAP of 0.1%, and a computational time of 22.3 s. Table 5 presents the comparison between the average scenario solution and the solution obtained under uncertainty conditions as proposed by [27]. This comparison consists of simulating what happens in a particular scenario where is present and calculating the objective function that reports evaluating the solution vector of the probabilistic scenario (ESC PROB) at. This value is compared with the one obtained by evaluating the solution vector of the average scenario in. The comparison is made for each of the scenarios in the tree.

Table 4. Scenario probability.

Scenario	ESC PROME	ESC PROB	ABS GAP	REL GAP (%)
1	$ 34,014,059,748	$ 33,956,245,553	$ 57,814,195	0.17
2	$ 35,324,659,234	$ 35,235,600,282	$ 89,058,952	0.25
3	$ 36,635,258,719	$ 36,514,955,012	$ 120,303,707	0.33
4	$ 37,945,858,205	$ 37,794,309,741	$ 151,548,464	0.40
5	$ 34,349,164,772	$ 34,190,370,952	$ 158,793,820	0.46
6	$ 35,659,764,257	$ 35,469,725,681	$ 190,038,576	0.53
7	$ 36,970,363,743	$ 36,749,080,411	$ 221,283,332	0.60
8	$ 38,280,963,228	$ 38,028,435,140	$ 252,528,088	0.66
9	$ 34,916,213,855	$ 34,583,930,512	$ 332,283,343	0.95
10	$ 36,226,813,340	$ 35,863,285,241	$ 363,528,099	1.00
11	$ 37,537,412,826	$ 37,142,639,970	$ 394,772,856	1.05
12	$ 38,848,012,311	$ 38,421,994,699	$ 426,017,612	1.10
13	$ 35,569,658,879	$ 35,112,758,888	$ 456,899,991	1.28
14	$ 36,880,258,365	$ 36,392,113,617	$ 488,144,748	1.32
15	$ 38,190,857,850	$ 37,671,468,347	$ 519,389,503	1.36
16	$ 39,501,457,335	$ 38,950,823,076	$ 550,634,259	1.39

In this sense, if scenario 13 occurs, the solution of the average scenario replaced in the objective function of scenario 13 presents a value of ESC PROM = $COP 35,569'658,879. On the other hand, the solution of the probabilistic model associated with scenario 13, if replaced in the objective function for this scenario, yields a result for ESC PROB = COP $35,112'758,888. The absolute difference GAP ABS = ESC PROB - ESC PROM is $COP 456'899,991. Therefore, for this scenario, the solution obtained in ESC PROB is 1.28% better than ESC PROM. Thus, the solution under uncertainty conditions is better than the average scenario solution.

Warehouse capacities correspond to the amount of product passing through the warehouse. The minimum capacity for establishing warehouses corresponds to the scenario where the yield per hectare is lower (Scenario 1). The maximum capacity of the warehouse corresponds to the amount of distribution in the highest yield scenario (Scenario 16). The harvest period is four months (in this study, it represents one year of production). The calculation of the daily capacities consists of dividing the annual quantity into the corresponding months. The warehouse with the highest capacity in the 16 scenarios is in the municipality of Ovejas, with a minimum capacity of 245 tons/day and a maximum capacity of 817 tons/day.

In addition, to observe the impact generated on the costs associated with the distribution of the cassava agri-food chain in Sucre, a new scenario is created that compares the current conditions of the CS. The new scenario prioritizes a producer with one hectare of land devoted to the crop with a yield of 5,625 tons/ha and a production of 5625 tons of sweet cassava. Given the current conditions, this product is sent using a tractor to the nearest town (in this case, the municipality of Sincé). Later, it is transported in a truck to the distributor (Corozal's public market). However, the model solution recommends shipping the product through warehouse number eight, located in Los Palmitos. Then, ship the product to the Corozal market. Distribution costs are shown in Table 5. In addition, warehouse administration and management costs are considered (20% of operating costs).

Table 5. Scenario probability.

Scenarios	Denomination	Costs
Current	Primary cost	$ 246,822
	Secondary cost	$ 55,068
	Cost - handling Agent	$ 776,250
	Total current	$ 1,078,140
Proposed	Primary cost	$ 277,107
	Secondary cost	$ 21,276
	Cost - Installation	$ 28,180
	Recruitment cost	$ 65,621
	Administrative costs (20%)	$ 78,437
	Proposed total	$ 470,621

6   Conclusions

This paper presents an unconstrained model for the location of agri-food supply chain facilities applied to a real case study corresponding to cassava production in the department of Sucre. The model incorporates the variations that occur in yields in tons per hectare due to the environmental conditions of the department, soil characteristics, and crop management. In addition, the model is multi-product and evaluates a chain in a department with deficiencies in the protection of environmental and mechanical risk factors of the product in the processes of packaging, storage, transportation, and post-harvest handling. The solution proposes the opening of four warehouses to provide strategic support to logistics operations in the SC. The expected costs correspond to COP $ 58,718'387,753. The results show a low computational time, a relative optimality tolerance of 10% (optcr = 0.1), and a relative gap equal to 0.001430. Based on the scenario recreated with the first cassava producer, the model generates a decrease of approximately 60% in distribution costs.

For future research, it is necessary to use scenarios to represent the individual variability of crop yields in each producer. Another uncertain factor in this type of model is the selling price. Similarly, it is necessary to include environmental parameters such as water availability and a method of post-harvest product preservation.

References

1. Chen, Z.-L.: Integrated production and distribution operations. In: Simchi-Levi, D., Wu, S.D., Shen, Z.J. (eds.) Handbook of Quantitative Supply Chain Analysis, pp. 711–745. Springer, Boston (2004). https://doi.org/10.1007/978-1-4020-7953-5_17
2. Chopra, S., Meindl, P.: Administración de la cadena de suministro. Pearson educación (2013)
3. Muñoz Aguilar, R.A., Roldan Zuluaga, S.: Competitividad Y Cadenas De Abastecimiento En El Sector Productivo Del Valle Del Cauca, Colombia (competitiveness and supply chain in the productive sector of Valle Del Cauca, Colombia). Revista Global de Negocios 4(1), 77–87 (2015)
4. Reina, M.L., Adarme, W.: Logística de distribución de productos perecederos: estudios de caso Fuente de Oro (Meta) y Viotá (Cundinamarca). Rev. Colomb. Ciencias Hortícolas 8(1), 80–91 (2017)
5. Simchi-Levi, D., Kaminsky, P., Simchi-Levi, E., Shankar, R.: Designing and Managing the Supply Chain: Concepts, Strategies and Case Studies. Tata McGraw-Hill Education, New York (2008)
6. Paam, P., Berretta, R., Heydar, M., Middleton, R.H., García-Flores, R., Juliano, P.: Planning models to optimize the agri-fresh food supply chain for loss minimization: a review. Ref. Module Food Sci. (2016)
7. Ahumada, O., Villalobos, J.R.: Application of planning models in the agri-food supply chain: a review. Eur. J. Oper. Res. 196(1), 1–20 (2009). https://doi.org/10.1016/j.ejor.2008.02.014
8. Salin, V.: Information technology in agri-food supply chains. Int. Food Agribus. Manag. Rev. 1(3), 329–334 (1998). https://doi.org/10.1016/S1096-7508(99)80003-2
9. Amorim, P., Günther, H.-O., Almada-Lobo, B.: Multi-objective integrated production and distribution planning of perishable products. Int. J. Prod. Econ. 138(1), 89–101 (2012). https://doi.org/10.1016/j.ijpe.2012.03.005
10. Daskin, M.S., Snyder, L.V., Berger, R.T.: Facility location in supply chain design. In: Langevin, A., Riopel, D. (eds.) Logistics Systems: Design and Optimization, pp. 39–65. Springer, Boston (2005). https://doi.org/10.1007/0-387-24977-X_2
11. Solimanpur, M., Kamran, M.A.: Solving facilities location problem in the presence of alternative processing routes using a genetic algorithm. Comput. Ind. Eng. 59(4), 830–839 (2010). https://doi.org/10.1016/j.cie.2010.08.010
12. Al-Sultan, K.S., Al-Fawzan, M.A.: A tabu search approach to the uncapacitated facility location problem. Ann. Oper. Res. 86, 91–103 (1999). https://doi.org/10.1023/A:1018956213524
13. Min, H., Zhou, G.: Supply chain modeling: past, present and future. Comput. Ind. Eng. 43(1), 231–249 (2002). https://doi.org/10.1016/S0360-8352(02)00066-9
14. Everingham, Y.L., Muchow, R.C., Stone, R.C., Inman-Bamber, N.G., Singels, A., Bezuidenhout, C.N.: Enhanced risk management and decision-making capability across the sugarcane industry value chain based on seasonal climate forecasts. Agric. Syst. 74(3), 459–477 (2002). https://doi.org/10.1016/S0308-521X(02)00050-1

15. Sun, M.: Solving the uncapacitated facility location problem using tabu search. Comput. Oper. Res. **33**(9), 2563–2589 (2006). https://doi.org/10.1016/j.cor.2005. 07.014

16. De Armas, J., Juan, A.A., Marquès, J.M., Pedroso, J.P.: Solving the deterministic and stochastic uncapacitated facility location problem: from a heuristic to a simheuristic. J. Oper. Res. Soc. **68**(10), 1161–1176 (2017). https://doi.org/10. 1057/s41274-016-0155-6

17. Hakli, H., Ortacay, Z.: An improved scatter search algorithm for the uncapacitated facility location problem. Comput. Ind. Eng. **135**, 855–867 (2019). https://doi.org/ 10.1016/j.cie.2019.06.060

18. Verter, V.: Uncapacitated and capacitated facility location problems. In: Eiselt, H.A., Marianov, V. (eds.) Foundations of Location Analysis. ISORMS, vol. 155, pp. 25–37. Springer, New York (2011). https://doi.org/10.1007/978-1-4419-7572-0_2

19. Ramshani, M., Ostrowski, J., Zhang, K., Li, X.: Two level uncapacitated facility location problem with disruptions. Comput. Ind. Eng. **137**, 106089 (2019). https:// doi.org/10.1016/j.cie.2019.106089

20. Mousavi, S.M., Vahdani, B., Tavakkoli-Moghaddam, R.: Optimal design of the cross-docking in distribution networks: heuristic solution approach. Int. J. Eng. **27**(4), 533–544 (2014). https://doi.org/10.5829/idosi.ije.2014.27.04a.04

21. Cortinhal, M.J., Lopes, M.J., Melo, M.T.: Dynamic design and re-design of multi-echelon, multi-product logistics networks with outsourcing opportunities: a computational study. Comput. Ind. Eng. **90**, 118–131 (2015). https://doi.org/10.1016/ j.cie.2015.08.019

22. Ardjmand, E., Park, N., Weckman, G., Amin-Naseri, M.R.: The discrete Unconscious search and its application to uncapacitated facility location problem. Comput. Ind. Eng. **73**(1), 32–40 (2014). https://doi.org/10.1016/j.cie.2014.04.010

23. Escobar, J.W.: Rediseño de una red de distribución con variabilidad de demanda usando la metodología de escenarios. Rev. Fac. Ing. **21**(32), 9–19 (2013)

24. Quinteros, M., Alonso, A., Escudero, L., Guignard, M., Weintraub, A.: Una aplicación de programación estocástica en un problema de gestión forestal. Rev. Ing. Sist. XX (2006)

25. Alonso-Ayuso, A., Escudero, L.F., Guignard, M., Weintraub, A.: On dealing with strategic and tactical decision levels in forestry planning under uncertainty. Comput. Oper. Res. **115**, 104836 (2020). https://doi.org/10.1016/j.cor.2019.104836

26. Ramos, A., Alonso-Ayuso, A., Pérez, G.: Optimización bajo incertidumbre. Universidad Pontificia Comillas (2011)

27. de Económico, S.: Encuesta Nacional Agropecuaria de los periodos 2007 a 2017 (2018)

28. Agronet: Base Agricola EVA 2007 - 2017 (2017). http://www.agronet.gov.co/ estadistica/Paginas/default.aspx. Accessed 4 Oct 2018

29. Govindan, K., Fattahi, M., Keyvanshokooh, E.: Supply chain network design under uncertainty: a comprehensive review and future research directions. Eur. J. Oper. Res. **263**(1), 108–141 (2017). https://doi.org/10.1016/j.ejor.2017.04.009

30. Martínez Bencardino, C.: Estadística y muestreo. e-libro, Corp. (2012)

Application of the CERT Values Measurement Model for Organizational Culture in the Management and Quality Company

Claudia Yadira Rodríguez-Ríos[✉] [iD], Abigail Calderón Narváez[iD], and Santiago Cárdenas Jiménez[iD]

Colombian School of Engineering Julio Garavito, Bogotá, Colombia
claudia.rodriguez@escuelaing.edu.co, {abigail.calderon, santiago.cardenas}@mail.escuelaing.edu.co

Abstract. At present, it has been shown that very few SMEs have knowledge of the Business Process Management BPM system, which offers a series of strategies and benefits oriented towards processes, using technology systems in terms of information management, evaluating the organizational culture and covering all the operational and business processes of the organization, in order to increase productivity and competitiveness, guaranteeing continuous improvement of internal processes following their life cycle, where they are documented, analyzed, improved, are implemented, and are monitored and controlled.

In this study, the BPM culture of an information technology SME, called Management and Quality, was evaluated based on the study carried out by Jan Vom Brocke, in which 4 values are established, which are: customer orientation, excellence, responsibility, and teamwork, called CERT values, the survey adapted to the context of the company and Colombia was applied; As a result, opportunities for improvement in excellence were found represented by the dimensions of continuous improvement and innovation, and in the formal structures, dimension of teamwork, recommendations were made for these findings.

Keywords: BPM culture · CERT values · Business Process Management (BPM)

1 Introduction

BPM is a comprehensive approach that is based on aspects such as: continuous improvement, process automation and organizational culture focused on processes, which is contrasted with the functional vision that originates in Taylorism and additionally, takes components of Total Quality Management (TQM) and the Process Reengineering (BPR) approach, contributing to the development of the systemic concept of process management [1–3].

The theory of BPM is currently a study of great importance and high applicability because many new companies have dedicated to implementing the theory developed by Jan Vom Brocke to improve both internal processes and their efficiency and effectiveness through organizational values. The four values defined by Jan Vom Brocke to measure the

© Springer Nature Switzerland AG 2021
J. C. Figueroa-García et al. (Eds.): WEA 2021, CCIS 1431, pp. 399–408, 2021.
https://doi.org/10.1007/978-3-030-86702-7_34

BPM culture are: Customer Service, Excellence, Responsibility and Teamwork. These are abbreviated by their acronym in English, CERT. The values were determined based on the Delphi methodology, which consists of bringing together experts in the field of BPM from different nationalities, in order to have a global understanding of the concept of BPM culture. Further, this study provides empirical evidence of the relevance of the CERT values identified for the development of BPM initiatives, and based on this, the most relevant and influential ones were selected to create a receptive ecosystem in terms of implementation of the BPM and the evaluation of the organizational culture [1].

Highlighting the importance of values for the development of organizational culture, it can be stated that these are defined as what a group considers desirable or appropriate in terms of the set of actions that are located in its thinking scheme. The above indicates that the mental models that are had in each group directly influence their behavior patterns and work organization, which will determine the performance and productivity of the organization since these people are the ones who determine, according to their values, business continuity [4, 5].

In this document, a study will be developed based on the application of the CERT values proposed by Jan Vom Brocke, which are focused on the BPM culture. The research will be carried out at the Management and Quality company that provides consulting, solutions and professional services in business architecture, analytics, applications, document management, data governance, information security, and IT governance, developing its operations in Colombia.

The model was applied within the department of project and service management and, to facilitate the understanding of the instrument's questions, a group training was developed where each of the members of the department met, once the doubts and questions about it. The survey was applied to measure the BPM culture, represented with the CERT values, in order to find opportunities for improvement and propose recommendations so that the company can implement action plans to optimize the processes and the BPM culture of the company.

The questions posed by Jan Vom Brocke in his study are 40, which were adapted to the context of the Management and Quality organization in order to obtain more accurate and congruent results with the current situation of the company [6].

2 Methodology

For the development of the research, a systematic search for information was made in scientific articles, which guided the research with a rigorous contextual description of the topics that should be addressed. The articles were selected to identify, differentiate and choose the material, based on the theoretical criteria of the research and thus determine the key concepts that allow establishing which aspects favor the BPM culture in a work team (Anguera, 1986; Serrano & Ortiz, 2012). In addition, scientific databases such as ScienceDirect, JSTOR, Emerald, ProQuest, and EBSCO were consulted. The keywords used were: BPM, teamwork, culture, communication, leadership, empathy, performance, mental models, responsibility, CERT Values.

Subsequently, the model proposed by the research initially carried out by Jan Vom Brocke was applied, the instrument was applied to the personnel of the Project Management and Services area of the Management and Quality company and its management team through the use of technological means, with in order to collect the necessary data for the evaluation and measurement of the CERT values, which constitute the instrument for measuring the BPM culture offering a broad overview of the state of the organizational culture in the company, so that the company can generate action and improvement plans that strengthen this important aspect of the organization [1, 6].

Regarding the questions in the survey designed by Jan Vom Brocke, it should be noted that the Likert scale is used to assess the responses, they are classified by the dimensions of the CERT values, which are made up of: Internal Customer and External Client in terms of customer orientation, Continuous Improvement and Innovation from the perspective of excellence, Accountability and Commitment for the perspective of Responsibility, Formal Structures and Informal Structures regarding Teamwork [6].

From the external customer perspective, questions were asked that are related to the management of stakeholders that do not belong to the organization, but play an important role within the business. Likewise, questions are developed to evaluate the management of internal clients, who are part of the organization and, therefore, they must be guaranteed good working conditions and promote their motivation.

In addition, questions were developed based on excellence that are divided into continuous improvement and innovation. Continuous improvement refers to the techniques used to optimize internal processes based on the learning obtained from previous experiences and innovation, which refers to the novel improvement proposals raised by the members of the organization, in order to generate value in the processes. Regarding the value of responsibility, it is intended to evaluate the fulfillment of the goals and tasks by the workers, as well as the commitment they have to carry out their work and thus contribute to business growth.

Finally, teamwork will be evaluated taking into account the formal structures, which refer to the communication that the workers have and the teamwork skills to solve different problems that may arise. On the other hand, there are informal structures, which refer to the interpersonal relationships that workers have, empathy with their colleagues, the interaction between work teams and other practices that contribute to the development of work and promote employee motivation.

The research carried out will be applied in such a way that it can be used as a conceptual framework in which the organizational culture of the companies will be evaluated and measured, taking into account that the processes constitute the center in which the businesses move, therefore, the support of each of the company's collaborators is of vital importance, based on the recognition and acceptance of the need to change the methodologies regarding the development of processes or their thinking at a general level, in order to promote the continuous improvement of the organization [2].

Regarding the present case in the Management and Quality company, the survey questions were adapted to facilitate the development of the study and obtain answers that are closer to the reality of the business and its particular characteristics. Additionally, in order for the workers to have more clarity about the survey, a previous training was developed directed by the researchers, in case the employees had doubts regarding the questions and to inform the purpose of the research.

3 Theoretical Framework

3.1 Business Process Management

Business Process Management (BPM) is an integrated management system based on the planning and establishment of processes, determination of the strategy and monitoring, which also has a technology component that allows it to properly manage processes by supporting the fulfillment of the strategic objectives of the organization, additionally, the management refers to the administration of the companies. The foregoing highlights the fact that BPM is associated with integrated systems, because these components make it a complete, holistic structure that is aligned with the same objectives [3].

It is also important to mention that, within the organization of the processes, where the positions are established, the people responsible for each of them and their corresponding functions generate an organizational structure oriented to these processes, which will directly affect the culture within the company. Company and consequently, the way in which all the activities that give life to the organization are carried out [3].

3.2 Organizational Culture from Systemic Thinking

Companies must be understood as a system in which not only missionary or operational processes related to their corporate purpose influence, but also those that comply with the exercise of providing support to these processes, since for their optimal functioning, interrelated acts must be developed that exhibit mutual effects; for this reason, it is necessary to mention that the systemic approach constitutes a conceptual framework with knowledge and tools that lead to the integration of both types of processes without fragmenting or seeing the system as isolated parts, which will allow observing patterns of thinking more clearly and identifying change agents that allow their modification to promote the improvement of the organization's performance.

One aspect that in many cases constitutes a barrier is that of mental models, which consist of ingrained assumptions, generalizations and images that influence the way of understanding the world and consequently, acting of human beings. Consequently, organizational mental models are also strongly rooted, and this can be evidenced, for example, in factors of resistance to change when trying to implement actions aimed at improving companies, or on the contrary, when outdated practices cannot be carried out to practice when they come across highly tactical and structured mental models [7, 8].

The discipline to work with organizational mental models begins with an introspection in which persons learn to analyze the internal conception of the world and make a scrutiny. After overcoming the internal barriers that skew the vision, it is important to foster the ability to constantly learn, which will lead to the formation of highly functional teams that promote trust by mutually socializing strengths and weaknesses, and aligning them towards strategic objectives. Which will produce better results [2, 8].

3.3 Organizational Culture in the Light of Business Process Management

One of the main factors that make up BPM corresponds to culture, which is understood mainly as a set of invisible values that act as guiding principles and are manifested in actions and structures that affect the effectiveness and efficiency of the processes that are established within the company [1, 2, 4].

The complexity within the concept of organizational culture lies in the multiculturalism of the work teams and, in many cases, in the diversity of national cultures, which requires greater flexibility in the organizational culture management strategies to maintain the motivation of team members. Additionally, several studies have indicated that the concept of culture within the BPM framework is not clearly specified in recent studies, so, in order to have greater clarity about the concept of organizational culture and its influence on the achievement of In the BPM objectives, four cultural values are defined that facilitate BPM management: Customer orientation, excellence, responsibility and teamwork, which are called CERT values for its acronym in English. Determining these values makes it easier to measure the degree to which an organization adopts the BPM culture [1, 6].

4 Results

For the development of the results, the data collected from the surveys completed by the members of the Management And Quality team were obtained, additionally, an analysis of reliability and validity of these was carried out, in order to obtain accurate results for the measurement of organizational culture. Once the data has been controlled, the level of the company regarding to each of the values is classified, along with the dimensions that compose them from the point of view and meaning of the BPM and the terminology of the CERT values [6].

The model was implemented making the use of technological tools and virtual media to the company's personnel, who have the following positions: consultant, specialist, assistant, general manager, project manager, senior consultant and analyst. Figure 1 synthesizes the results obtained in such a way that the 4 values can be viewed in a general way in a percentage classification for the measurement of the organizational culture and the opportunities for improvement that arise, in order to determine which of these has a lower score in the organization and propose action plans to increase these percentages.

In the previous figure, each of the results corresponding to each value can be fully evidenced, which presents a higher percentage in the areas of teamwork, and responsibility, this means that the company, broadly speaking, does a good communication management and distribution of work, together with the assignment of tasks to employees and a sense of commitment to responsibility, sharing a score of 83%. On the other hand, an opportunity for improvement in the company can be visualized with respect to the values with the best score within the study, which was the value of excellence with a percentage of 73%, which indicates that the company must implement plans action towards continuous improvement and innovation of processes, in order to create value in the performance of the organization increasing efficiency and effectiveness.

This can be achieved by creating an action plan focused on customer orientation, a value that plays an important role in improving processes, and that, in this case, presents a good percentage of participation in the model with an 82%, where it can relate the improvements within the internal and external processes. Based on the results seen above,

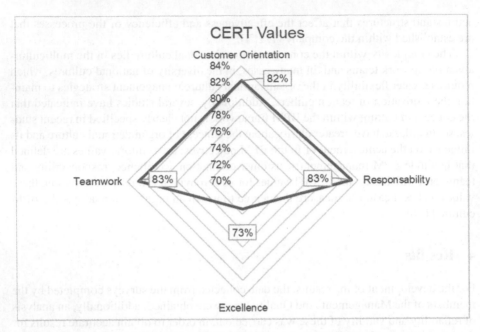

Fig. 1. General results of the measurement of CERT values.

if a company want to improve its efficiency and effectiveness, it must implement actions focused on improving the values with the lowest score to increase them, so that the BPM culture in the company is increased, to this, a more specific analysis must be done where a breakdown of the CERT values is made in the dimensions mentioned above, which are displayed in Table 1, and are taken as a reference for the action and improvement plan [6].

Table 1. CERT values dimensions.

Customer orientatión	Excellence	Responsability	Teamwork
External perspective	Continue Improvement	Accountability	Formal structures
Internal perspective	Innovation	Commitment	Informal structures

Source: (vom Brocke, 2011)

For the implementation of the actions to be taken, a radial graph was developed, which shows the representation of each dimension of the CERT values and their influence on the general results obtained previously, making a more detailed analysis focused on those with a lower rating.

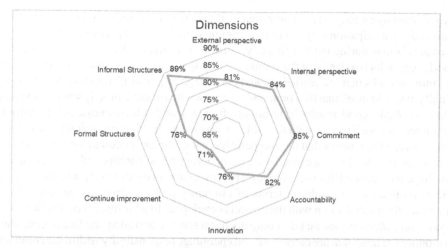

Fig. 2. Results of the dimensions of the CERT values

Once the specific analysis of the dimensions has been developed, shown in Fig. 2. it is possible to determine the representation of each of the dimensions taking into account the best scores and those that present opportunities for improvement, showing that the dimensions that make up the value of excellence are those that present a lower score compared to the others, which means that the company has a low tendency to implement innovation initiatives and continuous improvement management, obtaining scores of 76% and 71% respectively. Taking into account the above, it is important that the company develop programs for the creation of innovative ideas with work incentives, to promote the innovation of the processes in the organization, likewise, developing technological means and applications that facilitate the generation of ideas and that these function as communication channels where all ideas are taken into account. Regarding continuous improvement, the company must focus on the new success stories of other companies using tools such as benchmarking, in order to motivate the members of the organization to improve internal and external processes, making an analysis of the needs of the company, creating goals and objectives that measure the performance of the organization generating an increase in the performance of employees and consequently of the organization. Additionally, when making the specific analysis of the value of teamwork, despite the fact that it has a relatively high score, it has a low score within the formal structures of the organization, that is, the company does not have adequate communication channels between work areas and does not optimally distribute the tasks of each area for the fulfillment of the objectives and goals organizational.

On the other hand, the dimensions that present a higher score are the dimensions of informal structures (89%), commitment (85%), internal customer (84%), accountability (82%), external customer (81%). The above is evidence that employees have very good interpersonal relationships, increasing trust between them and creating an optimal work environment, in addition to having a good sense of commitment to the tasks of each employee with respect to the projects that are being developed and in this way meet the times stipulated by the external client. It can be seen that the organization takes into account its employees as an important value of the organization, taking into account their active participation within the organization's processes and promoting harmony and cordial relations during the working day, in addition to the rendering of accounts have a good score, which means that the company has a specific and adequate command line to monitor the tasks that are carried out and encourage responsibility within the company. Finally, it is evidenced that the company's processes are focused directly with the external client to obtain good results in terms of efficiency and effectiveness, additionally to guarantee their satisfaction with the projects developed. In addition, accountability has a good score, which means that the company has a specific and adequate line of command to monitor the tasks that are carried out and encourage responsibility within the company. Finally, it is evidenced that the company's processes are focused directly with the external client to obtain good results in terms of efficiency and effectiveness, additionally to guarantee their satisfaction with the projects developed. In addition, accountability has a good score, which means that the company has a specific and adequate line of command to monitor the tasks that are carried out and encourage responsibility within the company. Finally, it is evidenced that the company's processes are focused directly with the external client to obtain good results in terms of efficiency and effectiveness, additionally to guarantee their satisfaction with the projects developed.

5   Recommendations

Taking into account the results obtained, it can be seen that the Management and Quality company has a good level of application of the BPM culture, since it has high percentages for most of the CERT values, these are: responsibility, orientation to client and teamwork in terms of informal structures, however, an opportunity for improvement in the value of excellence was identified, since it has the lowest percentage among all the values measured in this company, so it is highly important to identify and develop actions aimed at improving the efficiency and effectiveness indicators, which will allow not only to increase the lowest percentages, but also to increase the values with the highest scores. In order to present the improvement opportunities presented by the value of excellence, the dimensions that compose it should be mentioned, which are: Continuous improvement and innovation.

Continuous improvement is an aspect that can be improved by generating feedback spaces from the external client regarding the projects developed by the organization, which will allow them to implement that feedback in future jobs and, in this way, offer a better service. Additionally, it is important that the company consider the use of tools that lead to the evaluation of the objectives that are set in order to see if they are really being met. A very useful tool for this purpose is the BPMN 2.0 notation to parameterize and monitor processes, in such a way that the company can have an indicator of how business practices are developing.

On the other hand, innovation management can be initially promoted through the training and development of the organization's staff regarding the implementation of agile methodologies such as SCRUM, since if all employees are trained and have knowledge of this tool that can be highly useful for business development, they can identify great innovation opportunities that can be applied in different areas such as: business practices, service development and improvements in existing services. Additionally, promoting the development of employees will allow them to feel more motivated and will significantly improve their perception of the organization, which will have a great influence on productivity and performance rates. These development initiatives are related to training, and should also be linked to the opportunities for employees to move up within the company and the work incentives available to them when they do excellent work. All of the above indicates that, by investing in the workforce, the company will have better results and will be on track towards its objective of growth and business development.

Regarding formal structures, it is important that the company considers the alignment of personal and strategic objectives in order to achieve business development, ensuring that employees can visualize the connection between the purpose and the business and also promoting their involvement within company levels.

Finally, for the values that obtained the highest scores within the development of this study, such as customer orientation, responsibility and teamwork, it is important to mention that these values can be optimized by implementing technological communication channels such as corporative social networks, allowing effective communication within all the areas that make up the company and that, likewise, this communication is fast. This will ensure that all departments are aligned and customer satisfaction can be guaranteed.

6   Conclusions

The purpose of this article and its greatest contribution is the research and application of the BPM culture measurement model proposed by Jan Vom Brocke, where it is possible to identify the degree to which the Management and Quality company promotes this culture taking into account the four main values that compose it and thus, determine in which it is at a good level, and in which it should be improved so that, in this way, the company can increase its efficiency and effectiveness to achieve a competitive advantage. These values allow to establish a notion about how current practices are being executed and if they are allowing the fulfillment of strategic purposes in order to identify improvement actions that promote continuous change.

The relevant contribution of the study carried out is the research and application of the BPM culture measurement model within companies, making a diagnosis of their organizational culture focused on management, responsibility, work methodology and innovation. In order to identify the shortcomings and opportunities for improvement, visualizing in turn some indicators such as the value of the company, its differentiation from the competition and its performance in which action plans are determined to ensure its fulfillment and that of goals and objectives. The concept of CERT values, seeks the identification of companies from a formal point of view of the management of organizations with the implementation of activities that promote constant change to get to apply this measurement in future research related to the management of processes to improve efficiency and efficacy.

References

1. Schmiedel, T., Recker, J., Vom Brocke, J.: The relation between BPM culture, BPM methods, and process performance: evidence from quantitative field studies. Inf. Manag. **57**(2), 48–50 (2020)
2. Vom Brocke, J., Schmiedel, T.: Culture in business process management: a literature review. Bus. Process Manag. J. **17**(2), 357–377 (2011)
3. Rodríguez, C.: Qué es business process management BPM. Rev. la Esc. Colomb. Ing. **25**(98), 23–29 (2015)
4. Schmiedel, T., Vom Brocke, J., Recker, J.: Which cultural values matter to business process management? Bus. Process Manag. J. **19**(2), 292–317 (2013)
5. Chiavenato, I.: Administración de los Recursos Humanos, 5th edn. McGraw-Hill, Bogotá (2000)
6. Schmiedel, T., Vom Brocke, J., Recker, J.: Development and validation of an instrument to measure organizational cultures' support of Business Process Management. Inf. Manag. **51**(1), 43–56 (2014)
7. Rodríguez, C., Luque, C., Lobatón, L.: Modelo para diagnosticar el nivel de madurez del equipo de trabajo bajo una cultura, BPM. In: Congreso internacional de ingeniería industrial UPTC, Tunja, pp. 1–11 (2017)
8. Senge, P.: La Quinta Disciplina, 1st edn. Granica, Buenos Aires (1990)

Engineering Applications

Methodology for the Implementation of Kalman Filters on Real Applications

Juan David Núñez$^{(\boxtimes)}$, Mónica Aydé Vallejo, and Héctor Botero

Facultad de Minas, Grupo de Investigación en Procesos Dinámicos - Kalman,
Universidad Nacional de Colombia, Medellín, Colombia
{jununez1,mavallejov,habotero}@unal.edu.co

Abstract. Some industrial variables cannot be measured directly due to environmental factors or high costs, then this variables need to be estimated by using Kalman Filters (KF). In order to solve this problem, this paper proposes a methodology that allows the complete design and implementation of KF estimators. A practical application shows that the implementation of the linear KF only consumes the 3.33% of the capacity of an AMD A8-5550M processor.

Keywords: State estimation · Kalman filter · Computational complexity · Industrial computer · Virtual sensor

1 Introduction

One of the main state estimators reported in the literature is the Kalman Filter (KF), which estimates the unknown state of a system based on a mathematical model and available measurements. The KF has the capability to deal with the noise of the sensors and with model uncertainty. Some reported KF applications are as follows: in [6] some computational requirements were established to carry out the execution of the KF algorithm. In that paper, the authors proposes two approaches: sequential processing and parallel processing, by making measurements of the computational time per cycle and the storage memory consumed. The paper concludes that the performance of KF can be improved, by making reductions in size of matrices with many zeros. In [5] computational requirements of a discrete KF for the algorithm of a dynamic robot were established from the amount of arithmetic operations. It was concluded that the Agee factorization method did not yield good results due to the complexity of models, specifically due to the calculation of the inverse of inertia matrix. In [1], a novel dual implementation of the KF was proposed for the simultaneous estimation of state and input, by using numerical simulation and experimental tests. It was determined that filters used in line are not an optimal solution and that KF presents observability problems when acceleration was measured. In [4] the performance of a Kalman filter was studied, by measuring noise covariance. The authors drew their conclusions by means of numerical simulation and it was concluded that

© Springer Nature Switzerland AG 2021
J. C. Figueroa-García et al. (Eds.): WEA 2021, CCIS 1431, pp. 411–421, 2021.
https://doi.org/10.1007/978-3-030-86702-7_35

the FMSE (Filter Calculated Mean Squared Errors) is the worst, and the IMSE (Ideal Mean Squared Errors) is the best, with positive (definite) deviation from the truth. And for the case with negative (definite) deviation from the truth, the IMSE is the worst, and FMSE is the best. In [2] a combination of KF with an observer based on ANFIS neural networks was implemented in order to estimate the states related to the angle of lateral slip of a vehicle. In that work, the implementation was carried out in a vehicle, by using low-cost sensors and a real time system. In [3] an algorithm that estimates the real time covariance matrix of the process noise was proposed. The methodology was applied on an LTI system, by taking the sequential measurements of the process. In accordance with the previous information, KF has been proved extensively through numerical simulation and laboratory scale implementations. However, the clear methodology to get the implementation of KF is still not evident. Therefore, this work develops a methodology which guides the design and processor implementation of KF estimators. This work is organized as follows: Sect. 2 explains the methodology proposed for the implementation of KF in processors. Section 3 analyzes a study case. Finally, Sect. 4 describes the conclusions.

2   Proposed Methodology

The proposed methodology can be easily assumed as the integration of two phases. The first one consists of a purely computational development. It does not include hardware equipment or implementations, and it comprises the development and validation of the model through the selection of the type of KF, and the simulations necessary to verify its correct operation. The second one corresponds to the implementation. It contains the hardware and software selection, the algorithm programming, and finally the implementation on a selected processor. To illustrate the aforementioned ideas the steps are shown in Fig. 1, which will be explained in the next section.

3   Study Case

Model Development. The plant consists of the TCLAB2 module created at Brigham Young University, by John Hedengren[1]. The plant corresponds to a thermal system, made up of two power transistors, which present changes in their temperatures according to the base current. Temperatures are taken by using two sensors, which are attached to the transistor encapsulation. The mathematical model, obtained by using energy balances, can be seen in Eq. (1).

---

[1] http://apmonitor.com/pdc/index.php/Main/ArduinoTemperatureControl.

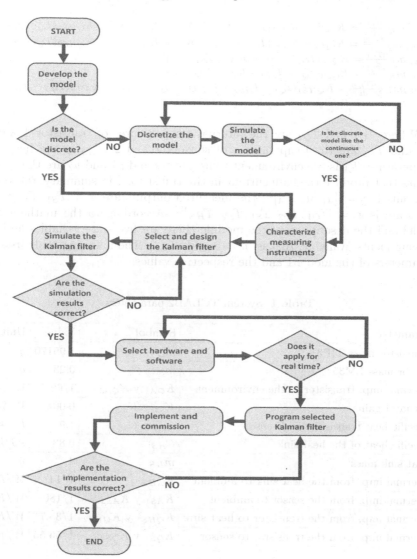

Fig. 1. Flowchart of the proposed methodology

$$C_{pQ} m_Q \frac{dT_{Q1}}{dt} = K_{u_1} u_1 - K_{QS1}(T_{Q1} - T_{S1}) - K_{QA1}(T_{Q1} - T_A) - K_{QHS1}(T_{Q1} - T_{HS})$$
$$C_{pQ} m_Q \frac{dT_{Q2}}{dt} = K_{u_2} u_2 - K_{QS2}(T_{Q2} - T_{S2}) - K_{QA2}(T_{Q2} - T_A) - K_{QHS2}(T_{Q2} - T_{HS})$$
$$C_{pS} m_S \frac{dT_{S1}}{dt} = K_{QS1}(T_{Q1} - T_{S1}) - K_{AS1}(T_{S1} - T_A)$$
$$C_{pS} m_S \frac{dT_{S2}}{dt} = K_{QS2}(T_{Q2} - T_{S2}) - K_{AS2}(T_{S2} - T_A)$$
$$C_{HS} m_{HS} \frac{dT_{HS}}{dt} = K_{QHS1}(T_{Q1} - T_{HS}) + K_{QHS2}(T_{Q2} - T_{HS}) - K_{AHS}(T_{HS} - T_A)$$

$$(1)$$

Where T_{Q1} and T_{Q2} are the internal temperatures of transistor 1 and 2. T_{S1} and T_{S2} are the temperatures of sensors 1 and 2. T_{HS} is the heat sink temperature. T_A is the environment temperature and $u1$ and u_2 are the system inputs that produce the base current in the transistors. In summary, the vector of inputs is $u = [u_1 \ u_2 \ T_A]^T$, the measured outputs are $y = [T_{S1} \ T_{S2}]^T$ and the state is $x = [T_{Q1} \ T_{Q2} \ T_{S1} \ T_{S2} \ T_{HS}]^T$. According to the mathematical model and the description of the module there are five state variables and two measurements available, that is, $n = 5$ and $r = 2$. The following table lists the parameters of the model 1 and the respective values.

Table 1. System TCLAB2 parameters

Parameter	Symbol	Value	Unit
Transistor mass TIP31	m_Q	1.95170	g
Sensor mass LM35	m_S	0.23	g
Thermal imp. transistor to the environment	K_{QA1} y K_{QA2}	1/62.5	W/K
Actuator gain	K_{u1} y K_{u2}	0.0053	$W/\%$
Specific heat transistors and sensors	C_{pQ} y C_{pS}	1.9	kJ/kgK
Specific heat of the heat sink	C_{HS}	0.88	kJ/kgK
Heat sink mass	m_{HS}	4	g
Thermal imp. from the heat sink to ambient	K_{AHS}	1/14	W/K
Thermal imp. from the sensor to ambient	K_{AS1} y K_{AS2}	1/180	W/K
Thermal imp. from the transistor to heat sink	K_{QHS1} y K_{QHS2}	1/35.7	W/K
Thermal imp. from the transistor to sensor	K_{QS1} y K_{QS2}	1/56.55	W/K

Model Discretization. The sampled time ΔT must be determined based on the settling time and the maximum frequency of measurements signals. The settling time can be obtained, by using a step response from the real system. In this case, two time constants were obtained (one for each measured temperature): $\tau_1 = 174\,\text{s}$ and $\tau_2 = 158\,\text{s}$. Therefore, the theoretical sampled time (ΔT_1) corresponds to 20% of the least time constant, which equals 34.8 s.

The next step, is to determine the sampling period, which allows to consider the maximum frequency of the measurement signals (ΔT_2). To do this, the maximum frequency of the measured output signals is obtained, by using the Fast Fourier Transform. In this case, we obtain that $f_{max} = 0.5\,\text{Hz}$. Therefore, we have that $f_s \geq 2(0.5)$, then $\Delta T_2 \leq 1\,\text{s}$. Finally, the sampled time was selected as the lowest value between ΔT_1 and ΔT_2 which equals $1\,\text{s}$. The discrete model, by using $\Delta T = 1\,\text{s}$, and the parameters of Table 1, can be seen in the Eqs. (2) and (3).

$$
\begin{bmatrix} T_{Q1}(k+1) \\ T_{Q2}(k+1) \\ T_{S1}(k+1) \\ T_{S1}(k+1) \\ T_{HS}(k+1) \end{bmatrix} = \begin{bmatrix} 0.9836 & 0 & 0.004606 & 0 & 0.007357 \\ 0 & 0.9836 & 0 & 0.004606 & 0.007357 \\ 0.03908 & 0 & 0.9483 & 0 & 0.000147 \\ 0 & 0.03908 & 0 & 0.9483 & 0.000147 \\ 0.007751 & 0.007751 & 0 & 0 & 0.9645 \end{bmatrix} \begin{bmatrix} T_{Q1}(k) \\ T_{Q2}(k) \\ T_{S1}(k) \\ T_{S2}(k) \\ T_{HS}(k) \end{bmatrix} +
$$
$$
\begin{bmatrix} 0.01417 & 0 & 0.004384 \\ 0 & 0.01417 & 0.004384 \\ 0.0002 & 0 & 0.01247 \\ 0 & 0.0002 & 0.01247 \\ 0 & 0 & 0.01996 \end{bmatrix} \begin{bmatrix} u_1(k) \\ u_2(k) \\ T_A(k) \end{bmatrix}
$$

$$\tag{2}$$

$$
[y_1(k), y_2(k)]^T = [T_{S1}(k), T_{S2}(k)]^T \tag{3}
$$

Comparison Between Continuous and Discrete Model. A comparison between continuous (1) and discrete model (2) was carried out. To do this simulation, a change in the input u_1 was introduced from 0 to 50%. The results are shown in Fig. 2. It should be noted that the initial conditions for both systems are the room temperature (25 °C) for each state variable. The discrete model is correct according to the result of Fig. 2 .

The discrete model is correct according to the result of the Fig. 2.

Measuring Instruments Characterization. The temperatures of the transistors were measured by two LM35 sensors, with TO-92 encapsulation, whose features of interest were taken from their data sheet and are listed below:

- Measuring range: −55 °C a 150 °C
- Accuracy: ± 0.5 °C
- Resolution: 0.25 °C
- Operating temperature: −55 °C a 150 °C

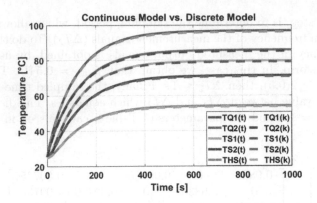

Fig. 2. Continuous and discrete system comparative

It is necessary to remember that the sensors need to be calibrates by using a calibration pattern. In this case the data sheet values were checked by calculating the variance using a series of data taken.

Selection and Design of KF. From the system described in (1) and (2), it is known that the model is linear. Therefore, a linear KF can be used, for which the initial values of the estimator and the noise covariance matrix of the model Q are defined.

$$\hat{x}_0^+ = \left[0, 0, 25, 25, 0\right]^T \quad ; \quad Q = P_0^+ = I_5 \tag{4}$$

In order to find the covariance matrix of the measurement noise R, samples were taken from the real sensors, and from these samples, the mean, the standard deviation σ, and the variance σ^2 were determined. Table 2 shows the results obtained for each sensor according to the duty cycle of the PWM, associated with the input u_1 and u_2. These statistical parameters were obtained, by using a Labview function block called *"Std Deviation and Variance.vi,"* which allows to calculate the aforementioned parameters. For each test, the total amount of samples taken was 2,000.

Table 2. Sensors characterization TS1 y TS2

Sensor	TS1 [°C]			TS2 [°C]		
Parameter	Mean	σ	σ^2	Mean	σ	σ^2
$u_1 = u_2 = 0\%$	25.4	0.055	0.0031	25.4	0.055	0.0031
$u_1 = u_2 = 30\%$	70.56	0.65	0.42	62.87	0.47	0.22
$u_1 = u_2 = 60\%$	110.98	0.52	0.27	97.69	0.58	0.33

The results obtained establish that the sensors present a low variance and standard deviation in room temperature. In contrast, these two parameters increased as the sensors were subjected to temperatures above 60 °C. Furthermore, the results suggest that the standard deviation is very close to the accuracy of the sensors, according to their data sheet, which sets for this parameter a value of 0.5 °C. Therefore, it was decided to take the highest value of the variances, and it was defined that $\sigma_1^2 = 0.42$ and $\sigma_2^2 = 0.33$. Finally, the covariance matrix of the measurement noise was calculated as follows:

$$R = \begin{bmatrix} 0.42 & 0 \\ 0 & 0.33 \end{bmatrix} \tag{5}$$

KF Simulation. The simulation was carried out, by using the continuous time system model (1), and, by including Gaussian noise in both the equation of state and the output equation in order to emulate modeling noise and measurement noise. The latter was modeled, by taking into account the related 0.5 °C accuracy in the characterization of the sensors. The parameters of KF were: the matrix Q presented in (4), the matrix R defined in (5), and the matrices F_{k-1}, G_{k-1} and H_k extracted from the model (2) and (3). The simulation was carried out, by using Euler's method, and the integration step h was $h = 15.8$, which corresponds to the tenth part of the plant time constant.

The changes introduced in the simulation were:

- Between $0 \leq t < 200$ s, the system had its inputs at 0% and no disturbance was performed.
- At $t > 200$ s, we make $u_1 = 50\%$ and $u_2 = 0\%$ and no disturbance was performed.
- At $t > 800$ s, we make $u_2 = 50\%$ and u_1 remains the same. No disturbance was made.
- At $t > 1800$ s, a disturbance is performed consisting of the change in value of the element (5,1) of the array F_{k-1}. It is changed from 0.007751 to 0.
- At $t > 2500$ s, KF was normalized, that is, the modified value of the F_{k-1} array was returned to its original value.
- At $t > 2800$ s, the entry was made $u_2 = 0\%$ and u_1 is kept at 50%. No disturbances were made.
- At $t > 3500$ s the entry u_1 was set to 0%. No disturbances were applied.
- The simulation ended at 4500 s with u_1 and u_2 at 0%.

The results can be seen in Fig. 3. In this Figure is evident that there is a correct estimation of the state until the disturbance occurs (second 1800), which is understood as a great dependence of the estimator towards the mathematical model of the system.

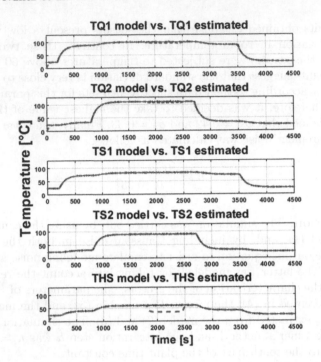

Fig. 3. Comparison between the system model and the estimated system.

Hardware and Software Selection. For this study case, we selected an AMD A8-5550 M processor, whose characteristics are: 4 cores, base clock 2.1 GHz, max clock 3.1 GHz, power 35 W, and cache L2 4 MB. However, it is convenient to know the processor power as a function of the number of floating point operations per second (FLOPS). For this reason, it is necessary to know the number of FLOP per cycle (F_i) of the linear KF, and the number of cycles per second (I_s) of the Kalman filter algorithm that the processor can perform. The F_i value was calculated as 1685 floating-point operations for each cycle of the KF. The I_s value was obtained, by running the linear KF on the processor, by closing all other applications, and by prioritizing the Labview program to be used in the operating system. The results obtained oscillate between 3448 and 14290 cycles per second, whose average value is located at 10834 cycles per second. Therefore, by knowing that the AMD A8-5550M performs on average more than 18 MFLOPS[2], it is concluded that the processor meets the necessary specifications for the real-time application.

KF Programming. Labview was the program used in the implementation of the KF because it uses a general-purpose graphical programming language, known as G-code, along with a built-in and associated compiler, linker, and

---

[2] www.amd.com/es/support.

debugging tools. This software was selected for its great versatility when creating a user interface, the number of functions associated with matrix and vector operations, and the ease of establishing communication between the TCLAB2 system and the Arduino *UNO* board.

Implementation and Commissioning. The results of the implementation and commissioning can be seen from Fig. 4a to Fig. 6, obtained, by using the following experimental protocol:

- Let the system and the estimator evolve from their initial conditions and keep it that way for 49 s, that is, with the inputs at $u_1 = u_2 = 0\%$.
- In second 50 $u_1 = 50\%$ and $u_2 = 0\%$ are set for 100 s.
- 151 s from the start of the test, $u_2 = 50\%$ is set, at that instant of time the two PWM's of the Arduino *UNO* are at 50% of their duty cycle.
- In second 350 a disturbance is made in the temperature sensor $TS1$ for 150 s.
- When the test hits 750 s it takes $u_1 = 0$ and u_2 is kept at 50% for 50 s and then equal to 0%.
- At 900 s into the test, a disturbance lasting 250 s is performed on the $TS2$ temperature sensor. The test ends at 1500 s.

From the test results, only the state variables T_{S1} and T_{S2} can be validated, which correspond to the measured variables, and the heat sink temperature T_{HS}, obtained from of offline measurements, by using temperature samples taken at the geometric center of the heat sink every 10 s. The internal temperatures of the transistors were only estimated because they cannot be measured. The results of $\hat{T}Q1$ and $\hat{T}Q2$ can be seen in Fig. 4a. The Figure shows the excessive noise in the estimate variable during the time interval in which the disturbances occurs (addition of noise in second 350 and 900). Said result is extended in all the state variables according to what can be seen in Fig. 4b.

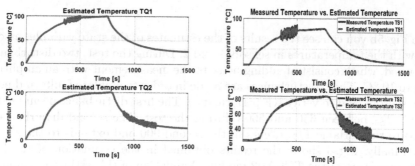

(a) Estimation of the internal temperature in the transistors 1 and 2

(b) Estimation of the temperature in the Sensors 1 and 2

Fig. 4. Kalman filter results with fixed R. a) left column. b) right column.

According to the previous results, it can be concluded that the KF does not cause any filtering effect on the estimate. This is due to the fact that the matrix R, defined in the Eq. (5), was calculated from the measurements related in Table 2, whose covariance values are small compared to the noise presented in the previous graphs, by causing a propagation of the measurement noise in the rest of the state variables. In order to solve this problem, it is decided to establish a dynamic R matrix that consists of taking 10 samples every second of the values transmitted by the sensors, and calculating the covariance of each group of samples. In this way, KF is shielded against this type of disturbance. Now, the results of the estimation with the previous problem solved can be seen from Fig. 5a to Fig. 6. The estimation of the internal temperatures of the transistors, that is $\hat{T}Q1$ and $\hat{T}Q2$, can be seen in Fig. 5a.

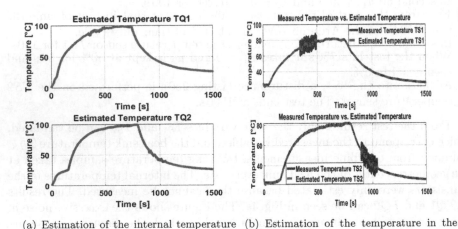

(a) Estimation of the internal temperature in the transistors 1 and 2

(b) Estimation of the temperature in the sensors 1 and 2

Fig. 5. Kalman filter results with dynamic R. a) left column. b) right column.

In Fig. 5b you can see the results of the estimates of the state variables associated with the temperatures in sensors 1 and 2. During the test, two disturbances are caused, which consist of adding noise to the measurement with an amplitude of up to 10 °C. These disturbances are made in order to emulate faults and noise in the sensors, and to verify KF performance. The first disturbance occurs in the variable T_{S1} between 350 and 500 s during the test. The second disturbance is caused to the variable T_{S2}, occurs in the second 900 and extends to the second 1050. Finally, Fig. 6 shows the results obtained in the estimation of the heat sink temperature of the TCLAB2 module. Validation of this estimate was made from temperature samples taken at the geometric center of the heat sink every 10 seconds, by using a thermocouple. The meter used had a resolution of 1°C and corresponds to a UNI-T UT61C multimeter.

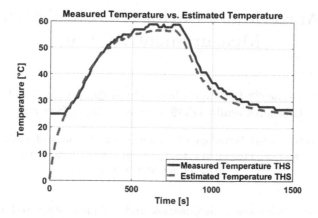

Fig. 6. Heat Sink temperature with dynamic R

4 Conclusions

In this article, a methodology was proposed for the implementation of KF on processors. The methodology was applied in a real case to estimate the internal temperatures and measurements of two transistors, based on the measured temperatures. The results obtained were completely satisfactory due to the coincidence between the data. Additionally, it was shown that the implementation of the linear KF only consumes on average 3.33% of the capacity of one of the cores of the AMD A8-5550M processor.

References

1. Azam, S.E., Chatzi, E., Papadimitriou, C., Smyth, A.: Experimental validation of the Dual Kalman filter for online and real-time state and input estimation. JVC/J. Vib. Control **23**(15), 2494–2519 (2015). https://doi.org/10.1177/1077546315617672
2. Boada, B., Boada, M., Diaz, V.: Vehicle sideslip angle measurement based on sensor data fusion using an integrated ANFIS and an Unscented Kalman Filter algorithm. Mech. Syst. Sign. Process. **72–73**, 832–845 (2016)
3. Feng, B., Fu, M., Ma, H., Xia, Y., Wang, B.: Kalman filter with recursive covariance estimation-Sequentially estimating process noise covariance. IEEE Trans. Ind. Electron. **61**(11), 6253–6263 (2014). https://doi.org/10.1109/TIE.2014.2301756
4. Ge, Q., Shao, T., Duan, Z., Wen, C.: Performance analysis of the kalman filter with mismatched noise covariances. IEEE Trans. Autom. Control **61**(12), 4014–4019 (2016). https://doi.org/10.1109/TAC.2016.2535158
5. Kozlowski, K.: Computational requirements for a discrete Kalman filter in robot dynamics algorithms. Robotica **11**(1), 27–36 (1993). https://doi.org/10.1017/S0263574700015411
6. Mendel, J.: Computational requirements for a discrete Kalman filter. IEEE Trans. Autom. Control **16**(6), 748–758 (1971)

Agro-Smart Caribe: Soil Moisture Measurement System

Eduardo Gomez$^{(\boxtimes)}$ ⓘ, Jorge Eliecer Duque ⓘ, Alvaro José Rojas ⓘ,
Cristian Camilo Jaik ⓘ, and Jose Angel Pertuz ⓘ

Universidad Tecnologica de Bolivar, Cartagena, Colombia
{egomez,jduque,arojas,cjaik,pertuzj}@utb.edu.co
http://www.utb.edu.co

Abstract. Advances in information and communication technologies
provide precision agriculture with more efficient tools for agricultural
monitoring systems and the possibility of crop irrigation automation.
This paper presents the implementation of a crop field monitoring system
based on wireless sensor networks (WSN) with moisture detectors, which
are remotely controlled for data collection. The implemented WSN performs information gathering functions from the sensor nodes to the base
station. The system is integrated into the internet cloud and together
with the hardware and software configuration, adequate energy efficiency
is obtained.

Keywords: Precision agriculture · Soil moisture · Wireless sensor
networks · Communication protocols · Internet of Things

1 Introduction

Agriculture as the basis for the development of civilizations is the most important
economic activity, and in addition to being a civilizing agent, it involves the
fulfillment of certain social objectives, of which the increase in food production,
economic viability and environmental sustainability are the most important,
however, in terms of water use, worldwide agricultural irrigation accounts for
70% of water consumption [1] and there is not a sufficiently optimized process
for this activity.

It is estimated that the world population will increase by just over 40% in
the next 30 years, which demands a 60% increase in food production [1], then it
becomes crucial to identify solutions that prioritize productivity and economic
benefits in agriculture. In response to the above, a wireless sensor network was
designed and implemented, whose main functionality is based on precision agriculture, to monitor soil moisture and improve the efficiency of water and energy
use, using low-power electronic devices and communication systems that optimize the overall performance within the agricultural irrigation processes.

Supported by UTB.

© Springer Nature Switzerland AG 2021
J. C. Figueroa-García et al. (Eds.): WEA 2021, CCIS 1431, pp. 422–434, 2021.
https://doi.org/10.1007/978-3-030-86702-7_36

2   Agriculture in the Colombian Caribbean

In Colombia, in 2016, the share of the agricultural sector in water demand represented 43.1% of the entire country. 90% of this sector is supported by soil moisture from rainfall and the rest represents the deficit that is met by crop irrigation [2]. Productivity is affected by poor technical assistance and some of the essential permanent crops have a water use efficiency of 50%. With the inclusion of technology, there is great potential for improvement in the country's production systems [3].

In a region it is important to know the local resources that allow an adequate quality of life and work for human beings. To frame the problem and the justification of the Agro-Smart Caribe project, it is necessary to describe the climate, soil and crops of the Caribbean Region.

The region includes territories of the departments of Atlantico, Cesar, Cordoba, Bolivar, Magdalena, Sucre, and La Guajira. In these areas, the climate is almost 70% tropical, due to its location is the hottest region of the country, throughout the year can reach temperatures of up to 30 °C [4].

Relative humidity fluctuates between 77% and 82.5%. Humidity is lower in the winter months, although it is still high. Rainfall, meanwhile, occurs mostly in summer, especially between October and December, decreasing in the winter. The driest month is March, while the rainiest is October [5].

The soils have high nutrient and sodium contents and low levels of organic carbon. Bolívar and Sucre are departments with slightly drier soils, with slightly faster drainage and less fertile conditions due to the lack of water reservoirs [6].

Agriculture in the region has 1.3 million hectares planted, of which 28.5% are cereals, 25.8% are bananas and tubers, 23.4% are agro-industrial crops, 12.4% are fruit crops and 10% are other crops (legumes, forestry, etc.). [7]

Droughts are prolonged and produce water shortages continuously in departments of the Region. In percentage terms: Guajira (67%), Magdalena (50%), Sucre (35%), Bolivar (32%), Cesar (28%), Atlantico (26%) and Cordoba (10%).

In the Colombian Caribbean, water demand represents 12.1% of the agricultural productivity unit (UPA) in the country [8]. An analysis of technical assistance in the region shows, worryingly, that only 8 out of every 100 producers received training in crop care [7].

Precision agriculture was born in the face of relevant difficulties of the last two decades in the rural sector, such as the reduction of the labor force, the increase in the average age of farmers and the negative impact of certain practices [9]. Figure 1 shows the general cycle of precision agriculture.

Among the technologies used for precision agriculture are wireless sensor networks (WSN). WSN are networks of autonomous terminals that communicate with each other. These networks facilitate the implementation of applications such as remote monitoring in large crop areas. Therefore, within the field of agriculture, for constant monitoring activities of crop conditions, it becomes a valuable technology in productivity. The implementation of a monitoring system guarantees the following advantages: high autonomy, a long useful life of the devices, appropriate coverage in the monitoring areas, lower cost, ease of

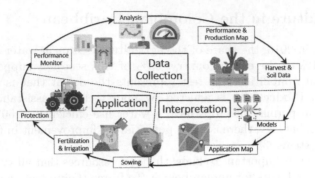

Fig. 1. Precision agriculture processes.

installation of devices, response time, low power consumption, accuracy, security, and the implementation of "IoT" (Internet of Things).

The Agro-Smart Caribe project, based on precision agriculture, contributes to the solution of the aforementioned problems. A prototype was developed for distributed soil moisture measurement dedicated to crops, based on wireless sensor networks together with a system capable of collecting, communicating, and storing data in the cloud.

3   Agro-Smart Caribe Architecture

To describe the monitoring solution implemented, the communication technology, hardware and software used to sense moisture in soils dedicated to crops is defined.

3.1   Communication Technologies

In the insertion of low-cost communication networks to assist agricultural processes, several types of data transmission protocols are identified with different characteristics that must be analyzed in search of a better solution according to the case study.

These communication protocols include: proximity technologies, personal area networks (PAN), wireless local area networks (WLAN), neighborhood and metropolitan area networks (WNAN and WMAN) and wide area networks (WAN). The latter are characterized by extending more than 50 km, which implies the use of licensed frequencies to avoid interference between different networks, as in the case of LoRaWAN, mobile communications (GSM) and Radio Frequency (RF) technologies.

Short-range technologies include Bluetooth, Ultra-wideband (UWB), Wi-Fi and Zigbee [10]. Table 1 shows a summary of the most important characteristics of the wireless technologies applied in agriculture.

Table 1. Main characteristics of wireless communication technologies.

Wireless communication technologies						
Technology	Frequency	Data rate	Range	Power	Cost	Application
GSM	Cellular bands	10 Mb/s	50 km	High	High	Mobile networks
Bluetooth	2.4 GHz	250 kb/s	20 m	Low	Low	Mobile credential
LoRa	<1 GHz	<50 kb/s	15 km	Low	Medium	Military, Space
Wi-Fi	2.4, 5 GHz	100 Mb/s	60 m	Medium	Low	LAN, Internet
ZigBee	2.4 GHz	250 kb/s	300 m	Low	Medium	Sensor networks

According to the information provided in Table 1, Zigbee technology was selected for the purposes of this project, since it has an adequate transmission coverage between devices, a sufficient data transfer rate, low energy consumption, low cost, good reliability and supports multiple devices in the same network. Additionally, it offers greater possibilities compared to other wireless protocols such as Bluetooth, since it allows using up to 65535 nodes distributed in subnets of 255 nodes, compared to the maximum 8 nodes possible in a Piconet subnet (Bluetooth). The Zigbee network architecture is presented in Fig. 2.

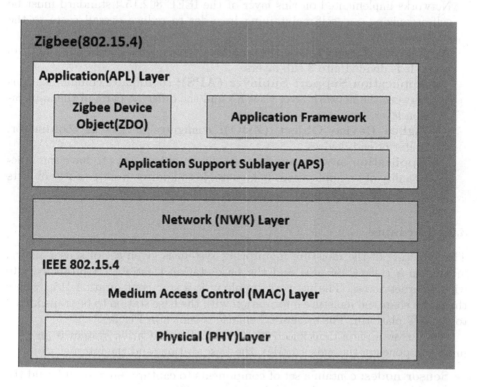

Fig. 2. Zigbee protocol stack

Each layer of the Zigbee protocol stack is described below:

- **Physical Layer:** the first concept of this protocol is to define the assigned bands and the number of channels for each band. There are 27 channels in total, one channel for the 868.3 MHz band, 10 for 915 MHz and 16 for 2.45 GHz. As an advantage, it is possible to maintain multiple communication channels on the same carrier frequency, by means of modulations such as BPSK, QPSK, and DSSS coding. For channel access, the method known as Carrier Sense Multiple Access with Collision Avoidance (CSMA-CA) is used, where the transmitter cannot use the channel if it detects that another node is using it to transmit. [11]
- **MAC Layer:** administers and manages access to the physical radio frequency channel, allowing the entry of nodes that are in the PAN or have been disconnected from it, thus managing RF data transactions between neighboring nodes. It also includes transmission retry and CSMA-CA acknowledgment, which generally makes use of the ACK frame between devices to verify errors when receiving packets [12].
- **Network Layer:** the network layer supports several topologies over which the transmission of information is carried out. The best known topologies are: star, cluster tree and mesh, as defined in the IEEE 802.15.4 standard. Networks implemented on this layer of the IEEE 802.15.4 standard must be self-organizing and self-maintaining in order to reduce overall costs to the consumer [13].
- **Application Layer:** this is the interface Layer between the node and its users. It is divided into 3 sub-layers:
  - **Application Support Sublayer (APS):** coordinates communications between the network layer (NWK) and the different parts of the application layer.
  - **Zigbee Device Object (ZDO):** configures devices as coordinator, router or end-devices.
  - **Application environment:** generally an object seeks to have the functionality of an application. It is possible to address from 1 to 240 objects per device, of which 30 can operate at the same time [12].

3.2 Hardware

The structure of the moisture monitoring system is given set of sensor nodes, located in a cultivation area and the base station located in a protected site with Internet access. The network topology is a star configuration [10], where the nodes share soil moisture information with the base station to be transmitted to the IoT platform. The system schematic is shown in Fig. 3.

The following is a description of the Agro-Smart Caribe system from its 3 main components: the sensor nodes, the base station, and the internet cloud.

- **Sensor nodes:** contain a set of components to capture, process and send the variable to be measured to the base station. The modules are:
  - **Processing module:** represents the core of the sensor node and is composed of an Arduino ADK board with a MEGA 2560 microcontroller.

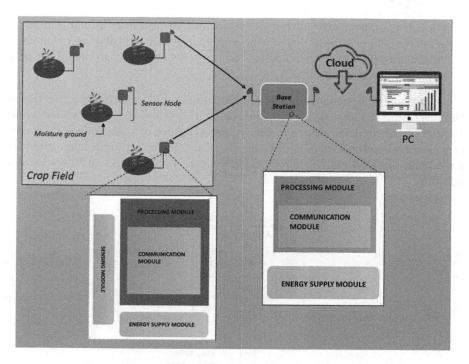

Fig. 3. General diagram of Agro-Smart Caribe

- **Communication module:** wirelessly communicates the sensor nodes with the base station. This module is based on the Zigbee protocol (IEEE 802.15.4) and the implemented device is the Xbee Pro S2C.
- **Sensing module:** it allows obtaining the physical magnitude of the humidity and then converting it to an electrical signal. It is composed of a FC-28 humidity sensor and a YL-38 conditioning card.
- **Power module:** comprises a rechargeable power supply, which corresponds to a 3.7 V lithium battery with a capacity of 5000 mAh.
- **Base Station:** facilitates the collection of the data sent by each sensor node and the processing and error control operations of the frames, and then transmits the data to the cloud. The components are:
  - **Power module:** a conventional AC power supply and an AC-DC adapter with the following characteristics are used: 110/5 V at 3000 mA.
  - **Communication module:**communicates the sensor nodes with the base station. This module is based on Zigbee technology and the implemented device is the Xbee Pro S2C in coordinator mode. There is also a wired/wifi connection for internet connection.
  - **Processing module:**a raspberry pi 3b+ device is used. It allows to control, management, process and transfer of data between the WSN and the cloud.

– **Cloud:** computer service that processes and stores data through a network of servers. The Agro-Smart Caribe system uses an IoT platform that must be configured and programmed to store, process and manage the information on soil moisture under study.

Additionally, accessories were used to connect and ensure the protection of the electronic devices along with improving the stability of the sensor nodes located in the field. As shown in Fig. 4, the structure of each node is composed of a Dexon thermoplastic IP55 box of 18 × 14 × 8 cm, a 150 cm long tube with a diameter of half an inch, a 24 AWG conductor of 150 cm and an Xbee-Arduino adapter.

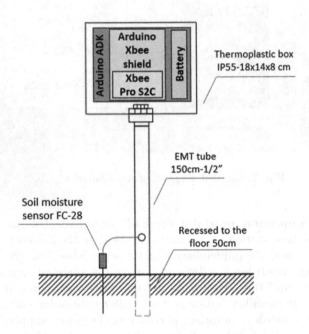

Fig. 4. Main components of a node structure

3.3   Software

To initiate the operation of the sensor network, a procedure is used that establishes a set of programmed steps in each device of the network. These programs are made with the objective of capturing, processing, storing and visualizing soil moisture data.

The processes implemented in the sensor network are illustrated in the flowchart in Fig. 5. It starts with the generation of an API broadcast frame [11] from the base station, which is sent to the sensor nodes using the Zigbee protocols. The nodes, upon receiving the request frame, proceed to measure the moisture of the ground through the FC-28 sensor. This data will be encapsulated in a new API frame and transmitted to the base station. The base station then stores the frames in its buffer and evaluates them to check if the information is correct. If there are errors or if the information is not received within a certain time, one or more unicast request frames are retransmitted to the corresponding node, where the number of possible retransmissions is defined by the user.

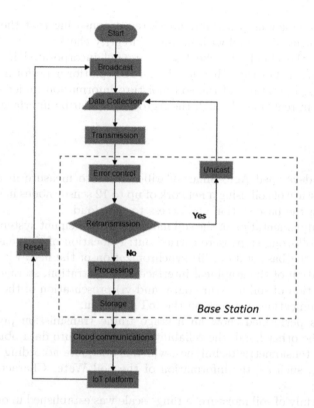

Fig. 5. General flowchart

For error control, the frames used in device communication are of fixed length. In this way the base station recognizes specific positions. Table 2 shows the structure of the designed frame and the position that each one occupies in the 16 bytes of the frame.

The frame fields called start byte, length, and the checksum (CRC) are used by the coordinator to detect errors and are unmodifiable in the process. This allows for better reliability of the moisture data provided by the sensor nodes.

Communication security is one of the strong points of ZigBee, implementing its security model according to the IEEE 802.15.4 standard. This provides access control mechanisms of the devices to the network with authentication, encryption

Table 2. Unicast frame structure

0x7E	MSB	LSB	0x90	ID Router	ID Network	Data	Checksum
1	2	3	4	5–12	13–15	16, 17	18
Start byte	Length		Frame type: transmission	Device addresses (global & local)		Content	Frame check

using symmetric key cryptography and integrity ensuring that the transmitted frames are not manipulated with message integrity checks.

To access the cloud, the client-server model incorporated in the TCP-IP protocols is used. On the other hand, the IoT platform performs the storage and processing operations of the soil moisture information under study, for its visualization in real time through the Agro-Smart Caribe interface.

4   Results

The project developed Agro-Smart Caribe allows to measure in a distributed way, the moisture of soil using a network of up to 12 sensor nodes in star topology together with the base station and access to the cloud.

For the implementation of the soil moisture measurement system Agro-smart Caribe, the following steps were carried out: i) location of the sensor nodes, ii) activation of the base station, iii) synchronization of the network elements, iv) parameterization of the graphical interface, v) registration, storage, processing, and visualization of soil moisture data, and vi) presentation of the performance of the communications network on the IoT platform.

The tests performed show an average frame transmission performance of 97.5%. On the other hand, the reliability of the moisture data obtained is 90% compared to tensiometric techniques, which is adequate according to studies on soil moisture, such as, the information of the Soil Water Characteristic Curve (SWCC) [14].

For the study of soil moisture, a range scale was established in order to define the soil type based on SWCC. Table 3 is presented below.

Table 3. Soil moisture classification

Moisture	Very low	Low	Medium	High
Bits	1023–850	850–400	400–300	300–200

Table 4 presents a test of the system in a plot with a configuration of 4 sensor nodes in star topology with the coordinator node and a sampling cycle of 3 h over a day.

The physical structure of the sensor nodes placed in the field is shown in Fig. 6. The communication (Xbee), processing (Arduino) and power (lithium

Table 4. Moisture record of the soil under study.

Cycle	1	2	3	4	5	6	7	8	9
Average (bits)	870	858	788	648	600	445	410	353	305

battery) modules are shown together with the thermoplastic box and the metal tube that protects the ground connection with the moisture sensors.

(a) Structure   (b) Location

Fig. 6. Sensor nodes

For the visualization of the basic configuration of the measurement system and the captured data, an interface was developed as shown in Fig. 7.

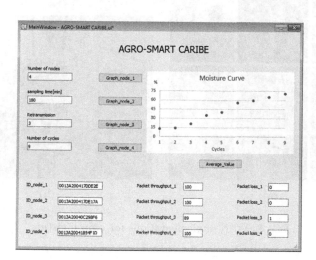

Fig. 7. Agro-Smart Caribe interface

5   Conclusions and Future Works

In the Colombian agricultural sector, agriculture accounts for 35% at the national level and 33% in the Caribbean region. In addition, the use of automated systems is lagging in the agricultural sector given that only 12 out of 100 producers have machinery dedicated to the production process, which translates into inadequate productivity for this region. For this reason, this area has enormous potential for agro-industrial exploitation given its diversification of agricultural flora and its size.

A project was developed to measure soil moisture in a distributed way called Agro-Smart Caribe, with a data reliability of 90%, an energy saving of 93% respect to other similar technologies and a loss of information packages of 2.5%, which allows a potential implementation in the rural Caribbean sector, providing farmers with an excellent monitoring and visualization of moisture in large areas for 24 h a day.

As a reference, the following illustrations show systems developed for soil moisture collection based on wireless sensor networks (WSN). Figure 8a shows the implementation of a WSN to measure moisture in a strawberry crop in Pasto, Colombia [15]. Figure 8b shows the use of this technology for the acquisition of crop parameters in Villa Clara, Cuba [16].

(a)   (b)

Fig. 8. WSN implementations for crop moisture.

The cost-benefit ratio starts at a value of less than US$130 for each node of the prototype developed. Given the technological need exposed together with government plans, it is possible to massify the Agro-Smart system to increase productivity in the Colombian Caribbean Region.

In the future it is necessary to continue with the development of the automated irrigation system for crops that allows water distribution and flow control, according to the moisture information provided by the prototype developed for this purpose, along with a hydraulic system, a control mechanism, local storage of information, scalability, agricultural irrigation system (drip, sprinkler, subway) and add the reading of other variables such as temperature, pH, solar radiation, along with the chemical and physical composition of the soil and water.

References

1. Meier, J., Zabel, F., Mauser, W.: A global approach to estimate irrigated areas - a comparison between different data and statistics. Hydrol. Earth Syst. Sci. **22**, 1119–1133 (2018). https://doi.org/10.5194/hess-22-1119-2018
2. Instituto de Hidrologia, Meteorologia y Estudios Ambientales IDEAM: Estudio Nacional del Agua 2018, 438 pp. IDEAM, Bogota (2019) ISBN: 978-958-54891-2-7
3. Junguito, R., Perfetti, J.J., Becerra, A.: Desarrollo de la agricultura colombiana. Fedesarrollo. Cuadernos de Fedesarrollo N°, vol. 48 (2014). ISBN: 978-958-57963-9-3
4. Observatorio del Caribe Colombiano: Plan Prospectivo y Estrategico de la Región Caribe colombiana. Hacia un plan de desarrollo para la región Caribe colombiana, Cartagena de Indias (2013). 978-958-58226-0-3
5. Rangel, J.O.: Colombia Diversidad Biotica XII. La region Caribe de Colombia, Bogotá D.C., 1046 pp. Universidad Nacional de Colombia Instituto de Ciencias Naturales (2012). ISBN: 978-958-761-215-8
6. Solano, J., Barros, J., Roncallo, B.: Requerimientos hidricos de cuatro gramineas de corte para uso eficiente del agua en el Caribe seco colombiano. Ciencia y Tecnología Agropecuaria **15**(1), 83–99 (2015). https://doi.org/10.21930/rcta.vol15_num1_art:399
7. Cano, C.: El desarrollo equitativo, competitivo y sostenible del sector agropecuario en Colombia. Bogota. Banco de la República (2016). ISBN: 978-958-664-339-9
8. Departamento Administrativo Nacional de Estadística DANE: Tercer Censo Nacional Agropecuario. Hay campo para todos (2016). ISBN: 978-958-624-108-3
9. Ochoa, D., Alexei, G., Forero, P., Aura, M., Cangrejo, A., Libia, D.: Present and trends of precision agriculture in the twenty-first century. Universidad Nacional de Colombia, Group ANGeoSc (2012)
10. Chikankar, P. Mehetre, D., Das, S.: An automatic irrigation system using ZigBee in wireless sensor network. In: 2015 International Conference on Pervasive Computing (ICPC), pp. 1–5 (2015). https://doi.org/10.1109/PERVASIVE.2015.7086997
11. Vivek, G., Sunil, M.: Enabling IOT services using WIFI - ZigBee gateway for a home automation system. In: 2015 IEEE International Conference on Research in Computational Intelligence and Communication Networks (ICRCICN), pp. 77–80 (2015). https://doi.org/10.1109/ICRCICN.2015.7434213
12. Prakash, S.: Zigbee based wireless sensor network architecture for agriculture applications. In: 2020 Third International Conference on Smart Systems and Inventive Technology (ICSSIT), pp. 709–712 (2020). https://doi.org/10.1109/ICSSIT48917.2020.9214086
13. Wang, J, Tang, J.: Design and implementation of WSN monitoring system for grain depot based on XBee/XBee Pro. In: 2011 International Conference on Electric Information and Control Engineering, pp. 4872–4874 (2011). https://doi.org/10.1109/ICEICE.2011.5777512

14. Velasquez, E., Kreinovich V.: Scale-invariance ideas explain the empirical soil-water characteristic curve. In: 2020 IEEE Symposium Series on Computational Intelligence (SSCI), pp. 958–962 (2020). https://doi.org/10.1109/SSCI47803.2020.9308136
15. Castro, N., Chamorro, L., Viteri, C.: Una red de sensores inalámbricos para la automatización y control del riego localizado. Rev. Cienc. Agr. **33**(1), 106–116 (2016). https://doi.org/10.22267/rcia.163302.57
16. Madruga, A., Estevez, A., López, R., Santana, I., García, C.: Red de Sensores Inalámbricos para la Adquisición de Datos en Casas de Cultivo. Ingeniería **24**(3), 224–234 (2019). https://doi.org/10.14483/23448393.14437

Entrepreneurial Intention in Vocational Technical Schools in Emerging Economies: A Case Study of Barranquilla, Colombia

David Ovallos-Gazabon[1]([⊠]), Nataly Puello-Pereira[2], Kevin Parra-Negrete[2], and Karol Martinez-Cueto[2]

[1] Punto Estratégico, 080020 Barranquilla, Colombia
dovallos@puntoestrategico.com.co
[2] Universidad de la Costa, 080001 Barranquilla, Colombia
{npuello,kparra7,kmartine8}@cuc.edu.co

Abstract. Entrepreneurship is a subject that according to literature has not been studied in technical institutions and institutions of education for work and human development. Because it has been done primarily in university institutions, primary and secondary schools. Based on the above, this research carries out a trend analysis and then analyzes the business intention given in the technical institutions in Barranquilla, Colombia. For this, the study is administered an online instrument to 738 students, considering the guide of the World Survey of University Business Spirits (GUESSS). The results obtained in the analysis indicate that the qualifications of the attributes that characterize the business intention of students of technical institutions are very similar to the Colombian average for the programs of university institutions, although there is no structure of business support.

Keywords: Entrepreneurship · Education for work · GUESSS · Business performance · Innovation · Competitiveness

1 Introduction

Current trends related to training and employment underscore the demand for changed processes to train human resources to boost competitiveness within this new economic context. Thus, issues such as globalization, scientific and technological change, new business structuring, transformed labor content, and employability and certification, among others, pose new additional challenges to education and training systems [1], especially concerning the creation of companies and the opportunities for independent growth.

A primary element to entrepreneurial behavior, company creation, and the identification of business opportunities is the existence of entrepreneurial intention, which may be defined as "the self-awareness of the conviction to start a business and conscious planning for its future execution" [2]. The entrepreneurial intention has been studied in recent years [3–6]; [7] however, research on entrepreneurial intention, entrepreneurship,

J. C. Figueroa-García et al. (Eds.): WEA 2021, CCIS 1431, pp. 435–446, 2021.
https://doi.org/10.1007/978-3-030-86702-7_37

and education place greater emphasis on higher education, and studies are generally conducted in mature or developed economies [6, 8–11]. References to the study of entrepreneurship in technical and technological education levels and education for work and human development are scarce.

The work conducted by [12] shows that according to the psychological literature, intentions are the best antecedent to predict planned behavior, especially if that behavior is rare, hard to observe, or involves unpredictable time lags. The creation of a new company requires substantial planning, and it represents the ideal planned behavior to be studied through an intention model because it offers a consistent and robust theoretical framework to explain how exogenous factors affect attitudes, intentions, and behaviors, enabling a greater understanding of the business process.

This study aims to analyze the entrepreneurial intention of students in the technical training institutions, using a methodology under the guidelines of the Global University Entrepreneurial Spirit Students' Survey (GUESSS). Sections 1.1 and 1.2 will address the concepts of "education and entrepreneurship" and "education for work and human development." The methods used shall be shown in Sect. 2, and the results obtained from the analysis shall be shown in Sect. 3, and finally, in Sect. 4, the main conclusions and potential research opportunities are listed.

1.1 Education and Entrepreneurship

One of the main drivers of a productive and competitive society is education, and there is a strong correlation between the level of development of countries and the strength of their education and scientific and technological research [13–16]. Thus, education is the vehicle to access equality and improved quality of life, which become the people's goals that perceive education as an opportunity for creating employment and acquiring resources [17].

In addition, the literature shows that the educational systems of developed countries focus on supporting and guiding entrepreneurial ideas and youth innovation from initial education, adopting a particular approach regarding the use of technologies and scientific research [18–26]. In the United States, the first business school course in entrepreneurship was taught at Harvard University in 1947 as a complement to Business Administration, and it is now the country with the oldest tradition in entrepreneurial education [27]. In Europe, entrepreneurship training was pioneered by the United Kingdom and France in the mid-70s and by the end of the decade, respectively [28]. Other countries such as Spain, France, Belgium, Poland, and Sweden implemented a more defined strategy related to the adoption of entrepreneurship skills as part of the objectives and contents of their educational systems [28].

Educational development in entrepreneurship and vocational education is gaining momentum as a strategy to fight unemployment and lack of opportunities [28]. Consequently, governmental organizations and academia show particular interest in understanding the entrepreneurial phenomenon [29–31] faced with implementing endogenous development strategies for countries and regions. In this respect, international evidence confirms that the highest levels of development are found in the countries that also show high levels of innovative entrepreneurship in their economies [32, 33].

Colombia is betting highly on entrepreneurship and innovation because they are the methods to solve people's problems by enhancing the quality of life and accumulating wealth. However, entrepreneurship training is limited to higher education levels, as shown by results such as those gathered by the research entitled "Emprendedores en crecimiento II" (Growing Entrepreneurs II) conducted by INNpulsa Colombia, the Colombian Confederation of Chambers of Commerce (CONFECAMARAS), and the School of Administration of Universidad de Los Andes. It shows that 3% of entrepreneurs are high school graduates; 36.8% hold an undergraduate degree; 31.8% pursued a specialist degree; 21.2% earned a master's degree; and 1.8% obtained a doctorate, disregarding other levels such as technicians and technologists.

Colombia is a developing country with an expanding economy and aims to bridge social, productive, and technological gaps to consolidate as a developed country. Consequently, significant adjustments were made in several systems, such as the educational system that is structured into kindergarten, preschool education, elementary education (five grades of primary education and four grades of secondary education), high school education (two grades so that students earn the bachelor's degree), and higher education. In addition, it also offers technical and technological education and education for work and human development (Act 1064 of 2006) (formerly known as "nonformal education"). This education is offered supplementarily to formal schooling to update or compensate for missing knowledge and offer training in academic or vocational matters without following the levels and grades of the formal education system [34]. Based on information published by the Colombian Ministry of Education, there are 4,420 institutions with 21,823 programs catering to 452,369 students across Colombia [35]. The Atlántico Department has 162 institutions that offer 1,208 programs for 44,795 students, from which 39,864 are from the District of Barranquilla divided into 924 programs [35].

1.2 Education for Work and Human Development

In Colombia, entrepreneurship culture has been transformed over the past few years by launching education reforms and introducing educational changes according to the employment market. These changes fueled entrepreneurship training through Act 1014 of 2006, which sets forth the creation of a mandatory class in schools, in addition to establishing the liaison with the Colombian Training Service (SENA), the entity in charge of supporting and providing advisory services to schools concerning entrepreneurship and education for work [28].

The purpose of vocational programs is to train people in specific areas within the productive sectors and develop specific employment skills related to the performance areas in the Colombian Classification of Occupations so that productive activities are carried out either individually or collectively as independent dependent entrepreneurs. To be registered, the program should last at least 600 (six hundred) hours. Moreover, at least 50% of the program should involve hands-on learning in face-to-face and computer based training sessions.

1.3   Trend Analysis

Through the literature and visualization generated by the VOSviewer software, Fig. 1 shows a heat map using a color key, indicating the trendy topic are, such as start-up, entrepreneur, business, teaching.

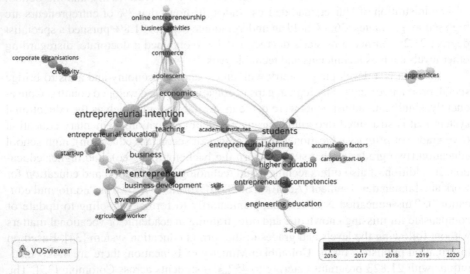

Fig. 1. .

2   Methods

An observational design was adopted because the subjects were selected based on their characteristics, mainly such as that they belonged to training programs offered by the institution, which has a population of almost 2,400 students. To determine the sample, we considered an N population of 2,400, a 99% confidence level, and a 5% margin of error. Based on this data, we obtained a sample of 522 individuals. However, upon applying the instrument, 783 members participated through the web. The instrument used was based on the Global University Entrepreneurial Spirit Students' Survey (GUESSS) [36]. The structure of the categories and variables analyzed is disclosed below (Table 1).

Table 1. Structure of the instrument employed

Categories	Variables	Type
Identification	ID number, Age	Open-ended
	Sex, Marital status	Close-ended
	Academic program	Open-ended
	Courses on entrepreneurship	Yes/No

(*continued*)

Table 1. (*continued*)

Categories	Variables	Type
Family and environment	Valuation of entrepreneurship within the family	Likert scale
	Valuation of entrepreneurship among friends	Likert scale
	Valuation of entrepreneurship across the region/community	Likert scale
	Family's opinion on entrepreneurship	Likert scale
	Friends' opinion on entrepreneurship	Likert scale
	Society's opinion on entrepreneurship	Likert scale
	Existence of family/friends that are entrepreneurs	Close-ended
	Valuation as an entrepreneur	Likert scale
	Attitude toward failure	Likert scale
Personal characteristics	Confidence	Yes/No
	Foresight	Yes/No
	Skills	Yes/No
	Open-mindedness	Yes/No
	Creative problem-solving	Yes/No
	Perseverance	Yes/No
	Achievement orientation	Yes/No
	Teamwork	Yes/No
	Communication	Yes/No
	Adaptation to change	Yes/No
	Innovation	Yes/No
	Attitude toward risk	Likert scale
	Creativity	Likert scale
	Leadership	Likert scale
	Competitive spirit	Likert scale
Entrepreneurial orientation	Intention to start a business upon conclusion of the academic program	Likert scale
	Entrepreneurial attraction	Likert scale
	Feasibility of starting a business	Likert scale
	Understanding of the political and funding context related to the enterprise	Likert scale
	Generation of business ideas	Yes/No
	Desire to start a business	Yes/No
	Capacity to partner up with others	Yes/No

(*continued*)

Table 1. (*continued*)

Categories	Variables	Type
Motivation	Independence/Autonomy	Likert scale
	Recognition and social status	Likert scale
	Profitability	Likert scale
	Challenge/Personal satisfaction	Likert scale
	Family tradition	Likert scale
	Lack of employment	Likert scale
	Management/Top management	Likert scale
	Equity investment	Likert scale
Institutional environment	Educational institution support	Likert scale
	Entrepreneurial training	Likert scale
	Success stories	Likert scale
	Vision upon conclusion of the academic program	Likert scale
	Vision 5 years after the conclusion of the academic program	Close-ended
	Useful entrepreneurial tools	Likert scale
	Vision of employment v. enterprise	Likert scale
	Creation of a network of contacts	Likert scale
	Development of entrepreneurial skills	Likert scale

Source: Own preparation based on [37]

3   Results

The institution currently offers different programs based on needs. It offers 13 programs and several courses according to the specific needs and requests of companies and other stakeholders. It has about 2,400 students and 92 faculty members, and administrative employees. The institution has no entrepreneurship center or office. No specific entrepreneurship-oriented content is offered within the program and courses.

3.1   Sample Characterization

The following section includes a brief characterization of the students that completed the survey of the institution because as there is no benchmark information for the institutions that offer education for work and human development (ITDH, in the Spanish acronym), we are unable to make comparisons using national and international data. See Fig. 2.

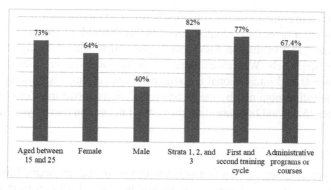

Fig. 2. .

3.2 Entrepreneurial Intention Index

As already mentioned, the method employed herein is developed under the GUESSS project, which calculates entrepreneurial intention by determining the students' intention to start their own business in the future. The index is an average of six attributes rated by students on a scale from 1 (strongly disagree) to 7 (strongly agree). See Fig. 3.

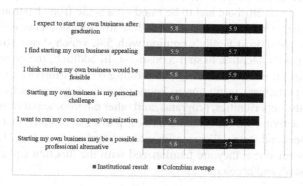

Fig. 3. .

3.3 Enterprise Context

3.3.1 Institutional Context

According to the GUESSS method, to assess the institutional context, we calculated the average between the ratings obtained for the three attributes assessed by the students on a scale from 1 (strongly agree) to 7 (strongly disagree).

Therefore, the institution has an average rating of 5.5 regarding the assessment of the institutional context. This shows that the institution provides a suitable environment and facilitates company creation among students. The attributes assessed upon rating the environment are broken down as follows: the item "The institution encourages students to become involved in entrepreneurial activities" is the best rated with 5.7, followed by "The institution fosters a favorable entrepreneurial environment by consolidating knowledge and skills" and "The institution fosters idea generation and company creation" rated 5.5 and 5.4, respectively. When we compared the national (universities involved in the GUESSS project) and international classification concerning institutional context, we found that the rating obtained by the institution (5.5) is above the Colombian average for universities (5.4), and both are well above the international average (4.2).

3.3.2 Family Context

Academic literature suggests that family is key to young entrepreneurs' intention to start a business. In this sense, according to the method used (GUESSS project), it is essential to examine the family context of the students surveyed to understand thus their decisions about the efforts made toward starting a business [38].

3.3.3 Social Context

As in the case of institutional and family context, the GUESSS method studies the social context for creating companies as a factor that may influence students' decision to start new businesses [39]. In order to analyze the social context, the students surveyed were asked about the expected social reaction should they disclose their plans to start a company. Each attribute had to be rated on a scale from 1 (strongly agree) to 7 (strongly disagree). The value obtained for fellow students stood out with 5.7, followed by the value for the closest family's opinion with 5.4, which shows strong agreement with the participant's intention to start a business. In addition, the community considers that enterprises are worth the risk, with a rating of 5.4. Moreover, we surveyed the students of the participant institution to know whether they were acquainted with the policies, methods, opportunities, programs, and other environmental elements that favor entrepreneurial activity. We found that 74.8% of participants stated that they are aware and clearly understand state policies to finance enterprises. Besides, 71.2% of the parties surveyed asserted that they are familiarized with the function and contributions of business incubators and accelerators.

3.4 Motivation and Attitudes Toward Company Creation

This section describes the attitudes identified among students that are necessary to face the entrepreneurial challenge. The main drivers are personal satisfaction, the desire to be self-employed and independent, and the desire to build up one's self-confidence by fulfilling the personal challenge of becoming an entrepreneur.

The study assessed the students' attitudes toward entrepreneurship. The results show the desire to start their own business as a life alternative (90.4%), to which end they mentioned that they are willing to invest their savings (86.%), which is not considered the only source of financing because they are aware of different sources (60.6%). They also consider partnering up with others to add complementarities (89.9%) and assign equity in exchange for financing (73.6%). See Fig. 4.

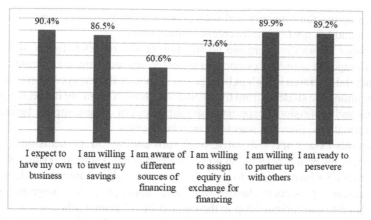

Fig. 4. .

Since failure is a possibility for any entrepreneur, they need to embrace failure and develop attitudes to carry on with their initiative. A total of 94.4% of the students mentioned that it is possible to learn from failure to generate new ideas without making the same mistakes; in this sense, 39.9% of students stated that they have already failed as entrepreneurs and that failure has consolidated their capacity to achieve entrepreneurial success. Only 34.6% of students would abandon the idea of starting a business for fear of failure. In general, motivation is high, and there is a healthy attitude toward company creation, in addition to high self-perception of their entrepreneurial competencies, latent business ideas, and a favorable institutional, family, and social context. All this validates that the intention to start a business upon the termination of the academic program and five years after finishing their studies is higher than the desire to work in a big company or an SME.

4 Conclusion

Entrepreneurship plays a significant role in Colombia's economic growth; this relationship is evidenced when comparing the figures reported by the Global Entrepreneurship Development Institute (GEDI) and the competitiveness ranking disclosed by the World Economic Forum. It is no surprise that the top ten positions in both rankings are held by countries like the United States, Switzerland, Sweden, Holland, and the United Kingdom. Colombia ranks 47th among the 147 countries analyzed in 2018 by the GEDI in entrepreneurship development, and it ranks 66th among the 137 countries analyzed regarding global competitiveness. Under this program, Colombia still has a long road ahead to enhance competitiveness through entrepreneurship.

The Colombian educational system is divided into preschool, elementary school, high school, technical school and higher education, and education for work and human development, offering employment opportunities. Technical vocational schools prepare students to face challenges in the productive sector but limit their actions to technical training; therefore, initiatives are needed to boost entrepreneurship because of its great advantages across the economy and society, such as employment generation, revenue generation, and life quality improvement, among others.

This paper shows that there are no substantial differences between the institution and the average for universities concerning entrepreneurial intention, confirming that entrepreneurial intention is high in both cases. Although the entrepreneurial intention is very high among the students from the institution, most of them are interested in gaining knowledge and professional experience as employees of a big company before dealing with the formal procedures to start their own businesses.

There is also a lack of collaborative work surrounding entrepreneurship in the sectorial context, so the goal or orientation is not clearly defined. There are no interinstitutional activities that coordinate efforts to pave the way for students' initiatives. It is essential to design research projects to classify, offer, and supply processes, programs, and other factors related to entrepreneurship in the context of vocational schools.

This research may be the starting point of a series of works aimed at classifying entrepreneurial intention among these institutions to generate a positive impact on the perception of entrepreneurship in this level of training and to maximize income and increase employment, among other benefits broadly analyzed in the entrepreneurship literature. The method under the guidelines of the Global University's Global University Entrepreneurship Student Survey (GUESSS), which calculates the entrepreneurial intention by determining the students' intention to start their own business in the future, is used primarily in universities. The main contribution of this article is the implementation of this method in the context of technical training institutions or institutions for human work and development, obtaining similar and better results in some cases.

Relevant results can be achieved in relation to entrepreneurship in technical training institutions or institutions for work and human development.

References

1. Aliaga, C., Schalk, A.: E2: Empleabilidad temprana y emprendimiento. Dos grandes desafíos en la formación superior en chile. Calid. en la Educ. 319 (2010). https://doi.org/10.31619/cal edu.n33.145
2. Soria-Barreto, K., Zuniga-Jara, S., Ruiz-Campo, S.: Educación e intención emprendedora en estudiantes universitarios: un caso de estudio. Form. Univ. **9**, 25–34 (2016). https://doi.org/10.4067/S0718-50062016000100004
3. Branchet, B., Křížková, A.: Gender and entrepreneurial intentions in a transition economy context: case of the Czech Republic. Int. J. Entrep. Small Bus. **25**, 260–281 (2015). https://doi.org/10.1504/IJESB.2015.069696
4. Liñán, F., Nabi, G., Kueger, N.: British and Spanish entrepreneurial intentions: a comparative study. Br. Spanish Entrep. Intentions Comp. Study 73–103 (2013)
5. Fuller, B., Liu, Y., Bajaba, S., Marler, L.E., Pratt, J.: Examining how the personality, self-efficacy, and anticipatory cognitions of potential entrepreneurs shape their entrepreneurial intentions. Pers. Individ. Dif. **125**, 120–125 (2018). https://doi.org/10.1016/j.paid.2018.01.005
6. Xiang, H., Lei, J.: Student entrepreneurial intentions in Chinese universities based on the ISO model. Qinghua Daxue Xuebao/J. Tsinghua Univ. **53**, 122-128+138 (2013)
7. Branchet, B., Alena, K., Ížková, N.A.: Gender and entrepreneurial intentions in a transition economy context: case of the Czech Republic. Int. J. Entrep. Small Bus. **25**, 260 (2015). https://doi.org/10.1504/IJESB.2015.069696

8. Wu, L.F.: Perceived value of entrepreneurship and its impact on university student's entrepreneurial intention. Wuhan Ligong Daxue Xuebao/J. Wuhan Univ. Technol. **32**, 200–204 (2010). https://doi.org/10.3963/j.issn.1671-4431.2010.01.047

9. Thandi, H., Sharma, R.: MBA students and entrepreneurship: an Australian study of entrepreneurial intentions and actualisation. J. Inst. Res. South East Asia **2**, 12–24 (2003)

10. Wang, H., Huang, Q.: A conceptal model of entrepreneurial intentions of IT professionals: from an organizational embeddedness perspective. In: International Conference on Management and Service Science, MASS 2011. School of Management, Zhejiang University, Hangzhou, China (2011). https://doi.org/10.1109/ICMSS.2011.5997935

11. Weber, S., Oser, F.K., Achtenhagen, F., Fretschner, M., Trost, S.: Becoming an entrepreneur. In: Becoming an Entrepreneur, pp. 1–322. Institute of Education, University of Zurich, Switzerland (2014). https://doi.org/10.1007/978-94-6209-596-0

12. Medina Brito, M., Bolívar Cruz, A., Lemes Hernández, A.: Un paso más en la investigación de la intención emprendedora del estudiante universitario: GUESSS. Rev. Estud. Empres. Segunda Época **2**, 63–80 (2014)

13. Suciu, C., Grigore, C., Nae, G.G.: Smart, creative, sustainable, inclusive regional development strategies in the age of knowledge & innovation based society & economy. In: Vision 2020: Innovation, Development Sustainability, and Economic Growth - Proceedings of the 21st International Business Information Management Association Conference, IBIMA 2013, pp. 1589–1594. Academy of Economic Studies, Bucharest, Romania (2013)

14. Chernykh, S.I., Parshikov, V.I.: Innovative education in Russia. Int. J. Econ. Financ. Issues **6**, 239–242 (2016)

15. Nicolae, S., Neagu, A.M.: Education and technology - the ways of access to the knowledge society: how far we are? In: Creating Global Economies through Innovation and Knowledge Management Theory and Practice - Proceedings of the 12th International Business Information Management Association Conference, IBIMA 2009, pp. 388–394. "Politehnica" University, Bucharest, Romania (2009)

16. Morton, C.S., Huang-Saad, A., Libarkin, J.: Entrepreneurship education for women in engineering: a systematic review of entrepreneurship assessment literature with a focus on gender. In: ASEE Annual Conference and Exposition, Conference Proceedings. Center for the Study of Higher and Postsecondary Education, University of Michigan, United States (2016). https://doi.org/10.18260/p.26725

17. Rodríguez Chaves, A.M.: La importancia del emprendimiento en la educación media en Colombia. http://hdl.handle.net/10654/14203, (2016)

18. Yan, Y.: The impact of education on economic growth in China. In: Proceeding of the International Conference on e-Education Entertainment and e-Management, ICEEE 2011, pp. 202–204 (2011). https://doi.org/10.1109/ICeEEM.2011.6137785

19. Na, C., XiangQian, Z.: Study on fair education, social mobility and long-term economic growth. Biotechnol. Indian J. **10**, 5900–5909 (2014)

20. Ramesh Rao, R., Jani, R.: Spurring economic growth through education: the Malaysian approach. Educ. Res. Rev. **4**, 135–140 (2009)

21. Ignazzi, C.A.: Lois d'échelle, croissance économique, éducation et crime au Brésil. Espac. Geogr. **43**, 324–337 (2014). https://doi.org/10.3917/eg.434.0324

22. Gylfason, T.: Natural resources, education, and economic development. Eur. Econ. Rev. **45**, 847–859 (2001). https://doi.org/10.1016/S0014-2921(01)00127-1

23. Ovallos Gazabón, D., Velez Zapata, J., Figueroa Cuello, A., Sarmiento Suarez, J., Barrera Navarro, J.: Knowledge and socioeconomic development. A review of the literature— Conocimiento y desarrollo socioeconómico. Una revisión de la literatura. Espacios, p. 38 (2017)

24. Ovallos Gazabón, D., et al.: Capacidades dinámicas y competitividad territorial. Un análisis para el departamento de Sucre. Editorial CECAR, Sincelejo, Sucre (2019). https://doi.org/10.21892/9789585547247

25. García, C.M., et al.: Formación para el emprendimiento en estudiantes de Administración de Empresas * Entrepreneurship training for students in Business Administration. Cent. Estud. en Diseño y Comun. **17**, 47–63 (2015)

26. Duran, S., Fuenmayor, A., Cárdenas, S., Hernández, R.: Emprendimiento Como Proceso De Responsabilidad Social En Instituciones De Educación Superior En Colombia Y Venezuela. Desarro. Gerenc. **8**, 58–75 (2017). https://doi.org/10.17081/dege.8.2.2560

27. Kliewe, T., Meerman, A., Baaken, T.: Challenges and solutions for fostering entrepreneurial universities and collaborative innovation. In: University Industry Innovation Network. University-Industry Interaction, Ámsterdam, The Netherlands (2013)

28. Rico, A.Y., Santamaría, M.: Análisis comparativo de los procesos existentes en el campo del emprendimiento en la educación media en Colombia y Ecuador. Voces y Silenc. Rev. Latinoam. Educ. **8**, 53–68 (2017). https://doi.org/10.18175/vys8.2.2017.04

29. Schlattau, M.: Institutions and entrepreneurial activity: a quantitative empirical analysis. In: Tilting at the Windmills of Transition. Societies and Political Orders in Transition, pp. 135–231. Springer, Cham (2021). https://doi.org/10.1007/978-3-030-54909-1_5

30. Álvarez, C., Urbano, D.: Una década de investigación basada en el gem: logros y retos. Acad. Rev. Latinoam. Adm. **16760**, 16–37 (2011)

31. Ovallos, D., Maldonado Pérez, D., De La Hoz Escorcia, S.: Creatividad, Innovación Y Emprendimiento En La Formación De Ingenieros En Colombia: Un Estudio Prospectivo. Rev. Educ. en Ing. **10**, 90–104 (2015)

32. Doepke, M., Zilibotti, F.: Culture, entrepreneurship, and growth. In: Aghion, P., Durlauf, S.N. (eds.) Handbook of Economic Growth, pp. 1–48. Elsevier (2014). https://doi.org/10.1016/B978-0-444-53538-2.00001-0

33. Liñán, F., Fernandez-Serrano, J.: National culture, entrepreneurship and economic development: different patterns across the European Union. Small Bus. Econ. **42**(4), 685–701 (2013). https://doi.org/10.1007/s11187-013-9520-x

34. Gobierno de Colombia: Sistema educativo colombiano

35. MEN: Sistema de Información de la Educación para el Trabajo y el Desarrollo Humano, Bogota (2020)

36. García-Rodríguez, F.J., Gil-Soto, E., Ruiz-Rosa, I., Gutiérrez-Taño, D.: Entrepreneurial potential in less innovative regions: the impact of social and cultural environment. Eur. J. Manag. Bus. Econ. **26**, 163–179 (2017). https://doi.org/10.1108/EJMBE-07-2017-010

37. Martins, I., Pérez, J., Álvarez, C., López, T., Moreno, J., Hugueth, A.: El espíritu emprendedor de los estudiantes en Colombia. Resultados del Proyecto Guesss 2018. Universidad EAFIT (2019)

38. Gaitán-Angulo, M., Viloria, A., Robayo-Acuña, P., Lis-Gutiérrez, J.P.: Bibliometric review on management of innovation and family enterprise. Int. J. Control Theory Appl. **9**, 247–253 (2016). ISSN 974-5572

39. Moreno-Gomez, J., Hugueth-ALba, A., Peña-Segura, K., Mejia-Neira, A.: EMPRENDIMIENTO en la Universidad de la Costa. Resultados proyecto GUESSS 2016. Educosta (2017)

Improvement of Visual Perception in Humanoid Robots Using Heterogeneous Architectures for Autonomous Applications

Joaquin Guajo[1]([✉]) [iD], Cristian Alzate Anzola[1] [iD], Daniel Betancur[2] [iD], Luis Castaño-Londoño[1] [iD], and David Marquez-Viloria[1] [iD]

[1] Department of Electronics and Telecommunication Engineering, Instituto Tecnológico Metropolitano ITM, Medellín, Colombia
{joseguajo152012,cristianalzate224500}@correo.itm.edu.co, {luiscastano,davidmarquez}@itm.edu.co
[2] Systems and Computer Science Research Group, Institución Universtaria de Envigado, Medellín, Colombia
danielbetancur@itm.edu.co

Abstract. Humanoid robots find application in a variety of tasks such as emotional recognition for human-robot interaction (HRI). Despite their capabilities, these robots have a sequential computing system that limits the execution of high computational cost algorithms such as Convolutional Neural Networks (CNNs), which have shown good performance in recognition tasks. This limitation reduces their performance in HRI applications. As an alternative to sequential computing units are Field-programmable gate arrays (FPGAs) and Graphics Processing Units (GPUs), which have a high degree of parallelism, high performance, and low power consumption. In this paper, we propose a visual perception enhancement system for humanoid robots using FPGA or GPU based embedded systems running a CNN, while maintaining autonomy through an external computational system added to the robot structure. Our work has as a case study the humanoid robot NAO, however, the work can be replicated on other robots such as Pepper and Robotis OP3. The development boards used were the Xilinx Ultra96 FPGA, Intel Cyclone V SoC FPGA and Nvidia Jetson TX2 GPU. Nevertheless, our design allows the integration of other heterogeneous architectures with high parallelism and low power consumption. The Tinier-Yolo, Alexnet and Inception-V1 CNNs are executed and real-time results were obtained for the FPGA and GPU cards, while in Alexnet, the expected results were presented in the Jetson TX2.

Keywords: CNN · Field programmable gate array (FPGA) · System-on-a-Chip (SoC) · High-level synthesis (HLS) · Humanoid robot

J. C. Figueroa-García et al. (Eds.): WEA 2021, CCIS 1431, pp. 447–458, 2021.
https://doi.org/10.1007/978-3-030-86702-7_38

1 Introduction

Humanoid robots are used in assistance-type applications related to domestic, educational, therapeutic services, among others [1]. This use arises from the sensations of comfort generated in humans in the interaction with this type of robot [2]. For the development of these interactions, they have sensory devices that provide them with the ability to perceive and understand the environment. In particular, the visual perception system of humanoid robots is composed of cameras integrated into their structure, which gives them a field of vision [3]. This field of vision allows them to be used in applications oriented to object recognition in real-time. In adition, machine learning algorithms have been used to replicate human cognitive ability for the use of robots in everyday environments. Among these algorithms are CNNs, which have proven to be relevant in projects where object recognition, localization, and detection are integrated, becoming efficient in terms of accuracy in the elaboration of these tasks [4].

Despite their advantages, CNNs involve a high computational cost for their implementation in the computing system of the humanoid robot. Therefore, developments have been implemented in external computational systems based on higher-capacity CPUs connected to the robot computational architecture [6]. The works presented by [7,8] concluded that the limitations in image processing were overcome integrating a external CPU based system. However, the robot autonomy was affected by the continuous connection, generating dependence in tasks that require a free movement in its environment. The limitations presented in terms of responsiveness and autonomy of humanoid robots is a challenging problem, therefore, the implementation of CNNs on GPU or FPGA based embedded systems is a suitable alternative. These devices have a high degree of parallelism and low power consumption in image and video processing applications, which could provide the humanoid robot with greater processing capacity and autonomy in tasks involving higher perception and understanding of the environment.

Different works have addressed the implementation of CNNs on FPGAs. In [10] explore weight and node-level parallelizations over convolutional layer computations. The system use maximum resources through data reuse and concatenation. On the other hand, the use of development environments has allowed researchers to control memory usage and parallelization techniques on these reconfigurable devices. In [11,12] information from a trained CNN network is synthesized in hardware through the Vivado HLS high-level synthesis tool. In [13] is presented a similar work, but they proposed an analytical design model called Roofline in their development. The model allows quantitatively analyzing the computational performance and memory bandwidth required for any solution of a CNN design.

For the implementation of CNNs on GPUs different acceleration techniques have been proposed for video and image processing. In [23] an acceleration method based on the treatment of binary weights is proposed, focusing on optimizing the arithmetic kernel in the storage of the weights. A similar approach is presented in [24], where the acceleration is realized through a resistive random access memory ReRam. This accelerator architecture was adapted for bit-by-bit convolution. In [9] is presented the comparison between the execution of a CNN SSD mobilenet DNN on Intel CPU centered IntelR NUC7i7BNH (NUC) and Jetson TX2 computational systems for an application focused on pedestrian detection on the NUgus humanoid robot. The DNN implementation on the NUC was performed on the CPU due to the incompatibility between Tensorflow and OpenCL, which prevents the implementation on the GPU side. Regarding the development on the Jetson TX2, the DNN implementation is performed on the GPU using CUDA. The results showed that the CPU of the NUC is faster than the GPU of the Jetson TX2 when executing the DNN, achieving 0.17 s in the NUC and 0.57 s in the Jetson TX2. In terms of power consumption, the NUC CPU consumes 40.52 W and the Jetson TX2 around 9.8 W. The results showed a high power consumption and inference times below what is established for a real-time application.

This paper proposes a visual perception enhancement system for humanoid robots using FPGA or GPU based embedded systems running convolutional neural networks. Our research work focuses on solving three problems: (I) improving the visual perception of the humanoid robot in an everyday environment while maintaining autonomy, (II) creating a system that can be replicable to humanoid robots such as Pepper and Robotis OP3, and (III) realizing a development that allows the integration of heterogeneous architectures with a high degree of parallelism, low power consumption and small size that execute a CNN and can be easily integrated to the structure of any humanoid robot. The rest of the document is organized as follows. In Sect. 2 the materials and methods that describe the acquisition of the image, communication with embedded systems, and use of CNN acceleration frameworks for each heterogeneous architecture. Results are presented in Sect. 3. Finally, the conclusions are given in Sect. 4.

2   Materials and Methods

The presented methodology considers that the goal is to design a visual perception enhancement system for humanoid robots based on an external computational system that executes a CNN. For this system, FPGA and GPU based embedded computational systems were evaluated. These heterogeneous architectures have a high degree of parallelism, low power consumption and a smaller size. For this work, Intel Cyclone V SoC and Xilinx Ultra96-V2 cards were used for FPGA evaluation, and Nvidia Jetson TX2 development board was used for GPU evaluation. Table 1 shows the embedded systems features, along with the acceleration framework and the CNN executed.

As a case study, a visual perception system for the NAO humanoid robot is presented. However, being an Ethernet connection between the robot and the embedded system, the presented system can be replicable in humanoid robots such as Pepper and Robotis OP3. This work was developed using a virtual NAO humanoid robot, where the virtual environment was created from Cyberbotics Webots [25], a mobile robotics simulation software that provides a rapid prototyping environment for modeling, programming and simulating mobile robots.

For the acquisition and transmission of the virtual image provided by Webots, Naoqi SDK and Choregraphe [20] programming software were used. For the transmission of the video from the robot, the encoding and sending of packets was performed using a TCP/IP socket. The video reception stage and the execution of the CNN are performed on each commercial embedded system selected. Figure 1 shows the diagram of the proposed system methodology.

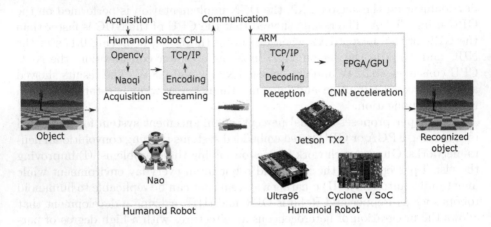

Fig. 1. Diagram of the presented system methodology

Table 1. Embedded systems, acceleration frameworks and CNNs executed

Company	Embedded system	CNN acceleration framework	CNN
Intel	Cyclone V SoC	PipeCNN	Alexnet
Xilinx	Ultra96	FINN	Tinier-Yolo
		DPU	Inception-V1
Nvidia	Jetson TX2	Darknet	Tinier-Yolo
		TensorRT	Inception-V1
			Alexnet

2.1 Image Acquisition and Transmission

The video acquisition system for the NAO humanoid robot was simulated using Webots, it was possible to create a virtual environment and subsequently perform a movement control using Choregraphe. Once the scene is captured by Choregraphe, video transmission to the FPGA or GPU embedded system is started.

Image Acquisition. The image acquisition system was based on the use of a virtual environment containing objects to be recognized by the NAO humanoid robot that was also located in the recreated scene. This virtual environment was created from the Webots simulator, where the image of the recreated scene is sent to Choreographe in order to edit interactive movements for the robot and start the transmission of the image to each embedded system. The communication between Webots and Choreographe is done using *naoqisim* software, which allowed the motion control of the NAO robot generated by Choreographe to be displayed in the Webots simulator. For the visualization in Choreographe of the image generated by Webots, Naoqi API is used, which contains libraries for the acquisition and communication of images by assigning an IP address and an Ethernet port.

Image Transmission to the Embedded System. In the development of this stage, TCP was used as the packet transmission protocol. Using Python libraries, it was possible to encode the image and then send it through an IP address and a Ethernet port. The *Base 64* library allowed the encoded and decoded of the image from *RFC 3548* standard. Using *Base 64*, the algorithms of *Base 16*, *Base 32* and *Base 64* were used to encode and decode arbitrary strings into text strings that could be sent over the network. Finally, the image displayed in Choregraphe is transmitted to each embedded system.

Image Reception on the Embedded System. For the reception of the virtual image provided by Webots on the FPGA and GPU, the libraries described in the previous section were used. Through the function *setsockopt string* the received data is manipulated and converted to a series of characters *string*. Subsequently, this series of characters is decoded and converted to the positional numbering system *Base 64*. Finally, the decoded image is read from the buffer stored in memory using the OpenCV function *cv2.imdecode*.

2.2 Implementation of CNNs on Acceleration Frameworks

The CNNs implementation on FPGA and GPU based embedded systems was performed using available acceleration frameworks. For the execution of CNNs on FPGAs the PipeCNN, FINN, and DPU frameworks were used. For the GPU, the Darknet and TensorRT frameworks were implemented. For our application, pre-trained models were used to evaluate the performance of these heterogeneous architectures and include them in the visual perception enhancement system for humanoid robots.

Implementation of CNNs on FPGA Boards. The FPGA implementation was performed for two different acceleration frameworks. The PipeCNN framework was adapted for the Cyclone V-SoC development system. PipeCNN is an FPGA CNN accelerator developed in OpenCL. PipeCNN uses two parameters to control the hardware resource cost and improve execution time. These parameters are the size of the data vectorization and the number of parallel computing units. This framework also uses high-level methodologies based on OpenCL, allowing highly efficient and configurable kernels to be adapted to a wide variety of CNN models. Another optimization used by PipeCNN is Fixed-Point arithmetic representation instead of Floating-Point, reducing the resource consumption considerably in the FPGAs, although the accuracy of the CNNs is also reduced. In addition, the free software application Quantized Neural Network was used for the Ultra 96 board. This application is based on the FINN framework presented by [14]. This framework allows the implementation of CNNs on Xilinx devices with a predefined architecture and high efficiency to focus more on the implementation. The implementation is done on an Ultra96 SoC board using the PYNQ framework. The PYNQ framework is used for rapid code development on the host. This framework allows high-speed applications to run side-by-side on hardware with Python-based software applications.

In the FINN framework, there are two types of CNN acceleration architectures implemented on FPGA. The main difference between them is based on the fact that the DF architecture is built for a single CNN topology, weights and activations already defined. The Tinier-yolo network architecture was implemented in the Ultra96 SoC. The input and output layers are executed in software (ARM) through Python, while the internal layers are executed in hardware (FPGA). The layers consist of operations such as convolutions and max pooling. The framework supports only quantized layers, meaning that weights and activations are represented from 1 to 3 bits. The Tinier-yolo is a modified version of the Tiny Yolo object detection system. Tinier-yolo is also trained with the PASCAL VOC database, but with 1 bit for weights and 3 bits for activations. Tinier-yolo has a 50.1% mAP compared to the 57.1% mAP of Tiny-yolo.

Finally, Xilinx DPU was used for the execution of the CNN Inception-V1 on the Ultra96-V2 FPGA. The DPU is a programmable engine dedicated to executing each of the convolutional layers present in a CNN through a register configuration module, data controller module, and convolution computation module. This DPU module is integrated as a programmable logic unit (PL) which connects to the processing system (PS). Like the FINN framework, along with the DPU, PYNQ is used for host-side application development through an AX14-based interface. Vitis IA is used to convert the model trained in Tensorflow to *.elf format. This format contains the weight information, which the ARM of the FPGA SoC reads, and from there, sends the tasks to the DPU for processing and transmission of the result back. There are *.elf files for trained models such as Mnist, Resnet50 and YoloV3. However, for comparison with the Jetson TX2 we have selected the CNN Inception-V1.

Implementation of CNNs on GPU Board. Two frameworks were used for the implementation of CNNs on the Jetson TX2 GPU. Inception-V1 and Alexnet networks were implemented using Nvidia TensorRT. TensorRT, Cuda and Cudnn were used for the inference stage. TensorRT is an optimizer of a model trained using Cuda and Cudnn, achieving low latency, ideal for real-time applications. This framework provides a quantization operation for the GPU inference engine. The computational latency is shortened due to floating arithmetic operations, and, in order not to reduce the model MAP, the weights were quantized to 16-bits in the inference stage.

TensorRT modifies the size of the images before and after the inference process. Since this modification is computationally expensive on the CPU, the framework uses *multithreading* on the CPU to speed up the process. TensorRT creates two threads on each CPU core, and each thread processes one batch of data. The Jetson TX2 has 6 CPU cores, so TensorRT creates 12 threads. GPU inference can only run on a single thread. Therefore, the framework takes inference as a mutual process, and the different threads must compete for the GPU. Finally, for the implementation of the Tinier-Yolo network, Darknet was used, which is an open source framework for running convolutional neural networks, where data processing is done through C and CUDA for computation between CPU and GPU.

3 Results

For the image acquisition and communication system, three different tests were performed varying the resolution of the acquired image and the encoding and decoding quality factor. In each test, data are taken on the number of frames per second (fps) and the transmission rate measured in kbps (kbits per second). The following Table 2 shows each of the results for each resolution. It can be seen that as the input image resolution increases, the frames per second decrease. However, the FPS obtained by setting the image to the standard resolution of the NAO camera (640×480) is much higher than expected for a real-time application. By focusing the research work on the NAO humanoid robot, this resolution is taken as the entry point to the given data processing system for each heterogeneous architecture when running the CNN.

Table 2. FPS and Kbps in image transmission and reception

Image resolution	Transmission		Reception	
	kbps	fps	kbps	fps
1920×1080 FullHD	91452.3	20	91121.1	19
640×480 VGA	10743.3	65	10534.6	63
224×224 Imagenet	11342.3	128	11134.6	123

On the other hand, concerning CNN implementations in embedded systems, results were obtained in frames per second and power consumption. To evaluate the performance of the object detection system implemented in FPGA, a CNN was implemented in the PipeCNN framework using an INTEL FPGA board. The implemented CNN is a quantized version of AlexNet containing eight convolution layers executed on the FPGA. A result of 205 ms per image was obtained, which means that the FPGA can process 4.87 images per second. As a first result, it is observed that this implementation is not in real-time because it is not in the range of 20 to 30 FPS. Table 3 shows different implementations of this same CNN in different platforms, and if our implementation is compared with the others, it is the one with the lowest performance in terms of FPS.

Table 3. Comparison on FPS for different platforms implemented by CNN Alexnet

	PipeCNN	PipeCNN [15]	CUDA [16]	AlexNet [17]	Ncsdk [16]
Platform	**Cyclone V-SoC**	DE5-net	Jetson TX2	Stratix-V	Movidius
Frame rate	**4.87**	66	70	864.7	11

Power consumption results were estimated with Intel Quartus®Prime Power Analyzer software. The maximum number of compute units that can be implemented on the Cyclone V SoC is four units. It can be seen from Table 4 that the resources used are below the total amount contained on the board. This occurs because the board contains only 4192 lab that are maxed out in this implementation. For this reason, it is not possible to increase the performance of the framework on the Cyclone V-SoC, unlike the implementation performed by [15] on the DE5-net platform which does achieve real-time ranking, since the platform is much larger in terms of resources.

Table 4. PipeCNN framework resources in the Cyclone V SoC Development Kit

PipeCNN			
Resources	Used	Available	Percentage of use
LUT	48173	110000	43.79%
FF	66830	219144	30.50%
RAM	285	514	55.45%
DSP	35	112	31.25%
Power consumption	2.056W		

For the second framework, the image was acquired with a high resolution webcam in real time. It was done with the help of the OpenCV libraries installed by default in the PYNQ framework. In Fig. 2, the boxes of the object position and the prediction of the identified objects are observed.

As a result, on the Ultra96, we obtain an execution time of 83 ms, equivalent to 12 frames per second, which is still below real-time execution. Table 5 shows implementations of this same CNN on different platforms where observe more FPS on the tinier-yolo implemented on the Ultra96 than on the Jetson Tx2, but worse performance compared to another FPGA implementation. However, this implementation is realized on a higher capacity FPGA than the one used in this implementation.

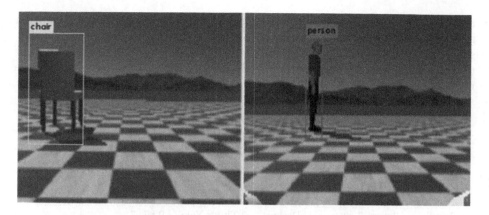

Fig. 2. Chair and person detection

Table 5. Comparison in FPS for different platforms implemented by CNN Tiny Yolo.

	Tinier yolo	Tiny Yolo [18]	Tiny Yolo [19]
Platform	**Ultra96**	Jetson TX2	VC707 board
Frame rate (fps)	**12**	5	21

The amount of resources used in the Ultra96 is the same for any implementation since the MO architecture is topology independent. It can be seen in Table 6 how the BRAM is at more than 90% of the available resources on the board, but for the rest of the resources it does not exceed 50%. This is expected since FPGAs have little internal memory storage capacity.

Table 6. Resources used in the implementation of the QNN framework at Ultra96

FINN framework			
Resources	Used	Available	Percentage of use
LUT	29754	70560	42.17%
Register	36050	141120	25.55%
Block RAM	200	216	92.59%
DSP	56	360	15.56%
Power consumption	3.1W		

The Table 7 shows the results obtained in the implementation of the CNNs in the heterogeneous architectures. The Inception-V1 CNN, when implemented on the FPGA and GPU, can be used in real-time applications in these embedded systems with low power consumption and smaller size. In the case of the Tinier-Yolo CNN, the results were well below those established for an application requiring fast response times. As a reference, we took the power consumption given by the Ultra96 when running a CNN presented in [22]. Regarding the Jetson TX2, for the execution of Inception-V1 (GoogleNet) and Alexnet, we show the power consumed presented by Nvidia in [26] during the execution of these networks in Max-Q clock cycle operation mode.

Table 7. General results

Company	Embedded system	Framework	CNN	Fps	Power consuption W
Intel	Cyclone V SoC	PipeCNN	Alexnet	4.87	2.056
Xilinx	Ultra96	FINN	Tinier-Yolo	12	3.1
		DPU	Inception-V1	30.3	8.16 [22]
Nvidia	Jetson Tx2	Darknet	Tinier-Yolo	9.86	7
		TensorRT	Inception-V1	28.5	4.8 [26]
			Alexnet	29.5	5.6 [26]

4   Conclusions

In this paper we present a system to improve visual perception in humanoid robots in autonomous applications by integrating heterogeneous architectures based on GPU or FPGA running a CNN. The Alexnet, Inception-V1, and Tinier-YOLO CNNs were used to reference architecture selection in the final implementation. We evaluated the performance of the Xilinx Ultra96-V2 FPGA, Intel Cyclone V SoC FPGA, and Nvidia Jetson TX2 GPU platforms when running these CNN models. The Ultra96 achieves 12 fps when running Tinier-YOLO at 3.1 W, while the Jetson TX2 achieves 9.86 fps and power consumption of 7 W, having as input an image size of 640×480 pixels, which is the standard resolution of the NAO humanoid robot camera. For our application on the CNN Inception-V1, real-time results were obtained for heterogeneous architectures with FPGA (Intel Cyclone V SoC and Ultra96-V2), while on Alexnet, expected behavior was obtained when running on the JetsonTX2. Despite the implementations of deep learning models in the conventional computational system of humanoid robots shown in the introduction, processing times during object recognition are affected by the high computational cost required by deep learning models such as CNNs. The integration of a CNN and a heterogeneous FPGA or GPU based architecture in humanoid robots can provide the automaton with real-time visual perception enhancement that can be exploited in human-robot interaction applications. In this research work, we have solved three problems: (I) reduce the execution time and improve the accuracy of object detection in an everyday environment while maintaining the autonomy of the robot, (II) create a system that can be replicable to humanoid robots such as Pepper and Robotis OP3 and (III) realize a development that allows to integrate heterogeneous architectures with a high degree of parallelism, low power and small size that execute a CNN and can be easily integrated into the structure of any humanoid robot through a backpack.

Acknowledgements. This study were supported by the AE&CC research Group COL0053581, at the Sistemas de Control y Robótica Laboratory, attached to the Instituto Tecnológico Metropolitano. This work is part of the project "Improvement of visual perception in humanoid robots for objects recognition in natural environments using Deep Learning" with ID P17224.

References

1. Fanello, S.R., et al.: Visual recognition for humanoid robots. Robot. Auton. Syst. **91**, 151–168 (2017)
2. Cha, E., Matarić, M., Fong, T.: Nonverbal signaling for non-humanoid robots during human-robot collaboration. In: 2016 11th ACM/IEEE International Conference on Human-Robot Interaction (HRI), pp. 601–602. IEEE (2016)
3. Shamsuddin, S.: Initial response of autistic children in human-robot interaction therapy with humanoid robot NAO. In: IEEE 8th International Colloquium on Signal Processing and its Applications, pp. 188–193. IEEE (2012)
4. Sermanet, P., et al. OverFeat: integrated recognition, localization and detection using convolutional networks. arXiv preprint arXiv:1312.6229 (2013)
5. Nguyen, H.V., et al.: DASH-N: joint hierarchical domain adaptation and feature learning. IEEE Trans. Image Process. **24**(12), 5479–5491 (2017)
6. Podpora, M., Gardecki, A.: Extending vision understanding capabilities of NAO robot by connecting it to a remote computational resource. In: Progress in Applied Electrical Engineering (PAEE), pp. 1–5. IEEE (2016)
7. Puheim, M., Bundzel, M., Madarász, L.: Forward control of robotic arm using the information from stereo-vision tracking system. In: IEEE 14th International Symposium on Computational Intelligence and Informatics (CINTI), pp. 57–62. IEEE (2013)
8. Noda, K., et al.: Multimodal integration learning of robot behavior using deep neural networks. Robot. Auton. Syst. **62**(6), 721–736 (2014)
9. Biddulph, A., Houliston, T., Mendes, A., Chalup, S.K.: Comparing computing platforms for deep learning on a humanoid robot. In: Cheng, L., Leung, A.C.S., Ozawa, S. (eds.) ICONIP 2018. LNCS, vol. 11307, pp. 120–131. Springer, Cham (2018). https://doi.org/10.1007/978-3-030-04239-4_11
10. Dundar, A., et al.: Embedded streaming deep neural networks accelerator with applications. IEEE Trans. Neural Netw. Learn. Syst. **28**(7), 1572–1583 (2016)
11. Sozzo, D.E.L., Emanuele, O.: The automation of high level synthesis of convolutional neural networks. . In: IEEE International Parallel and Distributed Processing Symposium Workshops (IPDPSW), pp. 217–244. IEEE (2016)
12. Zhang, C., et al.: Caffeine: toward uniformed representation and acceleration for deep convolutional neural networks. IEEE Trans. Comput. Aided Des. Integr. Circuits Syst. **38**(11), 2072–2085 (2018)
13. Zhang, C., et al.: Optimizing FPGA-based accelerator design for deep convolutional neural networks. In: Proceedings of the 2015 ACM/SIGDA International Symposium on Field-programmable Gate Arrays, pp. 161–170 (2015)
14. Blott, M., et al.: FINN-R: an end-to-end deep learning framework for fast exploration of quantized neural networks. ACM Trans. Reconfig. Technol. Syst. (TRETS) **11**(3), 1–23 (2018)
15. Wang, D., Xu, K., Jiang, D.: PipeCNN: an OpenCL-based open-source FPGA accelerator for convolution neural networks. In: 2017 International Conference on Field Programmable Technology (ICFPT), pp. 279–282. IEEE (2017)

16. Modasshir, M., Li, A.Q., Rekleitis, I.: Deep neural networks: a comparison on different computing platforms. In: 2018 15th Conference on Computer and Robot Vision (CRV), pp. 383–389. IEEE (2018)
17. Liang, S., et al.: FP-BNN: binarized neural network on FPGA. Neurocomputing **275**, 1072–1086 (2018)
18. Xu, S.: Real-time implementation of YOLO+ JPDA for small scale UAV multiple object tracking. In: international conference on unmanned aircraft systems (ICUAS), pp. 1336–1341. IEEE (2018)
19. Ma, J., Chen, L., Gao, Z.: Hardware implementation and optimization of tiny-YOLO network. In: Zhai, G., Zhou, J., Yang, X. (eds.) IFTC 2017. CCIS, vol. 815, pp. 224–234. Springer, Singapore (2018). https://doi.org/10.1007/978-981-10-8108-8_21
20. Pot, E., et al.: Choregraphe: a graphical tool for humanoid robot programming. In: RO-MAN 2009-The 18th IEEE International Symposium on Robot and Human Interactive Communication, pp. 46–51. IEEE (2009)
21. Mattamala, M., Olave, G., González, C., Hasbún, N., Ruiz-del-Solar, J.: The NAO backpack: an open-hardware add-on for fast software development with the NAO robot. In: Akiyama, H., Obst, O., Sammut, C., Tonidandel, F. (eds.) RoboCup 2017. LNCS (LNAI), vol. 11175, pp. 302–311. Springer, Cham (2018). https://doi.org/10.1007/978-3-030-00308-1_25
22. Cosmas, K., Kenichi, A.: Utilization of FPGA for onboard inference of landmark localization in CNN-based spacecraft pose estimation. Aerospace **7**(11), 159 (2009)
23. Andri, R.: YodaNN: an ultra-low power convolutional neural network accelerator based on binary weights. In: IEEE Computer Society Annual Symposium on VLSI (ISVLSI), pp. 236–241. IEEE (2016)
24. Ni, L., et al.: An energy-efficient digital ReRAM-crossbar-based CNN with bitwise parallelism. IEEE Jo. Explor. Solid-State Comput. Devices Circuits **3**, 37–46 (2017)
25. MICHEL, Olivier. Cyberbotics Ltd., Webots^{TM}: professional mobile robot simulation. International Journal of Advanced Robotic Systems, 2004, vol. 1, no 1, p. 5
26. Franklin, D.: NVIDIA Jetson TX2 Delivers Twice the Intelligence to the Edge (2017). https://devblogs.nvidia.com/jetson-tx2-delivers-twiceintelligence-edge/. Accessed 02 Nov 2019

Computational Design of a Road Safety Model Elaborated in Epoxy Material Reinforced with Glass Fibers and SiO2 Addition

M. Echeverri Peláez$^{(\boxtimes)}$ ⓘ, G. Suárez Guerrero ⓘ, J. Cruz Riaño ⓘ,
H. Kerguelen Grajales ⓘ, and E. Vallejo Morales ⓘ

Grupo de Investigación Sobre Nuevos Materiales, Escuela de ingeniería,
Universidad Pontificia Bolivariana, Medellín, Colombia
{mateo.echeverrip,gustavo.suarez,luis.cruz,herbert.kerguelen,
esteban.vallejomo}@upb.edu.co

Abstract. According to data from the World Health Organization (2018), road accidents are considered one of the main causes of mortality worldwide. The highest number of deaths occurs in motorcycle road accidents since the skull protection helmet does not effectively protect the life of the user. Globally, only 17% of countries have established standards to determine the quality of protective helmets. In this research, a Full-Helmet type road protection helmet was built to evaluate the mechanical behavior of a material made of epoxy resin reinforced with glass fibers and the addition of silicon nanoparticles, and to determine the efficiency of the design. Based on the Standard of the Colombian Institute of Technical Standards and Certification (ICONTEC-2017), an external pressure condition was determined on the front of the model, 0.01 MPa. The mechanical properties such as Young's modulus, Poisson's radius, densities, among others, were established. Computational implementations were made based on the Finite Elements technique. Likewise, computational tests were carried out incorporating conventional materials (ABS), in order to make comparisons of the effectiveness of the material between both designs. The results reflected an excellent mechanical contribution of the material reinforced with glass fibers and particles in comparison with the design implemented by means of conventional materials. As a result, approximately 30% of the ability to absorb mechanical impact energy was obtained. This research allows to present other alternatives of special materials to improve the mechanical properties of road protection helmets, with densities that do not increase the robustness or weight of the design.

Keywords: Road protection helmets · Nanomaterials · Finite elements · Modeling and computational simulations

1 Introduction

One of the great problems that have been presented at the road level is the high growth of traffic accidents and death of the driver despite wearing his road protection helmet. It has been detected that most of the helmets do not comply with the design standards

© Springer Nature Switzerland AG 2021
J. C. Figueroa-García et al. (Eds.): WEA 2021, CCIS 1431, pp. 459–467, 2021.
https://doi.org/10.1007/978-3-030-86702-7_39

established by governments with low product quality since they are manufactured with materials that do not withstand large impacts [1, 2].

The helmet is the most important safety accessory for a motorcyclist and his passenger. There are different types of helmets on the market, however, the user is usually guided by aesthetics and price without considering whether they are properly certified. Some regulatory helmets can be purchased in Colombia, even so, according to the Center for Experimentation and Road Safety (CESVI), out of every ten helmets sold in the country, six have major failures by not meeting minimum quality standards [3–5].

Currently, most helmets have a polymer of acrylonitrile, butadiene, styrene (ABS) as the main components. This thermoplastic provides good mechanical properties such as: impact resistance, toughness and rigidity, but only for certain functional conditions [6–8]. Traditionally, manufacturers improve impact resistance by increasing the proportion of polybutadiene in relation to styrene and acrylonitrile, to lower the manufacturing price, sacrificing quality [9, 10].

In this work, the evaluation of a helmet designed with epoxy resin reinforced with glass fibers was considered because it is lighter and cheaper compared to other compounds reinforced with synthetic fabrics made with Kevlar and carbon. Another advantage is that other component materials can be added to the fiber to improve its mechanical properties [11, 12].

To determine the functionality conditions, the standard of the Colombian Institute of Technical Standards and Certification (ICONTEC) was used, which was established under other international standards. The external pressure condition of 0.01 MPa was determined and the most appropriate point of the hull was established from the standard to execute the computational tests. The mechanical properties of the materials were established.

The computational implementation was carried out using the Finite Elements technique that allows solving the constitutive law of composite materials through a matrix variational formulation that can deliver the displacements and strains that occur in the impact phenomenon.

2   Conditions of Functionality

From the ICONTEC standard, the following functional conditions were established, see Table 1.

Table 1. Functional conditions for impact tests.

Conditions of functionality	Value
Acceleration	$9,8 \text{ m/s}^2$
Mass	15 kg
Impact area	10 cm^2
Pressure	0,01Mpa

In the same way, the Standard indicates the place where the impact should be generated, considering the reference plane, in the frontal area, as described (see Fig. 1).

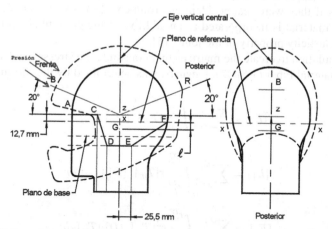

Fig. 1. Description of the reference plane, in the frontal area, in an area of 10 cm² to exert the impact.

The mechanical properties of the implemented materials are, see Table 2:

Table 2. Mechanical properties for impact tests.

Mechanical properties	Value
Epoxy material modulus of elasticity	3,4 GPa
Modulus of elasticity of fiberglass + SiO2	5.5 GPa
Poisson radius epoxy material	0,34
Poisson radius fiberglass + SiO2	0,19

3 Mathematical Model

A constitutive model defined by Hooke's law for composite materials was established by formulating:

$$\sigma_f = E_f \varepsilon$$
$$\sigma_m = E_m \varepsilon \tag{1}$$

where:
σ_f: Stresses in the direction of fiberglass.
σ_m: Epoxy matrix stresses.

ε: Strains in the direction of the fiber or matrix.

$E_{f, m}$: Elastic modulus of fiber + nanoparticles or matrix.

For the analysis of hull materials subjected to high impact pressures to model system conditions as if they were real accident environments [13, 14]. It is clarified that the nanoparticle material is incorporated as an additive in the glass fiber, so it only has a mechanical elasticity property of the joint [15].

The formulation to create the matrices that constitute the stresses and strains of the composite material Fiber (+ SiO2) + matrix, was determined by the formulation:

$$[E_0] = \sum_{j=1}^{n_L} \int_{r_j^{BT}}^{r_j^{TP}} [T_m] \ [D]_j [T_m]_j dr \tag{2}$$

$$[E_1] = \sum_{j=1}^{n_L} \int_{r_j^{BT}}^{r_j^{TP}} r[T_m] \ [D]_j [T_m]_j dr \tag{3}$$

$$[E_2] = \sum_{j=1}^{n_L} \int_{r_j^{BT}}^{r_j^{TP}} r^2[T_m] \ [D]_j [T_m]_j dr \tag{4}$$

Where:

n_L: Number of layers.

$[D]$: Stress-strain relationship at the point of interest within the layer.

$[T_m]$: Layer transformation matrix on element.

r: Coordinate at a point of interest within layer j.

The forces and moments of the deformed material are described by:

$$\left\{ \begin{array}{c} \{N\} \\ \{M\} \end{array} \right\} = \left\{ \begin{array}{cc} [E_0] & [E_1] \\ [E_1] & [E_2] \end{array} \right\} \left\{ \begin{array}{c} \{\varepsilon\} \\ \{k\} \end{array} \right\} \tag{5}$$

The stresses and strains of the simulation are obtained by:

$$\{\varepsilon\}_j = [T_m]_j [B] \{u_\epsilon\} \tag{6}$$

$$\{\sigma\}_j = [D]_j \left(\{\varepsilon\}_j - \left\{ \varepsilon^{th} \right\}_j \right) \tag{7}$$

Where:

$\{N\}$: Forces per unit length.

$\{M\}$: Moments per unit length.

$\{S_1\},\{S_0\}$: Vectors due to thermal loads.

$\{\varepsilon\}$: Strains.

$\{k\}$: Curvatures.

$\{u_e\}$: Element displacement vector.

$\{\varepsilon_{th}\}_j$: Thermal strains in layer j.

$[B]$: Matrix corresponding to membrane effects, bending, shear.

4 Design Considerations

The shape of the helmet was made from the standard dimensions established for a size M. This model was used since its shape can provide greater geometric safety. The form of the considered helmet design is presented below, (see Fig. 2).

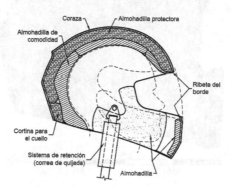

Fig. 2. Helmet design shape chosen for computational testing (Full-Helmet).

The geometry was built to the dimensions of the real Full-Helmet model. A coating of fiberglass, silicon nanoparticles and epoxy resin was implemented in the housing to this structure. Pressure conditions already described were established, (see Fig. 3).

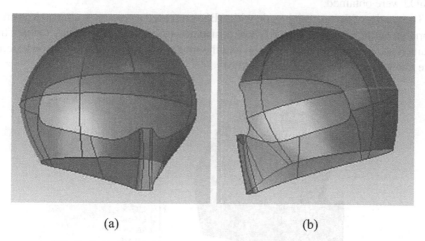

(a)   (b)

Fig. 3. Full-Helmet, developed for computational testing (a) y (b).

5 Computational Considerations

A numerical mesh was made with quadrilateral elements to numerically represent the geometry of the protective helmet. The Ansys program was used where the computational model was implemented (see Fig. 4).

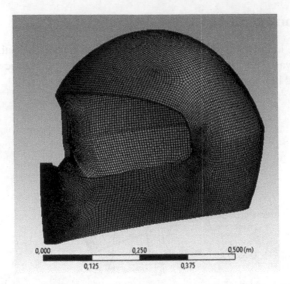

Fig. 4. Elaboration of the numerical mesh to represent the helmet computationally.

6   Results and Discussion

The results of the protective helmet made with ABS and made with Epoxy + Fiberglass + SiO2 were obtained.

The results of the material made with ABS, presented a greater strain and Von-mises efforts since the material supports less resistance to impact. The values of the strain obtained were approximately of 6e-4, and the maximum values of the von-mises effort were about 1.12E7 Pa, (see Figs. 5 and 6).

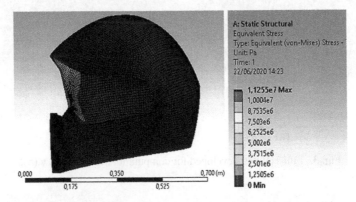

Fig. 5. Results of Von-Mises efforts of the helmet designed with ABS material.

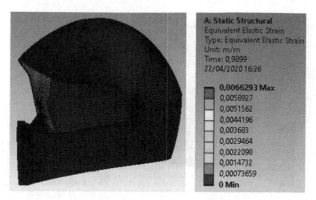

Fig. 6. Results of mechanical strain of the helmet designed with ABS material.

Similarly, simulations of the protective helmet with Epoxy + Fiberglass + SiO2 material were elaborated, which presented a mechanical behavior with less strain and Von-Mises efforts due to the contribution made by the composite material in the design. A maximum strain of 1e-3 was obtained, and the maximum values of the Von-mises stress were about 3.07E6 Pa, (see Figs. 7 and 8).

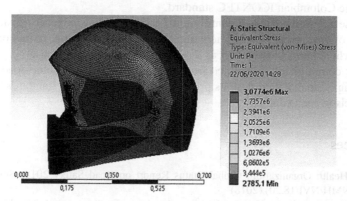

Fig. 7. Results of Von-Mises efforts of the helmet designed with epoxy + Ffberglass + SiO2 material.

The simulations reflected a significant contribution of the fiber-reinforced material + SiO2 compared to the design made with the ABS material. The composite material had a greater ability to dissipate impact energy, which would allow in a road accident to avoid significant damage to the wearer's skull. The mechanical behavior of ABS had a dissipation of mechanical energy in a differential way compared to the material hull made with glass fibers + SiO2, since the glass fibers can be oriented in a convenient way.

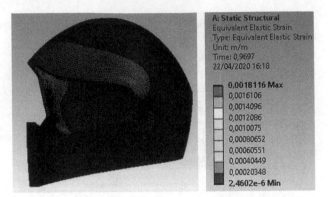

Fig. 8. Results of mechanical strain of the helmet designed with epoxy + fiberglass + SiO2 material.

7   Conclusions

The use of composite materials in designs where functional impact conditions are present has been applied in different road protection systems, among others.

The region selected to evaluate the design of the road protection helmet was made based on the Colombian ICONTEC standard.

The research is intended to contribute to a greater knowledge of impact behavior in designs of road protection helmets and thus, contribute to the reduction of traffic accidents where human loss occurs as a result of the failure of the case.

Greater commitment is expected from manufacturers that develop road protection helmet designs, so that their designs provide quality based on the standards that govern these models in each country.

References

1. World Health Organization: Global Status Report on Road Safety 2018: Summary (No. WHO/NMH/NVI/18.20) (2018)
2. Chaichan, S., et al.: Are full-face helmets the most effective in preventing head and neck injuries in motorcycle accidents? A meta-analysis. Prevent. Med. Reports **19**, 101118 (2020). https://doi.org/10.1016/j.pmedr.2020.101118
3. Becker, E.B., Anishchenko, D.V., Palmer, S.B.: Response to the impact of motorcycle helmets at various levels of severity for different standard certifications. In: Proceedings of the IRCOBI Conference, Lyon, France, pp. 9–11, September 2015
4. Fernandes, F.A., Alves de Sousa, R.J., Ptak, M., Wilhelm, J.: Certified motorcycle helmets: computational evaluation of the efficiency of standard requirements with finite element models. Math. Comput. App. **25**(1), 12 (2020). https://doi.org/10.3390/mca25010012
5. Aristizábal, D., González, G., Suárez, J.F., Roldán, P.: Factors associated with fatal trauma in motorcyclists from Medellín (Colombia). Biomedica **32**(1), 112–124 (2012)
6. Peters, E.N.: Plastics: Thermoplastics, Thermosets and Elastomers, pp. 335–355. Wiley-Interscience, New York (2002)

7. Dana, H.R., Barbe, F., Delbreilh, L., Azzouna, M.B., Guillet, A., Breteau, T.: Polymeric additive manufacturing with ABS structure: influence of the printing direction on the mechanical properties. J. Manuf. Process. **44**, 288–298 (2019). https://doi.org/10.1016/j.jmapro.2019.06.015

8. Ng, C.T., Susmel, L.: Notch the static strength of additively manufactured acrylonitrile butadiene styrene (ABS). Addit. Manuf. **34**, 101212 (2020). https://doi.org/10.1016/j.addma.2020.101212

9. Fernandes, F.A.O., De Sousa, R.A.: Motorcycle helmets: a cutting edge review. Anal. Prevent. Accidents **56**, 1–21 (2013). https://doi.org/10.1016/j.aap.2013.03.011

10. Gilchrist, A., Mills, N.J.: Modeling of the response to impact of motorcycle helmets. Int. J. Impact Eng. **15**(3), 201–218 (1994). https://doi.org/10.1016/S0734-743X(05)80013-2

11. Bajpai, P.K., Ram, K., Gahlot, L.K., Jah, V.K.: Manufacture of industrial safety helmet based on glass/jute/epoxy compound. Today's. Mater. Actas **5**(2), 8699–8706 (2018). https://doi.org/10.1016/j.matpr.2017.12.296

12. Clifton, S., Thimmappa, B.H.S., Selvam, R., Shivamurthy, B.: Polymer nanocomposites for high speed impact applications: a review. Composites Commun. **17**, 72–86 (2020). https://doi.org/10.1016/j.coco.2019.11.013

13. Suárez, G., Oller, S., Cruz, J.: Simulation of an industrial container designed under hydraulic pressure in a composite material with fiberglass. In: Computational Plasticity: Fundamentals and Applications-Proceedings of the 8th International Conference on Computational Plasticity, COMPLAS VIII, pp. 818–822 (2005).http: //hdl.handle.net/2117/16374

14. Kääntä, L., Kasper, G., Piirainen-Marsh, A.: Explanation of Hooke's law: definition practices in a CLIL physics classroom. Appl. Linguist. **39**(5), 694–717 (2018). https://doi.org/10.1093/applin/amw025

15. Suárez, H., Barlow, J.W., Paul, D.R.: Mechanical properties of ABS / polycarbonate blends. J. Appl. Polym. Sci. **29**(11), 3253–3259 (1984). https://doi.org/10.1002/app.1984.070291104

Modeling, Analysis and Simulation of Curved Solar Cell's Encapsulation Reinforcement

Gabriel Espitia-Mesa[1]([✉]), Efraín Hernández-Pedraza[1],
Santiago Molina-Tamayo[2], and Ricardo Mejía-Gutiérrez[1]

[1] Design Engineering Research Group (GRID), Universidad EAFIT,
Carrera 49 No 7 Sur–50, Medellín, Colombia
{gjespitia,ehernandep,rmejiag}@eafit.edu.co
[2] Mechanical Engineering Student, Universidad Nacional de Colombia,
Facultad de Minas, Avenida 80 No 65-223, Medellín, Colombia
smolinat@unal.edu.co

Abstract. Nowadays, the use of renewable energies has been boosted due to their accessibility. Costs are constantly being more accessible and efficiencies are increasing. This has raised an opportunity in photovoltaic applications, beyond roof solar installations, such as vertical or curved photovoltaic surfaces. This applications are tackled from construction and transportation sectors, as virtually any exposed surface to solar radiation may generate electrical energy. However, most commercial solar panels have a flat and rigid geometry, being difficult to adapt to amorphous surfaces. When analyzing a solar panel, this can be considered as multi-layer product, because it needs a reinforcement to compensate the fragility of the solar cells, glass to minimize the reflection of radiation. These layers play a key role, and have to be analyzed while considering curved solar applications. A Multi-Physics model is then necessary, while considering Mechanical, Electrical and Optical analysis. This paper presents the first of those three analysis, focusing in the reinforcement layer of a solar panel to estimate the implications of curved approaches. To do so, a 3D structural model is validated with finite element method. The effects of several parameters are considering, by analyzing the curvature radius and its variation by implementing different composite materials as reinforcement. The results may indicate a maximum curvature radius in solar modules to ensure the reliability of the solar cell, also an analysis of the variation of radius of curvature is presented given a particular composite reinforcement. This can introduce another perspective in modeling and manufacturing of this kind of systems from a multiphysics approach.

Keywords: Modeling photovoltaic module · Curved solar panel · Encapsulation · Reinforcement · Curved photovoltaic modules · Composite materials · Multiphysics analysis

© Springer Nature Switzerland AG 2021
J. C. Figueroa-García et al. (Eds.): WEA 2021, CCIS 1431, pp. 468–479, 2021.
https://doi.org/10.1007/978-3-030-86702-7_40

1 Introduction

Currently, the trend of energy consumption in the world is increasing due to the increase of the world's population and the invention of new electronic devices such as cell phones, vehicles, etc. This force countries to use non-conventional sources of energy, which are becoming more and more accessible. Photovoltaic (PV) energy can be considered as one of the Renewable Energies (REs) with higher potential in the future, thanks to its capacity to supply the worldwide energy demand [18]. In addition, it is expected that by 2021, the cost of solar PV will be even lower than wind power, giving it great potential for use in the coming decades [7].

Thus, it is possible to think new applications involving the use of surfaces exposed to solar radiation, where the current shape of solar panels limits their design and applicability. The possibility of having adaptable curved solar modules, allows to think on having photovoltaic surfaces for localized energy production, in order not to depend exclusively on solar farms. This localized applications are precisely on roofs, amorphous facades and transportation vehicles. Currently, only 0.3% of the energy consumed by vehicles is generated without causing any additional impact [14].

Most of the solar panels found commercially and in the literature have completely flat geometries. However, for applications in transportation systems and in buildings, it is possible to propose curved geometries that allow a better adaption to the required complex shapes. This fact has severe implications in terms of manufacturing and ultimately energy generation. For this reason, it is necessary to model the behavior of solar panels in more complex shapes. The study of these models is discussed below.

2 State of the Art

A solar panel is made up of solar cells connected together, which are usually made of silicon that allow the energy from solar radiation to be transformed into consumable electricity. The solar cell is assembled in a sandwich arrangement above and below. The material on top of the cell must have good optical properties so that the solar radiation can be absorbed as easily as possible, the set of these materials is called **encapsulation**. Similarly, the material at the bottom of the cell is called **reinforcement**, which must guarantee the structural integrity of the inner layer where **solar cells** are placed and protected. This layers can be seen in Fig. 1.

The proper functioning of a solar panel is given by the integration of different areas of physics that, articulated together, allow to know the efficiency and behavior of the photovoltaic unit. It can be seen then that electrical arrangement of cells, panel structural strength and optical properties of encapsulation have direct implications on the performance of solar panel, which has led to different multi-physics analyses of the photovoltaic module [15]. Thus, in order to estimate the global behavior of the solar array, it is necessary to know the implications

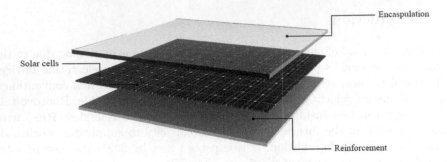

Fig. 1. Panel configuration

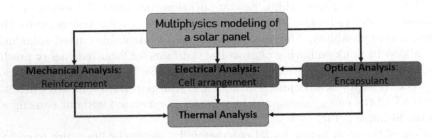

Fig. 2. Multiphysics modeling in solar panel

that each of the physical phenomena have on the operation of the panel. Figure 2 shows the relationship between each of these elements.

The photoelectric effect of solar cells transforms solar radiation into consumable electrical energy and heat, which has a significant negative implication on the overall efficiency of 75.58% while reflection losses are approximately 6.98% [6]. Energy losses due to heat are intrinsic to the photovoltaic panel and must therefore be reduced during operation. This energy in form of heat is harnessed by hybrid systems such as thermal collectors [17], air cooling for water generation [8] and heat exchangers [12]. Also, from the optical modeling and the design of the encapsulation, it is possible to apply passive cooling techniques, based on the use of spectral splitting and the elimination of high-energy solar photons [10, 11, 13].

The mechanical behavior of the PV module must ensure the strength of solar cells, the easy evacuation of heat from the panel reinforcement and the manufacturing of the PV module with curved surfaces. From the point of view of mechanical modeling, there have been different studies focused mainly on the structural study of the complete solar panel under bending conditions in which the objective is to try to predict the propagation of cracks generated in the cell [9, 16].

Also, thermo-mechanical studies have been carried out in order to estimate the influence of temperature on the structural capacity of the PV module assembly [5]. Similarly, reinforcement studies were found using composite materials and core materials such as honeycomb to predict thermal fatigue [1]. However, there is no evidence of a study focused precisely on the potential offered by composite

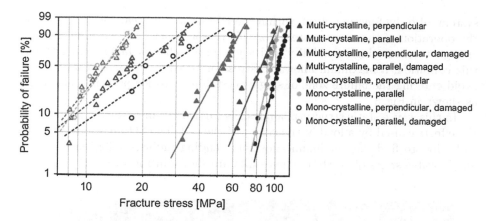

Fig. 3. Cell failure conditions [16]

materials for fabrication of panel reinforcements. The purpose of this article is to analyze the modeling of panel reinforcement material according to the operating and environmental conditions, this will allow to establish a starting point to estimate the complete performance of the photovoltaic system.

3   Analysis of Curved Solar Panels Operation

3.1   Solar Module's Operating Conditions

Considering that the implementation of curved photovoltaic generation surfaces is mainly oriented to the transportation and construction sectors, it is necessary to propose a general load scenario that allows knowing the state of the reinforcement. Solar panels in buildings are in a fixed position, while panels assembled in transport systems may be subjected to accelerations in different directions, so a 3-dimensional loading scenario is assumed in this way: loads to axes 1 and 2 will be associated with accelerations or loads due to plane motion, while direction 3 represents vertical impact loads due to the operation and displacement of photovoltaic system.

3.2   Estimation of the Radius of Curvature

The radius of curvature of panel will be based on the ability of the solar cell to deform and take the shape of the panel. In the assembly of this type of panels, it is necessary to preload the cell so that it adjusts to the shape of the reinforcement. In this way, it is necessary to estimate the maximum deformation that the cell can suffer allowing an adequate safety range, for this case, the SunPower C60 mono-crystalline cell will be taken as a reference with silicon properties.

In addition to the stresses generated in the cell by the preload, it is important to take into account that due to the operation there will be additional loads in system, also the function of cell within the PV array is critical and compromises the operation of the entire system, for this reason, safety factor should be high enough to ensure high reliability and a low probability of failure. To estimate this condition, a maximum allowable stress of 10 MPa is proposed in order to avoid entering the failure zone of single-crystalline cells for perpendicular loads as shown in Fig. 3

In this way, a static structural analysis is carried out in ANSYS™ to analyze the effects caused by a load in the center of the cell. The deformations obtained will allow to find the maximum allowable bending radius, taking into account an allowable stress of 10 MPa. The results are shown in Fig. 4.

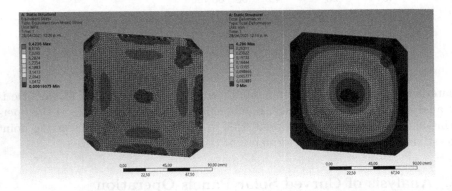

Fig. 4. Stress and Deformation in solar cell

A maximum stress of 9.4 MPa is obtained, which is less than the proposed allowable stress and presents a safety factor of 15 that adequately responds to the functional and structural requirements of solar cell. Likewise, a maximum deformation of 0.29 mm is obtained, which value allows the assembly of a reinforcement and cells with a curvature radius of 6.51 m, which is obtained from geometrical estimations.

3.3 Alternatives for the Reinforcement's Materials

The radius of curvature will be based on the ability of the solar cell to deform and take the shape of the panel. Based on the requirements, composite materials, these are an excellent choice for the manufacturing of panel reinforcement. It is observed that these materials are presented in the form of fabrics, which can be joined by the use of resins. Using these materials is highly dependent on commercial availability. Properties were found for Kevlar, Fiberglass and Carbon Fiber [2], the following table shows the properties found.

From the materials found, different analyses will be carried out including the loading conditions previously exposed, which will allow modeling the mechanical behavior of material, this is only a part of the multi-physical analysis previously exposed.

Properties	Kevlar	Glass fiber	Carbon fiber
E1 [MPa]	1960	36810	1360000
E2, E3 [MPa]	17900	9910	9800
v12, v13	0,08	0,25	0,28
v23	0,075	0,1	0,15
G12, G13 [MPa]	223	3727	4700
G23 [MPa]	1870	3030	4261
Thickness [mm]	0,37	0,38	0,3
Density [kg/m3]	1960	2000	1420

4 Modeling of Curved Solar Panels Reinforcement

4.1 Analytical Model of the Reinforcement

In order to model the behavior of the composite material, it was necessary to use macromechanics models, which allow relating the mechanical properties of the fabrics with respect to the characteristics of the lamination process. For this purpose, a fully planar geometry reinforcement was assumed in order to obtain the deformations generated due to the operating conditions. Also, a plane stress condition will be presented considering a panel without curvature, in which the panel will only have interaction with the loads in the direction 1. Thus, a uniaxial loading state of 1000 N is assumed for a flat glass fiber laminate consisting of 16 equally oriented layers. The governing equation [3], will be shown below.

$$\{\varepsilon\} = [S]\{\sigma\} \tag{1}$$

Furthermore, due to the behavior found between the Young's modulus between direction 1 and 2, a transversely isotropic material can be assumed, which leaves the above equation as follows:

$$\begin{Bmatrix} \varepsilon_1 \\ \varepsilon_2 \\ \varepsilon_2 \end{Bmatrix} = \begin{bmatrix} S_{11} & S_{12} & 0 \\ S_{12} & S_{22} & 0 \\ 0 & 0 & S_{66} \end{bmatrix} \begin{Bmatrix} \sigma_1 \\ \sigma_2 \\ \tau_{12} \end{Bmatrix} \tag{2}$$

The S variables of the above matrix are a function of the Poisson's, Young's and Shear Modules of material. A symmetrical laminate is considered for the plies, so they have a specific thickness, specific material properties and a ply orientation which for this case will be unidirectional over 1. The purpose is to find the deformation in direction 1 and compare it with a finite element analysis to validate the results obtained in the simulation. In this way, a numerical analysis in Matlab^{TM} is implemented, which allows to relate the proposed equations by the macromechanical models with respect to the mechanical properties of the fabrics. A deformation of 0.047 mm is then obtained for that stress condition, this result will be compared with simulation.

4.2   Finite Element Method (FEM) Validation

The purpose is to evaluate the condition analyzed in the analytical model in order to validate the results, these are shown in Fig. 5.

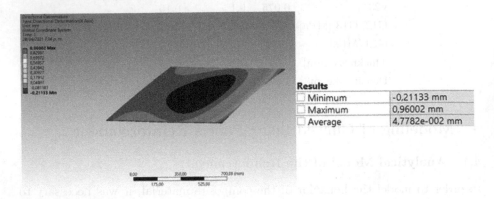

Results	
☐ Minimum	-0,21133 mm
☐ Maximum	0,96002 mm
☐ Average	4,7782e-002 mm

Fig. 5. Deformation analytical model

Finally, it is observed that the results obtained in the simulation correspond to those estimated in the analytical model, with respect to the average deformation of 0.047782 mm. With this value, there is an error of 1.7%. This fact allows us to propose more realistic load conditions for solar panel reinforcement, which will be discussed in next section.

5   Analysis and Simulation of Different Materials

Taking into account the validation of the simulation conditions for the flat panel, a more realistic scenario can then be proposed, including the curvature effects estimated above. A load condition will then be assumed for direction 1, 2 and 3 of 1000 N. The approximate thickness for the analysis is 6 mm for each of the materials, so that a total of 16 layers are used for Kevlar and Fiberglass, while 20 layers are used for Carbon Fiber. For this purpose, the ANSYS^{TM} composites ACP module is used, which allows establishing in detail different characteristics of the process, such as thickness and type of material. With these conditions, the effects on the deformation of Carbon Fiber, Glassfiber and Kevlar are analyzed and shown in Fig. 6.

It is observed that the distribution of deformations is very similar for the materials analyzed, presenting the same patterns, according to the load conditions assumed. Likewise, Kevlar is the material that shows the best behavior with a maximum total deformation of 1.20 mm, followed by Carbon Fiber with 1.5 mm and finally, Glassfiber with 1.73 mm, precisely in Directional Deformation Z. In order to be more specific, the directional deformations are analyzed in the established coordinate system, which are shown in the following table.

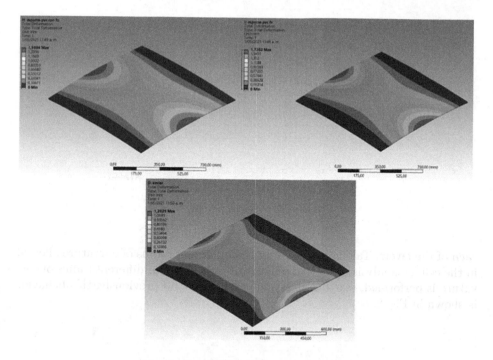

Fig. 6. Total deformation in materials

	Kevlar	Fiber glass	Carbon fiber
Directional Deformation X [mm]	0,059	0,045	0,032
Directional Deformation Y [mm]	0,0217	0,02509	0,022
Directional Deformation Z [mm]	1,201	1,7376	1,5
Mass [kg]	9,91	12,01	8,53

It can be seen that for the plane state, the magnitude of the deformation does not change substantially, while the load in the direction 3 does have an important effect of the total deformation. In addition, it is necessary to analyze the stresses in each layer, as shown in Fig. 7.

A very similar behavior is observed between Carbon Fiber and Glassfiber. The layers in contact with the cell receive a lower stress that increases according to the layer order. In contrast, Kevlar offers the lowest stresses in the intermediate layers of the reinforcement, while the outermost layers reach the maximum values. Likewise, shear stresses generated by the joint between the fabrics, which is an important factor in the failure of solar panels due to delamination which causes 10% of the failures of solar panels [4]. This behavior is shown in Fig. 7. Thus, it is observed that the shear stresses between layers have very low values. However, it can be seen that Kevlar is the material that behaves best under these conditions, maintaining lower stress values than the other materials throughout

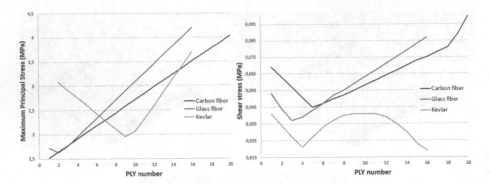

Fig. 7. Stresses per ply

each of the layers. Taking into account the minimum radius of curvature allowed in the cell, an analysis of the maximum stress obtained for different radius of curvature is performed, starting at a value of 6.5 m found previously, this behavior is shown in Fig. 8.

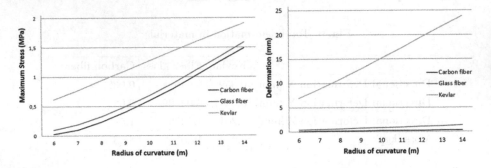

Fig. 8. Stresses, deformation v.s. Radius of curvature

It should be noted that the panel tends to become flatter at higher values of radius of curvature. Thus, as the panel becomes flatter, the stress values also increase. Similarly, a deformation analysis is carried out for each of the materials, which is shown in Fig. 8. A big difference can be seen in the deformation behavior of the material, where Kevlar achieves the highest values, while Glassfiber and Carbon Fiber behave in a very similar way. These graphs will be fundamental information to model the Multi-physical behavior of photovoltaic modules with curved geometry taking into account the mechanical nature, as well as to justify the final selection of the reinforcement materials according to the given operating conditions. The accuracy and confidence of the above results is based on the convergence graph in Fig. 9.

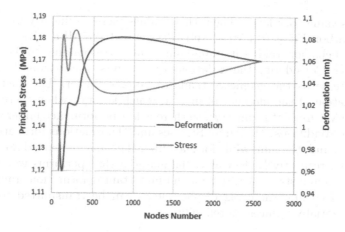

Fig. 9. Mesh convergence analysis

It is observed that from 2500 nodes, the values for stress and deformation are stabilized, which allows to establish the characteristics of the mesh in the FEM study to obtain adequate values with the lowest computational cost.

6 Conclusions

It can be seen that the structural performance of carbon fiber and glass fiber is very similar, starting from very low stresses in the first layers corresponding to 1.52 MPa and 1.72 MPa, respectively. The growth of the Maximum Principal Stress for these materials is linear, taking a maximum magnitude of 4.04 MPa for Carbon Fiber and 4.02 MPa for Glassfiber in the layer furthest from the cell. This behavior is different for Kevlar, which has high stress in the first layer corresponding to 3,08 MPa, descending to the lowest value of 2,06 MPa in 9th layer, and then reaching its maximum value in the last layer corresponding to 4,98 MPa, which is a similar stress to Carbon Fiber and Fiberglass. This fact makes Glassfiber and Carbon Fiber desirable to be used as first reinforcement layers, due to the fact that being in direct contact with the cell, it may cause less stresses decreasing the probability of cell failure.

Similarly, Kevlar is the material with the best deformation behavior in Z direction, with a maximum value of 1.2 mm, followed by 1.5 mm for Carbon Fiber and 1.7 mm for Glassfiber in first layers. The estimation of these values strongly depends on the loads in direction 3, associated with impact loads of the system, so their presence directly influences the final selection of the material. Regarding weight, Carbon Fiber is the best performer with a total of 8.53 kg, however, more layers are needed to complete the same thickness as in the previous ones, so costs may increase considerably. In relation to Shear Stresses, the values in first layer for Carbon Fiber, Glassfiber and Kevlar are respectively 0.069, 0.053 and 0.041 MPa. The subsequent intermediate layers have the minimum shear stress values per layer. Then, these values increase linearly until the last layer for Carbon Fiber (0.1 MPa) and Glassfiber (0.087 MPa). Kevlar presents a parabolic behavior, taking its minimum value corresponding to 0.019 MPa in the last layer. Considering the variation of the radius of curvature, Stresses and Strains increase as the geometry tends to become flatter. This fact is based on the variation of the moment of inertia, which is lower when there are large radius of curvature (flat geometry), so there is less performance under stress and deformation conditions. Maximum Stresses and Deformations for Carbon Fiber are 1.49 MPa and 0.34 mm, while for glass fiber the values obtained are 1.59 MPa and 1.32 mm, respectively. Kevlar is the material that performs worst, since it presents maximum stress of 1.91 MPa and important deformations ranging from 6.93 mm to 23.9 mm; these big displacements can be transmitted to the cell, which substantially reduces its reliability.

7   Future Work

With respect to the radius of curvature, it is observed that the cell size is the variable that has the greatest impact, so the use of split cells will allow the use of smaller radius of curvature without compromising the structural integrity, guaranteeing an adequate performance of the system under the operating conditions. Taking into account the heating of the cells and the fact that the panel reinforcement should promote the passive cooling of the system, heat transfer analyses should be carried out to evaluate the evacuation by conduction from the first layer to the last one, as well as the influence of the curved geometry in the last layer with respect to convective cooling. Similarly, the insulating capacity of the materials must be taken into account to avoid short circuits in the electrical arrangement of the cells. These facts will allow to consider the use of different types of materials, in precise orders to optimize the performance of the panel according to specific conditions.

Acknowledgements. Authors would like to thank Universidad EAFIT to support this research through the Research Assistantship grant from project 953-000012. This research has been also developed in the framework of the "ENERGETICA 2030" Research Program, with code 58667 in the "Colombia Científica" initiative, funded by The World Bank through the call "778-2017 Scientific Ecosystems", managed by the Colombian Ministry of Science, Technology and Innovation (Minciencias), with contract No. FP44842-210-2018.

References

1. Abdelal, G.F., Atef, A.: Thermal fatigue analysis of solar panel structure for micro-satellite applications. Int. J. Mech. Mater. Des. **4**(1), 53–62 (2008)
2. Ansari, M.M., Chakrabarti, A.: Effect of bullet shape and h/a ratio on ballistic impact behaviour of FRP composite plate: A numerical study
3. Barbero, E.J.: Introduction to Composite Materials Design. CRC Press, Boca Raton (2017)

4. Chowdhury, M.S., et al.: An overview of solar photovoltaic panels' end-of-life material recycling. Energy Strat. Rev. **27**, 100431 (2020)
5. Dietrich, S., Pander, M., Sander, M., Schulze, S.H., Ebert, M.: Mechanical and thermomechanical assessment of encapsulated solar cells by finite-element-simulation. In: Reliability of Photovoltaic Cells, Modules, Components, and Systems III, vol. 7773, p. 77730F. International Society for Optics and Photonics (2010)
6. Hanifi, H., Pfau, C., Turek, M., Schneider, J.: A practical optical and electrical model to estimate the power losses and quantification of different heat sources in silicon based pv modules. Renew. Energy **127**, 602–612 (2018)
7. Hauff, J.: Unlocking the sunbelt potential of photovoltaics. European Photovoltaic Industry Association and Others (2011)
8. Kabeel, A., Abdelgaied, M.: Performance enhancement of a photovoltaic panel with reflectors and cooling coupled to a solar still with air injection. J. Clean. Prod. **224**, 40–49 (2019)
9. Kaule, F., Wang, W., Schoenfelder, S.: Modeling and testing the mechanical strength of solar cells. Sol. Energy Mater. Sol. Cells **120**, 441–447 (2014)
10. Kim, S., Kasashima, S., Sichanugrist, P., Kobayashi, T., Nakada, T., Konagai, M.: Development of thin-film solar cells using solar spectrum splitting technique. Sol. Energy Mater. Sol. Cells **119**, 214–218 (2013)
11. Kiyaee, S., Saboohi, Y., Moshfegh, A.Z.: A new designed linear Fresnel lens solar concentrator based on spectral splitting for passive cooling of solar cells. Energy Convers. Manag. **230**, 113782 (2021)
12. Maadi, S.R., Khatibi, M., Ebrahimnia-Bajestan, E., Wood, D.: Coupled thermal-optical numerical modeling of PV/T module-combining CFD approach and two-band radiation do model. Energy Conver. Manag. **198**, 111781 (2019)
13. Mojiri, A., Taylor, R., Thomsen, E., Rosengarten, G.: Spectral beam splitting for efficient conversion of solar energy-a review. Renew. Sustain. Energy Rev. **28**, 654–663 (2013)
14. Murdock, H.E., et al.: Renewables 2020-global status report (2020)
15. Roy, S., Baruah, M.S., Sahu, S., Nayak, B.B.: Computational analysis on the thermal and mechanical properties of thin film solar cells. In: Materials Today: Proceedings (2021)
16. Sander, M., Dietrich, S., Pander, M., Ebert, M., Bagdahn, J.: Systematic investigation of cracks in encapsulated solar cells after mechanical loading. Sol. Energy Mater. Sol. Cells **111**, 82–89 (2013)
17. Wang, G., Yao, Y., Wang, B., Hu, P.: Design and thermodynamic analysis of an innovative hybrid solar PV-CT system with multi-segment PV panels. Sustain. Energy Technol. Assess. **37**, 100631 (2020)
18. Zobaa, A.F., Bansal, R.C.: Handbook of Renewable Energy Technology. WORLD SCIENTIFIC, New York (2011)

Variable-Prioritizing and Instrumentation for Monitoring of an Electrically-Powered Fluvial Vessel Through a FDM Approach

Felipe Mendoza[1]([✉]), Camilo Vélez[2], Santiago Echavarría[1],
Alejandro Montoya[2], Tatiana Manrique[3], and Ricardo Mejía-Gutiérrez[1]

[1] Design Engineering Research Group (GRID), Universidad EAFIT,
Carrera 49 No 7 Sur–50, Medellín, Colombia
{fmendoza,sechava4,rmejiag}@eafit.edu.co
[2] Departamento de Ingeniería de Producción, Universidad EAFIT,
Carrera 49 No 7 Sur–50, Medellín, Colombia
{cvelezg10,jmonto36}@eafit.edu.co
[3] Programa de Ingeniería Mecatrónica, Universidad EIA,
km 2 + 200 V ía al Aeropuerto JMC, Envigado, Colombia
dolly.manrique@eia.edu.co

Abstract. Monitoring is of strategic importance when concerning energy management in electric vehicles. Fully-electric boats and vessels are no exception. The proper selection of variables to be sensed, is a key issue when operating with limited energy resources. Underrating critical operational variables can impact vessel performance, and energy consumption, if they are not properly supervised. Yet, overstating variables implies additional computational costs and valuable energy wasted in acquisition and processing of non-critical information. This article implements a Function to Data Matrix (FDM) methodology to prioritize the variables to be sensed in a electro-solar fluvial vessel, based on its operational states. This approach enables to reduce the number of variables to monitor and keeping only the most relevant information. For the selected variables, electronic instrumentation, well suited to the fluvial application, is proposed together with the communication architecture for telemetry purposes.

Keywords: Electric vessel · Variable prioritizing · Data collection · FDM analysis · Electronic instrumentation · Sensors

1 Introduction

Nowadays, Data-Analytic is of high relevance in science, technology and industry. Sectors, such as transportation, benefits particularly from Data-Analytic and its applications being a key topic to be addressed in research [21]. From data it is possible to make decisions, correlate variables, understand processes and predict events. In the transportation sector and, particularly, in the design and

© Springer Nature Switzerland AG 2021
J. C. Figueroa-García et al. (Eds.): WEA 2021, CCIS 1431, pp. 480–492, 2021.
https://doi.org/10.1007/978-3-030-86702-7_41

manufacturing of new vehicles and new vehicular technologies, Data-Analytic is becoming crucial, since from each operating vehicle, a great amount of information can be obtained from both the vehicle and the environment [1, 19, 20].

During operation of fully-electric and hybrid vessels data acquisition takes high relevance when concerning energy management. For instance, from data, it is possible to build and simulate energetic models of the vessel to predict its behavior. Moreover, it is possible to manage efficiently the available energy, by means of a control strategy developed from data [2, 7, 11, 13]. Besides, data obtained can be used to monitor the ship performance and if deviations are found between measured data and forecasted data, predictive maintenance can be carried out [12, 16]. Finally, with the incorporation of emerging technologies such as the Internet of Things (IoT) it is possible to send these data to the cloud, enabling the possibility to monitor the vessel in real time [9, 17].

Nevertheless, large amount of information can be obtained when monitoring electrically powered vessels (electrical, mechanical, and performance variables are involved). Thus, variable-prioritizing becomes a key issue when concerning energy consumption in performing data acquisition and processing with limited energy resources. Larger number of variables usually does imply larger amount of energy required to properly process such data.

In this paper, a methodology to prioritize critical variables involved in an electro-solar vessel performance is presented. The methodology is based on a Function to data matrix (FDM) approach [3, 4, 6]. Trough FDM the critical variables to be monitored are ranked according to their relevance in each operating state of the vessel. The resulting variables' rank is used to propose consumption-sensitive electronics instrumentation to be implemented in the electro-solar vessel under study.

The rest of the paper is organized as follows: First, in Sect. 2, previous studies related to data management for vessel monitoring are presented. Next, in Sect. 3, the variables involved in the performance of the electro-solar vessel under study are properly described. Furthermore, in Sect. 4, FDM methodology to variable-prioritizing the data available in the vessel is developed. In Sect. 5, electronic instrumentation and sensors selected to acquire and process such data are presented. Finally, in Sect. 6 some conclusions are carried out.

2   Related Works

Concerning vessels' monitoring and the use given to acquired data, many studies have been carried out, implementing sensors and monitoring systems on vessels for different purposes. For instance, literature presents an on-board unit for monitoring a fleet of electric vehicles (EV) and electric boats [5]. Variables such as the location of the vehicles and electrical measurements on the batteries are broadcast trough GSM/GPRS and GPS signals to properly manage the fleet from a remote location. Other work presents a vessel remote tracking system, by means of a CubeSat (Cubic Satellite) [15]. The tracking system is also used for marine navigation safety and marine disaster management purposes.

Regarding data acquisition for parameter estimation, literature showed a full scale sensor measurements, used along with different statistical methods to predict vessel speed and, therefore, propulsion fuel efficiency [2]. The estimations are made from a dataset collected for 18 different variables trough two motion reference units (MRUs) and several other sensors (wind speed, etc.) installed on the ship. The estimation method with best results was the Generalized Additive Model (GAM) when compared against the baseline model. Furthermore, other works used a data-driven methodology to estimate vessel motion with measured data (*e.g.* wave height, peak wave period and peak wave direction), when transferring crew between offshore structures of a wind farm and the transporting vessels [8]. Dataset for motion estimation are from vessel telemetry. In other related work, power converter three-phase voltage and current measurements along with motor speed measurements are used by a monitoring system to estimate and broadcast power quality in an electrically powered vessel [10]. The monitoring system is designed using a methodology based on Internet of things (IoT) architecture.

Yet, managing large amount of data for monitoring purposes is still an issue. For instance some authors use machine learning techniques to design a decision support system to properly manage large amount of data provided by Vessel Telemetry Systems (VTeS) [18]. The decision support system allowed to fitly monitor energy consumption (fuel usage) in vessels and was trained from data sets obtained from an anchor handling tug supply boat (AHTS) and a tug boat. Other works use sensors, such as voltage sensors, current transformers and dielectric water level sensors to monitor the electric propulsion system in a fully-electric marine vessel [17]. A Contextual Data Prediction Technique (CDPT) algorithm is used to manage data and decides whether the vessel state requires attention from the operator. If not, the CDPT algorithm just keeps monitoring data. Information and decisions are broadcast trough an IoT architecture.

Despite the aforementioned applications, concerning vessels monitoring, none of them developed a systematic and deep analysis of the input information. This is a new issue as the ability to prioritize critical variables, involved in electro-solar vessels performance, may improve monitoring processes in terms of resources and computational costs. In the following sections, a variables ranking for an electro-solar vessel is performed through a Function to data matrix (FDM) approach.

3   Electro-Solar Boat Subsystems Description

In this section the subsystems involved in the electro-solar vessel are presented as well as the description of the variables that affect the performance of the boat. Let's consider an electro-solar boat with a data/control block diagram as depicted in Fig. 1. This diagram includes the most important variables of matter, energy and information that interacts between each subsystem and the environment.

The electro-solar vessel under study is mainly composed by five subsystems: **Naval architecture** comprehends the hull and the different elements

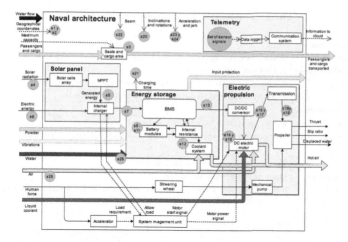

Fig. 1. Electro-solar vessel data/control block diagram.

of the vessel. The **Solar panel** includes the solar cells array and the MPPT (Maximum-power-point tracking) controller required to optimize the generated energy according to the P-V (power-voltage) curve. In the **Energy storage** subsystem, the battery pack and the BMS (Battery Management System) can be found. The BMS regulates the charging and discharging current and voltage in the battery and protects the battery from short circuits, over-voltage and under-voltage, and overheating. The **Electric propulsion** subsystem is composed by the electric motor, the MCU (Motor Controller Unit) and the outboard units. In the **Telemetry** subsystem, all the sensed variables are received by the data logger and are sent to the cloud.

The main energy flow would be: The photovoltaic module transforms solar energy into electrical energy. Energy is transferred to the energy storage subsystem. The stored energy is used by the electric propulsion subsystem which sends power to the electric motor and controls the motor speed according to the user's input signals. The motor transforms this electrical energy into rotational energy which is transmitted through the drive train to the propeller. Water displacement is generated producing a thrust force to propel the boat. In addition to this energy flow, there are secondary flows such as air flow, vibrations, water flow, etc., to be considered within each subsystem as shown in Fig. 1.

4   Electro-Solar Vessel Variable Prioritization

In this section the ranking process to prioritize the variables to be instrumented is described. For this purpose a Function to Data matrix methodology [6] is carried out. This methodology is divided in four steps: i) A mission essential analysis is done defining the main purpose or mission to be accomplished. ii) A goal to function (GTF) tree is established in order to determine the basic functions to achieve that mission. iii) An analysis of the data/control diagram (such

Table 1. Electric boat main requirements.

Mission objectives	
Main objective	Transport passengers with electric energy in a defined time
Secondary objectives	1. Perform multiple runs per day
	2. Charging with as much photovoltaic energy as possible
	3. To be a test bench for different scientific projects.
Functional requirements	
Time travel	Each trip should be completed in one hour or less
Energy consumption	To optimize the energy consumption while complying with the operation.
Restrictions	
Number of passengers	Transport maximum 13 passengers
Operation schedule	Operate between 6 am–6 pm
Battery health	The battery must be able to continue to store the energy required to operate the boat even over time.

as the one depicted in Fig. 1) and to properly define interactions between the different subsystems. iv) The function to data matrix where the basic functions and mission variables are linked by relevance index. In the following subsections, this FDM methodology is applied to the analysis of the vessel under study.

4.1 Vessel's Mission

The main purpose (mission) of the electric boat and the main requirements related to it are listed in Table 1. The main objective of the electric boat is to offer a transportation service energetically sustainable while being competitive with the current alternatives provided by internal combustion boats, in terms of travel time and number of passengers. In this sense, the main challenge is to manage the vessel's energy efficiently since the vessel must be able to perform more than one trip per day, must maintain an average speed that allows each trip to be made in an hour or less and also must transport the expected number of passengers. In addition, it is expected to make the best use of the photovoltaic energy generated by the solar panels. In order to properly manage energy flows throughout the vessel, monitoring and telemetry must be performed.

4.2 Goal to Function (GTF) Tree for the Vessel

From the main mission of the boat: *"To transport passengers with electric energy in a pre-defined time"*, the following functions are derived and presented in Fig. 2 as a GTF tree:

- *Maintain stability during the trip*: Safety during the trip must be the priority, therefore boat stability must be guaranteed.
- *Manage the vessel's consumption*: It must be ensured that the vessel's consumption allows it to reach its destination or the next charging station.
- *Control the speed of the boat*: The speed must be maintained ensuring that the vessel reaches its destination in time to meet the travel schedules.

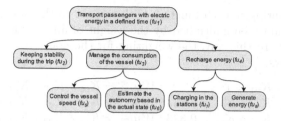

Fig. 2. Goal to function tree for electric boat operation.

- *Estimate the autonomy based in the actual state*: The energy consumption of the boat depends on several factors such as its weight. Thus, the current state of the variables must be considered in order to not overestimate or underestimate the energy consumption.
- *Recharge energy*: The energy to recharge the vessel's battery will come from two sources, the charging stations and the vessel's photo-voltaic panels.
- *Generate energy*: The boat will have photo-voltaic panels to charge the battery when the vehicle is in motion.
- *Charging in a given set of stations*: The main source for recharging the boat battery in terms of amount of energy and power are the charging stations. It must be ensured that the charging operations meet the autonomy and times requirements for the trip.

Based on the nomenclature for the functions presented in Fig. 2, the vector of functions L (Eq. 1) is composed by all the functions of the goal to function tree. The Prüfer sequence S (Eq. 2) [14], is constructed based on the set L and the GTF tree in Fig. 2.

$$L = [fu_1, fu_2, fu_3, fu_4, fu_5, fu_6, fu_7, fu_8] \tag{1}$$

$$S = [fu_1, fu_3, fu_3, fu_1, fu_4, fu_4, fu_1] \tag{2}$$

The vector of basic functions F_u is obtained with the Eq. 3:

$$
\begin{aligned}
F_u &= L - (L \cap S) \\
F_u &= [fu_2, fu_5, fu_6, fu_7, fu_8]
\end{aligned} \tag{3}
$$

Now, to establish the weighting for each basic function, the vector N_n (Eq. 4) is expressed as the number of functions on the same node for the functions in the vector L. In this analysis, is assumed that all functions in each node have the same importance. The vector K_v defined in the Eq. 5 represent the weight of each function in the specific node.

$$N_n = [1, 3, 3, 3, 2, 2, 2, 2] \tag{4}$$

$$K_v = \frac{1}{N_n} = [1, 0.333, 0.333, 0.333, 0.5, 0.5, 0.5, 0.5] \tag{5}$$

To find the weighting of each function with respect to the position in the GTF tree, its weight must be multiplied by the weight of all the functions preceding it up to the root. In this way, the weighting for the nodes in GFT presented in Fig. 2 is as follows:

$$
\begin{aligned}
&Wu_{(1)} = K_{v1} = 1 & | \; Wu_{(5)} = K_{v5} * K_{v3} * K_{v1} = 0.167 \\
&Wu_{(2)} = K_{v2} * K_{v1} = 0.333 & | \; Wu_{(6)} = K_{v6} * K_{v3} * K_{v1} = 0.167 \\
&Wu_{(3)} = K_{v3} * K_{v1} = 0.333 & | \; Wu_{(7)} = K_{v7} * K_{v4} * K_{v1} = 0.167 \\
&Wu_{(4)} = K_{v4} * K_{v1} = 0.333 & | \; Wu_{(8)} = K_{v8} * K_{v4} * K_{v1} = 0.167
\end{aligned}
\tag{6}
$$

Thus, the weight W_u for the basic functions F_u are:

$$
\begin{aligned}
Wu &= [Wu_{(2)}, Wu_{(5)}, Wu_{(6)}, Wu_{(7)}, Wu_{(8)}] \\
Wu &= [0.333, 0.167, 0.167, 0.167, 0.167]
\end{aligned}
\tag{7}
$$

Based on the functions defined on the GFT tree, the operational states of the vessel are defined. In general the operation of the boat will have 3 states:

- **Moving state** (OS_1). During this state the vessel is in motion and the photo-voltaic panels are delivering energy. This first mode of operation is called OS_1.
- **Charging state** (OS_2). In this state the boat is charging. During the charging state the photo-voltaic panels of the boat deliver energy to the vessel. This mode of operation is called OS_2.
- **Port docking state** (OS_3, OS_4). This state occurs when the boat is not performing power recharging operations. Two operational states are defined for this state, one called OS_3 when the generation from the boat's roof panels is being used and OS_4 when it is not being used.

Based on these four operational states and the basic functions F_u the matrix of operational states of the boat is developed (See Table 2).

4.3   Data/Control Diagram Analysis for the Electro-Solar Vessel

The monitoring system seeks to keep track for some energies and their interaction with the different subsystems, as presented in the functional diagram in Fig. 1 through sensors. The main aspects to be monitored in the different subsystems, as well as in the environment, are:

Table 2. Operational states matrix of the electro-solar vessel

Operational states	OS	fu_2	fu_5	fu_6	fu_7	fu_8	OS_{tm}
Moving	OS_1	1	1	1	0	1	29
Recharging in station	OS_2	0	0	1	1	1	7
Port docking state, generating energy	OS_3	0	0	1	0	1	5
Port docking state without generate	OS_4	0	0	1	0	0	4
N		4	3	2	1	0	

- **Propulsion system**: Measure mechanical powers delivered by the transmission system and motor, as well as voltage and current of the motor.
- **Energy storage**: Monitor variables such as charging energy, consumption energy and state of charge. Also record variables related to the state of health of the battery, such as its temperature or the estimated degradation.
- **Boat structure**: Monitor the inclinations, rotations and accelerations and draft during vessel operation, as well as the vessel's location.
- **Solar panel**: The amount of energy recharged at stations and the obtained through photo-voltaic generation from the panels on the boat's roof.
- **Environment**: Monitor environment variables such as solar radiance, ambient temperature, speed of water and wind.

Table 3. Function to data matrix analysis

OS_1 Moving

Variable	fu_2	fu_6	fu_7	fu_8	fu_9	Weighting
	0.333	0.167	0.167	0.167	0.167	
Vessel location	1	2	2	0	2	1.335
Vessel speed	3	3	3	0	1	2.168
Vessel weight	3	2	2	0	0	1.667
Solar radiance	0	0	2	0	3	0.835
Energy generated by the panels	0	2	2	0	2	1.002
Electric energy in station	0	0	0	0	0	0
Energy delivered by the charger	0	1	2	0	3	1.002
Battery voltage	0	3	3	0	2	1.336
Battery current	0	3	3	0	2	1.336
Battery state of charge	0	3	3	0	2	1.336
Battery state of health	0	1	3	0	2	1.002
Battery temperature	0	1	2	0	1	0.668
Energy delivered by the battery	1	2	3	0	1	1.335
Motor voltage	1	2	2	0	1	1.168
Motor current	1	3	3	0	1	1.335
Motor torque	1	2	2	0	0	1.001
Motor RPM	1	3	3	0	0	1.335
Drive system torque	1	2	2	0	0	1.001
Drive system RPM	1	3	2	0	0	1.168
Vessel inclinations and rotations	3	2	1	0	1	1.667
Charging time	0	0	0	0	0	0
Vessel draft	3	2	1	0	0	1.5
Vessel acceleration	2	3	2	0	0	1.501
Vessel's jerk	2	2	2	0	0	1.334
Ambient temperature	0	0	1	0	2	0.501
Water temperature	0	0	1	0	0	0.167

(a) FDM for the operational state OS_1

Variable	Threshold			
	OS_1	OS_2	OS_3	OS_4
	1.302	0.802	0.601	0.301
Vessel location	1.335	1.002	0.668	0.334
Vessel speed	2.168	–	–	–
Vessel weight	1.667	–	–	0.334
Solar radiance	–	1.169	0.835	0.501
Energy generated by the solar panels	–	1.336	1.002	–
Station electric energy	–	1.169	–	–
Energy delivered by the charger	–	1.169	–	–
Battery voltage	1.336	1.169	0.668	–
Battery current	1.336	1.169	0.668	–
Battery state of charge	1.336	1.336	0.835	0.501
Battery state of health	–	1.169	0.668	0.501
Battery temperature	–	0.835	0.668	0.334
Energy delivered by the battery	1.335	–	–	–
Motor voltage	–	–	–	–
Motor current	1.335	–	–	–
Motor torque	–	–	–	–
Motor RPM	1.335	–	–	–
Drive system torque	–	–	–	–
Drive system RPM	–	–	–	–
Vessel inclinations and rotations	1.667	–	–	–
Charging time	–	1.169	–	–
Vessel draft	1.5	–	–	–
Vessel acceleration	1.501	–	–	–
Vessel jerk	1.334	–	–	–
Ambient temperature	–	–	–	–
Water temperature	–	–	–	–

(b) Results of applying the threshold value of the variables to be monitored.

4.4   Function to Data Matrix - FDM

In this section the relevance of the variables to be monitored is evaluated according to each basic function, within each operational state of the boat. The evaluation is made with integer values between 0 and 3, where 0 means no relevance and 3 means strong relevance. The score for each variable is multiplied by the weight W_u previously assigned to each basic function. The weighting represents the sum of these multiplications for each variable. Table 3a present the FDM for the operational state OS_1 (Moving state).

From the results of the variables evaluation, a cut-off threshold was specified to determine which of these variables should actually be monitored for each operational state. These thresholds, denoted as Th and presented below, were determined as a 60% of the maximum weighting within each operational state [4].

$$\begin{bmatrix} Th_{OS_1} \\ Th_{OS_2} \\ Th_{OS_3} \\ Th_{OS_4} \end{bmatrix} = \begin{bmatrix} 1.302 \\ 0.802 \\ 0.601 \\ 0.301 \end{bmatrix} \tag{8}$$

The results of applying the threshold value in each operational state are shown in Table 3b. If the variables holds a dash symbol ('-'), it means the variable not being selected for the operation mode since its priority did not overcome the threshold value. Only priorities bigger or equal to the threshold are displayed. Variables that do not exceed the threshold for any of the operational states, are not selected as critical variables.

5   Electronic Instrumentation

In order to properly acquire and process the critical variables involved in the boat monitoring and as a complement information to the process realized trough this work the selection process of the electronic devices is described in the present section. In Table 4 the selected variables (as a result of the FDM prioritizing) are listed. The operation range is defined for each variable, as well as three commercial alternatives to be implemented.

Table 4. Variables ranges and instrumentation alternatives.

Variable		Range			Option 1	Electrical Features	Option 2	Electrical Features	Option 3	Electrical Features
		min	max	units						
Vessel Location		0	55	[km]	GPS-721-MRTU	Voltage: 5~30 [V]	GPS GV300CAN	Voltage: 12 [V]	GPS GN2000	Voltage: 12 [V]
Vessel speed		0	15	[m/s]		Resolution: 2.5 [m]		Resolution: 2.5 [m]		Resolution: 2.5 [m]
Vessel inclinations and rotations	Trim	0	6.5	[deg]	OPENIMU 300RI	IP67	IMU383ZA-400	Power: 250 [mW]	TARS-HCASS	Current: 100 [mA]
	Heel	-5	5	[deg]		Power: <400 [mW]		Angular rate: -400 to 400 [°/s]		Angular rate: -400 to 400 [°/s]
	Rudder	-20	20	[deg]		Angular rate: -400 ~ 400 [°/s]				
Vessel acceleration		0	0.5	[m/s^2]		Acceleration: -8 ~ 8 [g]		Acceleration: -8 to 8 [g]		Acceleration: -8 to 8 [g]
Vessel jerk		0	0.6	[m/s^3]		Magnetic field: -8 ~ 8 [Gauss]				
Vessel weight - Numer of passengers		0	13	[-]	MF02-N-221-A01	Force: 0.03~1 [kgf]	FSR01CE	Force: 5 [kgf]	Seat Membrane Occupancy	Force: 0.1~100 [N]
Solar radiance		4	4.5	[kWh/m^2]	RK200-4 Pyranometer	Range: 0~1.5 [kW/m^2]	SMP3 Pyranometer	Range: 0~2 [kW/m^2]	SR05-D1A3 Pyranometer	Range: 0~1.6 [kW/m^2]
Vessel draft		0	0.7	[m]	SUS316 level sensor	Power: 125 [mW]	Optical sensor GP2Y0A60SZ LF	Power: 165 [mW]	Ultrasonic distance sensor HC-SR04	Voltage: 3.3 [V]
						Range: 150~2000 [mm]		Range: 100~1500 [mm]		Range: 20~4000 [mm]
						Precision: 10~40 [mm]				Accuracy: 3 [mm]
Energy delivered by the charger		0	170	[kW]	BMS					
Battery voltage		276	386.4	[V]						
Battery current		0	765.3	[A]						
Battery state of charge		0	100	[%]						
Battery state of health		0	100	[%]						
Battery temperature		-20	54.48	[°C]						
Energy delivered by the battery		0	170.5	[kW]						
Motor current		0	470	[A]	VCU					
Motor RPM		0	12000	[rpm]						
Energy generated by the solar panels		0	5	[kW]	MPPT					
Charging time		1	2	[h]	CPU					
Station electric energy		N/A	N/A	[-]	Telemetry					

To select the most suitable sensor from the proposed alternatives, an analysis is carried out taking into account different features of the instruments. In Table 5 the IMU features and the analysis performed for its selection are presented. For each characteristic a weighting factor between 1 and 5 is assigned accordingly to its relevance. For each device all the characteristic are evaluated with a value between 0 and 1 and then a sum-product between the evaluation column and the relative weight column is calculated to obtain the final rating. This process is done for all the instruments and devices.

Figure 3 presents the architecture of all components, their location in the vessel and the communication protocol between the units, sensors and the principal processor.

Table 5. IMU selection matrix

			Device		
Characteristics	Weight	Relative weight	TARS-HCASS	IMU383 ZA - 400	OpenIMU 300RI
Price	5	0.16	0.28	0.00	0.72
Range	5	0.16	0.50	1.00	1.00
Resolution	5	0.16	0.50	1.00	1.00
Environmental	4	0.13	1.00	0.00	1.00
Communication	3	0.09	1.00	0.50	1.00
Accessibility	3	0.09	0.00	0.00	0.00
Size/weight	1	0.03	0.00	1.00	0.50
Voltage	3	0.09	1.00	0.50	1.00
Power	3	0.09	0.00	1.00	0.00
Total	32	1.00	0.51	0.53	**0.75**

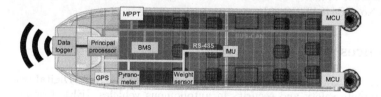

Fig. 3. Sensor architecture.

6   Conclusions

It is clear that monitoring the operation of any vehicle is nowadays an strategic task. Literature reinforces that the most important variables during the operation of a vessel, may be monitored in order to use their information in operational decision making. From the review of the state of the art it can be derived that none of the articles highlights a systematic approach on how to select the variables to be monitored or their relevance during a vehicle's operation, particularly for electro-solar vessels operation.

Concerning the data/control diagram of the vessel, as long as a more detailed analysis was made, more valuable information was obtained. It was also easier to understand the total number of variables that could be sensed from the data/control diagram. Nevertheless, no prioritization or variable hierarchy is established from the data/control diagram by itself.

With the FDM analysis, it was possible to obtain a reduction in the number of variables to be monitored in the vessel's operation. This was made explicit with the Goal To Function (GTF) tree where it was possible to rank the functions according to their relevance during the operation of the vessel. Consequently, from these analysis, it was possible to reduce by 50%, 42.3%, 30.7% and 23.1% the variables for the operational states OS_1, OS_2, OS_3 and OS_4 respectively. This is translated into a reduction of data to be sent and processed, reducing system operating costs and energy consumption in data-acquisition and processing.

To be able to robustly monitor these variables, an exploration of commercial instruments evidenced the feasibility of such a system. The alternatives can withstand the operation conditions of the vessel fulfilling with the resolution and operating ranges of the vessel.

In future studies it is recommended to further develop telemetry to send and store in databases the real-time information obtained from the instruments installed on the vessel in order to develop and improve models for the development of more advanced control systems.

Acknowledgements. Authors would like to thank Universidad EAFIT to support this research through the Research Assistantship grant from project 952-000029. This research has been also developed in the framework of the "ENERGETICA 2030" Research Program, with code 58667 in the "Colombia Científica" initiative, funded by The World Bank through the call "778-2017 Scientific Ecosystems", managed by the Colombian Ministry of Science, Technology and Innovation (Minciencias), with contract No. FP44842-210-2018.

References

1. Almeaibed, S., Al-Rubaye, S., Tsourdos, A., Avdelidis, N.P.: Digital twin analysis to promote safety and security in autonomous vehicles. IEEE Commun. Stand. Mag. **5**(1), 40–46 (2021). https://doi.org/10.1109/MCOMSTD.011.2100004
2. Brandsæter, A., Vanem, E.: Ship speed prediction based on full scale sensor measurements of shaft thrust and environmental conditions. Ocean Eng. **162**(May), 316–330 (2018). https://doi.org/10.1016/j.oceaneng.2018.05.029
3. Cárdenas-Gómez, I., Fernández-Montoya, M., Mejía-Gutiérrez, R.: Analysis of relevant variables to monitor a photovoltaic charging station through the function to data matrix (FDM) method. In: MOVICI-MOYCOT 2018: Joint Conference for Urban Mobility in the Smart City, pp. 1–6 (2018). https://doi.org/10.1049/ic.2018.0018

4. Echavarría, S., Mejía-Gutiérrez, R., Montoya, A.: Development of an IoT platform for monitoring electric vehicle behaviour. In: Figueroa-García, J.C., Garay-Rairán, F.S., Hernández-Pérez, G.J., Díaz-Gutierrez, Y. (eds.) WEA 2020. CCIS, vol. 1274, pp. 363–374. Springer, Cham (2020). https://doi.org/10.1007/978-3-030-61834-6_31

5. Fabbri, G., Calenne, F., London, M., Boccaletti, C., Cardoso, A.J., Mascioli, F.M.: Development of an on-board unit for the monitoring and management of an electric fleet. In: Proceedings - 2012 20th International Conference on Electrical Machines, ICEM 2012, pp. 2404–2410 (2012). https://doi.org/10.1109/ICElMach.2012.6350220

6. Fernández-Montoya, M., Mejía-Gutierrez, R., Osorio-Gómez, G.: A function to data matrix (FDM) approach for mission variables consideration. In: MATEC Web of Conferences, vol. 108, pp. 1–5 (2017). https://doi.org/10.1051/matecconf/201710810008

7. Geertsma, R., Negenborn, R., Visser, K., Hopman, J.: Design and control of hybrid power and propulsion systems for smart ships: a review of developments. Appl. Energy **194**, 30–54 (2017). https://doi.org/10.1016/j.apenergy.2017.02.060

8. Gilbert, C., Browell, J., McMillan, D.: A data-driven vessel motion model for off-shore access forecasting. In: OCEANS 2019 - Marseille, OCEANS Marseille 2019 2019-June (2019). https://doi.org/10.1109/OCEANSE.2019.8867176

9. Chih-Lin, I., Sun, Q., Liu, Z., Zhang, S., Han, S.: The big-data-driven intelligent wireless network: architecture, use cases, solutions, and future trends. IEEE Veh. Technol. Mag. **12**(4), 20–29 (2017). https://doi.org/10.1109/MVT.2017.2752758

10. Jinbao, Z., Weifeng, S., Ying, L., Ranran, D.: Design of power quality monitoring system for electric propulsion ship based on IoT technology. Chin. J. Ship Res. **14**(2), 118 (2019). https://doi.org/10.19693/j.issn.1673-3185.01197

11. Karagiannidis, P., Themelis, N.: Data-driven modelling of ship propulsion and the effect of data pre-processing on the prediction of ship fuel consumption and speed loss. Ocean Eng. **222**, 108616 (2021). https://doi.org/10.1016/j.oceaneng.2021.108616

12. Lazakis, I., Dikis, K., Michala, A.L., Theotokatos, G.: Advanced ship systems condition monitoring for enhanced inspection, maintenance and decision making in ship operations. Transp. Res. Procedia **14**, 1679–1688 (2016). https://doi.org/10.1016/j.trpro.2016.05.133. Transport Research Arena TRA2016

13. Nuchturee, C., Li, T., Xia, H.: Energy efficiency of integrated electric propulsion for ships - a review. Renew. Sustain. Energy Rev. **134**, 110145 (2020). https://doi.org/10.1016/j.rser.2020.110145

14. Prüfer, H.: Neuer Beweis eines Satzes über Permutationen. Arch. Math. Phys. **27**, 742–744 (1918)

15. Shao, T.Y., Kao, S.L., Su, C.M.: Taiwan AIS CubeSat tracking system for marine safety. In: Proceedings - 2019 International Conference on Intelligent Computing and Its Emerging Applications, ICEA 2019, pp. 70–73 (2019). https://doi.org/10.1109/ICEA.2019.8858312

16. Shuvo, S.S., Yilmaz, Y.: Predictive maintenance for increasing EV charging load in distribution power system. In: 2020 IEEE International Conference on Communications, Control, and Computing Technologies for Smart Grids (SmartGridComm), pp. 1–6 (2020). https://doi.org/10.1109/SmartGridComm47815.2020.9303021

17. Su, S., Ouyang, M., Li, T., Wang, Q.: Application of ship electric propulsion based on internet of things system and electronic system. Microprocess. Microsyst. **81**, 103748 (2021). https://doi.org/10.1016/j.micpro.2020.103748

18. Susanto, H., Wibisono, G.: Machine learning for data processing in vessel telemetry system: initial study. In: Proceeding - 2019 International Conference of Artificial Intelligence and Information Technology, ICAIIT 2019, pp. 496–501 (2019). https://doi.org/10.1109/ICAIIT.2019.8834655
19. Yang, S., Qian, S.: Understanding and predicting travel time with spatio-temporal features of network traffic flow, weather and incidents. IEEE Intell. Transp. Syst. Mag. **11**(3), 12–28 (2019). https://doi.org/10.1109/MITS.2019.2919615
20. Zheng, X., et al.: Big data for social transportation. IEEE Trans. Intell. Transp. Syst. **17**(3), 620–630 (2016). https://doi.org/10.1109/TITS.2015.2480157
21. Zhu, L., Yu, F.R., Wang, Y., Ning, B., Tang, T.: Big data analytics in intelligent transportation systems: a survey. IEEE Trans. Intell. Transp. Syst. **20**(1), 383–398 (2019). https://doi.org/10.1109/TITS.2018.2815678

A Framework for Multispectral Instance Classification Using Examples

Camilo Peláez-García[1]([✉]), Víctor-Alejandro Patiño-Martínez[1],
Juan-Bernardo Gómez-Mendoza[1][iD],
and Manuel-Alejandro Tamayo-Monsalve[1,2][iD]

[1] Universidad Nacional de Colomba, Sede Manizales, Bogotá, Colombia
{cpelaezg,vapatinom,jbgomezm,matamayom}@unal.edu.co
[2] Universidad Autónoma de Manizales, Manizales, Colombia
manuela.tamayom@autonoma.edu.co

Abstract. Multispectral imaging is currently being used in a wide variety of vision-based applications, with agricultural aimed challenges being regarded with particular interest. In this work, we present a framework for instance classification based on per-pixel information in various wavelengths, using a multi-example representation for each class. Reference class examples are constructed using the mean and covariance of the intensity of each wavelength found in regions selected from a small group of reference images. Spectral information is augmented using non-linear transformations of the original components obtained using the multispectral imaging system. The distance-to-class is computed as the minimum Mahalanobis distance measured with regard to every reference example in the class. Tests were conducted using multispectral images of coffee grains in diverse stages of maturity, where the number of examples used to represent each class was varied. The selected classes were conformed according to three fruit maturation stages: unripe (green), semiripe (yellowish) and ripe (red). Average classification rate based on distance-to-class criterion was over 96.689%, with a F1-score of 96.673%.

Keywords: Multispectral imaging · Mahalanobis distance · Coffee fruit classification

1 Introduction

Multispectral imaging systems have gained renewed importance in a wide variety of applications in recent years. The availability and cost-efficiency found in filter and illumination technologies makes it feasible to design and build low-cost systems for engineering applications [1]. With this kind of system, it is possible to extract information that lies in the non-visible part of the spectrum, along with the one acquired using traditional vision systems or by simple visual inspection done by humans. Thanks to this, products that normally require lengthy

This work has been supported by Universidad Nacional de Colombia and Universidad de Caldas.

J. C. Figueroa-García et al. (Eds.): WEA 2021, CCIS 1431, pp. 493–504, 2021.
https://doi.org/10.1007/978-3-030-86702-7_42

studies, different sensors, or destructive analysis have been derived from newly built multispectral systems [2,3].

Our case of regional interest focus on coffee fruit classification, which is currently carried out by the inspecting the color of the epidermis of the fruits in different stages of maturation [4,5]. This technique, along with the use of multispectral data of the fruits, is proving to be a promising way to achieve more consistent classification results than traditional ones and highlight features hidden to human vision.

Different authors have focused on analyzing fruits and vegetables using multispectral systems to highlight hidden features, useful when tackling tasks such as quality control, classification, or early disease detection purposes. Among them, Alexios [6] uses multispectral images for the inspection of citrus fruits, and Qin [7] uses the system for cancer detection in citrus fruits. In apples, Kleynen [8] seek external damage, Qin interal defects [9] and Chen [10] general detects in 3 different crops. Lunadei [11] studies quality levels in spinach, and Herrero [12] predicts ripening stage in peaches, to mention a few.

For more than two decades, the PCI research group at Universidad Nacional de Colombia has been conducting diverse researches in coffee characterization and classification, focused primarily in highlighting relevant features found in color. Among these works, we remark the color characterization of coffee fruits [13], the classification between ripe, unripe, semiripe and overripe [14], and more recently, the characterization of the color of coffee fruits based on multispectral images [15]. Based on these results, the maturation stage of a single coffee fruit can be identified by establishing the probability distribution of the data in the space of spectral characteristics, with which it is possible to characterize the class of fruit from the mean and variance of its data and differentiate it from the other classes according to the probabilistic distance between these values [16].

In this work, we tackle the challenge of classifying coffee beans by the means of spectral information acquired using a multispectral imaging system. The system uses 15 differentiated wavelengths and a capable sensor in order to capture images containing isolated coffee beans. Input data is augmented using four nonlinear transformations of the RGB color space. Then, we model each one of the three classes of interest (unripe, ripe and semiripe beans) using an example-based approach, in which every example is represented as a multivariate Gaussian function. Color is then classified according to the least Mahalanobis distance towards each of the reference examples. A graphic summary of our proposal is depicted in Fig. 1.

Figure 2 shows an approximation of the probability distribution function (PDF) of the test classes (unripe, ripe and semiripe) using the first two components of a principal component analysis of the data. Our hypothesis aims to prove that it is possible to improve the PDF approximation by increasing the number of reference examples used to model each class.

This document is organized as follows: in Sect. 2, a brief description of the proposed example-based classification approach used in our work is provided.

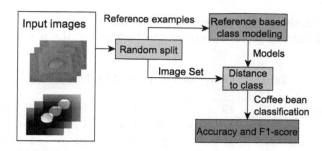

Fig. 1. Coffee bean classification workflow.

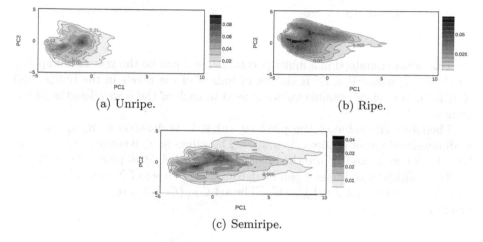

Fig. 2. Approximation of the probability density functions for a) unripe, b) ripe and c) semiripe classes, using ten examples per class.

Section 3 describes the experiments carried out in order to validate our method, along with a summary of the main results obtained. Finally, in Sect. 4 we draw the conclusion of our work.

2   Materials and Methods

2.1   Multispectral Imaging

The multispectral system used for image capture corresponds to a design based on narrow bandwidth LED illumination. The main feature of this system is the light generation of specific wavelengths together with a controlled illumination environment to discriminate reflectance at different points of the spectrum. This system has a monochromatic camera and a crown of 30 narrow bandwidth power LEDs divided into 15 different wavelengths that are 13 within the visible spectrum and 2 in the near-infrared NIR as shown in Table 1. Each of the LEDs is multiplexed in time to generate a reflectance image with each illumination.

Details of the multispectral system, the construction process, and the system's calibration within the visible spectrum can be found in the paper [17].

Table 1. LED wavelengths used in this work.

Wavelenght (nm)	410	450	470	490	505	530	560	590
Color	Violet	Royal blue	Blue	Azure	Cyan	Lime	Green	Yellow
Bandwidth (λ, nm)	30	20	20	20	30	30	10	20
Wavelenght (nm)	600	620	630	650	720	840	950	
Color	Amber	Red-orange	Red	Deep red	Far red	NIR	NIR	
Bandwidth (λ, nm)	20	10	20	20	30	50	50	

The values contained in a multispectral image I can be thought as a mapping $I : V \longrightarrow X$, where $V \in \mathbb{Z}^2$ is the set of indices of the pixels in the image, and $X \in \mathbb{R}^b$ is the set of possible values sensed in each of the b wavelengths of the image.

Therefore, the value of the pixel $(u, v) \in V$ is denoted as $\mathbf{x}_{u,v}$, and is a b−dimensional vector of intensity values. The values of u, v range from $(1, 1)$ to (H, W), where H and W are the image width and height in pixels, respectively.

The multispectral image I can be decomposed in a set of N mutually disjoint sets $C_n \subset I$, such that $I = \bigcup_{n=1}^{N} C_n$. The set $\mathcal{C} = \{C_n\}$ is a segmentation of the image I.

2.2   Color Feature Extraction

For the color-based transformations, RGB color space is recovered from the multispectral images using a LSE regression model from 15 different wavelengths covering the human visual spectrum plus two infrared components.

After the RGB image is obtained it is converted to La^*b^* for using the a^* and b^* components and to HSV for using the H and S components, for classifying the coffee fruits the 15 multispectral values and the other 4 calculated (a^*, b^*, H, S) are used, then a number of fruits is selected as reference for each class and the mean and covariance of the pixels on those fruits is calculated, those values are used for calculating the Mahalanobis distance in all the pixels of a new fruit, the classification program keeps the minimum distance between a new pixel to each class, and those minimum distances are finally added, the class with the less distance is the class to which the fruit belongs.

2.3   Reference Example Conformation

Reference examples are extracted from images in the image set. An example starts with a set (or region) C_i, extracted from an image I by a segmentation process. Then, the instance is built by the combination of a vector μ_i and a matrix $\mathbf{S}_i$, which correspond to the mean value and the covariance of the pixels contained in C_i.

Input images are masked using a manually annotated subset of pixels (the set C_i). We computed the mean using the sample mean formula

$$\mu_i = \frac{1}{N} \sum_{u,v \in C_i} \mathbf{x}_{u,v} \tag{1}$$

where N is the number of pixels in C_i. Also, we computed the covariance using

$$\mathbf{S}_i = \frac{1}{N} \sum_{u,v \in C_i} (\mathbf{x}_{u,v} - \mu_i)(\mathbf{x}_{u,v} - \mu_i)^{\mathsf{T}} \tag{2}$$

The rationale behind our approach is that intensity values inside regions do not vary greatly in each wavelength from pixel to pixel. Moreover, we assume that those data points can be approximated using a b-dimensional random variable in T with a Gaussian distribution depicted by $\mathcal{N}(\mu_i, \mathbf{S}_i)$. Similar approaches have been used to approximate statistic properties of data using probabilistic distances among objects [18], and modeling the images as a Gaussian mixture and comparing them using similitude metrics [19].

2.4   Distance-to-Class Measurement

In our work, we characterize classes by the means of one or more examples of the class, much like in k-nearest neighbor classification schemes [20, 21]. However, since each example is represented by a mean μ_i and a covariance $\mathbf{S}_i$, we chose to use the Mahalanobis distance as it takes into account the spatial distribution of the information contained in the examples.

Given a class U with K examples, denoted as C_k, and a b-dimensional measured intensity $\mathbf{x}_{u,v}$, the minimum distance to class U is

$$d_{U,x_{u,v}} = \min_i \sqrt{(\mathbf{x}_{u,v} - \mu_i)^{\mathsf{T}} \mathbf{S}_i^{-1} (\mathbf{x}_{u,v} - \mu_i)} \tag{3}$$

Since $\boldsymbol{\Sigma}_i$ is semidefinite positive, the function Eq. 3 is monotonic to its argument. Then, we chose to solve instead for

$$d_{U,x_{u,v}}^2 = \min_i (\mathbf{x}_{u,v} - \mu_i)^{\mathsf{T}} \mathbf{S}_i^{-1} (\mathbf{x}_{u,v} - \mu_i) \tag{4}$$

In order to account for possible rank-deficient covariances, the pseudo inverse $\mathbf{S}_i^{+}$ may be used instead of the inverse in Eq. 4. In those cases, numerical approximations of values of $\mathbf{x}_{u,v}$ that lie in the null space of the covariance will yield to arbitrarily large values of the distance.

2.5   Spectral Pixel-Based Region Classification

Given a test region C_i, and a class set $\mathcal{U} = \{U_k\}$, the class label k_i for the region C_i is calculated by solving

$$k_i = \underset{k}{\operatorname{argmin}} \sum_{u,v \in C_i} \left(d^2_{U_k, x_{u,v}} \right) \qquad (5)$$

Figure 3 shows a test image of a red coffee fruit that has been subject to classification using three classes: an unripe, a semiripe and a ripe class; each one of the classes represented by one example. Here, the total distance to class ripe was 5.4432×10^5, while distances to class semiripe and unripe were 5.1119×10^6 and 9.8555×10^6, respectively. It is clear that the distance to the ripe class is significantly smaller than the other two, hence the fruit is classified as ripe. Total distances to each class are calculated by summing all the distances from every pixel in the region to the examples of each of the test classes. The distribution of the distances from the pixels of the coffee fruit to each of the classes is shown in Fig. 3b.

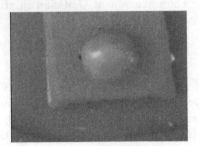
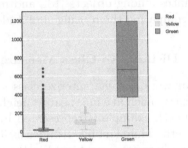

(a) RGB representation of a multispec-   (b) Pixel-wise Distance-to-class distri-
tral image of a ripe coffee fruit.   bution of the ripe coffee fruit.

Fig. 3. Ripe coffee fruit RGB representation and its distance-to-class distribution. (Color figure online)

2.6   Measurement and Scoring

The performance measurements used in our work are derived directly from the confusion matrix [22]. Their computation rely in classification true positives (TP), false positives (FP), true negatives (TN) and false negatives (FN).

Accuracy. Classification accuracy can be computed as

$$Acc = \frac{TP + TN}{TP + TN + FP + FN} \qquad (6)$$

F1-Score. Also known as balanced F-score or F-measure, can be computed as

$$F1 = \frac{2TP}{2TP + FP + FN} \tag{7}$$

2.7   Experimental Setup

Coffee Fruit Variety. The samples used in this paper were cherry coffee fruits of the Arabica type of the Caturra variety grown in the department of Caldas, Colombia. Experts classified those fruits through the fruit skin color in three main stages, i.e., unripe, semi-ripe, and ripe. These fruits have a green coloration in its first stage, which changes from green to yellow and then to red as the fruit ripens.

Test Images. For the experiments, we used 54 unripe coffee fruits (green), 54 semiripe coffee fruits (yellow), and 54 ripe coffee fruits (red).

Sensor Specifications. The MSI system uses a Flea3 FL3-GE-03S1M-C1 monochrome camera with a wide electromagnetic spectrum (300 nm to 1000 nm), which allows acquiring information from both the visible spectrum and a part of the near-infrared (NIR).

Lighting Specifications. The operation principle of the system is the narrow bandwidth illumination, coupled with a controlled illumination space to avoid interference from ambient light. The illumination crown has 15 pairs of 1-watt power LEDs with bandwidths between 10 and 50 nm, as described in Table 1.

Algorithms were coded in Python 3, using OpenCV 4 as backend for image loading and transformation. They were run using the Colaboratory platform from Google.

3   Results

3.1   One Example per Class Tests

In order to establish how classification performance changes regarding the selection of the reference examples, a robustness test was devised. In the test, the examples of two out of the three classes are kept constant whilst changing the reference example of the third class (denoted as class under testing). The reference example for the class is randomly chosen five different times. Each time, classification accuracy and F1-score are computed using the coffee fruits from the entire database, excluding only those that are chosen as reference examples. The results obtained in the test are presented in Table 2.

It is important to note that the largest deviation is in the change of the ripe fruit, given that in one of the iterations, the accuracy and F1-score values fell to 0.633540 and 0.529294, respectively.

Table 2. One example per class test results.

Class under testing	Accuracy		F1-score	
	Mean	StdDev	Mean	StdDev
Unripe (green)	0.932919	0.032095	0.932848	0.033124
Semiripe (yellow)	0.888199	0.007607	0.889834	0.007571
Ripe (red)	0.862112	0.127851	0.842580	0.175184

With only one coffee fruit as reference per class, the classification accuracy will vary a lot from 0.633 to 0.95, it is due to there is a wide variety on the color of the coffee fruits, and with only one, the system will be slanted, but even with the slanted problem, the system can get a high accuracy if a good representative coffee fruit is selected. The Fig. 4 shows the ripe fruits with the worst and best classification accuracy; with those fruits, we can identify which coffee fruit is more representative.

Table 3 illustrates the robustness of the classification scheme regarding changes in class example selection for one example per class test. In our tests, we evidenced a higher impact when varying the reference example for the ripe class than the one evidenced when changing the reference example for the other classes. Particularly, confusion between ripe and semiripe classes increased considerably in some cases when changing the reference fruit.

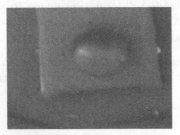

(a) RGB representation of the coffee fruit which has worst accuracy

(b) RGB representation of the coffee fruit which has the best accuracy

Fig. 4. Ripe coffee fruits used as reference for one example per class.

3.2   Multiple Examples per Class Tests

To test whether classification performance improves with respect to the number of reference examples used to represent each class, we varied such number to include two, three, four and five examples per class.

Figure 5a, 5c and 5b show the *RGB* representation of the unripe, ripe and semiripe fruits used in our best accuracy combination.

Table 3. Effect perceived in classification performance when changing the reference example. Class under testing highlighted in bold.

		Prediction outcome		
		Unripe	**Ripe**	Semiripe
Actual value	Unripe	48.0±0	0±0	0±0
	Ripe	0±0	37.4±20.92	15.6±20.92
	Semiripe	0±0	0.6±0.55	53.4±0.55

		Prediction outcome		
		Unripe	Ripe	Semiripe
	Unripe	52.0±1.22	0±0	1±1.22
	Ripe	0±0	49.0±0	5.0±0
	Semiripe	3.8±5.8	1±0	49.2±5.81

		Prediction outcome		
		Unripe	Ripe	**Semiripe**
Actual value	Unripe	47.0±1.58	0±0	7.0±1.58
	Ripe	0±0	47.4±3.36	6.6±3.36
	Semiripe	0±0	4.4±3.58	48.6±3.58

Our test starts by selecting the examples randomly from the database, maintaining the same number of samples for each class. In every case, we tested classification accuracy and F1-score when classifying the whole database (once again dropping out the examples used as class references). The results of the test are summarized in Table 4.

Table 4. Multiple examples per class test results.

Examples per class	Accuracy		F1-score	
	Mean	StdDev	Mean	StdDev
One	0.85912	0.09201	0.84791	0.11872
Two	0.85962	0.10544	0.85565	0.11067
Three	0.88301	0.04104	0.88009	0.04308
Four	0.89272	0.06457	0.89192	0.06636
Five	0.90473	0.03624	0.90486	0.03654
Six	0.91181	0.04548	0.91224	0.04534
Seven	0.90496	0.03413	0.90538	0.03422
Eight	0.90290	0.04283	0.90323	0.04278
Nine	0.92370	0.03663	0.92329	0.03690
Ten	0.92576	0.02941	0.92530	0.03012

The highest accuracy was attained when using 4 reference examples per class, giving us a 96.68 % classification rate. F1-score achieved its highest at 4 reference examples per class. In general, the tests done with 5 fruit have a higher accuracy and F1 score than 4 fruits as observed on the mean value of "Multiple examples per class test results". From Table 4, one can conclude that accuracy varies considerably when using a small number of reference examples per class. This variation decreases as the number of reference examples increase.

(a) Unripe coffee fruits used as reference for best accuracy.

(b) Ripe coffee fruits used as reference for best accuracy.

(c) Semiripe coffee fruits used as reference for best accuracy.

Fig. 5. Coffee fruits used as reference for best accuracy.

Figure 6a and Fig. 6b show the impact of increasing the number of examples per class in both accuracy and F1-score. It can be seen that increasing the number of examples per class improves the ability of the system to classify the beans correctly, while reducing the variability of the measurements.

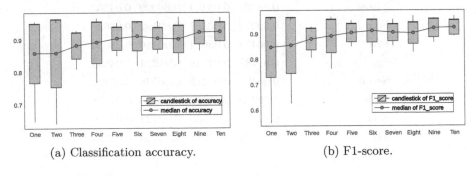

(a) Classification accuracy.

(b) F1-score.

Fig. 6. Classification performance vs. number of examples per class.

4　Conclusion

The results of the single-fruit experiment show that choosing an unrepresentative fruit as a base changes the results drastically. The test classes appear to be non-normally distributed, hence using one fruit to model each class yields high variability in accuracy and F1-score. Using a multi-fruit classification increases the accuracy and decreases the variation.

The coffee bean classification methodology proposed in this work can be coded statically once the reference examples have been chosen. Since the operations involved in our method are computed pixel-wise, the technique is likely deployable in either hardware with limited RAM memory and computational capabilities or in massively parallelized environments, where high processing speeds are required.

Acknowledgments. The authors want to thank both Universidad Nacional de Colombia and Universidad de Caldas for funding this work through the project Hermes - 48996 "Construcción del Prototipo de un Sistema de Visión Multiespectral Basado en Iluminación LED."

References

1. Deng, L., Mao, Z., Li, X., Hu, Z., Duan, F., Yan, Y.: UAV-based multispectral remote sensing for precision agriculture: a comparison between different cameras. ISPRS J. Photogramm. Remote Sens. **146**, 124–136 (2018)
2. Liu, J., et al.: Rapid and non-destructive identification of water-injected beef samples using multispectral imaging analysis. Food Chem. **190**, 938–943 (2016)
3. Lorente, D., Aleixos, N., Gómez-Sanchis, J., Cubero, S., García-Navarrete, O.L., Blasco, J.: Recent advances and applications of hyperspectral imaging for fruit and vegetable quality assessment. Food Bioprocess Technol. **5**(4), 1121–1142 (2012)
4. Ramos-Giraldo, P.J., Sanz-Uribe, J.R., Estrada-Estrada, J.H.: Sistema opto electrónico para la identificación de frutos de café por estados de maduración. Cenicafé **62**(1), 87–99 (2011)
5. Ramos-Giraldo, P.J., Sanz-Uribe, J.R., Oliveros-Tascón, C.E.: Identificación y clasificación de frutos de café en tiempo real a través de la medición de color (2014)
6. Aleixos, N., Blasco, J., Navarron, F., Moltó, E.: Multispectral inspection of citrus in real-time using machine vision and digital signal processors. Comput. Electron. Agricult. **33**(2), 121–137 (2002)
7. Qin, J., Burks, T., Kim, M.S., Chao, K., Ritenour, M.: Citrus canker detection using hyperspectral reflectance imaging and PCA-based image classification method. Sens. Instrum. Food Qual. Saf. **2**, 168–177 (2008)
8. Kleynen, O., Leemans, V., Destain, M.F.: Development of a multi-spectral vision system for the detection of defects on apples. J. Food Eng. **69**(1), 41–49 (2005)
9. Qin, J., Lu, R., Peng, Y.: Prediction of apple internal quality using spectral absorption and scattering properties. Trans. ASABE **52**(2), 499–507 (2009)
10. Mehl, P., Chao, K., Kim, M.S., Chen, Y.R.: Detection of defects on selected apple cultivars using hyperspectral and multispectral image analysis. Appl. Eng. Agricult. **18**, 219–226 (2002)
11. Lunadei, L., Diezma, B., Lleó, L., Ruiz-Garcia, L., Cantalapiedra, S., Ruiz-Altisent, M.: Monitoring of fresh-cut spinach leaves through a multispectral vision system. Postharvest Biol. Technol. **63**(1), 74–84 (2012)
12. Herrero-Langreo, A., Lunadei, L., Lleó, L., Diezma, L., Ruiz-Altisent, M.: Multispectral vision for monitoring peach ripeness. J. Food Sci. **76**(2), E178–E187 (2011)

13. Sandoval-Niño, Z.L., Prieto-Ortiz, F.A.: Caracterización de café cereza empleando técnicas de visión artificial. Revista Facultad Nacional de Agronomía-Medellín **60**(2), 4105–4127 (2007)
14. Montes-Castrillón, N.L. et al.: Real-time classification of coffee fruits using FPGA. Ph.D. thesis. Universidad Nacional de Colombia-Sede Manizales (2015)
15. Tamayo-Monsalve, M.A.: Diseño de un sistema de adquisición de imágenes multiespectrales basado en iluminación LED de potencia de ancho de banda estrecho (2020)
16. Du, Q., Chang, C.: A linear constrained distance-based discriminant analysis for hyperspectral image classification. Pattern Recogn. **34**(2), 361–373 (2001)
17. Tamayo-Monsalve, M.A., Osorio, G., Montes, N.L., López, S., Cubero, S., Blasco, J.: Characterization of a multispectral imaging system based on narrow bandwidth power LEDs. IEEE Trans. Instrum. Meas. **70**, 1–11 (2021)
18. Tavakkol, B., Jeong, M.K., Albin, S.L.: Object-to-group probabilistic distance measure for uncertain data classification. Neurocomputing **230**, 143–151 (2017)
19. Greenspan, H., Goldberger, J., Ridel, L.: A continuous probabilistic framework for image matching. Comput. Vis. Image Underst. **84**(3), 384–406 (2001)
20. Keller, J.M., Gray, M.R., Givens, J.A.: A fuzzy k-nearest neighbor algorithm. IEEE Trans. Syst. Man Cybern. **4**, 580–585 (1985)
21. Boiman, O., Shechtman, E., Irani, M.: In defense of nearest-neighbor based image classification. In: 2008 IEEE Conference on Computer Vision and Pattern Recognition, pp. 1–8. IEEE (2008)
22. Tharwat, A.: Classification assessment methods. Appl. Comput. Inform. **17**(1), 168–192 (2021)

Advanced Engineering Control Strategies Applied to Occupational Noise Management in Mining Dump Trucks

Diego Mauricio Murillo Gómez[1(✉)], Enney González León[2], Hugo Piedrahíta[3], Jairo Yate[3], and Camilo E. Gómez Cristancho[4]

[1] Asociación Colombiana de Higiene Ocupacional - Capítulo Antioquia, Medellín, Colombia
dmurillo@conhintec.com
[2] Conhintec - Control Técnico de Higiene Industrial y Ambiental, Medellín, Colombia
[3] Carbones del Cerrejón Limited, Dirección de Salud y Bienestar, Albania, Colombia
[4] Positiva Compañía de Seguros S.A., Vicepresidencia de Promoción y Prevención, Bogotá, Colombia

Abstract. This paper addresses the implementation of cutting-edge engineering techniques to reduce the exposure to occupational noise in drivers of mining dump trucks. For this, a project has been carried out in Cerrejón, which is one of the biggest open coal mines in the world. The target goal is oriented to reduce the noise values under the TLVs according to the exposure time. Although, a guideline methodology for noise control design is established by the international standard ISO 11690, the complexity of the problem yields to the development of state of the art signal processing algorithms and the implementation of knowledge frontier measurement/simulation techniques. The results indicate that the proposed approach allows to tackle noise problems of high complexity leading to a practical solution that benefits the exposed population as noise levels are lowered below threshold limit values.

Keywords: Noise control · Mining dump trucks · Occupational noise

1 Introduction

Occupational noise is one of the most significant physical risks in the mining industry [1–3]. The main reason is that the extraction of minerals requires the use of high energetic processes such as detonation, crushing, milling, grinding and heavyweight material handling, among others. These components are by their nature highly noisy [4,5]. In order to reduce the negative impact of noise, a set of national and international guidelines have been established whose general purpose is to generate recommendations, procedures and limits to control it [6–8].In Colombia, the national standards "Resolution 8321 and 1792" decreed by

Supported by Positiva Compañía de Seguros S.A.

J. C. Figueroa-García et al. (Eds.): WEA 2021, CCIS 1431, pp. 505–516, 2021.
https://doi.org/10.1007/978-3-030-86702-7_43

the Ministry of Health state the maximum time and the noise level that a worker is allowed to be exposed [9,10]. The acoustical indicator corresponds to the A-weighted Averaged Level (LAV) measured with a slow time constant. The limit for an ordinary 8-h workday is established in 85 dBA with a rate of change of 5 dBA i.e. the limit for a 12-h workday decreases to 82.1 dBA.

Cerrejón is one of the biggest open-pit coal mining in the world. It has a vast operation over an area of 50 squared kilometres, which involves dump trucks with a load capacity ranged between 190 and 320 tons. In terms of noise, one important Similar Exposure Group (SEG) corresponds to drivers of 240 tons dump trucks, which clusters more than 500 workers. Nowadays, the strategy to control the noise is mainly based on the use of hearing protectors. Nevertheless, in order to improve the acoustic comfort of the drivers, the department of industrial hygiene from Cerrejón has determined to carry out a noise control project to reduce the noise levels inside of the truck cabin. Due to the complexity of the problem, it is necessary to tackle several issues from noise source identification to cabin's intervention. Therefore, this paper presents a novel engineering framework that combines state of the art signal processing algorithms and knowledge frontier measurement/simulation techniques for that goal.

2   Methods

ISO 11690 [11] provides the foundation for an acoustic engineering control based on the sound path i.e. the noise source, the propagation medium or the receiver, respectively. At each component of this pathway, a set of alternatives can be implemented to reduce the impact of the noise according to its temporal and spectral characteristics. Nevertheless, the decision about in which step the control must be performed, depends on several aspects such as technical, financial, administrative and operational requirements, among others. It is important to point out that ISO 11690 establishes just the general strategies of control. Therefore, a rigorous knowledge of the physics and the engineering concepts involved are required for tackling noise problems of high complexity. For this project, a framework of 3 stages is proposed, which are described as follows: noise source identification, acoustic characterization and noise control design, respectively.

2.1   Noise Source Identification

The aim of this stage is to determine which are the most relevant acoustic sources in terms of their contribution to the total noise inside of the truck's cabin. Although this can be seen as a trivial step, the complexity of the enclosure and the operation involved do not allow to straightforward estimation. A frequency analysis based on 1/3 octave band resolution is not detailed enough to answer questions such as: what is the individual contribution of each acoustic source to the overall noise? The source identification is a crucial stage as provides insights about the characteristics of the acoustic sources. From that basis, it is possible to generate a precise engineering strategy of control by giving priority to the most relevant components. For this reason, it is proposed the implementation of a more robust analysis based on the Wavelet Transform [12]. This mathematical transformation is a powerful signal processing tool that has been widely used in different fields of science due to its capability of analyzing the characteristics of a signal both in time and frequency [13,14]. One of the more relevant applications is the analysis of non-stationary signals. The implementation is carried out by using the Undecimated Discrete Wavelet Transform (UDWT). This is performed by means of a perfect reconstruction filter bank using a family of orthogonal wavelets that decomposed the signal into sub-signals with different frequency content. The most common wavelets that satisfy the orthogonality properties are Daubechies, Symlets, Coiflets, and Discrete Meyer [15]. In its dyadic form, the wavelet dictionary D is built for powers of two for scaling s, holding the displacement parameter u.

$$D = \left\{ \psi_{u,s} = \frac{1}{\sqrt{s^j}} \psi\left(\frac{t-u}{2^j} \right) \right\}_{u \in R, s > 0}, \tag{1}$$

where $j = 1, 2, \cdots, N$. The result of the UDWT is a multilevel decomposition in which the signal is decomposed into approximation A and detail D coefficients for each level. This can be understood as an equivalent process to filter the signal through a set of low pass and high pass filters, respectively. UDWT performs a dyadic upsampling of each filter at each level of decomposition, thus eliminating the effects of aliasing. Figure 1 illustrates the implementation of the UDWT for two levels of decomposition.

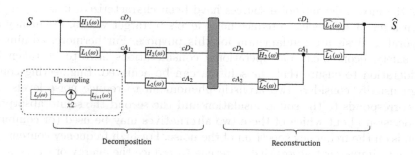

Fig. 1. Undecimated discrete wavelet transform implementation scheme.

2.2   Acoustic Characterization

Once the main acoustic sources have been identified, it is necessary to determine their relevant features so the most effective noise control alternatives can be implemented. The acoustic pressure is the standard quantity to characterize noise. However, because it is a scalar quantity, it does not provide information about the direction of propagation and it imposes some limitations such as the dependency on the distance [16]. Furthermore, if the noise is generated by several acoustic sources (which is common in many industries) or they are located within an reverberant enclosure, the acoustic characterization is not possible or at least not with the level of detail required for noise control design [17].

In the other hand, the acoustic intensity is a vector quantity with both magnitude and direction, thus providing an insight of the direction in which the energy flow is directed [18]. This allows to identify critical noisy elements of a complex system. The instantaneous acoustic intensity is defined as the rate of energy flow through unit surface area and it is calculated by taking the product between the acoustic pressure and the particle velocity. In the frequency domain, the averaged acoustic is expressed as:

$$\mathbf{I}(\mathbf{x}, \omega)) = \frac{1}{2}\mathbf{Re}\left\{p(\mathbf{x}, \omega)^* \mathbf{u}(\mathbf{x}, \omega)\right\}, \tag{2}$$

in which p corresponds to the acoustic pressure, $\mathbf{u}$ is the particle velocity, $(\cdot)^*$ denotes the complex conjugate, $\mathbf{x}$ is a position vector and $\mathbf{Re}$ relates to the real part. Furthermore, letters in bold identify vector quantities whereas italic letters scalar quantities. The particle velocity can be estimated based on Euler's equation [19] by approximating the gradient as the difference between neighboring sound pressure measurement sensors (p-p probe). The measurement of the particle velocity itself is also feasible by using more novel techniques. This device is referred as a p-u probe and it is implemented in this study due to its technical advantages. A comparison between a p-p and p-u probe can be found in [20].

2.3   Noise Control Design

Once the most relevant noise sources have been characterized, it is required to design a set of strategies to reduce noise levels to target values. Frequency and temporal analysis are fundamental for this purpose. Furthermore, administrative, safety, economical and operational considerations have to be taken into consideration to ensure that the solution can be achieved. Engineering control design usually considers two acoustic phenomena to reduce noise levels. The first corresponds to the sound insulation and the second the sound absorption. The decision about which of these two alternatives may be used (or combined) depends on the frequency spectrum of the noise. For high frequency content, it is feasible to implement absorptive materials to reduce the energy of the sound. If the energy it is mainly concentrated at low frequencies, the mass of the materials plays an important role in the insulation provided by the solution.

The calculation of the sound insulation provided by a given material can be performed by using a simplified model based on the mass law [21]. Coupled materials are also feasible to estimate allowing more complex configurations. Nevertheless, this simplified model has important assumptions and restrictions that increases the uncertainty of the result. For projects of high technical complexity, more robust approaches need to be implemented to guarantee the accuracy of the design. The Finite Element Method has been extensively used since the late 60s to analyze and solve problems in acoustics [22]. The implementation of this technique leads to a numerical solution of the wave equation for problems in which an analytical solution is not possible (due to the complexity of the domain or the boundary conditions, etc.). This simulation technique allows to evaluate and optimize, with high level of accuracy, a noise control design based on a defined environment without the need of physical prototypes.

3   Results

3.1   Noise Source Identification

The process started with the individual recording of the most relevant noise sources from the truck. This was performed by using a class 1 sound level meter with audio recording features. Each source was recorded independently to establish a set of profiles, which were input to the Wavelet algorithm. Measurements inside of the driver's cabin were performed based on the international standards ISO 6394:2008 [23]. The principal characteristics are presented as follows (Table 1):

Table 1. Frequency range of the most relevant acoustic sources

Acoustic source	Bandwidth [Hz]	Minimum frequency [Hz]	Maximum frequency [Hz]
Safety radio	3000	250	3250
Operation radio	18410	90	18500
Engine	245	5	250

Subsequently, noise measurements were made with the dump truck in motion as part of an everyday operation. The characterization corresponds to a complete cycle: loading, transporting and unloading inert material, respectively. The signals were recorded at a sampling frequency of 48 kHz and a bit depth of 24. A Wavelet algorithm was developed to estimate the individual contribution of the most relevant acoustic sources from these recordings. The process of noise extraction requires the selection of a mother Wavelet filter, which corresponds to the main characteristics of the desired source. Taking into consideration that two of the identified signals are radios, Daubechies 8 was selected due to its widely application in human voice processing [24]. Regarding the number of decompositions levels, a criterion based on the frequency distribution of the coding by sub-bands was adopted. By this approach, it was sought that the last approximation concentrated the acoustic energy of the engine. By implementing this condition, seven (7) decomposition levels were established where the last approximation represents the frequency band ranged 0 Hz and 187.5 Hz. Regarding to the threshold level, It was found that a value of 0.08 provides a suitable extraction of the desired signal. Lower values keep noisy elements from other acoustic sources. Higher values lead to a relevant degradation of the signal. Figure 2 illustrates the results due to the implementation of Wavelet algorithm.

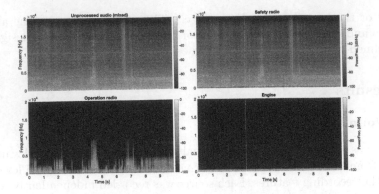

Fig. 2. Noise source separation.

Results indicates that the most relevant acoustic source corresponds to the engine of the dump truck (>10 dB compared to the others). Its main characteristics are a high concentration of energy at low frequencies and a relative stationary behaviour in time. Although the radios also provide an important contribution to the noise, their non-stationary features reduce the total influence. Furthermore, their non-stationary behaviour makes difficult the quantification of an error due to the lack of a exact reference signal [14]. Therefore, the evaluation of the algorithm was performed by listening tests in which the denoised signals were evaluated in terms of the expected signals. Finally, by taking into consideration that a noise control intervention directly to the engine is not feasible, it was decided to focus the design on the cabin truck. This strategy also provides insulation to other external acoustic sources and the environmental noise, which are relevant in a mining daily operation. The levels of the radio will be also minimized as a consequence of reducing the external noise due to the improvement in the signal/noise ratio.

3.2   Acoustic Characterization

Acoustic intensity measurements were carried out to evaluate the noise insulation performance of the driver's cabin truck and to establish possible elements for optimization. The procedure involved 3 scenarios: a non-installed new cabin, an installed cabin excited by an electroacoustic source and an installed cabin excited by the engine of the truck, respectively. For the first two cases, an electroacoustic transducer corresponding to a full range (40 Hz to 22 kHz) directional loudspeaker was used as a reference noise source. The excitation signal corresponded to white noise at a sampling frequency of 44.1 kHz. The general approach was to characterize each face of the cabin individually by locating the loudspeaker at 1 m of distance to each face. Inside of the cabin, an intensity scanning was performed simultaneously at that face (see Fig. 3). A reciprocal setup was also adopted (source inside of the cabin and the intensity probe outside).

Fig. 3. Acoustic intensity measurement - setup 2.

Figure 4 shows the measured particle velocity at the normal direction of the cabin truck. Only 1 kHz is illustrated due to the amount of data. The color scale is given in decibels (reference to 50 pico m/s) in which dark blue represent the lowest level (80 dB) and dark red the highest (105 dB).

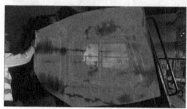

Fig. 4. Normal particle velocity - 1 kHz - left door of the cabin. (Color figure online)

The results indicate that the main components to optimize correspond to the sealing between the windows and the cabin's structure, the joint between the dashboard and the cabin's structure, open spaces to pass electrical cable, air ducts, glazing windows and the internal configuration of the cabin structure, respectively.

3.3 Noise Control Design

The noise control design was evolved by aiming to improve the acoustic insulation of the cabin based on the elements identified in the prior stage. The design was sectioned into 3 main elements: the acoustic materials, duct silencers and sealing, respectively. FEM was implemented to optimize the two first elements.

Materials. Numerical models were developed based on an incoming plane wave that propagates within an air domain divided with a layer of coupled acoustic materials. Several incident directions were simulated to obtain a representative value of the insulation. Perfectly Matched Layers (PML) [25] and Periodic Floquet boundary conditions were considered to ensure an infinite domain without reflections at the boundary and an infinite dimension of the acoustic materials. Furthermore, the domain was discretized by using 6 nodes per wavelength to ensure the convergence of the solution [26]. Three types of materials were used to improve the acoustic insulation of the cabin. They were installed as single elements or as coupled layers depending on to the area of the cabin to be intervened. The first material corresponded to a steel sheet of 2.5 mm, which was considered to increment the density of the structure in some areas where the pu probe showed a decrease in the performance. The second one was a rubber-based sheet of 4 mm. The aim was to mitigate resonances at low frequencies where the stiffness of the materials predominates the insulation. Finally, a porous absorptive material (thinsulate) was used to increase the insulation and absorption at medium and high frequencies. Figure 5 illustrates an example of the installation.

Fig. 5. Installation of the acoustic materials.

In terms of glazing windows, the existing configuration of double glass (3 mm + 3 mm) was replaced by a configuration of 4 mm + 5 mm. This not only leaded to improve the performance of the insulation in more than 6 dB, but to divide the critical frequency into different frequencies providing a better performance.

Air Ducts. Resistive duct silencers were mounted to reduce the noise due to the air flow generated by the AC system. Although the installation of this kind of elements reduces the air that goes inside of the cabin, it was verified that the thermal comfort was not affected. The design considered a box-shape silencer located at the main distribution compartment of AC system and a cylindrical silencer in the principal duct. Optimization of both silencers were carried out in FEM by using plane waves propagating inside of the silencer whose boundary conditions are assumed to be rigid (Neumann). The acoustic absorptive material was characterize by means of its air resistivity. Figure 6 shows an example of the installation.

Sealing. The acoustic sealing of the cabin was improved by installing custom-made elements focused on closing the air gaps, passings for electrical cables and reinforcing connections between the components of the cabin. Cable glands, conduits, gaskets, moulded seal plugs and neoprene tape were used for this purposed.

Fig. 6. Installation of the duct silencers.

3.4   Insulation Achieved

Figures 7 and 8 illustrate the insulation obtained once the design of control was installed. Left side of the figures shows the scenario before the control and the right side after the installation. Figures 9 and 10 show the changes on the LAeq due to the cabin's intervention. A general reduction of more than 9 dBA was achieved leading to exposure values below to the TLV. A mitigation of the acoustic energy in the broadband spectrum was obtained by tackling the low, medium and high frequency components. Finally, the estimated cost of the solution was approximately 3.500 USD, which represents a 50% of reduction compared to the price given by the provider of the truck.

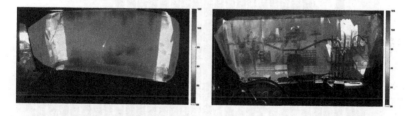

Fig. 7. Comparison acoustic insulation frontal view.

Fig. 8. Comparison acoustic insulation lateral view.

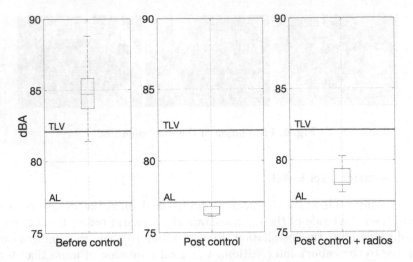

Fig. 9. Comparison of the overall LAEq due to the noise control.

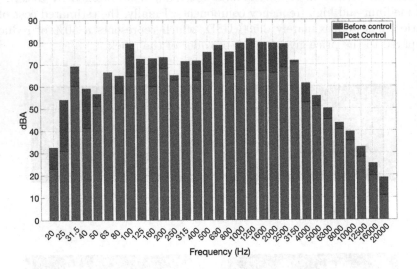

Fig. 10. Comparison of the energy spectrum due to the noise control.

4   Conclusions

An approach for tackling noise problems of high complexity is proposed. The methodology relies on the use of cutting edge signal processing techniques for source identification, measurements of acoustic vector quantities and numerical methods for optimization. The combination of these 3 elements leads to a robust scheme for engineering noise control.

A successfully case of study has been implemented in Cerrejón, which is one of the biggest open-pit coal mine in the world. The proposed design leaded to minimize the total exposure to noise in more than 9 dBA. An integral solution addressing the low, medium and high frequency energy content has been achieved.

Acknowledgments. Authors would like to thank to **Positiva Compañía de Seguros S.A.** for the support and technical assistance given to carried out this project, in particular, to Andrés Leonardo Tovar Rivera and Jawin Eduardo Gómez Freyle. Special regards to Marco Atencio from Cerrejón for his unwavering commitment and help.

References

1. Gerald, J., Paul, J.: Noise exposure and hearing conservation in U.S. coal mines - a surveillance report. J. Occup. Environ. Hyg. **4**, 26–35 (2007)
2. Edwards, A., Dekker, J., Franz, R., Dyk, T., Banyini, A.: Profiles of noise exposure levels in South African mining. J. South. Afr. Inst. Min. Metall. **11**, 315–322 (2011)
3. McBride, D.: Noise-induced hearing loss and hearing conservation in mining. Occup. Med. **54**, 290–296 (2004)
4. National Institute for Occupational Safety and Health - NIOSH: Information Circular 9492 - Equipment Noise and Worker Exposure in the Coal Mining Industry (2006)
5. Bauer, E., Kohler, J.: Cross-sectional survey of noise exposure in the mining industry. In: Proceedings of 31st Annual Institute of Mining Health, Safety and Research, Virginia (2000)
6. Elliott, H., Larry, H., Julia, D., Dennis, P., Marty, L.: The Noise Manual. AIHA, Virginia (2003)
7. Occupational Safety and Health Administration - OSHA: Section III: Chapter 5 (n.d.). https://www.osha.gov/dts/osta/otm/new_noise. Accessed 28 Nov 2020
8. National Institute for Occupational Safety and Health - NIOSH: Occupational Noise Exposure - Criteria for a Recommended Standard - Publication No 98–126 (1998)
9. Ministerio de Salud, Resolución 8321 - Normas sobre Protección y Conservación de la Audición de la Salud y el Bienestar de las Personas por Causa de la Producción y Emisión de Ruidos, Colombia (1983)
10. Ministerio de Trabajo y Seguridad Social y Salud, Resolución 1972 - Por la Cual se Adoptan Valores Límites Permisibles para la Exposición Ocupacional al Ruido, Colombia (1990)
11. International Organization for Standardization: International Standard ISO 11690-1: Recommended Practice for the Design of Low-Noise Workplaces Containing Machinery - Part 1: Noise control strategies, Switzerland (2020)
12. Narasimhan, S., Basumallick, N., Veena, S.: Introduction to Wavelet Transform: A Signal Processing Approach. Alpha Science International, Oxford (2011)
13. Daubechies, I.: The wavelet transform, time-frequency localization and signal analysis. IEEE Transform. Inf. Theor. **36**, 961–1005 (1990)
14. Gomez, A., Ugarte, J., Murillo, D.: Bioacoustic signals denoising using the undecimated discrete wavelet transform. Appl. Comput. Sci. Eng. **916**, 300–308 (2018)

15. Jyothi, R., Abdul, M.: Comparative analysis of wavelet transforms in the recognition of ancient Grantha script. Int. J. Comput. Theor. Eng. **9**, 235–241 (2017)
16. Bell, L., Bell, D.: Levels and spectra. In: Industrial Noise Control, pp. 37–66. Marcel Deeker, New York (1994)
17. Foreman, J.: Sound Analysis and Noise Control, Sound Fields. Springer, New York (1990). https://doi.org/10.1007/978-1-4684-6677-5
18. Fahy, F.: Sound Intensity, 2nd edn. CRC Press, London (2007)
19. Nelson, P., Fahy, F.: Fundamentals of Noise and Vibration, An Introduction to Acoustics. E & FN Spon, New York (2008)
20. Jacobsen, F.: A comparison of two different sound intensity measurement principles. J. Acoust. Soc. Am. **118**, 1510–1517 (2005)
21. Hopkins, C.: Sound Insulation. Direct Sound Transmission. Butterworth-Heinemann, Oxford (2007)
22. Astley, J., Crocker, M.: Numerical Acoustical Modeling (Finite Element Modeling). In: Handbook of Noise and Vibration Control. Wiley, New York (2007)
23. International Organization for Standardization, International Standard ISO 6394: Earth-moving machinery - Determination of Emission Sound Pressure Level at Operator's Position - Stationary Test Conditions, Switzerland (2008)
24. Popov, D., Gapochkin, A., Nekrasov, A.: An algorithm of Daubechies wavelet transform in the final field when processing speech signals. Electronics **7**, 120 (2018)
25. Rodriguez, A., Hervella, L., Prieto, A., Rodriguez, R.: An optimal perfectly matched layer with unbounded absorbing function for time-harmonic acoustic scattering problems. J. Comput. Phys. **223**(2), 469–488 (2007)
26. Murillo, D., Fazi, F., Astley, J.: Room acoustic simulations using the finite element method and diffuse absorption coefficients. Acta Acust. united Acust. **105**(1), 231–239 (2018)

Prerequisite Relationships of the OntoMath^{Edu} Educational Mathematical Ontology

Alexander Kirillovich[1,2]($\boxtimes$) (iD), Marina Falileeva[1] (iD), Olga Nevzorova[1] (iD),
Evgeny Lipachev[1] (iD), Anastasiya Dyupina[1] (iD), and Liliana Shakirova[1] (iD)

[1] Kazan Federal University, Kazan, Russia
[2] Joint Supercomputer Center of the Russian Academy of Sciences, Kazan, Russia

Abstract. We present the 2nd release of the OntoMath^{Edu} educational mathematical ontology. In this new release, the logical relationships between concepts have been complemented with prerequisite ones. The concept A is called a prerequisite for the concept B, if a learner must study the concept A before approaching the concept B. We adopted two approaches for defining prerequisite relationships: directly by establishing a relationship between two concepts and indirectly by arrangement the concepts by educational levels. Arrangement of concepts by educational levels, in turn, allows to extract an educational projection, i.e. projection of the ontology to an education system. Prerequisite relationships and educational projections will be used in developing of the digital mathematical educational platform of Kazan Federal University.

Keywords: Prerequisite · Ontology · Mathematical education · OntoMath^{Edu}

1 Introduction

In this paper, we present the network of prerequisite relationships of the educational mathematical ontology OntoMath^{Edu} [1–3]. This ontology is intended to be a Linked Open Data hub for mathematical education, a linguistic resource for intelligent mathematical language processing and an end-user reference educational database. The ontology is organized in three layers: a foundational ontology layer, a domain ontology layer and a linguistic layer. The domain ontology layer contains language-independent math concepts from the secondary school mathematics curriculum. The concepts are organized in two hierarchies: a hierarchy of objects (such as *Line segment*, *Triangle*, *Inscribed polygon*, or *Pythagorean Theorem*) and a hierarchy of reified relationships (such as *Relationship between a tangent line and a circle*). The linguistic layer contains multilingual lexicons, providing linguistic grounding for the concepts from the domain ontology layer. The foundation ontology layer provides the concepts with meta-ontological annotations. The current version of OntoMath^{Edu} contains 896 concepts from the secondary school Euclidean plane geometry curriculum.

OntoMath^{Edu} is a component of OntoMath digital ecosystem [4], an ecosystem of ontologies, text analytics tools, and applications for mathematical knowledge management, including semantic search for mathematical formulas [5] and a recommender system for mathematical papers [6]. OntoMath, in turn, underlines the Lobachevskii-DML

© Springer Nature Switzerland AG 2021
J. C. Figueroa-García et al. (Eds.): WEA 2021, CCIS 1431, pp. 517–524, 2021.
https://doi.org/10.1007/978-3-030-86702-7_44

digital mathematical library (https://lobachevskii-dml.ru/) [7] and a digital educational mathematical platform of Kazan Federal University under development.

For the ontology can be used for educational purposes, the logical relationships between concepts must be complemented with the prerequisite ones. These relationships reflect how the concepts of the ontology are studied in the actual educational process according to a corresponding national curriculum. The concept *A* is called a prerequisite for the concept *B*, if a learner must study the concept *A* before approaching the concept *B*. For example, comprehension of the *Addition* concept is required to grasp the concept of *Multiplication*.

Prerequisite relationships are used in such tasks as automatic reading list generation [8], curriculum planning [9, 10], evaluation of educational resources [11] and prediction of academic performance [12].

In this paper, we rely on the methodology, introduced at [3] and implement two approaches for establishing prerequisite relationships. The established relationships, in turn, are used to extract educational projections of OntoMath^{Edu}. The new release of the ontology is available on the GitHub: https://github.com/CLLKazan/OntoMathEdu.

2   Prerequisites, Educational Levels and Educational Projections

Prerequisite relationships are independent from taxonomic ones, i.e. it is possible for a class to be a prerequisite for its subclass as well as for a subclass to be a prerequisite to its superclass. For example, the *Triangle* concept is a prerequisite for both its subclass, the *Right triangle* concept and its superclass, the *Polygon* concept. In this respect, prerequisite relationships constitute a separate conceptual network that can be considered as an independent dimension of the ontology. Figure 1 represent a fragment of the network of the prerequisite relationships of the Russian education system.

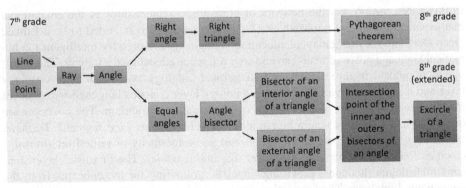

Fig. 1. Network of the prerequisite relationships of the Russian education system (fragment)

On the other hand, the prerequisite relation is highly interwoven with the relation of ontological dependence and the relation of aboutness. More specifically, the concept *A* should be considered as a prerequisite of the concept B, if *B* is a role depended on the type *A*, or *B* is a statement on the subject *B*. For example, the *Right triangle* concept is a prerequisite for the *Hypotenuse* and for the *Pythagorean theorem* concepts.

In contrast to logical relationships between concepts, prerequisite relationships are not universal and are relativized to particular education systems: for two concepts *A* and

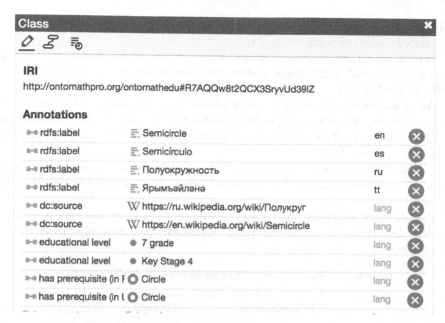

Fig. 2. The *Semicircle* concept, its prerequisites and its educational levels

B, the prerequisite relation can hold between them in one education system, but doesn't hold in another. In particular, for the concept *A* that is prerequisite of the concept *B* in one education system, the following options are possible with respect to another education system:

- *A* is a prerequisite of *B* too. For example, *Circle* is a prerequisite of *Circumference* in both the Russian and the UK education systems.
- *A* is a prerequisite of *C*, and *C* is a prerequisite of *B*. For example, in the UK education system, *Angle* is a prerequisite of *Alternate interior angles*, while in the Russian education system, *Angle* is a prerequisite of *Alternate angles* and *Alternate angles* is prerequisite of *Alternate interior angles*.
- *B* is a prerequisite of *A*. There aren't examples of this pattern in the current version of OntoMath^{Edu}, but such pair of concepts can be *Set* and *Function*, or *Circle* and *Disk*.
- *A* isn't a prerequisite of *B*, because *A* and *B* are learned independently. For example, in the UK education system, *Plane motion* is a prerequisite of *Area of a polygon*, while in the Russian education system it isn't, because *Plane motion* and *Area of a polygon* are independent in this system.
- *A* isn't a prerequisite of *B*, because *A* or *B* are not studied at all. For example, the prerequisite relation holds between *Angle* and *Complementary angles* concepts in the UK education system, but doesn't hold in the Russian education system, because the *Complementary angles* concept is not studied in it.

OntoMath^{Edu} provides two approaches for defining prerequisite relationships: a direct and an indirect ones.

Direct Approach. According to the direct approach, a prerequisite relationship is established directly between two concepts.

In order to relativize the relation to an education system, we intend using of "Descriptions and Situations" (D&S) design pattern, based on the top-level ontology DOLCE + DnS Ultralite [13–15].

As an alternative, the concepts can be linked by a subpropertis of the *has prerequisite* annotation property, corresponding to education systems, namely: *has prerequisite according to the Russian education system, has prerequisite according to the UK education system* and other.

Figure 2 represents the *Semicircle* concept in the WebProtégé editor. This concept has as its prerequisite the *Circle* concept in both the Russian and the UK education systems.

Establishment of direct prerequisite relationships between concepts is a labor-intensive task, and so the current version of OntoMath^{Edu} contains only 118 such direct relationships.

Table 1. Statistics of distribution of the concepts by educational levels.

Education level	Concepts
Russian education system	
7th grade	184
8th grade	122
8th grade (extended)	33
9th grade	37
9th grade (extended)	23
Additional program	18
Total	**417**
UK education system	
Key stage #1	27
Key stage #2	67
Key stage #3	30
Key stage #4	20
Total	**144**

Indirect Approach. According to the indirect approach, prerequisite relationships are established by arrangement of the concepts by educational levels.

Educational levels are the successive segments of the curriculum of an education system and roughly correspond to education grades. In the UK education system, the education levels are: *Key stage #1* (1st–2nd years of study), *Key stage #2* (3rd–6th years of study), *Key stage #3* (7th–9th years of study), and *Key stage #4* (10th–11th years of study). In the Russian education system, the education levels are: *7thgrade, 8thgrade, 8thgrade (extended), 9thgrade, 9thgrade (extended)*, and *Additional program*.

Every concept can belong to only one education level of a given education system. For example, the *Semicircle* concept, represented at Fig. 1, belongs to *7th grade* of the Russian education system, and *Key stage #4* of the UK system. Table 1 provides statistics of distribution of the concepts by educational levels.

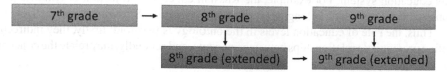

Fig. 3. Education levels of the Russian education system (fragment)

Just like concepts, educational levels are also related by the prerequisite relation. The level *L1* is called a prerequisite for the level *L2*, if a learner must study the content of the level *L1* before approaching the content of the level *L2*. In terms of the direct prerequisite relationships between concepts, a prerequisite relationship between two levels can be interpreted as follows: For any concept *C* belonging to the level *L*, all the direct prerequisite for this concept belong to either *L*, or prerequisite levels for *L*, or to their prerequisites and so on. Figure 3 represents some levels of the Russian education system and the prerequisite relationships between them.

```
OntoMath^Edu ontology

Russian projection                          UK projection

Polygonal line      Line segment      Kite       Dart

Complete                              Complementary
quadrangle          Square            angles

Bounded part of a Plane

Tool for measuring segment lengths

Mutual arrangement of a segment and a line
```

Fig. 4. Fragment of the educational projections of OntoMath^Edu

In OntoMath^Edu, both education system and education level are considered as types of points of view. A point of view is used to relativize non-universal statements. Another example of points of view are definition systems, because one and the same concept may be defined in different ways. Education systems, education levels and points of view are represented as instances of the *Education system*, *Education level* and *Point of view* classes respectively, and the first two classes are defined as subclasses of the last one. Education levels are linked to their education systems by the *belongs to education system* object property; the concepts are linked to their education levels by the *educational level* annotation property; and prerequisite relationships between education levels are represented by the *prerequisite of an educational level* object property.

Educational Projections. Arrangement of concepts by educational levels allows to extract a projection of the ontology to an education system (educational projection). The educational projection of the OntoMath^{Edu} ontology to an education system S is a fragment of the ontology, containing all the concepts, that belong to educational levels of this education system. For example, the Russian education projection of OntoMath^{Edu} consists in the concepts, belonging to 7th *grade*, 8th *grade*, 8th *grade (extended)*, etc.

Thus, the role of education levels in the ontology is two-fold: firstly, they indirectly define prerequisite relationships between concepts, and secondly, they relate the concepts to education systems.

Figure 4 represents an example of concepts, belonging to the Russian projection (the blue rectangle), the UK projection (the green rectangle) and both projections, as well as the concepts, that don't belong to either one of them.

Currently, the Russian educational projection contains 417 concepts, the UK educational projection contains 144 concepts, and 133 concepts belong to both projections.

3   Applications

In this section, we describe two experimental applications of the presented prerequisite relationships, education levels and projections.

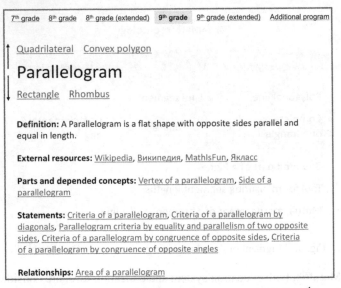

Fig. 5. The reference database entry for the *Parallelogram* concept on the 9th grade (prototype)

Personalized reference database. This application is a part of the service for semantic annotation of educational math texts. The service identifies mentions of the OntoMath^{Edu} concepts in text and links them to the corresponding entries in the database. A student interested in a particular concept may follow the link and open the corresponding database entry. The entry provides the detailed information about the concept, including the concept name, its definition, the position in the conceptual network and the relations with other concepts.

However, providing a student with all available information may lead to information overload and obscure the interesting facts. For example, if the student has just learned the concept of *Right triangle*, and knows nothing about the notions of *sinus* and cosines, he/she would be only confused by a list of trigonometric theorems. To mitigate this information overload, the personalized reference database provides the student only with such information, that is relevant to the his/her educational level. Figure 5 represents the database entry for the *Parallelogram* concept on the 9th *grade*.

Adaptive knowledge testing and recommender system. This application is based on the assumption that when a student demonstrates a lack of knowledge on some concept this lack may be caused by a lack of knowledge on some of its prerequisites. In this case, any efforts to learn this concept would futile before all the prerequisites were learned. Relying on this assumption, the system first test the knowledge on the given concepts, and then on the prerequisites for those for which the student demonstrated the poor results, then the prerequisites of the prerequisites and so on. After that, it recommends the list of the concepts to be learned starting with the unlearned prerequisites.

4 Conclusion

In this paper, we implemented two approaches for defining prerequisite relationships: directly by establishing a relationship between concepts and indirectly by arrangement the concepts by educational levels. Arrangement of concepts by educational levels, in turn, allows to extract an educational projection, i.e. projection of the ontology to an education system. Prerequisite relationships and educational projections will be used in developing of digital mathematical educational platform of Kazan Federal University.

Further development of the network of prerequisite relationships will be undertaken by the following directions. (1) At first, we are going to develop an automatic method for extracting prerequisite relationships from educational texts and then employ this method to complement the manually developed relationships with automatically extracted ones. (2) At second, we are going to develop educational projections for other national education systems, including the Colombian one. As the first step in this direction, we provided the concepts of the ontology with Spanish annotations. (3) Finally, prerequisite relationships and educational projections will be used in developing of digital mathematical educational platform of Kazan Federal University.

Acknowledgements. The main part of this work, the new release of OntoMath^{Edu}, was funded by Russian Science Foundation according to the research project no. 21-11-00105. The methodology implemented in this release had been previously developed by the authors at KFU and JSC with support of RFBR according to the project #19-29-14084 and the state assignment to SRISA RAS respectively. We would also thanks S. Gnanaprakasam and N. Paramasivam (Springer) for preparing our paper.

References

1. Kirillovich, A., Nevzorova, O., Falileeva, M., Lipachev, E., and Shakirova, L.: OntoMath^{Edu}: a linguistically grounded educational mathematical ontology. In Benzmüller, C. and Miller, B. (eds.) CICM 2020. LNAI, vol. 12236, pp. 157–172. Springer (2020)

2. Kirillovich, A., Nevzorova, O., Falileeva, M., Lipachev, E., Shakirova, L.: OntoMath^{Edu}: towards an educational mathematical ontology. In: Brady, E., (eds) et al. Workshop Papers at 12th Conference on Intelligent Computer Mathematics (CICM-WS 2019). CEUR Workshop Proceedings, vol. 2634. CEUR-WS.org (2020)
3. Falileeva, M., Kirillovich, A., Shakirova, L., Nevzorova, O., Lipachev, E., Dyupina, A.: OntoMathEdu educational mathematical ontology: prerequisites, educational levels and educational projections. In: Gorbunov-Posadov, M., (eds.) et al. Proceedings of the 22nd Conference on Scientific Services & Internet (SSI-2020). CEUR Workshop Proceedings, vol. 2784, pp. 346–351. CEUR-WS (2020)
4. Elizarov, A., Kirillovich, A., Lipachev, E., Nevzorova, O.: Digital Ecosystem OntoMath: Mathematical Knowledge Analytics and Management. In: Kalinichenko, L., Kuznetsov, S.O., Manolopoulos, Y. (eds.) DAMDID/RCDL 2016. CCIS, vol. 706, pp. 33–46. Springer, Cham (2017). https://doi.org/10.1007/978-3-319-57135-5_3
5. Elizarov, A., Kirillovich, A., Lipachev, E., and Nevzorova, O.: Semantic formula search in digital mathematical libraries. In: Proceedings of the 2nd Russia and Pacific Conference on Computer Technology and Applications (RPC 2017), pp. 39–43. IEEE (2017)
6. Elizarov, A.M., Kirillovich, A.V., Lipachev, E.K., Zhizhchenko, A.B., Zhil'tsov, N.G.: Mathematical knowledge ontologies and recommender systems for collections of documents in physics and mathematics. Dokl. Math. **93**(2), 231–233 (2016)
7. Elizarov, A.M., Lipachev, E.K.: Lobachevskii DML: towards a semantic digital mathematical library of Kazan university. In: Kalinichenko, L., et al. (eds.) Selected Papers of the XIX International Conference on Data Analytics and Management in Data Intensive Domains (DAMDID/RCDL 2017). CEUR Workshop Proceedings, vol. 2022, pp. 326–333. CEUR-WS.org (2017)
8. Gordon, J., Aguilar, S., Sheng, E., Burns, G.: Structured generation of technical reading lists. In: Tetreault, J., et al. (eds.) Proceedings of the 12th Workshop on Innovative Use of NLP for Building Educational Applications (BEA 2017), pp. 261–270. ACL (2017)
9. Agrawal, R., Golshan, B., Papalexakis, E.: Data-driven synthesis of study plans. Technical report TR-2015–003, Data Insights Laboratories (2015)
10. Auvinen, T., Paavola, J., Hartikainen, J.: STOPS: a graph-based study planning and curriculum development tool. In: Proceedings of the 14th Koli Calling International Conference on Computing Education Research (Koli Calling 2014), pp. 25–34. ACM (2014)
11. Rouly, J.M., Rangwala, H., Johri, A.: What are we teaching?: Automated evaluation of CS curricula content using topic modeling. In: Dorn, B., et al. (eds.) Proceedings of the 11th Annual International Conference on International Computing Education Research (ICER 2015), pp. 189–197. ACM (2015)
12. Polyzou, A., Karypis, G.: Grade prediction with models specific to students and courses. Int. J. Data Sci. Anal. **2**(3–4), 159–171 (2016). https://doi.org/10.1007/s41060-016-0024-z
13. Borgo, S., Masolo, C.: Ontological foundations of DOLCE. In: Poli, R., Healy, M., Kameas, A. (eds.) Theory and Applications of Ontology: Computer Applications, pp. 279–295. Springer, Dordrecht (2010). https://doi.org/10.1007/978-90-481-8847-5_13
14. Borgo, S., Masolo, C.: Foundational choices in DOLCE. In: Staab, S., Studer, R. (eds.) Handbook on Ontologies. IHIS, pp. 361–381. Springer, Heidelberg (2009). https://doi.org/10.1007/978-3-540-92673-3_16
15. Gangemi, A., Mika, P.: Understanding the Semantic Web through Descriptions and Situations. In: Meersman, R., Tari, Z., Schmidt, D.C. (eds.) OTM 2003. LNCS, vol. 2888, pp. 689–706. Springer, Heidelberg (2003). https://doi.org/10.1007/978-3-540-39964-3_44

Author Index

Acuña, Leonardo Castellanos   239
Álvarez Q., Juan M.   202
Amaya, Hector Daniel Bernal   275
Andrades, Carlos Eduardo   290
Anzola, Cristian Alzate   447
Arias-Vergara, Tomás   72
Arroyave, Juan Rafael Orozco   72

Baena, Mauricio Torres   315
Ballesteros, Dora Maria   38
Barreneche, Juan Guillermo   190
Benítez, Angela Victoria Fonseca   225
Bernábe-Loranca, María Beatriz   327
Betancur, Daniel   447
Blanco-Diaz, Cristian Felipe   213
Botero, Héctor   411
Bula, Gustavo Alfredo   374

Calderón-Ochoa, Andrés F.   347
Camacho, Steven   38
Camargo, Julian   275
Cárdenas, Elsa Adriana   25
Castaño-Londoño, Luis   447
Ceberio, Martine   13
Colmenares, Gabriel Maldonado   147
Contreras, Angel Fernando Garcia   13
Contreras, Juan David   299
Coronado-Hernández, Jairo R.   315, 335, 347

D'amato, Juan P.   263
Dominguez, Leonardo   263
Duarte-Forero, Edgar   374
Duarte-González, Mario Enrique   213
Duque, Jorge Eliecer   422
Durango-Giraldo, Geraldine   160
Dyupina, Anastasiya   517

Echavarría, Santiago   480
Escobar, John Wilmer   315
Escobar-Grisales, Daniel   171
Escobar-Restrepo, Bryan   49
Espitia-Mesa, Gabriel   468
Estevez, Eduardo   84

Falileeva, Marina   517
Fernandez, Luis David Pabon   133

García M., José I.   202
Garcia, Elvis Eduardo Gaona   275
Garcia, Jose Isidro   299
García-Valdez, Mario   3
Gatica, Gustavo   315
Gavilanez, Tomas S.   84
Giraldo M., Lillyana M.   60
Goez-Mora, Jhon E.   180
Gómez Cristancho, Camilo E.   505
Gómez, Edgar A.   84
Gomez, Eduardo   422
Gómez, Felipe Silva   250
Gomez, Julian   299
Gómez, Manuel   97
Gómez-Mendoza, Juan-Bernardo   493
González León, Enney   505
González, María José   239
González-Velázquez, Rogelio   327
Grajales, H. Kerguelen   459
Granillo-Martínez, Erika   327
Guacaneme, Yolanda Parra   250
Guajo, Joaquin   447
Guarnizo-Mendez, Hector Fabian   225
Guerrero, G. Suárez   459
Guerrero-Mendez, Cristian David   213
Guzmán, José   3
Guzmán, Tomás Francisco   250

Heck, Thiago Gomes   290
Hernández-Pedraza, Efraín   468
Herrera, Milton M.   362
Herrera-Fontalvo, Zulmeira   335

Infante, Cristian Andrés Triana   225

Jaik, Cristian Camilo   422
Jaramillo, Carlos Marcelo   25
Jaramillo-Isaza, Sebastián   213
Jimenez, Carolina Campillo   110
Jiménez, Santiago Cárdenas   399

Kirillovich, Alexander 517

Lara, Sandra Janneth Perdomo   225
Lipachev, Evgeny 517
López-Pabón, Felipe Orlando   121

Magre, Luz Alejandra 239
Manrique, Tatiana 480
Marquez-Viloria, David 447
Martinez, Estibaliz 25
Martinez-Cueto, Karol 435
Martínez-Santos, Juan Carlos 110
Medina, Sandra Johanna Morantes 225
Mejia, Maryori Sabalza 110
Mejía-Gutiérrez, Ricardo 468, 480
Mendoza, Felipe 480
Mendoza-Ortega, Gean Pablo 386
Merelo-Guervós, Juan J. 3
Molina-Tamayo, Santiago 468
Montoya, Alejandro 480
Morales, E. Vallejo 459
Morales-Mercado, Jorge 347
Morillo-Torres, Daniel 315
Murillo Gómez, Diego Mauricio 505

Narváez, Abigail Calderón 399
Narváez, Ray 239
Nevzorova, Olga 517
Nieto Aristizabal, Jenny Kateryne 147, 190
Niño, Johana Cómbita 335
Núñez, Juan David 411

Olarte-Jiménez, Leonardo J. 335
Orjuela-Castro, Javier Arturo 362
Orozco-Arroyave, Juan Rafael 49, 121, 171
Orrego, Christian 60
Otero-Diaz, Jeysser Johan 362
Ovallos-Gazabon, David 435

Parra-Gallego, Luis Felipe 72
Parra-Negrete, Kevin 435
Patiño-Martínez, Víctor-Alejandro 493
Peláez, M. Echeverri 459
Peláez-García, Camilo 493
Peñaranda, Edison Andres Caicedo 133
Perez, Alejandro 263
Pertuz, Jose Angel 422
Piedrahíta, Hugo 505

Portnoy, Ivan 347
Powell-González, Jairo E.   327
Puello-Pereira, Nataly 435

Rasia, Julia 290
Rasia, Luiz Antonio 290
Renza, Diego 25, 38
Riaño, J. Cruz 459
Rivadeneira, Pablo S. 180
Rodriguez, Jorge Luis Diaz 133
Rodríguez-Ríos, Claudia Yadira 399
Rojas, Alvaro José 422
Romero-Conrado, Alfonso R. 315
Rubiales, Aldo 263
Ruiz-Meza, José 386

Sabogal, Andrés Felipe 97
Salas, Carlos 239
Salgado, Rodrigo 386
Sanabria O., John A. 202
Sepúlveda-Cano, Lina Maria 60
Shakirova, Liliana 517
Soto, Manuel 386
Stramana, Franco 263

Tamayo-Monsalve, Manuel-Alejandro 493
Thirumuruganandham, Saravana Prakash 84
Tobón, Catalina 160
Torregroza, Angelica 386

Ugarte, Juan P. 97
Ugarte, Juan Pablo 160

Vallejo, Mónica Aydé 180, 411
Vásquez, Christian Camilo Cano 225
Vásquez-Correa, Juan Camilo 171
Vega, Juan Felipe Botero 49
Vélez, Camilo 480
Villa, Luisa Fernanda 60
Villamil, Juan David Jaiquel 225

Weber, Serena Sarah 25

Yate, Jairo 505

Zafra, Sebastian Mesa 225
Zapata, Mabel Catalina 190

Printed in the United States
by Baker & Taylor Publisher Services